The Federal Mafia

HOW IT ILLEGALLY IMPOSES AND UNLAWFULLY COLLECTS INCOME TAXES

— A Shocking and Comprehensive Analysis —

WITH
WAYS FOR FIGHTING BACK

by
IRWIN SCHIFF

Freedom Books

4616 W. SAHARA AVENUE
SUITE 340
LAS VEGAS, NV 89102
(702) 877-2833
FAX (702) 877-0521

This book is designed to provide the author's findings and opinion, based on research and analysis of the subject matter covered. This information is not provided for purposes of rendering legal or otherwise professional services, which can only be provided by knowledgeable professionals on a fee basis.

Further, there is always an element of risk in standing up for one's lawful rights in the face of an oppressive taxing authority backed by a biased judiciary.

Therefore, the author and publisher disclaim any responsibility for any liability of loss incurred as a consequence of the use and application, either directly or indirectly, of any advice or information presented herein.

ISBN 0-930374-09-6

95 96 97 10 8 7 6 5 4

DEDICATION

...To Earl J. Teeman, an electrician from Ohio who was murdered by Brazilian bandits in 1979 after he fled the United States following his illegal conviction of failing to file income tax returns.

...To Jack and Wanda Biggers of Houston, Texas, who in February 1987 killed themselves after the IRS illegally seized and sold their home.

...To Everett O. Lasher of Seattle, Washington, who shot himself in Tax Court after being told that he was going to be (illegally) fined $5,000 for raising "frivolous" arguments before that "court."

While these four Americans did not die in concentration camps or in some Siberian gulag, their deaths were not entirely dissimilar from those who did.

BOOKS BY IRWIN SCHIFF

The Federal Mafia
— How It Illegally Imposes and Unlawfully Collects Income Taxes —

The Great Income Tax Hoax

How An Economy Grows and Why It Doesn't

The Social Security Swindle
— How Anyone Can Drop Out —

How Anyone Can Stop Paying Income Taxes

The Kingdom of Moltz

The Biggest Con: How The Government Is Fleecing You

— CONTENTS —

INTRODUCTION

The revelations in this book will shock those Americans who naively assume that their government operates pursuant to law and according to a Constitution. When it comes to income taxes—an activity that deeply affects every American—the only difference between the government in our country and that found in any fascist state is merely one of style and degree, not substance.

This observation will hardly surprise those Americans who have had their assets seized and businesses destroyed by IRS agents acting without court orders. Nor will it surprise those who have gone to prison for committing tax "crimes" that, by law, do not exist. But to the average American who is totally unaware of such activities, my comparison will seem blasphemous, if not downright silly.

However, I promise you that before you finish reading this book you will be convinced that:

    1. No American is legally required to file an income tax return;

    2. No American is legally required to pay federal income taxes;

    3. All IRS seizures of money and property in payment of income taxes are *illegal* and not authorized by law;

    4. No law gives IRS agents the right to seize or otherwise acquire personal records (including bank records) for income tax purposes;

    5. All government prosecutions (including those for tax evasion) in connection with alleged income tax "crimes" are *illegal*, and are not authorized by law; and finally,

    6. The United States government, with the cooperation of a culpable federal judiciary, has been extracting income taxes from the American public *in total violation of the law.*

In short, if you think you are living in a country governed by law and a Constitution, this book will convince you that you are living in a fool's paradise.

Irwin A. Schiff

— CHAPTER 1 —
SURPRISE!
THE INCOME TAX IS VOLUNTARY

"Our system of taxation is based upon voluntary assessment and payment, not upon distraint."

—**The Supreme Court**
Flora v. United States, **362 U.S. 145, pg. 176**

In 1986, 99.5 million Americans were tricked into filing and paying federal income taxes when legally, they didn't have to do either. If this statement shocks you, it is only because you and the rest of the nation have been thoroughly deceived by the federal government (with federal courts playing the key role), and an army of accountants, lawyers, and other tax preparers. All of these have a vested interest in keeping you ignorant concerning the real nature of federal income taxes.

That an entire nation of supposedly intelligent human beings could be so thoroughly hoodwinked, must rank as the greatest and most spectacular hoax of all time, with the phenomenon of millions of Americans scurrying to IRS offices each April 15th comparable to lemmings marching into the sea.

The fact is, no provision of the Internal Revenue Code requires anyone to *file* or *pay* income taxes. This tax, unlike other internal revenue taxes, is strictly voluntary. This is because a compulsory income tax would violate the Constitution's *three taxing clauses,* the Bill of Rights and the 16th Amendment—all of which impose *restrictions on the government's power and ability* to tax income in ways few Americans understand. So, in order for the income tax **not to be unconstitutional** it had to be written on a *non-compulsory basis.* However, in order to deceive Americans of this, as well as provide federal courts and the IRS with deceptive passages on which to hang illegal prosecutions and illegal seizures, the Internal Revenue Code was written to make paying income taxes *appear* mandatory. The government succeeded in doing this by tricking the public into believing that those enforcement provisions of the Code, *that apply to other, non-voluntary taxes* (such as alcohol and tobacco taxes), also apply to income taxes when in fact, *they do not.* However, despite such trickery, the IRS still admits that our "income tax laws"[1] are purely *VOLUNTARY!*

Indeed, every official IRS pronouncement on this issue admits to the voluntary nature of the income tax, as the following quotations and government documents prove.

"The IRS' primary task is to collect taxes under a *voluntary* compliance system." (emphasis added)
— *Jerome Kurtz*
Internal Revenue Annual Report, 1980

"Our tax system is based on individual *self-assessment* and *voluntary* compliance." (emphasis added)
— *Mortimer Caplin*
Internal Revenue Audit Manual, 1975

"Each year American taxpayers *voluntarily* file their tax returns and make a special effort to pay the taxes they owe." (emphasis added)
— *Johnnie M. Walters*
Internal Revenue 1040 Booklet, 1971

"Because the American tax system is based on *voluntary* compliance and *self-assessment,* each year taxpayers make their own determination of their tax liability[2] and file returns reporting the correct tax. (emphasis added)
— *WELCOME to the United States of America Form 1-357, Re. 7-19-80, the United States Department of Justice, Immigration and Naturalization Service*

Additional proof of the voluntary nature of income taxes can be found in the IRS' own regulations. For example, under Section 601.601 which deals with "Objectives and Standards for Publication" we find the following:

The purpose of publishing revenue rulings and revenue procedures in the Internal Revenue Bulletin is to promote correct and uniform applications of the tax laws by the Internal Revenue Service employees and to assist taxpayers in attaining maximum *voluntary* compliance. (emphasis added)

On July 8, 1981 the Controller General of the United States issued a report entitled *Illegal Tax Protesters Threaten Tax System* (GGD-81-83)[3] which, on its cover, warned that illegal tax protesters threatened our tax system because . . .

...they represent a threat to our nation's *voluntary* tax system. (emphasis added)

Figure 1-1 contains the entire introductory statement of Commissioner Jerome Kurtz that appeared in the 1979 IRS Annual Report in which Kurtz mentions the voluntary nature of income taxes no less than six times, and comments that in 1978 "individuals *voluntarily* [emphasis added] reported nearly $1.1 trillion in income...." Don't you think that Kurtz knows the difference between "voluntary" and "mandatory," and if he thought that people were required to file he certainly wouldn't claim they did so "voluntarily"? How many of those who Kurtz claimed filed "voluntarily," actually believed they did so "voluntarily," as opposed to believing that they were *required* to do so?

Figure 1-2 is an excerpt from the Federal Register, Vol. 39, No. 62, dated March 29, 1974 which explains that the IRS' "mission...is to encourage...*voluntary* compliance."

Figures 1-3 are reproductions from the IRS' latest issue of *Understanding Taxes,* a slick teaching syllabus sent to our public schools so that the brainwashing of the American public can start at an early age. The syllabus seeks to dupe students into believing that they are required to pay income taxes by using such deceptive language as [note F]: "taxpayers are responsible for paying income taxes as income is earned through withholding." Why doesn't it say that taxpayers are *required?* The syllabus reluctantly admits the voluntary nature of the income tax no less than *three* times (at A, E and H) but, referring to the statements at A and B:

(a) How can students "understand the [meaning of] "voluntary compliance" if there are "consequences" for "non-compliance"? (Note how the government specifically avoids saying that "penalties" apply!)

(b) How can there be *legal* "consequences" if "taxpayers *voluntarily* report income to the government..."

1979 Annual Report

Commissioner of Internal Revenue

FIGURE 1-1

Doesn't it seem strange that the IRS uses the word "voluntary" *six* times in the introduction to their own Annual Report, but does not use the term *once* in your Privacy Act Notice?

This year I'm pleased to report that a number of organizational changes have been implemented and appear to be accomplishing the intended goals. The changes were undertaken last year to implement recommendations made in a study conducted by senior IRS career executives.

The change most directly affecting taxpayers was the modification of our administrative appeals procedure by consolidating the former two levels of appeal into a single appeal structure at the regional level. This system is now fully in effect and is resulting in the more expeditious handling of controversies at less expense to both taxpayers and the IRS. We continue to hold appeals conferences at all locations where district conferences were formerly held with the result that taxpayers have conveniently available to them a regional appeals officer with full settlement authority.

We believe the change in settlement procedures of docketed Tax Court cases is working effectively to utilize our resources better and to provide a more orderly procedure for handling the increasing volume of docketed cases.

The streamlining of our smallest districts has been accomplished smoothly. We are realizing savings at no loss of service to taxpayers.

Separating functions involving service to the public from those involving compliance has increased our emphasis on taxpayer service as well as permitted better integration of our collection activities with related compliance functions.

Notwithstanding our increased emphasis on taxpayer problems, it seems clear that some of these will continue to "slip through the cracks." If this occurs in even a very small percentage of the huge number of matters we handle the number of such cases will be large. To address this problem we instituted our problem resolution program (PRP) on an experimental basis in 1977 to provide a separate function to handle persistent taxpayer problems — those not satisfactorily resolved through normal channels. PRP is now fully operational in all of our 58 districts and 10 service centers with problem resolution officers who have the ability and know-how to cut through red tape quickly on behalf of taxpayers. About 72,000 taxpayer problems were successfully resolved through this pro-

cedure in 1978 and a number of systems changes identified by this program have been made to improve IRS efficiency and responsiveness.

A sample followup with taxpayers whose problems were handled through PRP found a high degree of satisfaction but I will not be satisfied as long as some taxpayer complaints and problems persist. Therefore, as the year ended we were planning to set up an ombudsman-like position in my immediate office to have broad authority over PRP and to serve as an advocate for taxpayers.

Our forms and instructions are a matter of continuing concern. The challenge of presenting and explaining a complex law in an understandable way is formidable and we devote substantial effort to this problem. In addition to our normal work in this area we have formed a high-level task force to consider longer-range possibilities. We have engaged a private firm to review all the individual tax return forms, schedules and instructions and to make recommendations for redesign and rewriting. This effort should be completed in the fall of 1980 when we will start evaluating and testing any recommended alternatives.

While it is important that we constantly look for ways of simplifying the burden of reporting, frequent changes should be avoided. There is great value in taxpayers' familiarity with our forms. I'm, therefore, pleased that the 1979 forms follow the 1978 forms except for a few changes required by new legislation.

There is no doubt that better taxpayer assistance, more sensitive responsiveness to taxpayer complaints and problems and simpler tax forms and instructions are of great importance in achieving a high level of <u>voluntary</u> compliance with our tax laws. But our enforcement efforts also are crucial. Any significant noncompliance is a matter of deep concern to the IRS. Congress and the taxpaying public. Beyond the tax revenues lost when income is not reported is the basic question of fairness to taxpayers who <u>voluntarily</u> obey the laws.

Since the mid-Sixties the IRS has regularly measured compliance on filed returns through its taxpayer compliance measurement program (TCMP). As an adjunct to our audit program, TCMP is an effective tool to measure the unreported income detectible by normal audit procedures and to develop the

computer formulae used to identify returns for audit. It does not, however, measure the unreported income of those who fail to file returns nor certain types of income not readily detectible by normal audit procedures, such as income from illegal sources.

In 1978 I appointed a study group to prepare estimates of unreported income. The group's report, *"Estimates of Income Unreported on Individual Income Tax Returns,"* was released in August 1979. This report, using data for the 1976 tax year, marks our first effort to measure unreported individual income.

The report estimates that individuals failed to report $75 billion to $100 billion in income from legal activities, with a resulting revenue loss of $13 billion to $17 billion. Unreported income from certain illegal sources — narcotics, illegal gambling and prostitution — was estimated to be between $25 billion and $35 billion, and cost the government approximately $6 billion to $9 billion in lost tax revenues.

To put these figures in context, in the same tax year individuals <u>voluntarily</u> reported nearly $1.1 trillion in income and paid a total of $142 billion in income taxes.

The report lends considerable weight to conclusions drawn from past TCMP studies that <u>voluntary</u> reporting is highest when incomes are subject to tax withholding. Incomes subject to information reporting show a lower compliance level but still much higher than incomes subject to neither withholding nor information reporting.

In fairness to the millions of taxpayers who <u>voluntarily</u> file, report all their income and pay the tax due, we must strengthen current compliance efforts and, where called for, plan innovative actions to find and tax unreported income.

A Treasury legislative proposal, currently under consideration by Congress, to withhold taxes from certain independent contractors would be a major step in dealing with one area of low compliance.

Our program to match information documents filed by payers of wages, dividends, interest and certain other payments with income tax returns has become an increasingly important tool to identify cases of underreporting of income and nonfiling of returns. The number of documents matched has been increasing substantially and with the full

implementation of the combined annual wage reporting system will reach 400 million or about 80 percent of the total filed.

Our document matching activity has been separate from our examination program and has not affected the selection of returns for audit or their actual audit. However, in the next filing season, a printout of the information documents processed will be associated with returns selected for the examination program so that the information will be available to tax return classifiers and to return examiners. Since these documents will also be used during TCMP audits, the accuracy of the results of that program should also be improved.

In last year's report I noted our increasing concern about the use of abusive tax shelters – those which take positions beyond a reasonable interpretation of the law – and our increased audit effort in this area. As a result of that effort we have, at various stages of the examination and appeals process, about 200,000 tax returns involving about $4.5 billion of questionable deductions. This program requires a substantial commitment of resources but it is a commitment we will continue to make, and even increase if necessary. The great abuse we are finding in this area, if allowed to continue unchecked, could result in a serious decline in taxpayers' perception of the fairness and evenhandedness of our administration of the tax system and consequently in their <u>voluntary</u> compliance.

Many abusive tax shelters depend for their successful marketing on the participation of professional tax advisors. We intend to continue an exploration, begun this year, into the ethical and legal standards that should govern such participation.

Tax administration today calls for us to increase our abilities to serve the majority of taxpayers who comply with the law. A crucial aspect of this service is to enforce the law vigorously against the few who attempt to subvert it. We believe this year's report reflects that commitment.

Jerome Kurtz
Jerome Kurtz
Commissioner of Internal Revenue

Even the Supreme Court in *Flora v. United States,* (as previously noted) recognized and commented on the voluntary nature of the income tax.

You can check with as many dictionaries as you like, and you will find that the word "voluntary" means something done of one's own free will, and without legal obligation. So if compliance with "income tax laws" is required, why would commissioner after commissioner claim that filing is voluntary if it were not? Do you really believe that "voluntary compliance" can mean the same thing as "compulsory compliance"? And if compliance with "income tax laws" is *required,* i.e. *compulsory,* why would all of these government documents claim otherwise?

THE MEANING OF VOLUNTARY COMPLIANCE AND SELF ASSESSMENT

While the reader might need to have the meaning of "self assessment" explained, the meaning of "voluntary compliance" should be perfectly clear. "Voluntary compliance" can only mean that compliance with "income tax laws" is voluntary and that you can comply or not comply as you choose. Actually the term "voluntary compliance" makes no sense. If something is "voluntary," then the word "compliance" is superfluous. If, on the other hand, "compliance" is compulsory, then any use of the word "voluntary" is nonsensical. It should be perfectly evident why the government contrived this self-contradictory expression. Have you ever heard of it in

FIGURE 1-2

DEPARTMENT OF THE TREASURY
Internal Revenue Service
ORGANIZATION AND FUNCTIONS

This material supersedes the statements on organization and functions published at 37 FR 20961–20990, 38 FR 23341 and 23342, and 38 FR 30011 and 30012.

Dated: March 25, 1974.

[SEAL]   DONALD C. ALEXANDER,
Commissioner of Internal Revenue.

1100 ORGANIZATION AND STAFFING

1110 ORGANIZATION AND FUNCTIONS OF THE INTERNAL REVENUE SERVICE

SEC. 1111 *Establishment of the Internal Revenue Service.*
SEC. 1111.1 *Mission.*
The mission of the Service is to encourage and achieve the highest possible degree of voluntary compliance with the tax laws and regulations and to maintain the highest degree of public confidence in the integrity and efficiency of the Service. This includes communicating the requirements of the law to the public, determining the extent of compliance and causes of non-compliance, and doing all things needful to a proper enforcement of the law.

FEDERAL REGISTER, VOL. 39, NO. 62—FRIDAY, MARCH 29, 1974

FIGURE 1-3

UNIT 1
UNDERSTANDING YOUR ROLE AS A TAXPAYER

LESSON A
INCOME TAX & YOU

PURPOSE
To help students understand the importance of voluntary compliance with income tax laws and the consequences for citizens and society of noncompliance.

Students will explain how income taxes provide revenue for goods and services that benefit the general public, including students.

Students will define noncompliance with federal income tax laws as illegal and list the results of noncompliance as:

■ Loss of tax revenue
■ A need for additional resources for enforcement
■ Higher taxes for those who do comply

Students will identify the right of citizens to participate in the formulation of tax policy as well as the obligation of citizens to comply with tax policy decisions.

VIDEO SUMMARY
Seventeen-year-old Jake Daniels has calculated that with the income from his new job in a bicycle shop he can buy a car in time to take pretty fellow employee Samanthe to the harvest dance. But Jake's calculations failed to allow for taxes. With a newly discovered respect for the subject of taxes, Jake learns about the importance of voluntary compliance with income tax laws.

LESSON B
TAXPAYER RIGHTS AND RESPONSIBILITIES

PURPOSE
To help students understand that they have basic rights and responsibilities as taxpayers.

OBJECTIVES
Students will discuss the taxpayer's responsibilities related to filing a tax return.

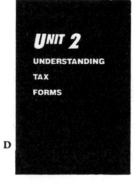

UNIT 2
UNDERSTANDING TAX FORMS

LESSON A
FROM W-4 TO W-2

PURPOSE
To help students understand that taxpayers are responsible for paying income taxes as income is earned through withholding.

OBJECTIVES
Students will explain how taxpayers use Form W-4 to tell their employers how much to withhold from their pay for taxes.

Students will, given sufficient information, correctly complete Form W-4.

Students will identify the importance of the information contained in a Form W-2 received from an employer.

Students will describe the use of Form 1099-INT.

LESSON B
FILING A RETURN/ FORM 1040EZ

PURPOSE
To help students understand that taxpayers voluntarily report their income to the government by "filing" a tax return, that there are several ways to do this, and that the simplest of these is using Form 1040EZ.

OBJECTIVES
Students will define the expression "filing a tax return."

Students will determine, given sufficient information, whether an individual is required to file a return.

Students will identify the specific tax return form that each of a selection of taxpayers should use.

Students will complete Form 1040EZ accurately.

LESSON C
FORM 1040A AND BEYOND

PURPOSE
To help students understand the correct use of Form 1040A and, in general, the purpose of Form 1040.

OBJECTIVES
Students will complete Form 1040A accurately.

Students will describe the function of Form 1040.

UNIT 3
UNDERSTANDING STATE AND LOCAL TAXES

LESSON
STATE AND LOCAL TAXES

PURPOSE
To help students understand that state and local governments need revenue to provide goods and services for their residents.

OBJECTIVES
Students will list kinds of taxes collected by state and local governments and identify the nature of the taxes – consumption, income, or wealth.

Students will give examples of goods and services provided by state and local tax revenues.

connection with anything else? The government feared that if it correctly used the solitary word "voluntary" to describe federal income taxes, the nature of the tax would become immediately apparent. So it added the word "compliance," seeking, in this way, to fool the public by the mandatory meaning that word conveys. The government relied on an ingenuous public not to notice that the preceding word, "voluntary," rendered the latter word, "compliance," meaningless. And the American public, in overwhelming measure, didn't let the government down!

Actually, the government is very careful not to *officially* misrepresent the voluntary nature of the tax nor to *officially* tell the public that anything about it is "required." Instead, the government relies on a myriad of misleading techniques that enable it to accomplish the same thing.

One such example is shown in Figure 1-3. Note how the government, even when telling school children that the income tax is voluntary, *simultaneously* seeks to persuade them that it is not. It does this by discussing the tax in terms that make it *sound* compulsory, but really do not make it so. With practice, you will be able to spot these deceptions in all government documents. For now, I will help you—though little help should be necessary on this point.

Note that instead of telling readers that Americans are *required* to file and pay income taxes (if this were really the case), the government seeks to mislead them on this issue by appearing to warn them (at B) about the "consequences for citizens and society of *noncompliance*"; and that (at C) the "*Students* will define *noncompliance* with federal income tax laws as illegal and list the results of noncompliance." Notice it will be the "students" who will define "noncompliance...as illegal,"—**not the government!** The government, of course, knows that "noncompliance" is not illegal so it can not "define" it in this manner. But the government is nevertheless able to convey this by its use of some verbal sleight of hand that neither the teacher or students will ever notice. The government has truly raised the level of deception to a veritable art form.

At D, the government seeks to mislead students by using such mumbo-jumbo as citizens having an "obligation . . . to *comply* with tax policy decisions." Try figuring out what that means, while you also try figuring out what an inferred *legal* "obligation to comply" means—when "compliance" is admittedly voluntary.

Continuing with its deception, the government states (at I) that "Students will determine, given sufficient information, whether an individual is required to file a return." So this is how the government deceitfully infers that filing is "required" knowing full well that it is not, and provides another example of the technique referred to

earlier. The government, of course, knows full well that it can not legally tell the students who "is required to file" (unless it says, "nobody"). So it relies on the students misleading each other—under the influence of their own trusted teacher, who is also totally convinced that filing is mandatory and therefore files regularly. **Since the teacher will not be dissuaded from this belief, regardless of how many times the syllabus says that such filing is voluntary, he or she**[4] **will be instrumental in fooling her pupils.**

Using the public to fool the public is an important aspect of the government's program of deception. In addition, it would never dawn on those school children (who undoubtedly infuse Washington politicians with the same honesty that they associate with George Washington and the cherry tree) that their own government would deliberately seek to deceive them in the manner the syllabus is intended to do. As the government relies on the nation's school teachers to mislead children right in their own classrooms, so too does the government rely on and utilize the nation's media—converting it into a virtual monolithic government propaganda agency. This vast media network is harnessed to work the American public into a virtual filing frenzy around April 15th, little realizing that it has been actually duped into duping the public in like manner.

Interestingly enough (at G), the syllabus correctly states that employees (though the syllabus uses the tricky legal term "taxpayers") "use form W-4 to tell their employers how much to withhold from their pay for taxes." This is an accurate acknowledgement by the IRS that under the "law," it is the employee who supposedly "tells" the employer how much to deduct, and not the other way around. In practice, however, the IRS totally disregards this principle and sends unsigned, computerized letters (see Figure 2-2 in Chapter 2) to employers telling them to disregard what their employees "tell" them to deduct, and to deduct instead, what nameless and faceless IRS employees instruct them to deduct. This is a clearcut example of how a correct IRS policy statement is illegally disregarded by the Service in practice.

"STRENGTHENING VOLUNTARY COMPLIANCE"

In a 200 page study entitled *Internal Revenue Service Strategic Plan* (Document 6941 5-85) the IRS provided the nation with a sterling example of "double think," since the document outlined new and "strategic initiatives for strengthening voluntary compliance." Now ask yourself—precisely how does a government go about "strengthening" something that is "voluntary"? Roscoe Egger, the IRS Commissioner responsible for the "Strategic Plan," explained that one of the principle reasons for the "Plan" was the problems caused by so called "tax protesters." However, throughout that document Mr. Egger consistently refers and admits to the voluntary nature of the income tax. For example:

External environmental indicators and internal compliance measures reflect a continuing decline in the extent to which taxpayers are willing or able to *voluntarily* comply with the federal tax laws.

Tax law changes are occurring with greater frequency...to achieve national socio-economic goals... These frequent changes have materially increased the complexity of tax administration, and may adversely affect *voluntary* compliance.

With the decline in *voluntary* compliance in a period of budgetary constraints, the IRS must find ways to increase "presence" and to selectively apply resources to produce effective results.

The enactment of state statutes designed to ensure the filing of appropriate returns in connection with the pursuit of business activities clearly strengthens *voluntary* compliance.

It is important that Public Affairs do more to assist in improving *voluntary* compliance.

Issues: (1) What steps can the IRS take to stem or reverse this decline in *voluntary* compliance?
(emphasis added throughout)

Obviously, one of the "steps" that the government decided to take to "stem"...and "reverse"...the "decline in voluntary compliance," was to step up the illegal prosecutions of those unwilling to "volunteer."

In Figure 1-4 I have reproduced the entire introduction to the chapter entitled "Strengthening Voluntary Compliance" just in case you thought *Animal Farm* was fiction.

FIGURE 1-4

STRENGTHENING VOLUNTARY COMPLIANCE

INTRODUCTION

The tax gap for 1981 was estimated to be over $81 billion, with over two-thirds ($55 billion) attributable to unreported individual income taxes. The seriousness of this situation is underscored by estimates that in five years, the portion of the gap attributable solely to unreported income of individuals, will reach $98 billion, larger than all the components of the current tax gap combined.

The initiatives that follow are designed to translate the Strategic Directions on Strengthening Voluntary Compliance into action and concentrate particularly on the problem of non-compliance by individual income taxpayers. These include the "nonfarm business" or self-employed taxpayers, whose noncompliance stands out as a growing concern within the area of unreported income.

In all, fifteen initiatives will be pursued with the intent of strengthening voluntary compliance. Many recommend or support specific projects that concentrate on bolstering compliance through no-cost or relatively low-cost initiatives. These proposals look outside, as well as within IRS for solutions.

The Service will attempt to broaden its knowledge about taxpayers' attitudes and perceptions about tax laws and IRS' administration of laws in order to devise more pertinent and effective programs and communications. Expanded use of computer technology for tax assistance as well as more efficient enforcement programs will be explored. The need for adequate planning is stressed in order to be prepared for future technological changes expected to impact tax administration.

Externally, the Service will be looking to other federal agencies, state governments and non-government organizations to join in cooperative efforts to promote compliance with the tax laws. These efforts involve improved enforcement efforts and better tax education, particularly for self-employed taxpayers.

In summary, the Strategic Initiatives for Strengthening Voluntary Compliance recognize that the Service must look to diverse and innovative solutions that do not demand major staffing commitments. These initiatives should make substantial inroads against the compliance decline and, together with other projects planned or underway, will prove effective in strengthening voluntary compliance.

48   May 9, 1984

CONFUSING THE PUBLIC ON THE MEANING OF "VOLUNTARY COMPLIANCE"

In addition to using deliberately deceptive (though technically not false) language in its official publications, IRS employees (from the top to the bottom) lie profusely (though some are obviously just merely ignorant concerning the "law" that they believe they are enforcing) in letters and conversations with the public and in all tax prosecutions and civil litigation. In all of my civil and criminal litigation I never once have come across an attorney for either the IRS or the tax division of the Justice Department who told the truth about federal income taxes. (Numerous examples appear in following chapters.)

On top of all of this, the government gets total support from a duplicious federal judiciary, who will not only boldly lie from the bench about alleged "requirements" under our income tax "laws," but in furtherance of the government's mammoth deception, it helps it intimidate the public by conducting illegal trials and by knowingly sending innocent people to jail. So, if our all-powerful federal judiciary is willing to collectively lie about this tax, and to close ranks in sending innocent people to jail—who's going to challenge it on this issue?

It should also be obvious, that if I have to devote the next 200+ pages of this book trying to convince you of something that the government has already told you at least a dozen times is voluntary—then somebody has done a number on your psyche!

The Red Light Story

If you ask the IRS (or anyone else in government for that matter) the meaning of "voluntary compliance" you will get a lot of double talk. When I first concluded that filing income tax returns was voluntary (based on some of the government documents and statements shown herein), I decided to check out my conclusion with the IRS. I called and asked, "Is filing an income tax return based on voluntary compliance?" "It is," I was told. "In that case," I said, "I don't want to volunteer." "You have to volunteer," I was informed. "If I have to volunteer," I replied, "wouldn't that make compliance compulsory and not voluntary?" "No," the agent answered, "voluntary compliance is similar to our motor vehicle laws; you voluntarily stop at a red light—but if you don't, you get a ticket!" I objected to this reasoning by pointing out that if I could be ticketed, stopping at a red light (or obeying other traffic regulations) was compulsory, and not based on "voluntary compliance" at all. "No," the agent insisted, "you stop voluntarily." His reasoning was based on the absurd logic that since nobody was physically in the car

FIGURE 1-5

INTERNAL REVENUE INVESTIGATION

HEARINGS

BEFORE A

SUBCOMMITTEE OF THE

COMMITTEE ON WAYS AND MEANS

HOUSE OF REPRESENTATIVES

EIGHTY-THIRD CONGRESS

FIRST SESSION

ON

ADMINISTRATION OF THE INTERNAL REVENUE LAWS

PART A

FEBRUARY 3, 4, 5, 6, 9, 10, 25, 26, 27, MARCH 2, 3, 4, 5, 6, 10, 11, 12, AND 13, 1953

Printed for the use of the Committee on Ways and Means

UNITED STATES
GOVERNMENT PRINTING OFFICE
WASHINGTON : 1953

29091

INTERNAL REVENUE INVESTIGATION

One of my assistants refers to policy and personnel, and of course, under this new structure, we are concerned here in Washington, as I pointed out, largely with policy and in administering the industry, rather than directing the personnel. That is left primarily to the district commissioners or, rather, the assistant district commissioners.

Mr. CURTIS. An alcohol tax matter that would go to the Appeals Section——

Mr. AVIS. There is just no such thing. That is where this structure differs.

Let me point this out now: Your income tax is 100 percent voluntary tax, and your liquor tax is 100 percent enforced tax. Now, the situation is as different as day and night. Consequently, your same rules just will not apply, and therefore the alcohol and tobacco tax has been handled here in this reorganization a little differently, because of the very nature of it, than the rest of the over-all tax problem.

Mr. CURTIS. In other words, the alcohol and tobacco tax setup, while it is a part of the Bureau generally, has more or less an autonomy of its own, with the power and authority vested in it; is that right?

Mr. AVIS. I think that is a fair statement; yes, sir, Mr. Curtis.

Chairman KEAN. How about legal matters; does the counsel of the Bureau advise with you?

Mr. AVIS. Well, we have an Alcohol and Tobacco Tax Division counsel, and he reports to the Chief Counsel of the Bureau, and he is part of the general counsel's setup in the Treasury. But for convenience, so that when I get a problem, for example, over the telephone and it is a question of whether a big factory or a plant's operations are to be set up, I can grab my lawyer across the hall and find out what the law is, don't you see; and he, for convenience, is located right in the adjoining suite to me here in Washington. And the same thing applies in the field. In other words, it is a specialized field, and the lawyers that service alcohol tax are generally attached to the assistant district commissioner's office, as far as space is concerned. They still report to their boss, who is the divisional counsel.

Chairman KEAN. There is a lawyer in every one of the 17 areas?

Mr. AVIS. Yes.

Chairman KEAN. He is under the lawyer who deals with you, who is under the man in Mr. Davis' office at the moment, who is under the man in the Treasury Department?

Mr. AVIS. That is Mr. Tuttle; I think he is the new man.

Mr. CURTIS. But your lawyers are confined to problems relating to alcohol tax and tobacco tax?

Mr. AVIS. Yes; because it is so highly specialized, sir.

Mr. Chairman, I think we have covered the rest of my statement, but I will read it.

The reorganization plan abolished the district supervisors and established in their place 17 assistant district commissioners, Alcohol and Tobacco Tax Division, who, subject to the general supervision of the district commissioners, have substantially the same functions, powers, and duties that the former district supervisors had.

making me stop, then I stopped "voluntarily." If that is true, then all criminal laws are based on "voluntary compliance," since nobody physically prevents anyone from committing murder, rape, bank robberies, etc., etc. But law enforcement people never claim that those laws are based on "voluntary compliance."

The agent, of course, was trying to confuse me—although he himself might have been confused. The IRS obviously indoctrinates all new agents with the "red light" story, so that they will be able to confuse the public if the question ever comes up.

Figures 1-5 and 1-6 prove that the government realizes that while income taxes are based on "voluntary compliance," other tax statutes are not. Figure 1-5 contains testimony by Dwight E. Avis, then head of the Alcohol and Tobacco Tax Division of the IRS, given to a House of Representatives Subcommittee of the Committee on Ways and Means when it held hearings on the administration of the internal revenue laws. He states on page 12:

> Let me point this out now: Your income tax is 100% *voluntary tax,* and your liquor tax is 100 percent *enforced tax.* Now, the situation *is as different as night and day.* Consequently, your same rules just will not apply... (emphasis added.)

I also recently wrote to the Department of the Treasury, Bureau of Alcohol, Tobacco and Firearms and asked them if those taxes were based on "voluntary compliance." Look what they wrote back (Figure 1-6). They left no doubt that their "collection...is created by an enactment of law...(and so)...*compliance automatically becomes mandatory...*(and that)...in response to [my] specific question, the collection

---

FIGURE 1-6

DEPARTMENT OF THE TREASURY
BUREAU OF ALCOHOL, TOBACCO AND FIREARMS
WASHINGTON, D.C. 20226

MAR   3

C:R:D:MAW
5600

Mr. Irwin A. Schiff, 08537-014
P.O. Box 1000-702
Loretta, Pennsylvania   15940

Dear Mr. Schiff:

This is in response to your letter dated February 5, 1988, in which you state that you were informed that the collection of tobacco and alcohol taxes were based on voluntary compliance and, if not voluntary, ask if they are collections based on compulsary compliance.

The collection of taxes on tobacco and alcohol products is created by an enactment of a law by our legislative branch of the Government. Once a law is enacted, requiring the collection of taxes on tobacco and alcoholic products, compliance automatically becomes mandatory and it is the Bureau of Alcohol, Tobacco and Firearms' responsibility to administer those Federal laws.

With the above in mind and in response to your specific question, the collection of tobacco and alcohol taxes orginates from statutes and, as a result, compliance is complusary.

Should you have any additional questions, please feel free to contact me at the letterhead address or telephone me at (202) 566-7531.

Sincerely yours,

Mary Wood

Mary A. Wood
Specialist, Distilled Spirits and
Tobacco Branch

of tobacco and alcohol taxes originates from statutes and, as a result, *compliance is mandatory.*'' Did you notice that I didn't get any "red light" story from them?

Along the same lines, it is obvious that if the Ten Commandments were based on "voluntary compliance," the Bible would have referred to Moses' stone tablets as the Ten Suggestions.

THE MEANING OF SELF-ASSESSMENT

As you will soon discover, federal income taxes, by law, have to be assessed just like city property taxes.[5] City property taxes, however, are assessed by city assessors, and not by property owners assessing themselves, on the basis of "self-assessment." Cities and towns are **empowered by law** to assess and levy property taxes—and do not have to rely on the willingness of property owners to **voluntary** assess themselves under a system of "self-assessment." But in accordance with the "self-assessment" nature of the income tax, unless Americans voluntarily elect to assess income taxes against themselves (by sending in a tax return and swearing they owe a tax that by statute they can not

possibly owe)–the federal government **has no statutory authority to make such an income tax assessment on its own initiative.** And without such a voluntary "self-assessment," no income tax, **by law,** can be owed to the federal government. How the government has been **breaking the law** in order to illegally assess income taxes on its own initiative (thus disregarding the principle of "self-assessment") is covered in Chapter 5.

While the government can make assessments with respect to other (mandatory) federal taxes, it is **legally barred** from doing so in connection with income taxes. As a matter of fact, the federal government does not even have the legal authority to even **estimate** how much income tax a non-filer supposedly owes—let alone harass or prosecute him if he chooses not to voluntarily self-assess himself to pay the tax altogether.

Now that you know the real nature of federal income taxes, we will turn to examining why the tax is **voluntary** and why it is based on **self-assessment**. The federal government would dearly love to have it otherwise, but— thanks to a Constitution (that is all but dead)—it can't.

NOTES TO CHAPTER 1

---

1. It is actually incorrect to speak of "income tax laws," since there really aren't any. Laws, by definition, are based on compulsory compliance and include penalties for non-compliance. "Laws" based on "voluntary" compliance are not "laws," by definition. Neither the Internal Revenue Code nor the U.S. Criminal Code (as you will discover) contain any penalties in connection with income taxes— which is why compliance with it is voluntary.

2. An example of a false government inference, and from the Justice Department no less. There is no such thing as an income tax "liability" (see Chapter 6), yet this fraudulent claim is constantly repeated in government documents.

3. "Tax protesters" is the word that the government coined to throw the public off the track regarding Americans who have discovered the truth about income taxes: that, *under the law,* they are not required to file and pay the tax. By this label the public is supposed to believe that "tax protesters" protest the law pursuant to weird and irresponsible ideas; when, in fact, they all obey the law. If they "protest" anything, it is the illegal enforcement.

However, not all "tax protesters" have an equal understanding as to why they are not required to file or pay. Some actually find it inconceivable that the law is actually enforced as illegally as it is, so they incorrectly theorize as to how the government surreptitiously got "jurisdiction" over them, which they then take unnecessary and often bizarre steps to avoid. Others explain their non-tax status in terms far more complex than necessary, and in so doing, actually attribute far more legality to the income tax than it deserves. While some "tax protesters" may be in the wrong pew, they are all in the right church. In describing what "tax protesters" allegedly believe, the government never ascribes to them the reasons presented in this book, but always attributes to them reasons that sound weird and irresponsible. For example, look how Commerce Clearing House describes tax protesters in the *Standard Federal Reporter,* 73rd Edition:

> According to the IRS, the Congress, and the courts, tax protestors represent a major threat to our voluntary compliance system of reporting revenue. To attack the variety of protest activities, significant deterrents to the use of tax protest tactics have been

added to the law in the form of an immediately assessable penalty against individuals filing tax protest documents, an imposition of damages for instituting proceedings in the Tax Court primarily for delay, and the imposition of damages where an appeal from the Tax Court is filed merely for delay. Arguments to the effect that the income tax is unconstitutional, or that compliance with the income tax law infringes upon one or more of the tax protestor's constitutional rights, have been summarily rejected by the courts. The constitutional rights which are allegedly violated include the right to freedom of religion, the Fifth Amendment privilege against self-discrimination, the Thirteenth Amendment's prohibition of involuntary servitude, and the claim that the Tax Court is an unconstitutional court. Some arguments have centered on the Federal Reserve System. Other forms of protest which frequently occur include the submission of a blank tax form by a protestor, the assertion that wages do not constitute income, erroneous claims of deductions, credits, or adjust-ments to income, and claims by organizations that they qualify as churches.

(As quoted from Paragraphs 400-402A.08)

Note that in describing "tax protesters," the Commerce Clearing House itself admits that the income tax is *voluntary,* but then refuses to ascribe this as one of the reasons "tax protesters" believe they are not required to pay the tax. Why do you suppose this is?

4. This book contains references to many individuals, including teachers, lawyers, students, etc., which obviously include members of both sexes. For ease in reading, however, (not meant to be discriminatory) I will use simply "he" or "she" rather than the coupled "he/she" when necessary, throughout the remaining chapters.

5. Obviously no one can be required to pay estimated taxes or submit to withholding, since this would amount to paying federal income taxes before they were assessed. (See Chapter 4 for more information.)

— CHAPTER 2 —

WHY AN INCOME TAX MUST BE VOLUNTARY

"Anything repugnant to the Constitution is null and void."
—Chief Justice John Marshall,
Marbury v. Madison, 1 Cr. 137 (1803)

There are a number of reasons why our income tax must be voluntary. Here are a few of them:

1. A compulsory income tax would violate all three taxing clauses of the Constitution, and would be *unconstitutional on this basis alone.*

2. The inquisitorial nature of an income tax would be repugnant to both the letter and spirit of the Bill of Rights—and the government could extract such a tax only by *disregarding the first Ten and other amendments.*

3. A compulsory income tax would also be *violative of the 16th Amendment*—the very Amendment which allegedly gave rise to the current tax.

4. Since nowhere in the Code is the word "income" defined, (Remember an "income tax" is a tax on "income," not on its sources) how can a valid law presume to tax *an abstract accounting concept* which the law itself does not (and can not) define—and which Congress *does not have the authority to define?*

5. The "law" applicable to income taxes is so incomprehensible that even tax professionals have to rely on a myriad of tax services to explain it. Thus, pursuant to a fundamental legal principle known to every law student, a *compulsory* income tax would have to be declared—by any court of integrity—"void for vagueness."

WHY THE INCOME TAX VIOLATES ALL OF THE TAXING CLAUSES IN THE CONSTITUTION

The Constitution provides for two broad classes of taxes—direct taxes and indirect taxes. All federal taxes (if compulsory) **must fall** into either one class or the other. The Constitution also lays down specific conditions pursuant to which each class must be levied. And federal taxes **not levied** pursuant **to these conditions would be automatically unconstitutional.**

DIRECT AND INDIRECT TAXES[1]

The Constitution makes important distinctions between direct and indirect taxes and sets up different conditions for their imposition. Few Americans are aware of these different forms of taxation, let alone their constitutional distinctions. Historically, with one notable exception (the 1895 *Pollack* decision) federal courts have obscured and/or misconstrued these distinctions. Today's courts, however, ignore them altogether—as if they didn't even exist.[2]

One such class of taxes, referred to in the Constitution as "direct taxes," is provided for in Article 1, Sections 2 and 9, clauses 3 and 4, which states that all "direct taxes shall be apportioned among the several states" pursuant to "a census or enumeration...directed to be taken." The only thing that the Constitution says twice, is that **direct taxes must be apportioned.**

Direct taxes are those paid directly to government and are imposed directly on individuals. They may be levied as a simple head or pole tax, or related to some other standard such as wealth, rank, profession or income. Federal taxes that fall into this category are income, estate and gift taxes; however, the U.S. Congress has, since 1861, totally ignored the constitutional restrictions that apply to direct taxes. All such taxes, however, according to the Constitution, have to be imposed in proportion to state population. This means that before any direct tax can be constitutionally imposed, the U.S. Congress has to do the following things before it can begin collecting such a tax. It first would have to:

1. Decide and incorporate within the law the exact dollar amount it intended to collect—such as, $100 million, $648 million, $1.10 trillion, etc., etc.;

2. Apportion a fixed percentage of that total against each state in proportion to its population;

3. Determine the different tax rates that would apply in each state, so that each state could collect the total amount apportioned.

Thus the government's ability to collect income taxes by way of apportionment would be far more complicated and harder (**And for darn good reasons!** Our Founding Fathers weren't fools, but represented the best minds that have ever been assembled on this continent) than how it goes about extracting direct taxes today.[3]

Indirect Taxes

Indirect taxes permit the government to tax people indirectly, by placing taxes on the things they buy. However the people can avoid such taxes by refusing to buy the things taxed. This, as our Founding Fathers recognized, gives to indirect taxes a self-correcting mechanism which guards against their abuse. However, since direct taxes can not be avoided, they possess *no similar self-correcting mechanism.* Our Founding Fathers believed that *some* protection had to be written into the law—and apportionment was the method devised. However, by tossing these protective provisions out the window, federal courts freed the government from all *effective* constitutional restrictions that apply to direct taxes, and permitted it to levy (with ease) direct taxes to whatever abusive and destructive levels it desired.[4]

The Constitution provides for indirect taxes (referring to them as "duties, imposts and excises") in Article 1, Sect. 8, Clause 1, and mandates that they must be levied on the basis of geographic uniformity. This simply means that an excise tax imposed on a product in one state must be imposed on a similar basis in all states. But unlike direct taxes, no total amount has to be first determined, nor does any specific amount have to be allocated to any state. Our Founding Fathers assumed that the government could run on indirect taxes alone, and would levy direct taxes only in time of war and other emergencies. They believed this because they gave the new government very few peacetime powers and duties. The bulk of what the federal government now spends money on is for expenditures nowhere authorized in the Constitution. (See pages 44-54 of *The Great Income Tax Hoax.)*

So all federal taxes can only be lawfully levied on either one basis or the other. If they represent a direct tax, they must be apportioned. If they represent an indirect tax, they must be geographically uniform. Since the income tax is levied neither as an apportioned, direct tax nor as a "duty, impost, or excise," it falls into none of the taxing clauses of the Constitution and because of this **it can not be levied as a mandatory tax!**

A COMPULSORY INCOME TAX IS REPUGNANT TO THE BILL OF RIGHTS

It would appear that the Bill of Rights now holds little interest for Americans since they are perfectly willing to jettison it in favor of the government's ability to extract income taxes from them. Had the Founding Fathers realized how little future generations of Americans might value these Rights, they probably wouldn't have bothered appending them to the Constitution.

How Federal Income Taxes Obliterated the 4th and 5th Amendments

In pursuit of income taxes, the government was willing to obliterate the three most important provisions in the Bill of Rights while eliminating the Constitution's most important feature. Those eliminated provisions are:

1. The Fourth Amendment, which mandates that the "right of the people to be secure in their persons, houses, and **papers**...shall not be violated" except "upon probable cause" supported by a valid warrant;

2. The Fifth Amendment provision which bars the government from compelling an American "to be a witness against himself"; and

3. The Fifth Amendment provision barring the government from depriving an American "of life, liberty, or property, without due process of law."

The Due Process Clause Of the Fifth Amendment

There can be no question that the "due process clause" is the most important feature of the Constitution, without which the rest of it isn't worth a hill of beans. This provision is what formerly set Americans apart from the rest of the peoples of the world—allowing Americans to walk freer and taller. In essence, what this provision says is that an American's property belongs to him and not the state, and before the state can take property away from an American, his government is required to first give him a hearing, before an impartial judge, and only then take his property pursuant to a court order. That's what "due process of law" means. The essence of "due process" is **a hearing**...a fair one, before an **impartial** judge... since a hearing before a partial and biased judge would be a "hearing" in name only...and would only make a **mockery of the right.** At such a hearing, the United States would have to prove its claim to property before it could take it, and the citizen would have an opportunity to refute the government's claim. That was how the Founding Fathers envisioned it. Constitutionally, that's the way it is supposed to be—but that's not the way it is anymore. **The "due process" clause is dead!**

America Without "Due Process"

To appreciate the importance of this clause, picture an America with every right guaranteed by the Constitution except this one. Americans would have the right of assembly, free speech, religion, and any other right you can think of, but the government could, if it wished, confiscate private property without hearings of any kind. Suppose the government could send U.S. marshals, armed not with court orders but only with guns, to drive Americans from their land and homes, which the government could then sell to satisfy alleged claims. Or suppose the government could send agents directly to banks and clean out accounts based only on the agent's unsupported claim that the money is owed the government. Or suppose they could send people to jail without trials. What would the Constitution be worth then? Would that sound like America? In case you are unaware of it, however, **this is America today.**[5]

IRS agents (not U.S. marshals, though they are occasionally involved) now seize property including land and homes without benefit of court hearings or court orders and auction them off to satisfy fictitious government claims. These government agents even go so far as to seize property belonging to one party to satisfy the alleged tax "owed" by another. In these instances denial of due process is compounded, since no proof is ever presented to any court that:

1. The tax allegedly owed is, in fact, owed, and
2. The property seized belonged not to the person possessing it, but to some other person allegedly owing the tax.

Such seizures get special media attention when IRS agents, for example, wipe out entire bank accounts belonging to children on the pretext that the money actually belonged to the parents, who they claim owed the government back income taxes and/or penalties. The public's indignation is aroused only because the children's money was earned babysitting, or mowing lawns or shoveling sidewalks. The IRS has received a lot of unfavorable publicity following a rash of such seizures (involving amounts of, for example, $17.00 and $22.00), and as a result, announced that, henceforth, it would limit such seizures to accounts containing only $100.00 or more! It should be observed that such seizures only evoke public criticism because the amounts are so small and belong to children. But the press and the public never question the **obvious illegality of such seizures on other grounds.** The press never even bothers reporting and or criticizing such seizures when the amounts involved are much larger and involve adults. (For more on this see Chapter 7.)

An October, 1988 *Reader's Digest* article by Sen. David Pryor (D., Ark.), Chairman of the Senate Finance Subcommittee on Internal Revenue Service Oversight, reported about Thomas L. Treadway, "owner of a successful trash management business" in Pipersville, PA. The article explained that on the very day the IRS informed Mr. Treadway that he owed the government $247,000, it began seizing his assets. Also "Claiming that Treadway was diverting assets to his friend and companion Shirley Lojeski, revenue officer George Jessup also seized $22,000

from her bank account and put a lien on her horse farm." Senator Pryor points out that, "There was absolutely no evidence to support the charge. But the seizure made it impossible for Lojeski to buy feed for her horses and she was threatened with foreclosure when she did not make her mortgage payments." Later, an IRS Appeals Officer found the assessment unreasonable, and the IRS was also forced to remove the liens on Miss Lojeski after she successfully brought suit in federal court. The court, however, denied Treadway and Lojeski recovery of any of the $75,000 they spent in legal and accounting fees, and it took the IRS four months to remove its liens.

While the Senator's article highlights this particular citizen's nightmare, there are thousands upon thousands (but even one would be too many) that go unreported, unpublicized and unnoticed. This occurs, on a daily basis, in a country that boasts of a commitment to due process and civil rights.

The Senator reported in that article that, "The IRS can seize a person's property or garnish his income just ten days after its official notice that a tax is due—even if the taxpayer disputes the assessment." He also reported that, "A judgment or court order is not required," and that "there is presently no formal process to appeal a wrongful collection action." Senator Pryor's misconception concerning what the IRS can and can not lawfully do, illustrates just how little our lawmakers know about the laws they pass—to say nothing about their lack of understanding regarding the meaning of constitutional rights. **There are no laws that allow the IRS to seize property in the manner described by Senator Pryor.** And if there were, they would be void for being repugnant to the Constitution—pursuant to the principle expressed by John Marshall in the famous *Marbury* v. *Madison* decision.[6]

EXTORTION—FEDERAL STYLE

In 1982, Congress added new penalty provisions to the Code, as embodied in sections 6700, 6701, 6702, 6703, and 6682 (Figure 2-1). Note that the section 6701(B) penalty relates to "an understatement of the liability" of a tax, while 6702(C) provides a penalty for those filing returns which do "not contain information on which the substantial correctness of the self-assesment may be judged" or where "on its face indicates that the self-assessment is substantially incorrect." Note too, that section 6703(D) places the burden of proof "as to whether or not any person is liable" for section 6700(A), 6701(B), and 6702(C) penalties, on the government. The following should be noted with respect to the wording of these sections:

1. For the first time, a specific reference and acknowledgement in the "law" itself that income taxes are

---

FIGURE 2-1   TITLE 26—INTERNAL REVENUE CODE   § 6700

A § 6700. **Promoting abusive tax shelters, etc.**

(a) Imposition of penalty

Any person who—
    (1)(A) organizes (or assists in the organization of)—
        (i) a partnership or other entity,
        (ii) any investment plan or arrangement, or
        (iii) any other plan or arrangement, or
    (B) participates in the sale of any interest in an entity or plan or arrangement referred to in subparagraph (A), and
    (2) makes or furnishes (in connection with such organization or sale)—
        (A) a statement with respect to the allowability of any deduction or credit, the excludability of any income, or the securing of any other tax benefit by reason of holding an interest in the entity or participating in the plan or arrangement which the person knows or has reason to known is false or fraudulent as to any material matter, or
        (B) a gross valuation overstatement as to any material matter,

shall pay a penalty equal to the greater of $1,000 or 10 percent of the gross income derived or to be derived by such person from such activity.

B § 6701. **Penalties for aiding and abetting understatement of tax liability**

(a) Imposition of penalty

Any person—
    (1) who aids or assists in, procures, or advises with respect to, the preparation or presentation of any portion of a return, affidavit, claim, or other document in connection with any matter arising under the internal revenue laws,
    (2) who knows that such portion will be used in connection with any material matter arising under the internal revenue laws, and
    (3) who knows that such portion (if so used) will result in an <u>understatement of the liability</u> for tax of another person,

shall pay a penalty with respect to each such document in the amount determined under subsection (b).

C § 6702. **Frivolous income tax return**

(a) Civil penalty

If—
    (1) any individual files what purports to be a return of the tax imposed by subtitle A but

which—
        (A) does not contain information on which the <u>substantial correctness</u> of the <u>self-assessment</u> may be judged, or
        (B) contains information that on its face indicates that the <u>self-assessment is substantially incorrect</u>; and

    (2) the conduct referred to in paragraph (1) is due to—
        (A) a position which is frivolous, or
        (B) a desire (which appears on the purported return) to delay or impede the administration of Federal income tax laws,

then such individual <u>shall</u> pay a penalty of $500.

§ 6703. **Rules applicable to penalties under sections 6700, 6701, and 6702**

(a) Burden of proof   **D**

In any proceeding involving the issue of whether or not any person <u>is liable</u> for a penalty under section 6700, 6701, or 6702, the burden <u>of proof</u> with respect to such issue shall be on <u>the Secretary</u>.

§ 6682. **False information with respect to withholding** **E**

(a) Civil penalty

In addition to any criminal penalty provided by law, if—
    (1) any individual makes a statement under section 3402 which results in a decrease in the amounts deducted and withheld under chapter 24, and
    (2) as of the time such statement was made, there was no reasonable basis for such statement,

such individual shall pay a penalty of $500 for such statement.

(b) Exception

The Secretary may waive (in whole or in part) the penalty imposed under subsection (a) if the taxes imposed with respect to the individual under subtitle A for the taxable year are equal to or less than the sum of—
    (1) the credits against such taxes allowed by part IV of subchapter A of chapter 1, and
    (2) the payments of estimated tax which are considered payments on account of such taxes.

These are laws?! What college professor will claim that such language is enforceable as "law"? With respect to Section 6702: What is "frivolous", or constitutes "a desire to delay or impede, and just who will make these determinations? With respect to Section 6682: What is a "reasonable basis" and just who will make that determination? Talk about "void for vagueness!" Who will now claim that we are a society of law and not men?

based solely on "self-assessment." This direct acknowledgement never appeared in the law before—since the principle was derived solely from the fact that the Code authorized *no other form of income tax assessment*. But now section 6702 officially confirms it—for whatever good that'll do. But this official acknowledgement regarding the "self-assessment" of income tax does not appear anywhere else in the Code with respect to *any other* federal tax!

2. Note that section 6702 states that the penalty only relates to "the tax *imposed* [emphasis added] by subtitle A," but not to any tax "liability" created in that subtitle. The reason for this omission is covered in Chapter 6 and reveals why section 6702, if mandatory, would be illegal—which is how it is being enforced.

3. Note the use of the word "shall" in "shall pay a penalty of $500." "Shall" in each case really means "may," because any other construction in connection with income taxes (see Chapter 3) would render the section unconstitutional.

4. Note further that section 6701 only applies "to an understatement of [a tax] liability"; which as Chapter 6 explains, means it can not apply to income taxes; while section 6703 applies only when a "person is liable for a penalty" under sections 6700, 6701 and 6702. But since no one is made "liable" for a penalty in any of those sections, section 6703 can't apply to any of them.

Figure 2-2 will, however, illustrate with what lawlessness these provisions are enforced by the government, and should dispel forever any naive belief that taxing statutes are enforced with any degree of honesty by the federal government. First of all, note that Mr. Ollman is informed that his "Form W-4 does not meet the requirements of Section 3402..." This claim is false since Mr. Ollman's Form W-4 *does meet* the requirements of Section 3402 (see Chapter 8). In any case, Mr. Olman is also informed that his "Form W-4 is not acceptable because we have no record of your 1986 income tax return on file." On this basis, Mr. Ollman is further informed that he is being made subject to a $500 civil penalty for false information with regard to withholding." It should be obvious from these two statements that the IRS had absolutely no evidence to substantiate its claim. The government *arbitrarily* claimed that the information on Mr. Ollman's 1987 W-4 was "false" simply because it had "no record of [his] 1986 income tax return on file." One does not need a high I.Q. to figure out that this provides *absolutely no basis* for concluding that *any* information on Mr. Ollman's 1987 W-4 was "false"—let alone provide a basis for a $500 civil penalty. In addition, Mr. Ollman signed his W-4s under "penalty of perjury"— would he have risked criminal prosecution for perjury if he, for a moment, did not believe the information that he supplied on his W-4 was truthful? And if the government

claims that the information was "false," then why did it not charge Ollman with perjury? In addition, did the faceless and nameless IRS agent who wrote Ollman's employer claiming that Ollman's Form W-4 was "incorrect" (and requesting that it be disregarded) ever similarly swear *under penalty of perjury* as to the truthfulness of *his* claim? So how can an unsigned and unsworn to statement of a phantom government employee (maybe a charlady) take precedence over a signed and sworn declaration of a private citizen? I challenge anyone to explain that! Also note that besides illegally extracting a $500 penalty (plus interest charges) the government has also instructed Ollman's employer to "disregard" his sworn W-4 and to "withhold tax as if the employee was single and claiming 1 withholding allowance." This is the document, remember, that the government told those students in Figure 1-3, note D (Chapter 1) by which employees "tell their employers how much to withhold from their pay." But obviously that statement was a lie! (So, what else is new?) If the government doesn't like what employees "tell" employers, then employers are told to disregard what they are told by employees. Therefore, since employees have no control over their wages, then who really owns their wages—them or the United States government? And, if the United States government now owns and controls the wages of American employees, then what have American employees become?

But the government did not only take $500 from Mr. Ollman, it seized (based on the claim of some Revenue Officer whose signature is hardly legible and who might now be employed pumping gas, see Figure 2-3) $1,936.80 in such penalties, plus interst (overlooking the additional $3,714.24 it illegally seized for taxes Ollman didn't owe)! Do you realize that there are thousands of people now serving time for stealing a whole lot less?

As shown by Figure 2-4, if victims do not pay up in 10 days, the IRS can begin confiscating anything they can get their hands on (including the victim's wages), to satisfy the totally fraudulent penalty imposed. To maintain a fiction of "due process," the government in its beneficence gives victims the "right" to bring a law suit in federal court to recover the funds illegally seized. However, since any such federal law suit would cost the victim far more in time and money (in courts that have already been stacked against him) than the fine itself, this amounts to nothing more than naked, mafia-like federal extortion. And if, in such a lawsuit, the victim raises valid legal arguments to contest the government's illegal seizure of his property, he risks being fined another $5,000 for raising "frivolous" arguments. Welcome to Amerika![7]

And while this goes on in America on a daily basis, college law professors give esoteric lectures to the nation's law students on the protection afforded Americans by the "due

FIGURE 2-2 Letter (A) is the letter sent to Mr. Ollman by the IRS claiming that his W-4 "did not meet the requirements of Section 3402"—it did. The letter also informs him that he will be fined $500. Letter (B) was sent to Mr. Ollman's employer, the U.S. Post Office, directing it to disregard "how much" Mr. Ollman told his employer "to withhold from his pay."

A.

Department of the Treasury
Internal Revenue Service

MEMPHIS, TN 37501

```
In reply refer to: 49753770
MAR. 18, 1988  LTR 1385C
129-42-0251  0000 00 300
                        02627
```

HOWARD HAL OLLMAN
BOX 52 2802
MIAMI FL 33152

```
        Form W-4 Dated:   Mar. 01, 1987
        Form W-4 Claimed:  Exempt
        Employer's Name:   United States Post Office
Employer Identification Number:  41-0760000
Control Document Locator Number:  49542-213-02714-7
```

Dear Howard Hal Ollman:

We reviewed your Form W-4 Employee's Withholding Allowance Certificate, that your employer forwarded to us in accordance with Section 31.3402(f)(2)-1(g) and Section 31.3402(f)(2)-1T of the Employment Tax Regulations.

Your Form W-4 does not meet the requirements of Section 3402 of the Internal Revenue Code and the related Employment Tax Regulations for the reason(s) given. We have, therefore, directed your employer to disregard (or to continue to disregard) your Form W-4 and withhold as if you were single and claiming 1 withholding allowance(s) until he or she receives a new Form W-4 from you claiming no more than that number of withholding allowances. If you choose to claim less than this number, you may do so without sending the new Form W-4 to us.

To file a new Form W-4 claiming more than that number of withholding allowances, or claiming exemption from withholding, you must furnish a written statement explaining your change in circumstances or any other reasons justifying the change. Send your new Form W-4 and your supporting statements directly to the address shown at the end of this letter or give it to your employer. If you send the Form W-4 to us, attach it to the enclosed copy of this letter. If you give it to your employer, he or she has been instructed not to honor it, but to send a copy of your new Form W-4 and supporting statement immediately to us. In the meantime, your employer must withhold on the basis of 1 withholding allowance(s) until he or she receives further instructions from us.

Your Form W-4 is not acceptable because we have no record of your 1986 income tax return on file.

                    ATTENTION

Section 6682 of the Internal Revenue Code provides a $500 civil penalty for false information with regard to withholding. Based on the information available to us, we are assessing the $500 penalty.

B.

Department of the Treasury
Internal Revenue Service

MEMPHIS, TN 37501

```
In reply refer to: 49753770
MAR. 18, 1988  LTR 1650C
41-0760000  0000 00 000
                        03015
```

UNITED STATES POST OFFICE
MN POSTAL DATA CENTER
TWIN CITIES MN 55111

```
Employee's Name:  Howard Hal Ollman
Employee's Social Security Number:  129-42-0251
Date Form W-4 Filed or Received in IRS:  Mar. 01, 1987
Form W-4 Claimed:  Exempt
Control Document Locator Number:  49542-213-02714-7
```

Dear Employer:

We have reviewed the Form W-4, Employee's Withholding Allowance Certificate, filed by your employee named above and have determined that it is incorrect. It does not conform with the requirements of Internal Revenue Code section 3402 and related Employment Tax Regulations. Therefore, disregard this employee's Form W-4 and withhold tax as if the employee is single and claiming 1 withholding allowances until you receive a new Form W-4 from your employee claiming no more than this number of withholding allowances.

If you receive or have already received a new Form W-4 claiming exemption from withholding or claiming more than this number of withholding allowances, do not honor it and do not send a copy to us. But if the employee gives you a statement justifying the change, send a copy of the new Form W-4 with the supporting statement immediately to our office address shown at the end of this letter. Please attach it to a copy of this letter. Continue withholding based on 1 withholding allowances until we notify you to do otherwise.

Copies of Forms W-4 sent direct to our office are considered filed with the IRS and should not be submitted again with your Forms 941, 941E, or 941M.

Please give a copy of this letter to your employee. We have also separately notified your employee of our instructions to you. If this employee no longer works for you, disregard this letter.

If you have any questions about this matter and want to call us at 901-365-5948, a W-4 representative will help you. This is not a toll-free number. Since there will be a long-distance charge if you are beyond the immediate dialing area of the service center, you may prefer to write to us. Attach this letter to your reply and include your telephone number, area code, and the most convenient time for us to call, if additional information is needed.

process" clause of the Constitution, and the American Civil Liberties Union (ACLU) jumps up and down and pounds its chest to remind us that it is ever watchful, lest our constitutional rights be eroded or violated.

So despite the due process clause of the Constitution and all of the slogans and trappings of justice with which American courthouses and courtrooms are adorned, the United States "acquires" property on a basis that differs little from how Ghengas Kahn "acquired" property or how some large and pugnacious caveman might have "acquired"

a thigh bone from someone smaller and less robust, living in the next cave.

In addition to all of the above, the IRS, when determining the tax a non-filer allegedly owes (which the law doesn't authorize it to do) often adds to that amount a 50 percent "civil fraud" penalty, the elements of which differ little from those constituting criminal tax evasion. Assuming that, in this latter case, the individual does not, within 90 days, choose to contest this penalty in a kangaroo "Tax Court" (which is not really a court at all, but merely another

FIGURE 2-3

Form **668-W** (Rev. September 1986)	Department of the Treasury — Internal Revenue Service **Notice of Levy on Wages, Salary, and Other Income**

Date: 11-24-87   District: Ft. Lauderdale, Fl.   Telephone number of IRS Office D. Tucker (305) 536-4872

Name and Address of Taxpayer

TO: Minneapolis Postal Data Center
U.S. Postal Service
Twin Cities, MN. 55111-9635
Att: Gen. Accounting - Payroll

Howard H. Ollman
8625 NW 8th St.
Miami, Fl. 33126
15675 sw 82 Cir Lan 33193-M17
#37   EL 591
                     1-5850

REPLY: IRS
51 SW 1st Ave, Room 400
Miami, Fl. 33130
Att: D. Tucker Stop 3180

Identifying Number(s)
129-42-0251
129-42-0251(N)

Kind of Tax	Tax Period Ended	Unpaid Balance of Assessment	Statutory Additions	Total
1040	12-31-82	$ 3,636.86	$ 77.38	$ 3,714.24
941	12-31-82	500.00	50.87	550.87
1040	12-31-83	500.00	232.94	732.94
1040	12-31-84	500.00	152.99	652.99
			Total amount due ▶	$5,651.04

Interest and late payment penalty have been figured to ___12-20-87___.

As required by the Internal Revenue Code, notice and demand for the above amount were made on the taxpayer, who neglected or refused to pay. The amount is unpaid and still due. Chapter 64 of the Internal Revenue Code provides a lien for the tax and statutory additions. Items levied to pay this are: (1) all wages and salary for personal services of this taxpayer that you now possess or for which you become obligated, from the date you receive this notice of levy until a release of levy is issued, and (2) other income belonging to this taxpayer that you now possess or for which you are obligated. These wages, salary, and other income are levied on only to the extent that they are not exempt from levy under Code section 6334 as shown in the instructions. Demand is made on you to pay the total amount due.

Signature of Service Representative

Title REVENUE OFFICER

administrative agency masquerading as a court) district courts will permit the IRS to proceed to confiscate property on the basis of **totally unproven civil fraud allegations,** and if the victim seeks a **hearing** in a district court to contest those allegations, **it will be denied.** The courts will then permit the IRS to seize property on the basis of totally unproven civil fraud allegations even though the statute (see Figure 2-5) clearly states that the government has the burden of proving civil fraud, but the government will be allowed to seize property even though the government *never meets that burden!*

Now in all the above instances, the government **seized property in payment of alleged income** taxes and **related fines and penalties** *without court hearings of any kind.* So it shouldn't take a particularly keen legal mind to figure out that any law that would authorize such seizures **would have to be illegal in view of the Constitution specifically prohibiting such governmental behavior.** So why isn't the law authorizing such seizures illegal—or unconstitutional? Why? Because there are no laws that authorize it! Remember, the income tax is **voluntary,** so if there were such laws, the payment of income taxes would be *mandatory,* not *voluntary.*

Nowhere in the Internal Revenue Code is the IRS (i.e., the government) authorized to seize property in the manner described above. The people responsible for drafting the Internal Revenue Code were smart enough not to put anything like that in the law, since if the Code did authorize such seizures, the Code would be unconstitutional for

---

FIGURE 2-4

```
                              004116  107  6501              RPT           ACR    REF #616
      Department of the Treasury
      Internal Revenue Service    P  900 240 802     If you have any questions, refer to this information:
                                                     Date of This Notice:  04-18-88      504    8819
                                                     Taxpayer Identifying Number: 129-42-0251   SV
      Past Due                                        Form       Tax Year Ended    Document Locator
      Final Notice (Notice of Intention to Levy)                                         Number
      Read Carefully
                                                       CIV PEN    12-31-87      49254-467-52020-8

           lll.ll.ll.ll.lll.ll.ll.ll.lll.ll.ll.ll.lll

      HOWARD H OLLMAN                                 Call:    1-800-424-1040
      PO BOX 522802
      MIAMI   FL  33152-2802                          or

                                                      Write:  Chief, Taxpayer Assistance Section
                                                              Internal Revenue Service Center
                                                              ATLANTA, GA  39901

                                                      If you write, be sure to attach the bottom part of this notice.
```

THIS IS YOUR FINAL NOTICE. YOUR FULL PAYMENT OF THE FEDERAL TAX SHOWN BELOW HAS STILL NOT BEEN RECEIVED. IF FULL PAYMENT IS NOT RECEIVED WITHIN TEN DAYS FROM THE DATE OF THIS NOTICE, WE WILL BEGIN ENFORCEMENT PROCEEDINGS.

A NOTICE OF FEDERAL TAX LIEN MAY BE FILED, WHICH IS A PUBLIC NOTICE THAT THERE IS A TAX LIEN AGAINST YOUR PROPERTY. AS PROVIDED BY SECTION 6331 OF THE INTERNAL REVENUE CODE, YOUR PROPERTY OR RIGHTS TO PROPERTY MAY BE SEIZED. THIS INCLUDES SALARY OR WAGES, BANK ACCOUNTS, COMMISSIONS, OR OTHER INCOME. REAL ESTATE AND PERSONAL PROPERTY SUCH AS AUTOMOBILES, MAY ALSO BE SEIZED AND SOLD TO PAY YOUR TAX.

[handwritten: AND WITHOUT ANY HEARING!]

TO PREVENT THIS ACTION, SEND FULL PAYMENT TODAY BY CHECK OR MONEY ORDER PAYABLE TO INTERNAL REVENUE SERVICE. WRITE YOUR TAXPAYER IDENTIFYING NUMBER ON YOUR PAYMENT. INCLUDE THE BOTTOM PART OF THIS NOTICE WITH YOUR PAYMENT SO WE CAN QUICKLY IDENTIFY AND CREDIT YOUR ACCOUNT.

WE HAVE CALCULATED PENALTY AND INTEREST AMOUNTS TO TEN DAYS FROM THE DATE OF THIS NOTICE. IF PAYMENT IS NOT RECEIVED BY THEN, ADDITIONAL INTEREST AND PENALTIES WILL BE CHARGED. THE FAILURE TO PAY PENALTY INCREASES FROM ONE HALF PERCENT PER MONTH TO ONE PERCENT PER MONTH AFTER THIS NOTICE.

IF YOU RECENTLY PAID THE AMOUNT DUE, OR IF YOU CANNOT PAY THIS AMOUNT IN FULL, CONTACT THE OFFICE SHOWN ABOVE TODAY.

```
TAX FORM NUMBER                                              CIV PEN
TAX PERIOD ENDED                                             12-31-87

BALANCE OF PRIOR ASSESSMENTS                                 $500.00
LATE PAYMENT PENALTY                                           $0.00
INTEREST                                                       $2.92

TOTAL AMOUNT DUE                                             $502.92
```

ENCLOSURES: **Reply within 10 days**
ENVELOPE   **to avoid enforcement action**
                               and additional penalties.

reasons that should already be apparent. "How," you ask, "can the IRS get away with it?" It can—only because federal judges are perfectly willing to disregard both the law, the Constitution, and their oaths of office.

HOW THE INCOME TAX VIOLATES THE "FIFTH"

There is probably more misunderstanding about the Fifth Amendment than anything else in the Constitution, due in large measure to the publicity it has received through television. Numerous labor racketeers, underworld characters, politicians, and other personalities have been seen and heard on the tube saying, "I plead the Fifth Amendment and respectfully refuse to answer the question on the grounds that the answer would tend to incriminate me," or words to that effect. Thus the public has come to regard the Fifth Amendment only with protection against "self-incrimination" and nothing more. However, apart from there being more to the Amendment than this, such a perception distorts it even further, since "self-incrimination" has nothing to do with this right. As a matter of fact, self-incrimination, is not even mentioned in the Amendment which states that "no person shall...be compelled in any criminal case to be a *witness against himself.*"

So the amendment declares that Americans cannot be compelled to be witnesses and give information about themselves, **whether or not such information is incriminating.** This means that under no circumstances can the United States require Americans to give information which can be used against them for alleged violations of civil or criminal statutes. Although the Fifth Amendment only mentions "criminal" matters, the Supreme Court (in *McCarthy* v. *Arndstein*, 266 US 34) ruled that the Fifth Amendment "applies alike to criminal and civil proceedings."

Self-incrimination has nothing to do with this Fifth Amendment right because Americans may not know what is incriminating in the information they give. Suppose some junkie spotting you on Times Square at 3:00 p.m. on Christmas Day, later tells the police that he met you there at that time for the purpose of purchasing drugs from you. Suppose later, the police ask you if you were at Times Square at that time—and you say, yes. You have obviously incriminated yourself without knowing it.

The Founding Fathers' abhorrence for compelling individuals to give information about themselves undoubtedly goes back to their abhorrence of the medieval rack, which was used to extract confessions and other information. Any process, therefore, by which the United States compels Americans to give information about

---

FIGURE 2-5
(from the Internal Revenue Code)

§ 7454. Burden of proof in fraud, foundation manager, and transferee cases

(a) Fraud

In any proceeding involving the issue whether the petitioner has been guilty of fraud with intent to evade tax, the burden of proof in respect of such issue shall be upon the Secretary.

---

themselves, which can later be used against them **in any manner**—either criminally or by way of civil fines and penalties—is nothing more than a manifestation of the "rack" syndrome, and is clearly barred by our Constitution.

How Americans Got Conned Out of a Right

The public's confusion concerning its Fifth Amendment right and the better known privilege against self-incrimination is due to the United States' success in getting the public to accept a limited privilege in exchange for a broad right. What enabled the government to do it is related to the American legal principle that "the state is entitled to everyone's testimony."

This is a good principle, designed to protect the innocent and convict the guilty. Suppose, for example, that you were charged with a crime, but the testimony of another could establish your innocence. Shouldn't you have the right to compel that person to testify to help prove your innocence? The answer is yes—which is why both parties to a trial have the power to subpoena witnesses. Without being subpoenaed, many potential witnesses might refuse to testify, but a subpoenaed witness risks being held in contempt of court for such refusal. Similarly, congressional committees (as well as grand juries) have the power to subpoena witnesses in connection with congressional investigations. However, in such investigations, those subpoenaed are not considered "targets:" Their testimony is wanted only because it might reflect on others or on the subject under investigation.

However, if, in this situation, questions are asked which answers might be self-incriminating to the witness, he or she can refuse to answer. In such instances, the witness claims, not his Fifth Amendment *right* not to be compelled to be a witness against himself (since in this case he was not subpoenaed for that purpose) but his Fifth Amendment *privilege* against self-incrimination, since in that setting, he has no right *not* to be a witness. Note that in one case we have the claim of a *right* which can have no exceptions, while in the other case we have the claim of a *privilege* which can have exceptions, such as the granting of immunity to compel testimony.

What has all this to do with income tax returns? Well, when you fill out a return, you agree to waive this right (you mean you didn't know?) and give the government permission to use all that informtion you supply against you—either criminally or civilly—in any manner it wishes. But not only that, you also give the United States permission to turn this information over to the States so that they can use it against you too! And you also give the United States permission to turn the information over to foreign governments so that they *too* can use the information against you. And you also give the United States permission to share your "private" financial affairs with numerous individuals and committees of government. This was how President Nixon was able to use IRS audits against those on his "enemies list" and how the Republicans found out about Senator Eagleton's psychological problems (which they then leaked to the press), from the medical deductions shown on his returns.

Figure 2-6 contains excerpts from Section 6103 of the Internal Revenue Code entitled "Confidential Disclosure of Return and Return Information." This is an extensive section of approximately 12 pages (of tightly spaced type) listing those individuals, committees and governments with whom the United States can share the contents of your tax return. For example, Section 6103(d)(2)(A) states that your return will be "open for inspection" by state governments in connection with their tax collection activities. And who can state governments share this information with? Section 6103(f)(1) lists specific committees of Congress such as: the House's Committee on Ways and Means, and the Senate's Committee on Finance and Congress' Joint Committee on Taxation, whose chairmen are authorized to request returns. But 6103(f)(3) provides that any other committee can get permission by resolutions passed by each body (and I have no doubt that this isn't too difficult to do). Paragraph 6103(g)(1) entitled "Disclosure to President and Certain Other Persons," authorizes the President or "such employee or employees of the White House Office, as the President may designate by name," to get "a return or return information." This section further authorizes the head of any federal agency and the FBI to get returns from the prior three years of anyone who is being considered for "appointment to a position in the executive or judicial branch." Section 6103(h) is one of the sections that provides that returns and return information can be turned over to the Department of Justice for use against filers.

For example, Section 6103(h) (2) provides that:
In a matter involving tax administration, a return or returns shall be open to inspection by or disclosure to officers and employees of the Department of Justice (including United States attorneys)...in, any

FIGURE 2-6
(portions extracted from the Internal Revenue Code)

Section 6103:

(d) Disclosure to State tax officials

(1) In general

Returns and return information with respect to taxes imposed by chapters 1, 2, 6, 11, 12, 21, 23, 24, 31, 32, 44, 51, and 52 and subchapter D of chapter 36 shall be open to inspection by, or disclosure to, any State agency, body, or commission, or its legal representative, which is charged under the laws of such State with responsibility for the administration of State tax laws for the purpose of, and only to the extent necessary in, the administration of such laws, including any procedures with respect to locating any person who may be entitled to a refund. Such inspection shall be permitted, or such disclosure made, only upon written request by the head of such agency, body, or commission, and only to the representatives of such agency, body, or commission designated in such written request as the individuals who are to inspect or to receive the returns or return information on behalf of such agency, body, or commission. Such representatives shall not include any individual who is the chief executive officer of such State or who is neither an employee or legal representative of such agency, body, or commission nor a person described in subsection (n). However, such return information shall not be disclosed to the extent that the Secretary determines that such disclosure would identify a confidential informant or seriously impair any civil or criminal tax investigation.

(2) Disclosure to State audit agencies

(A) In general

Any returns or return information obtained under paragraph (1) by any State agency, body, or commission may be open to inspection by, or disclosure to, officers and employees of the State audit agency for the purpose of, and only to the extent necessary in, making an audit of the State agency, body, or commission referred to in paragraph (1).

(f) Disclosure to Committees of Congress

(1) Committee on Ways and Means, Committee on Finance, and Joint Committee on Taxation

Upon written request from the chairman of the Committee on Ways and Means of the House of Representatives, the chairman of the Committee on Finance of the Senate, or the chairman of the Joint Committee on Taxation, the Secretary shall furnish such committee with any return or return information specified in such request, except that any return or return information which can be associated with, or otherwise identify, directly or indirectly, a particular taxpayer shall be furnished to such committee only when sitting in closed executive session unless such taxpayer otherwise consents in writing to such disclosure.

FIGURE 2-6 (continued)

(3) Other committees

Pursuant to an action by, and upon written request by the chairman of, a committee of the Senate or the House of Representatives (other than a committee specified in paragraph (1)) specially authorized to inspect any return or return information by a resolution of the Senate or the House of Representatives or, in the case of a joint committee (other than the joint committee specified in paragraph (1)) by concurrent resolution, the Secretary shall furnish such committee, or a duly authorized and designated subcommittee thereof, sitting in closed executive session, with any return or return information which such resolution authorizes the committee or subcommittee to inspect. Any resolution described in this paragraph shall specify the purpose for which the return or return information is to be furnished and that such information cannot reasonably be obtained from any other source.

g) Disclosure to President and certain other persons

(1) In general

Upon written request by the President, signed by him personally, the Secretary shall furnish to the President, or to such employee or employees of the White House Office as the President may designate by name in such request, a return or return information with respect to any taxpayer named in such request.

(h) Disclosure to certain Federal officers and employees for purposes of tax administration, etc.

(1) Department of the Treasury

Returns and return information shall, without written request, be open to inspection by or disclosure to officers and employees of the Department of the Treasury whose official duties require such inspection or disclosure for tax administration purposes.

(2) Department of Justice

In a matter involving tax administration, a return or return information shall be open to inspection by or disclosure to officers and employees of the Department of Justice (including United States attorneys) personally and directly engaged in, and solely for their use in, any proceeding before a Federal grand jury or preparation for any proceeding (or investigation which may result in such a proceeding) before a Federal grand jury or any Federal or State court.

(i) Disclosure to Federal officers or employees for administration of Federal laws not relating to tax administration

(1) Disclosure of returns and return information for use in criminal investigations

(A) In general

Except as provided in paragraph (6), any return or return information with respect to any specified taxable period or periods shall, pursuant to and upon the grant of an ex parte order by a Federal district court judge or magistrate under subparagraph (B), be open (but only to the extent necessary as provided in such order) to inspection

by, or disclosure to, officers and employees of any Federal agency who are personally and directly engaged in—

(i) preparation for any judicial or administrative proceeding pertaining to the enforcement of a specifically designated Federal criminal statute (not involving tax administration) to which the United States or such agency is or may be a party,

(ii) any investigation which may result in such a proceeding, or

(iii) any Federal grand jury proceeding pertaining to enforcement of such a criminal statute to which the United States or such agency is or may be a party,

solely for the use of such officers and employees in such preparation, investigation, or grand jury proceeding.

proceeding before a federal grand jury...or any Federal or State court.

So, the information given the IRS on income tax returns can be turned over to the Department of Justice and is used by it to get indictments and convictions against those who file. (The use of tax return information against filers *even in non tax cases,* is provided for in section 6103[i]) Do you really think that the United States has the legal power to force you to give such information to the Department of Justice? Of course not. But although the section appears to allow the Justice Department to use income tax returns in this manner (which it uses in practically all tax prosecutions), the section actually bars such use.

While it might not have come as a shock to you to discover that in filing a tax return you have "voluntarily" waived your right not to be a witness against yourself, federal courts have always known this, while in practice, they pretend not to. As long ago as 1928, in a case that should have ended the income tax (see Chapter 10) an honest Fourth Circuit Court of Appeals reversed an individual's conviction for failing to file an income tax return, because the court pointed out:

There can be no question that one who files a tax return under oath is a witness within the meaning of the Amendment.
Sullivan v. United States, 15 F2d 809

In 1976, the Supreme Court expressed the exact same view in *Garner* v. *United States,* 424 US 48 when it held:

The information revealed in the preparation and filing of an income tax return is, for Fifth Amendment analysis the testimony of a "witness" as that term is used herein.

Obviously, the witness referred to in both cases is the person filing the return and the person against whom such "testimony" will be used—is himself. So it should be clear that all those who file income tax returns, "willingly" surrender their Fifth Amendment right and agree to become witnesses against themselves.

But what about those, such as myself, who don't want to surrender that right—what happens to them? Well, they are sent to jail (some getting as much as five years, on five counts) as "tax protesters" by federal judges pledged to uphold the Constitution—a more meaningless oath can hardly be imagined—for allegedly violating Section 7203 (Figure 2-7) of the Internal Revenue Code, a section that does not even mention income taxes and could not apply to that tax for reasons (and there are others) that you already know.

And while all this is going on, college law professors lecture the nation's law students about the sanctity of this constitutional provision, while the ACLU thinks it's more important to fight for the rights of Nazis to march in Skokie, Illinois.

Your Miranda Warning

Since the government is going to use all the information on your income tax return against you, you are entitled to the same Miranda warning that all law enforcement officers give to those they arrest. Those arrested are warned that anything they say from that point on can and will be used against them. A taxpayer's "Miranda warning" is buried in a place that the IRS hopes the public will never look—in the

---

FIGURE 2-7

§ 7203. Willful failure to file return, supply information, or pay tax

Any person required under this title to pay any estimated tax or tax, or required by this title or by regulations made under authority thereof to make a return (other than a return required under authority of section 6015), keep any records, or supply any information, who willfully fails to pay such estimated tax or tax, make such return, keep such records, or supply such information, at the time or times required by law or regulations, shall, in addition to other penalties provided by law, be guilty of a misdemeanor and, upon conviction thereof, shall be fined not more than $25,000 ($100,000 in the case of a corporation), or imprisoned not more than 1 year, or both, together with the costs of prosecution. In the case of any person with respect to whom there is a failure to pay any estimated tax, this section shall not apply to such person with respect to such failure if there is no addition to tax under section 6654 or 6655 with respect to such failure.

"Paperwork and Reduction Act Notice" (Figure 2-8) that appears in the 1040 booklet that accompanies a return. Note that the notice says the return information may be given to:

the Department of Justice and to other Federal agencies, as provided by law. We may also give it to States, the District of Columbia, and U.S. commonwealths or possessions to carry out their laws. And we may give it to foreign governments because of tax treaties they have with the United States.

Now it should be obvious that the only reason that any one of the above agencies of government would want information from your tax return is to use that information against you—so how can you be *required* to supply it?

WHY YOU CAN GO TO PRISON FOR SENDING IN AN HONEST RETURN

Did you know that you could go to jail and/or be subject to fines and other penalties for sending in a totally accurate income tax return? Well you can. This apparent anomaly can occur in the following situations. Suppose that, though you send the federal government a totally accurate return, you leave material out of your State income tax return, and because State authorities can check your State return against your federal return (remember, you gave them permission), they discover the errors and/or omissions in your State return, and fine and/or prosecute you under State law, on the basis of the *accurate information* they got from your federal return.

Or, suppose you own income-producing property in Italy or some other foreign country, but haven't been entirely forthcoming in reporting it there (if such income is taxable there), while you have reported everything here. If the Italian government checks with the IRS, they could discover possible violations of Italian law, so the next time you visited Italy you could be picked up for tax evasion *there*, because you accurately reported your total income *here*. That illustrates for you how dangerous filing federal income tax returns can be. Even filing truthful ones can get you in trouble!

HOW THE INCOME TAX MAKES A MOCKERY OF THE FOURTH AMENDMENT

The Fourth Amendment to the Constitution states, in relevant part, that:

The right of the people to be secure in their person, houses, *papers*, and effects, against unreasonable searches and seizures shall not be violated. [emphasis added.]

A reasonable search is one where the government has probable cause to believe that one possesses something illegal, such as untaxed cigarettes, gambling paraphernalia, counterfeit or ransom money, or perhaps a murder weapon. A search warrant signed by a judge, based upon a showing that a reasonable probability exists that such items could be found in the place sought to be searched, allows law enforcement personnel to search private premises for the specific item which, if found, might indicate that a crime has been committed. But an IRS "search" through your books and records is a "fishing expedition"—pure and simple. That is, the government doesn't have any probable cause to believe that you did something wrong or that you swore falsely on your return, and, in addition, your books and records don't represent items of contraband. The IRS merely wants to fish through your personal records to see whether or not you **may** have done something wrong—such as swearing falsely on your return. Such "fishing expeditions" are **barred** by the Constitution as was clearly stated by the Supreme Court in the definitive *Boyd* decision, which held that:

> It does not require actual entry upon premises and search for and seizure of papers to constitute an unreasonable search and seizure within the meaning of the Fourth Amendment; a compulsory production of a private party's books and papers, to be used against himself or his property in a criminal or penal proceeding, or for a forfeiture, is within the spirit or meaning of the Amendment.

> **Boyd v. United States, 116 US 616**

Thus, the Supreme Court has ruled that your Fourth and Fifth Amendment rights provide ample grounds for keeping your financial records out of the hands of the IRS.

But the IRS knows this full well, and any taxpayer can easily avoid an IRS audit by simply refusing to attend or by using my two "magical questions" (see Chapter 9). For example, Section 342.12 of the IRS' own *Handbook For Special Agents* (Figure 2-9) states:

> An individual *may refuse* to exhibit his books and records for examination on the ground *that compelling him to do so violates his right against self-incrimination under the Fifth Amendment* and constitutes an *illegal search* and seizure under the Fourth Amendment ([8]) [emphasis added.]

In addition, this excerpt even acknowledges that

FIGURE 2-8

Privacy Act and Paperwork Reduction Act Notice

The Privacy Act of 1974 and Paperwork Reduction Act of 1980 say that when we ask you for information, we must tell you:

a. Our legal right to ask for the information.
b. What major purposes we have in asking for it, and how it will be used.
c. What could happen if we do not receive it.
d. Whether your response is voluntary, required to obtain a benefit, or mandatory under the law.

For the Internal Revenue Service, the laws include:

• Tax returns and any papers filed with them.
• Any questions we need to ask you so we can:

  Complete, correct, or process your return.

Figure your tax.
Collect tax, interest, or penalties.

Our legal right to ask for information is Internal Revenue Code sections 6001 and 6011 and their regulations. They say that you must file a return or statement with us for any tax you are liable for. Your response is mandatory under these sections. Code section 6109 and its regulations say that you must show your social security number on what you file. This is so we know who you are, and can process your return and papers.

You must fill in all parts of the tax form that apply to you. But you do not have to check the boxes for the Presidential Election Campaign Fund.

We ask for tax return information to carry out the Internal Revenue laws of the United States. We need it to figure and collect the right amount of tax.

We may give the information to the Department of Justice and to other Federal agencies, as provided by law. We may also give it to States, the District of Columbia, and U.S. commonwealths or possessions to carry out their tax laws. And we may give it to foreign governments because of tax treaties they have with the United States.

If you do not file a return, do not provide the information we ask for, or provide fraudulent information, the law provides that you may be charged penalties and, in certain cases, you may be subject to criminal prosecution. We may also have to disallow the exemptions, exclusions, credits, deductions, or adjustments shown on the tax return. This could make the tax higher or delay any refund. Interest may also be charged.

Please keep this notice with your records. It may help you if we ask you for other information. If you have questions about the rules for filing and giving information, please call or visit any Internal Revenue Service office.

A: You are required to file only if you wish to "obtain a benefit." If you do not want the "benefit" (whatever it is) you are obviously not "required" to file.
B: What "must" you file — a "return or statement?" The Notice does not say. In addition, are you concerned about "any tax" or the *income* tax? To what Federal tax, therefore, does the "any" apply? Does the Notice state *anywhere* that individuals are *required* to file *income* tax returns? Are you required to file returns for taxes you are not *liable* for? The Notice says *no*.
C: Can the Federal government *require* that you give information to all these government agencies so that they can use such information against you?
D: The "criminal prosecution" refers only to giving "fraudulent information." Where does the Notice tell you that you can be charged criminally or be subject to civil fraud penalties for giving *no* information?

individuals don't even have to turn over their records in response to an IRS summons!

Despite these acknowledgements, federal judges still order Americans to turn over books and records (especially if those summoned are unfamiliar with the above passages, and don't know how to claim their constitutional rights; though, even then, such claims are often ignored) to the IRS and often impose civil fines on those who don't. One individual told me that a New York district court judge fined him $150.00 per day for every day that he refused to turn over his private records to the IRS.

The point is that if there were any provision in the Internal Revenue Code that required Americans to turn over their private papers and records to the IRS, such a provision would render the Code unconstitutional, just as those IRS manuals say. But since no such provision is contained in the Code, it is not unconstitutional on this ground.

Incidentally, since the IRS' own manuals admit that Americans can not be compelled to turn over books and records, because the information can be used against them—the same reason also applies to income tax returns. If the government can't compel you to turn over books and records, obviously, it can't compel you to turn over a **summary of them,** which, after all, is what **an income tax return really is!**

How Surrendering One Right Compels You to Lose Another

It is possible (as the IRS manuals admit) to avoid audits completely. I have never been audited in my life (see Figure 2-10 for newspaper accounts of such IRS audit attempts). However, the government **punishes** those Americans who do not choose to be audited!

Once you file an income tax (waiving your Fifth Amendment right), swearing that you had a given amount of taxable "income" (you didn't, but were tricked into thinking so) less your related exemptions and deductions, the IRS takes the position that **unless you can prove your deductions,** they can re-compute your tax based only on the gross income you reported and can *disallow* all of your claimed exemptions and deductions! Thus if you refuse to submit to an audit on *constitutional grounds,* as those IRS manuals claim you have a perfect right to do, you are **punished for doing so** by having a higher tax (and additional penalties) levied against you. So, if the United States can fine you (by imposing higher taxes and other penalties) for claiming the constitutional rights *it claims you have*—then, obviously, you *don't* have those rights *at all!*

Handbook for Special Agents

FIGURE 2-9

342.12 *(1-18-80)*   9781
Books and Records of An Individual

(1) An individual taxpayer may refuse to exhibit his/her books and records for examination on the ground that compelling him/her to do so might violate his/her right against self-incrimination under the Fifth Amendment and constitute an illegal search and seizure under the Fourth Amendment. [*Boyd v. U.S.; U.S. v. Vadner*] However, in the absence of such claims, it is not error for a court to charge the jury that it may consider the refusal to produce books and records, in determining willfulness. [*Louis C. Smith v. U.S.; Beard v. U.S.; Olson v. U.S.; Myres v. U.S.*]

(2) The privilege against self-incrimination does not permit a taxpayer to refuse to obey a summons issued under IRC 7602 or a court order directing his/her appearance. He/she is required to appear and cannot use the Fifth Amendment as an excuse for failure to do so, although he/she may exercise it in connection with specific questions. [*Landy v. U.S.*] He/she cannot refuse to bring his/her records, but may decline to submit them for inspection on constitutional grounds. In the Vadner case, the gov-

ernment moved to hold a taxpayer in contempt of court for refusal to obey a court order to produce his/her books and records. He refused to submit them for inspection by the Government, basing his refusal on the Fifth Amendment. The court denied the motion to hold him in contempt, holding that disclosure of his assets would provide a starting point for a tax evasion case.

342.15 *(1-18-80)*   9781
Waiver of Constitutional Rights

(1) The privilege against self-incrimination must be specifically claimed, or it will be considered to have been waived. [*Lisansky v. U.S.*] In Nicola v. U.S. the taxpayer permitted a revenue agent to examine his books and records. The taxpayer was indicted for income tax evasion and invoked his constitutional rights under the Fifth Amendment for the first time at the trial, by objecting to the revenue agent's testimony concerning his findings. The court said, on the question of waiver:

"But he did not refuse to supply the information required. Did he waive his privilege? The constitutional guarantee is for the benefit of the witness and unless invoked is deemed to be waived. Vajtauer v. Commissioner of Immigration (supra). Was it necessary for the defendant to invoke it in the first place before the revenue agent or could he wait until his trial

on indictment for attempting to evade a part of his income tax? (Cases cited) *** it was necessary for him to claim immunity before the Government agent and refuse to produce his books. After the Government had gotten possession of the information with his consent, it was too late for him then to claim constitutional immunity."

(2) A taxpayer who makes verbal statements or gives testimony to agents during an investigation, or at a Tax Court trial, may still rely upon his/her constitutional privilege and refuse to testify at trial of his/her indictment for tax evasion. [*U.S. v. Vadner*] However, any statements inconsistent with his/her innocence may be used against him/her as admissions. [4 Wigmore, *Evidence,* (3d Ed.), Sec. 1048]

(3) If a witness has testified at a trial and voluntarily revealed incriminating facts, he/she cannot in the same proceeding avoid disclosure of the details. [*Rogers v. U.S.; Ballantyne v. U.S.*] However, waiver of constitutional rights will not lightly be inferred, and no specific language is required in asserting them. [*George Smith v. U.S.; Quinn v. U.S.; Emspak v. U.S.*] In the language of the Quinn case:

"It is agreed by all that a claim of privilege does not require any special combination of words. Plainly a witness need not have the skill of a lawyer to invoke the protection of the Self Incrimination Clause. *** As everyone agrees, no ritualistic formula is necessary in order to invoke the Privilege."

ADDITIONAL CONSTITUTIONAL RIGHTS ABOLISHED BY THE INCOME TAX

While the Constitution does not specifically say anything about an American's right to privacy, such a right has always been acknowledged.[9]

An American's right to privacy was provided for in the Ninth Amendment which states:

The enumeration in the Constitution, of certain rights, shall not be construed to deny or disparage others retained by the people.

Thus the Ninth Amendment guarantees a number of other rights which We the People retained for ourselves—one of them being the right to privacy. However, after filling out income tax returns, Americans have little privacy left. Suppose one's next door neighbor happens to be an IRS agent. It would be a simple matter for him to get your tax return to audit. After doing so, your next door neighbor would now know how much money you have in the bank, how much stock and bonds you own (by the interest and dividends you declare), whether you are seeing a doctor and/or psychiatrist (and perhaps *why*), how charitable you are (if, at all), and what charities you support, the companies in which you invest and those in which you might own an

interest (even a silent one), the banks you use, whether or not you were formerly married and to whom (by the alimony checks you either send or receive), whether you came from wealthy parents or grandparents who provided you with trust income, whether you have a foreign bank account, who your dentist is and whether or not you possibly wear dentures, how much of a mortgage you have, your religion, the professional magazines you subscribe to, whether you have property in other places, whether you have other children you are supporting, whether you are smart enough to sell stocks at a gain, or dumb like the rest of us and only take losses, whether you trade futures and how good you are at it, whether your trips were for business or pleasure, how much you have in treasury bills and mutual funds, what financial arrangement you are making for your retirement, the amount of pension money you receive, and so on and so on. The point is, how much privacy do you have left after you send in a tax return? The answer is none! Chances are the United States knows more about you than the Soviet Union knows about any one of its citizens. And you allegedly have a right to privacy and they don't!

Americans are also conned into believing that they have to give their Social Security number to just about anyone who asks—*but they don't*. Those who usually ask for your number include: stockbrokers, banks, employers, and those who pay commissions or royalties, etc. In this way, the government can simply punch a number into a computer

FIGURE 2-10
The Hartford Courant—Friday, December 17, 1976

Nonpayer's IRS Interview Taxing for Agents

By MARK MELADY

NORTH HAVEN -- Irwin A. Schiff, who passionately refuses to pay income tax because he claims his only source of income is federal promissory notes — more widely known as dollarbills — was summoned by the IRS Thursday for an examination of some tax records.

He showed up to answer the summons with four friends, five members of the press, two cardboard boxes marked "tax records and other secret stuff" and a copy of the U.S. Constitution.

The entourage was met by three apprehensive IRS agents and everyone adjourned to a little office, whereupon Schiff cordially said to the agents, "Sit down, make yourself comfortable, I've got some questions to ask."

From the proceedings that followed it was impossible to determine who was the summonor and who was the summonee.

Schiff, a Hamden investment and insurance specialist, has not paid any income tax since 1973. High among his multitude of reasons for skipping the annual mandatory event, is his insistence that he hasn't earned any money.

Federal reserve notes, commonly accepted as U.S. currency, are defined by Schiff as "accounts receivable."

Besides that, Schiff contends, paying income tax would implicate him in treasonous taxing and monetary policies that subvert our republican form of government and will lead to rioting, pillaging and bloodshed.

Rioting and pillaging aside, what the three IRS agents really wanted to see Thursday was a few re-

cords.

In May the IRS tried to go over Schiff's personal income through a conventional audit. When agent John F. O'Brien showed up at Schiff's home, however, he found reporters sitting around munching bagels and Schiff smiling over a tape recorder.

The audit attempt ended when Schiff asked O'Brien if anything he said during the audit could be used against him in court. O'Brien said it could. Schiff said that would violate his fifth amendment rights. O'Brien said he would be back.

But instead the IRS turned its keen attention to the corporation of which Schiff is president, Irwin A. Schiff Inc.

O'Brien began writing letters addressing Schiff as "Gentlemen" and attempting to arrange a convenient time to conduct an audit of Schiff Inc.

Schiff, the person, responded with "Dear John" letters telling O'Brien to be mindful of his dress because TV people would probably be present. He refused to meet in "the murky bowels" of the IRS.

The inability of both parties to agree on a time and place led to the IRS summons demanding Schiff be at the IRS office, murky or not, at 10 a.m. Thursday.

So there was Schiff, with a handkerchief in his breast pocket and the Constitution in his hand, lecturing polite O'Brien, who had dutifully sat down, about the law. The law, said Schiff, gives a taxpayer the right to investigate why the IRS has issued him a summons.

The law, according to Schiff, also prohibits the IRS from compelling a taxpayer to turn over records of a corporation in which   he is a sharehold-

er if the real intent is to audit the shareholder's personal income.

O'Brien told Schiff that one of the reasons the IRS was examining the record of Schiff Inc. was to review Schiff's personal income. Schiff felt compelled to read the agents the law concerning conspiracy to deprive someone of his Constitutional rights.

To enhance his investigation, Schiff said he had developed a public servant questionnaire, which he produced.

Schiff's first question to O'Brien was where he lived.

"You don't have to answer that," counseled agent Frank Trager, a grade school chum of Schiff's.

"I don't want to answer these questions," said O'Brien.

"You want to plead the Fifth then," said Schiff as he wrote on the questionnaire, "Fifth Amendment plea."

Meanwhile IRS Group Manager Peter Abbagnaro had excused himself from the room to see if he could find an IRS regulation that could reduce the number of people in the room, namely Schiff's four friends and the five members of the press.

He found one after a while and reported back to the gathering that the IRS had the right to set the time, place and conditions for an examination.

The negotiations over the conditions of the meeting turned out to be moot, however, because Schiff claimed he needed to question a supervisory agent who was not present to complete his investigation.

and find the total amount that each American earns, and from what sources. If the United States can legally require this kind of reporting from those who pay out money, why can't it require the same thing from those who take money in? In this way the United States might "require" all sellers of goods and services to get Social Security numbers of those to whom they sell their goods and services to. Not only could that number be punched in to get a total of what every American earns, but also what they spend it on![10]

Unfortunately, the majority of Americans undoubtedly believe that the federal government has the legal power to do this, not withstanding the rights Americans retained in the Ninth Amendment. The fact of the matter is that there is nothing in our tax laws that requires Americans to give their Social Security number to anyone except the Social Security Administration—and that is only for the purpose of claiming benefits. If our tax laws really required turning over all this kind of information to the government, such laws would be an unconstitutional invasion of an American's constitutional right to privacy—and anyone who can't see that should be declared legally blind.

Since no law requires such reporting, though Americans have been fooled into thinking there is, the law is not unconstitutional on this ground.

Notice (Figure 2-11) that the instructions from the Department of Health and Human Services (HEW), say that neither one's card nor Social Security number is "required" to be given to one's employer. The instructions merely say that one "show" it to him. But HEW doesn't say that one is "required" to do so. Naturally, those reading the card will get that impression—which is what the government wants—but the instructions themselves say no such thing. Presumably an employee can simply "flash" his card at his new employer as he walks in. Notice, however, that HEW specifically states that while private organizations may ask you for your card, "such use is [not] required by law." Then why do banks and brokerage firms insist that you give them your number, by telling you that the law "requires" them to get it? Obviously, the government misleads them so that they, in turn, can mislead you. Notice further that even "Federal, State or local government(s)" that ask you for your number "must tell you whether giving it is mandatory or voluntary" (along with a few other things). This obviously applies to the federal government as well, when it asks for your number on a tax return. But since it doesn't tell you whether giving it "is mandatory or voluntary"—it is breaking the law. But what does breaking one more law mean to the federal government?

FIGURE 2-11
(Reproduced as printed on the back of the stub containing my Social Security card and information.)

Your Social Security Card
The Social Security number shown on your card is yours alone. Record your number elsewhere for safekeeping.

If you lose your card or change your name, you will need to file a new application and submit evidence of identity to obtain a replacement or corrected card. You may also have to submit evidence of U.S. citizenship or legal alien status. Contact any Social Security office immediately to find out what you need to do to obtain a replacement or corrected card with the same number.

Show your card to your employer when you start a new job and make sure your employer copies the number and name correctly so that your earnings will be recorded correctly.

Some private organizations use Social Security numbers for recordkeeping purposes. Such use is neither required nor prohibited by Federal law. The use of a person's Social Security number by such an organization for its own records is purely a private matter between the organization and the person. Knowing your number does not allow these organizations to get information from your Social Security records.

Any Federal, State, or local government agency that asks for your number must tell you whether giving it is mandatory or voluntary, tell you of its authority for requesting the number, and tell you how the number will be used.

If you are an alien legally in the U.S. but you do not have permission to work in this country, your Social Security card will be marked "NOT VALID FOR EMPLOYMENT." U.S. immigration officials will be notified if the number is used for unauthorized employment.

Contact any Social Security office immediately if you:
● are unable to work because of a severe disability expected to last a year or more.
● are 62 or older—to ask about possible retirement benefits.
● are within 3 months of age 65, even if you don't plan to retire—to sign up for Medicare.

OTHER AMENDMENTS
ABOLISHED BY THE INCOME TAX

In order for the government to continue illegally extorting income taxes from a misinformed and intimidated public, it must abolish, whenever possible, any likelihood of its learning the truth. It seeks to do this by stamping out such First Amendment rights as: freedom of speech and the press, the "right of the people peaceably to assemble and to petition the government for a redress of grievances." It also does it by conducting illegal trials in violation of the Sixth Amendment, and by imposing excessive fines in violation of the Eighth Amendment. It has thrown out the Tenth Amendment completely; since in enforcing the tax, the United States recognizes not a single right that has been "reserved to the States respectively, or to the people," and has also discarded the Thirteenth Amendment, which outlawed "involuntary servitude" along with slavery.

Abolishing First Amendment Rights

Figure 2-12 is the actual reproduction from my trial

FIGURE 2-12   F-71W   DECEMBER 18, 1985

```
                                                            6

 1              THE COURT:  Let me finish and I'll ask
 2    you if you have any questions.
 3              Fourth, the defendant shall, during
 4    the period of probation, not associate or maintain
 5    any relationship with any group which advocates or
 6    promotes the noncompliance or violation,
 7    noncompliance or the violation of tax laws.
 8              Fifth, the defendant shall not
 9    participate nor involve himself, nor promote any
10    meeting, in the form of groups formed or brought
11    together in the form of seminars, media events of
12    any sort, or any kind of activity on any group basis
13    which advocates or which promotes the noncompliance
14    with, or the violation of the tax laws.
15              My purpose in the terms and conditions
16    of probation, Mr. Schiff, is as an alternative to a
17    longer period of incarceration to attempt to rectify
18    what you have done in the past with respect to the
19    spreading of the seed of noncompliance in violation
20    of the tax laws.  And it is intended as an
21    alternative to isolating you from that kind of
22    activity, not only for the sake of the community and
23    its members whom you might otherwise, and in my
24    judgment, have mislead to their potential detriment,
25    but is also intended to afford you the kind of
```

transcript of the special conditions of probation as they were being imposed upon me in open court by Federal Judge Peter C. Dorsey. Note that pursuant to the Fifth condition, I am not to "participate nor involve" myself in, "nor promote any meeting...formed or brought together in the form of seminars, media events of any sort, or any kind of activity on any group basis which advocates or which promotes the noncompliance with, or the violation of tax laws."

Note that Judge Dorsey has set up two different conditions, one dealing with promoting "**noncompliance** of tax law" and the other dealing with promoting "**violation** of tax law." What's the difference? Obviously, if promoting "**noncompliance** of tax law" was the same thing as promoting "**violation** of tax law," Judge Dorsey would not have made the distinction. So even if I merely **attended** a meeting, let alone speak, that was **not** "brought together" to promote "**violation** of the tax laws" but merely "**noncompliance**" of them, I run the risk of being "violated" and sent back to prison. But on what basis is a group "brought together" to promote "noncompliance" of laws which, admittedly, are based on "voluntary compliance?" Would I risk being sent back to jail if I organized a meeting in which I merely read those government documents shown in Chapter 1? Wouldn't the government argue that people had been "brought together" for the purpose of "promot(ing) noncompliance?" If not, why would Judge Dorsey have included such language in his conditions? And parole and probation "violation" hearings are conducted without juries, with the guilt of the alleged violator left solely to the discretion of the judge conducting the hearing—and in my case that would be Judge Dorsey. It should also be observed that this condition was cleverly worded so as to avoid any appearance of overtly depriving me of my right to speak—since this First Amendment right has been well publicized and there is an abundance of case law protecting it. However, by tying my probation to such unlitigated and conveniently vague and arbitrary conditions as "participate...involve...promote... brought together..." my right to speak was as effectively curtailed (actually, more so) than if that right had been directly abridged—which the court, for obvious reasons, was not inclined to do.

The point is that while parolees and those on probation do not have all the rights of other Americans (principally they have travel and reporting restriction, they can't own firearms, associate with other felons and vote), their First Amendment rights are still supposed to be unimpaired.[11] But what is even more ludicrous is, that while the Court seeks to curtail basic freedoms in relationship to an alleged advocacy and promotion of "noncompliance"—which must obviously be something less serious than the advocacy and promotion of "violation of law,"—the Supreme Court in

Brandenburg v. *Ohio*, 395 U.S. 444 (1969) ruled that *even the "advocacy" of violation of law is constitutionally protected* and that any state statute that sought to "punish" such advocacy "falls within the condemnation of the First and Fourteenth Amendments." So what would that make a Federal court's attempt to seek curtailment of First Amendment rights—under threat of imprisonment— contingent on an even *lesser* standard?[12]

To really see how far down the road of despotism the United States has travelled, compare what the court is trying to do here to the following observations by Justice Louis Brandeis in another Supreme Court decision, *Whitney* v. *California*, 274 U.S. 357, 376-77, in which he stated:

> Every denunciation of existing law tends in some measure to increase the probability that there will be violation of it.
> Those who won our independence by revolution were not cowards. They did not fear political change. They did not exalt order at the cost of liberty. To courageous, self-reliant men, with confidence in the power of free and fearless reasoning applied through the processes of popular government, no danger flowing from speech can be deemed clear and present...the remedy to be applied is more speech, not enforced silence.

Apparently, we are no longer governed by people who believe in such principles. I included passages from both of these Supreme Court cases in my appeal to the district court when I sought to have these obviously illegal conditions vacated, but to no avail. If my conviction is not reversed on other grounds[13] I will have to challenge these conditions in higher courts.

However, it is also clear from the following remarks of the court why the government engineered my conviction in the first place:

> "My purpose in the terms and conditions of probation, Mr. Schiff, is an alternative to a longer period of incarceration to attempt to rectify what you have done in the past with respect to the spreading of the seed of noncompliance in violation of the tax laws."

Of course, I have never advocated "violation of the tax laws" (and the court knew it) and there cannot be any such thing as "spreading the seed of noncompliance" in connection with laws which even the government admits, are based on "voluntary compliance." And in addition, such prohibitions had nothing to do with the underlying offenses for which I was allegedly convicted. It is also clear from Judge Dorsey's remarks just *why* I was convicted of those offenses. The government could *now* threaten me with imprisonment for conduct which is not only *not otherwise punishable* under our laws—but, in reality, is *constitutionally protected!*

PROOF THAT THE FIRST AMENDMENT IS DEAD IN AMERICA

On August 8, 1985 and again on August 26, 1987 the Seventh Circuit Court of Appeals affirmed restraining orders (*U.S.* v. *White,* 769 F.2d 511 and *U.S.* v. *Kaun,* 827 F2d 1144) enjoining the Minnesota Society for Educated Citizens from (among other things) teaching that "wages, salaries or other compensation for labor or services are exempt from federal income taxation or any other such frivolous claim with respect to the scope of federal income taxation."

Well, as a matter of fact, the Society was right (if anything, it didn't go far enough) and so its claim was certainly not "frivolous"—but even that is beside the point. Even if wages were income, how can an American be enjoined from arguing otherwise? Does an American have the right to put out a pamphlet declaring that the sun revolves around the earth, that black is white, or that he or she is the living God? Would the government care? Would anybody really care or pay attention? Americans certainly have the right to be wrong and/or even allege nonsense. Presumably if one advocates nonsense, no one pays attention or somebody else will refute it. So what would motivate a federal court to totally disregard the First Amendment and ban a pamphlet claiming that wages are not taxable as income?[14] Because the pamphlet obviously *made sense* and undoubtedly **proved** that wages are not income within the meaning of the law. So, while American courts presumably protect First Amendment rights to the extent that practically anything is printable—such protection does not include the right of people to argue that *wages are not income.*

To sustain their outrageous gag orders, the courts invoked Code Sections 6700 (Figure 2-1) and 7408, shown in Figure 2-13. You will note that Code section 6700 clearly deals with the marketing of such tax shelters as those associated with gas and oil exploration, real estate syndication, computer leasing, coal and other such limited partnerships, where participants make investments on the basis of promoters promising write-offs of as much as five for one. That is, where individuals are solicited on the basis that a $10,000 investment could generate as much as $50,000 in initial tax deductions. Applying this Section to the marketing of *printed matter* relating to what the author or authors *believe* are taxable within the meaning of the tax laws *themselves,* clearly amounts to nothing more than blatant judicial fraud. But as you can further see, section

7408 only applies to those taxes for which one can be "liable," and as Chapter 6 makes clear; this *can not apply to income taxes.* So, in discarding the First Amendment, the courts invoked two Code sections that were not even applicable.

FIGURE 2-13
(from the Internal Revenue Code)

§ 7408. Action to enjoin promoters of abusive tax shelters, etc.

(a) Authority to seek injunction

A civil action in the name of the United States to enjoin any person from further engaging in conduct subject to penalty under section 6700 (relating to penalty for promoting abusive tax shelters, etc.) or section 6701 (relating to penalties for aiding and abetting understatement of tax liability) may be commenced at the request of the Secretary. Any action under this section shall be brought in the district court of the United States for the district in which such person resides, has his principal place of business, or has engaged in conduct subject to penalty under section 6700 or section 6701. The court may exercise its jurisdiction over such action (as provided in section 7402(a)) separate and apart from any other action brought by the United States against such person.

(b) Adjudication and decree

In any action under subsection (a), if the court finds—

(1) that the person has engaged in any conduct subject to penalty under section 6700 (relating to penalty for promoting abusive tax shelters, etc.) or section 6701 (relating to penalties for aiding and abetting understatement of tax liability), and

(2) that injunctive relief is appropriate to prevent recurrence of such conduct,

the court may enjoin such person from engaging in such conduct or in any other activity subject to penalty under section 6700 or section 6701.

In 1634, an ecclesiastical court found the great Italian scientist, Galileo, guilty of teaching that the earth revolved around the sun, instead of the other way around. So it put Galileo under house arrest (where he remained the last seven years of his life) and barred him from making such frivolous claims. So it is clear, that in many respects, American courts—the Constitution notwithstanding—are no better than the one Galileo faced in the 17th century.

It is also amusing to note that in the *Kaun* decision the court stated: "The government may ban forms of communications more likely to deceive the public than to inform it." Obviously, if this doctrine were applied to the federal government itself almost *nothing*—either verbal or written—would ever make it out of Washington, D.C. For a chilling insight into arbitrary and totally asinine and hyper-critical federal court decisions, I recommend these gems (and their underlying cases) to you, and to the ACLU— **where were you when these cases were being decided?**

In my book, *The Great Income Tax Hoax,* I made *the same argument.* So why wasn't my book banned? My argument was made in a formalized book which sold in bookstores and on which I was able to focus some publicity. The government could not risk enjoining its distribution in the same way that it might a pamphlet or a packet of material put out by a small local group whose efforts might be maligned by some autocratic judge as being the nonsensical and anti-social work of disgruntled and misguided "tax protesters." In my case, instead of banning my books (which it would dare not do), the government, *instead,* sought to both discredit them and impede their distribution **by imprisoning me** on trumped up charges of tax evasion.

Ignoring a Little Known and Publicized Right

The First Amendment also provides that Americans can "petition the Government for a redress of grievances." After I was convicted in 1980 of failing to file income tax returns for the years 1974 and 1975 (I did file returns, but claimed the Fifth Amendment to each question. So I was sent to jail, not for filing, but for claiming a constitutional right!), I petitioned the government pursuant to this right, and explained that I had been imprisoned for failing to file income tax returns; therefore, I asked my government (by sending copies to the President, the Commissioner of Internal Revenue, the Supreme Court, and my congressman) to explain to me:

1. How I could file a federal income tax return without waiving any of my constitutional rights.
2. Whether the government could compel me to pay a tax levied in violation of the three taxing clauses of the Constitution.
3. That if the tax were not being levied in violation of those clauses, then to please identify for me the specific constitutional clause or clauses that governed its imposition.

Nobody answered me but you might want to petition your government by similarly exercising your First Amendment right, and see how far *you* get!

AMERICA—SERFDOM REINSTITUTED

At my "Untax Seminars" which I conducted all around the country, I would have fun finding someone in the audience who owned a service business, to question. One time I asked the owner of an auto repair service: "What would you do if you got a call from the U.S. Army telling you that they were sending over some trucks that needed repairs and they wanted you to do it. Would you do it?"

"Well, if they were going to pay me, sure."
"No, they're not going to pay you, but they want you to fix them anyway. Would you do it?"
"Of course not."
"Why not?"
"Because, I don't work for nothing."
"Are you sure about that?"
"Of course, I'm sure."
"How many employees do you have?"
"Twelve."
"Do you withhold taxes from those employees and remit them to the government?"
"Yes, I do."
"Does the government pay you for doing it?"
"No, they don't."
"Well, if the government can make you collect taxes for nothing, why can't it make you repair trucks for nothing?"

And, of course, nobody could answer that question.

The fact is that if the government could legally make Americans, at considerable expense to themselves, collect taxes for nothing, then it could make them provide almost any other service for nothing too. The constitutional amendments that would protect the public from such attempted government behavior are the Fifth, Ninth, Tenth and more specifically the Thirteenth, which says in relevant part that:

> Neither slavery nor *involuntary servitude,* except as a punishment for a crime...shall exist within the United States. [emphasis added.]

If the United States could make you perform services for nothing, then it would be holding you in "involuntary servitude" in direct violation of this Amendment, which, among other things, is why there is no law requiring employers or anyone else to withhold income taxes for the government. I never withheld income taxes including Social Security taxes (which, despite its name, is just another income tax.[15]), nor did I ever provide W-9's to those to whom I paid commissions, nor did I ever report such payments to the government. The government knew it and never did anything about it. Collecting taxes is the government's business, not mine. (How to go about doing this is more fully explained in Chapter 8.)

But in a larger sense, taxes have made serfs out of all Americans, whether they perform unpaid services for the government or not. In 1944, the 1974 Nobel Prize winner for economics, Fredich A. von Hayek, wrote *The Road to*

Serfdom. Well, Americans are no longer on that road, they've arrived!

Unlike medieval serfs who generally had 25 percent of their productivity confiscated by the Lord of the Manor, Americans now have about 50 percent of their earnings confiscated by government in the form of one kind of tax or another. Americans are only directly conscious of the taxes taken from their pay and they generally overlook the taxes they pay in the form of the employer's portion of Social Security which is also taken out of the worker's productivity; property taxes passed on to them in the form of higher rent, and other city and state excise, sales and income taxes; the considerable federal excise taxes they pay when they purchase gasoline, tobacco, and alcoholic products, and imported goods; and such nondeductible business expenses as the cost of going to and from work, and the substantially higher interest rates (which are nothing more than another disguised federal tax[16]). Americans must now pay over what they paid up until a generation ago; and without taking into consideration additional civil fines and penalties.

If you add up all of the above, you will see that fully half of what the average American earns today is confiscated from him in the form of one kind of tax or another. What does this mean?

It means that the average American now works for the government, not for himself. The half of his earnings that government now *permits him to keep* just about covers his *necessities* of food, clothing, shelter, transportation, and insurance. In many cases, it doesn't even cover that! That is why the nation's homeless have now risen to epidemic proportions; that is why so many wives are now forced to work; and why singles in increasing numbers are forced to move back in with ma and pa, or look for roommates. In other words, the money which many Americans now get to keep is little more than what is absolutely essential for them **just to keep on working!** The government confiscates that portion of their productivity that might have gone for comforts and luxuries and in many cases, even necessities.

Remember, even plantation owners provided their slaves with food, clothing, shelter and medical care. If this is all that Americans can now buy with the money they earn (while turning the rest over to government), then what have Americans become?

It was Karl Marx who concocted the surplus value theory of labor, according to which greedy capitalists exploited the working classes by confiscating from them their surplus labor value, while leaving them with only enough to buy back life's barest necessities. While Marx's theory does not at all describe the economics of a free market, it pretty much describes what has happened in America, except the exploiters are not greedy capitalists—**it is government!**

PURSUIT OF WHAT HAPPINESS?

The Declaration of Independence states that "all men are created equal" and that "they are endowed by their Creator with certain unalienable Rights" and that among those rights are "Life, Liberty, and the **Pursuit of Happiness.**" Well, how can any Americans "pursue happiness" (forgetting the other two) if they have to be pack rats for Uncle Sam? We are being mislead into believing that we must save all of our receipts, to keep detailed records (which otherwise we might not have any interest in doing), and must organize our lives and investment decisions around arbitrary and capricious tax laws.

When the Tax Reform Act of 1986 became law, every major weekly news and business magazine ran feature stories as to what Americans would now have to do to take advantage of or accommodate to the new law. I remember one magazine listing some 18 things, including re-mortgaging one's home to accommodate more favorably to new interest provisions, rearranging one's retirement program, and manipulating information with respect to one's vacation home. But no one questioned the right of the government to suddenly force Americans to incur new costs and make all kinds of financial changes in their lives, simply because the government **decided to change the tax laws.**

A few years ago, while listening to President Reagan give a State of the Union speech, he practically knocked me over when he said:

> You know, America is not like other countries. In America the government can only exercise those powers given to it in the Constitution. And in America it is the government that is the servant of the people, and the people its master.

And I said, "Does he really believe that?" I mean, that is the way it was *supposed* to be. That's the way our Founding Fathers envisioned government and they referred to it as being, "the servant of the people." But that was at a time when Americans knew something (and cared) about individual liberty, the role of government, and what powers were granted to it under the Constitution. Sadly, Americans don't have the vaguest idea about such things anymore, nor do they understand the concept of individual liberty and how it exists in opposition to government power. If the federal government would only do today what it is authorized to do by the Constitution, the federal budget would be reduced by some $500 billion in the twinkling of an eye.

And as far as the government in America being the "servant of the people," since when do masters account to their servants concerning how they spend their money? And what master ever went trembling to his servant with his books and records fearful lest his servant might not find everything in order and to his liking? Can you conceive of Daniel Boone, Davey Crockett, Wyatt Earp, or any one of America's Founding Fathers ever doing such a thing? What kind of jellyfish have Americans been turned into?

THE SIXTEENTH AMENDMENT— GOVERNMENT IGNORES THAT TOO

The Sixteenth Amendment provides that:
The Congress shall have power to lay and collect taxes on incomes, from whatever source derived, without apportionment among the several States, and without regard to any census or enumeration.

Since the Constitution had to be *specifically amended* to provide for an income tax, your suspicions should be aroused concerning the *underlying legality of such a tax.* The Constitution did not have to be amended to provide for other kinds of taxes such as alcohol and tobacco taxes. So why did it have to be amended to provide for an income tax? The government and its courts have always contended that the 16th Amendment provided the legal basis for the current tax[17], and I doubt that there is a law student in the country who isn't taught that the current income tax is based on the Sixteenth Amendment. The truth is, however, that the income tax is enforced in *defiance* of that Amendment.

The Supreme Court Declares An Income Tax Unconstitutional

In what was undoubtedly its finest hour, the Supreme Court in 1895 declared the income tax of 1894 unconstitutional. In *Pollack* v. *Farmer's Loan & Trust Company*[18] the Supreme Court did an exhaustive review of the taxing provisions in the Constitution, their historic underpinnings, and a number of prior Supreme Court decisions involving federal taxes, and refused to go along with them. In so doing, it declared the Income Tax Act of 1894 unconstitutional, for want of apportionment.

So for the next 17 years, congressmen, starting initially with extremists on the left (who saw it as a soak-the-rich tax and presented it that way[19]), but gathering more and more support over the years, finally passed the tax in 1909 and the legally ratified it in 1912. However, recent research casts substantial doubt on the legality of that ratification.[20]

You will note from the Amendment's language, that Congress apparently believed that it had amended the apportionment provisions of the Constitution with respect to income taxes, and that's what every law school student in the country is taught (if they are taught anything at all about the law's history). But that isn't so!

The constitutionality of the tax was almost immediately attacked, which culminated in the *Brushaber* decision, decided January 24, 1916. This is the decision that the United States always cites when it claims that the Supreme Court declared an income tax constitutional—except it never discloses the reasons supporting that decision.

The Supreme Court Rules That The Sixteenth Amendment Did Not Amend The Constitution but Merely Established The Income Tax as an Indirect, Excise Tax

Strange to say in *Brushaber* v. *Union Pacific RR*, 240 US 1 the Supreme Court ruled that "the Amendment contains nothing repudiating or challenging the ruling in the Pollack case" (see page 19 which means that the Pollack decision is still good law); nor that the Amendment *changed the Constitution* or gave the government *any new taxing powers* (see pages 11, 12, 13, and 14).

What the Supreme Court said in *Brushaber* (an extremely confusing case to understand) was that:

1. "Taxation on income was in its nature an **excise** [tax] entitled to be enforced as such" (at pages 16 and 17), and

2. "The whole purpose of the Amendment was to relieve all income taxes when imposed from apportionment from a **consideration of the source** whence the income was derived." [emphasis added.]

Essentially, what the Supreme court said was that an "income" tax was an *excise* tax that could be levied on "income" *separated* from its "source." As you will discover, this only occurs in connection with corporate income and can not occur in connection with money received by individuals. When individuals pay an "income" tax, they actually do not. They, unlike a corporation, pay a tax directly on **sources** of "income," such as wages, dividends, interest, alimony, etc., etc. As a result, individuals do not pay an "income" tax at all—that is, a tax on "income" "relieve(d)...from a consideration of the source" but they pay a tax *directly on their* **sources** **of income.** The Supreme Court said in *Brushaber* that the Sixteenth Amendment was designed to eliminate a direct tax **on** wages, dividends, interest, and only tax profits "derived" **from** such sources. A tax *on* interest is not the same thing as a tax on the profits derived *from* interest—though the government seeks to enforce the income tax as if they *both meant the same thing!*

In other words, the Sixteenth Amendment gave the government the right to levy an *excise* tax on income *separated from its sources* (which only occurs when a corporation determines its profit on the basis of a profit and loss statement). So an "income" tax can only be levied as an *excise tax* on corporate profits in the exact same manner as "income" was taxed in connection with The Corporation Excise Tax of 1909—the forerunner of the current income tax.

So instead of levying the income tax as an excise tax on corporate profits, as laid down by *Brushaber;* the government levies the tax, with respect to individuals, as a direct tax *on* their *sources* of income (which, pursuant to Pollack, can only be done on the basis of apportionment); and with respect to corporations, as a direct tax on their profits, and not as an *excise* on them. So nobody, neither individuals nor corporations, has to pay such a tax.

The Income Tax Law Does Not Even Define What It Purports To Tax

As you can see, the Sixteenth Amendment only gave the government the right to tax "income" (whatever that term legally means), but did not give the government the right to tax wages, interest, rent, alimony, dividends, or anything else, without apportionment. If you notice, all government documents claim to tax "income *from*" something, and do not claim to be putting a tax *on* anything—which is a subtle but technically accurate distinction that few even *notice or understand!* So the question is—what exactly is the "income" that the government was given the power to tax without apportionment? Well in *United States* v. *Ballard,* 535 F2d 400 (1940 at page 404) the Circuit Court of Appeals correctly observed that "The general term 'income' is not defined in the Internal Revenue Code." The absence of any such definition in the Code and the *legal inability of Congress to supply one* is a factor of fundamental importance that few in America are **even remotely aware of.** The Supreme Court in *Eisner* v. *Macomber, 252* US 189 (at page 206) explains why this is so:

> In order, therefore, that the clauses cited from Article I of the Constitution may have proper force and effect...it becomes essential to distinguish between what is and is not 'income'...**Congress cannot by any definition it may adopt conclude the matter,** since it cannot by legislation alter the Constitution. (emphasis added)

The reason that the Court said that is because the meaning of what is taxable as "income" as used in the Constitution (the 16th Amendment) **can only be defined by the Supreme Court,** and once that Court defines it, **that**

concludes the matter, and that is the **only thing** that can constitute "income" as that term is used in the Constitution. "Income" *is a constitutional term*—so its meaning **can not legally be changed or tampered with** (to any degree!) **by Congress,** which is why, Congress can not, as it now does, keep changing its meaning by saying that one year one thing is taxable as "income," while the following year something else is taxable as "income."

Suppose the Constitution gave Congress the right to tax "horses"—could Congress keep changing its meaning so that different animals or things fall within the definition of a "horse?" Could Congress one year define a horse as an animal that walks on two legs, but in another year define it as an animal that walks on four legs but has a large hump on its back, etc., etc.? The point is that once the Supreme Court defined what a "horse" was, that would, for tax purposes, conclude the matter—and all that Congress could do from that point on is simply change the *rate of tax* on horses, but not the definition of a horse. The same holds true concerning what is constitutionally taxable as "income."

When the current income tax law was being originally debated in the United States Senate, Iowa Senator Cummins, the bill's chief Senate advocate, was asked by Senator Williams of Mississippi, "Does the Senator think that it is useless in a tax bill to try to define the thing you propose to tax?" Cummins answered, "Mr. President, I do think in this instance that it is worse than useless; I think it is dangerous."[21]

However, I do not see how Congress can legally pass *a tax bill* without itself clearly defining that which it seeks *to tax.* This principle was established as early as 1904 when the Supreme Court said in *Spreckles Sugar Refining Co.* v. *McClain,* 192 US 397 (at page 416) that a "citizen is exempt from taxation, unless the same is imposed by clear and unequivocal language." (This alone should brand the income tax illegal).

In any case, during the period between 1912 and 1921, the Supreme Court sought to hammer out the meaning of "income" and in *Merchant's Loan & Trust Company* v. *Smietanka,* 255 US 509 (1921) laid out its most comprehensive definition (at pages 518, 519) when it held:

> There would seem to be no room to doubt that the word [income] must be given the **same meaning** in all of the Income Tax Acts of Congress that was given to it **in the Corporation Excise Tax Act** and that what that meaning is **has now become definitely settled by decisions of the court.** (emphasis added)

So by 1921 what "income" (as used in the Sixteenth Amendment) meant, had finally become "settled by

FIGURE 2-14

§ 6053. Reporting of tips

(a) Reports by employees

Every employee who, in the course of his employment by an employer, receives in any calendar month tips which are wages (as defined in section 3121(a) or section 3401(a)) or which are compensation (as defined in section 3231(e)) shall report all such tips in one or more written statements furnished to his employer on or before the 10th day following such month. Such statements shall be furnished by the employee under such regulations, at such other times before such 10th day, and in such form and manner, as may be prescribed by the Secretary.

decisions" of the Supreme Court. And that word had "the same meaning" as the word meant "in the Corporation Excise Tax Act" of 1909. So if you have no "income" that would be subject to tax under the Corporation Excise Tax of 1909, *you can have no "income" that is subject to an income tax today!* And **nothing that was received by private persons was taxable as "income" under that Act, so nothing received by private persons can be taxable as "income" today!** But, while corporations have "income" that could be subject to an "income" tax, their "income" (actually their profit) is not subject to the current tax, because it has not been constitutionally imposed either in the form of a uniform excise tax[22] or as an apportioned direct tax. In essence, America doesn't even have an "income" tax—it has a PROFITS TAX! And since an individual does not generate an accounting "profit" (in order to do that individuals would have to be permitted to deduct *all expenditures* such as food, clothing, shelter, medical costs, depreciation of themselves over their working life, and the amortization of the cost of their own education and training) he can have no "profit" that can be subject to a "profits" tax—that he has been conned into thinking is an "income" tax.

PROOF THAT THERE IS A "PROFITS" TAX—NOT AN "INCOME" TAX

It has been widely publicized that many American corporations pay no income tax at all. I believe that General Dynamics, a corporation that generates approximately $7 billion in annual income, was (and perhaps still is) one of those. Well those American corporations that pay no income taxes *certainly have an income*—or else they would have to close their doors. So, why don't they pay a tax on that *income*—if we have an "income" tax? They don't pay any income taxes because they don't show a *profit!* If they show a profit they pay a tax *on that profit*—which is proof that what we have is a **profits tax**—not an income tax. Yet

individuals, unlike corporations, are conned into paying a tax on their income—regardless of whether or not they have a profit!

What is being **illegally enforced** against individuals is an *unapportioned direct tax* on their sources of income, and what is being **illegally enforced** against corporations is an *unapportioned direct tax* on their profits, instead of a *uniform excise tax* on those profits. All of this, of course, would be as illegal as a three dollar bill if the tax were not **voluntary,** both with respect to individuals and corporations—which, of course, explains why the government insists that the income tax is based on "voluntary compliance"!

ADDITIONALLY, THE "LAW" SHOULD BE "VOID FOR VAGUENESS"

As if all of the above weren't enough to brand the income tax illegal, the "law" itself (if it weren't voluntary) would be "void for vagueness"—as expressed in *Spreckles,* supra. There is literally not a man alive who really understands this "law" or could figure out everybody's tax without help from explanatory materials—which lay people simply do not have or even know about. Why should the public have to hire experts to help them figure out their taxes? If they have to, then the law must be obviously void on its very face.

Just try figuring out what section 6053 means. (Figure 2-14) This section has to do with withholding taxes from tip income. Nobody has to do it, but the IRS relies on this section to claim that people do. Notice that this section only applies to "tips received as *wages*" and not tips received as *gratuities*—the basis on which tips are received. But if you tried to figure out what this section means by referring to the sections being referred to within the section itself, you would be hopelessly lost before you ever got into the third referred-to section.

In addition, people can only challenge arbitrary and capriciously-determined IRS deficiency assessments by going to "Tax Court," if they don't want to first pay the claimed additional taxes and *penalties* on them and sue in a district court for a refund. Though the IRS wins in 85 percent of those cases, the people still win 15 percent of the time. This means that in at least 15 percent of those cases the IRS must not have known what the laws meant. And people who challenge Tax Court decisions in the Appeals Court occasionally get their "Tax Court" decisions reversed—which means that even "Tax Court" judges don't know what the law means. So if IRS professionals and "Tax Court" judges" don't know what the law is, how is the public supposed to know? Do you think that people have this kind of trouble figuring out what they owe in connection with the liquor, gasoline and tobacco taxes?

Incidentally, if a citizen decides to challenge the imposition by the IRS of additional taxes and penalties in "Tax Court," that "court" has 232 Rules *of its own* that a citizen is presumed to know. You can be sure that those IRS lawyers who will be opposing you in "Tax Court" know them. You can also be sure that they know how to use each and every one of them against those confused and befuddled taxpayers who happen to wander in.

Now that you know that the payment of income taxes *is* voluntary, and *why* it is voluntary, let's turn to the "law" itself, and see just how the IRS, the Department of Justice and the Federal judiciary all go about *subverting it*—and what you can do about it!

NOTES TO CHAPTER 2

1. For a thorough, in-depth analysis of the history of the income and other federal taxes and how and why the Constitution made these taxing distinctions, and how federal courts at first scuttled, then retrieved and then again scuttled these constitutional distinctions, read: Schiff, Irwin, *The Great Income Tax Hoax.* (Hamden Ct.: Freedom Books, 1985).

2. Yet, "No provision of the Constitution is designed to be without effect," *Marbury* v. *Madison,* 1 Cr. 137. Today, however, numerous provisions of the Constitution are **totally** without effect.

3. The last time the federal government apportioned a direct tax occurred on August 5, 1861. To see the actual laws apportioning federal taxes in 1798, 1813, 1815 and 1861 see Chapter 6 of *The Great Income Tax Hoax,* "Federal Real Estate Taxes—How They Were Levied and Collected."

4. Theoretically, another restraint might be that they would be voted out of office if they raised direct taxes too high. But Congress, by putting some 40,000,000 Americans on a monthly federal dole, has largely eliminated this restraint. Millions of well-organized and voting Americans are now far more interested in how much money and other benefits they get from the federal government than how much money the government takes in taxes from other Americans to pay for those benefits.

5. Trials given to so called "tax protesters" for example are "trials" in name only. Judges merely go through the motions (there a few exceptions but not many) and routinely misstate the law. In my case Federal Judge Peter C. Dorsey reinstructed my jury (after it had announced itself deadlocked) that it could find me guilty of tax evasion even if the government did not prove all elements of the crime and even if the government did not prove a single act of tax evasion—yet despite such an outrageous recharge, the Second Circuit upheld my conviction. In addition, no federal judge, by law, has jurisdiction to prosecute anyone for any alleged income tax "crime" (see Chapter 11). In reality, Americans are now literally thrown in jail without lawful trials of any kind.

6. Based upon its uncovering so much IRS abuse, Pryor's Subcommittee recommended the much heralded Taxpayer Bill of Rights, which never made it out of Congress in its original, publicized form. Initially the Bill was supposedly going to require IRS agents to truthfully tell taxpayers their "rights" in connection with income taxes. That would have meant that the IRS would have to inform the public that they did not have to file or pay the tax—which is why, predictably, this was eliminated from the Bill's final version, Besides, there is a law now on the books that the IRS and the courts already ignore that would have accomplished the Bill's intended purpose. In addition, taxpayers already have a Bill of Rights that theoretically gives them all the protection they need; it's the one in the Constitution, but that's the last place Congress would look.

7. According to Senator Pryor's article, there were 2.1 million of such salary liens alone last year. Thus it would be pretty safe to assume that there were at least three million IRS liens of all types that were illegal; though some, in payment of mandatory taxes pursuant to court orders (which the IRS does get on rare occasions) could have been legal. Since America suffered approximately three million robberies in 1986, it would appear that the United States Government alone committed at least as many robberies as all the nation's other crooks and thieves *combined.*

8. Notice how the handbook misstates the reason. The issue is one of being "a witness against oneself," not one of "self-incrimination."

9. Fundamental right to privacy is rooted in Amendments: 1, 4, 5, and 9. *Ben Shalom* v. *Secretary of the Army,* D.C. Wis 1982, 489 F. Supp. 964; by the 9th and 14th Amendments, *Martin* v. *Covington,* Ky. DC. Ky 1982.541 F. Supp. 803; is on an equal or possibly more elevated pedestal than certain other constitutional rights and should be treated with as much deference as free speech, *Merricken* v. *Cressman,* D.C. Pa. 1973, 364 F.Supp. 913.

10. And if you don't think that this is where the nation is heading, then you're oblivious to what's going on.

11. In *Sobel* v. *Reed,* 327 F. Supp. 1294 (1971) the court stated "While there are differences between prisoners and parolees... there are none that diminish the protection enjoyed by the latter under the First Amendment;" citing *Hyland* v. *Procunier,* 311 F.Supp. 749; *United States Exrel Sperling* v. *Fitzpatrich* 426 F2d 1161; but here the courts are *not talking about First Amendment rights exercised to expose illegal government taxing activities. For those purposes,* the courts have no problem sharply curtailing First Amendment rights.

12. To see how Judge Dorsey sought (and apparently succeeded) in illegally imposing these conditions during my parole (when they had not been made parole conditions) see Chapter 10.

13. See Chapter 10 for an update on my attempt to both vacate my conviction and/or vacate my conditions of probation.

14. As Justice Brandeis noted in *Whitney,* supra, "Compare Thomas Jefferson: 'We have nothing to fear from the demoralizing reasonings of some, if others are left free to demonstrate their errors and especially when the law stands ready to punish the first criminal act produced by the false reasonings; *these are safer corrections than the conscience of the judge'.*" [emphasis added.]

15. See Schiff, Irwin, *The Social Security Swindle: How Anybody Can Drop Out.* (Hamden, CT, Freedom Books. 1984)

16. Not too long ago Americans could get mortgages between 4-6%. Now they pay from 10-15%. The difference is a federal tax. When Congress creates budget deficits, because it has neither the courage nor the integrity to tax the public to the same extent with which it spends their money, it literally creates money out of thin air. (They don't really "borrow," see Chapter 2 of the Biggest Con) which is the inflation that forces up both prices and interest rates. The higher interest rates that Americans are now paying are the result of continual government budgetary deficits. So instead of Congress taxing the public openly and honestly, it taxes them covertly and dishonestly in the form of higher interest payments they are forced to pay in lieu of direct taxation.

17. This is what the courts had universally contended until relatively recently. Since so called "tax protesters" can now present irrefutable evidence that the income tax is enforced in violation of that Amendment, the courts have shifted their ground and now contend that the 16th Amendment is *unnecessary* for the collection of income taxes. A case in point is *Firacola* v. *Commissioner,* 751 F.2d 85, in which the Second Circuit claimed that "In the case of

New York ex rel. Cohn v. Graves, 330 U.S. 308 (1937), the Supreme Court in effect overruled Pollack, and in so doing rendered the Sixteenth Amendment unnecessary..." How could a lone court decision render the "Sixteenth Amendment unnecessary"—even overlooking the fact that the decision in question *had absolutely nothing to do with federal income taxes?* Yet such an asinine contention by the Second Circuit was actually used against me in my recent "trial!"

18. Actually this case involved two Supreme Court decisions, 157 US 429 and 158 US 601 and The Great Income Tax Hoax devotes an entire chapter, 45 pages, just analyzing this magnificent but much maligned decision alone.

19. In 1916 only 362,970 Americans out of a population of 102 million paid the tax—or less than 4/10 of one percent. The $4,000 family exemption eliminated most Americans from the tax—which is why they voted for the Amendment. They had been told that an income tax "Would only fall on rich people." Would they have voted for the Amendment if they thought that working men and women would be taxed at rates of 30% and 40%, plus *excessive civil penalties?* The original rates for the tax started at 1% and worked its way up to 7% on amounts over $500,000—which is the equivalent of $20 million in today's depreciated, funny money.

20. See Benson, William, *The Law That Never Was.* (South Holland, Michigan: Constitutional Research Associates, 1985).

21. For a more extensive treatment of these revealing (and sometimes unbelievable) debates, see *The Great Income Tax Hoax,* pages 150-167.

22. *The Philadelphia Inquirer* (P.O. Box 8263, Philadelphia, PA 19101) ran a series in 1988 entitled, "The Great Tax Giveaway," in which it exposed how hundreds of exceptions to the 1986 tax law were written into that law to eliminate taxes for particular friends of our lawmakers. (These articles were compiled into a 36 page supplement which, I'm sure, you can still get by writing to the Inquirer). The point is, these exceptions prove that the current income tax was not imposed **uniformly.** Since it was neither imposed *uniformly* or on the basis of *apportionment,* **it was imposed in violation of all of the taxing clauses of the Constitution,** and therefore would be unconstitutional if it were mandatory!

— CHAPTER 3 —
THE INTERNAL REVENUE CODE: A MASTERPIECE OF DECEPTION

"When there is an income tax, the just man will pay more and the unjust man less on the same amount of income."
—The Republic, (Book 1) Plato

In order to appreciate the enormity of the government's deception with respect to income taxes, we have to examine the "law" itself.[1] All statutes (including those dealing with taxes) when enacted by Congress are identified by number as General Statutes of the United States. Those that relate to taxes are integrated into the Internal Revenue Code, or more accurately, the Internal Revenue Code of 1954 and become identified by section or subsection. General Statutes are also grouped by subject matter into "Titles" which may or may not be further enacted into positive law. The U.S. Criminal Code, for example, is referred to as Title 18, while The Internal Revenue Code is referred to as Title 26. However, while Title 18 was formally enacted by Congress into positive law and can be legally referred to as Title 18, the Internal Revenue Code has never been so enacted and can not legally be referred to as Title 26. However, the U.S. Department of Justice and the courts completely close their eyes to this distinction and treat the Internal Revenue Code of 1954 just as though it were positive law.

Now the Internal Revenue Code is divided into six major subtitles, labeled as follows:
1. Subtitle A: Income Tax
2. Subtitle B: Estate and Gift Taxes
3. Subtitle C: Employment Taxes and Collection of Income Tax At Source
4. Subtitle D: Miscellaneous Excise Taxes
5. Subtitle E: Alcohol, Tobacco, and Certain Other Excise Taxes
6. Subtitle F: Procedure and Administration

There are 54 chapters in those six subtitles and they contain approximately 400 parts, subparts and subchapters which are further broken down into approximately 8,000 Code sections. By far the largest chapter in the Code is the first one which deals with income taxes. It contains 1,399 separate Code sections—not counting subsections. For example, in the 1985 Code, section 103 (of Chapter 1) entitled "Interest on certain government obligations" had approximately 343 subsections, sub-subsections, subsub-subsections, and subsubsub-subsections! By contrast, the smallest chapter in the Code, Chapter 41, entitled "Public Charities," had only one Code section. But that Code section had approximately 50 subsections, sub-subsections, subsub-subsections, and subsubsub-subsections!

WHO ARE RESPONSIBLE?

It would be important for this nation, I suggest, to track down those responsible for writing the Internal Revenue Code, since it is clear that it was deliberately written to deceive us. It would be extremely enlightening, I suggest, to discover under whose direction it was done, and who and how many were involved.

Consider these facts. While no Code section requires anyone to file income tax returns, the Code makes it appear otherwise. While no Code section creates an income tax "liability," the Code makes it appear otherwise. While no Code section requires anyone to pay this tax, the Code make it appear otherwise. While no code section authorizes the IRS to get any documents in connection with income taxes, the Code makes it appear otherwise. While no Code section authorizes the IRS to seize any money or property in connection with income taxes (with the sole exception of money withheld from wages and not remitted to the Government), the Code makes it appear otherwise. While no Code section contains any criminal or civil penalties in connection with income taxes, the Code makes it appear otherwise.

To successfully perpetrate a scam of this magnitude, hundreds of Code sections had to be written and pieced together in such a way that, while no section technically misstated the law or violated the Constitution, the sections, individually and collectively, had to be written to allow the Government to do just that. Those responsible knew exactly what they were doing. They were creating the greatest deception the world has ever seen.

KEY CODE SECTIONS

We begin our understanding of how this was accomplished by initially focusing on four key Internal Revenue Service Code sections: 6001, 6011, 6012, and 6020, all of which are shown in Figure 3-1. Code sections 6001 and 6011 are the two sections which the Government has quoted (falsely) for years in its Privacy Act Notice (Figure 2-8). The government sought to mislead the public into believing that these two sections created some type of filing "requirement" in connection with income taxes. While you can see how the IRS scrupulously avoided using the

FIGURE 3-1

§ 6001. Notice or regulations requiring records, statements, and special returns

Every person <u>liable</u> for any tax imposed by this title, or for the collection thereof, shall keep such records, render such statements, make such returns, and comply with such rules and regulations as the Secretary may from time to time prescribe. Whenever in the judgment of the Secretary it is necessary, he may require any person, by notice served upon such person or by regulations, to make such returns, render such statements, or keep such records, as the Secretary deems sufficient to show whether or not such person is liable for tax under this title. The only records which an employer shall be required to keep under this section in connection with charged tips shall be charge receipts, records necessary to comply with section 6053(c), and copies of statements furnished by employees under section 6053(a).

§ 6011. General requirement of return, statement, or list

(a) General rule

When required by regulations prescribed by the Secretary any person <u>made liable</u> for any tax imposed by this title, or for the collection thereof, shall make a return or statement according to the forms and regulations prescribed by the Secretary. Every person required to make a return or statement shall include therein the information required by such forms or regulations.

(f) Income, estate, and gift taxes

For requirement that returns of income, estate, and gift taxes be made <u>whether or not</u> there is tax <u>liability</u>, see subparts B and C.

§ 6012. Persons required to make returns of income

(a) General rule

Returns with respect to income taxes under subtitle <u>A shall be made</u> by the following:

(1)(A) Every individual having for the taxable year gross income which equals or exceeds the exemption amount, except that a return shall not be required of an individual—

the taxable year, less than the sum of twice the exemption amount plus the basic standard deduction applicable to a joint return, but only if such individual and his spouse, at the close of the taxable year, had the same household as their home.

§ 6020. Returns prepared for or executed by Secretary

(a) Preparation of return by Secretary

If any person shall fail to make a return required by this title or by regulations prescribed thereunder, but shall consent to disclose all information necessary for the preparation thereof, then, and in that case, the Secretary may prepare such return, which, being-signed by such person, may be received by the Secretary as the return of such person.

(b) Execution of return by Secretary

(1) Authority of Secretary to execute return

If any person fails to make any return (other than a declaration of estimated tax required under section 6015) required by any internal revenue law or regulation made thereunder at the time prescribed therefor, or makes, willfully or otherwise, a false or fraudulent return, the Secretary shall make such return from <u>his own knowledge</u> and from <u>such information</u> as he can obtain through testimony or otherwise.

(2) Status of returns

Any return so made and <u>subscribed</u> by the Secretary shall be prima facie good and sufficient for all legal purposes.

(i) who is not married (determined by applying section 7703), is not a surviving spouse (as defined in section 2(a)), is not a head of a household (as defined in section 2(b)), and for the taxable year has gross income of less than the sum of the exemption amount plus the basic standard deduction applicable to such an individual,

(ii) who is a head of a household (as so defined) and for the taxable year has gross income of less than the sum of the exemption amount plus the basic standard deduction applicable to such an individual,

(iii) who is a surviving spouse (as so defined) and for the taxable year has gross income of less than the sum of the exemption amount plus the basic standard deduction applicable to such an individual, or

(iv) who is entitled to make a joint return and whose gross income, when combined with the gross income of his spouse, is, for

mandatory term "required," the Notice, nevertheless, claims that these two sections "say" that individuals "must file a return or statement." So, obviously, if neither of these sections "say" any individual "must file a return or statement"—it would automatically prove that there is no such filing "requirement" anywhere in the Code.

Read sections 6001 and 6011. Can you find anywhere in either section a statement that anyone "must file a return or list"? Does it "say" that anyone is "required" to do so? Does either section even mention "income taxes"? So how can anyone claim that these sections "require," or "say," anything about filing income tax returns—or indeed, that they even pertain to income taxes?

A Significant Comparison

Compare those sections with Code sections 4371 and 4374; and 5071(a) and 5703(b) (Figure 3-2). These Code sections deal with taxes on foreign insurers and tobacco products and are contained in Chapters 34 and 52 of subtitles D and E respectively. Note how Chapter 34 is entitled "Policies Issued by Foreign Insurers," while Chapter 52 is clearly labeled "Cigars, Cigarettes, and Cigarette Papers and Tubes." Note how both Sections 4374 and 5703(b) specifically state that the taxes "imposed" in section 4371 and 5701..."**Shall be paid on the basis of a return.**"

Income taxes are imposed in the very first section of the Code. Section 1 states that a tax is "imposed on the taxable income of every" married individual (1a), heads of households (1b), unmarried individuals (1c), married individuals filing separately (1d), and estates and trusts (1e) "a tax determined in accordance with the following tables"—which is then shown in each section. Code section 11 imposes the tax on corporations. You can see that nowhere in sections 6001 or 6011 [unlike Code sections 4374 and 5703(b)] does it state that, "The taxes imposed by section 1 shall be ...paid on the basis of a return." Obviously, then, these two sections have *absolutely nothing to do with income taxes* as the IRS Privacy Act Notice suggests. As a matter of fact, if either section can be said to apply to *any* tax, they would apply to those insurance and tobacco taxes imposed by Code sections 4371 and 5701, but *not* income taxes imposed by Code section 1 and 11.

HOW CODE LANGUAGE SEEKS TO MISLEAD THE PUBLIC

Code section 6001 states that "Every person liable for any tax imposed by this title..." shall do various things. Here the key word is "liable." If one is not "liable" for the tax

"imposed" then Code section 6001 admittedly doesn't apply. Well, it is clear that section 5703(a)(1) makes manufacturers or importers of tobacco products "liable for the taxes imposed in section 5701," so section 6001 can apply to those taxes. But as you will see in Chapter 6 of this book, there is no section of the Internal Revenue code that makes anyone "liable" for income taxes—so section 6001 can not apply to income taxes as the IRS Privacy Act Notice misleadingly implies.

What about Section 6011? Well, this section also states that it only applies to those "made liable for any tax imposed by this title." So, obviously, for the reason stated above, it can not apply to income taxes either. But section 6011 is deceptive in numerous other ways that should be explained. The section states that it only applies when persons are "required" to make "returns or statements" pursuant to certain "regulations prescribed by the Secretary." But notice it does not identify any of those regulations. So how could anyone know if any of those regulations "required" the filing of income tax returns—or any other types of Federal returns? Would the average American have at home the three volumes of Treasury Regulations containing some 6,000 pages of "regulations" which he or she might leisurely comb through in order to check whether the law "required" them to file income tax returns? Even if Americans had their own copies, most of them would not know that no Treasury Regulation could require the filing of a return for a tax for which no "liability" was ever created by Congress.

Public Easily Mislead

If any member of the public happened to have section 6011 pointed out to him, he could be easily mislead into believing that this section really did require the filing of an income tax return—especially if the one pointing it out to him happened to be an IRS agent, a Department of Justice attorney or a Federal Judge. It is the public's ability to be misled in this manner that allows the government to illegally enforce the income tax.

Believe it or not, there are no "regulations prescribed by the Secretary" that require the filing of an income tax return! At least four reasons are:

1. Since no statute makes anyone "liable" for income taxes, no regulation can exist that would require the filing of a tax return in connection with a tax for which no one has a statutory "liability" to pay.
2. If regulations "required" people to be witnesses against themselves in the manner that filing income tax returns forces them to be, such "regulations" would be automatically void as unconstitutional, pursuant to the Fifth Amendment (for reasons you already know).

FIGURE 3-2

§ 4371. Imposition of tax

There is hereby imposed, on each policy of insurance, indemnity bond, annuity contract, or policy of reinsurance issued by any foreign insurer or reinsurer, a tax at the following rates:

(1) Casualty insurance and indemnity bonds

4 cents on each dollar, or fractional part thereof, of the premium paid on the policy of casualty insurance or the indemnity bond, if issued to or for, or in the name of, an insured as defined in section 4372(d);

(2) Life insurance, sickness, and accident policies, and annuity contracts

1 cent on each dollar, or fractional part thereof, of the premium paid on the policy of life, sickness, or accident insurance, or annuity contract, unless the insurer is subject to tax under section 819;

(3) Reinsurance

1 cent on each dollar, or fractional part thereof, of the premium paid on the policy of reinsurance covering any of the contracts taxable under paragraph (1) or (2).

§ 4374. Liability for tax

The tax imposed by this chapter shall be paid, on the basis of a return, by any person who makes, signs, issues, or sells any of the documents and instruments subject to the tax, or for whose use or benefit the same are made, signed, issued, or sold. The United States or any agency or instrumentality thereof shall not be liable for the tax.

§ 5701. Rate of tax

(a) Cigars

On cigars, manufactured in or imported into the United States, there shall be imposed the following taxes:

(1) Small cigars

On cigars, weighing not more than 3 pounds per thousand, 75 cents per thousand;

(2) Large cigars

On cigars weighing more than 3 pounds per thousand, a tax equal to 8½ percent of the wholesale price, but not more than $20 per thousand.

Cigars not exempt from tax under this chapter which are removed but not intended for sale shall be taxed at the same rate as similar cigars removed for sale.

§ 5703. Liability for tax and method of payment

(a) Liability for tax

(1) Original liability

The manufacturer or importer of tobacco products and cigarette papers and tubes shall be liable for the taxes imposed thereon by section 5701.

(2) Transfer of liability

When tobacco products and cigarette papers and tubes are transferred, without payment of tax, pursuant to section 5704, the liability for tax shall be transferred in accordance with the provisions of this paragraph. When tobacco products and cigarette papers and tubes are transferred between the bonded premises of manufacturers and export warehouse proprietors, the transferee shall become liable for the tax upon receipt by him of such articles, and the transferor shall thereupon be relieved of his liability for such tax. When tobacco products and cigarette papers and tubes are released in bond from customs custody for transfer to the bonded premises of a manufacturer of tobacco products or cigarette papers and tubes, the transferee shall become liable for the tax on such articles upon release from customs custody, and the importer shall thereupon be relieved of his liability for such tax. All provisions of this chapter applicable to tobacco products and cigarette papers and tubes in bond shall be applicable to such articles returned to bond upon withdrawal from the market or returned to bond after previous removal for a tax-exempt purpose.

(b) Method of payment of tax

(1) In general

The taxes imposed by section 5701 shall be determined at the time of removal of the tobacco products and cigarette papers and tubes. Such taxes shall be paid on the basis of return. The Secretary shall, by regulations, prescribe the period or the event for which such return shall be made and the information to be furnished on such return. Any postponement under this subsection of the payment of taxes determined at the time of removal shall be conditioned upon the filing of such additional bonds, and upon compliance with such requirements, as the Secretary may prescribe for the protection of the revenue. The Secretary may, by regulations, require payment of tax on the basis of a return prior to removal of the tobacco products and cigarette papers and tubes where a person defaults in the postponed payment of tax on the basis of a return under this subsection or regulations prescribed thereunder. All administrative and penalty provisions of this title, insofar as applicable, shall apply to any tax imposed by section 5701.

3. "Regulations" can not broaden or extend the law, so if one were "required" to file, it would be the law itself that would be cited, and not just mere "regulations," and finally

4. Section 6011 does not even appear in Subtitle A—the subtitle dealing with income taxes.

So, on what basis can anyone claim that section 6011 relates to the income tax? Also notice how this section actually avoids making any false claims or statements (as occurred in Figure 1-3). It merely relies on making false inplications, while leaving it to others to make the false claims on its behalf. This technique is repeated throughout the Code (and all government documents related to income taxes). I would use up too many pages pointing out other examples, so let me specifically deal with this one, then you will able to spot the others yourself.

Section 6011 starts off by saying, "When required by regulations etc., etc." However, no claim is made that such a "requirement" is *actually contained* in any regulation, let alone the law. The public is merely mislead into believing that such a "requirement" must be contained in *some* law or regulation, but section 6011 never actually makes this claim. There is only a fraudulent implication that such a regulation or statute exists. But if such a regulation or statute really existed, it would have been named! Code Sections 4413, 4414, 5601, 5604, and 5852 (Figure 3-3) make this clear.

"RETURNS," WHEN USED IN THE CODE, RARELY MEAN *INCOME TAX* RETURNS

When I first read the Internal Revenue Code, I automatically assumed that every time the word "return" appeared, it meant an income tax return, since that was the only type of "return" I had ever heard of. That is precisely the mistake the government intends for everybody to make, since, unlike income tax returns, certain other returns are required to be filed. Mandatory Code language only applies to *them*—not to income tax returns. If the public is unaware of other types of returns, then anytime it sees a mandatory Code inference or claim regarding a "return" it incorrectly assumes that it relates to income tax returns—when it does not! For example, sections 5701 and 5703(b), (Figure 3-2), clearly provide for:

1. The filing of tax returns by foreign insurers and manufacturers of tobacco products, and

2. the payment of taxes on the basis of such returns, while also

3. establishing a tax "liability" with respect to those taxes. **There are no similar provisions in the entire Internal Revenue Code in connection with income taxes!**

LACK OF PROPER PLACEMENT AND "CROSS-REFERENCES"

Note that sections 4371, 4374, 5701 and 5703 are contained within the very subtitle and chapter that deals with those taxes. If Sections 6001 and 6011 dealt with income taxes they would be included in Subtitle A, the subtitle dealing with that tax—the way provisions relating to other taxes are grouped in the Code.

For example, Code Sections 4401(a), 4401(c), 4403, and 4405 (Figure 3-4) provide other examples of this principle and further demonstrate why neither section 6001 or 6011 can apply to income taxes. Those four Code references deal with wagering taxes, the federal tax imposed on bookmakers. Note that all four references are contained in Chapter 35 entitled "Taxes on Wagering," which is in Subtitle D, so there is no question that these provisions apply to wagering taxes. Note how subsection 4401(a) "imposes" the tax, and subsection (c) immediately informs us who "shall be liable" for the tax so imposed. In addition, section 4403 clearly establishes a requirement that those "liable" for the tax shall keep certain records, both pursuant to that section and section 6001! So now we also see how section 6001 is made applicable to wagering taxes. However, there is no similar cross-reference anywhere in Subtitle A that section 6001 applies, *in like manner,* to income taxes What does that tell you? This is additional proof that section 6001 does not apply to income taxes. If it did, a similar cross-reference would appear in Subtitle A.

Penalty Provisions: When Applicable, When Not

Note that Code section 4405 specifically makes the provisions of Subtitle F applicable to wagering taxes. It is in Subtitle F that all of the general enforcement and penalty provisions of the Code appear (such as for tax evasion), so 4405 makes these penalties applicable to the wagering taxes provided for in Subtitle D. However, **there is no cross-reference anywhere in Subtitle A making the penalty and other provisions of Subtitle F similarly applicable to the income taxes found in Subtitle A!** A similar cross-reference to Subtitle F can be seen in Code section 4414 (Figure 3-3) and is found in connection with other taxes, as provided for in Code sections 4484, 4998(6), 5148, 5560, and 5684(c) (Figure 3-5). The fact that such a cross-reference is missing in connection with income taxes but is not missing in connection with other internal revenue taxes is proof that the Code contains *no penalty provisions in connection with income taxes.* Naturally—that tax is "voluntary," so how can penalty provisions apply?

FIGURE 3-3

§ 4413. Certain provisions made applicable

Sections 4901, 4902, 4904, 4905, and 4906 shall extend to and apply to the special tax imposed by this subchapter and to the persons upon whom it is imposed, and for that purpose any activity which makes a person liable for special tax under this subchapter shall be considered to be a business or occupation referred to in such sections. No other provision of sections 4901 to 4907, inclusive, shall so extend or apply.

(Aug. 16, 1954, ch. 736, 68A Stat. 527.)

§ 4414. Cross references

For penalties and other general and administrative provisions applicable to this subchapter, see sections 4421 to 4423, inclusive; and subtitle F.

§ 5601. Criminal penalties

(a) Offenses

Any person who—

(1) Unregistered stills

has in his possession or custody, or under his control, any still or distilling apparatus set up which is not registered, as required by section 5179(a); or

(2) Failure to file application

engages in the business of a distiller or processor without having filed application for and received notice of registration, as required by section 5171(c); or

(3) False or fraudulent application

engages, or intends to engage, in the business of distiller, warehouseman, or processor of distilled spirits, and files a false or fraudulent application under section 5171; or

(4) Failure or refusal of distiller, warehouseman, or processor to give bond

carries on the business of a distiller, warehouseman, or processor without having given bond as required by law; or

(5) False, forged, or fraudulent bond

engages, or intends to engage, in the business of distiller, warehouseman, or processor of distilled spirits, and gives any false, forged, or fraudulent bond, under subchapter B; or

(6) Distilling on prohibited premises

uses, or possesses with intent to use, any still, boiler, or other utensil for the purpose of producing distilled spirits, or aids or assists therein, or causes or procures the same to be done, in any dwelling house, or in any shed, yard, or inclosure connected with such dwelling house (except as authorized under section 5178(a)(1)(C)), or on board any vessel or boat, or on any premises where beer or wine is made or produced, or where liquors of any description are retailed, or on premises where any other business is carried on (except when authorized under section 5178(b)); or

(15) Unauthorized withdrawal, use, sale, or distribution of distilled spirits for fuel use

Withdraws,[2] uses, sells, or otherwise disposes of distilled spirits produced under section 5181 for other than fuel use;

shall be fined not more than $10,000, or imprisoned not more than 5 years, or both, for each such offense.

(b) Presumptions

Whenever on trial for violation of subsection (a)(4) the defendant is shown to have been at the site or place where, and at the time when, the business of a distiller or processor was so engaged in or carried on, such presence of the defendant shall be deemed sufficient evidence to authorize conviction, unless the defendant explains such presence to the satisfaction of the jury (or of the court when tried without jury).

§ 5604. Penalties relating to marks, brands, and containers

(a) In general

Any person who shall—

(1) transport, possess, buy, sell, or transfer any distilled spirits unless the immediate container bears the type of closure or other device required by section 5301(d),

(2) with intent to defraud the United States, empty a container bearing the closure or other device required by section 5301(d) without breaking such closure or other device,

(3) empty, or cause to be emptied, any distilled spirits from an immediate container bearing any mark or brand required by law without effacing and obliterating such mark or brand as required by section 5206(d),

(4) place any distilled spirits in any bottle, or reuse any bottle for the purpose of containing distilled spirits, which has once been filled and fitted with a closure or other device under the provisions of this chapter, without removing and destroying such closure or other device,

(5) willfully and unlawfully remove, change, or deface any mark, brand, label, or seal affixed to any case of distilled spirits, or to any bottle contained therein,

(6) with intent to defraud the United States, purchase, sell, receive with intent to transport, or transport any empty cask or package having thereon any mark or brand required by law to be affixed to any cask or package containing distilled spirits, or

(7) change or alter any mark or brand on any cask or package containing distilled spirits, or put into any cask or package spirits of greater strength than is indicated by the inspection mark thereon, or fraudulently use any cask or package having any inspection mark thereon, for the purpose of selling

Figure 3-3 (continued)

other spirits, or spirits of quantity or quality different from the spirits previously inspected,

shall be fined not more than $10,000 or imprisoned not more than 5 years, or both, for each such offense.

(b) Officers authorized to enforce this section

Any officer authorized to enforce any provision of law relating to internal revenue stamps is authorized to enforce this section.

§ 5852. General transfer and making tax exemption

(a) Transfer

Any firearm may be transferred to the United States or any department, independent establishment, or agency thereof, without payment of the transfer tax imposed by section 5811.

(b) Making by a person other than a qualified manufacturer

Any firearm may be made by, or on behalf of, the United States, or any department, independent establishment, or agency thereof, without payment of the making tax imposed by section 5821,

(c) Making by a qualified manufacturer

A manufacturer qualified under this chapter to engage in such business may make the type of firearm which he is qualified to manufacture without payment of the making tax imposed by section 5821.

(d) Transfers between special (occupational) taxpayers

A firearm registered to a person qualified under this chapter to engage in business as an importer, manufacturer, or dealer may be transferred by that person without payment of the transfer tax imposed by section 5811 to any other person qualified under this chapter to manufacture, import, or deal in that type of firearm.

(e) Unserviceable firearm

An unserviceable firearm may be transferred as a curio or ornament without payment of the transfer tax imposed by section 5811, under such requirements as the Secretary may by regulations prescribe.

(f) Right to exemption

No firearm may be transferred or made exempt from tax under the provisions of this section unless the transfer or making is performed pursuant to an application in such form and manner as the Secretary may by regulations prescribe.

NOTE!!!
No such treats, penalties or "enforcement" provisions appear anywhere in the Internal Revenue Code in connection with income taxes! Doesn't that tell you something?

FIGURE 3-4

§ 4401. Imposition of tax

(a) Wagers

(1) State authorized wagers

There shall be imposed on any wager authorized under the law of the State in which accepted an excise tax equal to 0.25 percent of the amount of such wager.

(2) Unauthorized wagers

There shall be imposed on any wager not described in paragraph (1) an excise tax equal to 2 percent of the amount of such wager.

(b) Amount of wager

In determining the amount of any wager for the purposes of this subchapter, all charges incident to the placing of such wager shall be included; except that if the taxpayer establishes, in accordance with regulations prescribed by the Secretary, that an amount equal to the tax imposed by this subchapter has been collected as a separate charge from the person placing such wager, the amount so collected shall be excluded.

(c) Persons liable for tax

Each person who is engaged in the business of accepting wagers shall be liable for and shall pay the tax under this subchapter on all wagers placed with him. Each person who conducts any wagering pool or lottery shall be liable for and shall pay the tax under this subchapter on all wagers placed in such pool or lottery. Any person required to register under section 4412 who receives wagers for or on behalf of another person without having registered under section 4412 the name and place of residence of such other person shall be liable for and shall pay the tax under this subchapter on all such wagers received by him.

§ 4403. Record requirements

Each person liable for tax under this subchapter shall keep a daily record showing the gross amount of all wagers on which he is so liable, in addition to all other records required pursuant to section 6001(a).

§ 4405. Cross references

For penalties and other administrative provisions applicable to this subchapter, see sections 4421 to 4423, inclusive; and subtitle F.

FIGURE 3-5

§ 4484. Cross references

(1) For penalties and administrative provisions applicable to this subchapter, see subtitle F.
(2) For exemption for uses by Indian tribal governments (or their subdivisions), see section 7871.

§ 4998. Cross references

(1) For additions to the tax and additional amount for failure to file tax return or to pay tax, see section 6651.
(2) For additions to the tax and additional amounts for failure to file certain information returns, registration statements, etc., see section 6652.
(3) For additions to the tax and additional amounts for negligence and fraud, see section 6653.
(4) For additions to the tax and additional amounts for failure to make deposit of taxes, see section 6656.
(5) For additions to the tax and additional amounts for failure to collect and pay over tax, or attempt to evade or defeat tax, see section 6672.
(6) For criminal penalties for attempt to evade or defeat tax, willful failure to collect or pay over tax, willful failure to file return, supply information, or pay tax, and for fraud and false statements, see sections 7201, 7202, 7203, and 7206.

§ 5148. Cross references

(1) For penalties for willful nonpayment of special taxes, see section 5691.
(2) For penalties applicable to this part generally, see subchapter J.
(3) For penalties, authority for assessments, and other general and administrative provisions applicable to this part, see subtitle F.

§ 5560. Other provisions applicable

All provision of subtitle F, insofar as applicable and not inconsistent with the provisions of this subtitle, are hereby extended to and made a part of this subtitle.

§ 5684. Penalties relating to the payment and collection of liquor taxes

(c) Cross references

(1) For provisions relating to interest in the case of taxes not paid when due, see section 6601.
(2) For penalty for failure to file tax return or pay tax, see section 6651.
(3) For additional penalties for failure to pay tax, see section 6653.
(4) For penalty for failure to make deposits or for overstatement of deposits, see section 6656.
(5) For penalty for attempt to evade or defeat any tax imposed by this title, see section 7201.
(6) For penalty for willful failure to file return, supply information, or pay tax, see section 7203.

FOOLING THE PUBLIC WITH "SHALL"

Starting in 1987 the IRS, in order to increase the public's misconception still further, added a new Code section to its Privacy Act Notice that allegedly "says" Americans have to file income tax returns—Code section 6012 (Figure 3-1). Well, you already know that this section can have nothing to do with "telling" Americans that they are "required" to file such returns. Apart from all of the reasons which you already know, if this section "told" Americans that they are "required" to file, it would have appeared in the Privacy Act Notice long ago and would not have suddenly surfaced in 1987. Besides, if the Code really did provide a filing requirement for income taxes, it would only have to be contained in one Code section. The government would not have to cite three! So the question that needs addressing is how is section 6012 designed to fool the public into thinking that they are "required" to file tax returns? By answering this question, we will uncover still other techniques used by the government to fool the public.

Notice first that the section is entitled "Persons required to make returns of income." Since you already know that no person is "required" to make or file income tax returns, you already know that you are looking at a Code section specifically designed to mislead you. But you will again discover that it is cleverly worded so as to contain no false statements. First of all, the public would not know that the section's descriptive title is not a part of the law itself. Since a Code section's descriptive title is not part of the law (as provided for in Code section 77806(b), it is routinely designed to mislead the public as to what the law itself actually says.[2] So despite the Section's title, section 6012 has nothing to do with who is "required" to make returns of income." If anything, the section only deals with who is *not* "required."

Did you notice that nowhere in that section does it state that anybody is "required" to file an income tax return? The section only enumerates categories of people who, the section declares, "shall not be required." Since those who wrote this section knew that no one is required to file an income tax return why would they list specific categories of people who allegedly are *not* "required" to file? They did so, to mislead the public into thinking that if certain categories of people are *not* "required" to file, then all other people (not in those categories) must *be* "required"!

Surprise! "Shall" Means "May" (In Connection With Income Taxes)

If persons are "required" to file income tax returns, then why didn't Section 6012 come right out and say so? Why did it pussy-foot around and only say that such returns "shall be made"? Because those writing the Code knew that in the context the word "shall" was not "mandatory," while "required" would be. Using "required" would have brought Section 6012 into direct conflict with both the "law" and the Constitution—something that the government always manages to avoid. Those writing the Code realized that the public would not recognize these differences, and federal judges could be counted on to ignore them. And, the government was right on all counts. But regardless of how many times duplicitous federal judges contend that the word "shall" in Section 6012 really means "required," it is crystal clear that it does not.

Notice how the government conspicuously avoids using the word "required" in the most relevant part of that section. Also, there is abundant case law that demonstrates that the word "shall" as used in section 6012 can not mean "required." There are other significant factors that will be addressed which further prove that.

The public simply is unaware that the courts have consistently ruled (when the issue didn't involve federal income taxes) that the word "shall," which, in many statutes is mandatory, is not mandatory *when such a construction would bring the statute in conflict with the Constitution.* Since a mandatory construction of "shall" as used in Section 6012 would do just that—it *must* be construed as "may."

For example in *Fort Howard Paper Co.* v. Fox River Heights Sanitary Dist., 26 NW 2nd 661 the court ruled:

The word "shall" in a statute may be construed to mean "may," particularly in order to avoid a constitutional doubt.

Other courts have similarly stated:

If necessary, to avoid unconstitutionality of a statute, "shall" will be deemed equivalent to "may."[3]

"Shall" in a statute may be construed to mean "may" in order to avoid constitutional doubt.[1]

Even the Supreme Court in *Cairo and Fulton R.R. Co.* v. *Hect*, 95 US 170 ruled:

As against the government the word "shall" when used in statutes is to be construed as "may," unless a contrary intention is manifest.

Therefore, even the Supreme Court has ruled that the word "shall" as used in section 6012 must be construed as "may," since no other intention is "manifest." If the "manifest" intention of that section were to establish a mandatory construction, then clearly "required" would have been used and not "shall."

In *Ballou* v. *Kemp*, 92 F2d 556, the . . . Circuit Court of Appeals gives added insight as to how we can determine when "shall" in a statute really means "may."

The word "shall" in a statute may be construed as "may" where the connection in which it is used or the relation to which it is put with other parts of the same statute indicates that the legislature intended that it should receive such a construction. [emphasis added]

Section 6012 refers to people being "not required." If, in "the same statute" others are supposedly "required," then pursuant to *Ballow*, the statute would have said so.

In addition to all of the above, note Code sections 4901, 4902 (Figure 3-6). In section 4902, the Code is dealing with a mandatory tax, the Federal wagering tax. Here the Code says *"shall be required to pay."* Notice that when the Code is dealing with a mandatory tax, it is not at all squeamish about using the word "required." It did not merely say "shall pay." Not only won't you find any place in the Code language which states that persons "shall be required to pay" income taxes, but you won't even find *a line* in the Code that states persons "shall pay" that tax either! Doesn't that tell you *something?*

Even if it could be established that Code Section 6012 did require the filing of income tax returns, where does it state anywhere in that section that any taxes "shall be paid" with such returns? It's clearly stated in Code section 5703(b). Why not in section 6012? And where does section 6012 refer to penalties in the event returns are *not* filed pursuant to that section? The Code sections in Figure 3-3 clearly provide for such penalties. Why not section 6012?

SECTION 6012 IS VITIATED BY SECTION 6011(f)

And finally, refer to Code Section 6011(f) (Figure 3-1), which is the section immediately preceding section 6012. This three line section makes absolutely no sense from the public's standpoint. It was obviously included in the Code just to protect the government—in case anyone challenged those Code sections as they applied to those listed taxes as being unconstitutional. Note that the section allegedly seeks to establish a filing "requirement" for income, estate and gift taxes (all of which are imposed unconstitutionally) "whether *or not*. . .(one has). . .a tax liability" with regard to those taxes. Why, then, would anyone *care about* or *bother with* Code sections dealing with them, let alone file returns with respect to them? Would anyone not engaged in the manufacture of tobacco and/or liquor products or who is not a bookmaker (and thus not "liable" for those taxes) care a hoot about what the Code says relevant to those taxes

FIGURE 3-6

§ 4901. Payment of tax

(a) Condition precedent to carrying on certain business

No person shall be engaged in or carry on any trade or business subject to the tax imposed by section 4411 (wagering) until he has paid the special tax therefor.

(b) Computation

All special taxes shall be imposed as of on the first day of July in each year, or on commencing any trade or business on which such tax is imposed. In the former case the tax shall be reckoned for 1 year, and in the latter case it shall be reckoned proportionately, from the first day of the month in which the liability to a special tax commenced, to and including the 30th day of June following.

§ 4902. Liability of partners

Any number of persons doing business in co-partnership at any one place shall be required to pay but one special tax.

(except maybe for comparison purposes)? Would anyone not engaged in those businesses feel bound to file the tax returns required of those who are, and thus made "liable" for those taxes?

Section 6011(f) proves that Section 6012 (as well as those other sections referred to) is *meaningless* and that its *only purpose is to deceive the public* on precisely the same basis as its recent inclusion in the Privacy Act Notice was intended to do. Apart from everything else, in order to understand the irrelevancy of Section 6012 to income taxes, one would *also* have to know about Section 6011(f), which was *not* referred to in that Notice. The use of one Code section to vitiate another is a particularly vicious ploy, because it allows federal judges to distort the legal meaning of one section, while they disregard the existence and impact of the other.

So it is clear from all of the above that the word "shall" when used in a statute, can mean "may." Clearly then, this is the construction that *must* be given to it when it is used in connection with income taxes, *if the constitutionality of the Code is to be preserved.* "Shall" can only mean "required" in section 6012 if **the constitutionality of the Code is of no particular significance.**

SECTION 6020—A KEY INGREDIENT IN THE INCOME TAX HOAX

Another extremely important Code section in the government's program of deceit is Code Section 6020. This is the section that the government violates so it can prepare bogus income tax returns for those who lawfully choose not

Figure 3-7

to voluntarily file any returns on their own. Four such bogus returns (which one court labeled "dummy" returns) are shown in Figure 3-7 as "prepared" for me by the government. Would you believe that based solely on those "dummy" returns the United States (in 1983) seized over $200,000 from me for the years 1976, 1977 and 1978 (A, B and C) while the "dummy" for 1979, (D), was created so the United States could extort another $44,199.99 from me now. On October 9, 1986 I brought suit in Federal court to recover the money illegally seized from me in 1983, and in August 1986, I petitioned "Tax Court" to challenge the IRS' latest extortionary efforts. Both suits are currently in litigation.[5]

A FRAUDULENT IRS "NOTICE"

Note the unsigned "notice" that I received from the IRS in Figure 3-8. (Letters and "notices" sent by the IRS concerning income taxes are usually unsigned. Since all of them are purely extortionary [despite the cleverly worded "escape" language] the IRS takes the added precaution of seeing to it that no one in particular can be held responsible for them). This IRS "notice" sent to me seeks information

concerning my 1984 income tax return, but notice how it cleverly avoids:

1. putting me "on notice" of anything.
2. stating that I might be legally "required" to file an income tax return (form 1040), or
3. claiming that there are any penalties in connection with not filing income tax returns.

What The Notice Should Have Said

If I were really required to file an income tax return this is how its "notice" would read.

This is to advise you that pursuant to Internal Revenue Code section 6012 (Notice that while the "notice" does mention other Code sections, it avoids citing any section that allegedly requires the filing of 1040's. Isn't that strange and shouldn't that tell you something?) all those having gross income of over $1,000 or more (and who are not otherwise subject to the exceptions provided in that section) are required to file income tax returns.

FIGURE 3-8

Department of the Treasury Internal Revenue Service ANDOVER, MA 05501

IRWIN SCHIFF
144 SHEPARDS KNOLL
HAMDEN CT 06514

608 06010000   0002269 S PC-P   914 023321 ACR

If you have any questions, refer to this information:
Date of This Notice: 05-12-86 518 8618
Taxpayer Identifying Number: 047-16-2491
Form 1040 Tax Period Ended: 12-31-84

*Call: 1-800-424-1040
or
Write: Chief, Collection Branch
Internal Revenue Service Center
ANDOVER, MA 05501
If you write, be sure to attach the bottom part of this notice.

```
****************************************************
* YOUR TAX FORM IS OVERDUE - LET US HEAR FROM YOU NOW *
****************************************************
     WE HAVE NOT RECEIVED YOUR ANSWER TO ANY OF OUR REQUESTS FOR FORM
1040   US INDIVIDUAL INCOME TAX RETURN        FOR THE TAX PERIOD
ENDED   12-31-84. IF YOU DO NOT CONTACT US IMMEDIATELY, WE MUST
CONCLUDE THAT YOU DO NOT INTEND TO FILE THE FORM OR TO GIVE US A REASON
FOR NOT FILING IT.  THEREFORE, THE ACTIONS WE MAY TAKE ARE TO :
     1. SUMMON YOU TO COME IN WITH YOUR BOOKS AND RECORDS (AS PROVIDED
BY SECTIONS 7602 AND 7603 OF THE INTERNAL REVENUE CODE);
     2. FILL IN THE TAX FORM FOR YOU BASED ON THE INFORMATION WE HAVE
(CODE SECTION 6020(B)); OR
     3. CONSIDER CRIMINAL PROSECUTION THAT INCLUDES A FINE,
IMPRISONMENT, OR BOTH FOR PERSONS WHO WILLFULLY FAIL TO FILE A TAX
FORM OR TO PROVIDE TAX INFORMATION (CODE SECTION 7203).
     WE DO NOT WANT TO TAKE THESE ACTIONS, SO WE URGE YOU TO FILE THE
FORM OR CONTACT US IMMEDIATELY AND EXPLAIN WHY YOU ARE NOT REQUIRED TO
FILE IT, OR FURNISH PROOF THAT IT HAS BEEN FILED.  BE SURE TO REFER TO
THIS NOTICE.  IF YOU GO TO YOUR LOCAL IRS OFFICE, TAKE THIS NOTICE AND
ANY OTHER INFORMATION NEEDED.  IF YOU FILED THE FORM, TAKE YOUR COPY OF
IT; IF YOU PAID THE TAX, TAKE YOUR RECEIPT OR CANCELED CHECK.
```

We have not received your answer to any of our requests for your form 1040 for the period ended 12-31-84.

This is to put you on notice that if we do not within 45 days of the date of this notice, receive from you a 1040 pursuant to Section 6012, then you could be subject to additional civil fines and penalties pursuant to Code Sections 6653 and 6661 and/or criminal prosecution for willfully failing to file income tax returns pursuant to section 7203, or for tax evasion with respect to such taxes, pursuant to section 7201.

In view of the grave penalties the law imposes on those who are required to file income tax returns but who fail to do so, we urge you to take notice of the legal obligations established under section 6012.

Obviously, if the law really did impose a filing requirement on anyone, that is the type of letter the IRS would send out—not the mickey-mouse one it actually sends. Their letter is merely designed to mislead the public into believing that there is a filing requirement with respect to income taxes (while not actually saying so). It intimidates recipients into believing that the Code provides penalties for not filing income tax returns—without saying that either!

The reason that the IRS always asks people why they "are not required to file" (instead of *telling* them why they *are)* is that most people don't know why they "are not required," so such a question generally intimidates them into filing. Those replies that do furnish the IRS with the correct answer by saying "The Code imposes no filing requirement nor income tax liability on me" are generally ignored by the IRS!

If the Code clearly made people liable to file income tax returns, would the IRS go around *bothering* people and creating needless work for itself by asking people to "explain" to them why they are "not required to file" income tax returns? Why didn't the IRS send me a "notice" asking me to "explain" to them why I am "not required to file" wagering tax returns, tobacco tax returns or any of the other returns that I might "not be required to file?" **How transparent does this hoax have to be?**

A FALSE AND FRAUDULENT CLAIM

The main reason I bring this "notice" to your attention is because it states that one of "THE ACTIONS WE MAY TAKE" if I didn't send in a 1040, is that the IRS legally could (and would) allegedly "FILL IN THE TAX FORM FOR (ME) BASED ON THE INFORMATION WE HAVE [CODE SECTION 6020(B)]." So this "notice"

from the IRS claims that it has the authority, pursuant to Code Section 6020(b), to prepare a 1040 for me, if I didn't elect to send one in voluntarily. I wonder how many millions of computer-generated letters the government sends out containing this false and fraudulent claim?

When I first discovered that the IRS had prepared those four "dummy" returns for me, I asked both the Justice Department and the IRS, by way of discovery,[6] to explain the IRS' legal authority to do so. The lawyers for both the Justice Department and the IRS claimed that their authority was section 6020(b). The Justice Department's claim came in response to admission number 28 (one of the 136 admissions that I submitted to it on March 19, 1987) which stated:

Admit that the purported tax returns prepared by the Defendant for the Plaintiff, were allegedly made pursuant to I.R.C. 6020(b),

to which the Justice Department responded, "Admitted." The claim from the IRS' lawyers came in response to Interrogatory No. 2 (as shown in the Appendix). Both answers are both false and fraudulent. False, because section 6020(b) gives the IRS no such authority, and fraudulent because even if it did, the dummy returns prepared by the IRS are clearly not the type that are even remotely envisioned, contemplated or authorized by that section—and only charlatans would claim otherwise. Also note that those dummy returns are devoid of any entries that the IRS claimed in its "notice" that it was authorized to "FILL IN...BASED ON THE INFORMATION WE HAVE." Such a claim was blatantly false as those blank returns prove. So all Government claims that section 6020 allows the IRS to prepare income tax returns not authorized by taxpayers themselves are false for the two following reasons.

1. The section itself states that it only applies when "any person shall fail to make a return *required* by this title...," since income tax returns are not "required" returns, section 6020(b) can not apply to them.

2. Even if income tax returns were covered by that section, any return prepared pursuant to it, has to be "subscribed to" (signed) as stated in subsection 6020(b)(2) and contain "information" from which a tax can be calculated—attributes that none of those "dummies" have. So any claim that the "returns" shown in **Figure 3-7** are the type authorized by section 6020(b) is fraudulent on its very face.

Interestingly enough, in 1975 an optometrist from Rochester, Pennsylvania, Dr. Raymond M. Hartman,[7] claimed before the "Tax Court" that the IRS was required to prepare a tax return for him pursuant to Code section 6020(b) before it could allege a "deficiency," which is what the IRS claimed to have done in my case. But look at what the "Tax Court" said then in *Hartman* v. *Commissioner*, 65 T.C. 542 (1975), (Figure 3-9), concerning Hartman's bizarre claim. [The comments in brackets are mine]:

Does section 6020(b)(1) require the Commissioner to make a return for every taxpayer who fails or refuses to do so before a deficiency can be determined pursuant to section 6201? We think not.

...there was nothing to show that Congress ever intended the statute to operate as the taxpayer...would have us hold. [which is *precisely* how it is "held" *today*.] When section 6020(b) is lifted out of the Code and read literally, as petitioner has done [how else was he supposed to read it?], its scope is broad and its meaning and purpose hazy. [But when the Government seeks to use it, "its meaning and purpose" suddenly become *clear*.] But the Internal Revenue Code cannot be so read [then why doesn't the government provide instructions on how one is supposed to read it?] for each section is not a self-contained whole, but rather a building block of complex, interrelated statute. Based on its location in Chapter 61 [i.e., it is not contained within those sections, Subtitle A, dealing with income taxes] and the lack of any cross-references (other than the word "return"), section 6020(b) is not to be read as a prerequisite to the Commissioner's proceeding under section 6201(a)(1).

I couldn't have said it better myself!

Based on the above, and on the following legal decisions, all of those government lawyers had to know that their representations to me were false and fraudulent:

1. "A return filed unsigned is no return at all," Vaira v. C.I.R., 444 F2d 770, citing *Dixon* v. *Commissioner*, 28 T.C. 338.

2. Since the returns prepared by the IRS contained no information from which a tax could be determined, they were *not returns* as clearly held in *U.S.* v. *Verkuilen* 82-2 U.S.T.C.; *Schiff* v. *Commissioner* U.S.T.C. 1984-223, and numerous other cases that could be cited.

3. In *Phillips* v. *C.I.R., 1986 T.C. 433 the court specifically ruled that ___ such* "dummy" returns do not have "the status of a return."

FIGURE 3-9

(542)   RAYMOND M. HARTMAN   545

He then argues:

By law all taxes, deficiencies, determinations or penalties must be based on *taxes shown on a return* prepared either by the taxpayer, who is the [petitioner] herein, or by the Secretary or his delegate, who is the [respondent] herein.

Petitioner concedes (and correctly so) that he filed no "return" within the meaning of the statute. *Edward A. Cupp, supra.* Thus, the question before us is: Does section 6020(b)(1) require the Commissioner to make a return for every taxpayer who fails or refuses to do so before a deficiency can be determined pursuant to section 6201? We think not.

In *United States v. Harrison,* an unreported case (E.D.N.Y. 1972, 30 AFTR 2d 72-5367, 72-2 USTC ¶ 9573), affd.—F.2d— (2d Cir. 1972, 31 AFTR 2d 73-967, 73-1 USTC ¶ 9295), cert. denied 411 U.S. 965 (1973), the District Court ably traced the legislative history of section 6020(b), a history extending back to the 1860's, and concluded that there was nothing to show that Congress ever intended the statute to operate as the taxpayer there, and petitioner here, would have us hold. When section 6020(b) is lifted out of the Code and read literally, as petitioner has done, its scope is broad and its meaning and purpose hazy. But the Internal Revenue Code cannot be so read, for each section is not a self-contained whole, but rather a building block of a complex, interrelated statute. Based on its location in chapter 61 and the lack of any cross-references (other than to the word return), section 6020(b) is not to be read as a prerequisite to the Commissioner's proceeding under section 6201(a)(1) (ch. 63). *United States v. Harrison, supra.*

Petitioner also argues that there has been no valid determination of a deficiency because there was no return filed by him. Section 6211(a) reads as follows:

SEC. 6211. DEFINITION OF A DEFICIENCY.
(a) IN GENERAL.—For purposes of this title in the case of income, estate, gift, and excise taxes, imposed by Subtitles A and B, and chapter 42, the term "deficiency" means the amount by which the tax imposed by subtitle A or B or chapter 42 exceeds the excess of—
(1) the sum of
(A) the amount shown as the tax by the taxpayer upon his return, *if a return was made by the taxpayer* and an amount was shown as the tax by the taxpayer thereon, plus
(B) the amounts previously assessed (or collected without assessment) as a deficiency, over—

AUTHOR'S NOTE: A "deficiency" assessment made pursuant to section 6211 is a "supplemental" assessment as provided for in section 6204. And a "deficiency" assessment can only be made to correct an (original) assessment made pursuant to section 6201 which was "imperfect or incomplete."

So it can be easily established, that, based upon any *one* of the reasons described above, all of those Justice Department and IRS lawyes had to know that those unsigned "dummy" returns were *meaningless* and could serve *no legal purpose whatsoever* even though they all sought to represent otherwise. That's exactly the kind of "integrity" the public can generally expect from *all* government lawyers involved—either criminally or civilly—with federal income taxes.

NOTES TO CHAPTER 3

1. Most Americans, of course, never read the actual income tax "laws" for themselves, but accept what government and professional tax preparers tell them. This helps explain how and why they have been so thoroughly hoodwinked.

2. To see some really outrageous examples of this technique see Schiff, Irwin, *The Social Security Swindle: How Anyone Can Drop Out* (Hamden, CT., Freedom Books, 1984) pp 24, 25.

3. *Gow* v. *Consolidated Coopermines Corp.*, 165 Atl. 136

4. *George Williams College* v. Village of Williams Bay, 7NW 2d 6.

5. In my suit in Federal court, the United States is defended by the Tax Division of the U.S. Department of Justice, represented by trial attorney, Deborah S. Meland. However, all documents signed by her are submitted by and under the authority of Stanley A. Twardy, the U.S. Attorney for the State of Connecticut and Jeremiah F. Donovan an Assistant U.S. Attorney in that department. However, often documents are received from the Assistant Attorney General, himself, and the Chief of the Trial Division of the Northern Region

In my "Tax Court" suit the Commissioner of Internal Revenue is represented by Powell W. Holly, Jr., the District Counsel and Joseph F. Long, an attorney in that department. However most documents are also submitted under the authority of William F. Nelson, Chief Counsel, of the Internal Revenue Service and with the approval of Agatha L. Vorsanger, its Regional Counsel. So in these two law suits I am opposed by two different teams of government lawyers both of whom are supposed to know something about federal income taxes. It is principally due to the documents they supplied and *refused* to supply, and the information, *disinformation* and information they refused to give (pursuant to "discovery") that enabled me to write this book. (As particularly detailed in Chapter 9.)

6. Discovery is the process by which parties in civil litigation can gather information from each other prior to trial.

7. On February 28, 1988, a virtual 12-man swat team complete with guns drawn (absolutely barred in the collection of income taxes) descended on Dr. Hartman's home and cleaned it out, leaving one bed. Then they went to his office and chained it closed. They prevented Dr.Hartman from getting to his patient's records, and shut down his practice. Despite the government having a court order (which is not usual in income tax cases), Dr. Hartman was not liable to the United States for one single penny as alleged in the government's fraudulent judgement! The United States wanted to crush Dr. Hartman since the good doctor knows a lot more about income taxes than any of his fellow citizens in Rochester, PA. The United States will go to any length to prevent Dr. Hartman and others from infecting other people with the truth.

— CHAPTER 4 —

INCOME TAXES HAVE TO BE ASSESSED

"In a recent conversation with an official at the Internal Revenue Service, I was amazed when he told me that, 'If the taxpayers of this country ever discover that the Internal Revenue Service operates on 90 percent bluff, the entire system will collapse'."
—Senator Henry Bellmon (1969)

Income taxes, by statute, have to be assessed just like local property taxes. Would you pay—or have any obligation to pay—those taxes before they were assessed?

Chapter 63 of the Code, entitled "Assessment" contains a subchapter containing 7 Code sections. This extremely important subchapter is largely ignored by the IRS, the Justice Department, and the federal judiciary when they deal with Federal income taxes.

Section 6201(a), (Figure 4-1) the first section that appears in that chapter, states (in relevant part) that the Secretary (meaning the Secretary of the Treasury, whose Department is responsible for the collection of Federal Taxes):

is authorized and required to make the inquiries, determinations, and *assessments of all taxes...* imposed by this title...which have not been duly paid *by stamp...*

While this section deals with Federal taxes "paid by stamp" (such as tobacco and alcohol taxes), the next section, Section 6201(a)(1) deals with "Taxes shown on return," and provides that with respect to those taxes:

The Secretary shall assess *all taxes* determined by the taxpayer or by the Secretary **as to which returns or lists are made** under this title.

So, sections 6201(a) and (a)(1) make clear that:

1. All Federal taxes (including income taxes) have to be assessed.
2. Before an income tax can be assessed, the Secretary must first be in possession of a "return or list."
3. Without the Secretary having either a valid income tax "return or list," no income taxes against anyone *can be assessed.*

Section 6203 (Figure 4-2) further provides that the assessment "shall be made by recording the liability of the taxpayer in the office of the Secretary" and that the Secretary "shall furnish" taxpayers copies of the record of assessments. It is therefore clear that no one can "owe" an

FIGURE 4-1

§ 6201. Assessment authority

(a) Authority of Secretary

The Secretary is authorized and required to make the inquiries, determinations, and assessments of all taxes (including interest, additional amounts, additions to the tax, and assessable penalties) imposed by this title, or accruing under any former internal revenue law, which have not been duly paid by stamp at the time and in the manner provided by law. Such authority shall extend to and include the following:

(1) Taxes shown on return

The Secretary shall assess all taxes determined by the taxpayer or by the Secretary as to which returns or lists are made under this title.

(2) Unpaid taxes payable by stamp

(A) Omitted stamps

Whenever any article upon which a tax is required to be paid by means of a stamp is sold or removed for sale or use by the manufacturer thereof or whenever any transaction or act upon which a tax is required to be paid by means of a stamp occurs without the use of the proper stamp, it shall be the duty of the Secretary, upon such information as he can obtain, to estimate the amount of tax which has been omitted to be paid and to make assessment therefor upon the person or persons the Secretary determines to be liable for such tax.

FIGURE 4-2

§ 6203. Method of assessment

The assessment shall be made by recording the liability of the taxpayer in the office of the Secretary in accordance with rules or regulations prescribed by the Secretary. Upon request of the taxpayer, the Secretary shall furnish the taxpayer a copy of the record of the assessment.

income tax until the assessment has been *recorded* "in the office of the Secretary." If one could "owe" an income tax before it was assessed and recorded, then **there would be no point at all in the law providing for assessments and their official recording.** In addition, this section's supporting Regulation, 301.6203-1, provides that:

> The assessment shall be made by an assessment officer signing the *summary record of assessment.* The summary record, through *supporting records,* shall provide *identification* of the taxpayer, the character of the *liability* assessed, the taxable period, if applicable, and the *amount* of the assessment. The amount of the assessment shall, in the case of tax shown on a return by the taxpayer, be the amount so shown, and in all other cases the amount of the assessment shall be the amount shown on the supporting list or record. *The date of the assessment is the date that the* summary *record is signed* by an assessment officer. If the taxpayer requests a copy of the record of assessment, *he shall be furnished a copy* of the pertinent parts of the assessment which set forth the name of the taxpayer, the date of the assessment, the character of the liability assessed, the taxable period, and the amounts assessed. [emphasis added]

Actually, section 6201 incorporates the very language and procedures used by Congress in its very first direct taxing Act, in which, on July 14, 1798, it "laid upon the United States" a $2,000,000 tax "assessed upon dwelling-houses, lands and slaves." This Act[1] provided that the Secretary of the Treasury had to assess "upon the dwelling-houses, lands and slaves, according to the valuations and enumerations to be made pursuant to the act." Then "surveyors of the revenue" were "to make out lists containing the sums payable, according to such assessments." The law directed that a federal tax collector "after receiving his collection list, advertise, by notifications, to be posted up in at least four public places...that the said tax has become due." So, pursuant to that Act taxes were not due until assessments were made and the amount assessed communicated to those presumably owing the tax. **This requirement of communicating to those owing the tax, the amount allegedly owed is still preserved in the law today!** It is contained in Code Section 6303 (Figure 4-3) as well as other sections. That section states that the Secretary:

> shall as soon as practicable, and within 60 days after the making of an assessment of a tax pursuant to Section 6203, **give notice** to each person liable for the unpaid tax, **stating the amount and demanding payment.**

So, from all of the above, you now know that before you can even owe an income tax, the amount of that tax must first be *assessed* against you, and then a *demand* made upon you for the amount assessed. But, before an income tax can even be assessed, the government must first have an income tax return prepared by the taxpayer. And without having such a return **an income tax can not even be assessed, let alone owed!**

This means at the very least that no one can be legally required to have income taxes taken from his or her pay, or be required to pay an estimated tax, since all such payments would obviously be made *before* income tax returns are prepared and *before* any assessment could possibly be made and recorded. In addition, all such payments are made without any *demand* having been made upon taxpayers as required by section 6303. Thus the following points regarding federal income taxes (which all departments of the federal government have carefully concealed from the American public) should now be clear:

1. No one can be legally compelled to have income taxes taken from their pay and no one can be legally compelled to pay estimated taxes, since such payments would necessarily occur before any income tax liability[2] pursuant to Code sections 6201, 6203 and 6303 could possibly have been established.

2. All payments as described above, therefore, would have to be "voluntarily" made.

3. All government letters to employers "directing" them to withhold more of their employees' salary than employees elect to have withheld must be illegal. Employees, can not be required to have *anything* at all taken from their pay, since pursuant to Code sections 6201, 6203 and 6303, no employee could possibly "owe" an income tax subject to withholding.

FIGURE 4-3

§ 6303. Notice and demand for tax

(a) General rule

Where it is not otherwise provided by this title, the Secretary shall, as soon as practicable, and within 60 days, after the making of an assessment of a tax pursuant to section 6203, <u>give notice to each person liable for the unpaid tax, stating the amount and demanding payment</u> thereof. Such notice shall be left at the dwelling or usual place of business of such person, or shall be sent by mail to such person's last known address.

(b) Assessment prior to last date for payment

Except where the Secretary believes collection would be jeopardized by delay, if any tax is assessed prior to the last date prescribed for payment of such tax, payment <u>of such tax shall not be demanded</u> under subsection (a) until after such date.

4. All $500 fines levied by the government on individuals on the grounds that they did not authorize enough taxes to be taken from their pay are, obviously, illegal. Since no American could have been required to **have any money at all withheld,** for the reasons stated above.

SELF ASSESSMENT AND VOLUNTARY COMPLIANCE

You should now have an even clearer picture of what "voluntary compliance" is all about. Let's take a closer look at the meaning of "self assessment" to get an even better idea of how both concepts are directly tied in to the statutes themselves.

1. When a taxpayer sends in his tax return and pays his tax he has "determined" his tax pursuant to Code section 6201(a)(1). He has authorized the Secrtary to "assess" the tax he swore "under penalty of perjury" he owed.

2. This is the tax that the Secretary now proceeds to assess. In essence, the taxpayer assessed the taxes on himself (since no one told him he owed it or demanded he pay it) i.e. he "self-assessed" the tax.

No notice and demand pursuant to Code section 6303 is now required to be sent, since the tax has already been *voluntarily paid without regard to any notice and demand.*

When You Legally Owe a Tax, The Government *Tells You*— You Don't Have to *Tell Them!*

If you think about it, you never have to compute other federal taxes such as liquor, gasoline, tobacco, telephone, etc., etc. yourself,[3] so how can you be compelled to compute an income tax? When you buy a tankful of gasoline you pay federal taxes but you don't calculate them nor swear under penalty of perjury that you paid the correct amount. You also pay federal taxes when you purchase cigars, cigarettes, liquor, pay your phone bill, and purchase imported products. When you pay those taxes you don't give the government any information that it can use against you, swear under penalty of perjury that you paid the correct amount, or run the risk of being charged with tax evasion. This is proof that the government can collect federal taxes without forcing Americans to surrender constitutional rights. Local governments always compute the tax you owe (with the exception of state and local income taxes which all state and local governments also enforce illegally). Property taxes, sales taxes, excise taxes, licenses and other state fees are computed for you.[4] There is probably something illegal about any tax that taxpayers must compute themselves and where the amount due is not easily determined.

Americans are free, if they so choose, to self-assess an income tax against themselves and to voluntarily pay that amount. But suppose an American doesn't want to assess an income tax against himself or pay the tax, what then? Can the government on its own initiative assess such a tax against him and then force him to pay it? The answer is a very definite (read my lips!)—No! The Code section that proves this is 6201(2), entitled "Unpaid taxes payable by stamp." You will note that this section authorizes the Secretary:

> **to estimate** the amount of tax which has **omitted to be paid** (by stamp) and to make assessment therefore upon the person or persons the Secretary determines to be liable for such tax.

So the Secretary is specifically authorized "to estimate" the amount of tax which was *omitted* to be paid "by means of a stamp;" but the Secretary was *not* similary authorized to "estimate" the amount of tax that was *omitted* to be paid *on the basis of a return.* This omission was not accidental. It should also be noted that section 6201 is the only section of the code which deals with the making of *all original* tax assessment—payable either by stamp or by returns. The section specifically authorizes the Secretary to make the assessments of all taxes payable by stamp that were "omitted to be paid." However, the Secretary was not similarly authorized to "estimate" those taxes "omitted" to be paid *on the basis of tax returns*—and no such similar authorization can *be found anywhere else in the Internal Revenue Code!* Therefore, it should be clear that the Secretary has no lawful authority to "estimate" and assess income taxes that individuals (or corporations) have elected not to pay and for which they filed no returns. Therefore it should now be clear that the millions of letters that the IRS has sent to Americans who never sent in tax returns, claiming that they owed a specific amount of income taxes, were all fraudulent.

SUPPLEMENTAL ASSESSMENTS

While the Code does not authorize the IRS to even estimate (let alone assess) income taxes against those who do not send in tax returns, the Code does authorize the Secretary to estimate and assess *higher amounts* than what taxpayers say they owe on the tax returns **they do send in.** In other words, if you send in a tax return in which you swear you owe $1.00 in income taxes, the government can assess that amount, **then it can recompute your tax, and by disallowing claimed deductions and by attributing to you more income than you reported, it can make a *supplemental assessment* of $1,000,000.** However, without your sending in a tax return (thus authorizing the government to make that *original* assessment) the government has *no statutory authority to estimate any income taxes you allegedly owe or to assess even one dollar of income taxes against you!*

Section 6204 of Chapter 63 (Figure 4-4) entitled "Supplemental assessments" makes this clear. It states that the Secretary may "make a supplemental assessment whenever it is ascertained that any assessment is imperfect or incomplete in any material respect." However, Treasury Regulation 301.6204-1 clarifies this language further and clearly draws the distinction between "original" and "supplemental" assessments. This entire regulation reads as follows:

> If an assessment is incomplete or incorrect in any material respect, the district director or the director of the regional service center, subject to the restrictions with respect to the assessment of deficiencies in income, estate, gift, chapter 41, 42, 43, and 44 taxes, and subject to the applicable period of limitation, may make a **supplemental** assessment for the purpose of completing the **original** assessment. [emphasis added]

So, not only do income taxes have to be assessed, but they have to be assessed **in a certain order.** The overwhelming majority of the American public is not even aware that income taxes have to be assessed (otherwise they wouldn't pay this tax *in advance,* before assessments according to the law are made) let alone that they must be assessed **in a certain order.**

Deficiency Assessments

By far the most common type of supplemental assessment is the "deficiency assessment," which is defined in section 6211(a) as "The amount by which the tax imposed by Subtitle A (the income tax) exceeds the excess of—

A. the amount shown as a tax "by the taxpayer upon his return" if he filed one, and
B. any amount previously assessed or collected without assessment
C. less any credits

It should be clear, therefore, that the government is precluded, by statute, from determining a deficiency unless it receives a tax return from the taxpayer (a) on which he claims he owes a tax, or (b) from whom the government has collected some taxes "without assessment." The latter occurs when taxpayers voluntarily make payments through withholding or by sending in estimated payments prior to sending in returns.

Assessing Deficiencies

The IRS is authorized by section 6212 (Figure 4-5) to send out proposed deficiency assessments, which it does by

---

FIGURE 4-4

Sec. 6204. Supplemental assessments.

(a) General rule.

The Secretary may, at any time within the period prescribed for assessment, make a <u>supplemental</u> assessment whenever it is ascertained that <u>any assessment</u> is <u>imperfect</u> or <u>incomplete</u> in any material respect.

---

way of A NOTICE OF DEFICIENCY, shown in Figure 5-1. If the taxpayer disagrees with the claimed deficiency, he has to challenge it by petitioning "Tax Court." If the taxpayer does not petition that "court" within 90 days of receiving his NOTICE OF DEFICIENCY, the government is authorized to assess the deficiency pursuant to Section 6213(c) (Figure 4-5). If the taxpayer petitions "Tax Court" the amount determined by that "court" as a deficiency can be assessed pursuant to section 6215(a) (Figure 4-5).

Notice that both sections 6213(c) and 6215(a) provide that the deficiencies "shall be assessed, and shall be paid upon notice and demand from the Secretary." Thus the only time that the Code states that income taxes "shall be paid" is in connection with *supplemental* assessments! This language is never used in connection with *original* assessments. But once a taxpayer swears (by way of filing a tax return) that he has income subject to tax, the government, pursuant to Code sections 6211, 6212, 6213 and 6215, can on its own initiative (at least it would so appear) assess a deficiency and the Code further provides that such deficiencies "shall be paid." Neither of these conditions apply to *original* assessments as provided in Code section 6201.

It is the government's *statutory ability* to initiate supplemental assessments (as opposed to its *inability* to initiate original ones) that is the key to understanding how the government has been able to deceive an entire nation into thinking that its procedures are legal, and has enabled it to extort untold billions from the public.

Professed Government Ignorance

The Government so takes for granted the total unfamiliarity of the American public with income tax assessments, that it feels it can make the most outlandish representations concerning the matter if the subject is even raised. For example, note the Government's answer (see Response #5 in the Appendix) when I asked the Justice Department's team of lawyers to admit that an assessment made pursuant to section 6213(c) (which had to be the section used against me since I did not petition "Tax Court" for the years at issue) can not be made as an original

FIGURE 4-5

Code Section 6212:

§ 6212. Notice of deficiency

(a) In general

If the Secretary determines that there is a deficiency in respect of any tax imposed by subtitles A or B or chapter 41, 42, 43, 44, or 45 <u>he is authorized to send notice of such deficiency</u> to the taxpayer by certified mail or registered mail.

Code Section 6213:

§ 6213. Restrictions applicable to deficiencies; petition to Tax Court

(c) Failure to file petition

If the taxpayer does not file a petition with the Tax Court within the time prescribed in subsection (a), the deficiency, notice of which has been mailed to the taxpayer, <u>shall be assessed, and shall be paid upon notice and demand</u> from the Secretary.

Code Section 6215:

§ 6215. Assessment of deficiency found by Tax Court

(a) General rule

If the taxpayer files a petition with the Tax Court, the entire amount redetermined as the deficiency by the decision of the Tax Court which has become <u>final shall be assessed and shall be paid upon notice and demand</u> from the Secretary. No part of the amount determined as a deficiency by the Secretary but disallowed as such by the decision of the Tax Court which has become final shall be assessed or be collected by levy or by proceeding in court with or without assessment.

assessment. They answered that they did not know what I meant by an "original assessment"! And in its reply on the same issue the IRS' team of lawyers stated (see Response #2, Appendix) "There can be no assessment without a previous deficiency determination." This, of course, placed the cart squarely before the horse. Treasury Regulation 301.6204-1 makes it perfectly clear that an assessment must be made *before* a deficiency can be determined. How could a whole team of IRS lawyers, including its Chief Counsel not know that?

What is real funny about all of this is that IRS deficiency determinations are assumed by the courts to be "presumptively correct," which is why the burden is on taxpayers to prove them incorrect. But how can IRS deficiency determinations (and the assessments that result from them) be "presumptively correct" when it is clear from the government's answers to my discovery questions that two high-powered teams of government tax lawyers didn't even know; (1) what original or supplemental assessments were, and (2) how such supplemental (deficiency) assessments were to be made?

In summation, it should be clear from all of the above that a deficiency assessment can only be made for the purposes "of correcting or completing the original assessment." And if there has been no original assessment, then the IRS lacks any authority to even allege a deficiency—since there is nothing to "correct" or "complete." It should further be clear that, by statute, the Government can not make either an assessment or a deficiency assessment against anyone who has neither (1) filed a tax return or (2) nor made any payments by way of withholding or estimated payments for any given taxable year.

This means that there is nothing in the Internal Revenue Code that can legally reach anyone who neither files an income tax return nor voluntarily makes any payments to the government by way of either withholding or by paying estimated taxes. Such people are simply not "taxpayers" as the word is used in the Code and nothing in the Code can apply to them. So, as far as income taxes are concerned, such people are "home free." But how the government *illegally* subjects them and others to the tax, will be treated in the next chapter.

NOTES TO CHAPTER 4

1. A copy of this entire Act is included in Appendix C of *The Great Income Tax Hoax.*

2. For the purpose of this chapter, to make these Code sections intelligible, and to further demonstrate how the government both disregards and distorts them, I have assumed that under certain conditions it is possible for one to be "liable" for income taxes. This, however, is a false premise as you will see in Chapter 6 of this book.

3. The only federal taxes that the public computes itself are estate, gift and income taxes; three taxes that are enforced in violation of the taxing clauses of the Constitution.

4. The only exception I can think of, apart from income taxes, is a gross receipts tax. However, such a tax is simple to calculate.

— CHAPTER 5 —

A CRIMINAL CONSPIRACY

"Government, even in its best state, is but a necessary evil; in its worst state, an intolerable one."
—**Thomas Paine**

In previous chapters you discovered how those federal employees who control and run the IRS (and those in power who assist them) mislead you. Now you will discover why most of them should be in jail.

The federal establishment (as this chapter will document and prove) has managed to fashion an elaborate swindle complete with false statements, false journal entries and the knowing violation of law (coupled with extortion) that equals anything the private sector has to offer. But the irony is that its perpetrators are the same people who put others in jail for committing **the same or lesser crimes.**

I should also point out that it is misleading for me to accuse the IRS of doing this, that and the other thing, but I do so purely out of habit and custom. It is misleading because it is not really the IRS that does these things, *but the United States itself.* Blaming the IRS for its "excesses" (a euphemism for "criminal behavior") as Senator Pryor and others do, gets the United States and its various culpable departments (including Congress and the courts) off the hook. The IRS only does what these departments let them get away with. So blaming the IRS is like blaming a broken jaw on the fist that hit it—and not on the fellow who threw the punch. The public has been somehow conditioned to forget that the IRS is merely an arm of the United States, so when the IRS breaks the law it is really the United States that's doing it, not the "IRS." Suppose your next door neighbor allowed his dog to jump over the fence and dig up your flower beds, chew up your newspapers, and bite your children while he looked on. Would you blame the dog or its master for such behavior? The reason that the IRS can break the law is that it knows that the courts and the Justice Department will let it get away with it. So the courts and the Justice Department are the real culprits (along with the Congress) not the IRS. Now that I have clarified that, let us proceed to discover why, in America, *organized crime begins with the Federal Government.*

FIRST, A FRAUDULENT NOTICE OF DEFICIENCY

In December of 1982, I received the IRS' NOTICE OF DEFICIENCY shown in Figure 5-1, which was merely the first page of a 10-page document in which the IRS revealed how it had determined the tax "deficiency" it claimed I owed. It had calculated my taxes from bank records (which had been illegally acquired), while its basis for determining my civil fraud (which was imposed arbitrarily and clearly in violation of the statutes) is shown in Figure 5-2. The notice was clearly a total fraud because up until then no *original* assessment had ever been made against me pursuant to Code Sections 6201 and 6203. Obviously, there could not be a "deficiency" calculated pursuant to Sections 6204 and 6211. The numbering of the relevant assessment sections, indicative of the statutory sequence in which assessments must be made, make this clear. I knew that I had never been assessed for the years in question because when I wrote to the District Director asking that he:

Please notify me (pursuant to Code Section 6203) if any income taxes have been assessed against me for the years 1976, 1977, or 1978...

I received the reply shown in Figure 5-3.

It used to be that within about a month after making such an inquiry, people would get such a reply—if no return had been filed. If a return had been filed, they would receive an assessment document similar to the 4340's shown in Figure 5-9, showing the amount assessed, which would be for the amount they showed as the tax due on their returns, i.e., what they had "self-assessed" and also paid.

Write For Copies of Your Assessment

Notice that pursuant to Code Section 6303 (Figure 4-2) the law states, "Upon the request of the taxpayer, the Secretary shall furnish the taxpayer a copy of the record of the assessment. (In this case the "shall" is mandatory—but here the government will argue that it is not—since his furnishing you with the document doesn't interfere with his constitutional rights.) But now that individuals have discovered the secret of income tax assessments, and the importance of a notification that "no assessment has been made" against them, the IRS has grown reluctant to make this admission. Now it often sends back excuses as to why it can't provide the information, or it may even ask you for

FIGURE 5-1

Internal Revenue Service
District Director

CERTIFIED MAIL
No. _143,724_

Date: DEC 0 2 1982

Mr. Irwin A. Schiff
2405 Whitney Ave.
Hamden, CT   06518

Department of the Treasury
135 High Street - Stop 190
Hartford, CT   06103

Social Security or
Employer Identification Number:
047-16-2491
Tax Year Ended and Deficiency:
Additions to the Tax
Internal Revenue Code of 1954

Tax Year Ended	Deficiency	Section 6653(b)	Section 6654
December 31, 1976	$19,006.00	$ 9,503.00	$ 709.00
December 31, 1977	$18,678.00	$ 9,339.00	$ 663.00
December 31, 1978	$53,447.00	$26,724.00	$1,706.00

Person to Contact:
Thomas J. Smith
Contact Telephone Number:
722-3060

CERTIFIED MAIL

Dear Mr. Schiff:

We have determined that there is a deficiency (increase) in your income tax as shown above. This letter is a NOTICE OF DEFICIENCY sent to you as required by law. The enclosed statement shows how we figured the deficiency.

If you want to contest this deficiency in court before making any payment, you have 90 days from the above mailing date of this letter (150 days if addressed to you outside of the United States) to file a petition with the United States Tax Court for a redetermination of the deficiency. The petition should be filed with the United States Tax Court, 400 Second Street NW., Washington, D.C. 20217, and the copy of this letter should be attached to the petition. The time in which you must file a petition with the Court (90 or 150 days as the case may be) is fixed by law and the Court cannot consider your case if your petition is filed late. If this letter is addressed to both a husband and wife, and both want to petition the Tax Court, both must sign the petition or each must file a separate, signed petition. You can get a copy of the rules for filing a petition by writing to the Clerk of the Tax Court at the Court's Washington, D.C. address shown above.

If you decide not to file a petition with the Tax Court, we would appreciate it if you would sign and return the enclosed waiver form. This will permit us to charge your account quickly and will limit the accumulation of interest. The enclosed addressed envelope is for your convenience. If you decide not to sign and return the statement and you do not timely petition the Tax Court, the law requires us to bill you after 90 days from the above mailing date of this letter (150 days if this letter is addressed to you outside the United States)

If you have any questions, please contact the person whose name and telephone number are shown above.

Sincerely yours,

Roscoe L. Egger, Jr.
Commissioner
By

Enclosures:
Copy of this letter
Waiver
Envelope
paf
District Director, Hartford District

District Director

Letter 892(DO) (Rev. 3-79)

FIGURE 5-2

I:R:90D   -7-   Statement continued

Mr. Irwin A. Schiff

15) Additions to the Tax:

All or part of the underpayment of tax required to be shown on the return for the taxable years 1976, 1977 and 1978 is due to fraud. Consequently, the 50% addition to the tax is charged for each of those years, as provided by Section 6653(b) of the Internal Revenue Code.

Since you underpaid your estimated tax for the taxable years 1976, 1977 and 1978, the addition to the tax is charged for each of those years, as provided by Section 6654 of the Internal Revenue Code.

some kind of identification—hoping that you will get discouraged.

For example, Lynn Poll, Chief, Correspondence Section of the IRS, Ogden Utah wrote to someone who asked for copies of their assessments as follows:

A record of assessments for the years ...cannot be determined until such time as you file your income tax returns and any subsequent examinations of the tax years are made. The amount of tax owed depends on a number of different items such as filing status, income, exemptions, etc....

Any further requests should be made after you have filed your income tax returns or examinations have been completed.

In effect, Miss Poll's letter, while actually admitting that no assessments can be made without a taxpayer's return, seeks to avoid saying so by the delusive use of the word "determined" and the phrase "and any subsequent examinations of the tax years are made." (I am not suggesting for a moment that Miss Poll ever drafted the short, two paragraph letter she sent out. She merely sent the letter that head honchos of the IRS spent hours drafting to deviously cover the situation.)

If the IRS writes to you claiming that they can not determine whether an assessment has been made against you or words to that effect, simply write back as follows:

"Look, just tell me whether or not your records show if an income tax assessment has been made against me pursuant to Code section 6201 as of... (the current date of your letter)..., yes, or no. If your records show no such assessment, please advise me of that. Whether I may or may not have filed a return is beside the point, since I understand that the Secretary can make an assessment against me (utilizing the provisions of Section 6020) *even if I didn't file a return.*

Please note that pursuant to Code section 6203, the Secretary "Upon the request of the taxpayer shall furnish the taxpayer a copy of the record of the assessment." So pursuant to that section, please either furnish me with such a record or notify me that none has been made, either pursuant to section 6201 or as a consequence of the Secretary not exercising section 6020(b).

Please note that my letter from the IRS was dated January 25, 1983—almost *two months* after the IRS informed me of a "deficiency" in my assessment. Remember, that while the IRS' NOTICE OF DEFICIENCY doesn't mention

FIGURE 5-3

Internal Revenue Service   Department of the Treasury

Internal Revenue   North-Atlantic Region   310 Lowell St., Andover, Mass. 01812
Service Center

Mr. Irwin A. Schiff   Person to Contact:
P. O. Box 5303   Disclosure Office
Hamden, CT 06518   Telephone Number:
                                             617-681-5618
                                             Refer Reply to:
                                             83D009
                                             Date:
                                                 January 25, 1983

Dear Mr. Schiff:

In response to your request dated 12/21/82 for a record of assessment of your individual income taxes for 1976, 1977 and 1978, a search was made of the Individual Master File and our records show that as of this date, January 25th, there is no record of assessments for these periods (1976, 1977 & 1978).

This information is furnished to you in accordance with Internal Revenue Code Section 6203.

                                             Sincerely yours,

                                             HENRY F. CAMACHO
                                             Disclosure Officer

"assessment" the "deficiency" referred to in its NOTICE means (pursuant to sections 6204 and 6211) a *deficiency in my assessment.* But how could there have been "deficiencies" in my assessments on December 2, 1982 when some two months later, on January 25, 1983, the IRS informed me that no assessment against me for those years **had ever been made?** If I didn't have the documents to prove this, you never would have believed it, would you?

Of course, most people who get these deficiency notices and who have not filed tax returns for the year or years in question would not know that:

1. Before a "deficiency" assessment can be legal an *original assessment* pursuant to section 6201 would had to have been made.
2. Since no original assessment could have been made if no return was filed, the claim of a "deficiency" in such cases is totally contrary to what the statutes provide.
3. THE IRS' NOTICE OF DEFICIENCY they receive therefore is both fraudulent and **extortionary.**

This, of course, is exactly the type of notice that automatically should get jail sentences for all IRS Commissioners and District Directors who send them out in the instances where no returns have been filed. In such cases there is *absolutely no question* that such Commissioners and District Directors are merely seeking to use the U.S. mail to defraud. And, in addition, such fraudulent and extortionary letters (coupled with other letters, phone calls and actions) cut across state lines, and thus would make all those government officials who participate, prime candidates for civil law suits under RICCO (Racketeer Influenced and Corrupt Organizations Act) and hopefully members of the public will begin filing such suits against them. So if you did not file a tax return but still receive a NOTICE OF DEFICIENCY, be sure to write the IRS **subsequent to the date** of that NOTICE for a copy of your record of assessment. You will have to be informed that no assessment has yet been made, proving conclusively that your NOTICE OF DEFICIENCY **was a total fraud.** Some day you might want to prove the obvious implications of this to some federal judge.

A DOCUMENT FRAUDULENT ON ITS FACE

The Missing Code Section

The real clue to the fraudulent character of a NOTICE OF DEFICIENCY is its missing Code section. No Code section is shown over the "Deficiency" column. You will note that the Notice identifies the two Code sections which presumably authorized the "Additions to the Tax." These are not really "additions" to the tax, but outright "penalties"[1]—penalties levied pursuant to Sections 6653(b) and 6654. The penalty of $45,566 levied allegedly pursuant to 6653(b) is for *civil fraud*—where the elements of the fraud alleged are identical with the type of criminal fraud alleged in a criminal indictment for tax evasion pursuant to section 7201[2]. However, here the United States expects its victims to pay such fraud penalties without *its ever having proved them*—albeit only exacting a fine instead of a prison term. And if the Government can allegedly do this with respect to *monetary* penalties, why can't it do the same thing with respect to *criminal* penalties? If the Government can seize property in connection with fraud charges it never proves, then why can't it send people to prison on the same basis? What would be the rationale that could justify the former but not the latter?

But if in that document the Government could identify the two Code sections that allegedly made me liable for the penalties **why didn't the Government also identify the Code Section that made me liable for the underlying tax?** *This omission* was no mere *accident*. Obviously, if the Government could have cited such a section it would have (more on this in the next chapter). The inclusion in the Government's NOTICE OF DEFICIENCY of Code sections that authorized the penalties, but *not* the section that authorized the underlying tax; should, in and of itself, provide all the proof that anyone needs regarding the United States' **CRIMINAL EXACTION OF INCOME TAXES.**

The United States Refuses to Answer

Immediately upon receiving the Government's extortionary "Notice," I sent Secretary of the Treasury, Donald T. Regan, the letter shown in Figure 5-4. The Secretary did not even acknowledge, let alone answer, any of the questions. Obviously, writing correct answers would only confirm the criminal nature of his conduct and that of all of his underlings.

MORE FRAUDULENT IRS DOCUMENTS

Approximately four months later on April 5, 1983, the Government sent me the three documents shown in Figure 5-5, which the Government would later try to pass off as a "demand" for taxes due. The document can be seen to be fraudulent on the following grounds.

1. The documents are entitled "Statement of Tax Due on Federal Tax Return," but notice that the statement does not identify the kind of tax allegedly "due." If it were income taxes, then why didn't they say so? While a "Form Number 1040" was *filled in* (indicating that this form is used for other kinds of taxes) such an entry is pointedly vague and evasive.

2. If the taxes were really "due" the Code section pursuant to which they were "due" should obviously have been cited.

3. Note that assessment dates of "04-01-83" are indicated. This substantiates that the taxes allegedly "due" had to have been assessed, but it was only done a few days before these "Statements" were sent out.

4. Notice that there is no "demand" that any of these amounts are to be paid. The fact that it states "should be paid" is the equivalent of saying that it "must," "shall" or "may" be paid. The fact that the government again avoided using the mandatory "required" and opted for the innocuous "should" was no accident. The Government conscientiously does this all the time, knowing full well how the public is fooled by such permissive language. See Figure 5-6 for another blatant and more dramatic example.

Where Did The Interest Come From?

Note that the assessment of my taxes was claimed to have been made on 04-01-83 and these bills were prepared on April 5, 1983—only **4 days** after the taxes were assessed! Presumably, I didn't owe any taxes before the assessments were made, since if I did, *what purpose would the assessments have served!* So how could I be charged $52,071.23 in interest on a bill that was only four days old? Also note that of the $191.846.23 that the government claimed I owed as of 04-01-83 only $91,131 was for taxes—the rest was for *false* penalty charges! (This is further developed in Chapter 9.)

FIGURE 5-4

Freedom Books

P.O. BOX 5303 HAMDEN, CONNECTICUT 06518 PHONE (203) 281-6791

If a nation values anything more than freedom, it will lose its freedom; and the irony of it is that if it is comfort or money that it values more, it will lose that too.—Somerset Maugham.

December 7, 1982

Donald T. Regan, Secretary of the Treasury
Department of the Treasury
Main Treasury Building
15th Street & Pennsylvania Avenue, NW
Washington, D.C. 20220

Dear Mr. Secretary:

I received the attached notice from Roscoe L. Egger, Jr., Commissioner of the Internal Revenue Service, who acts under your authority.

I am writing directly to you to determine whether you are aware that your agents - Commissioner Egger and Connecticut District Director, James E. Quinn - are assessing taxes and fraud and interest penalties contrary to law and whether they are violating these laws with your knowledge and approval.

I would, therefore, like your answers to the following questions with respect to the attached "Notice of Deficiency."

1. Is the assessment of taxes shown on this document levied pursuant to Section 6303 of the Internal Revenue Code?

2. Has the liability of $91,131.00 shown as a "deficiency" been recorded in your office pursuant to Section 6203 of the Internal Revenue Code?

3. Has there been any tax liability recorded in your office with respect to any taxes due from me for the years 1976, 1977, and 1978?

4. If not taxes have been assessed against me and recorded in your office, can I have a "deficiency assessment?"

5. Am I to understand that this 90 Day Letter makes me liable for $91,131.00 in taxes?

6. Are you authorized, by law, to determine a tax deficiency before you have even determined a tax liability, as provided for in Section 6201?

7. What section of the Internal Revenue Code authorizes you, as Secretary, to determine a tax deficiency before you even determine a tax, record the liability, and notify the taxpayer as provided for in Sections 6201, 6203, and 6303?

8. Am I to assume that you have authorized Mr. Egger to assess fraud and interest penalties against individuals who refuse to voluntarily disclose tax information to the government in accordance with Section 6020(a) of the Internal Revenue Code?

9. Was my tax liability as calculated by Mr. Egger determined in accordance with Section 6020(b) of the Internal Revenue Code?

10. Does Section 6020(b) provide that fraud and interest penalties apply if "the Secretary makes a return from his own knowledge?"

11. I note that Section 6020(a) states that a taxpayer can "consent to disclose information necessary for the preparation of [the return]," but nowhere in Section 6020 does it state that there are penalties if a taxpayer does not consent to disclose information. Have you, therefore, authorized the Commissioner to assess fraud and interest penalties against those who elect to follow the law as contained in Section 6020(a) of the Internal Revenue Code?

12. Has Section 6020(a) of the Internal Revenue Code been revoked? Is there a new section that provides for fraud and interest penalties if a taxpayer does not consent to disclose information necessary for the preparation of his return?

13. Can you provide me with any section of the law that says that there are interest and fraud penalties if a taxpayer does not consent to give the Internal Revenue Service information from which a tax can be computed?

14. Is compliance with IRS rules and regulations voluntary or mandatory? If it is your view that compliance is compulsory please provide me with any published IRS material that confirms this.

15. Were you, as Secretary of the Treasury, given any authority by Congress other than to encourage voluntary compliance with Internal Revenue laws and regulations?

I would further like to remind you that Section 6214(a)(1) & (2) makes it a crime for you to knowingly demand of me a sum which is greater than authorized by law. The question is, does the Internal Revenue Code authorize you to demand of me - through your agents, Mr. Egger and Mr. Quinn - $91,131.00 as a tax deficiency; $45,566.00 in fraud penalties; and $3,078.00 in interest penalties as a result of my not having filed tax returns for the years 1976, 1977, and 1978 as provided for in Section 6020(a) of the Internal Revenue Code?

Respectfully,

Irwin A. Schiff

FIGURE 5-5

Department of the Treasury
Internal Revenue Service
Director 310 LOWELL ST.
ANDOVER, MA 01812

Date of This Notice: IDRS# 06010000 23C 04-01-83 **SRC: 000**

DLN — For IRS Use Only 670
06251-091-13204 30 76 12 570

If you find it necessary to inquire about your account, please refer to this number. ▶ 047-16-2491

APR - 5 1983

IRWIN A SCHIFF
60 CONNOLLY PARKWAY
HAMDEN CT 06518

Form Number: 1040

Tax Period Ended: 12-31-76

Assessment Date: 04-01-83 ◀

Statement of Tax Due On Federal Tax Return

This is a notice of tax due on your return identified above. The amount shown as Balance Due should be paid within 10 days from the date of this notice. Please make your check or money order payable to Internal Revenue Service and send it with this notice to the address shown above.

Reference	Assessment	Credit	Balance Due
04-01-83 TAX	19,066.00 ◀ what kind?		
04-01-83 FR PEN	9,503.00		
04-01-83EST PEN	700.00		
04-01-83 INT	12,619.35		
Penalty — Failure to Pay	.00		$41,837.35

IDRS# 06010000 23C 04-01-83 **SRC: 000**

DLN — For IRS Use Only 670
06251-091-13205 30 77 12 570

If you find it necessary to inquire about your account, please refer to this number. ▶ 047-16-2491

APR - 5 1983

IRWIN A SCHIFF
60 CONNOLLY PARKWAY
HAMDEN CT 06518

Form Number: 1040

Tax Period Ended: 12-31-77

Assessment Date: 04-01-83 ◀

Statement of Tax Due On Federal Tax Return

This is a notice of tax due on your return identified above. The amount shown as Balance Due should be paid within 10 days from the date of this notice. Please make your check or money order payable to Internal Revenue Service and send it with this notice to the address shown above.

Reference	Assessment	Credit	Balance Due
04-01-83 TAX	18,678.00 ◀ what kind?		
04-01-83 FR PEN	9,339.00		
04-01-83EST PEN	663.00		
04-01-83 INT	11,080.99		
Penalty — Failure to Pay	.00		$39,760.99

IDRS# 06010000 23C 04-01-83 **SRC: 000**

DLN — For IRS Use Only 670
06251-091-13206 30 78 12 570

If you find it necessary to inquire about your account, please refer to this number. ▶ 047-16-2491

APR - 5 1983

IRWIN A SCHIFF
60 CONNOLLY PARKWAY
HAMDEN CT 06518

Form Number: 1040

Tax Period Ended: 12-31-78

Assessment Date: 04-01-83 ◀

Statement of Tax Due On Federal Tax Return

This is a notice of tax due on your return identified above. The amount shown as Balance Due should be paid within 10 days from the date of this notice. Please make your check or money order payable to Internal Revenue Service and send it with this notice to the address shown above.

Reference	Assessment	Credit	Balance Due
04-01-83 TAX	53,447.00 ◀ what kind?		
04-01-83 FR PEN	26,724.00		
04-01-83EST PEN	1,706.00		
04-01-83 INT	28,370.99		
Penalty — Failure to Pay	.00		$110,247.89

FIGURE 5-6

Internal Revenue Service
District Director

Date: April 18, 1983

▷ Irwin A. Schiff
   60 Connolly Parkway
   Hamden, Connecticut 06518

Department of the Treasury
  0 Court Street Room 205
  New Haven, Connecticut 06510

**Social Security or
Employer Identification Number:**

047-16-2491
Person to Contact:

J Holmberg
Contact Telephone Number:

773-2053

FINAL NOTICE
Reply Within 10 Days to Avoid Enforcement
Action and Additional Penalties

Dear Mr. Schiff:

   Although notices and demands have been made for payment of your Federal taxes shown on the back of this letter, we have no record of receiving the amount due. This is your final notice before we proceed with enforcement action.

   To prevent such action, send us, within 10 days from the date of this letter, your check or money order for the total amount due, payable to the Internal Revenue Service. Show your taxpayer identifying number (social security or employer identification number) on it and enclose this letter to assure prompt and accurate credit. An envelope is enclosed for your convenience. The copy of this letter is for your records.

   If you have recently paid the amount due but your payment has not been credited to your account, or if you cannot pay this amount in full, contact the person whose name and telephone number are shown above within 10 days from the date of this letter.

   If we do not receive your payment or if you do not contact our office, enforcement action may be taken at any time after 10 days from the date of this letter without any further notice to you. Salary or wages due you may be levied upon, as provided by section 6331 of the Internal Revenue Code, by serving a notice of levy on your employer. Bank accounts, receivables, commissions, or any other kind of income you have are also subject to levy. Property or rights to property, such as automobiles, may also be seized and sold to satisfy your tax liability.

Enclosures:
Envelope
Copy of this letter

Sincerely yours,

District Director

Form Number	Tax Period	Tax Balance	Accumulated Penalty	Accumulated Interest
1040	12-31-76	Tax Assessed	19,006.00	
		Fraud penalty	9,503.00	
		Estimated Tax Penalty	709.00	
		Interest.	13,117.35	
		Total this period		42,335.35
1040	12-31-77	Tax Assessed	18,678.00	
		Fraud penalty	9,339.00	
		Estimated Tax Penalty	663.00	
		Interest	11,554.28	
		Total this period		40,234.28
1040	12-31-78	Tax Assessed	53,447.00	
		Fraud penalty	26,724.00	
		Estimated Tax Penalty	1,706.00	
		Interest	29,683.20	
		Total this period		111,560.20
	Total 1976 through 1978			194,129.83

Above totals computed to April 28, 1983. Interest continues to accrue at 16% annually.

The Most Fraudulent Document
Of Them All—The IRS' FINAL NOTICE

Approximately 10 days after receiving my "Statement of Tax Due," I received the Final Notice shown in Figure 5-6. First of all, observe how the NOTICE starts off by stating that "although *notices* and *demands* have been made for payment of your Federal taxes." Well, you can see that up until that moment the government had not sent me one previous document "demanding" payment of any tax. A real "notice and demand" will be discussed in great detail in Chapter 7, but such a notice was never sent to me. The reason that the government uses this specific language is because of Code Section 6331 which states that:

If any person liable to pay any tax neglects or refuses to pay the same within 10 days after *notice and demand,* it shall be lawful for the Secretary to collect such tax

by distraint—that is involuntarily. So by falsely claiming that "notices and demands have been made" upon me, the government seeks to set me up for the illegal seizures that are to follow as threatened in the fourth paragraph of its FINAL NOTICE.

But additional clues as to the fraudulent character of this NOTICE is that, though it threatens to seize my property for not paying a federal tax, the type of federal tax I allegedly owe is never even mentioned in that document. Most people, of course, when they get a FINAL NOTICE automatically assume that the "Federal taxes" referred to mean *income* taxes—but the NOTICE says no such thing! And while a "Form Number 1040" is mentioned, the Code section establishing the "tax liability" of which it speaks is not identified. And note how the operation of interest alone has increased my alleged "tax liability" from $191,846.23 to $194,129.83 (or by $2,233.60) in just 27 days! This amounts to 2-1/2 percent of the basic tax the government claimed I owed!

More Letters Ignored

In response to the Government's threat to begin seizing my property (in violation of law), I sent a nine-page letter to the District Director, James Quinn, with a copy to James Holmberg, the IRS revenue officer, over whose signature the threatening FINAL NOTICE was sent. That letter incorporates a good deal of the material covered in this book, so there is no question that the District Director knew that he was breaking the law. Perhaps that is why he refused to answer any of the questions I raised either in that letter or in my follow-up letter, both of which have been included in the Appendix.

I also paid a visit to the local IRS office and asked to speak to James Holmberg the revenue officer who had presumably calculated the taxes, penalties and interest shown on the Notice. I had brought along a check book and offered to immediately pay the full amount due. I told them that I only wanted to know the Code Section making me liable for the tax so I could put it on my check stub. "So would you please tell me the Code section that makes me liable for these taxes?," I asked of Holmberg and his colleagues. But neither one could tell me. I told them that I was in no hurry and would wait until they found the Code section. I thought that for $194,129.83 the least the government could do was to cite the law that made me "liable." For that kind of money, I felt that I shouldn't have to take the *word* of a low level government employee that such a tax liability actually existed. Mr. Holmberg stepped out of the room and when he returned he told me that no one then in the office could find the Code section. I told him to call the District Director's office in Hartford, or the IRS' main office in Washington. Here I was prepared to hand over $194,129.83 to the government and all I wanted to know was the Code section that made me "liable" for the tax, yet Holmberg said that he was too busy to get the information! So, I left without paying the government the money it claimed I owed, but for which they refused to show me the law (Code section) pursuant to which I "owed" it. In case you don't believe me, try that yourself the next time the IRS claims you owe income taxes. Ask them to produce the law that makes you "liable" for the taxes they claim you "owe." Be prepared for a long wait. Bring along a sandwich or two.

MORE FRAUD AND EXTORTION, WITH THE HELP OF THE COURTS

It's hard to believe, but at that time I was so naive that I actually believed that the Constitution was still in effect. I thought the government could not take property without a court order. I thought that there were limits beyond which federal courts would not go in ignoring the law. Unfolding events were to prove me wrong on all counts.

An attorney warned me that despite the lack of proof that I owed the government a dime, the IRS could still confiscate my property. I was only to find out later how the IRS illegally seized property by subverting Code section 6331 (Figure 5-7). Meanwhile, I was convinced that the government's claim that I had been assessed for taxes for those years was fraudulent (three years later my suspicions would be confirmed), and I believed that they could not produce a valid assessment certificate. I believed that coupled with that and my ability to present to any court how the income tax was being levied contrary to the taxing clauses of the Constitution and the Sixteenth Amendment itself, that I could get a restraining order and permanent injunction against such threatened seizures. These constitutional arguments were clearly made, but

Connecticut District Court Judge Ellen Burns, following the usual procedure of federal judges, ignored them all and rationalized her decision not to intervene with a truncated quote from a Supreme Court decision whose actual meaning she distorted, but which actually supported and verified my argument.[3] But Judge Burns refused to intervene by falsely claiming that she lacked the jurisdiction to do so.[4] But what turned out to be of even greater significance (for the purposes of this book) is that a day or two before the hearing, the government produced a "quick" ASSESSMENT CERTIFICATE of the "Summary Assessments," as shown in Figure 5-8, and claimed that my assessment was "included within the (lumped) 82 individual income tax, penalty and interest items which totaled $721,505.20." The

explanation for this was contained in an accompanying two-page letter from Glenn L. Archer, Jr., the (then) Assistant Attorney General of the Justice Department and D. Patrick Mullarkey, Chief, Civil Trial Section, Northern Region. That letter four other documents that accompanied the ASSESSMENT CERTIFICATE are included in the Appendix.

First of all, note that nowhere in the ASSESSMENT CERTIFICATE does my name appear. What proof did either my attorney or I have that my "assessment" was actually contained within that composite entry of 82 individual items as claimed by Archer and Mullarkey? It was not until some three years later that I discovered that Treasury Regulation 301.6203-1 provided that:

FIGURE 5-7

§ 6331. Levy and distraint

(a) Authority of Secretary

If any person liable to pay any tax neglects or refuses to pay the same within 10 days after notice and demand, it shall be lawful for the Secretary to collect such tax (and such further sum as shall be sufficient to cover the expenses of the levy) by levy upon all property and rights to property (except such property as is exempt under section 6334) belonging to such person or on which there is a lien provided in this chapter for the payment of such tax. Levy may be made upon the accrued salary or wages of any officer, employee, or elected official, of the United States, the District of Columbia, or any agency or instrumentality of the United States or the District of Columbia, by serving a notice of levy on the employer (as defined in section 3401(d)) of such officer, employee, or elected official. If the Secretary makes a finding that the collection of such tax is in jeopardy, notice and demand for immediate payment of such tax may be made by the Secretary and, upon failure or refusal to pay such tax, collection thereof by levy shall be lawful without regard to the 10-day period provided in this section.

(b) Seizure and sale of property

The term "levy" as used in this title includes the power of distraint and seizure by any means. Except as otherwise provided in subsection (e), a levy shall extend only to property possessed and obligations existing at the time thereof. In any case in which the Secretary may levy upon property or rights to property, he may seize and sell such property or rights to property (whether real or personal, tangible or intangible).

(c) Successive seizures

Whenever any property or right to property upon which levy has been made by virtue of subsection (a) is not sufficient to satisfy the claim of the United States for which levy is made, the Secretary may, thereafter, and as often as may be necessary, proceed to levy in like manner upon any other property liable to levy of the person against whom such claim exists, until the amount due from him, together

with all expenses, is fully paid.

(d) Requirement of notice before levy

(1) In general

Levy may be made under subsection (a) upon the salary or wages or other property of any person with respect to any unpaid tax only after the Secretary has notified such person in writing of his intention to make such levy.

(2) 10-day requirement

The notice required under paragraph (1) shall be

(A) given in person,

(B) left at the dwelling or usual place of business of such person, or

(C) sent by certified or registered mail to such persons's last known address,

no less than 10 days before the day of the levy.

(3) Jeopardy

Paragraph (1) shall not apply to a levy if the Secretary has made a finding under the last sentence of subsection (a) that the collection of tax is in jeopardy.

(e) Continuing levy on salary and wages

(1) Effect of levy

The effect of a levy on salary or wages payable to or received by a taxpayer shall be continuous from the date such levy is first made until the liability out of which such levy arose is satisfied or becomes unenforceable by reason of lapse of time.

(2) Release and notice of release

With respect to a levy described in paragraph (1), the Secretary shall promptly release the levy when the liability out of which such levy arose is satisfied or becomes unenforceable by reason of lapse of time, and shall promptly notify the person upon whom such levy was made that such levy has been released.

(f) Cross references

(1) For provisions relating to jeopardy, see subchapter A of chapter 70.

(2) For proceedings applicable to sale of seized property see section 6335.

A Criminal Conspiracy

75

the assessment shall be made by an assessment officer signing the summary record of assessment. The summary, *through supporting records,* shall provide *identification of the taxpayer,* the character of the liability assessed, the taxable period, if applicable, and the amount of the assessment. The amount of the assessment shall, in the case of tax *shown on a return by the taxpayer, be the amount so shown,* and in all other cases the amount of the assessment shall be the amount shown on the *supporting list or record.* The date of the assessment is the date the summary record is signed by an assessment officer. If the taxpayer requests a copy of the record of assessment, *he shall be furnished* a copy of the *pertinent parts* of the assessment which set forth the *name of the taxpayer,* the date of assessment, the character of the liability assessed, the taxable period, if applicable, and the amount assessed. [emphasis added]

As you can see, Messrs. Archer and Mullarkey supplied none of the identifying and supporting documentation as called for by Regulation 301.6203-1. Unfortunately, both my attorney and I, and *possibly* the Judge were completely taken in by the Justice Department's fabricated claim, which contributed to Judge Burns' refusal to intervene so as to prevent the government's intended illegal seizures. However, that letter from Archer and Mullarkey would ultimately provide me with the key that would unlock the door to the government's elaborate *modes operandi* which had enabled it to *illegally* assess income taxes against those who never filed income tax returns. The following is the irrefutable evidence of this criminal conspiracy.

THE IRS FORM 4340 REVEALS ALL— IF YOU CAN UNDERSTAND IT

Actually it was those six IRS Form 4340s (Figure 5-9) that I received in connection with the years 1974, 1975, 1976, 1977, 1978, and 1979 (A, B, C, D, E, and F) that revealed the government's underhanded plot. When I first saw the forms for the years 1976, 1977 and 1978, I frankly didn't completely understand them, and while I suspected they were fraudulent, I couldn't definitively explain why. I realized, of course, that the first entry that declared "Return Filed" had to be erroneous, **since I had filed no returns for any of the years shown.** I also knew that, despite its fraudulent claim, neither had the government. When I subsequently demanded to see those "returns," the government produced the "dummies." In addition, since a long time had elapsed between my receiving these various form 4340s and my letter from Archer and Mullarkey, I didn't really comprehend the significance of column (g) entitled "23C Date." At the time of Archer's letter, I was beset by so many other concerns that the statement in his

FIGURE 5-8

QUICK
ASSESSMENT CERTIFICATE
SUMMARY RECORD OF ASSESSMENTS

CLASS OF TAX	CURRENT ASSESSMENTS TAX & PENALTY (a)	INTEREST (b)	DEFICIENCY AND ADDITIONAL ASSESSMENTS (Resulting From Regular Audit Examinations) TAX & PENALTY (c)	INTEREST (d)	NO. OF ITEMS (e)	TOTAL ASSESSMENTS (f)
1. SERVICE CENTER: ANDOVER		2. DATE: APRIL 1, 1983		3. PREPARED BY: MM		4. NUMBER: 482
WITHHELD INDIVIDUAL INCOME AND FICA	2,425 39					2,425 39
INDIVIDUAL INCOME-OTHER			519,611 69	201,893 51	82	721,505 20
CORPORATION INCOME AND EXCESS PROFITS			375,399 70	193,352 17	11	568,751 87
EXCISE						
ESTATE AND GIFT			58,566 49	12,677 00	1	71,243 49
TAX ON CARRIERS AND THEIR EMPLOYEES						
FEDERAL UNEMPLOYMENT TAX ACT						
TOTAL ASSESSMENTS	2,425 39		953,577 88	407,922 68	94	1,363,925 95

5 JEOPARDY ASSESSMENTS AGAINST PRINCIPAL TAXPAYERS (Included in the assessments above)		6. PREPARED FROM ACCOUNTING ASSESSMENT JOURNALS DATE AND NUMBER	THROUGH	DATE AND NUMBER
		4-1-83 8-1936	4-1-83	8-1940
NUMBER OF PRINCIPAL TAXPAYERS		4-1-83 8-5505		
TOTAL ASSESSED AGAINST PRINCIPAL TAXPAYERS		4-1-83 8-5507		

CERTIFICATION

I certify that the taxes, penalties, and interest of the above classifications, hereby assessed, are specified in supporting records, subject to such correction as subsequent inquiries and determinations in respect thereto may indicate to be proper.

7. DATE: APRIL 1, 1983	8. SIGNATURE (For Service Center Director of Internal Revenue)	Assessment Officer

U. S. TREASURY DEPARTMENT · INTERNAL REVENUE SERVICE   FORM 23C (REV. 9-67)

FIGURE 5-9   A

Certificate of Assessments and Payments

Name of Taxpayer		Address (Number, street, city, and state)			EIN or SSN		
Irwin A. Schiff		144 Shepards Knoll, Hamden, CT 06514			047-16-2491N		1040
Date (a)	Explanation of Transactions (b)	Assessment (Abatement) (c)	Credit (Credit Reversal) (d)	Balance (e)	DLN or Account Number (f)	23C Date (g)	Period Ending (h)
04-20-83	Additional Tax Assessed	16,406.25			06647-111-20000	04-20-83	7412
	Fraud Penalty	8,203.13					
	Failure to Pay Tax Penalty	525.00					
	Restricted Interest	17,502.54					
08-14-84	Payment		176.68				
11-15-84	Lien Fee	18.00					
03-25-85	Payment		8,619.31				
04-26-85	Payment		19.02				
09-19-85	Payment		2,174.10				
10-28-85	Payment		7,271.23	24,394.58			
04-20-84	First Notice						

I certify that the foregoing transcript of the taxpayer named above in respect to the taxes specified is a true and complete transcript for the period stated, and all assessments, penalties, interests, abatements, credits, refunds, and advance or unidentified payment relating thereto as disclosed by the records of this office as of the date of this certification are shown therein.

Signature of Director (required for certification) SUPERVISOR PAYMENT & CERT. UNIT	Location INTERNAL REVENUE SERVICE CENTER NORTH ATLANTIC REGION, ANDOVER, MA 01812	Date 03-24-88

Form **4340** (Rev. 7-80)   Use and issue first "Rev. 7-74"   PS/gd   Department of the Treasury - Internal Revenue Service

                                                                                    B

Certificate of Assessments and Payments

Name of Taxpayer		Address (Number, street, city, and state)			EIN or SSN		
Irwin A. Schiff		144 Shepards Knoll, Hamden, CT 06514			047-16-2491N		1040
Date (a)	Explanation of Transactions (b)	Assessment (Abatement) (c)	Credit (Credit Reversal) (d)	Balance (e)	DLN or Account Number (f)	23C Date (g)	Period Ending (h)
04-20-83	Additional Tax Assessed	3,226.39			06647-111-20001	04-20-83	7512
	Fraud Penalty	1,613.20					
	Failure to Pay Tax Penalty	139.68					
	Restricted Interest	3,138.24					
05-17-84	Payment		6,927.08				
03-25-85	Payment		1,380.69				
05-15-86	Restricted Interest	190.26		.00			
04-20-84	First Notice						

I certify that the foregoing transcript of the taxpayer named above in respect to the taxes specified is a true and complete transcript for the period stated, and all assessments, penalties, interests, abatements, credits, refunds, and advance or unidentified payment relating thereto as disclosed by the records of this office as of the date of this certification are shown therein.

Signature of Director (required for certification) SUPERVISOR PAYMENT & CERT. UNIT	Location INTERNAL REVENUE SERVICE CENTER NORTH ATLANTIC REGION, ANDOVER, MA 01812	Date 03-24-88

Form **4340** (Rev. 7-80)   Use and issue first "Rev. 7-74"   PS/gd   Department of the Treasury - Internal Revenue Service

FIGURE 5-9 (continued)   C

Certificate of Assessments and Payments

Name of Taxpayer	Address (Number, street, city, and state)		EIN or SSN		
Irwin A. Schiff	P.O. Box 5303, Hamden, CT 06518		047-16-2491 ✚ 1040		

Date (a)	Explanation of Transactions (b)	Assessment (Abatement) (c)	Credit (Credit Reversal) (d)	Balance (e)	DLN or Account Number (f)	23C Date (g)	Period Ending (h)
11-09-82	Return Filed	.00			0821133102306	12-27-82	7612
04-01-83	Additional Tax	19,006.00			0625109113204	04-01-83	
	Fraud Penalty	9,503.00					
	Estimated Tax Penalty	709.00					
	Interest	12,619.35		41,837.35			
04-01-83	First Notice						

I certify that the foregoing transcript of the taxpayer named above in respect to the taxes specified is a true and complete transcript for the period stated, and all assessments, penalties, interests, abatements, credits, refunds, and advance or unidentified payment relating thereto as disclosed by the records of this office as of the date of this certification are shown therein.

Signature of XXXiXXXXX (required for certification)	Location	Internal Revenue Service Center North-Atlantic Region Andover, Massachusetts 01812	Date
Alin H. Tanner Supvr., Account Unit			May 12, 1983 AT/jm

Form **4340** (Rev. 7-80)   *Use and issue first "Rev. 7-74"*   ＊U.S. GOVERNMENT PRINTING OFFICE 1982 522-064/5953   Department of the Treasury - Internal Revenue Service

                                                                              D

Certificate of Assessments and Payments

Name of Taxpayer	Address (Number, street, city, and state)		EIN or SSN		
Irwin A. Schiff	P.O. Box 5303, Hamden, CT 06518		047-16-2491 ✚ 1040		

Date (a)	Explanation of Transactions (b)	Assessment (Abatement) (c)	Credit (Credit Reversal) (d)	Balance (e)	DLN or Account Number (f)	23C Date (g)	Period Ending (h)
11-09-82	Return Filed	.00			0821133102305	12-27-82	7712
04-01-83	Additional Tax	18,678.00			0625109113205	04-01-83	
	Fraud Penalty	9,339.00					
	Estimated Tax Penalty	663.00					
	Interest	11,080.99		39,760.99			
04-01-83	First Notice						

I certify that the foregoing transcript of the taxpayer named above in respect to the taxes specified is a true and complete transcript for the period stated, and all assessments, penalties, interests, abatements, credits, refunds, and advance or unidentified payment relating thereto as disclosed by the records of this office as of the date of this certification are shown therein.

Signature of XXXXXXX (required for certification)	Location	Internal Revenue Service Center North-Atlantic Region Andover, Massachusetts 01812	Date
Alin H. Tanner Supvr., Account Unit			May 12, 1983 AT/jm

Form **4340** (Rev. 7-80)   *Use and issue first "Rev. 7-74"*   ＊U.S. GOVERNMENT PRINTING OFFICE 1982 522-064/5953   Department of the Treasury - Internal Revenue Service

FIGURE 5-9 (continued)   E

Certificate of Assessments and Payments

Name of Taxpayer	Address (Number, street, city, and state)		EIN or SSN	
Irwin A. Schiff	P.O. Box 5303, Hamden, CT 06518		047-16-2491 1040	

Date (a)	Explanation of Transactions (b)	Assessment (Abatement) (c)	Credit (Credit Reversal) (d)	Balance (e)	DLN or Account Number (f)	23C Date (g)	Period Ending (h)
11-09-82	Return Filed	.00			0821133102304	12-27-82	7812
04-01-83	Additional Tax	53,447.00			0625109113206	04-01-83	
	Fraud Penalty	26,724.00					
	Estimated Tax Penalty	1,706.00					
	Interest	28,370.89		110,247.89			
04-01-83	First Notice						

I certify that the foregoing transcript of the taxpayer named above in respect to the taxes specified is a true and complete transcript for the period stated, and all assessments, penalties, interests, abatements, credits, refunds, and advance or unidentified payment relating thereto as disclosed by the records of this office as of the date of this certification are shown therein.

Signature of XXXXXXX (required for certification) Supvr., Account Unit	Location Internal Revenue Service Center North-Atlantic Region Andover, Massachusetts 01812	Date May 12, 1983 AT/jm

Form **4340** (Rev. 7-80)   Use and issue first "Rev. 7-74"   ☆U.S. GOVERNMENT PRINTING OFFICE 1982 522-064/5953   Department of the Treasury - Internal Revenue Service

                                                                                          F

Certificate of Assessments and Payments

Name of Taxpayer	Address (Number, street, city, and state)		EIN or SSN	
Irwin Schiff	144 Shepard's Knoll Drive, Hamden, CT 06518		047-16-2491 1041	

Date (a)	Explanation of Transactions (b)	Assessment (Abatement) (c)	Credit (Credit Reversal) (d)	Balance (e)	DLN or Account Number (f)	23C Date (g)	Period Ending (h)
11-21-84	Return Filed	.00		.00	08211-048-29472	05-20-85	7912

I certify that the foregoing transcript of the taxpayer named above in respect to the taxes specified is a true and complete transcript for the period stated, and all assessments, penalties, interests, abatements, credits, refunds, and advance or unidentified payment relating thereto as disclosed by the records of this office as of the date of this certification are shown therein.

Signature of XXXXXX (required for certification) SUPERVISOR PAYMENT & CERT. UNIT	Location INTERNAL REVENUE SERVICE CENTER NORTH ATLANTIC REGION, ANDOVER, MA 01812	Date 07/28/87

Form **4340** (Rev. 7-80)   Use and issue first "Rev. 7-74" PS/gd   ☆U.S. G.P.O. 1980-620-255/6088   Department of the Treasury - Internal Revenue Service

letter that said;

> This document is commonly referred to by its form number 23-C, with the term "23-C date" referring to the assessment date, here April 1, 1983

did not really make a significant impression on me; and, as I am ashamed to admit, I also apparently mislaid that letter. However, it resurfaced when the United States was kind enough to send me another copy while I was in federal confinement and pursuing discovery in connection with my civil law suit. Since the government sent me another copy, I had an opportunity to reread and study Archer's letter in the somewhat less pressured atmosphere of a federal correctional facility. In addition, when I read it *this time*, I had in front of me those three 4340s, which I didn't have in May 1983 when I first received Archer's letter and documents.

Irrefutable Proof That Both The Assistant Attorney General and His Trial Chief of the Northern Region, Conspired to Mislead Both Me and the Court in May 1983

You will note that the 4340s covered by Archer's letter (C, D & E) show "23C Date" assessments both for 12-27-82 and 04-01-83, yet his letter (and "supporting" documents) of May 17, 1983 only refer to *one* 23C assessment, that of April 1, 1983. Why didn't he mention the prior one that the government claimed was made on 12-27-82? Wouldn't there had to have been similar documentation for those assessments too? Why didn't our crime-fighting Assistant Attorney General also include them in his letter? Because, at that very moment, Archer was involved in a conspiracy which was no less criminal than those for which he and others in his Department were sending people to jail.

WHY DID THE UNITED STATES CLAIM THAT IT MADE A ".00" ASSESSMENT "AGAINST ME" ON 12-27-1982?

Take a long hard look at those three ".00" assessments that the United States claimed were made on 12-27-82 and ask yourself, why would it make such an assessment? Remember, the whole purpose of an assessment is to record what somebody legally owes by way of taxes. Why, therefore, would the government go to all that trouble of officially recording (three times!) that I owed it **nothing** on 12-27-82? How many *other people* owed the government "nothing" on 12-27-82? (All of the nation's children come immediately to mind!) Why didn't the government assess them with nothing too? Does your city or town make property assessments against all those who owe the city or

town nothing? **Do you think that there is a Code section that instructs the Secretary to go around making assessments against all those people who *owe* the government *nothing* as of a certain date?** If the government concluded that on 12-27-82 I owed no taxes, does anyone seriously believe that there could have been one legitimate reason for the government to record such a "liability?" Frankly I don't believe that such an asinine assessment was ever made. And I don't believe that there is a ".00" assessment recorded anywhere on any ASSESSMENT CERTIFICATE as was *certified* too, on those form 4340s. And, as a matter of fact, the government has refused to produce any such certificates or supporting records. The Justice Department falsely claims that they were *already* produced—though they can't produce a document that says so! If they had been produced they certainly would have been mentioned in Archer's letter, but were not. So why did the government cause a false certification to be placed on a document, claiming that an "assessment" was made, which, obviously, was not made?

Making Government Records Look Legitimate

As explained in Chapter 4, before an income tax assessment (which, remember, must be based on "self-assessment") can be made, the government must have an income tax return filed by the taxpayer, without which, they have no lawful basis to proceed further. And, as already explained, once they have that return they can make an *original* assessment pursuant to Code section 6201, and then make "supplemental" (i.e. deficiency) assessments pursuant to Code sections 6204, 6211(a) and 6212(a). So to make their "back office" records look "legitimate," official IRS records must show;

> 1. The date that a tax return was filed, since without a recorded entry of a return being filed, no further progress is possible.
> 2. A record reflecting an *original* assessment, since without such an assessment, the IRS would not have a statutory basis to support additional "deficiency" assessments which it can make on its own initiative.
> 3. The dates on which supplemental or "additional" assessments and payments are subsequently made.

Now you know why my form 4340s had to contain false entries both with respect to "Return(s) Filed" and alleged "original" assessments which had to be entered before supplemental assessments could be legally shown. Further proof of this is provided by the entry "Additional Tax" which was claimed for all of those assessments made subsequent to the zero assessments claimed to have been made on 12-27-82. But those "additional tax" assessments didn't provide for "additional" taxes at all, since no assessments are shown **prior to those entries!** Obviously, those "Additional Tax(es)" shown were not for "additional" taxes at all, but were falsely labeled to hide the fact that they were in fact *original* assessments—which the IRS knows that it has no authority to make! So it falsified its records to make original assessments look like "supplemental" (i.e. "additional") ones! In a nutshell, the IRS has been making *original* assessments in the guise of *supplemental* ones, and concocted an elaborate scheme involving false documents, false entries and false regulations in order to pull it off. **In other words, the federal government has been robbing the American public blind on a scale never before conceived by man.** However, before leaving this incredible government scam, there are a few more aspects of it that should be explored.

A LUDICROUS
AND FRAUDULENT REGULATION

To solidify its mind-blowing swindle and to help throw everybody off the track[5], the Treasury wrote an outlandish Regulation 301.6211-1 (which together with Treasury Regulation 301.6331-1 really provide the two bows on the government's whole fraudulent package) which really took a lot of chutzpa, but the Treasury actually got away with it. What this Regulation states in part is that:

> If no return is made, or if the return...does not show any tax, for the purpose of the deficiency "the amount shown as the tax by the taxpayer upon his return" shall *be considered zero.*(!) [emphasis added]

While regulations are not laws, those made pursuant to the law and which do not "broaden or narrow the specific provisions" of the law are accorded the status of law—but this regulation contradicts both law and fact. But assuming for the moment that this regulation is "law" (and that's how it is treated), ask yourself these questions. "How *can* a law assume a fact that isn't so?" "What *kind* of law would *assume* a fact **that isn't so?**" Laws tell you what you are required to do—they don't allege facts—**especially false ones.** So, how, if individuals do not file tax returns, can we have a law that (1) assumes they did, and (2) further assumes that they showed zero amounts on the returns they *didn't* file?

I always said, that if the government can assume that you filed a tax return *when you didn't*, why couldn't you assume that you paid the tax, *when you didn't?* One makes about as much sense as the other, don't you think?

Compare the law, Section 6211 (see page 64) with its Regulation. Is there any inkling that the law itself ever contemplated such a ridiculous assumption?

Where is there any suggestion in the "law" that anything not shown "as the tax *by the taxpayer*" can be assessed? Where does the law provide that the government is free to make *assumptions* as to what taxpayers show or don't show on their returns? And if the law contemplated such a ridiculous assumption, it would have been contained in the law itself. Since the law specifically took into consideration "if a return was made," the law could have taken into consideration "if a return was *not* made, then the amount shown on the taxpayer's return will be considered to be zero" if that was what the *law* intended. But the law did not say, or even *suggest* any such thing. So obviously, the Regulation was deliberately made to subvert the law. Once you understand this you can feel confident that you now know more about assessments and deficiencies than did the former Chief Justice Warren Burger. In a dissenting opinion (*Laing v. United States*, 423 US 161), the former Chief Justice wrote:

> The term "deficiency" is defined in §6211(a), 26 USC §6211(a) (1970 ed. and Supp. IV) [26 USC §6211(a)], essentially as the excess of the tax imposed by the Code over the amount shown on the taxpayer's return as filed. If, however, the taxpayer files no return, or shows no tax on the return he does file, *the deficiency is the amount of the tax imposed by the Code.* Treas. Reg. 301.6211-1(a) CFR 301.6211-1(a) (1975). (Emphasis added.)

Thus the Chief Justice demonstrates that he had swallowed Treas. Reg. 301.6211-1 and believed that for persons who had not filed, the amount they allegedly owed and the amount of their alleged "deficiency" was one and the same! (He also demonstrates his lack of understanding of the existence of Code Section 6501(c)(3) and/or its purpose and significance). So here is incontrovertible proof that the perversion (or misunderstanding) of income tax "law" reaches the highest rung of the judicial ladder![6]

As I stated earlier, the law as expressed in the Code contains nothing that is inconsistent with or repugnant to either itself or to the Constitution. However, when the United States needs to get around or subvert the law, it writes a regulation which the Courts will dutifully support, even if it is contrary to the law and common sense.

THE ICING ON THE CAKE

The irony of this is that, even if the regulation were valid, *it would make no difference,* since the government would still not be able to lawfully assess the zero that it desperately wants to assume that taxpayers put on those returns they *didn't* file. Remember, the Secretary can only make an original assessment pursuant to Section 6201 or a supplemental (deficiency) pursuant to Sections 6213(c) or

6215. But a 6201 assessment, as clearly shown by the Regulation 301.6201-1 must either be an assessment of the amount shown by the taxpayer on his return, or an *amount determined by the Secretary "from his own information."* For example, as shown by my NOTICE OF DEFICIENCY (Figure 5-1), the government claimed that on Dec. 2, 1982, I owed income taxes for various years, so why didn't it simply assess those amounts pursuant to section 6201? Why didn't the government, for example, assess a tax of $19,006.00 against me as of 12-27-82, instead of assessing the $19,006.00 as an "Additional Tax" three months later on 4-1-1983? Because it couldn't assess the $19,006.00, the IRS had to make it look like it was assessing this amount as an "additional" deficiency assessment on 4-1-1983. If the government had no authority to make a $19,006.00 assessment against me on 12-27-82, it also had no authority to make a ".00" assessment against me either, since it would have required the same Code section to assess either one. And if the government could not legally assess one amount against me—how could it legally assess the other? You might want to write the former Chief Justice and, based upon his claim in *Laing*, ask him. You now know more than enough to shoot down anything he might tell you—that is, even if he knew where to begin!

SOME ADDITIONAL OBSERVATIONS

Note that the 4340s shown for the years 1974 and 1975, (A & B) unlike all the others show no "returns filed" at all. Why do you think that happened? Well, the government sent me to jail because it claimed that I had filed no returns for those years, so I guess it would have felt a little squeamish about recording in its official records that "Returns (were) Filed" for years it sent me to jail for not filing!

In connection with the 4340 supplied to me for the year 1979 (F), the attorneys handling the case for the IRS in Tax Court keep insisting (Figure 5-10) that despite the certification on that 4340 that an assessment was made against me on "5-20-85," that no such assessment was ever made. Then why was it shown on my 4340?

I have already brought all the evidence of these illegal government procedures before the courts (Connecticut District Court and "Tax Court"—see Chapter 9) in which I am fighting my two law suits in the forms of Motions to Dismiss and Motions for Summary Judgment. More on these suits will follow.

So doesn't all of the above prove to you that any war on organized crime must first start with the federal government? But don't think that our government's criminal activities stops with the making of illegal assessments. Wait until you see how **it shifts into high gear in the making of illegal seizures!**

FIGURE 5-10

DISTRICT COUNSEL
Internal Revenue Service

NORTH-ATLANTIC REGION
William R. Cotter Federal Building
135 High Street - Room 259
Hartford, Connecticut 06103

CC:HAR-TL
JFLong

Irwin A. Schiff
Reg. No. 08537-014
P.O. Box 1000
Loretto, Pennsylvania 15940

      Subject: Irwin A. Schiff v. Commissioner
              Docket No. 33728-86

Dear Mr. Schiff:

    You will find enclosed a copy of the certified transcript for your taxable year 1979. This transcript confirms that there has been no assessment made against you for income tax for 1979.

    If you have any questions you can contact me at (203) 240-4253.

                    Sincerely,

                    POWELL W. HOLLY, JR.
                    District Counsel

        By: _____
             JOSEPH F. LONG
             Attorney

NOTES TO CHAPTER 5

1. In continually *minimizing* the actual level of federal income taxes, the public is also made to forget the exhorbitant penalties that are often added. For example, the rate of tax over $10,000 on our basic income tax is 28%. If that person is self-employed, the rate on his additional income tax (fraudulently called Social Security or self-employment taxes) is 14% for a total income tax rate at this level of 42%. If the Government now arbitrarily imposes a 50% fraud penalty and an additional 5% penalty for under-payment, the total amount confiscated at this level is 65% of an ordinary man's productivity. And when we add to this the substantial interest penalties (at usurious rates, compounded daily) that are often added, we get levels of confiscation (and forgetting *all the other* taxes this taxpayer *also* pays) extracted in the name of taxation that can take virtually all that a person earns! I have actually seen an IRS tax notice where the original tax due was $1,500, but where penalties and interest had swollen the amount due to about $10,000. At certain levels this amount becomes too large (with the continual running of interest) to pay off (with after tax dollars): at which time the government doesn't have a taxpayer, but a virtual slave. When income taxes started, the rates were from 1% to 6%. So even a 50% penalty would only take from 1/2 to 3-1/2 percent of one's income. But based on current tax rates, penalties are **50 times higher,** and can take an **added 25%** of income—**before** the addition of substantial interest penalties—even from income near the poverty level. This situation, therefore, cannot be regarded as the payment of "taxes" borne by a free people, but is more akin to the tribute exacted from a vanquished nation by some foreign despot, but at levels that even a foreign conqueror would not attempt.

2. In *Spies* v. *United States,* 317 U.S. 492 (1943) an often cited, unanimous decision, the Supreme Court ruled that to be guilty of tax evasion a defendant had to be guilty of an "affirmative act"; such as concealing his income or assets, keeping a double set of books, and destroying records all done for the purpose of evading taxes. And that an individual could not be guilty of tax evasion on the basis of "omissions" alone; such as for merely omitting to file returns or paying the tax. Therefore, the elements of criminal and civil tax fraud are exactly the same, only the *burden of proof* is different. In criminal tax fraud the Government has to prove guilt beyond a reasonable doubt, while in civil fraud the government has to prove it on the basis of "clear and convincing" evidence whether the penalty is litigated in tax court (*Solomon* v. *Commr.,* 732 F2d 1459, 1461-62) or in a refund suit in a district court (*Paddock* v. *U.S.,* 280 F2d 563). However if the penalized citizen does not himself initiate these court actions, the government **never has to prove its fraud allegations.** And it can

seize the money without even having done so! Notice that in assessing $45,566 in fraud penalties, the IRS did not allege any *affirmative act* of fraud I might have committed but arbitrarily stated that my failure to file and failure to pay (which they fraudulently termed an "underpayment") was "due to fraud." And notice that they expected me to pay this amount without ever having proved that I actually committed the fraud alleged! This, as you will see, was not only violative of section 6653(b) itself, but was also contrary to *Spies,* all case law on the issue, and the "due process" clause of the Constitution. Here the Government merely accuses me of what amounts to a crime, but instead of imposing a jail sentence on me, fines me instead and expects me to pay the fine without it ever having proved the criminal act on *any* basis whatsoever! This will give you some idea of how the Government abuses its authority to assess penalties and why the Constitution is dead. For more on *Spies* and how it was disregarded in even the criminal charges that were applied to me, see Chapter 11.

3. In justifying her decision, Judge Burns used the following partial sentence from Brushaber, *supra;* "Nothing could make this clearer than to recall that in the Pollack Case in so far as the law taxed incomes from other classes of property than real estate and invested property, that is, income from 'professions, trades, employments, or vocations (158 U.S. 637), its validity was recognized;" ***However, she neglected to finish the sentence*** which went on as follows: "indeed it was expressly declared that no dispute was made upon that subject and attention was called to the fact **that taxes on such income had been sustained as excise taxes in the past.**" So the "validity" of the tax that Judge Burns sought to establish by this quote **only applied when the tax was levied** as an **excise tax—** which is **exactly the point** I made in my request for a restraining order. For a more detailed account of this incident, see *The Great Income Tax Hoax,* pp 346-366.

4. The way this works is as follows. When Federal judges *don't have* jurisdiction, such as for conducting criminal trials in connection with income taxes, they claim they *do.* And when they *have* civil jurisdiction to prevent unlawful seizures in connection with the income tax, they claim they *don't.*

5. Actually, the scheme is so massive in scope and so diabolially contrived, involving as it does numerous Code sections and Treasury Regulations, that it was practically impossible to fully detect, document and expose.

6. Section 6501(C)(3) is discussed in Chapter 10.

— CHAPTER 6 —
NO LAW ESTABLISHES
A "LIABILITY" FOR INCOME TAXES
(THE HEART OF THE ISSUE)

"Liberty cannot be preserved without a general knowledge among the people, who have ... a desire to know; ... that most dreaded and envied kind of knowledge. I mean of the characters and conduct of their rulers."

—John Adams
A Dissertation on the Canon and Feudal Law [1765]

When *How Anyone Can Stop Paying Income Taxes* was published, I believed it contained sufficient information to convince everyone that filing income tax returns was voluntary, and that no one was required to have income taxes taken from their pay or to pay estimated taxes. However, when I wrote that book, I believed that the Code did authorize the government (albeit unconstitutionally) to estimate, assess and bill individuals for income taxes, even when they did not file tax returns on their own—and only *then* did I suggest that individuals might be required to pay the tax. I corrected this **false belief** in *The Great Income Tax Hoax.*

But even then, when I focused on the voluntary nature of the income tax (in connection with filing and paying the tax before it was billed and demanded), people would ask, "But where does the law say that it is voluntary?" I always thought that was a dumb question—but it came up often enough, nevertheless. Naturally, I couldn't point to a specific Code section that stated the tax was voluntary, because the "law" was not written that way. It was the *absence of mandatory language* (once one learned how to read the Code) that established its voluntary character (which turned out to be even more "voluntary" than I recognized at that time). But there was no Code Section that I could point to that said so. Later, I discovered the proof that such people wanted. It turns out to be the single most important fact anyone can learn about federal income taxes. In a nutshell...

THE INTERNAL REVENUE CODE ESTABLISHES NO SUCH THING AS AN INCOME TAX "LIABILITY." THEREFORE, SINCE ALL MANDATORY AND ENFORCEMENT PROVISIONS OF THE CODE RELATE TO A TAX "LIABILITY," NONE OF THESE ENFORCEMENT PROVISIONS CAN APPLY TO INCOME TAXES.

If you leaf through the Code (or check the index) you will find numerous sections that refer to a tax liability, but none apply to income taxes. So, if no section of the Code makes anyone "liable" for an income tax, **THEN EVERYTHING IN CONNECTION WITH THAT TAX HAS TO BE VOLUNTARY!**

"LIABILITY"—THE KEY TO MANDATORY COMPLIANCE

Each and every enforcement provision of the Code is made contingent upon the taxpayer being "liable" for the tax in question. As you have already seen, even the restraining power of the court in section 7408 (Figure 2-13) is contingent upon the existence of a tax "liability," and you have seen how the Code clearly establishes such a tax liability (Figures 3-2 and 3-4). The courts have ruled that "liability" for taxation must clearly appear," *Seagraves* v. *Wallace*, 69 F.2d 163; quoting *Miller* v. *Standard Nut Margarine*, 284 U.S. 498, 508; *U.S.* v. *Updike*, 281 U.S. 489; and *U.S.* v. *Merriam* 263 U.S. 179, 187, 188. Some additional Code sections that create tax liabilities other than those already referred to (in certain cases the words "shall be paid" was deemed the equivalent of "liability") are sections: 1461, 4162(c), 4481(b), 4495(c), 4941(a), 4971(a), 4973(a), 4975(a) and (b), 4978, 4986(b), 4995(a)(1)(B), 5054(a)(1), (2), (3), (4), 5005, 5043, 5044, 5061, 5811, 5821, 7272, 7273, and 7501.

Only a "Liability" Can Create Legal Obligations

It is *only* when you are "liable" for a tax that you need worry about the laws that pertain to it. If you are not "liable" for a tax you can obviously ignore all laws related to it, since they wouldn't apply to you. As you now know, there is a federal wagering tax on the gross bets made by bookmakers (Figure 3-4). If you're not a bookmaker you're obviously not "liable" for wagering taxes, so you would be totally unconcerned about all laws related to that tax. Isn't that so? Knowing you are not a bookmaker and not *liable* for wagering taxes, could the IRS subpoena your bank records and/or seize your property in connection with that tax? Or, could the government charge you with willfully failing to file wagering tax returns? Of course not. So everything that our government does to compel people to pay income taxes is no more legal than if the government sought to make people pay federal wagering, alcohol or tobacco taxes, knowing full well that they weren't *liable* for those either.

If, on the other hand, you are "liable" for a given federal tax, the government can impose numerous other conditions on you which are related to that tax liability. For example: tobacco manufacturers who are specifically made "liable" for tobacco taxes by section 5703(a)(1), are further required to make tax payments by section 5703(b); secure a permit by section 5712; secure a bond by section 5711; keep a "true and accurate inventory" by section 5721; make reports by secton 5722; adhere to packaging restrictions by section 5723; keep records by section 5741; and be subject to specific criminal and civil penalties by sections 5762 and 5763.

Similarly, distillers of alcoholic beverages who are made liable for alcohol taxes by sections 5005(a), (b), (c), and (d) are further required to pay the tax by section 5007; adhere to restrictions with respect to installing or removing stills, by sections 5101, 5102, 5103, 5105 (which also provides penalties for non compliance); keep records by sections 5114 and 5124; adhere to packaging restrictions by section 5116; adhere to registration requirements by section 5171; adhere to bonding requirements by section 5173; adhere to restrictions as to plant locations by section 5178; post signs as required by section 5180(a), be subject to penalties for non-compliance by section 5180(b); furnish "keys as may be required for internal revenue officers to gain access to the premises" by section 5203(a); allow any IRS "revenue officer at all times, as well by night as by day" to enter any part of the plant by section 5203(b); allow IRS revenue officers "to break up the ground" in any part of the distillery "to search for pipes...to examine whether such pipes or other conveyance conceals any distilled spirits, mash, wort, or beer, or other liquor" by section 5203(d); and be subject to specific fines and criminal penalties for violating any number of infractions as provided by the following sections and subsections—5203(e), 5505(i), 5601, 5602, 5603, 5606, 5607, 5608, 5609, 5610, 5611, 5612, 5613, 5614, 5615, 5661, 5662, 5663, 5671, 5672, 5673, 5681, 5682, 5683, 5684, 5685, 5686, 5687, 5688, and 5690. All this plus the penalty provisions of subtitle F which are made specifically applicable to Chapter 51 (which provides for alcohol taxes) by secton 5560.

Section 5555(a), for example, is really specific and provides as follows:

> Every person liable for any tax imposed by this Chapter (51), or for the collection thereof, shall keep such records, render such statements, make such returns and comply with such rules and regulations as the Secretary may prescribe.[1]

Now there are **simply no comparable sections as those listed above anyplace** in Subtitle A which similarly impose obligations, requirements, civil or criminal penalties, or cross-references to Code sections that do for *any* alleged violation of *income tax laws!* As I stated before, the government has been fraudulently using Code sections that only apply to certain *mandatory* federal excise taxes (such as alcohol and tobacco) *to enforce payment of income taxes.* It has managed to get away with this only because we have a perfidious federal judiciary and (with only a few exceptions) an incompetent, ineffectual and duplicitous legal establishment.

All government measures designed to compel Americans to file income tax returns, keep records, turn over records, turn over property, pay, withhold and collect income taxes, etc., etc., have all been based on nothing more than plain criminal fraud. In essence, our government has been getting **the bulk of its revenue in a manner not unlike how Jessie James, John Dillinger or Genghis Khan got theirs.**

In addition, many Americans have been prosecuted and given long jail sentences for income tax "crimes" which, by law, do not exist. If any justice exists in America, then the ones responsible for those illegal prosecutions will be brought to the bar of justice.

PROOF THAT NO "LIABILITY" FOR INCOME TAXES EXISTS ANYWHERE IN THE INTERNAL REVENUE CODE

While I stated in *The Great Income Tax Hoax* that no section of the Code made anyone liable for income taxes, I was asking my readers to take my word for it—or to check the Code out for themselves. But now, thanks to my latest criminal prosecution and to my two civil law suits, my readers won't have to do either. As a result of that litigation, the government has supplied me with all the information that anybody should need.

A U.S. ARRAIGNMENT—NAZI STYLE

On April 5, 1985, while on a media tour to promote my recently released book, *The Great Income Tax Hoax*, three IRS agents pounced upon me as I was about to enter the studios of radio station KFBK, Sacramento, California, for a scheduled talk show appearance. They pinned me against a wall, handcuffed and arrested me. They all carried concealed pistols, which they were not authorized to carry (per section 7608) except in connection with the "enforcement of Subtitle E and other laws pertaining to liquor, tobacco, and firearms." But what does violating one more law mean to the IRS?

I was subsequently released on bond, and on April 17, I appeared for arraignment before Magistrate Owen Eagan in Connecticut Federal District Court in Hartford. The government had charged me with three counts of tax evasion for the years 1980, 1981 and 1982 and one count of failing to file a corporate tax return for 1980 pursuant to the indictment shown in Figure 6-1. However, on April 8th, approximately 10 days prior to my arraignment, I submitted a written motion to the court asking it to dismiss the indictment due to the court's lack of subject matter jurisdiction.[2] I supported this motion with two memorandums of law. One memorandum cited sufficient case law to remind the court of two things it already knew, (1) that whenever a federal court's jurisdiction is challenged the party invoking its jurisdiction (in this case the federal government) must prove it by clear and convincing evidence, and (2) that a federal court's jurisdiction can never be assumed by the court. Two short excerpts from two of the cases in my Memorandum of Law illustrate this:

> Jurisdiction cannot be assumed by a District Court nor conferred by agreement of the parties, but it is incumbent upon plaintiff to allege in clear terms, the necessary facts showing jurisdiction which must be proved by convincing evidence.
> —*Harris* v. *American Legion,* 162 F. Supp. 700

> The authority which the statute vests in the court to enforce the limitations of its jurisdiction precludes the idea that jurisdiction may be maintained by mere averment or that the party asserting jurisdiction may be relieved of his burden by any formal procedure. If his allegation of jurisdictional facts *are challenged by his adversary* in any appropriate manner, *he must support them by competent proof.* And where they are not so challenged, the court may still insist that the jurisdictional facts be established or the case dismissed, and for that purpose the court may demand that the party alleging jurisdiction justify his allegations by a preponderance of the evidence. [emphasis added]   —*The Supreme Court*
> *McNutt* v. *General Motors Acceptance,* 56 S.Ct. 780

There is ample case law to support the principle that once jurisdiction is challenged the court has no authority to do anything but take action on that motion. As the Supreme

Court held in *The State of Rhode Island* v. *The State of Massachusetts,* 37 U.S. 709 once the question of jurisdiction is raised "it must be *considered* and *decided,* before any court can move one step further." With this in mind let us see how a Connecticut District Court dealt with this issue in my case. My motion claimed that the court lacked subject matter jurisdiction to try me for alleged income tax crimes because:

1. The indictment failed to identify the statute that required the filing of a corporate income tax return, and thus failed "to state a charge cognizable in the courts of the United States."

2. "No section of the Internal Revenue Code (erroneously referred to in my indictment as 26 U.S.C. 7201 and 7203) makes individuals liable for the payment of income taxes" and so I was not required to file a return or pay the tax purely as a matter of law.

3. "Section 7402 specifically grants civil jurisdiction only." I pointed out to the court that it was never given jurisdiction by Congress to conduct a criminal tax trial, because "Title 26" only conferred civil, not criminal jurisdiction on federal courts. What could be plainer than that!

4. The court had no jurisdiction to prosecute me (either for evasion or for not filing) for a tax which was not imposed pursuant to any of the taxing clauses in the Constitution. That since the income tax was imposed neither as "a uniform excise tax in accordance with Article I, Sec. 8, Clause 1 nor as an apportioned direct tax pursuant to Article 1, Sect. 2, Clause 3 and Article 1, Sect. 9, Clause 4," a criminal prosecution pursuant to such a tax would be manifestly unconstitutional.

I supplied the court with an eighteen page Memorandum of Law just to support that last contention.

Government Fails To Respond

In total violation of the principle explained in the three cases cited above, both the prosecution and the court paid absolutely no attention to my jurisdictional claim—as shown by the following excerpts from the arraignment tape that was supplied to me by the court.[3]

Magistrate Eagan:
It is my understanding this morning that we were taking the criminal docket. The first matter will be criminal number N-85-20. This is a case that is assigned to the Honorable Peter C. Dorsey for trial. It is the matter of the United States of America vs. Irwin A Schiff. Is that correct?

M. Hartmere, Asst. U.S. Attorney:
That's correct, your Honor.

FIGURE 6-1

FILED

UNITED STATES DISTRICT COURT APR 3 4 04 PM '85

DISTRICT OF CONNECTICUT S. DIST COURT
NEW HAVEN CONN

```
UNITED STATES OF AMERICA      :
                              :   CRIMINAL NO. N-85-20(RCZ)
          v.                  :   26 U.S.C., §§7201, 7203
                              :   (Income Tax Evasion; Failure
IRWIN A. SCHIFF               :    to File Corporate Returns)
```

I N D I C T M E N T

The Grand Jury charges:

COUNT ONE

That during the calendar year 1980, IRWIN A. SCHIFF, the defendant herein, a resident of Hamden, Connecticut, had and received taxable income of approximately $26,529.13; that upon said taxable income he owed to the United States of America income tax of approximately $6,485.96; that he was required by law on or before April 15, 1981, to make an income tax return to the Internal Revenue Service, and to pay such income tax; that well knowing the foregoing facts, the said IRWIN A. SCHIFF on or about April 15, 1981, in the District of Connecticut, did willfully and knowingly attempt to evade and defeat the said income tax due and owing by him to the United States of America for the said calendar year by failing to make such income tax return to the said Internal Revenue Service, and by failing to pay to the Internal Revenue Service said income tax, and by concealing and attempting to conceal from all proper officers of the United States of America his true and correct taxable income.

In violation of Section 7201, Internal Revenue Code; Title 26, United States Code, Section 7201.

[handwritten annotations: "WHAT LAW?", "PURSUANT TO WHAT LAW?"]

COUNT FOUR

That during the fiscal year ended August 31, 1981, IRWIN A. SCHIFF, the defendant herein, was the president and responsible officer of Irwin A. Schiff, Inc., a corporation not expressly exempt from tax, with its principal place of business at Hamden, in the District of Connecticut, and by reason of such facts IRWIN A. SCHIFF was required by law after the close of the fiscal year ended August 31, 1981, and on or before November 15, 1981, for and on behalf of the said corporation, to make an income tax return to the District Director of Internal Revenue for the Internal Revenue District of Connecticut, at Hartford, in the District of Connecticut, or to the Director, Internal Revenue Service Center, Northeast Region, Andover, Massachusetts, stating specifically the items of the corporation's gross income and the deductions and credits allowed by law; that well knowing all of the foregoing facts, IRWIN A. SCHIFF did willfully and knowingly fail to make said return to the said District Director of Internal Revenue, to the said Director of the Internal Revenue Service Center, or to any other proper officer of the United States.

In violation of Section 7203, Internal Revenue Code; Title 26, United States Code, Section 7203.

[handwritten annotation: "WHAT LAW?"]

A TRUE BILL

_____
FOREMAN

_____
ALAN H. NEVAS
UNITED STATES ATTORNEY

_____
MICHAEL HARTMERE
ASSISTANT UNITED STATES ATTORNEY

Eagan:
And this matter is here on indictment?

Hartmere:
Yes, it is your Honor.

Eagan:
And has a copy of this indictment been given to Mr. Schiff?

Hartmere:
Yes, your Honor I believe he has been provided with a copy.

Eagan:
All right, fine...

Schiff:
Your Honor, I submitted last Monday to this court and to the U.S. Attorney, a Motion to Dismiss the indictment on four grounds of lack of jurisdiction. So far the government hasn't responded to that motion. Therefore, I move for a summary judgment on the grounds that since I filed a motion that this court has no jurisdiction, because the income tax falls into none of the taxing clauses of the Constitution, and because I have no liability for the tax; and since the government hasn't responded to the contrary, I move that the procedure here be dismissed. However, if the government wants more time to respond, I'll agree to giving it a continuance.

Eagan:
All right, Mr. Schiff, if you'll excuse me, we'll be seated for a minute. I'll go through the whole procedure with you and I'll explain it to you. [He totally ignores the jurisdictional issue I raised in my written motion, and which I just orally re-urged.]

Schiff:
Well before we can proceed, your Honor, I think what we have to *establish* is whether or not you have *any jurisdiction to proceed.* Now, it's very simple. I have in front of me Section 7402 and it very clearly says, "For general jurisdiction of the district courts of the United States in *civil* actions involving internal revenue, see section 1340 or Title 28 of the United States Code." Now if I can show the court where it has *civil* jurisdiction, I think it's appropriate for the government to show the court where it has criminal jurisdiction...

Eagan:
All right, Mr. Schiff, if you'll sit down for just a second please. Mr. Schiff this is a preliminary hearing, this is not a trial of the matter nor am I here to hear motions addressed to jurisdiction. I will give you sufficient time to address your motion to the trial judge and he will be the one...Mr. Schiff, please...

[Eagan again totally ignores my claim that the court lacks jurisdiction to continue, even though the government has yet to utter a single word in its own behalf. If Eagan had no authority to address this issue, then he should have rescheduled it before someone who did. But my written motion was submitted to the court days before my "arraignment," so the Honorable Peter C. Dorsey obviously knew that it had to be held before someone who could deal with the subject. The reason that the court *chose this method to avoid dealing with this issue,* will soon become apparent. But let's continue with my "arraignment."]

Schiff:
Your Honor, are you going to ask me to plead?

Eagan:
Yes, I am.

Schiff:
You'll be asking me to plead to a legal fiction...to plead to something that's not a crime...Suppose Michael Hartmere indicted me for eating a banana, would you expect me to plead guilty or not guilty to that? And if I pleaded not guilty, would I not be suggesting that I believed that eating a banana was a crime? Before we continue...

Eagan:
No, before we continue you will sit down and you will listen to my explanation of what we are doing. Please be seated, Mr. Schiff.

[The court and the prosecutor (actually, in this case, one in the same) were conspiring to get me to plead to a legal fiction so that the United States could illegally prosecute me. For example, suppose that Michael Hartmere, the U.S. prosecutor who fraudulently engineered my indictment, was similarly able to pull the wool over the grand jury's eyes and get it to indict me for having eaten a banana. Suppose further, that I had never eaten a banana in my life. Would that mean that because of that fact at any subsequent arraignment, I should simply plead not guilty, or that I could be "required" to *even enter a plea* for that "crime"? Why should I needlessly have to defend myself (which takes both time and money) from charges that I was guilty of doing something that I didn't do, but which was not a crime anyway? By pleading "not guilty," one also subjects himself to the authority of (and in this case a hostile one) a federal judge who, once he has you in his clutches, (i.e. become subject to his "jurisdiction") can exercise arbitrary and awesome power over you. He can establish unrealistic bail requirements, decide that you should be confined right through your trial and can keep you in jail—*without a trial*—by holding you in continuous contempt of court. And once you are under the court's jurisdiction (which can only occur after you submit to its jurisdiction by refusing to challenge it [and possibly prevailing] by simply entering a standard plea) you can indeed be found guilty of something you never did and which is not even a crime. This can occur because once the court assumes jurisdiction, it is in a position to make false rulings on matters of law (in which defendants are also denied oral argument) and falsely charge the jury on the law itself—which occurs all the time in tax cases.

In addition, the prosecutor can totally fabricate its prosecution by using purjurious testimony—a perfectly routine procedure in all "tax protestor" cases. To put it in the context of my banana example (though a better illustration might be, being accused of speaking ill of the President), once you plead not guilty to eating a banana, the government is now in a position to get witnesses to falsely testify that you did, while the court is now in a position to falsely instruct the jury that eating a banana is a crime. Since a jury is made up of individuals who generally know *absolutely nothing* about tax law, they can be made to believe anything the "judge" decides to tell them. So, in case you thought my banana illustration was a little far fetched, this is *precisely* what happens in all "tax protestor" cases. Such people are all tricked at their arraignments, and then fraudulently prosecuted for doing something that is no more illegal than eating a banana. But let's leave the subject of bananas and get back to my "arraignment."]

Eagan:
Now, before we continue you will sit down and you will listen to my explanation of what we are doing. Please be seated Mr. Schiff.

Schiff:
Well, I think that jurisdiction has to be established your Honor...

Eagan:
All right...

Schiff:
And I think the record ought to show...

Eagan:
The record is going to show everything that should be shown. Mr. Schiff, my name is Owen Eagan. I am the United States magistrate. I am here for the preliminary purposes of taking a plea in this case.

Schiff:
May I just ask is this an adversary...

Eagan:
You may shut up for just a second and let me finish. I'm here to take a plea to this particular case. The only plea that I can

and will accept is a plea of not guilty.

[In the above exchange I sought to get Eagan to admit that an arraignment is an adversary proceeding between me and the government, with the court merely "judging" between us, based upon the legal arguments we make. I had already made (and legally supported) an argument that the court had no jurisdiction—which *also included Eagan's authority to arraign me!* Obviously, that authority had to be established before Eagan could utter *one arraignment word!* The court was thus duty bound to hear contrary arguments from my adversary (the government) and to render its decision accordingly. But it is clear from the arraignment tape (as my trial itself would prove) that my adversary *was also the court!* Note Eagan's comment that he was only there to take "a plea of not guilty." But the court was on notice that I intended to argue jurisdiction. So why wasn't it prepared to hear it? But you already know the answer to that. So the court concocted a ruse to avoid addressing the issue as the law required it to do.]

Continuing with the "arraignment"...

Schiff:
I'm perfectly willing to plead guilty. I will plead guilty. Can I plead guilty?

Eagan:
No, you may not.

Schiff:
Why can't I?

Eagan:
Because I have no authority to take a guilty plea.

Schiff:
Well then let's get a judge in here who can accept a guilty plea.

Eagan:
Mr. Schiff, please sit down at this time...please...

Schiff:
I'm perfectly willing to plead guilty to save the United States and myself the expense of a trial. I admit, your honor, that I haven't filed and I haven't paid, and if I have a tax liability and if Mr. Hartmere will show this court where I can have a tax liability (as a matter of law) I'm prepared to plead guilty.

Eagan:
All right, now I've given you your opportunity to talk so you please sit down and listen...

Schiff:
But I'm prepared to plead guilty. [Can you believe that this is actually happening in an American court?]

Eagan:
Please sit down.

[Suppose I had been charged with murder, rape, bank robbery, counterfeiting, arson, mail fraud or any other crime you can think of and I asked the court, "Look, just show me the law which makes what I'm charged with a crime, and I'll plead guilty." Don't you think that under those circumstances any *legitimate* court would have produced the law? In my case, "the law" was the Code section that made me "liable" for the tax. Yet neither the government nor the court *could* or would produce the law!]

Eagan (continuing):
It's my obligation today to take a plea to an indictment that was handed down by a grand jury on April 3 of this year in New Haven. The only authority I have is the authority to accept a plea of not guilty ...and that is the only authority I have. My other **obligations are to make sure** that you get a copy of the charging documents; **that you understand what the charge is;** and you understand what the maximum penalty might be. Now the way that I accomplish this is to have the U.S. Attorney explain to you and to me what the charges are and what the maximum possible penalty is. After that, I must advise you of what your rights are. [But apparently not of my right to be tried only by a court that has jurisdiction!]

[Additional explanation followed in which Eagan explained that he would cover such things as: the Speedy Trial Act, the filing of pre-trial motions, my competency to stand trial, whether I had an attorney, and whether he had any conflict of interest. Following that, I again asked of the court...]

Schiff:
Is this an adversary or inquisitory proceeding?

Eagan:
Well, the procedure is a preliminary procedure in a criminal process. All criminal process is adversary in nature.

Schiff:
Well, who is my adversary in this courtroom, your Honor?

Eagan:
Your adversary is the United States government.

Schiff:
Is that Mr. Hartmere?

Eagan:
Hartmere is only an agent of the government. He is not your adversary.

Schiff:
But he represents my adversary, is that correct?

Eagan:
He represents the government.

Schiff:
Therefore, I assume that if I raise an issue, before you can judge, my adversary would have to respond?

Eagan:
No, that's not so. Dispositive motions—and that's what you are talking about, have a time and a place. [I hadn't the vaguest idea what he meant by a "dispositive motion." But I knew that Eagan wasn't telling the truth about the issue of jurisdiction which I knew was validly before the court.] Once the plea is entered, dispositive motions may be filed and they will be addressed to the trial judge.

Schiff:
If you're telling me that you can only take a not guilty plea, I could have mailed it on a postcard.

Eagan:
No, the rules require that a personal appearance...Rule 10...

Schiff:
Why?

Eagan:
That's the way Congress deems it legal.

Schiff:
But this is supposed to be my hearing, isn't that right? It's not a court martial?

Eagan:
This is a preliminary hearing for the purpose of taking a not guilty plea.

Schiff:
But it's also a hearing to see if you have the jurisdiction to take a plea.

Eagan:
There's no question in my mind whether I have jurisdiction or not. I have jurisdiction.

[So here the court, without any shame at all, openly violates a fundamental principle of federal law—it *assumes* jurisdiction and without the plaintiff being asked to offer any comment at all (let alone assume its burden of proof) on the matter!]

Schiff:
Where do you have it from?

Eagan:
I don't think I have to sit here and explain it to you Mr. Schiff. Mr. Schiff, please sit down and we're going to go through the normal procedure...

Schiff:
Your Honor, the courts have ruled that when the issue of jurisdiction is raised...the jurisdictional facts must be established or the case dismissed..."Jurisdiction can not be assumed but must be clearly shown" *Brooks* v. *Yalkie* 200 F2d 663. Sir, you cannot assume jurisdiction. When I raise the issue of jurisdiction, the government (my adversary) must prove you have it. [So far the government, my adversary, hadn't uttered one word in opposition to my four claims, yet Eagan decided the matter in its favor! *Talk about having a friend at court!*]

Eagan:
For the preliminary purpose of this hearing I am denying your motion, if that's what you want. I have jurisdiction. I will proceed...

Schiff:
You haven't proven it. On what basis do you have it?

Eagan:
I don't have to prove anything to you, Mr. Schiff.

Schiff:
Your Honor, if I can prove that you have *civil* jurisdiction pursuant to section 7402, why don't you simply ask Mr. Hartmere to tell you where you have *criminal* jurisdiction? *Isn't that simple enough?*

Eagan:
I think I explained this to you before. The dispositive motions must go to the trial judge. The trial judge is the only one who can rule on...

Schiff:
Well, then let's get a judge in here.

Eagan:
Mr. Schiff, you are not running this court. We will run the court in the normal way that it has always been run, under the laws and under the Constitution of this country. [It's a good thing that Eagan pointed this out, otherwise no one would have guessed it!]

Schiff:
Your Honor, I wasn't...

Eagan:
Mr. Schiff, SIT DOWN!

[This should give you a rough idea of how justice "works" in federal courts, as opposed to how it supposedly works in theory. It is clear that the court was willing to proceed even though it obviously knew it had no jurisdiction (otherwise the court and/or the prosecutor would have offered some proof) to do so.]

My willingness to immediately plead guilty came up *again* as follows...

Schiff:
I am willing to plead guilty.

Eagan:
I don't want a guilty plea.

Schiff:
Why not?

Eagan:
Because I cannot accept a guilty plea.

[Therefore, I should have insisted that, that was the plea I wanted to make. This would have forced a rescheduling of my arraignment before the judge. Then I could have undergone a change of heart and forced oral argument on each of the jurisdictional issues I raised. This is what Judge Dorsey wanted to avoid—oral argument. In that situation the government would have to support its baseless jurisdictional claims in open debate, where its reasoning could be challenged and where both its answers and the court's would be *recorded*. Judge Dorsey, for obvious reasons, wanted to make any jurisdictional claims and statements from within the safety of his own *written* decision. By employing that technique, both his and the government's answers to my jurisdictional questions wouldn't have to be **defended in open court.** By contrast, the court, by limiting its remarks and answers to its own written opinion, could with relative safety and impunity, base its decision on arguments that were patently false, incomplete and invalidly supported.[4]]

Schiff:
Well then let's get a judge in here who can accept a guilty plea. Why should I be put to the expense of a trial? I can't afford a trial.

Eagan:
Do you want to plead guilty?

Schiff:
I will plead guilty, if the government will only show me where the Code makes me *liable* for the tax.

Eagan:
NO. You don't want to plead guilty. What you want to do is argue. [Can you believe this?]

Schiff:
I don't want to argue. I'm perfectly willing to plead guilty. [Here, I further reminded the court, that none of the Code sections I was charged with violating even mention income taxes, and that the government had also refused to address that issue too.] Does Mr. Hartmere suggest that I am evading an alcohol tax?

Eagan:
Mr. Schiff, you are just back at the same thing all over again.

Schiff:
Well why don't you ask him where in the (Code I am required to file an income tax return and pay an income tax)

Eagan:
No, I'm not going to ask him anything about that.

And further on...

Schiff:
You want me to give jurisdiction to the court by entering a not guilty plea? Not guilty to what? Where's the crime?

Eagan:
Mr. Schiff, you're arguing the case.

Schiff:
I'm not arguing.

Eagan:
The proper place to argue that defense, is to Judge Dorsey and it's through a Motion to Dismiss (which I had already filed but which the court was now ignoring!). Let me get on with this. I will give you the dates where you can argue it and to whom you can argue it.

[First of all, I wasn't "arguing" the case. I wasn't arguing whether I had filed tax returns or not, or whether I had paid the taxes or not (as a matter of fact I had already admitted to not doing either) or whether or not I "concealed" any income. that would have been "arguing the case." I was only arguing the issue of *jurisdiction,* not "the case." And an *arraignment is just the place to make that argument.* Eagan's claim that I would have an opportunity to "argue it" later was another sham. Once the court got by the "arraign-

ment" with its "magistrate" ploy, it refused to grant me oral argument on this issue as Eagan falsely claimed it would do. The reasons for this have already been explained.]

Schiff:
This is the proper place to argue jurisdiction.

Eagan:
This particular proceeding is not the proper place. [Eagan's statement was a blatant lie as my next statement and his response prove.]

Schiff:
Jurisdiction can be raised during any part of the judicial process.

Eagan:
You raised it. I've denied your Motion to Dismiss this case.

[A moment before he instructed me to submit my Motion to Judge Dorsey. Now he denies the Motion he just told me to submit. And if Eagan only had the authority to accept a not guilty plea, (as he repeatedly claimed) then where did he get the authority to deny my Motion to Dismiss For Lack of Subject Matter Jurisdiction?]

Schiff:
Without hearing from my adversary?

Eagan:
Without hearing from your adversary.

Schiff:
Then this is not an adversary proceeding?

Eagan:
I don't need to hear from your adversary to know that I have jurisdiction to take your not guilty plea and send you on to Judge Dorsey for the trial to take place.

Schiff:
Is this a star chamber proceeding or is this an American court where I am supposed to have a hearing?

Eagan:
It is a courtroom where you will have a hearing. It is not a political podium for you to give addresses to the court.

[Eagan's statements and admissions prove him to be wrong on all counts. This was no "courtroom." I was not to be given a "hearing." And his comment that I was turning his "courtroom" into a "political podium" was Freudian: reflective of his obvious understanding that my "trial" was really political in nature.]

Explaining The Charges

In addition to giving an accused an opportunity to challenge jurisdiction, an arraignment (as mentioned by Eagan) is where an accused supposedly has the charges explained to him so he can make an informed plea of either guilty, not guilty, or nolo contendere. By entering one of these standard pleas, the accused accepts the legality of the charges and the court's jurisdiction.

As you can see, I offered to *immediately plead guilty* to save both the government and myself further time and expense, if the U.S. prosecutor (sitting at counsel table with two IRS agents as assistants) would merely *cite the Code section that made me liable* for an income tax. But the government and the court refused to take me up on my offer! An accused clearly can not make an intelligent and informed plea of not guilty (thereby not only saving himself the time and expense of a trial, but perhaps securing a lighter sentence then he would otherwise get if he proceeded to trial and lost) unless he understands the charges against him. Thus it is the duty of the court to explain those charges and answer any questions the accused might have concerning them.

While many an accused can understand the charges from the language of the indictment or information[5] and are apparently willing to enter a plea based solely on the information contained in them, this is not true in all cases. Those who signify confusion and doubt concerning what exactly they have been charged with, can not have their questions and doubts ignored by the court.

But in addition to the court's refusal to explain the basis of its claimed jurisdiction, Eagan was also asking me to plead to criminal charges involving a tax for which no legal basis (i.e. "liability") had been cited in the indictment. And Eagan refused to clarify that matter when I raised it in connection with his asking me if I understood the charge. Incredulously, he claimed that by raising these questions I was again attempting to "argue" my case! So I asked the court point blank to just show me the law that made me "liable" and I would plead "guilty." What could be more judicially expedient than that? But both the U.S. prosecutor and the court refused to do it!

I further pointed out to Eagan that the indictment did not even allege an offense that one could plead to, since it also did not cite the law that allegedly required me to file the income tax return I was charged with not filing. But again Eagan refused to compel the government to identify that law

too! I explained to Eagan that given these omissions in the indictment and his refusal to compel the prosecutor to clarify them for me, it was impossible for me to enter an informed plea.

Then Eagan took the absurd position that "since" I was "refusing to plea," he would enter a plea of "not guilty" for me! I insisted that I was not refusing to plea at all, and reminded him of my repeated offer to plead guilty, if the court would merely show me where I could be guilty of the charges alleged *simply as a matter of law!* But still the government and the court refused to produce the law!

My indictment accused me of violating Code sections 7201 and 7203, neither of which even *mentions* income taxes, so how can anyone plead to alleged income tax "crimes" based on these Code sections alone? My indictment stated (in connection with the first three counts) that I did "willfully and knowingly attempt to evade and defeat the said income tax due and owing," but didn't cite the Code section which made such a tax "due and owing." Was I supposed to take the prosecutor's word that some unidentified law existed that did that? Similarly, the fourth count of my indictment accused me of violating section 7203 by failing to file a corporate income tax return "as required by law"; but neither the indictment nor section 7203 identifies any law containing any such alleged "requirement"! Was I supposed to take the prosecutor's word for that, too? How could I (or anyone else) intelligently plead to these four counts? But most important, neither section 7201 or 7203 could possibly apply to me unless they involved a tax *for which I was liable!* The existence of either an actual or potential tax "liability" is obviously crucial to any lawful indictment and information involving a federal tax (something that all income tax indictments and informations are not). Therefore, my ability to plead to the charges depended on whether or not I could be *legally liable* for the tax I was accused of evading and for which I was accused of failing to file a return. However, no such reference appears anywhere in my indictment, and as proven by my "arraignment" tape neither the government nor the court could supply it! If there was any law that made me liable for such a tax or established such a filing requirement, you'd better believe **they would have been indicated in my indictment.** Those Code sections would be cited in all indictments and informations involving income taxes. **But they never are! Now you know why!**

So Magistrate Eagan refused to cite the Code section that made me "liable" for the tax I was charged with evading and for which I allegedly failed to file a return. Therefore he *refused* to explain the charges to me as he admitted he was *required to do.* Therefore, it was impossible for me (as it would be for anyone else) to make an intelligent and informed plea. Yet he pled me not guilty on the absurd ground that I had "refused to make a plea"! The irony is that after the court illegally extracted a guilty plea from the jury, it fined me $28,000 in court costs (although the trial obviously cost the government a whole lot more) in addition to a $30,000 fine. Yet I had offered to plead guilty at my arraignment to save myself and the government these expenses! But the government and the court wouldn't accept my guilty plea in exchange for merely citing the law that made what I had been accused of a crime! This proves that the perfidy of federal courts knows no bounds!

It should also be clear from all of the above that as far as my "trial" was concerned, the prosecution and the bench were one in the same. It will also be perfectly obvious to any student of the law, that I went to trial **without ever having been arraigned.**

LUDICROUS CLAIMS FROM THE GOVERNMENT AND THE COURT

As a result of the court's refusal to hear oral argument at my arraignment on the issue of jurisdiction and on the question of my tax "liability," I submitted (through the attorney I ultimately retained to represent me) additional motions attacking jurisdiction and the motion shown in the Appendix, in which I offered to plead guilty if the government or the court would simply cite the law that made me liable for the tax. The responses to that motion (which are also included in the Appendix) by both the government and the court, should convince anyone that federal judges and U.S. prosecutors have been criminally engaged in prosecuting Americans for crimes that they both knew did not exist.

Note that the government's six line response does not even attempt to address, let alone refute, the issues I raised in that motion. In its claim that "whether or not the defendant is liable for income taxes under appropriate provisions of law is a matter of proof at trial," will be immediately recognized by every law student in the country as being blatantly absurd. Issues of law are decided by the court before a case even goes to jury, since if there is no case as a matter of law, then the facts that the jury might be called upon to judge are immaterial.[6]

The issues that I raised in that pre-trial motion were purely matters of law—as any eighth grader would have had no trouble figuring out—and had absolutely nothing to do with any fact that a jury had to decide. I maintained in that motion that there was no law that made me liable for the tax I was charged with evading or for which I was charged with failing to file a return. I was *challenging the court* (not the jury!) *to produce that law!* The government could not produce it, proving conclusively that my trial was illegal.

The government's shameless claim that producing the law "is a matter of proof at trial" was errant nonsense. The response by the court was no less ignoble. The Honorable Peter C. Dorsey also claimed that "Defendant's Motion to Dismiss on grounds that the Internal Revenue Code does not, as a matter of law, make him liable for the payment of income tax is denied.[7] At trial, the jury shall determine the factual matters raised by this claim." There were, of course, no "factual matters" raised by my motion; only legal ones as the Honorable Peter C. Dorsey well recognized. And Judge Dorsey's inability to produce a Code section that made me liable for an income tax made him aware that he was proceeding to trial on a matter for which he clearly had no jurisdiction.

MORE DUPLICITY ON THE PART OF GOVERNMENT LAWYERS

When, during civil discovery, I asked the Justice Department's team of lawyers to supply me with the Code section that made me liable for income taxes, look at the reply I received (Figure 6-2). The Justice Department had the nerve to suggest that these Code sections made me liable for income tax. I have already covered section 1 in a previous chapter, and have reproduced Code sections 3, 61, 62 and 63 in Figure 6-3. Notice that the word "liability" does not appear anywhere in those four sections, nor does it appear in section1. Sections 1 and 3 simply impose the tax (as does section 4401(a) as shown in Figure 3-4), but nowhere in those sections does it state (as does Sec. 4401(c), Figure 3-4) who is liable for the tax imposed. Sections 61, 62 and 63, on the other hand, only claim to define gross, adjusted gross and taxable income.[8]

It is perfectly obvious that none of the five Code sections supplied by the Justice Department's team of lawyers, which allegedly establish an income tax "liability," did so. It should also be obvious that if such a "liability" did exist, it would only have had to be stated in one Code section. The Justice Department would not have needed to cite *five!*

To nail down the government's duplicity even further, look how the IRS' team of lawyers answered the same question. (Figure 6-4 #5) And it took me almost an entire year to pry that answer out of them! Notice that the IRS' team of laywers didn't even suggest that any of the Code sections cited by the Justice Department's team had anything whatever to do with establishing an income tax "liability"! What does that tell you?

This alone establishes that either one or both teams were not telling the truth. The fact, is, neither of them were, as is proven by the IRS' answer. The IRS' team (as represented by messrs. Holly and Long) didn't even pretend to cite a Code section. They based their claim solely on the fact that

FIGURE 6-2

IN THE UNITED STATES DISTRICT COURT FOR THE

DISTRICT OF CONNECTICUT

IRWIN A. SCHIFF,   )
)
            Plaintiff,   )
)
    v.   ) CIVIL NO. N-86-354-(WWE)
)
UNITED STATES OF AMERICA,   )
)
            Defendant.   )

RESPONSE OF THE UNITED STATES TO THE
PLAINTIFF'S REQUEST FOR PRODUCTION
OF DOCUMENTS, GOVERNMENT RECORDS,
STATUTES AND REGULATIONS

The United States, by its attorney, Stanley A. Twardy, Jr.,
United States Attorney for the District of Connecticut, for its
response to the plaintiff's Request for Production of Documents,
Government Records, Statutes and Regulations states as follows:

- 6 -

REQUEST:

   (11) The statute that the Defendant claims made the Plaintiff
liable for income taxes for the years 1976, 1977, and 1978.

RESPONSE:

   (11) The United States' response to the plaintiff's eleventh
request is that Title 26 of the United States Code (26 U.S.C.),
Sections 1, 3, 61, 62, and 63, establish the circumstances under
which an individual is liable for federal income taxes.

   Production of the foregoing documents is being accomplished
by mailing copies thereof to the plaintiff as indicated on the
attached Certificate of Service.

                                        STANLEY A. TWARDY, JR.
                                        United States Attorney

                          By: _____
                                        JEREMIAH F. DONOVAN
                                        Assistant United States Attorney

                                        DEBORAH S. MELAND
                                        Trial Attorney, Tax Division
                                        U.S. Department of Justice
                                        Post Office Box 55
                                        Ben Franklin Station
                                        Washington, D.C. 20044
                                        Telephone: (202/FTS) 724-6549

                                                        39/0085-A

my "history of unsuccessful litigation proves that there is such a thing as income tax liabilty."! How's that for incestuous legal logic? What their letter does prove is all of the "litigation" referred to, was obviously conducted in kangaroo federal courts where I was opposed by government prosecutors having no more "integrity" than those who produced the above two specious responses!

The fact that a United States magistrate, a United States District Court judge, a United States prosecutor, and two teams of governmental lawyers could not produce a Code section that established an income tax liability should convince you that **there is no such thing as an income tax "liability."** Knowing that, you are in a position to understand why all government seizures of property in connection with income taxes are illegal—as will be conclusively laid out in the next chapter.

— IMPORTANT —

The fact that you are not "liable" for income taxes should enable you, through bankruptcy, to discharge all back income taxes the government claims you owe. This flies in the face of the prevailing wisdom that a bankruptcy will not discharge income taxes. Fortunately in Bankruptcy Court (unlike Tax Court and refund suits in district courts—see Chapter 9) the burden of proof is on your creditors: they have to establish that you are "liable" for the debts they claim. Before the Bankruptcy Court you should claim that, while the government claims you owe income taxes, you claim (and you could swear to this) that you don't. (Naturally this only applies to income taxes—not withholding taxes). You claim that you are not "liable" for the income taxes, and that no law (Code section) makes you "liable" for any such taxes. The government would then have to prove to the Bankruptcy Court (by providing the law) that you were "liable" for the income taxes claimed. Since the government will not be able to do that, the bankruptcy judge should have no alternative but to throw out the government's claim—**thus discharging all of the back income taxes the government claims you owe!**

FIGURE 6-3

Sec. 3. Tax tables for individuals.

(a) Imposition of tax table tax.

(1) In general. In lieu of the tax imposed by section 1 there is hereby imposed for each taxable year on the tax table income of every individual whose tax table income for such year does not exceed the ceiling amount, a tax determined under tables, applicable to such taxable year, which shall be prescribed by the Secretary and which shall be in such form as he determines appropriate. In the tables so prescribed, the amounts of tax shall be computed on the basis of the rates prescribed by section

§ 61. Gross income defined

(a) General definition

Except as otherwise provided in this subtitle, gross income means all income from whatever source derived, including (but not limited to) the following items:

(1) Compensation for services, including fees, commissions, fringe benefits, and similar items;

(2) Gross income derived from business;
(3) Gains derived from dealings in property;
(4) Interest;
(5) Rents;
(6) Royalties;
(7) Dividends;
(8) Alimony and separate maintenance payments;

(9) Annuities;
(10) Income from life insurance and endowment contracts;
(11) Pensions;
(12) Income from discharge of indebtedness;
(13) Distributive share of partnership gross income;
(14) Income in respect of a decedent; and
(15) Income from an interest in an estate or trust.

§ 62. Adjusted gross income defined

(a) General rule

For purposes of this subtitle, the term "adjusted gross income" means, in the case of an individual, gross income minus the following deductions:

§ 63. Taxable income defined

(a) In general

Except as provided in subsection (b), for purposes of this subtitle, the term "taxable income" means gross income minus the deductions allowed by this chapter (other than the standard deduction).

FIGURE 6-4

DISTRICT COUNSEL

Internal Revenue Service

NORTH-ATLANTIC REGION
William R. Cotter Federal Building
135 High Street - Room 259
Hartford, Connecticut 06103

CC:HAR:TL
JFLong

JUN 0 3 1988

Mr. Irwin A. Schiff
Reg. No. 08537-014
P.O. Box 1000 - 702
Lorretto, PA 15940

          Subject: Docket No. 33278-86
                    Income Tax 1979

Dear Mr. Schiff:

     On March 7, 1988, you served us with a document entitled
Petitioner's Third Series of Interrogatories. It is our position
that you have failed to comply with Tax Court Rule 70(a) and that
therefore no response is required at this time. In the spirit of
cooperation I am responding to the aforementioned request for
interrogatories as if it were an informal request for
information.

     1. and 2. Object on the ground that this is an attempt to go
behind the statutory notice of deficiency.

     3. and 4. Object on the ground that the respondent is not
required to explain the law to the petitioner.

     5. For 1974 and 1975 you were convicted of willful failure
to file tax returns, sentenced to prison and later found liable
for the civil fraud penalty. You are presently involved in
refund litigation for 1976, 1977, and 1978 in the United States
District Court. Your 1979 year is the subject of this litigation, and you are presently incarcerated for willfully
attempting to evade income tax in violation of I.R.C. § 7201 for
1980, 1981 and 1982. I submit <u>that your history of unsuccessful
litigation proves that there is such a thing as income tax
liability</u>.

                              Sincerely,

                              POWELL W. HOLLY, JR.

             By: _____
                  JOSEPH F. LONG
                  Attorney

NOTES TO CHAPTER 6

1. In this section "shall" is mandatory. Since Americans never had a constitutional right to distill alcoholic beverages for commercial purposes, such a tax has always been exacted from distillers since the birth of the nation.

2. Jurisdiction is a federal court's legal authority to hear the case brought to it. The court might not have jurisdiction over the person, such as one living in a foreign land, or it might not have jurisdiction over the subject matter. Before a court can acquire a criminal jurisdiction Congress must (1) first make an act a crime, (2) fix punishment to it, and (3) declare the court that will have jurisdiction over it. (See *United States* v. *Hudson,* 11 U.S. 32) Not one of these elements was present in my case. And while the issue of jurisdiction can be raised at any time, once the issue *is raised* it must be *addressed and settled.* Obviously, a defendant should not have to suffer any further expense and inconvenience if the court has no jurisdiction to proceed. Lawyers, however, have a tendency to postpone attacking jurisdiction by saying "we can always raise that issue later." Naturally, their clocks keep ticking as long as the issue is not resolved. Courts take the same position when they are determined to railroad the accused, which is generally the situation when they are hearing "tax protester" cases.

3. For those wanting to experience first-hand how drum head justice is administered in federal courts (and for those who might refuse to believe that such an "arraignment" could ever take place in an American court and so might think I made the whole thing up), the entire 45-minute "arraignment" can be secured from Freedom Books on cassette tape (as recorded by the court) for $7.00, including postage and handling.

4. In case you're thinking "he would be accountable to an appellate court," forget it. Appellate courts are a part of the federal income tax conspiracy, and in these situations, back up district courts. This is easily accomplished with the ol' "frivolous" ploy, or its slightly longer variation, "these arguments have been rejected time and time again." Or it could be flat out "denied" without any opinion. Then where are you going to go—to the Supreme Court? Do you really think it would grant certiorari? Or to put it another way, do you really think that, that Court doesn't know what's going on? In 1985 I sent each Supreme Court justice his own copy of *The Great Income Tax Hoax* and not only didn't I get back *one* thank you note, but on top of that, *it denied me certiorari in 1986.*

5. An information is a written accusation of a crime, made by a U.S. attorney, which permits the government to prosecute an individual without benefit of a grand jury indictment. It is used when the crime alleged is a misdemeanor as opposed to being a felony. It has been used a great deal by the government against "tax protesters" in illegal 7203 prosecutions, since the government claims that not filing an income tax return is a misdemeanor pursuant to Section 7203. It's not, of course, but that has been the government's illegal contention. Now that the government has become even more tyranical by seeking to make failure to file a felony pursuant to Section 7201, informations are used less frequently. "The use of [informations] has a long history. For example, in the reign of Henry VII," writes Justice Blackstone, in 4 Bl. Comm. 310, "...a century, so as to continually harass the subject and shamefully enrich the crown.": which pretty much describes how informations are used by the Justice Department today.

6. However, in criminal trials juries can take it upon themselves to judge both the law and the facts pursuant to a principle known as "jury nullification." See the Supreme Court's acknowledgement of this principle in *Georgia* v. *Brailsford,* 3 Dall 1 (1774). However, today federal judges totally mislead juries concerning their alleged obligation to follow the law as given to them by the court. Some federal judges even make jurors swear to do so, thus making a total mockery out of the American jury system. For more on this see *The Great Income Tax Hoax,* pages 378-381.

7. All of my pre-trial motions were denied without oral argument.

8. These claims, however, are all false. Since section 61 uses the word "income" to define "gross income," it violates the basic principle governing definitions, and therefore does not define "gross income" at all.

— CHAPTER 7 —
HOW THE FEDERAL MAFIA
ILLEGALLY SEIZES PROPERTY

"To lay with one hand the power of the government on the property of the citizen, and with the other bestow it on favored individuals...is nonetheless robbery because it is done under the form of law and is called taxation."

—**United States Supreme Court**
Loan Association v. Topeka **(1874)**

Apart from ruining people's lives with illegal prosecutions and imprisonment, there is probably no more reprehensible activity that the U.S. government engages in, than in the illegal confiscation of property (including wages) in payment of taxes that nobody owes. While the former would appear to be more contemptible, the latter is experienced by far more people and can have consequences just as tragic. Severe financial deprivation, caused by loss of wages, loss of savings, loss of homes, and loss of businesses, often leads to divorce, depression, and nervous breakdowns. How many suicides, directly and indirectly result from such despicable government behavior can only be speculated upon. But I am sure the number is far greater than anyone would suspect.

I have received numerous calls from people whom the federal government was literally squeezing to death. One such call came from a railroad worker in Oklahoma who the government claimed owed over $25,000 in taxes, penalties and interest. The government had garnisheed his wages (using a Notice of Levy), and had left him with only $75.00 a week, which was not enough for him to even live on. This individual knew that he didn't owe the government one penny of that amount and, as a subscriber to *The Schiff Report,* he also knew that the Notice of Levy issued by the government did not even apply to him. Yet he was legally powerless to stop this illegal confiscation of his wages which had suddenly reduced him, practically, to the status of a pauper. He had brought copies of my Report (which clearly documents the illegality of such "notices" and the reason that employers are not required to honor them) to the attention of his employer's legal department but to no avail. What he was permitted to keep from his own wages would not even cover his mortgage payment, so he was facing the loss of his home. If he stayed with the railroad he would be unable to support himself and his family on $75.00 a week; while, if he left, he would lose valuable seniority with little prospect of being able to earn anywhere near what his salary was at the railroad. He doubted whether he could find a job in that small Oklahoma town that would even cover his basic living expenses. He did not know what to do or where to turn. One day I received a letter from him saying that by the time I received it, he would be dead. He had become so frustrated and despondent over his situation that he decided

to end his life. I was, therefore, apprehensive when I immediately called him and was relieved when he answered the phone. I extracted a promise that he would never again consider doing such a thing, and gave him some fresh ideas to try. I never heard from him again, since shortly thereafter I had to turn myself in to begin my own three year prison term.

Also about that time, I got another call from a man in New York City who ran a small service business. A month or so before, the IRS, without warning, walked into his bank and totally cleaned out his account of some $25,000. Besides the checks that started bouncing, he could not meet his payroll, so his employees left. Now, he informed me, he couldn't even pay his rent, and so would shortly be out of business completely. He also claimed (for reasons I don't now recall) that he did not owe the government the amount claimed, and wanted my advice as to what he could do. In many instances, victims are not left with enough money to consult a lawyer, let alone retain one. The IRS, of course, took his $25,000 without a hearing or court order. Suppose that in six months or so, this individual could prove that he didn't owe those taxes; that they were actually owed by someone having the same name. What then? In that case, the government would simply refund his money plus interest. But what about the value of his business that went down the drain? "T.S." the government would say, "That's the way the cookie crumbles," if it bothered to say anything at all.[1]

HOW THE GOVERNMENT MAKES LAWLESSNESS LOOK LEGAL

All IRS seizures for income taxes claim to be made pursuant to Code Section 6331 (Figure 7-1). Yet, you now know enough to be able to immediately recognize why this section doesn't apply to income taxes **on any basis!** Please test yourself accordingly by reading paragraph (a) of that section. Did the reason immediately jump out at you? If it didn't, then you should reread the last chapter. But, I'm sure you spotted that because the fourth word in the section's opening paragraph is "liable." Section 6331 can have (as fully explained in the last chapter) **absolutely nothing whatsoever to do with income taxes!** This alone establishes that all government seizures in connection

FIGURE 7-1

§ 6331. Levy and distraint

(a) Authority of Secretary

A.

If any person liable to pay any tax neglects or refuses to pay the same within 10 days after notice and demand, it shall be lawful for the Secretary to collect such tax (and such further sum as shall be sufficient to cover the expenses of the levy) by levy upon all property and rights to property (except such property as is exempt under section 6334) belonging to such person or on which there is a lien provided in this chapter for the payment of such tax. Levy may be made upon the accrued salary or wages of any officer, employee, or elected official, of the United States, the District of Columbia, or any agency or instrumentality of the United States or the District of Columbia, by serving a notice of levy on the employer (as defined in section 3401(d)) of such officer, employee, or elected official. If the Secretary makes a finding that the collection of such tax is in jeopardy, notice and demand for immediate payment of such tax may be made by the Secretary and, upon failure or refusal to pay such tax, collection thereof by levy shall be lawful without regard to the 10-day period provided in this section.

(b) Seizure and sale of property

The term "levy" as used in this title includes the power of distraint and seizure by any means. Except as otherwise provided in subsection (e), a levy shall extend only to property possessed and obligations existing at the time thereof. In any case in which the Secretary may levy upon property or rights to property, he may seize and sell such property or rights to property (whether real or personal, tangible or intangible).

(c) Successive seizures

Whenever any property or right to property upon which levy has been made by virtue of subsection (a) is not sufficient to satisfy the claim of the United States for which levy is made, the Secretary may, thereafter, and as often as may be necessary, proceed to levy in like manner upon any other property liable to levy of the person against whom such claim exists, until the amount due from him, together with all expenses, is fully paid.

(d) Requirement of notice before levy

(1) In general

Levy may be made under subsection (a) upon the salary or wages or other property of any person with respect to any unpaid tax only after the Secretary has notified such person in writing of his intention to make such levy.

(2) 10-day requirement

The notice required under paragraph (1) shall be—
(A) given in person,
(B) left at the dwelling or usual place of business of such person, or
(C) sent by certified or registered mail to such persons's last known address,

no less than 10 days before the day of the levy.

(3) Jeopardy

Paragraph (1) shall not apply to a levy if the Secretary has made a finding under the last sentence of subsection (a) that the collection of tax is in jeopardy.

(e) Continuing levy on salary and wages

(1) Effect of levy

The effect of a levy on salary or wages payable to or received by a taxpayer shall be continuous from the date such levy is first made until the liability out of which such levy arose is satisfied or becomes unenforceable by reason of lapse of time.

(2) Release and notice of release

With respect to a levy described in paragraph (1), the Secretary shall promptly release the levy when the liability out of which such levy arose is satisfied or becomes unenforceable by reason of lapse of time, and shall promptly notify the person upon whom such levy was made that such levy has been released.

FIGURE 7-2

Form 17A
Revised May 1953
U. S. Treasury Department
Internal Revenue Service

CHARLES H LEHIGH
1415 WE 'AIN
ELDORADO ...<K   AUG 15. 510100 55
OH 22753   1954   1953
INT TO 8/15/55
JEOPARDY ASSESSMENT – SEC 273(A)
IRC OF 1939 – SEC 6861 IRC 1954

DISTRICT DIRECTOR'S COPY

Statement of
Income Tax
Due

	Amount paid	Balance due
AUG 55 247,012.96		
AUG 55 20,996.10		
AUG 55 14,815.93		
ASS 55P 21,400.78		304,225.76

87.88

Dated· Aug 16 1955

This bill for the amount shown as "Balance Due" is being sent to you in accordance with law. The law also requires that interest at 6 percent per year until date of payment be added unless this amount is paid within 10 days from date of this notice.

Amounts shown in "Assessment" above are for tax unless identified as penalty by letter "P" or interest by letter "L"

Please return this notice with remittance to District Director of Internal Revenue at

Little Rock, Arkansas

TY ITEM 26

with income taxes are illegal, and I should not have to proceed any further than this to prove it! But the government's fraudulent use of Section 6331 is so massive on so many different levels, that a far greater analysis of this section is called for.

If you haven't already done so, please read Section 6331 in its entirety. Did you notice that it doesn't even *mention* income taxes? Since it doesn't mention income taxes, and since Section 6331 isn't in Subtitle A, on what basis can anyone claim that it even *applies* to income taxes? The answer is none whatsoever!

Actually, no other tax is even mentioned in that section. But, since Subtitle F (in which this section appears) was made specifically applicable to other taxes by cross-reference, (as shown in Figure 3-5) Section 6331 applies to those taxes even though they are not mentioned. This cannot be said for income taxes, since no similar cross reference appears in Subtitle A! So who and what are the only persons and taxes to which Section 6331 can apply? Well the first line in that section tells you. Section 6331 only applies to "any person *liable* to pay any tax (who) neglects or refuses to pay the same within 10 days **after notice and demand**..." So, this section can't apply to income taxes for *two* reasons. One, because no one can be "liable" for that kind of tax, and two, because no one allegedly liable for such a tax, is **ever** sent a "notice and demand" as required by that section!

THE MISSING "NOTICE AND DEMAND"

Figure 7-2 reveals IRS Form 17A, a document that few Americans have ever seen, though its use is mandated by no less than seven Internal Revenue Code Sections—6155(a), 6156(d), 6213(c), 6215(a), 6303 (Figure 4-3), 6321, 6861(a) and (f) in addition to Section 6331. Form 17A is extremely important, since the IRS is barred by Section 6331 from seizing any property unless it first sends one out. And since, as I have already stated, the IRS rarely sends them out in connection with income taxes, it is **additionally** barred by this provision of Section 6331 from seizing any property in connection with income taxes!

It stands to reason that before the government can seize any property in connection with a tax allegedly due, it must first make a formal, unequivocal, and lawful demand for its payment—and Form 17A is the statutory notice specifically designed and authorized to do that. Now the reason this form is rarely used in connection with income taxes, is that since such a tax cannot be legally "owed", how can it be legally "demanded"? As the Supreme Court said in *Flora* v. *United Staes,* supra, our income tax system is based upon "*voluntary*" assessment and *payment,* not upon *distraint.*" *Therefore, no "demand" for such a tax can be legally made,*

nor seizures threatened for non-*voluntary* payment. However there is another reason why it is rarely used. By not making a lawful demand on the proper statutory notice, the government is able **to extort billions in fictitious interest penalties** *in addition* **to the taxes fraudulently extorted!**

A Bogus Demand

In order to fool the public that valid "demands" pursuant to Sections 6303 and 6331 have been made, the government sends out the bogus "notices" shown in Figure 5-5, captioned "Statement of Tax Due On Federal Tax Return." These are actually statements designed to be used in connection with Code Section 6014 (Figure 7-3). That section authorizes the Secretary, in certain cases, to

---

FIGURE 7-3

§ 6014. Income tax return—tax not computed by taxpayer

(a) Election by taxpayer

An individual who does not itemize his deductions and who is not described in section 6012(a)(1)(C)(i), whose gross income is less than $10,000 and includes no income other than remuneration for services performed by him as an employee, dividends or interest, and whose gross income other than wages, as defined in section 3401(a), does not exceed $100, shall at his election not be required to show on the return the tax imposed by section 1. Such election shall be made by using the form prescribed for purposes of this section. In such case the tax shall be computed by the Secretary who shall mail to the taxpayer a notice stating the amount determined as payable.

(b) Regulations

The Secretary shall prescribe regulations for carrying out this section, and such regulations may provide for the application of the rules of this section—

(1) to cases where the gross income includes items other than those enumerated by subsection (a),

(2) to cases where the gross income from sources other than wages on which the tax has been withheld at the source is more than $100,

(3) to cases where the gross income is $10,000 or more, or

(4) to cases where the taxpayer itemizes his deductions or where the taxpayer claims a reduced standard deduction by reason of section 63(c)(5).

Such regulations shall provide for the application of this section in the case of husband and wife, including provisions determining when a joint return under this section may be permitted or required, whether the liability shall be joint and several, and whether one spouse may make return under this section and the other without regard to this section.

compute an individual's tax *when the Secretary is requested to do so by the taxpayer.* As you can see, Section 6014 provides that "the Secretary...shall mail to the taxpayer a notice stating the amount determined as payable." Instead of sending out the legally constituted "notice and demand" that the IRS is required to do, according to Section 6331 and 6303, it has been fraudulently sending out, *in its place,* the statement designed to meet the requirements of Section 6014! Understanding this will enable you to see through the language contained in the bogus statements which the government has been using, as compared to the language contained and required in the legitimate, statutory notice.

The taxes shown on the bogus "Statements" sent to me, only refer to an alleged "Tax Due," which, presumably, I might have shown on the "Tax Returns" I *didn't file,* and/or which, I *might* have asked the government *to compute for me* based upon information I *might* have supplied, but *didn't!* If I had done the above, the Secretary (pursuant to Section 6014) would have sent me those statements, indicating the amounts "I should" pay if I believed (incorrectly!) that I owed the taxes for the years shown!

The reason that the government can get away with this outrageous subtrafuge is that the language of both forms is similiar enough so the public can't tell the difference—especially when it is totally unaware of both the **existence** and **purpose** of either form! But an examination of both forms will reveal their significant differences, and, in addition, will reveal how the government is able to use the bogus forms (unlike the legitimate ones) **to extract additional billions in non-existent interest penalties!** As you can see, Form 17A is entitled "Statement of Income Tax Due," which unequivocally notifies the recipient that the amount indicated is "due and owing." The bogus statement claims that the amount shown is only a "Statement of Tax Due On Federal Tax Return." The difference should be obvious. The second form merely informs individuals of the amount that they could have shown on the "Federal Tax Return," that they asked the Secretary to calculate for them. This does not mean that this amount is actually "due and owing" or that it is being "demanded." If this distinction escapes you, then just recognize that Form 17A does not even lend itself to such confusion!

As previously explained, a Form 17A informs the recipient that an income tax is "due." The bogus form does not! The bogus form merely informs recipients of the "Tax Due" on the returns they apparently *wanted to send in.* So the amounts shown on both forms are hardly the same, and, obviously, the IRS had no authority to send me the forms it did. Since I had never made a Section 6014 request!

In addition Form 17A clearly refers to itself as a "bill." This bill,..." it states, is "for the amount shown as 'Balance Due'." Now everybody knows what a bill is. When you get a bill, you're supposed to pay it. However the "Statement of Tax Due On Federal Tax Return" does *not claim to be a bill*—so why should anybody think he or she is required to pay it? Form 17A specifically calls the recipient's attention to the fact that "The law also *requires* that interest at 6 percent" will be added "unless this amount is paid within 10 days from the date of this notice." So Form 17A uses threatening legal language to back up its demand. Such language is *entirely absent in the bogus form!* But most important, in employing that language, Form 17A informs recipients that not only are they "required" by law to pay the "bill," but if not, *interest will be added!* You will notice that not only does no such mandatory language appear in the "Statements" sent me on April 5th—**but $52,071.23 in interest charges had already been added!** So now you see why the government never uses valid notices and demands. It couldn't bilk the public out of bogus interest penalties if it did! The statutory notice states that, unless the bill is paid, interest **will be** added. By using bogus notices, the government is able to *include* **bogus interest penalties (from the date tax returns are allegedly due) in its bogus "bills"!!**

NOW IS ANYONE PREPARED TO ARGUE THAT THOSE RESPONSIBLE FOR SENDING OUT THESE BOGUS AND EXTORTIONARY "NOTICES" (AND THOSE WHO *ENFORCE THEM*) SHOULD NOT BE TRIED AND JAILED AS COMMON THIEVES AND CRIMINALS?

It is clear that Form 17A is the official notice designed to meet the requirements of the eight Code sections previously listed, and it is also clear that the requirement that it be sent out prior to levy is disregarded by the IRS and ignored by federal courts.[2] However, on certain occasions in the past, the IRS apparently *made the mistake* of sending some out. For example, the one shown in Figure 7-2 was reproduced as it appeared in *United States* v. *Lehigh,* 201 F. Supp. 224. It was identified in that decision as being the statutory "Statement of Income Tax Due." In another decision, *United States* v. *Pavenick,* 197 F. Supp. 257 (1961), the court stated:

Therefore, upon proof of demand, the Government lien arises at the time of assessment by the collector. §3670, 3671, I.R.C. 1939. However, the evidence presently before me does not suffice to establish the Government's asserted lien because proof of its demand for payment of the amounts assessed has not been furnished. *The mailing of Form 17, Statement of Taxes Due* (First Notice and Demand) [emphasis (but not parentheses) added.]

Here the court correctly points out that a taxpayer must receive two demand notices before the government can seek to seize his property. The "First Notice and Demand" is the Form 17 which must be sent pursuant to Code Sections 6303(a) (Figure 4-3) and 6331(a), and the Second Notice is the Secretary's notification "in writing of his intention to make such levy," as provided in 6331(d). The IRS' FINAL NOTICE as shown in Figure 5-8 is that "Second" Notice. However, the IRS **never even sends out the required first notice!**

TREASURY DECISION 1995

If there is any doubt that Form 17 is the specific government document designed to meet the requirements of Code Section 6303 and 6331 (and those other six Code sectons), then Figure 7-4 should dispel that doubt. Figure 7-4 contains Treasury Decision 1995 entitled "Assessed Taxes—Notice and Demand, Form 17." This Treasury Decision specifically *provides and requires* the Service to send out a Form 17 "before the delinquent taxpayer

---

FIGURE 7-4

INTERNAL REVENUE.

(T. D. 1995.)

Assessed taxes—Notice and demand, Form 17.

Notice of and demand for assessed taxes to be issued promptly to secure tax lien, penalty, and interest in case of nonpayment.

TREASURY DEPARTMENT,
OFFICE OF COMMISSIONER OF INTERNAL REVENUE,
Washington, D. C., June 12, 1914.

To collectors of internal revenue:

It appears that certain collectors hold that notice of assessment and demand, Form 17, is not necessary to create a liability to 5 per cent penalty and interest at 1 per cent per month in the case of income tax remaining unpaid after June 30 or other due date. This view as to the requirements of the law is clearly wrong and contrary to the instructions (art. 197, Regs., 33) issued on the subject.

The necessity of issuing Form 17 is twofold —first, to determine the date when 5 per cent penalty accrues and interest at 1 per cent per month begins to run, and, second, to complete the Government's lien on property belonging to the taxpayer.

In special excise and income-tax assessments a notice on Form 647 is required to be given in all cases where the required return is filed in due time. This, however, is simply a preliminary notice of assessment, to be followed, in case of nonpayment, by a formal notice and demand which the law clearly contemplates and which the courts hold to be necessary before the delinquent taxpayer becomes chargeable with penalty and interest.

In all cases, therefore, where an assessed tax remains unpaid after it becomes due a notice on Form 17 should be at once issued, to be followed, when necessary, by Forms 21 and 69, in their order. The fact that a claim for abatement is pending or the tax is in litigation does not relieve the collector from issuing the notices, demands, etc., required by law.

A misunderstanding on the part of certain collectors as to these requirements has occasioned a considerable loss to the Government of penalty and interest, especially where claims for abatement were pending.

W. H. OSBORN,
Commissioner of Internal Revenue.

becomes chargable with penalties and interest." Since, to my knowledge, this Treasury Decision has never been rescinded, revoked, nor overruled by the Treasury Department, **it is binding on the IRS and must be obeyed.**

IF YOU DIDN'T GET A FORM 17, WHAT THEN?

It is clear that, by law, the government is required to send individuals a Form 17 before it can levy any property pursuant to Section 6331. This is known as a "condition precedent," and the seizure of any property without this "condition precedent" having been met, **automatically invalidates the seizure** and entitles all such parties to a return of all property and cash seized (plus interest). There is ample case law to support this. See *United States* v. *Coson,* 286 F.2d 453 (9th Cir. 1961); *Bauer* v. *Foley,* 404 F.2d 1215 (2d Cir. 1968); on rehearing; 408 F2d; 1331 (2d Cir. 1969); *L.O.C. Indus. Inc.* v. *United States,* 423 F. Supp. 265 (M.D. Tenn. 1976); *Mrizek* v. *Long,* 176 F. Supp. 830 (N.D. Ill. 1959); *Shapiro* v. *Sec. of State,* 499 F2d, 527, 531 N.12 (D.C. Cir. 1974) aff'd 424 U.S. 614 (1976). and re *Baltimore Pearl Hominy Co.,* 5 F2d 553, in which the Fifth Circuit held that "The purpose of requiring a demand as a condition precedent to the tax becoming a lien is protection of the taxpayer."

In *Coson,* supra, the court said:

> No notice or demand concerning these taxes had been given to or served upon Coson. This procedural pre-requisite to the securing of a Government lien for such taxes is made plain by the statute...The procedure for making such demand is set forth in §6303(a).

> It will be noted that our decision here is based upon our holding that the Government's lien was irregular, insufficient and valueless from a procedural stand-point for failure *to serve the statutory notice and demand* in connection therewith and for failure to comply with required procedures. [emphasis added.]

In affirming a lower court's action in removing a government tax lien, the *Coson* court clearly stated that "the lack of proper notice or demand was fatal to the acquisition of the Government's lien against *Coson.*"

In *Bauer,* supra, the court invalidated a government lien when proper notice and demand was not given despite the government's claim that the court should uphold its "long standing administrative practice" of not doing so. The court said:

> The Government's principal objection to the court's

holding concerns that portion of the opinion which says that §6303(a) requires that the assessment notice be given "to each person liable for the unpaid tax, stating the amount and demanding payment thereof" and that the consequences of failing to give such separate notice is that it invalidates the lien subsequently filed. The government asserts that such an application of §6303(a) would be contrary to the customary practices of the Internal Revenue Service allowed for many years, and if it were compelled to change its collection methods to comply with this court's holding, the result would be nothing short of devastating to the present procedures...

The Government is particularly troubled about what we said about the notice of assessment and demand for payment and cites authorities to support its contention that a long standing administrative practice in dealing with a statutory provision is of considerable importance and should be upheld. These authorities, however, were considering statutory provisions capable of different interpretations. Section 6303(a) is not such a statute. Its language is perfectly clear: "* * * the Secretary shall * * * give notice to each person liable for the unpaid tax * * *," it goes on to specify how the notice shall be given. But it clearly provides for a notice separately addressed or directed to *each person* liable for the tax.

It should be noted that it was the government's position (but here rejected by the court) that if it had to "comply with the court's holding," *which was that it obey the law,* that such a requirement would be "devastating" to its collection procedures!

In *Shapiro* v. *Secretary of State,* supra, the court held (on page 531) that:

> It should be noted that Section 6331(a) requires that the Commissioner provide a taxpayer prior notice of the demand for payment. The power to levy is *inoperative* until the subsequent "failure or refusal" of the taxpayer to pay the required amount.

> In the present case there are allegations that the Commissioner *failed to provide the taxpayer the required notice prior to serving "Notices of Levy"* on the taxpayer's New York banks. If so, then the Commissioner may well have *violated Shapiro's right to due process.* [emphasis added.]

Thus the courts have ruled that the taking of property pursuant to Section 6331 without first sending out the statutory notice and demand for payment, violates one's constitutional right to due process of law!

I wish to specifically point out, however, that in this decision, as in all of the others cited, there were peculiar circumstances which led the courts to rule as they did. In *Bauer*, for example, the issue was whether the notice to one partner was notice to all partners and roughly the same issue was present in the *Coson* case. In *Shapiro*, the issue involved a jeopardy assessment in which the IRS failed to send out *even its bogus notice*. However, the basic legal principle laid down in all of these court decisions must apply in all cases where the IRS fails to send out **the requisite statutory notice and demand (Form 17)** prior to seizure; though one can not help but feel that if this were the only issue presented in all of the above cases, these same courts might well have dismissed all such claims as "frivolous."

Be that as it may, the principle laid down in these decisions stands and, I submit, can be utilized in those situations where the IRS has seized property without first sending out the statutory notice and demand, i.e. Form 17. If this happened to you, then you are in a position to **sue the government for funds illegally deprived.** (Chapter 10)

A PUBLIC BEREFT OF LEGAL PROTECTION

A simple analysis of Section 6331 and how the federal government perverted it, not only reveals the government's criminal character (and that of its courts) but also reveals the total unreliability of the nation's legal establishment in letting the government get away with it. While only devoting the last hour or so to this book, you now know—as surely as you know your own name—that those two million salary seizures, to which Senator Pryor referred, **were all illegal** on at least *two* fundamental grounds! If you could learn that much in only an hour or so of light reading, doesn't it make you wonder what our lawyers read? As long as I have raised that question, let me address it.

TAX SERVICES— PLAYING AN IMPORTANT ROLE

Apart from the crucial role played by a duplicious federal judiciary, the next most important element in explaining the government's fantastic success in pulling off its outrageous income tax scam, has been the vital role played by the nation's influential tax services and law book publishers. Lawyers, tax preparers, and the public are misled (misinformed) by a multi-million, if not a milti-billion, dollar publishing industry. One need only visit any law library and see the walls of books devoted to nothing else but income taxes, to appreciate the vast amount of money that private publishers reap from the income tax. If the public currently understood the correct nature of this tax, these same shelves would be bare and law libraries a whole lot smaller. So it is obvious that publishers of income tax literature have a substantial, vested stake (right along with the government) in keeping the public in the dark about the true (voluntary) nature of the income tax.

In checking the nation's tax services, I found absolutely no mention of Form 17 or 17A in either of the tax services published by Prentice Hall or the Commerce Clearing House—two of the nation's leading services. I checked out tax services across the country and found only one reference to Form 17.[3] That reference was in the most prestigious and authoritative service of all. *Mertens Law of Federal Income Taxes*, published by Callaghan & Company of Wilmette, Illinois. However, even the one lone reference I found in the 17 volume set of *Mertens*, was obliquely made and unnecessarily misleading—which I believe was intentional. The *Mertens* reference is contained in *Mertens*, Vol. 9, Sect. 49.187 and is as follows:

There is no requirement in the Code that an assessment is incomplete until the sending of a notice of assessment to the taxpayer by means of Form 17, or otherwise. Nor does the code require that the Form be sent by registered mail, where notice is sent by mail.

At *least Mertens* mentions the Form. However, it doesn't say that it is *required* to be sent out prior to levy—only that it does not have to be sent out "registered"!

Let me illustrate how misleading the *Mertens* reference is. When I first read it I assumed that what it said was that a Form 17 did not have to be sent out *at all*. Since *Mertens* apparently cited *Filipini* v. *United States*, 200 F. Supp. 286, as its apparent authority for this claim, I decided to check that case out to see how that court could have reached such a conclusion. When I read that case, I discovered that the court mentioned Form 17 **no less than eight times** and never for a moment suggested that it did not have to be sent out. In fact the court said:

Although the statute requires that the statutory notice of deficiency be sent by registered mail, see Section 272(a) there is no such requirement as to Form 17.

The section which *requires* that notice of an assessment and demand for tax shall be given a taxpayer is Section 6303(a) of the 1954 I.R.C. (made applicable to the 1939 I.R.C. by Section 7851(a)(6)(B) of the 1954 I.R.C. This section allows such notice either to be left at the dwelling place of the taxpayer or his usual place of business, or to be mailed to him at his last known address. Such a decision *does not*, however, *specify that the Form 17 be sent by registered mail*, where notice is sent by mail, nor are we aware of any other section or any regulation which imposes such a *mailing requirement*. (emphasis added.)

There can be no question that *Filippini* stands for the proposition that Section 6331(a) "requires" that a Form 17 be sent out. Therefore my impression after reading *Filippini* was that *Mertens* had deliberately misrepresented that decision. However when I reread *Mertens,* I discovered that I had read the entry incorrectly and that *Mertens* had correctly reported what *Filippini* held, which was only that the Form 17 did not have to be sent out by registered mail—*not that it was not "required" to be sent out!* What *Mertens* should have said, if it wanted to correctly inform its readers regarding the mandatory sending of a Form 17, would have been as follows:

Prior to any levy being made, the Service has to send out a notice and demand, Form 17. However, this notice, unlike a deficiency notice, does not have to be sent out by registered mail—it need only be sent to the taxpayer's last known address.

If I received the wrong impression from the *Mertens'* entry (that a Form 17 did not have to be sent at all), others, I'm sure, also got the same wrong impression, and there was no reason for it. But a careful reading of the *Mertens* will reveal, without question, that this prestigious service deliberately set out to mislead the public concerning the necessity of a notice and demand in general and a Form 17 in particular.

Apart from the misleading reference noted above, *Mertens* states that "There is no requirement in the Code that an assessment is incomplete until the sending of a notice of assessment to the taxpayer by means of Form 17." Here *Mertens* makes an entirely irrelevant observation. Of course, there is nothing in the Code that an "assessment is incomplete" without a Form 17 because that Form has nothing to do with the assessment! (which is covered in Code Sections 6201 and 6203). It relates to the requirement contained in Section 6303 that after an assessment is made it must be communicated to the taxpayer and demanded of him before any summary seizure (pursuant to Section 6331) can take place. So *Mertens* is able to infer (without actually making a false statement) that since a Form 17 is not "required" to complete an assessment (pursuant to Section 6201 and 6203)—**it apparently is not required by Sections 6303 and 6331 either!** Such an inference is false and, I suggest, deliberate, since it is in character with the entire entry. In the same vein, *Mertens* makes a misleading (though, again, cleverly not false) inference in claiming that "There is no requirement in the Code..." with respect to a "Form 17." Well the Code doesn't identify any other tax form either, including a 1040! So why should *Mertens* have made such an observation with respect to a "Form 17," if not to again mislead readers with another irrelevant observation? But what I would ask *Mertens* is, if there is no requirement in the law or regulations with respect to a Form

17, then why was it created **and why did *Mertens* feel compelled to mention it at all?**

Despite its tangential nature, this entry in the definitive *Mertens Tax Service* (and its source in *Filippini*) confirms and clearly establishes that a Form 17 must be sent by the IRS prior to its being able to exercise any of its alleged levying powers—albeit, not registered!

However, I could not find even one reference to Form 17 in any of Mertens explanations of the seven other Code Sections to which it also obviously applies.

In addition, all three of these aforementioned influential tax services contain indices supposedly listing all IRS tax forms. They are listed two ways; by form number and alphabetically by subject. Yet in none of these six indices is either a Form 17 or a "notice and demand" listed. Doesn't that strike you as a little odd?

Another example that demonstrates how tax practitioners and students of law, as well as the public, are misled by law book authors and publishers is shown by the entry in *IRS Practice and Procedure,* a highly regarded and quoted work by Long Island University Law Professor Michael Saltzman. In discussing the nature of a *"Demand,* once the formal act of assessment takes place," Professor Saltzman quotes Code Section 6303 almost in its entirety and then goes on to state:

Although there is an explicit statutory requirement that a taxpayer receive notice of the assessment and demand for payment of the amount assessed, a demand need not be formal—that is, by way of official government form.

As his authority for that statement, Professor Saltzman cites (by way of a footnote) seven court decisions. It is conceivable that Professor Saltzman is himself unfamiliar with Form 17, Treasury Decision 1995, the sole *Mertens* entry, and all of the cases that I cited in which Form 17 is identified as the statutory notice and demand. However, what is inconceivable is that the professor should uncritically (and without comment) accept court decisions that obviously contradict both the sense and language of the law and even *offend common sense!* His willingness to do this demonstrates that America, despite the popular belief to the contrary, is realy a society of men, not law. As Professor Saltzman demonstrates—it is not what a law clearly says, that counts, but what men (lawyers in black robes) *claim* the law says!

No less than eight Code sections specifically call for a "notice and demand," and even Professor Saltzman grants in the very same sentence in which he claims that a demand "need not be formal—that is, by way of official government form," that there is an "explicit statutory demand for payment of the amount assessed." Given such an admitted "explicit statutory requirement," is it conceivable that **no official form exists or was ever created** to meet that "explicit statutory requirement"? Is it *conceivable* as Professor Saltzman would have us believe, that a notice and demand required by *no less than eight Code sections* could be informally (and lawfully) scribbled out in pencil and sent out on a piece of Kleenex? But if a notice need not be sent, "by way of official government form", why *not* on a piece of Kleenex? Instead of pointing out how nonsensical such a claim must be, Professor Saltzman reports such absurd opinion (albeit judicial) as being "the law"!

WHAT IS AN IRS "LEVY" ANYWAY?

When I first read Section 6331 (as a result of being threatened with having my assets seized pursuant to that section, as stated in my FINAL NOTICE) I was totally at a loss to understand it. My understanding of American justice and an American's right to "due process" (theoretical as it turned out) did not square with what I initially thought I read in that section. On what basis, for example, could our government legally seize property "by any means" as provided in the first line of paragraph 6331(b). Did this mean, even by "illegal means"? That wording certainly seemed to suggest so. But how could that be, if the Constitution was still in force? After analyzing that section further, I discovered that the IRS' vaunted levy power was largely a myth—a legal optical illusion! This I discovered *without even knowing any of the material that I have so far covered in this chapter!*

Such broad seizure powers could not be constitutional (which is why Section 6331 doesn't provide for them)—given the superior authority of the Fifth Amendment with which such a comprehensive summary procedure would obviously clash. After I was sure of my conclusion I called several lawyers to find out what they knew about IRS levies. They all (incorrectly) believed that it was somehow related to a court order (but they were not quite sure exactly how), and they all believed it was perfectly legal (one's constitutional right to due process not withstanding) but they didn't exactly know why. "By law, the IRS can seize property (including wages and bank deposits) without a hearing or court order" I was told. "But what about the Fifth Amendment and due process?" I would ask. "Well, for some reason that doesn't apply to taxes," would be the answer. "But the Fifth Amendment doesn't say that the government can seize property without due process *except* for taxes, does it?" I would question. "Well that's the way the courts have interpreted it, so that's the way it is," I would be told. The point is, not one lawyer I spoke to really understood what an IRS levy was or why it could be lawful, given the due

process clause of the Constitution!

SEIZURE BY ANY MEANS

I had automatically assumed (as did everybody else that I spoke with) that a "levy" is a noun, but it is not; it is really a verb. All the Internal Revenue Code says about it (see subsection b) is that it "includes the power of distraint and seizure by any means." But what else does it "include"? Nowhere in the Code does it say! So we can only conclude that the term "levy" only "includes" (i.e. means) the power to "seize" and *nothing* more; since nowhere in the Code is any other meaning given to it. But since this term includes "the power of distraint" it cannot apply to income taxes since the Supreme Court ruled (as you already know) in *Flora* v. *United States,* supra, that the payment of income taxes is voluntary and cannot be based "upon distraint." So, based upon *Flora* alone, that "term" and procedure cannot apply to income taxes! **What could be plainer or simpler than that?**

But there are other troubling questions about this procedure. Just who decides that a citizen's property can be *confiscated pursuant to that section?* And are such persons legally delegated to make such a determination? And if so, how would anyone know this? And how does one get to see the documents delegating that authority to the person or persons allegedly making that determination?

You will note from Figures 7-5 and 7-6 that a Levy and a Notice of Levy are only signed by one lone revenue officer—who 12 months previous might have been employed pumping gas—and who could be back pumping gas one week after signing your Notice of Levy! The IRS can also levy property in connection with civil fraud penalties. Who decides that (1) civil fraud was committed, and that (2) property can be seized to satisfy those unproven civil fraud charges? In addition to everything else, how can one be "liable" for unproven civil fraud charges before the IRS meets its burden of proof as provided for in Section 7454 (Figure 7-7). On what basis then, can anyone suggest that such a process could possibly be legal if the Constitution is still in force? The fact that Section 6331 doesn't even apply to income taxes would render all such questions moot, if the

government did not disregard the law in the first place. As I explained earlier, those who wrote the Code were careful not to write into it anything that would conflict with the Constitution. They simply relied on the government's ability to circumvent the law and the Constitution whenever it suited its purpose—which is exactly what the government has done in connection with Section 6331.

LEVY V. NOTICE OF LEVY

You should have already noted, based upon Figures 7-5

FIGURE 7-5

FIGURE 7-6

Form 668-A
(Rev. May 1986)

Department of the Treasury-Internal Revenue Service
Notice of Levy

Date 6/30/87

District Hartford, Ct.

Telephone number of
IRS Office
773-2190

TO

Frances Silberberg
144 Shepard Knoll Drive
Hamden, Ct. 06514

Name and Address of Taxpayer

Irwin Schiff
60 Connolly Pkwy.
Hamden, Conn. 06514

Identifying Number(s)

047-16-2491N

REPLY:
150 Court St. Rm. 609
New Haven, Ct. 06510

Kind of Tax	Tax Period Ended	Unpaid Balance of Assessment	Statutory Additions	Total
1040	12/31/74	$24,394.58	$12,684.42	$37,079.00

Total amount due ▲ $37,079.00

THIS LEVY WILL NOT ATTACH TO ANY INDIVIDUAL RETIREMENT ACCOUNT, IRA, RETIREMENT PLAN BENEFITS, NO SELF EMPLOYED INDIVIDUALS, OR ANY OTHER QUALIFIED PLAN IN YOUR POSSESSION OR CONTROL

Interest and late payment penalty have been figured to 7/31/87

Chapter 64 of the Internal Revenue Code provides a lien for the above tax and statutory additions. Notice and demand, as required by the Internal Revenue Code, have been made on the taxpayer for the above amount that the taxpayer has neglected or refused to pay. This amount is still due, owing, and unpaid. All property, rights to property, money, credits, and bank deposits now in your possession and belonging to this taxpayer (or for which you are obligated) and all additions provided by law. Demand is made on you either to pay this tax liability or to pay any smaller amount that you owe this taxpayer. Please make your check or money order payable to the Internal Revenue Service. Write on your payment the taxpayer's name, the identifying number(s) shown above, and the words "LEVY PROCEEDS". **Complete the back of Part 3 of this form and mail it to us with your payment in the enclosed envelope.** Keep Part 1 for your records and give Part 4 to the taxpayer within 2 work days. **If you do not have funds due this taxpayer, please complete the back of Part 3 of this form and return all copies in the enclosed envelope.**

Title _____ Revenue Officer

Part 1 · ADDRESSEE'S COPY

FORM 668-A (Rev. 5-86)

Form 668-B
(Revised January 1983)

Department of the Treasury — Internal Revenue Service
Levy

Originating Internal Revenue District (City and State)

Hartford, Connecticut

Due from

Frances Silberberg, as nominee of
Irwin Schiff
144 Shepard Knoll Drive
Hamden, Conn. 06514

Kind of Tax	Tax Period Ended	Date of Assessment	Taxpayer Identification Number	Unpaid Balance of Assessment	Statutory Additions	Total
1040	12/31/74	04/20/84	047-16-2491N	$ 24,394.58	$ 12,684.42	$ 37,079.00

Total amount due ▲ $ 37,079.00

The amounts shown above are now due, owing, and unpaid to the United States from the above taxpayer for internal revenue taxes. Notice and demand have been made for payment. Chapter 64 of the Internal Revenue Code provides a lien for the above tax and statutory additions. Section 6331 of the Code authorizes collection of taxes by levy on all property or rights to property of a taxpayer, except property that is exempt under Code section 6334. Therefore, under the provisions of Code section 6331, so much of the property or rights to property, either real or personal, as may be necessary to pay the unpaid balance of assessment shown, with additions provided by law, including fees, costs, and expenses of this levy, are levied on to pay the taxes and additions.

Dated at New Haven, Connecticut ____ June 30th ____, 19 87.
(Place)   (Date)

Signature of Revenue Officer   Date
Thomas Pieron   6/30/87

Part 4 — To be given to person in possession of taxpayer's property

Form 668-B (Rev. 1-83)

FIGURE 7-5A

Excerpts from the Internal Revenue Code

✳ ✳ ✳ ✳ ✳ ✳ ✳ ✳ ✳ ✳ ✳ ✳

SEC. 6331.   LEVY AND DISTRAINT.

(b)   Seizure and Sale of Property.—The term "levy" as used in this title includes the power of distraint and seizure by any means. Except as otherwise provided in subsection (d)(3), a levy shall extend only to property possessed and obligations existing at the time thereof. In any case in which the Secretary may levy upon property or rights of property, he may seize and sell such property or rights to property (whether real or personal, tangible or intangible).

(c)   Successive Seizures.—Whenever any property or right to property upon which levy has been made by virtue of subsection (a) is not sufficient to satisfy the claim of the United States for which levy is made, the Secretary may, thereafter, and as often as may be neccessary, proceed to levy in like manner upon any other property liable to levy of the person against whom such claim exists, until the amount due from him, together with all expenses, is fully paid.

(d)   Salary and Wages.—

(3)   Continuing levy on salary and wages.—

(A)   Effect of levy.—The effect of a levy on salary or wages payable to or received by a taxpayer shall be continuous from the date such levy is first made until the liability out of which such levy arose is satisfied or becomes unenforceable by reason of lapse of time.

(B)   Release and notice of release.—With respect to a levy described in subparagraph (A), the Secretary shall promptly release the levy when the liability out of which such levy arose is satisfied or becomes unenforceable by reason of lapse of time, and shall promptly notify the person upon whom such levy was made that such levy has been released.

SEC. 6332.   SURRENDER OF PROPERTY SUBJECT TO LEVY.

(a)   Requirement.—Except as otherwise provided in subsection (b), any person in possession of (or obligated with respect to) property rights to property subject ot levy upon which a levy has been made shall, upon demand of the Secretary, surrender such property or rights (or discharge such obligation) to the Secretary, except such part of the property or rights as is, at the time of such demand, subject to an attachment or execution under any judicial process.

(b)   Special Rule for Life Insurance and Endowment Contracts.

(1)   In general.—A levy is an organization with respect to life insurance or endowment contract issued by such organization shall, without necessity for the surrender of the contract document, constitute a demand by the Secretary for payment of the amount described in paragraph (2) and the exercise of the right of the person against whom the tax is assessed to the advance of such amount. Such organization shall pay over such amount 90 days after service of notice of levy. Such notice shall include a certification by the Secretary that a copy of such notice has been mailed to the person against whom the tax is assessed at his last known address.

(2)   Satisfaction of levy.—Such levy shall be deemed to be satisfied if such organization pays over to the Secretary the amount which the person against whom the tax is assessed could have had advanced to him by such organization on the date prescribed in paragraph (1) for the satisfaction of such levy, increased by the amount of any advance (including contractual interest thereon) made to such person on or after the date such organization had actual notice or knowledge (within the meaning of section 6323 (i)(1)) of the existence of the lien with respect to which such levy is made, other than an advance (including contractual interest thereon) made automatically to maintain such contract in force under an agreement entered into before such organization had such notice or knowledge.

(3)   Enforcement proceedings.—The satisfaction of a levy under paragraph (2) shall be without prejudice to any civil action for the enforcement of any lien imposed by this title with respect to such contract.

(c)   Enforcement of Levy.

(1)   Extent of personal liability.—Any person who fails or refuses to surrender any property or rights to property, subject to levy, upon demand by the Secretary, shall be liable in his own person and estate to the United States in a sum equal to the value of the property or rights not so surrendered, but not exceeding the amount of taxes for the collection of which such levy has been made, together with costs and interest on such sum at an annual rate established under section 6621 from the date of such levy (or, in the case of a levy described in section 6331 (d)(3), from the date such person would otherwise have been obligated to pay over such amounts to the taxpayer). Any amount (other than costs) recovered under this paragraph shall be credited against the tax liability for the collection of which such levy was made.

(2)   Penalty for violation.—In addition to the personal liability imposed by paragraph (1), if any person required to surrender property or rights to property fails or refuses to surrender such property or rights to property without reasonable cause, such person shall be liable for a penalty equal to 50 percent of the amount recoverable under paragraph (1). No part of such penalty shall be credited against the tax liability for the collection of which such levy was made.

(d)   Effect of Honoring Levy.—Any person in possession of (or obligated with respect to) property or rights to property subject to levy upon which a levy has been made who, upon demand by the Secretary, surrenders such property or rights to property (or discharges such obligation) to the Secretary (or who pays a liability under subsection (c)(1)) shall be discharged from any obligation or liability to the delinquent taxpayer with

respect to such property or rights to property arising from such surrender or payment. In the case of a levy which is satisfied pursuant to subsection (b), such organization shall also be discharged from any obligation or liability to any beneficiary arising from such surrender or payment.

SEC. 6333.   PRODUCTION OF BOOKS.

If a levy has been made or is about to be made on any property, or right to property, any person having custody or control of any books or records, containing evidence or statements relating to the property or right to property subject to levy, shall, upon demand of the Secretary, exhibit such books or records to the Secretary.

SEC. 6334.   PROPERTY EXEMPT FROM LEVY.

(a)   Enumeration.—There shall be exempt from levy—

(1)   Wearing apparel and school books.—Such items of wearing apparel and such school books as are necessary for the taxpayer or for members of his family;

(2)   Fuel, provisions, furniture, and personal effects.—If the taxpayer is the head of a family, so much of the fuel, provisions, furniture, and personal effects in his household, and of the arms for personal use, livestock, and poultry of the taxpayer, as does not exceed $500 in value;

(3)   Books and tools of a trade, business or profession.—So many of the books and tools necessary for the trade, business, or profession of the taxpayer as do not exceed in the aggregate $250 in value.

(4)   Unemployment benefits.—Any amount payable to an individual with respect to his unemployment (including any portion thereof payable with respect to dependents) under an unemployment compensation law of the United States, of any State, or of the District of Columbia or of the Commonwealth of Puertos Rico.

(5)   Undelivered mail.—Mail, addressed to any person, which has not been delivered to the addressee.

(6)   Certain annuity and pension payments.—Annuity or pension payments under the Railroad Retirement Act, benefits under the Railroad Unemployment Insurance act, special pension payments received by a person whose name has been entered on the Army, Navy, Air Force, and Coast Guard Medal of Honor roll (38 U.S.C. 562), and annuities based on retired or retainer pay under chapter 73 of title 10 of the United States Code.

(7)   Workmen's compensation.—Any amount payable to an individual as workmen's compensation (including any portion thereof payable with respect to dependents) under a workmen's compensation law of the United States, any State, the District of Columbia, or the Commonwealth of Puerto Rico.

(8)   Judgements for support of minor children.-—If the taxpayer is required by judgment of a court of competent jurisdiction, entered prior to the date of levy, to contribute to the support of his minor children, so much of his salary, wages, or other income as is necessary to comply with such judgment.

(9)   Minimum Exemption for Wages, Salary, and Other Income.—Any amount payable to or received by an individual as wages or salary for personal services, or as income derived from other sources, during any period, to the extent that the total of such amounts payable to or received by him during such period does not exceed the applicable exempt amount determined under subsection (d).

SEC. 6343.   AUTHORITY TO RELEASE LEVY AND RETURN PROPERTY.

(b)   Return of Property.—If the Secretary determines that property has been wrongfully levied upon, it shall be lawful for the Secretary to return—

(1)   the specific property levied upon,

(2)   an amount of money equal to the amount of money levied upon, or

(3)   an amount of money equal to the amount of money received by the United States from a sale of such property.

Property may be returned at any time. An amount equal to the amount of money levied upon or received from such sale may be returned at any time before the expiration of 9 months from the date of such levy. For purposes of paragraph (3), if property is declared purchased by the United States at a sale pursuant to section 6335(e) (relating to manner and conditions of sale), the United States shall be treated as having received an amount of money equal to the minimum price determined pursuant to such section or (if larger) the amount received by the United States from the resale of such property.

✳ ✳ ✳ ✳ ✳ ✳ ✳ ✳ ✳ ✳ ✳ ✳ ✳

Applicable Sections of Internal Revenue Code

6321.   LIEN FOR TAXES.
6322.   PERIOD OF LIEN.
6325.   RELEASE OF LIEN OR DISCHARGE OF PROPERTY.
6331.   LEVY AND DISTRAINT.
6332.   SURRENDER OF PROPERTY SUBJECT TO LEVY.
6333.   PRODUCTION OF BOOKS.
6334.   PROPERTY EXEMPT FROM LEVY.
6343.   AUTHORITY TO RELEASE LEVY AND RETURN PROPERTY.
7426.   CIVIL ACTIONS BY PERSONS OTHER THAN TAXPAYERS.

For additional information concerning this notice, please contact the person whose signature appears above the taxpayer identifying number.

FIGURE 7-6A   **AS PRINTED ON THE REVERSE**
                                                             SIDE OF THE LEVY

Applicable Sections Under The Internal Revenue Code

Sec. 6321.   Lien for Taxes
Sec. 6322.   Period of Lien
Sec. 6323.   Validity and Priority Against Certain Persons
Sec. 6324.   Special leins for Estate and Gift Taxes
Sec. 6325.   Release of Lien or Discharge of Property
Sec. 6331.   Levy and Distraint
Sec. 6332.   Surrender of Property Subject to Levy
Sec. 6334.   Property Exempt from Levy
Sec. 6335.   Sale of Seized Property
Sec. 6339.   Legal Effect of Certificate of Sale of Personal Property
             and Deed of Real Property
Sec. 6343.   Authority to Release Levy and Return Property

Sec. 6331.   Levy and Distraint
(a)   **Authority of Secretary.** — If any person liable to pay any tax neglects or refuses to pay the same within 10 days after notice and demand, it shall be lawful for the Secretary to collect such tax (and such further sum as shall be sufficient to cover the expenses of the levy) by levy upon all property and rights to property (except such property as is exempt under section 6334) belonging to such person or on which there is a lien provided in this chapter for the payment of such tax. Levy may be made upon the accrued salary or wages of any officer, employee, or elected official, of the United States, the District of Columbia, or any agency or instrumentality of the United States or the District of Columbia, by serving a notice of levy on the employer (as defined in section 3401 (d)) of such officer, employee, or elected official. If the Secretary makes a finding that the collection of such tax is in jeopardy, notice and demand for immediate payment of such tax may be made by the Secretary and, upon failure or refusal to pay such tax, collection thereof by levy shall be lawful without regard to the 10-day period provided in this section.
(b)   **Seizure and Sale of Property.** — The term "levy" as used in this title includes the power of distraint and seizure by any means. Except as otherwise provided in subsection (d) (3), a levy shall extend only to property possessed and obligations existing at the time thereof. In any case in which the Secretary may levy upon property or rights to property, he may seize and sell such property or rights to property (whether real or personal, tangible or intangible).
(c)   **Successive Seizures.** — Whenever any property or right to property upon which levy has been made by virtue of subsection (a) is not sufficient to satisfy the claim of the United States for which levy is made, the Secretary may, thereafter, and as often as may be necessary, proceed to levy in like manner upon any other property liable to levy of the person against whom such claim exists, until the amount due from him, together with all expenses, is fully paid.

Sec. 6332.   Surrender of Property Subject to Levy.
(a)   **Requirement.** — Except as otherwise provided in subsection (b), any person in possession of (or obligated with respect to) property or rights to property subject to levy upon which a levy has been made shall, upon demand of the Secretary, surrender such property or rights (or discharge such obligation) to the Secretary, except such part of the property or rights as is, at the time of such demand, subject to an attachment or execution under any judicial process.
(c)   **Enforcement of Levy.** —
(1)   **Extent of Personal Liability.** — Any person who fails or refuses to surrender any property or rights to property subject to levy, upon demand by the Secretary, shall be liable in his own person and estate to the United States in a sum equal to the value of the property or rights not so surrendered, but not exceeding the amount of taxes for the collection of which such levy has been made, together with costs and interest on such sum at an annual rate established under section 6621 from the date of such levy (or, in the case of a levy described in section 6331 (d) (3), from the date such person would otherwise have been obligated to pay over such amounts to the taxpayer). Any amount (other than costs) recovered under this paragraph shall be credited against the tax liability for the collection of which such levy was made.
(2)   **Penalty for Violation.** — In addition to the personal liability imposed by paragraph (1), if any person required to surrender property or rights to property fails or refuses to surrender such property or rights to property without reasonable cause, such person shall be liable for a penalty equal to 50 percent of the amount recoverable

under paragraph (1). No part of such penalty shall be credited against the tax liability for the collection of which such levy was made.
(d)   **Effect of Honoring Levy.** — Any person in possession of (or obligated with respect to) property or rights to property subject to levy upon which a levy has been made who, upon demand by the Secretary, surrenders such property or rights to property (or discharges such obligation) to the Secretary (or who pays a liability under subsection (c) (1) shall be discharged from any obligation or liability to the delinquent taxpayer with respect to such property or rights to property arising from such surrender or payment. In the case of a levy which is satisfied pursuant to subsection (b), such organization shall also be discharged from any obligation or liability to any beneficiary arising from such surrender or payment.

← — THE MISSING PARAGRAPH —

Sec. 6334.   Property Exempt from Levy
(a)   **Enumeration.** — There shall be exempt from levy -
(1)   **Wearing Apparel and School Books.** — Such items of wearing apparel and such school books as are necessary for the taxpayer or for members of his family;
(2)   **Fuel, Provisions, Furniture, and Personal Effects.** — if the taxpayer is the head of a family, so much of the fuel, provisions, furniture, and personal effects in his household, and of the arms for personal use, livestock, and poultry of the taxpayer, as does not exceed $1,500 in value;
(3)   **Books and Tools of a Trade, Business or Profession.** — So many of the books and tools necessary for the trade, business, or profession of the taxpayer as do not exceed in the aggregate $1,000 in value.
(4)   **Unemployment Benefits.** — Any amount payable to an individual with respect to his unemployment (including any portion thereof payable with respect to dependents) under an unemployment compensation law of the United States, of any State, or of the District of Columbia or of the Commonwealth of Puerto Rico.
(5)   **Undelivered Mail.** — Mail, addressed to any person, which has not been delivered to the addressee.
(6)   **Certain Annuity and Pension Payments.** — Annuity or pension payments under the Railroad Retirement Act, benefits under the Railroad Unemployment Insurance Act, special pension payments received by a person whose name has been entered on the Army, Navy, Air Force, and Coast Guard Medal of Honor Roll (38 U.S.C. 562), and annuities based on retired or retainer pay under chapter 73 of title 10 of the United States Code.
(7)   **Workmen's Compensation.** — Any amount payable to an individual as workmen's compensation (including any portion thereof payable with respect to dependents) under a workmen's compensation law of the United States, any State, the District of Columbia, or the Commonwealth of Puerto Rico.
(8)   **Judgments for Support of Minor Children.** — If the taxpayer is required by judgment of a court of competent jurisdiction, entered prior to the date of levy, to contribute to the support of his minor children, so much of his salary, wages, or other income as is necessary to comply with such judgment.
(9)   **Minimum Exemption for Wages, Salary, and other Income.** — Any amount payable to or received by an individual as wages or salary for personal services, or as income derived from other sources, during any period, to the extent that the total of such amounts payable to or received by him during such period does not exceed the applicable exempt amount determined under subsection (d).

Sec. 6343.   Authority to Release Levy and Return Property
(a)   **Release of Levy.** — It shall be lawful for the Secretary, under regulations prescribed by the Secretary, to release the levy upon all or part of the property or rights to property levied upon where the Secretary determines that such action will facilitate the collection of the liability, but such release shall not operate to prevent any subsequent levy.

Form **668-B** (Rev. 1-83)

and 7-6, that there are two procedures that Section 6331 authorizes which presumably allow the government to get taxpayer property without a court order. In one procedure a Form 668-A is used (Figure 7-5), while in the other procedure a Form 668-B is authorized (Figure 7-6). The "Notice of Levy," Form 668-A, is by far the more important of the two, since it is the one the IRS illegally uses to extort cash from third parties such as banks, insurance companies, mutual funds and employers in connection with employee wages. The "levy," Form 668-B is used when IRS revenue agents steal physical assets (such as cars, homes, boats, etc.,—and even cash) directly from the general public. In order for you to appreciate the magnitude of the government's fraudulent use of a "Notice" of levy, you first need to know more about what a "levy" is (as distinguished from a mere notice of one) and how the IRS disregards the law in connection with that procedure.

More on the Meaning of Levy

First of all, note that the term "levy" is used 24 times in Section 6331 (Figure 7-1) while the term "notice of levy" appears only once (note A). It is also clear that with the exception of that lone entry, all provisions of Sections 6331, 6332, 6333, 6334, and 6343 (Figure 7-5A) deal only with the act of "levy" (which we know can only mean "seizure by any means") and not with the mere "Notice" of one. By way of confirmation, Figure 7-9 contains a number of excerpts from the IRS' *Legal Reference Guide for Revenue Officers*, which specifically distinguishes between both procedures.

Paragraph 333.1 of the *Guide,* for example (not shown in Figure 7-9) while first distinguishing between a "levy" and a "notice of levy," goes on to say with respect to a "levy," that:

> It should be borne in mind that a levy requires that the property levied upon him be brought into legal custody *through seizure.* There must be actual or constructive physical appropriation of the property levied upon. Mere intent to reduce to possession and control is insufficient. (citing *Freeman* v. *Mayer,* 152 F. Supp. 383).

The *Freeman* v. *Mayer* decision referred to, has a lot of very interesting things to say about levies. It points out, for example, that in *United States* v. *Stock Yards Bank of Louisville, Kentucky,* 231 F2d 628, 630; that court made the eye-opening observation that the Internal Revenue Code:

> "does not set out any method for accomplishing a levy upon property."

What that statement means is that private citizens cannot check any law to see if the IRS seized their property (pursuant to a levy) legally or illegally! How

---

FIGURE 7-7

§ 7454. Burden of proof in fraud, foundation manager, and transferee cases

(a) Fraud

In any proceeding involving the issue whether the petitioner has been guilty of fraud with intent to evade tax, the burden of proof in respect of such issue shall be upon the Secretary.

(b) Foundation managers

In any proceeding involving the issue whether a foundation manager (as defined in section 4946(b)) has "knowingly" participated in an act of self-dealing (within the meaning of section 4941), participated in an investment which jeopardizes the carrying out of exempt purposes (within the meaning of section 4944), or agreed to the making of a taxable expenditure (within the meaning of section 4945), or whether the trustee of a trust described in section 501(c)(21) has "knowingly" participated in an act of self-dealing (within the meaning of section 4951) or agreed to the making of a taxable expenditure (within the meaning of section 4952), or whether an organization manager (as defined in section 4955(e)(2))[1] has "knowingly" agreed to the making of a political expenditure (within the meaning of section 4955),[2] or whether an organization manager (as defined in section 4912(d)(2)) has "knowingly" agreed to the making of disqualifying lobbying expenditures within the meaning of section 4912(b), the burden of proof in respect of such issue shall be upon the Secretary.

---

does that grab you? The *Freeman* court immediately seeks to mollify that condition by observing that:

> The procedure of accomplishing a levy may be spelled out from the *reported cases.* A "levy" requires that property be *brought into legal custody through seizure,* actual or constructive, *levy being an absolute appropriation in law of the property levied on, mere notice of intent to levy is unsufficient. United States* v. *O'Dell,* 6 Cir., 1947, 106 F2d 304, 307. Accord, In re *Holdsworth,* D.C.N.J. 1953, 113F. Supp. 878, 888; *United States* v. *Aetna Life Ins. Co. of Hartford Conn.,* D.C. Conn. 1942, 146 F. Supp. 30, 37, in which Judge Hincks observed that he could *"find no statute which says that a mere notice shall constitute a 'levy.'* There are cases which hold that a warrant for distraint is necessary to constitute a levy." [emphasis added.]

The above paragraph itself proves that the IRS even seizes property in violation of the actual levy provisions of Section 6331—*in addition to disregarding those basic provisions with which you are already familiar!* Before we turn to these additional violations, however, there is another revelation here that should be addressed.

FIGURE 7-8

Form **668-A** (Rev. February 1981)	Department of the Treasury — Internal Revenue Service **Instructions for Responding to a** **Notice of Levy**

This Notice of Levy, Form 668-A, attaches funds due the taxpayer named on it. We would appreciate your following these instructions.

    1. In the space above your name and address, please sign, date, and note the time received.

    2. If you have funds due the taxpayer, please make your check or money order payable to the Internal Revenue Service and mail it with Part 1 of this from in the enclosed envelope. Keep Part 2 for your records and give Part 3 to the taxpayer within 2 working days.

    3. If you do not have funds due this taxpayer, please so indicate on the front of this form, fill in the information requested below, and return all copies in the enclosed envelope.

Thank you for your cooperation.

Taxpayer telephone number		Present address of taxpayer, if different from below
Last date you paid funds to the taxpayer	Amount	
Date next funds are due	Amount	Additional information which you believe may assist us
Name and address where funds are sent		
		(If more space is needed, continue on the back)

Name and address of Taxpayer

    ⌐ IRWIN SCHIFF
    60 CONNALLY PARKWAY
    HAMDEN, CONNECTICUT 06518 ⌐

Part 5 — Instructions for responding   Form 668-A (Rev. 2-81)

Notice that the "instructors" do not even state, let alone demand, that any funds be sent to the IRS! The government just assumes that third parties will be sufficiently intimidated to send in the funds, even though there is nothing in the instructions asking them to do any such thing.

FIGURE 7-9

The IRS's *Legal Reference Guide For Revenue Officers* [MT 58 [10][0]-14) states:

332 *(10-29-79)*   58(10)0
Constitutional Limitations
(1) During the course of administratively collecting a tax, an occasion may arise where service of a levy or notice of levy is not adequate to seize property of the taxpayer. However, it cannot be emphasized too strongly that constitutional guarantees and individual rights must not be violated. Property should not be forceably removed from the person of a taxpayer. Such conduct may expose a revenue officer to an action in trespass, assault and battery, conversion, etc. *Larson v. Domestic and Foreign Commerce Corp.,* 337 U.S. 682 (1949), *rehearing denied,* 337 U.S. 682 (1949). *Maule Industries v. Tomlinson,* 224 F. 2d 897, (5th Cir. 1949). If there is reason to suspect a failure to honor a notice of levy or an interference with a levy, the matter should be referred for proper legal action against the offending party. Remedies available to the Government, as contained in the Code and other statutes, are more than adequate to cope with the problem.
(2) The Supreme Court in *G.M. Leasing Corp. v. United States,* 429 U.S. 336 (1977) held that warrantless entries into the private premises of a person by the Internal Revenue Service for the purpose of seizing property to satisfy a tax liability is a violation of that person's reasonable expectation of privacy under the Fourth Amendment to the Constitution. Before levies or seizures of property located on private premises are made, permission of the occupant of the premises on which the seizure is to take place must be obtained. If the occupant refuses to permit the entry, the matter should be referred to District Counsel so that a court order authorizing the entry may be obtained.

334.2 *(10-29-79)*   58(10)0
Final Demand
Where a notice of levy is served upon a third party and there is no response within ten days, it is followed by service of a Final Demand (Form 668-C). IRC 6332(a) states that except as otherwise provided in subsection (b), (which contains a special rule for life insurance and endowment contracts) a person in possession of property or rights to property upon which levy has been made shall, upon demand, surrender such property. The demand is contained in the Notice of Levy (Form 668-A). A Notice of Final Demand (Form 668-C) is not required to be served under the Code, although use of the form as an administrative tool is generally uniform. In the event the Final Demand is not responded to, a suit will ordinarily be required to reach the property.

AMERICA: A SOCIETY OF MEN, NOT LAW

The above observation by the *Freeman* court confirms a statement I made earlier, that America is really a society of men, not law; despite the popular Pollyanna belief to the contrary. What the above excerpt from *Freeman* says is that the only way Americans can determine whether or not their property was legally "levied on" is based, not upon what any *law says,* but upon "reported cases"—that is, based upon the opinions of lawyers, men who somehow managed to ascend to the bench. I doubt if 5 percent of the 2 million Americans who had their wages levied upon last year, know how to even check (or would have the time to check) such "reported cases." So in addition to Americans being "presumed to know the law" they are apparently also "presumed to know 'reported cases'."

Three paragraphs back I cited some "reported cases." You'd better learn how to locate and understand them, since, according to *Freeman* that is the only way you can know whether or not the government seized your property legally or illegally. But...

Even Reading "Reported Cases" Won't Help

In the paragraph immediately following the one quoted above, District Judge Modarelli (who should be lauded for writing this well-researched, candid and correct [he held against the IRS] decision), the good judge states:

The Court of Appeals sustained as to the "set-off" aspect of the case (referring to the Second Circuit's decision in *Brust* v. *Starr,* 237 F2d, 135), but reversed on other aspects. *On reading the appeal decision several times, it is not clear on what grounds the District Court was reversed.* [emphasis added.]

So here a forthright district court judge admits to not being able to understand an appellate court's "reported case" even though he read it "several times"! So how can John Q. Public, with no legal training, be presumed to understand "reported cases" (even if he could find them) when even federal judges don't? Yet this is how the public is supposed to determine if a levy has been lawfully made! Can you believe it? Not to worry—it gets worse!

Even if you could find the "reported cases" and understand them, that won't help, because, as Judge Modarelli points out on the next page:

The courts which have had occasion to construe the scope of this section (as to how levies are lawfully made) *are not in agreement...*

There is conflict among the circuits as to the proper way to assert the lien. The Fourth Circuit, disagreeing with the Sixth and Seventh, has ruled that where the Government has made a levy upon an indebtedness to the taxpayer, service of notice by the Government upon the taxpayer's debtor is sufficient...The case noted in opposition insist that a warrant for distraint is necessary in addition to the notice to the debtor. [emphasis added.]

Modarelli continues discussing how notices of levy are to be legally implemented through four more paragraphs and finally concludes that the more correct view (although, as you will shortly see [and already know], both views are incorrect) that "warrants for distraint" are required when such assets as bank accounts, wages, commissions, etc., etc., are sought to be seized pursuant to a "notice" of levy.

However, what the good judge fails to see is the utter absurdity of his protracted analysis! Since all U.S. judges were themselves once lawyers, Modarelli apparently sees nothing wrong with a legal analysis that is no more relevant than how many angels can dance on the head of a pin. In the final analysis, the more U.S. judges can't agree on the law, the more litigation this creates and the more the U.S. legal industry can extract from the public. Of course, U.S. lawyers and former lawyers (now judges) see nothing wrong in this—the legal industry thrives on it.

Of course, the vast majority of Americans haven't the vaguest idea that such uncertainties exist in our courtrooms especially as regards a routine issue of law. Remember, here we are not talking about some complicated question of constitutional law, but a simple procedure pursuant to which the government confiscates the wages and bank accounts of well over two million people each year—and our judges claim they aren't *exactly sure how this is to be lawfully done?* How much more are they not sure of? Think about that, the next time someone tells you that America is a society of law and not men.

But the real reason that our "judges" seem to be having trouble with the law is that they are trying to infuse it with something it doesn't have—**a legal way for the government to acquire property from third parties without a court order!** The judiciary appears confused only because it isn't exactly sure what is the best **illegal** way for the government to do this. If what the government was doing was *really provided by law, do you really think our judges would have so much trouble figuring it out?*

HOW LEVIES ARE SUPPOSED TO BE MADE

As explained in the *Freeman* decision:

1. "A 'levy' requires that the property levied upon be brought into legal custody through seizure."

2. "A levy [is] an absolute appropriation in law of the property levied on," and

3. "Mere notice of intent to levy is insufficient" to constitute a levy.

This being the case one is hard pressed to understand what a "constructive" seizure might be as contrasted to one which must be "actual" and as distinguished from a mere "notice'" of "intent to levy"? Note that Judge Hincks is quoted as saying that he could "find no statute which says that a mere notice shall constitute a 'levy'." Note that the *Freeman* court also observed that "there are cases which hold that a warrant for distraint is necessary to constitute a levy"; however, there is absolutely no mention of such warrants any place in Section 6331 (or any other Code section for that matter). So on what lawful basis could the courts have contrived documents and a procedure to affect a levy which is nowhere mentioned in the Code?

A Notice of Seizure

The law (Section 6502, Figure 7-10) also provides that "The date on which a levy...is made shall be the date on which the notice of seizure...is given." An example of an IRS seizure notice is shown in Figure 7-11. Your understanding and awareness of this document is crucial to your understanding of how the government has totally subverted Section 6331. So let there be no doubt about this. Under the law, as provided in Section 6331, there can be no levy (i.e. no levy is made) **unless a notice of seizure (pursuant to Section 6502) is given to the person whose property has been allegedly made subject to levy.** And if a person's property is taken allegedly by levy but without a notice of seizure being given, then only one of two possibilities exist. Either:

1. Such property was not taken (or is sought to be taken) by levy, or

2. Such property was taken by levy—illegally.

An Example of a Levy

A levy pursuant to Section 6331 might be said to have occurred in the following example. Assume that one Mr. D. Linquent, had an income tax liability (which, as you know, is impossible), and had also been sent a Form 17 (which, as you know, never happens) which D. Linquent ignored. Assume further that a Final Notice was also sent to D. Linquent which he also ignored. Now assume that IRS revenue officer, Greb DeMonay, knowing all of this, spots D. Linquent's automobile parked on a public street. Greb now calls for a tow truck and has D. Linquent's car towed to a government warehouse or parking lot. He then pays D.

Linquent a visit and hands him a Notice of Seizure which explains that "Under the authority in Section 6331 of the Internal Revenue code, and by virtue of a levy from the District Director of the district shown below, I have seized the property below for non-payment of past Internal Revenue taxes," the total of which is shown on that document. The Notice of Seizure would identify the car seized along with any other property which might have been in the car at the time of seizure (such as cash, jewelry, cameras, golf clubs, etc., etc.) and which might also have been subject to seizure.[4]

Note, however, that the "Kind of Tax" is shown as a "1040" tax. Did you ever hear of a 1040 tax? Such mislabeling, I submit, is part of the government's overall ruse in connection with income taxes. It compels the payment of a tax it knows to be voluntary, under the guise that it is really compelling the payment of another tax, a "1040" tax!

Greb DeMonay would, in all probability, also hand D. Linquent a completed Form 668-B which is actually unnecessary. The statute does not call for such a document

and there would seem to be no reason for it. The Notice of Seizure tells the victim all that he might be required to know. No doubt the reason that a 668-B is given is to make levy and Notice of Levy procedures appear as similar as possible—to give the public as little chance as possible to distinguish between them. However, the law itself calls for a Notice of Levy to be used in connection with that procedure, and only a Notice of Seizure to be used in connection with an actual levy. So there is absolutely no need or legal purpose for a Form 668-B, except as a means of confusing the public.[5]

In any case, the above illustration might be termed a lawful levy as contemplated by Section 6331. However, my use of the word "lawful" is contingent upon three things being present: (1) a lawful assessment, (2) a legal liability, and (3) a prior, lawful demand. In all IRS levies in connection with income taxes, elements 2 and 3 are never present, while in my case, all three elements were lacking. But assuming that all three elements were present in our illustration, then the seizure of D. Linquent's car, one could argue (given other considerations that will be addressed later), could be said to be legal, on the basis that: a statutory

FIGURE 7-10

§ 6502. Collection after assessment

(a) Length of period

Where the assessment of any tax imposed by this title has been made within the period of limitation properly applicable thereto, such tax may be collected by levy or by a proceeding in court, but only if the levy is made or the proceeding begun—

    (1) within 6 years after the assessment of the tax, or
    (2) prior to the expiration of any period for collection agreed upon in writing by the Secretary and the taxpayer before the expiration of such 6-year period (or, if there is a release of levy under section 6343 after such 6-year period, then before such release).

The period so agreed upon may be extended by subsequent agreements in writing made before the expiration of the period previously agreed upon. The period provided by this subsection during which a tax may be collected by levy shall not be extended or curtailed by reason of a judgment against the taxpayer.

(b) Date when levy is considered made

    The date on which a levy on property or rights to property is made shall be the date on which the notice of seizure provided in section 6335(a) is given.

FIGURE 7-11

Department of the Treasury
Internal Revenue Service
Form 2433 (Rev. March, 1985)

Notice of Seizure

Name and Address
Raymond M Hartman
201 Jefferson St
Rochester, PA 15074

Under the authority in section 6331 of the Internal Revenue Code, and by virtue of a levy from the District Director of Internal Revenue of the district shown below, I have seized the property below for nonpayment of past due internal revenue taxes.

Due from	Amount	Internal Revenue District (City and State)
Raymond M Hartman 201 Jefferson St Rochester, PA 15074	$14,426.32	

Description of property

liability existed; no force was used; no property was trespassed upon; and no property was coerced or extorted from third parties. And since the property was "actually brought into...(IRS)...custody and control through seizure," and not by someone merely "handing over" the property to the IRS, all the elements constituting a 6331 "levy" would have been satisfied.

ILLEGAL IRS LEVIES—
THE USUAL KIND

Now, just because the IRS might have the legal authority to seize a car while it was parked unattended on a public thoroughfare, does that mean the IRS has the same authority to seize automobiles parked on private property over the objection and resistance of their owners, or by intimidating or threatening individuals into giving up property belonging to others and/or for which they have a fiduciary relationship? The answer to that, of course, is no, as explained in Sections 332 and 334.3 of the *Legal Reference Guide for (IRS) Revenue Officers* (Figure 7-9). Note that Section 332 (among other things) states that:

An occasion may arise where service of *a levy or notice of levy* is not adequate to seize property of the taxpayer. However, it cannot be emphasized too strongly that *constitutional guarantees* and individual rights **must not be violated. Property should not be forcibly removed from the person of a taxpayer.** Such conduct may expose a revenue officer to an action in trespass, assault and battery, conversion, etc....If there is reason to suspect a *failure to honor a notice of levy* or an *interference with a levy*, the matter should be referred for proper legal action against the offending party...[emphasis added.]

Before levies or seizures of properties located on private premises are made, **permission of the occupant of the premises on which seizure is to take place must be obtained.**

While Section 334.3(2) says, in part:

As previously indicated, **force should not be used in seizing property of a taxpayer.**

Who would have believed, based upon how IRS revenue officers actually operate, that such material is contained in their own manuals? This is merely another example of how the IRS, in practice, disregards and violates its own professed, published policies. As I pointed out earlier, the IRS is careful never to put in print anything that suggests policies that might be violative of law and/or constitutional rights. Its policy, howver, is simply to ignore in practice what it preaches in print.

IRS Storm Troopers in Action

The August 13, 1982 issue of *Parade Magazine* carried a feature story describing an IRS raid involving approximately forty men on the farm house of Dwight Snyder. The article reported that:

U.S. marshalls, state patrolmen, IRS revenue officers and IRS special agents—some brandishing M-16 automatic rifles, shotguns and sidearms...[and] all of his vehicles, his machinery, tools, and stock were seized from a pickup truck and tractor down to towel holders, soap dishes, sink strainers, toothbrush holders and a half-empty box of staples.

I wonder if they got any school books? The article didn't say. But in any case, do you think the IRS got Snyder's permission to come onto his property in this fashion?[6]

Another incident described in the article (and one which got considerable press coverage because a photographer was present) involved a couple from Fairbanks, Alaska. The IRS claimed that Stephen and Mona Oliver owed the government $4,700 and had (illegally) filed a notice of levy on their wages. The Olivers disagreed with the assessment and had sought a court hearing, whereupon the IRS decided to teach them a lesson..

...by grabbing their 1970 Volkswagon while it was parked in downtown Fairbanks. The Olivers, however, locked themselves in the car and refused to hand over the keys, whereupon IRS agents smashed the windows, dragged Mona Oliver out of the car and across a sidewalk littered with broken glass and towed their car away—in full view of astonished bystanders and a local newspaper photographer.

Apparently these IRS revenue officers neglected to read that manual. In any case, these IRS agents should have been arrested for assault and battery and car theft but they weren't because such IRS maurauders are protected by the Justice Department and the courts.

In addition IRS revenue and special agents are not authorized to carry guns in connection with the collection of income taxes. Section 7608 (Figure 7-12) points out that though IRS revenue officers might have statutory authority to carry guns in connection with the enforcement of alcohol, tobacco and firearms taxes, they have no such authority when it comes to income taxes. **Somebody should have told that to those men who paid a visit to Snyder's farm.**

In order to get around the weapons (and enforcement) impediment, note the statement in paragraph 334.3 of the

Reference Guide in which IRS agents are encouraged to use "Local or other law enforcement authorities" to assist them in performing their duties. This method of intimidation being recommended should be obvious. Since IRS revenue officers aren't authorized to enter onto private property, to use force or carry weapons in connection with income tax levies, they are encouraged to **dupe** local law enforcement people into helping them. What Greb DeMonay might do is stop by the local constabulary and show the local police the levy documents and suggest that he believes that he might "run into trouble serving them" and so might ask an officer to accompany him. Since local cops and/or sheriffs will generally be ignorant concerning the actual legal status of Forms 668-B and 2433 (the Notice of Seizure), they can easily be misled into believing that they are the equivalent of court orders that must be obeyed. So they could be persuaded to accompany Greb DeMonay to the home of the intended victim whose car or tractor Greb is determined to pinch. In this manner, local police provide the guns and show of force to intimidate private citizens into giving up their own property (thus such property is not really "seized", but is actually "handed over"). They are not required to do so. If these levy documents were legally enforceable, Greb would have been accompanied by one or more U.S. marshals. He would not need the extortionary presence of the local police—who, incidentally, if they supply it, should be sued for doing so. Now that you have seen how the IRS violates basic levy procedures, let us enter a new dimension of federal fraud, one that really boggles the imagination.

THE FRAUDULENT NOTICE OF LEVY

My first contact with the IRS' summary seizure procedures began when I got a letter (Figure 7-13) and copy of a Notice of Levy from the American National Bank of Hamden, Connecticut informing me that it had already turned over $10,100 of my money to the IRS—thereby cleaning out both accounts. Note that its letter advises me that if I had "any objections or legal reason why this levy is invalid" that I should "contact the Revenue Officer mentioned in the Levy"! Of course, the bank as a fiduciary, should have made these determinations before turning over any money entrusted to its care! Once the IRS gets its hands on it, of course, it will say that the "levy" is valid. The bank should have, at least, allowed me to present some of these arguments to them *before* they handed over the money. But they did not. This, I believe, is typical of how banks handle such Notices—completely abandoning their fiduciary responsibilities.

In order to mislead and intimidate third parties into turning over assets, the IRS prints Code Sections on the back of its "notices" which are designed to mislead the public into believing that dire consequences await them if they do not immediately give the government the money it wants.

When I received my copy of the Notice of Levy I instinctively knew it was a fraud—but not in the variety of ways so far discussed in this chapter. But I lacked definitive proof of this. Besides, banks and other third parties, being

---

FIGURE 7-12

§ 7608. Authority of internal revenue enforcement officers

(a) **Enforcement of subtitle E and other laws pertaining to liquor, tobacco, and firearms**

Any investigator, agent, or other internal revenue officer by whatever term designated, whom the Secretary charges with the duty of enforcing any of the criminal, seizure, or forfeiture provisions of subtitle E or of any other law of the United States pertaining to the commodities subject to tax under such subtitle for the enforcement of which the Secretary is responsible may—

(1) carry firearms;

(2) execute and serve search warrants and arrest warrants, and serve subpoenas and summonses issued under authority of the United States;

(3) in respect to the performance of such duty, make arrests without warrant for any offense against the United States committed in his presence, or for any felony cognizable under the laws of the United States if he has reasonable grounds to believe that the person to be arrested has committed, or is committing, such felony; and

(4) in respect to the performance of such duty, make seizures of property subject to forfeiture to the United States.

(b) **Enforcement of laws relating to internal revenue other than subtitle E**

(1) Any criminal investigator of the Intelligence Division or of the Internal Security Division of the Internal Revenue Service whom the Secretary charges with the duty of enforcing any of the criminal provisions of the internal revenue laws or any other criminal provisions of law relating to internal revenue for the enforcement of which the Secretary is responsible is, in the performance of his duties, authorized to perform the functions described in paragraph (2).

(2) The functions authorized under this subsection to be performed by an officer referred to in paragraph (1) are—

(A) to execute and serve search warrants and arrest warrants, and serve subpoenas and summonses issued under authority of the United States;

(B) to make arrests without warrant for any offense against the United States relating to the internal revenue laws committed in his presence, or for any felony cognizable under such laws if he has reasonable grounds to believe that the person to be arrested has committed or is committing any such felony; and

(C) to make seizures of property subject to forfeiture under the internal revenue laws.

subject to IRS audits and thus IRS intimidation, are reluctant to say no to the IRS, and so generally give them whatever they want—especially, as in these cases, where they are being asked to turn over other people's money! What is easier than that—especially when federal courts will protect such parties from justifiable lawsuits brought by those to whom fiduciary obligations were breached. Note that in all third party cases the IRS doesn't really "seize" a thing. Thus no levy pursuant to Section 6331 is actually made.

But I knew (based on certain constitutional and statutory considerations) that I could not owe the money claimed, and I also knew that the bank was not required to turn over any money based on its receipt of a mere "notice." At that time I did not know, for instance, that the courts had even ruled (as quoted in *Freeman*) that "mere notice of intent to levy" does not constitute a levy, which, of course, is precisely what a "Notice of Levy" is and why no one is required to honor it. Had I known about that case, I would have incorporated a reference to it in my letter of May 26th (Figure 7-14) which would not really have made any difference, since the bank **had already turned over my money.** However, based upon your increased understanding of this subject over what I knew in May, 1983, you will be able to make a more formidable presentation than I did. And you might have an opportunity to do so before your bank turns over *your* money. In any case, it is pretty clear that a "notice" of levy is not the "levy" referred to in all those threatening 6332 subsections (Figure 7-5A). And it was merely on this limited knowledge that I wrote to the bank. Incidentally, before continuing, read the back of that notice (Figure 7-5A) and see if you notice anything unusual about it. Also see how much mickey-mouse language you can spot in those Code sections that are reproduced.

A "Notice of Levy" is Not a "Levy"

Subsequent to my getting a copy of that notice, I did something that everybody should do when they get a communication from the IRS citing or quoting a Code Section. They should read the Code Section referred to. When I got over my initial shock in connection with Section 6331 which was that it was flagrantly unconstitutional and contained a summary procedure that I never knew existed, I noticed something extremely peculiar that I had not initially noticed. There was a strange inclusion in Section 6331's first paragraph (see Figure 7-1 or 7-6-A):

Levy may be made upon the **accrued salary or wages** of any officer, employee, or elected official, **of the United States**, the District of Columbia, or any agency or instrumentality **of the United States** or the District of Columbia, by serving a notice **on the employer** (as defined in Section 3401[d]) of such

FIGURE 7-13

AMERICAN NATIONAL BANK
2992 Dixwell Avenue, Hamden, Connecticut 06518
Area Code 203 281-1060

May 24, 1983

Irwin Schiff
144 Shepard's Knoll Drive
Hamden, CT 06514

RE: Notice of Levy/Amount $197,044.19

Dear Mr. Schiff:

Today we were served with a Levy on your account (s) by the Internal Revenue Service in the amount of $197,044.19. Accordingly, we have deducted two separate amounts from two of your accounts. One for the sum of $5.400.00, deducted from account #611540-3; and the second for the sum of $4.700.00, deducted from account #105089-4 as per the enclosed miscellaneous debits.

Further enclosed is a copy of the Levy for your use. Should you have any objections or legal reasons why this Levy is invalid, please contact the Revenue Officer mentioned in the Levy.

Very truly yours,

Elizabeth K. Ryder
Vice President

EKR/dl

Enclosures

officer, employee, or elected official.

When I first noticed that provision, I was sitting in my living room contemplating that section with my son Peter, and I said, "Pete, why should there be a special reference to government employees right in the middle of that first paragraph?" "And why," I remember asking, "should that reference not only make a distinction between government employees and all other employees, but why should it make a further distinction between their accrued salaries and any other asset they might own or be entitled to?" Obviously the above reference only makes a "notice of levy" applicable to a government employee's accrued salary—but not to any **other asset**: such as bank accounts, cars, homes, mutual funds, or anything else he/she might own. *Why was this double distinction made?* Initially, neither my son nor I could come up with any plausible explanation. See if you can come up with the answer, before I give it to you.

For about 15 minutes we wrestled with this question but nothing made any sense. Then suddenly the light bulb went on in my head. Section 6331 deals with "levy and distraint," and "levy" means "seizure by any means." What is the one asset that the government can't seize? An asset already in its possession! The government can't seize (i.e. levy) property it already has, can it? Suppose the government wanted to apply the accrued salary of one of its own employees against their alleged delinquent tax liability. It wouldn't "seize" such funds since it would already have them! All it would

FIGURE 7-14

Freedom Books

P.O. BOX 5303   HAMDEN, CONNECTICUT 06518   PHONE (203) 281-6791

If a nation values anything more than freedom, it will lose its freedom; and the irony of it is that if it is comfort or money that it values more, it will lose that too...

May 26, 1983

Elizabeth K. Ryder
Vice President
American National Bank
2992 Dixwell Avenue
Hamden, CT 06518

Dear Ms. Ryder:

Your letter of May 24, 1983 informs me that you allowed my two bank accounts to be cleaned out because you "were served with a Levy on your account (s) by the Internal Revenue Service in the amount of $197,044.19". You were served with no such thing!

What you got was a <u>Notice of Levy</u> - not a Levy! The penalty sections shown on the reverse side of that fraudulent Notice of Levy apply only to levies themselves and not to "notices".

The Notice of Levy is fraudulent on numerous other grounds such as:

1. The Notice does not specify the kind of tax allegedly owed.

2. The Notice does not even identify the section of the law which established the liability for the tax allegedly owed.

3. By comparison I attach a Tax Notice for the city of Hamden which clearly identifies both the type of tax and the statutory authority for levying it. It is no accident that such material is absent from the IRS's fraudulent notice.

4. Chapter 64 referred to in the Notice deals with the <u>collection</u> of a variety of Federal Taxes but does not establish any "liability" for "income taxes", if that is the tax that I allegedly owe.

5. The Notice was not signed or sworn to by anyone authorized to deprive me of $10,100.00.

6. I also attach merely page 4 of a 15 page letter that I sent to the commissioner in which I asked him to identify the code section that creates an "income tax liability" and a "requirement" that such a liability be paid (a); or where is he authorized to collect a tax on "income" by distraint (b); or what section states that "income taxes" shall be paid on the basis of a return (c). His letter to me of May 11, 1983 (copy attached), shows that he refuses to answer these questions.

7. Today I sent him a shorter letter which I am sure he will not answer either, since there is no section of the Internal Revenue Code that establishes an "income tax liability" or would establish that I owe or need pay this outrageous $197,044.19 tax bill.

8. I also have attached a sworn statement that I have <u>no tax liability</u> to the Federal Government for the years 1976, 1977 and 1978 and until you get a similar sworn statement or a court order to the contrary I suggest that you restore my funds to me forthwith or I will take immediate legal action which, I assure you, will prove extremely costly to the bank.

Very truly yours,

Irwin A. Schiff

Author's note:

While I sued the bank, it wasn't until years later that I discovered that my lawsuit was dismissed due to the failure of my attorney to timely file a response to a defense motion to dismiss—though the suit probably would have been dismissed anyway, because it was heard by the same judge who dismissed my suit against Simon and Schuster. Incidentally, while I sued in State court, it was remanded to federal court—where, of course, such law suits don't stand a chance. I believe, however, that I might have been able to keep the suit in State court had I not made the mistake of raising certain federal issues. Had my lawsuit just charged violations of state banking laws, I believe, I could have kept the lawsuit out of federal court, and the outcome might have been different.

But in any case, I feel that in all such instances, you might be better off filing a complaint with the State Banking Commission rather than sue. I believe that by turning over depositor money without a court order, a bank would be in violation of state banking laws and fiduciary obligations spelled out in such laws and regulations.

The Great Income Tax Hoax (pages 397-398) describes what you might do at bank stockholders' meetings (by buying one share of stock in your bank [which you can sell after the meeting] you qualify) to insure that your bank doesn't turn over your funds (or anybody else's) to the IRS without a court order.

have to do is notify its employee of this—which it could do by letter or notice. A Notice of Seizure (necessary when levies [seizures] are made) would be inappropriate and unnecessary in this situation, which is why the statute does not provide that a "Notice of Seizure" be used in connection with a "Notice of Levy." And, since the IRS never issues Notices of Seizure in conjunction with Notices of Levy, such "Notices" cannot constitute levies on any basis. If no Notice of Seizure is given, no actual levy pursuant to Section 6331 is "made"—as explained in Section 6502(b) (Figure 7-10). Now you know the reason for a Notice of Levy, and also **the only time where it can lawfully be used!**

This situation is actually analagous to an employee being indebted to his employer for an amount in excess of his accrued wages. If that employee quits or is fired, his employer might inform him that he is not going to pay him the wages he has coming, but will apply them against that debt. In that situation, the employer doesn't need a court order permitting him to keep those wages. He simply keeps it without benefit of any order. If the employee feels that he is entitled to those wages, he has to bring suit against his employer. The employer has nothing to fear if he can, in fact, prove that debt. So what the law provides through issuing a Notice of Levy is no different from what *any* employer *can do* in a situation where an employee allegedly owes them money. Since the government has a document that allows it to do what *any* employer can do, it has *diabolically adopted that document* to acquire property from the rest of the public, in situations where it **actually needs a court order and couldn't get the property by levy!** Remember whenever the government gets money from third parties such as banks, etc., etc., it never "seizes" it. It gets handed over to them. And no one is ever required to "hand over" property **except pursuant to a court order.** What is especially contemptible in this situation, is that all those third parties turning over money to the government generally occupy and *breach* a fiduciary relationship in doing so.

So the federal government has been using a document that doesn't apply to the general public at all, to take billions from the public in payment of taxes that aren't even owed! If the federal government had only used a *portion* of that ingenuity against the Russians, we could have won the cold war long ago without having to become the world's biggest debtor in the process. Since so much ingenuity went into this diabolical scam, we must examine it in greater detail.

SNEAKING THE "NOTICE OF LEVY" PAST THE PUBLIC

Starting right at the beginning, the first thing the

government had to do was to slip the real purpose of a Notice of Levy past the public. Since members of the general public (the victims in this case) hardly ever read the Internal Revenue Code, this presented no real problem. (Only those who profit from the government's illegal income tax activities generally read the Code, and they can be trusted to see no evil, hear no evil or speak no truth about that evil). Leaving nothing to chance, the compilers of the Code sought to throw everyone off the track by using the misleading term "employer" in the place where only the "United States" could possibly fit. Notice that the line in paragraph (a) (Fig. 7-6A) regarding a Notice of Levy states:

Levy may be made...[upon all manner of government employees]...by serving a notice of levy *on the employer* (as defined in section 3401[d]) of such officer, employee or elected official.

The average person reading this paragraph would get the impression that the word "employer" as used in that sentence *means a private employer!* Who would believe that the government has to **"serve"** a document on itself! Obviously, if the federal government wanted to notify one of its own employees that it intended to apply his/her accrued wages to taxes they allegedly owed the government, it would simply notify that employee. **It would not need to "serve"** *anything* on itself! If the writers of the Code did not *intend* to deceive the public, that line would have read as follows:

Levy may be made upon the accrued salary or wages of any officer, employee, or elected official of the United States, the District of Columbia, or any agency or instrumentality of the United States, by sending to such employee (as defined in Secton 3401(d) a notice of levy.

What the government has done here is similar to what it did in connection with the document designed to be used in connection with Section 6014 (Figure 7-3), which it then used as a bogus notice and demand. Here the government is using against the general public a document *designed solely to be used in connection with its own employees.* As far as the legal significance of this "notice" is concerned, the statute could just have easily called for a letter. In which case the last phrase of that line (as indicated above) could have read, "by sending to such employee...a letter to this effect."

In addition, the way this line is worded, anyone reading it who was not a government employee would quickly skim over it (as I initially did) thinking that it did not apply to them anyway! And on this basis too, the general public is thrown off the scent.

So by covertly burying the real meaning and purpose of a

Notice of Levy in this confusing and misleading manner, the government assumed that the public would be none the wiser. And the government would never again mention a Notice of Levy within the body of Section 6331 nor in any of the enforcement provisions that were to follow.[7]

But for added insurance the government was prepared to carry its deceit a good deal further.

THE MISSING PARAGRAPH!

When I suggested that you read the back of the Notice of Levy (Figure 7-5A) to see if you saw anything peculiar, I wanted you to notice whether or not you spotted **the missing paragraph.** Notice that your honest government, in claiming to present Section 6331 in its entirety, **left out paragraph (a)!** Thus the only relevant paragraph dealing with such a Notice is omited from the government's presentation of the statutes presumably relevant to it! Why do you suppose that happened? Take a wild guess! You will notice that this paragraph was not omitted from the back of Form 668-B (Figure 7-6A) where it is *not* relevant! And the federal government has the nerve to prosecute others for mail and stock fraud. **It wrote the book!**

INTIMIDATING THE PUBLIC

Besides making sure that no third party discovers the truth about a Notice of Levy and why it didn't apply to them [by omitting paragraph (a)], the government also misleads and intimidates the public concerning its legal obligations with respect to that document. For one thing, note that what banks, employers and other third parties get is form No. 668-A and not Form 668-B. This alone proves that third parties are not involved in a "levy" situation. Notice that Section 6332 (Fig. 7-5A) is captioned "SURRENDER OF PROPERTY SUBJECT TO LEVY," that is property that can only be taken pursuant to Form 668-B, **not Form 668-A**—the form banks, employers and other third parties actually receive!

So the alleged threats and consequences that might befall "Any person who fails or refuses to surrender any property or rights to property, subject to levy...shall be liable etc., etc." (first line paragraph 6632(c)[1]) doesn't even apply here because no "levy" is involved! The same type of deception can be noted in the last three lines of paragraph 6332(c)(2). In this situation no "levy" could have possibly been "made" since no Notice of Seizure pursuant to Section 6502 was ever "given." Thus these constant references on the back of that Notice to Levy are not even applicable here, simply because it is clear that no actual "levy" is involved!

This should be clear for a number of reasons beside the fact that no Notice of Seizure is ever "given" in connection

with a Form 668-A. For one thing, pursuant to both *Freeman* v. *Mayer* and the *Reference Guide for Revenue Officers* (Figure 7-9) "a levy requires that the property levied upon be brought into legal custody through seizure." This is exactly what happened with D. Linquent's car. It was "seized" and brought into "legal custody" when it was placed in a government enclosure. But, as noted before, when an IRS agent goes into a bank with a Notice of Levy, does he actually seize any funds? Does he go over to where the bank presumably keeps that particular individual's money and "seize" it out of some box or receptacle? Of course not. As in **all third party cases**, the bank (and other third parties) simply hand over or send the government a check through the mail in the amount requested! Such funds are never "brought into legal custody *through seizure*". They are actually received by the government in the nature of a gift! **But if property is not "seized", no levy takes place!**

Since, from all of the above, it must be crystal clear that in connection with a Notice of Levy absolutely no levy is involved, none of those conditions shown on the back of such Notices can apply. This not only applies to the penalties (that don't apply) but to the alleged protection afforded to third parties as well. In order to encourage third parties to hand over assets that, (1) don't belong to them, and (2) the government is not legally entitled to, third parties are misled into believing that they have legal immunity when they hand over such property to the government—even if it means breaching a contract and violating a fiduciary responsibility. This, of course, is sheer nonsense. Such immunity, as stated in Section 6332 only applies to "property subject to levy upon which a levy has been made." Since this condition is not present when a Notice of Levy is mailed to third parties, such immunity does not apply! Unfortunately federal "courts" have been giving culpable third parties the protection that the law doesn't provide. But this practice may not go on indefinitely—**now that the public knows the truth!**

Strange to say, **all of those penalties and immunity features can only apply to IRS revenue offices themselves, and not to the general public at all!** Isn't that surprising! Revenue officers are the only ones in possession of property "upon which a levy has been made" and which has been brought "into custody through seizure"! They are the only ones who legally must turn over such property "upon demand by the Secretary" and they are the only ones who might be "discharged from any obligation or liability to the delinquent taxpayer" for having done so! This is part of the overall technique used by the government to mislead the public concerning income taxes: simply present law to the public that only applies to certain people in certain situations, and mislead the public into believing that the law presented actually applies to them and to income taxes. The government knows no shame.

I believe that I have already nailed down the fact that a Notice of Levy is not a levy. This issue goes to the core of our government's deceit and the culpbility of our judiciary (who continue to maintain that a levy and a Notice of Levy are one in the same). I don't want to beat a dead horse, but I need to call your attention to a few other significant distinctions which are contained in the *Legal Reference Guide for Revenue Officers* and on a Notice of Levy itself.

A Significant Distinction

Note that the statement in paragraph 332 of the *Legal Reference Guide,* that if someone "fails to *honor* a notice of levy or an *interference* with a levy" the IRS has to get a court order, i.e., "the matter should be referred for proper legal action against the offending party." And again in connection with the Notices of Levy (Section 334.2) revenue officers are told, "In the event the Final Demand is not responded to, a suit will ordinarily be required to reach the property." That section states that:

A Notice of Final Demand (Form 668-C) is not required to be served under the Code [this also can be said of Form 668-B], although use of the form as an administrative tool [not unlike a rack] is generally uniform.

You bet its use is not "required" by the Code, since those who wrote it took the precaution of leaving out such unlawful procedures!

But notice the clear cut distinction shown by the IRS' use of the phrase *"honor* a notice of levy" as opposed to *"interference* with a levy." Despite the deceitful claims of federal judges that both procedures are inherently the same, this language proves that **the government knows that both procedures are inherently different.** "Failure to *honor* a notice of levy" can only mean refusing to turn over property in response to it. Obviously there can be no "interference" with a Notice of Levy unless somebody tried to stop the postman from delivering one—but that's not the kind of "interference" contemplated here. "Interference" with a levy, on the other hand, can occur in a variety of ways; all designed to prevent the IRS from carting away one's goods. Locking oneself in one's car as the Olivers did, comes immediately to mind. Refusing to allow IRS agents onto one's property—and calling the cops if they refuse to leave—might be another way. Thus, such distinctions clearly show the inherent differences between the two procedures. Then how can federal judges claim that both procedures are the same? You answer that one for yourself.

FRAUDULENTLY INVOLVING THIRD PARTIES

There is another important distinction between the operation of a levy and a Notice of Levy that should not be overlooked. In the case of a levy, **no member of the public gets involved or is put at risk.** A levy is a procedure strictly between the government and the allegedly errant taxpayer. There is nothing on a Notice of Seizure, for example, that asks, requests, threatens, or orders anyone to do anything to help the government get the property it seeks.

A Notice of Levy is different. It arrogantly expects third parties (who may even occupy a fiduciary relationship with respect to the intended victim) to get involved in a questionable collection process by turning over property belonging to others based on information the IRS claims is accurate! Apart from the fact that the information in all Notices of Levy is flat-out false and deliberately deceiving, how can the government put third parties (especially fiduciaries) in such a situation? Certainly such third parties should be expected to check out such information (but they don't!) before acting—and be liable (especially banks) if they don't. They certainly should be expected not to turn over any property without first being absolutely certain that:

1. The information contained in a Notice is 100% accurate, and
2. They are required under the law to turn over the property in question.

Yet any third party who responsibly checks out the information contained in a Notice of Levy would find that it's practically all false, and that they are under no legal obligation to "honor" such Notices. It should be perfectly obvious that from purely a legal point of view, third parties can throw any Notice of Levy they receive right into the nearest trash can.

The minimum number of false and misleading statements contained in a typical Notice of Levy are the following:

1. "Chapter 64 of the Internal Revenue Code provides a lien for the above tax and addition."
2. "Notice and demand...has been made on the taxpayer."
3. "This amount is still due" and owing.
4. "All property...in your possession and belonging to this taxpayer...are levied upon."
5. "Demand is made on you...to pay this tax liability."

How can any responsible third party be expected to accept all of these allegations at face value and accordingly turn over property entrusted to their care? If such allegations are false, why shouldn't third parties (especially banks) be liable for their actions? Yet why should third parties be put to the trouble (and risk) of having to verify such information? Relying on an order *signed by a judge* is one thing, but on what basis *should anyone rely on the signature and representations contained in a Notice of Levy? Who signed it anyway?* A former filling station attendant?

But let's briefly analyze these false statements. That first statement is designed to throw third parties off the track in a manner they would hardly suspect. Not only doesn't Chapter 64 provide "a lien" with respect to either an income or a "1040" tax and their "statutory additions," it certainly does not provide that the public is required to turn over property pursuant to a Notice of Levy! **And that's really all that is important!**

Secondly, as far as a "1040 tax" is concerned, no notice and demand would ever have been "made on the taxpayer" which he "refused to pay," as this Notice fraudulently claims.

Thirdly, since the payment of income taxes is based upon "voluntary compliance," no amount can be "due and owing."

Fourthly, as stated in *Freeman,* "Mere *intent* to reduce to possession" is no levy. *So no property is being "levied upon" by this "Notice."* And fifthly, the person whose property is being demanded cannot have a "1040" (or income) tax **liability** as is fraudulently claimed in this Notice.

In addition to all of this, the IRS asks such third parties to complete a Form (Figure 7-8) which comes attached to the Notice of Levy. Note the language used in this form, i.e., "we would appreciate...please make your check or money order payable...please indicate on the front..." How does this constitute a "seizure"? Note that the form also instructs third parties who turn over funds to the government to "give Part 3 to the taxpayer within 2 working days." Suppose the third party takes 3 "working days" or 7 "working days" or neglects to send the form to the "taxpayer" altogether. What then? Can the "taxpayer" sue? Who, and on what grounds?

Note further that there is nothing on a Form 668-A that specifically tells third parties that they are legally "required" pursuant to any Code section to turn over any money to the government pursuant to that Notice! And what should be particularly noted is, that while a Notice of Seizure refers to Section 6331 (as does even the front of Form 668-B), **no such reference appears anywhere on the face of a Notice of Levy! What does that tell you?**

How much more evidence does anyone need to be convinced that a Notice of Levy is a complete fraud and cannot be lawful or mandatory on any basis?!

The final bit of trickery in this nefarious scheme was the adoption of Treasury Regulation 301.6331-1 (Figure 7-15). This supposedly provided a legal basis to enforce Notices of Levy on the same basis as levies themselves. While it may have accomplished this, it also revealed the utter contempt federal judges have for both the law and their own oath of office.

A TREASURY REGULATION ILLEGAL ON ITS FACE

To put the icing on its "Notice of Levy" scam, the government wrote Treasury Regulation 301.6331-1. Notice that this regulation openly changes and extends the law in connection with a Notice of Levy. The law itself is specific: a Notice of Levy can only apply to the accrued wages and salary of government employees—period. The regulation blithely extends this wording to all manner of persons and to all manner of property! It states:

> "Levy may be made by serving a notice of levy on any person in possession of, or obligated with respect to, property or rights to property subject to levy, including receivables, bank accounts, evidences of debt, securities, and salaries, wages, commissions, or other compensation."

It is perfectly clear that under the law, a Notice of Levy can only apply in that one narrow circumstance with which you are now very familiar. Any regulation that seeks to change the law as Treasury Regulation 301.6331-1 does is born dead. That's basic. That, as they say in the trade, is hornbook law. Any freshman law sudent can tell by even a cursory examination of the law and its alleged regulation that Treasury Regulation 301.6331-1 was D.O.A., but federal judges keep on pretending that this cadaver is actually still alive and kicking!

WHERE DO LAWS COME FROM ANYWAY?

If Americans were asked where federal laws come from, they would undoubtedly say "From acts of Congress." It would probably never dawn on them that federal laws could come from any other place. This undoubtedly stems from their notion that the constitutional provision which states that "Congress shall make all laws" still prevails. Americans are largely oblivious to the fact that this constitutional provision, like so many others, is, as a practical matter, dead.

American "laws" are largely made by the judicial and

FIGURE 7-15

SEIZURE OF PROPERTY FOR COLLECTION OF TAXES

§ 301.6331-1 Levy and distraint.

(a) *Authority to levy—(1) In general.* If any person liable to pay any tax neglects or refuses to pay the tax within 10 days after notice and demand, the district director to whom the assessment is charged (or, upon his request, any other district director) may proceed to collect the tax by levy. The district director may levy upon any property, or rights to property, whether real or personal, tangible or intangible, belonging to the taxpayer. The district director may also levy upon property with respect to which there is a lien provided by section 6321 or 6324 for the payment of the tax. For exemption of certain property from levy, see section 6334 and the regulations thereunder. As used in section 6331 and this section, the term "tax" includes any interest, additional amount, addition to tax, or assessable penalty, together with costs and expenses. Property subject to a Federal tax lien which has been sold or otherwise transferred by the taxpayer may be seized while in the hands of the transferee or any subsequent transferee. However, see provisions under sections 6323 and 6324 (a)(2) and (b) for protection of certain transferees against a Federal tax lien. Levy may be made by serving a notice of levy on any person in possession of, or obligat-

A

ed with respect to, property or rights to property subject to levy, including receivables, bank accounts, evidences of debt, securities, and salaries, wages, commissions, or other compensation. Except as provided in § 301.6331-2(c) with regard to a levy on salary or wages, a levy extends only to property possessed and obligations which exist at the time of the levy. Obligations exist when the liability of the obligor is fixed and determinable although the right to receive payment thereof may be deferred until a later date. For example, if on the first day of the month a delinquent taxpayer sold personal property subject to an agreement that the buyer remit the purchase price on the last day of the month, a levy made on the buyer on the 10th day of the month would reach the amount due on the sale, although the buyer need not satisfy the levy by paying over the amount to the district director until the last day of the month. Similarly, a levy only reaches property in the possession of the person levied upon at the time the levy is made. For example, a levy made on a bank with respect to the account of a delinquent taxpayer is satisfied if the bank surrenders the amount of the taxpayer's balance at the time the levy is made. The levy has no effect upon any subsequent deposit made in the bank by the taxpayer. Subsequent deposits may be reached only by a subsequent levy on the bank.

B

C

executive branches of government, even though they were never given such powers under the Constitution. The judiciary, in effect, makes law when it enforces its own opinions (even when they conflict with the law) rather than the law itself. The executive, in effect, makes law, when it enforces its own regulations even when they too conflict with the law. In many cases, neither court decisions nor department regulations have any relation to any law passed by Congress.

With respect to income taxes, both branches enforce "laws" that don't even exist. For example, there are no laws that provide that anyone has to pay income taxes or file income tax returns nor provide any punishment whatsoever (either civil or criminal) because of such taxes. Yet people are harrassed and have their assets seized by the Treasury Department, are prosecuted by the Justice Department and are fined and imprisoned by the judiciary all because of income tax "laws." **Where, therefore, did these "laws" come from?**

In passing laws, Congress never fills in all of the details, but leaves that up to the executive department charged with their enforcement. For example, while Congress provided for a notice and demand with respect to federal taxes, it never stated the form number it should have or what specific information it should contain. It left that up to the Treasury Department to handle by Treasury Regulations.

"CASE" LAW

An understanding of the legal relationship between statutory law and case law (i.e. court decisions), can be derived from the following excerpt from *Consumer Products Safety* v. *GTE Sylvania* 447 U.S. 102 (at page 108) in which the Supreme Court, in explaining statutory construction said:

> We begin with the familiar canon of statutory construction that the starting point for interpreting a statute is the language of the statute itself. Absent a clearly expressed legislative intention to the contrary, the language must ordinarily be regarded as conclusive.

So, it is clear that "case" law (court decisions) is supposed to take a back seat to statutory law; especially the Supreme Law of the Land—the United States Constitution. But in actual practice case law does not take such a back seat!— especially when the issues involve the *expansion of federal fiscal and monetary power*. Here are but *two* such examples.

Charles Griffith brought an action in the United States District Court of Ohio (*Griffith* v. *C.I.R.*, 598 F. Supp. 405) to prevent the IRS from seizing his assets (as it threatened to

do in his Final Notice) in order to collect a $500 penalty that had been assessed against him for allegedly filing a false W-4. As stated in the court decision;

> According to plaintiff's complaint, on September 3, 1982 the Internal Revenue Service (IRS) sent plaintiff a letter claiming that his W-4 did not meet the requirements of the Internal Revenue Code Sect. 3402 and informing him that his employer be directed to disregard [notice the court did not say "ordered" to] the W-4 form and withhold monies from his paycheck as if he were single and claiming one (1) withholding allowance. By letter dated September 14, 1982 plaintiff informed the IRS of his reasons for completing the W-4 **in the alleged illegal manner.** However the IRS notified his employer to proceed withholding as if plaintiff were single...and was assessed a penalty of five hundred dollars ($500) under 26 U.S.C. 6682(a). (Emphasis added.)

Note that the court suggests that Griffith completed his W-4 in an "allegedly illegal manner." How exactly does one complete a W-4 in an "illegal manner"? Did Griffith hit the personnel clerk over the head with a hammer, strip her clothes off and then complete his W-4 on her naked body? And if it were completed in an "allegedly illegal manner," why wasn't he arrested? It is clear that Griffith's W-4 *did* "meet the requirements of Section 3402." Griffith obviously knew (as you now know) that he was not liable for income taxes, and so probably claimed "exempt" in accordance with Section 3402(n) (see Chapter 8). Note that the court states that the "plaintif informed the IRS of his reasons for completing the form." So why didn't the court state those reasons in its decision, since Section 6682 only applies (Figure 2-1) when such *reasons are not "reasonable"*? But not only did the court refuse to consider whether Griffith's reasons were "reasonable," it refused to even mention them! I wonder why? Who, therefore, decided that Griffith's "reasons" were not "reasonable"? An IRS cleaning lady?

In finding against Griffith the Honorable Judge White wrote:

> Plaintiff's claim that the manner of collection of the penalty violates his Fifth Amendment rights is without merit. He has attempted to show that the government cannot prevail in the collection of the penalty because to do so prior to a hearing would deprive him of his Fifth Amendment constitutional rights. [Who can argue with that!]. *Case law dictates otherwise...* The power of the government to levy is essential to the *self assessment* tax system because it *encourages voluntary compliance.* [emphasis added.]

So the court, in deciding to allow the IRS to seize Griffith's property without any hearing whatsoever, admits that it does so on the basis of what "case law dictates"—never mind what the statute itself "dictates" or what the Constitution "dictates" (Section 6682 only allows the penalty if there is no "reasonable basis" for the claim, which the court here refuses to even consider.)

It should also be noted that in this case, Griffith represented himself against the government. He undoubtedly believed he could do so, since he was convinced (and rightly so) that he had several statutes, the Constitution and logic all on his side. But he learned (as we all do so sooner or later), that these often do not count for much in federal court. Incidentally, did you happen to get the feeling when you read the above, that you were reading something right out of *Alice in Wonderland?*

Clearly, Griffith's argument is not only "not without merit"; it is legally correct. But federal judges can easily dispatch such arguments by labeling them "frivolous" or stating they are "without merit."

The Overriding Power of Case "Law"

Paragraph 40.12[3] (Feb. 1987) captioned "Voluntariness of Filing Income Tax Returns," is part of an 85-page section entitled "Tax Protesters" which appears in the Justice Department's Criminal Tax Manual. This paragraph (quoted below in its entirety) is designed to help the government prosecute and convict "tax protesters" who claim that filing income tax returns is voluntary and not mandatory.

Protesters commonly argue that the filing of income tax returns is voluntary and not required. The circuit courts have rejected this argument. "Every income earner is required to file an income tax return." *United States* v. *Pilcher,* 672 F.2d 875, 877 (11th Cir. 1982), cert. denied, 459 U.S. 973 (1982). If the taxpayer has received more than the statutory amount of gross income, then he or she is obligated to file a return. *United States* v. *Richards,* 723 F.2d 646, 648, (8th Cir. 1983). See also *United States* v. *Hurd,* 549 F2d 118 (9th Cir. 1977). "Persons who meet the requisite statutory definition are required to pay income taxes." *United States* v. *Tedder,* 787 F2d 540, 542 (10th Cir. 1986).

That paragraph is loaded with legal *disclaimers* and omissions that few would detect. For one thing, if the Justice Department believes that filing is mandatory, **why didn't it just cite the Code section that says so?** If such a section existed, why not just quote it, and forget all those court decisions (case "law") which conclude nothing, since

there is not a Supreme Court case in the lot? So the Justice Department cites no statute that makes filing mandatory, but bases its entire claim merely on the fraudulent opinions (case "law") of "circuit court" judges *who allegedly claim that it is!*

Why are there no Supreme court cases cited, even though in the last 25 years hundreds of appeals have been sent up to that body on this very issue? Because the Supreme Court knows what its decisions would have to be! So the Supreme Court refuses to hear such appeals (cert. denied) so that circuit courts can be free to break the law (and/or disregard its *Sullivan* decision) in the manner illustrated above!

The last time the Supreme Court heard an appeal from an illegal failure to file conviction was in 1928. At that time (*United States* v. *Sullivan,* 274 U.S. 259), the Supreme court authorized the filing of Fifth Amendment returns. Approximately 35 years later, district courts deliberately misinterpreted that decision and began throwing people in jail (including myself) for relying on it—i.e. for filing Fifth Amendment returns!

The reason that all of the above statements are fraudulent is that none of them actually ever say that anyone is really required to file an income tax return. But they all seek to convey that false impression.

For example, in none of the above decisions is any court quoted as saying, "anyone whose earnings (through wages, dividends, interest, rents and similar items) is of a sufficient amount, is required to file an income tax return," since it is only in this context, that individuals actually file! Remember, the Supreme Court has already ruled that the word "income" as used in all tax statutes only means *corporate profits.* Thus, by definition, no individual can have "income" within the meaning of the statute. Once this is understood, it becomes clear how the above court decisions are worded to deceive. For example:

1. since *no individual* incurs a corporate profit, *no individual* can be the "income earner" to whom the "required" as used in the first case, can apply.
2. Since *no individual* receives "more than the statutory amount of gross income" *no individual* can be the "taxpayer" who is "obligated" to "file" the return referred to in the second case.
3. Since *no individual* falls within the category of "persons" who supposedly "meet the requisite statutory definition" of who and what constitutes a "taxpayer" within the meaning of the Code; there are *no individuals* who "are required to pay income taxes" within the language used in the third case.

So, while none of the above cases actually state that

individuals are required to file income tax returns, a copy of that paragraph introduced as evidence in any tax evasion trial involving the filing of an allegedly fraudulent return *should be more than enough to abort that trial!!*

So that's how the actual validity of "case" law contradicts statute or the Constitution—or sometimes both.

The Lawfulness of Regulations

As far as the significance of regulations is concerned, the following passages from *H. Wetter Manufacturing Company* v. *United States,* 458 F2d 1033, (at page 1033) should put them in their proper perspective.

Because Congress has delegated to the Secretary only the power to issue regulations for the enforcement of the revenue laws, and because this power is limited to carrying into effect the will of Congress as expressed by the statutes, the express words of the statute must control when they conflict with the regulation. The Secretary **may not broaden or narrow the specific provisions of the revenue laws.** In 1967, this Court approved the observation of the Eighth Circuit that "[t]he Commissioner has no more power to add to the Act what he thinks Congress may have overlooked than he has to supply what Congress has deliberately omitted", *General Electric Co.* v. *Burton,* 372 F2d 108, 111 (6th Cir. 1967). *A court may not enforce a regulation which is plainly inconsistent with the revenue statute.* [Emphasis added and additional citings omitted.]

Where the provisions of an act are unambiguous, and its direction specific, the Secretary of *the Treasury has no power to amend the statute by regulations. Koshland* v. *Helvering,* 298 U.S. 441, 447, 56 S.Ct. 767, 80 L.Ed. 1268 (1936). [emphasis added]

Clearly this is what the Treasury has done with respect to Regulation 301.6331-1 in violation of the above principle. Since, where a Notice of Levy applies is "expressed by the statute," the Secretary has no authority to "amend the statute" as was done by Regulation 301.6331-1. But in this case, not only do federal courts knowingly allow the Treasury Department to make law by regulation, they then proceed to allow the Treasury to violate even their own illegal regulations! Thus, federal lawlessness is carried to its ultimate conclusion![8]

THE IRS' ILLEGAL USE OF A "CONTINUOUS" LEVY

An important but little understood (by the public) aspect

of Notices of Levy is their inability to reach "after acquired property." This principle is covered in Sections 6331(b) and (c) (Figure 7-1).

After Acquired Property

Note that Section (b) states that "a levy shall extend only to property possessed and obligations existing at the time thereof." Proceeding on the false assumption that private, third parties can even be subject to Notices of Levy, Section (b) means that third parties can only be required to surrender to the government only those assets that are *immediately* due and owing to the taxpayer. Note further that in such cases no *"seizure" takes place.* Third parties are not required by law to give the government *anything* that becomes due the "taxpayer" *one second after the receipt of a Notice of Levy.* The Notice of Levy can only apply to those "obligations existing" and "possessed" at the *moment the Notice is received.* While an understanding of this principle is really quite simple; IRS violations of it are *massive*—yet easy to detect. However, my failure to do both cost me $204,303.25 in 1983!

The government's illegal use of a continuous levy is its chief weapon in robbing the public. It is also its principle means of reducing millions of normally law abiding and honorable Americans into becoming nothing more than despicable thieves and informers for the IRS. The following examples are designed to thoroughly familiarize you with this aspect of Notices of Levy, so that the government (with the help of private, third parties) will not be able to do to you what it did to me.[9]

Example Number One

Assume that Greb DeMonay walked into D. Linquent's bank at precisely 10:00 a.m. on January 31, and handed the manager a Notice of Levy with respect to D. Linquent's account. Let's further suppose that D. Linquent had $169.72 in that account, all the money to his name. Greb can only leave the bank with that amount. Suppose that while Greb was waiting around for the bank to give him a check, D. Linquent, not knowing that this was happening, walks into the bank and deposits another $25.00 to his account. Suppose that Greb, seeing D. Linquent at the teller's window, concludes that he indeed made another deposit. Could Greb tell the bank to make its check for an amount (let's assume that D. Linquent deposited cash) that included that last deposit? Well, he could "tell" them, but if the bank complied, it would have conspired (and maybe unknowingly) to steal that $25.00. Since that deposit represented after acquired property, it would have required another subsequent Notice to reach it. To get that $25.00 Greb would have to go back to his car where he might keep his supply of Notices and write up a new one to cover that

$25.00. During this time, of course, D. Linquent would have time to withdraw his $25.00 to prevent it from falling into the hands of the IRS. However, let us suppose that D. Linquent, being in a hurry and not knowing that any of this was going on, simply deposits his money and leaves the bank. Suppose that Greb had inadvertently left all of his Notices at the office and feared that before he could get back with another one, a check might be presented for payment that could eat up that last deposit. So he tells the bank that this last deposit is indeed covered by the Notice previously presented, and that the bank would be liable to the government for its loss if it were not immediately handed over. In this situation, most bank managers would probably yield to such intimidation and would turn over all the money. Obviously the bank's manager is more fearful of an IRS audit than a small depositor. If he thought about it, he might say to himself, "Is D. Linquent really going to sue the bank for $25.00, when we only turned over the funds standing to his account (which we were required to do), on the *very day* the Notice of Levy was presented? I mean, is anybody *really* going to check the specific time everything happened?"

So now Greb walks out of the bank with another $25.00 that under the law he was not entitled to get! So what if he got it on the basis of giving out false information combined with a little intimidation (i.e. extortion)? Under the law, he is allowed to seize property "by any means," and this presumably means fraud, trickery, and intimidation. And the Notice of Levy was designed to do that job!

Example Number Two

An old West Coast friend of D. Linquent's, I.M. Noble, had himself, on many occasions, been helped by D. Linquent. Suppose, hearing of D. Linquent's financial problems, Noble decides to repay these past favors. He decides to suprise D. Linquent by wiring $10,000 right into D. Linquent's account just as D. Linquent had, on more than one occasion, wired him money when he needed it. Suppose Noble's $10,000 is received by the bank the next day and accordingly is put into D. Linquent's account. The Notice of Levy received by the bank the day before would not apply to these funds. The actual legal significance of the Notice of Levy to those funds is, as if that Notice had never been received. Greb would have to beat D. Linquent to the bank with a new Notice (pursuant to Section 6331[c]) in order to swindle him out of this $10,000. But D. Linquent has no idea that the funds are there. In my view, if the bank did not immediately call D. Linquent, and (1) inform him of that, and (2) advise him that it would be wise for him to withdraw the funds before the IRS presented the bank with a new Notice of Levy, the bank, at least in the first instance (and perhaps in the second too), would have violated a fiduciary obligation owed its client.

Remember the bank (as any third party) is under no obligation to help the government steal depositor's (nor anyone else's money). Its *maximum obligation* under both the law and regulation is simply to hand over to the government whatever property it might have at the instant it receives the Notice of Levy—*and nothing more!* At the same time, it has a substantial legal basis [if not a fiduciary obligation] to *refuse to hand over any property at all without a court order!*

In all matters, the bank has a contractual fiduciary obligation, to preserve for its client the funds entrusted to its care—as long as it can do this without breaking any laws. And there is no law (though the public might think otherwise) that says a bank (or anybody else) can't immediately mail out funds for the *admitted purpose* of trying to prevent their seizure by the IRS!—or by making a phone call that "you had better come and get your money before the IRS does!" Naturally, such action could not be done once the Notice of Levy is received. But, in my view, any fiduciary who *did not act* in that manner when *he had the opportunity,* would have *violated a contractual fiduciary responsibility* and should, accordingly, be held *accountable* for any resulting *loss* to his principle.

Let's suppose that D. Linquent, not being informed by the bank that these funds had arrived, makes no attempt to withdraw them. Let's further supose that Greb, while at that bank on some other matter, discovers that D. Linquent's account now holds $10,000. He runs out to his car and prepares a new Notice of Levy which he gives to the bank. Whereupon the bank, obediently and in short order, hands him a check covering those funds.

If such a scenario occurred, in my view, the bank would be *liable on two grounds*—for not notifying D. Linquent initially, and for its negligence in allowing Greb to discover that such funds were in D. Linquent's account.

For Greb to legally obtain such information, he would have had to subpoena it from the bank pursuant to a Section 7602 IRS summons (Chapter 9), which D. Linquent would have had an opportunity to quash. The bank by negligently allowing such information to leak out without either a court subpoena or an IRS summons, would be, I'm sure, in violation of the banking laws, as well as having violated D. Linquent's rights under the Code. But there is no doubt that banks as well as other fiduciary third parties, do give out such information to the IRS all the time—out of fear and/or to curry its favor, to the detriment of those whose assets they hold in trust. This is reason enough why such Notices cannot be applicable to the public—and why, under the law, they aren't applicable anyway!

But shouldn't third parties who respond to such fraud, trickery and intimidation be held accountable for property they turn over to the IRS, when, under the law and regulation (as you will soon see) they are not required to do so; and when, what they turn over, generally involves property that, when under the laws of contract and agency they have a fiduciary obligation to protect?[10]

Example Number Three

Suppose the bank, (or other third party) not fully understanding its responsibilities upon receiving a Notice of Levy, holds off doing anything until it can clarify its responsibility with legal counsel. Let's further suppose that by the time the bank hears from its counsel (who informs the bank that it is required to turn over D. Linquent's funds to the IRS) the additional $10,000 arrives and the bank puts a hold on that too. Suppose the bank, being informed by counsel that it is required to turn over all of D. Linquent's funds, does so without making any distinction between the money held before or after the Notice was received, and so turns over all the funds to the IRS. Obviously, in any subsequent lawsuit against the bank, D. Linquent would be entitled to recover the $10,000, plus interest, plus costs and perhaps damages resulting from his not having the $10,000 available. The bank, if it had used outside counsel, might possibly recover from them the losses it sustained as a result of counsel's negligence in not making these distinctions known.

Example Number Four

Let's now assume that I.M. Noble, instead of trying to surprise D. Linquent, calls him immediately after he wires the funds to assure him that help is on its way. Suppose that D. Linquent, realizing the danger to his money, gets up bright and early the next day and runs to the bank to await its arrival. Suppose further that the bank itself was having problems with the IRS over some deductions it had taken on some prior returns which were then under audit. Further assume that to win points with the IRS, the bank's manager, Ima Snitcher, calls Greb and tells him about the new money now in D. Linquent's account, while also reminding Greb of the bank's current problems with the IRS. Let's further assume that in that conversation, Snitcher gives every indication of being fully cognizant of the fact that the bank was under no obligation to turn any of this money over to the IRS, since it was never presented with any Notice that could reach it. Let's cut in on this conversation when Ima is saying...

"Look, D. Linquent is at the bank right now and insisting that we give him his money, but we can stall under some pretext until you get over here with a new Notice, okay?"

"Be there as soon as I can," Greb replies.

"And you will mention this to Frank N. Stein who is now auditing us, won't you?", Snitcher queries.

"I'll arrange to have lunch with him tomorrow," assures Greb. So in this manner Ima Snitcher and Greb DeMonay steal all of D. Linquent's money, since they both have something to gain from this conspiracy.

Obviously, if D. Linquent could prove that the above conversation took place, not only would he be entitled to get back his $10,000 plus costs and interest and substantial punitive damages, but Snitcher and DeMonay would be eligible to be indicted (under a number of state and federal criminal statutes) for embezzlement and other crimes.

After Greb shows up at the bank with that new Notice, and Snitcher sorrowfully explains to D. Linquent that under the circumstances the bank has no choice but to turn over the $10,000 to him, what can D. Linquent do besides tear his hair out? Sue the bank? Sue the government? First of all, before he could sue the government he would first have to make application for a refund. (See Chapter 10). But before he could do that he would first have to pay up all the money the government claims is owed for the year or years in question. Let's suppose that for the year at issue, the government claims that D. Linquent owes it $16,789.36— $483 in taxes and $16,306.36 in added penalties and interest. Since the government got only $679 for his car and $53.00 for a pair of andirons and a portable TV that were in the trunk, this only comes to $10,732 which still leaves a balance of $5,574.36 he would have to pay before he could claim a refund and then sue if his refund claim were denied. He could sue the bank, but how would he know that he was hiring a lawyer who knew what he was doing. And how would he prove his case? He has no proof that the conversation between Greb and Ima ever took place. Besides where would he get the money to pay a lawyer. He still has some family heirlooms, but because of sentimental value he refuses to part with them. Though actually broke, he still can't make a deal with the IRS. Besides if he sued the bank, chances are it would be thrown out of court by some federal judge who would rule that the bank had no choice, under the law, but to turn over his money to the government.

There is no doubt that situations containing one or more or all of the above elements occur every day in America between the IRS, third parties and a victimized public. My experience was somewhat similar to that portrayed in the last example. In my case a major U.S. corporation conspired openly with the IRS (but unlike D. Linquent, I have the actual proof) to rob me of $204,303.25. In stealing this money from me, this corporation violated our contract and the assurances it had given me to my financial detriment. Also, two federal courts protected this corporate scoundrel from having to make financial restitution to me. Before we examine the facts in my case, please verify for yourself that Treasury Regulation 301.6331-1(a) covers a continuous levy (Notes B and C) in the manner I have just described.

STEALING MONEY FOR UNCLE SAM

On April 29, 1982 I contracted with Simon & Schuster, a division of Gulf & Western Corporation, one of the nation's largest publishers, to take over the distribution of *How Anyone Can Stop Paying Income Taxes.* That book, which was released on February 2, 1982, sold out its first printing of 30,000 copies in nine weeks and became a national best seller before Simon & Schuster (S & S) ever took over its distribution.

For distributing the book (largely through book stores, since Freedom Books continued making mail order sales directly to the public), S & S was to receive 25 percent of gross receipts and was to turn the rest over to me. However, before S & S determined the amount actually due, the receipts were to be subject to a discount formula, designed to protect S & S from book returns. An example of how this worked is shown in Figure 7-16. In return, I was responsible for supplying all the books and paying all promotional expenses. This included substantial outlays for such things as advertising, publicity agents and the expense involved in media tours.

A fairly comprehensive account of the swindle perpetrated by S & S in cooperation with the government is provided in letter (Figure 7-17) sent by S & S's Assistant General Counsel Karen R. Mayer, to Robert Percy, Esq., District Counsel of the IRS on November 28, 1983. Figure 7-18 will verify that during this period, S & S only received three Notices of Levy; one on May 23, one on December 2 and the last one, on December 27.

As noted in paragraphs 2 and 3 of that letter, on May 3, 1983 I transferred my interest in my contract with S & S, to Howy Murzin who co-authored the book. So, when S & S received its first Notice of Levy on May 23, 1983, they owed me nothing as of that date. This would have been true *even if I hadn't transferred my interest to Mr. Murzin.* Because S & S paid me on a monthly basis, and as of that date S & S was current, they owed me nothing. The next "determination" of monies due me (actually due Mr. Murzin) would not have occurred until May 31 (the last day of the month) and that amount would have been paid to Mr. Murzin the following week.

So, on the date that S & S received the Notice of Levy, no money was owed to either Mr. Murzin or myself, regardless of whether or not I had assigned away my interest. Assuming that I had never assigned my interest, it would still have been possible for S & S to continue making

FIGURE 7-16

SIMON & SCHUSTER
DISTRIBUTION AGREEMENT
FREEDOM BOOKS
ACCOUNTING REPORT MONTH OF MARCH 1983
HOW ANYONE CAN STOP PAYING INCOME TAX

	SALES UNITS	SALES DOLLARS	RETURNS UNITS	RETURNS DOLLARS	NET SALES UNITS	NET SALES DOLLARS
46082	6,385	$36,802	1,134	$6,378	5,251	$30,424.00
30374	-	-	3	17	(3)	(17.00)
	6,385	36,802	1,137	6,395	5,248	30,407.00

Less: Distribution Fee - 25% Net Sales ($30,424.00)   7,606.00
      Returns & Handling Fee @.10¢ per copy (1,137)   113.70
      Promotional Copies @ .10¢ per copy   .20
      Unreimbursed Transportation   -0-
      Advertising & Promotion Publicity   -0-
      Stickering @ .03 per copy   -0-
      Reserve for Returns - 35% Gross ($36,802.00   12,880.70   20,600.60

Balance   9,806.40

                        90 Days Due 60% 6/30/83   5,883.84
                        30 Days Due 20% 7/31/83   1,961.28
                        30 Days Due 20% 8/31/83   1,961.28
                                                            $9,806.40

FIGURE 7-17

RETURN RECEIPT REQUESTED

Simon & Schuster

Karen R. Mayer
Assistant General Counsel

November 28, 1983

Robert Percy, Esq.
District Counsel
Internal Revenue Service
Cotter Federal Building
135 High Street
Room 259
Hartford, CT 06103

RE: IRWIN SCHIFF

Dear Mr. Percy:

In further response to the Final Demand served upon
Simon & Schuster, Inc. on July 11, 1983, please be advised
of the following facts:

1. The IRS Notice of Levy (Form 668-A) was served on
May 26, 1983.

2. Prior to that date (on May 3, 1983), we were advised
by Mr. Schiff that he had assigned all his rights under the
distribution agreement dated as of April 29, 1982 to Howy
Murzin (Mr. Murzin notified us that he had assigned his
rights back to Mr. Schiff by letter dated July 20, 1983).

3. Based on our understanding that an effective assignment had preceded service of the Notice, our General Counsel,
Alexander Gigante, responded to the Notice of Levy by letter
dated June 6, 1983 stating that we held no property of Mr.
Schiff at the time we were served with the Notice.

4. Thereafter, we learned that on May 26, 1983 a check
for $4,467.00 had been issued to Mr. Schiff c/o Freedom
Books. This amount represented a release of the reserve for
returns that was being held against sales. We also learned
that on May 31, 1983 another check for $8,513.53 had been
issued to Mr. Schiff c/o Freedom Books. This amount represented amounts payable as of May 31, 1983 with respect to
sales of Mr. Schiff's book through January 1983. Neither of
these checks had been paid as of May 26, 1983, the date of
service of the Notice. The checks have since been voided.

5. Based on the fact that the two checks totaled
$12,980.53 and had not been paid to Schiff, Mr. Gigante sup-
plemented his letter of June 6, 1983 with another letter
dated June 15, 1983 advising the IRS that this money was due
to Schiff.

6. We were served with a Final Demand on July 11,
1983.

7. By letter dated July 13, 1983, I confirmed a telephone conversation with Mr. Holmberg (the Internal Revenue
Service officer assigned to collect Mr. Schiff's taxes) that
we would not comply with the Final Demand and that the IRS
would not invoke penalties against us as a result of our
decision.

8. The distribution agreement was terminated by mutual
agreement as of October 17, 1983.

9. On November 10, 1983, I received a phone call from
you concerning our failure to comply with the Final Demand
and requesting further information regarding the disposition
of monies payable to Schiff.

10. As a result of this conversation, we have now made
the following determinations:

(a) On May 31, 1983, $8,513.53 became payable
with respect to sales through January 1983. (The distribution
agreement provides for payments to be made on an installment
basis.)

(b) The total dollar amount attributable to sales
made through May 31, 1983 is $35,428.37. As noted above,
of this amount, $8,513.53 became payable on May 31, 1983
(after the Notice of Levy was received) and the remaining
$26,914.84 became payable thereafter.

(c) An additional $13,560 is attributable to
sales that have occurred since May 31, 1983 through October
31, 1983.

(d) Thus, at the present time, $48,988.37 remains
unpaid on Mr. Schiff's account.

(e) We have held and continue to hold a 35%
reserve against future returns equivalent in dollars to
$156,624. Mr. Schiff has taken the position that the reserve
is too high based on actual returns received. Obviously, a
portion of this reserve is attributable to sales prior to
service of the Notice and the remainder to sales after
service of the Notice.

(f) Although the IRS has taken a different view,
it has been our concern that the Notice of Levy served on
May 26, 1983 might not extend to monies earned from sales
after that date.

(g) It is also our view that turning over any
assets to the IRS without a court order, particularly in
light of the questions with respect to the assignment, even
unpaid amounts attributable to sales made before May 26,
1983, could subject us to unnecessary liability.

Although we do not believe that the existing Notice
applies to monies earned on sales after May 26, 1983, we
intend to initiate an interpleader action in New York in
order to secure a judicial determination with respect to all
funds held by us. However, before doing so, we will wait to
hear from you as to your position with respect to this
matter.

At this time, it seems appropriate to mention that we
have consistently taken an extremely conservative position
with respect to Mr. Schiff's account. No monies that may be
payable to the IRS have yet been paid to Mr. Schiff. Our
prudence in this regard has in fact protected assets that
otherwise might not have been available to the IRS.

Under these circumstances, including Mr. Holmberg's
assurances, we believe that all our actions have been proper.

I trust that I can count on your cooperation to ensure
that all parties' rights are adequately protected.

Sincerely,

Karen Mayer

uninterrupted monthly payments to me even in the face of a barrage of IRS Notices. This assumes, however, that I was dealing with a reliable and honorable firm, which, as events will show, Simon and Schuster is not. This could have been accomplished in a number of ways. For example: after truthfully telling the IRS that they were holding no money of mine on May 23, 1983, S & S could have *wired* me the money that became due on May 31, 1983, since those funds would not have been covered by the Notice they received on May 23.

What S & S Should Have Done

In order for S & S to have been "required" to turn over any of this money, they would have had to receive a new Notice between the time they "determined" what they owed me (i.e., when the amount due became "fixed and determinable" pursuant to Treas. Reg. 301.6331-1(a)[1]) and when they wired me those funds. The time involved could have been reduced to minutes if not seconds. Or S & S could have arranged to have a sufficient amount of cash on

---

FIGURE 7-18   - 2 -

    3.   The United States is producing copies of the following Notices of Levy which were used in aid of its efforts to collect the tax liability of Irwin A. Schiff for the years ending December 31, 1976, December 31, 1977, and December 31, 1978.

Date	Levy Source
May 18, 1983	Confederation Life Association
May 18, 1983	Bankers National Life Ins. Co.
May 18, 1983	United Life Accident Ins. Co.
May 18, 1983	Security Connecticut Life
May 18, 1983	National Benefit Life
May 18, 1983	Connecticut Casualty Co. a/k/a CNA Insurance
May 18, 1983	Massachusetts Mutual Life
May 18, 1983	Travelers Insurance Co.
May 18, 1983	The Old Security Life Ins. Co.
May 23, 1983	Simon & Schuster
May 23, 1983	American National Bank
December 2, 1983	Simon & Schuster
December 27, 1983	Simon & Schuster

Production of the foregoing documents is being accomplished by mailing copies thereof to the plaintiff as indicated on the attached Certificate of Service.

                          STANLEY A. TWARDY, JR.
                          United States Attorney

By: _____
                  JEREMIAH F. DONOVAN
                  Assistant United States Attorney

Deborah D. Meland
DEBORAH S. MELAND
Trial Attorney, Tax Division
U.S. Department of Justice
Post Office Box 55
Ben Franklin Station
Washington, D.C. 20044
Telephone: (FTS/202) 724-6549

6/0292-C

hand when it "determined" the amount owed me, and saw to it that it was immediately handed over to me personally (while I stood next to the calculator), or to a messenger sent by me. Even if a Notice of Levy did manage to slip through (which would have been near impossible) it still could only have affected one month's payment.

S & S would have been under no obligation to explain to the IRS when or how its "liability" to me became "fixed and determinable" or on what basis it was discharging that liability. All S & S was required to do, under the law, (hypothetically, of course) was to hand over to the government any money due me after the amount had been "determined" and before it was paid out—assuming it received a Notice of Levy in the interim. That's all they had to do under the "law", and nothing more. Now that you see how an honorable firm might have handled it, let's see what Simon and Schuster did.

You will note (as explained in paragraphs 2 and 3 of S & S's letter of November 28), that S & S's General Counsel, Alexander Gigante, correctly informed the IRS on June 6, 1983 that S & S "held no property of Mr. Schiff at the time we were served with the Notice." That, of course, should have ended the matter right then and there. Not only had S & S not made any "determination" as to what they might have owed me as of that date, but they also had in their possession an "effective assignment" of my interest. S & S had no legal obligation to question that assignment, and the law imposed no obligation (nor could it) on S & S to do so. That's all they had to tell the government. Case closed.

S & S should have simply continued making monthly payments pursuant to the terms of our contract and my assignment of that contract to Mr. Murzin. If the government believed that a fraudulent transfer had taken place to avoid the payment of income taxes, it was free under the law to proceed against Mr. Murzin or myself or both of us—but that was not a concern of S & S. It was now safely out of the picture.

But instead of honoring the terms of our contract and the assignment they had determined was "effective," S & S sent instead, the letter shown in Figure 7-19 to Mr. Murzin. Note that S & S wanted Mr. Murzin to "secure an indemnity bond or an irrevocable letter of credit." For what purpose? S & S, as of that date, had absolutely nothing at risk. The Notice they received had nothing to do with what it might owe Howy Murzin, only me. Clearly the IRS Notice posed no problem that required such a costly bond or letter from Howy. But even if there had been some exposure, it would only have been for an amount coming due between May 1 and May 23. So, what was the $100,000 supposed to protect? Apparently S & S wanted protection

with respect to *possible future payments*. But, no Notice of Levy or payments pursuant to such Notices had ever been received or made! So S & S's high-powered legal department wanted Howy to purchase a very costly indemnity bond which, at that point, could only have "indemnified" them against nothing! Since my relations wth S & S had always been good, and since we were even talking about their distributing or publishing a few other books of mine, I allowed such considerations to cloud my thinking concerning the need for such a bond and/or letter of credit. Despite my doubts, Howy and I actually tried to get the bond or the letter of credit. However, we found that neither was available to cover such a contingency, and even if there were, the cost of such would have been prohibitive.

FIGURE 7-19

Simon&Schuster

Karen R. Mayer
Assistant General Counsel
June 7, 1983

Mr. Howy Murzin
1153 SW First Way
Deerfield Beach, FL 33441

RE: HOW ANYONE CAN STOP PAYING INCOME TAXES
By Irwin Schiff with Howy Murzin

Dear Mr. Murzin:

As you are no doubt aware, Mr. Schiff has notified us that he has assigned his right to receive distribution fees in connection with the above book to you. A copy of the notice is enclosed. (We are still waiting to receive a replacement notice that corrects certain inadvertent errors in the original.) Since the execution of this notice, we have been served with a Notice of Levy for Mr. Schiff by the IRS.

Please be advised that we will not make any payments to you under the asssignment referred to in the enclosed notice unless and until you provide us with a complete indemnification and an indemnity bond or letter of credit as provided below.

Your signature in the space below shall confirm your agreement to indemnify Simon & Schuster, Inc., its parent, affiliates, subsidiaries or divisions against any tax, interest or penalties which Simon & Schuster, Inc., its parent, affiliates, subsidiaries or divisions might be responsible for as a result of payments made to you pursuant to the enclosed notice or any similar notice.

To secure your obligation hereunder, you shall within 10 business days hereof obtain an indemnity bond or an irrevocable letter of credit in the amount of $100,000 in favor of Simon & Schuster, Inc. We shall have the right to approve the terms and conditions of the indemnity bond or letter of credit. We shall have the additional right in our sole discretion to require an increase in the amount of the indemnity bond or letter of credit and to withhold future payments until such increased bond or letter has been secured to our satisfaction.

I look forward to receiving an executed copy of this letter at your earliest convenience.

Sincerely,

Karen Mayer

AGREED AND ACCEPTED:

_____
Howy Murzin
enc.
cc: Irwin Schiff

How Is The Public To Know?

At this point, you must understand, dear reader, that you know far more about Notices of Levy than I did in the summer of 1983. So, while all of this undoubtedly seems rather cut and dried to you—as indeed it is, in the summer of 1983 this was still new to me and I did not have anyone to explain it to me as I have explained it to you. At that time I was also laboring under the ludicrous belief that all of the lawyers involved in this matter, including my own, actually knew what they were doing. Naturally, when the fancy legal department of a multi-million dollar corporation tells you that in this situation, it needs a $100,000 indemnity bond, and when your own lawyer doesn't tell you differently, you think, maybe there's something to it.

In my own defense I should also point out that, at that time, practically all of my concentration was directed toward trying to finish two books that I wanted to get out in time for the forthcoming tax season, now only five months away. (I succeeded with *The Social Security Swindle* which came out in January 1983). I was also engaged in writing and publishing the 16 page *Schiff Report,* which came out eight times a year, not to mention overseeing an insurance business and promoting my other three books. Given this schedule, I didn't really devote as much time as I should have to analyzing the situation with S & S. Another disarming factor was S & S's assurance that they would not turn over any money to the IRS without a court order. Based on that, I did not feel that I was in any immediate danger of losing that money.

While my primary assumption at that time, as to why S & S was not legally required to turn over any money, was based on my recognition of the Notice's fraudulent character; federal courts still treated the document as if it were legitimate. And since "establishment lawyers" are more concerned with what courts say than what the law does, my representations to S & S along these lines were less than totally persuasive. Still, I made some impact since S & S did not initially turn over any money to the IRS—but they **weren't turning over any money to me either.** In retrospect, I believe I would have had more success with S & S if I had merely concentrated on Code Sections 6331(b) and (c) rather than on (a). However, because I saw the very regulation that would have clarified this as being fraudulent, I didn't even bother reading beyond Note A! This regulation would have clearly explained to S & S's legal department why it could have ignored the Notice of Levy—even if it were valid—on other grounds. But, because of the newness of this subject to me, my work load, and my reliance on what lawyers around me were saying, I didn't see the situation with the same clarity with which I perceive it now. And few laymen, I suspect, would have seen it any differently.

Worthless Assurances From S & S

Karen Mayer, S & S's Assistant General Counsel, continued to assure me that all monies due either Howy or myself would be placed in a segregated, interest-bearing account, pending a determination by a court. I was told, on more than one occasion, that the IRS had been apprised of S & S's determination to do nothing without a court order, and that the IRS had accepted this position. How could the IRS have done otherwise, since this is exactly what is stated in its *Legal Reference Guide* (paragraph 334.2)?

Written confirmation of these assurances can be found in letters sent by Miss Mayer to the IRS on July 13, 1983 (Figure 7-20), in a letter to me on August 24, 1983 (Figure 7-21), in a letter from the IRS to S & S dated October 6, 1983 (Figure 7-22), and in a letter S & S sent to my lawyer on October 19, 1983 (Figure 7-23). The IRS' letter of October 6 indicates that the IRS had absolutely no expectation of getting any money from S & S without a court order and that S & S was in no danger of incurring any penalties for taking that position. This understanding by S & S is clearly reflected in their letter to James Holmberg on July 13 and as confirmed in paragraph 7 of their letter to the IRS on November 28.

Thus it is crystal clear that as late as November 28, 1983, some six months after it first received the Notice of Levy and four months after getting a "Final Demand," S & S knew they were under no legal order to turn over any funds to the IRS. This overlooks the five months of receipts that they were still holding (all examples of after acquired property) that they could have turned over to me, pursuant to Sections 6331(b) and (c), without any fear whatsoever. So, all subsequent claims made by S & S in connection with my eventual lawsuit, that they were required to turn over $204,000.00 to the goverment, were pure rubbish.

A DUMB MOVE

Because neither Mr. Murzin nor myself were getting any money from immediate book store sales (since all such receipts were now being held by S & S), we decided to terminate our contract with them and distribute the book ourselves. Also, relying on S & S's word to await a court order, and, believing that I was in a better position to handle such litigation than was Mr. Murzin, he assigned his interest back to me! This shows you how much faith we had in our legal position! We were so convinced that in any court suit we could prove that (1) I was not liable for any income taxes, and (2) the Notice of Levy was not compelling on S & S, that we were willing to put the entire amount on the line by placing it back in my name *even in the face of the IRS' threat!* We did this only because *we had been assured by Simon and Schuster that it would only turn over the money to*

FIGURE 7-20

Simon&Schuster

Karen R. Mayer
Assistant General Counsel
July 13, 1983

Mr. James Holmberg
Revenue Officer
150 Court Street
Room 205
New Haven, CT 06510

RE: IRWIN SCHIFF

Dear Mr. Holmberg:

This will confirm our telephone conversations of July 11 and July 13 following service of the IRS Final Demand. As discussed, Simon & Schuster is a disinterested stakeholder and does not wish to incur liability to any party as the result of improper payments to either the IRS or Irwin Schiff. Accordingly, we have elected not to comply with the Final Demand and will await a court order advising us (i) whether any property was owing to Mr. Schiff at the time of service of the Notice of Levy and (ii) if so, the proper disposition of such property.

As discussed, our decision to await a court order is by no means an attempt to evade our legal responsibilities. Further, you have assured me that the IRS fully understands our position and will not invoke any penalty provisions, such as the 50% penalty referred to in Section 6332 of the Internal Revenue Code, as a result of our failure to comply with the Final Demand.

Thank you for your cooperation in this matter.

Sincerely,

cc: Irwin Schiff
     Alexander Gigante

FIGURE 7-21

Simon&Schuster

Karen R. Mayer
Assistant General Counsel
August 24, 1983

Mr. Irwin Schiff
Freedom Books
P. O. Box 5303
Hamden, CT 06518

Dear Irwin:

Steve Dorsky asked me to answer your letter of August 4.

As you know, we have taken a conservative position with respect to the IRS Notice of Levy and have decided not to release any monies that may be payable to you in connection with our distribution of HOW ANYONE CAN STOP PAYING INCOME TAXES except under court order. While this decision is obviously holding up your receipt of money, it has not, to my knowledge interfered with normal distribution of your book. We, therefore, do not believe that we have breached our agreement with you as a result of what we consider to be a prudent response to the IRS Notice.

If you wish to seek another distributor or publisher for your next two books or the paperback edition of HOW ANYONE CAN STOP PAYING INCOME TAXES, you are free to do so since we have elected not to exercise our options under paragraphs 11 through 13 of our distribution agreement dated as of April 29, 1982.

On a related matter, you asked me to provide you with information regarding the status of your account. I am advised that as of August 31, 1983, $34,306.03 will be payable to you in connection with HOW ANYONE CAN STOP PAYING INCOME TAXES. This money is being held as part of our general business accounts, in keeping with our customary accounting practices.

Sincerely,

cc: Steve Dorsky

FIGURE 7-22

Internal Revenue Service

District Director

Department of the Treasury
150 Court Street Room 205
New Haven, Connecticut 06510

Person to Contact:
J. Holmberg
Telephone Number:
(203) 773-2053
Refer Reply to:

Simon & Schuster, Inc.
c/o Simon & Schuster Building
1230 Avenue of the Americas
New York, New York 10020

ATTN: Karen Mayer

Date:
October 6, 1983

Dear Ms. Mayer:

This letter will confirm our conversation of September 29, 1983 regarding Irwin Schiff. A Notice of Levy, Form 668-A, and attested copy of the Federal Tax Lien, Form 668, were served upon Simon & Schuster on May 26, 1983, to attach to funds held as of that time or in the future belonging to Irwin A. Schiff of Hamden, Connecticut. These documents were served with Alexander Gigante, Vice President and General Counsel and receipted by him. My understanding is that funds are being held by Simon & Schuster in this regard and will be held until the question of payment of these funds is decided by the courts.

In question at this time is the disposition of a quantity of books written by Mr. Schiff and currently in the possession of Simon & Schuster. It was not the intention of the Service to attach to these books and, in fact, a notice of seizure would be required to take possession of these assets. The Service makes no claims against these books and they may be distributed in any way mutually agreeable between Mr. Schiff and Simon & Schuster.

If there are any further questions in this regard, please feel free to contact me.

James Holmberg
Revenue Officer

cc: I. Schiff

FIGURE 7-23

Simon&Schuster

Karen R. Mayer
Assistant General Counsel

October 19, 1983

Esq.

RE: HOW ANYONE CAN STOP PAYING INCOME TAXES by Irwin Schiff

Dear Mr.

In response to your letter of October 11, 1983 and in an effort to resolve amicably the dispute that has arisen between Mr. Schiff and us, this will confirm that our distribution agreement for the above book will terminate on October 17, 1983. Please be advised that our acknowledgement of this termination does not constitute an admission that we have breached the agreement in any respect. In accordance with paragraph 6(a) the representations and warranties contained in the distribution agreement survive termination.

To respond to the other matters raised in your letter, I have authorized all unsold books to be shipped to Freedom Books. They should be shipped (freight collect) by the end of this week or the beginning of next. All unfulfilled orders will be forwarded to Mr. Schiff. And all future returns will be forwarded to Mr. Schiff freight collect. Mr. Schiff will be responsible for stickering all books to reduce returns to S&S.

Our accounting department is reviewing your question concerning the reserve for returns and I will provide a response soon. Finally, as stated in my letter of October 13, I have instructed our accounting department to establish a separate, interest-bearing account. Because of the difficulty of establishing an escrow account, the account will be in our name but will be segregated. I will, in addition, instruct our accounting department to make monthly reports to you on behalf of Mr. Schiff.

Please indicate your acceptance of the foregoing on behalf of Mr. Schiff by signing this letter in duplicate in the space provided.

Sincerely,

Karen Mayer

ACCEPTED AND AGREED:

the IRS pursuant to a court determination! That shows you how incredibly naive (or stupid) we were. We actually believed *we could trust Simon and Schuster*—and/or get tax justice in a federal court. Unfolding events proved us wrong on both counts.

S & S Changes Its Position

It is amazing the change that came over S & S once it ceased making money on our book. Suddenly it believed that it was not only obligated to turn over all our money to the government without a court order but that it was further obligated to give the government complete details concerning how and when this money would become due and payable! Note that paragraph 9 (Figure 7-17) refers to a conversation that took place approximately three weeks after we terminated our distribution agreement. I don't know what else was said in that conversation, but S & S was obviously agreeable to helping the government steal all of our money.

Note paragraph 10(d) in which Miss Mayer states, "at the present time, $48,988.37 remains unpaid on Mr. Schiff's account." All of this, of course, became payable *after the Notice of Levy was received* and was thus payable to me *as of the date of her letter.* Incredibly, Miss Mayer even admits this, (paragraph 10(b)) "this amount [$8,513.53] became payable on May 31, 1983" or 8 days **after** the Notice was received! As you can see, every bit of that $48,988.37 had been "determined" as becoming due either on May 31, 1983 or later! Thus, based upon this very admission, S & S was *contractually obligated to send that entire $48,988.37 to Mr. Murzin or myself. But, S & S was determined to steal this money in order to curry favor with the IRS. This is made plain in the second paragraph. Here, Simon and Schuster's thievery is openly admitted.* **Its culpability can not even be disputed.**

LARCENY—CLEAR CUT!

Also note paragraph 10(e) in which Miss Mayer admits that the reserve I had been complaining about was *indeed too high.* It should have been lowered and the funds released to me. Note that S & S had an option to "determine" when to release those funds. Any reputable firm would have exercised that option only when *no Notice of Levy was applicable*, and would have immediately dispatched the money to me. But not an untrustworthy and disreputable company like Simon and Schuster. *They went so far as to ask the IRS to send them a new Notice to cover the reserve that would be released!* (last paragraph S & S letter of December 22, 1983 (Figure 7-24). That paragraph *alone* contains enough information (especially when combined with other admissions) to have earned for both Robert Percy and Karen Mayer, indictments for conspiring to embezzle.

Further note the revealing comments contained in paragraph 10(f) (Figure 7-17). This paragraph reveals that it had been S & S's "concern" not to "extend monies earned" after "the Notice of Levy served on May 23, 1983" and that the IRS had "taken a different view." This indicates that S & S realized that they were considering turning over our funds in violation of Sections 6303(b) and (c), but what is also extremely revealing is their comment about the IRS taking "a different view."

Here is concrete proof that the IRS knowingly tries to intimidate third parties into handing over property in violation of Code sections 6331(b) and (c)! And, if the IRS attempts this when they are dealing with supposedly sophisticated in-house counsel of a major corporation, you can imagine the extortion they practice when they deal with lay members of the public!

So, instead of protecting assets which Simon and Schuster was contractually and morally obligated to do and paying them out to their rightful owners, S & S elected instead to protect them for the benefit of the government! (third paragraph, at Note A). Pursuant to what law did S & S think they had such an obligation? Such is the power of the IRS to make major U.S. corporations bow, bend, grovel and scrape—literally turning them into common thieves and hoods. This illustrates why **the IRS must not be permitted to go after assets in the hands of third parties without bona fide court orders. Third parties are simply too prone to turn over assets** (which don't belong to them but which have been entrusted to their care) to the IRS even when they know they don't have to, simply *because they are fearful of the IRS due to their own tax vulnerability.* This is why the term "Gestapo" appropriately describes the IRS. It is continually exerting *illegal pressure* for the benefit of the government! How ludicrous can a situation be?[11]

Shortly after their letter of November 28, on December 2, 1982, S & S got their second Notice of Levy. On December 22, in violation of all their promises to me and Howy (on which we had relied), S & S turned over $34,974 to the IRS even though it had received no court order to do so, and when all such funds were clearly payable to either Howy or myself before S & S got its second notice. This is admitted in paragraphs 1 and 2 of that letter (Fig. 7-24). In the next paragraph S & S even admits that it intends to make payment of funds to the IRS "that would otherwise have fallen due to the taxpayer." Such is the power of the IRS to turn people, who perceive of themselves as being law abiding, upright and honorable, into downright thieves! Miss Mayer even tells the IRS that she intends to send them "a schedule indicating the amounts and dates of payments." Did Simon and Schuster have a tax problem that Miss Mayer was trying to solve with my money?

Note that in the fifth paragraph of that letter Miss Mayer states that S & S had "determined" that what they were holding "against future returns...should be reduced from 35% to 12-1/2%" and that such a determination was made "following the December 2 service of the Notice of Levy." So, admittedly, on the date that "determination" was made, that money belonged to me and not to the government! And, it should have been sent to me as called for by our contract!

This admission also proves that Simon and Schuster realized that they could not include this amount in the check sent to the IRS on December 22, 1983—since it was not subject to any Notice of Levy received before the "determination" was made. If they believed that they had such an obligation, they would have included that amount in the check sent on December 22. Miss Mayer even acknowledges this in her final paragraph wherein she says, "Because the determination to release this reserve was made **after the service of the Notice of Levy, we are unable to release this money to the IRS at this time.**" If the "money" could not have been released to the IRS "at (that) time" it means that the money was obviously mine and not theirs or the IRS'— **and should have been released to me!**

On the basis of this letter, if not on the basis of the letter of November 22 alone, my lawyer, who, at this time, was supposedly handling all of these matters for me, should have filed a restraining order to prevent S & S from turning over any more money. He should also have filed a restraining order as well, to enjoin them from giving the IRS any information in the absence of an IRS summons (pursuant to Section 7602) which I would have had an opportunity to quash. But, this is how the public is served by lawyers who generally don't know what they are doing when it comes to income taxes—and the IRS takes full advantage of this. On December 27, acting upon the information supplied to the IRS by Karen Mayer in her letter of December 22 (which actually requested a new Notice), the IRS sent S & S their third and final Notice. On December 30, 1983, in reponse to that Notice, Karen Mayer sent the government another $98,365 (Figure 7-25). Thus, on that date, Karen R. Mayer, acting for Simon & Schuster, openly embezzled another $98,365 from me on behalf of Uncle Sam.

TALK ABOUT HANDING OVER AFTER ACQUIRED PROPERTY!

On January 18, 1984 Miss Mayer, after keeping the IRS informed, sent them the letter shown in Figure 7-26.

On January 18, 1984 Miss Mayer sent the government a check for $14,031.

On February 28, 1984 Miss Mayer sent the IRS another

check for $4,670.

On April 11, 1984 Miss Mayer sent the IRS another check for $4,078.

And on May 15, 1984 Miss Mayer sent the IRS its final check in the amount of $46,185.25, together with a final statement covering my account (Figure 7-27 A & B).

Obviously all four payments represented after acquired property and represented additional amounts embezzled from me by Miss Mayer acting on behalf of S & S. It should be noted (as shown in their final statement) that Simon and Schuster earned $99,341 for distributing my book for 15 months. The $15,005.94 shown for "Advertising & Promotion" was what I had reimbursed S & S. This does

FIGURE 7-24

Simon&Schuster

REGISTERED EXPRESS MAIL
RETURN RECEIPT REQUESTED

Karen R. Mayer
Assistant General Counsel
December 22, 1983

Robert Percy, Esq.
District Counsel
Internal Revenue Service
Cotter Federal Building
135 High Street
Room 259
Hartford, CT 06103

RE: IRWIN SCHIFF

Dear Mr. Percy:

In response to the Final Demand served upon Simon & Schuster, Inc. on December 16, 1983, please find enclosed a check payable to the Internal Revenue Service in the amount of $34,974. This amount consists of:

1. $30,507 representing amounts attributable to sales prior to service of the Notice of Levy (December 2, 1983) and payable prior to the Levy; and

2. $4,467 representing a partial release of the reserve for returns which was made in May 1983 but was unpaid.

Please note that there is an additional $18,482 which is attributable to sales made prior to service of the Levy but which, pursuant to the terms of our distribution agreement with Irwin Schiff d/b/a Freedom Books dated as of April 29, 1982, is not payable until after service of the Levy. We intend to pay this amount to the IRS as it would otherwise have fallen due to the taxpayer. Within the next week or so, I will send you a schedule indicating the amounts and dates of payment.

Please be advised that following the December 2 service of the Notice of Levy, we determined that the reserve that we have been holding against future returns on Mr. Schiff's account should be reduced from 35% to 12½%. This determination was made on the basis of actual returns experience and in response to repeated requests from Mr. Schiff. Accordingly, we have authorized the release of $103,365 from the $152,157 reserve that we have been holding (the latter figure represents the $156,624 reserve we had been holding minus the $4,467 release of the reserve enclosed with this letter). Of the $103,365 release of reserve, $98,365 is currently due. However, because the determination to release this reserve was made after the service of the Notice of Levy, we are unable to release this money to the IRS at this time. Please note that of the remaining $53,792 reserve that we will be holding, $5,000 will be payable over the next five months. The remaining balance of $48,792 will be netted out against future returns at the time of the final accounting, pursuant to the terms of paragraph 5(b) of the distribution agreement. This final accounting will take place on May 1, 1984.

Sincerely,

Karen Mayer

FIGURE 7-25

Simon&Schuster

Karen R. Mayer
Assistant General Counsel
December 30, 1983

REGISTERED EXPRESS MAIL
RETURN RECEIPT REQUESTED

Robert Percy, Esq.
District Counsel
Internal Revenue Service
Cotter Federal Building
135 High Street
Room 259
Hartford, CT 06103

RE: IRWIN SCHIFF

Dear Mr. Percy:

In response to the Notice of Levy served on us on
December 27, 1983, enclosed please find a check for
$98,365, payable to the order of the Internal Revenue
Service.

Sincerely,

cc: Irwin Schiff

JAN   6 1984

FIGURE 7-26

Simon&Schuster

Karen R. Mayer
Assistant General Counsel
January 18, 1984

Robert Percy, Esq.
District Counsel
Internal Revenue Service
Cotter Federal Building
Room 259
Hartford, CT 06103

RE: IRWIN SCHIFF

Dear Mr. Percy:

As promised in my letter of December 22, 1983, the
following is a schedule of amounts and dates of payments due
Mr. Schiff:

          1/31/84 - $14,031
          2/25/84 - $ 4,670
          3/31/84 - $ 4,305

Please be advised that on or about January 31, 1984, we
expect to make payment of the $14,031 to the IRS. The two
remaining payments may be reduced somewhat if the 12½%
reserve that we are currently holding against returns proves
to be inadequate. The resultant amounts, if any, will be
paid to the IRS when they otherwise would have been paid to
Mr. Schiff. As mentioned in my letter of December 22, the
12½% reserve against returns will be netted out against
actual returns on May 1, 1984.

Please call if you have any questions.

Sincerely,

cc: Irwin Schiff

Simon&Schuster Inc.
Simon & Schuster Building
1230 Avenue of the Americas
New York NY 10020
212 245 6400

not take into account approximately $50,000 I directly spent in these areas, **nor the cost to me of writing and publishing the 67,482 copies that S & S sold.** To earn its $99,341, Simon & Schuster paid me $65,312 and patriotically stole another $204,303.25 from me, for the benefit of Uncle Sam.

I SUE

On January 5, 1984 my attorney sued Roscoe L. Egger, Jr., Commissioner of the Internal Revenue; Donald Regan, Secretary of the Treasury; James R. Quinn, District Director—IRS Connecticut; James Holmberg, IRS Revenue Officer, and Simon & Schuster. Discovering later that the suit against these federal employees was premature, they were subsequently dropped as defendants.

As against S & S, my attorney initialy raised the following issues in his complaint:

1. That pursuant to an agreement S & S was given an "exclusive right" to distribute my book.

2. That pursuant to that agreement S & S had agreed to distribute my book "throughout the United States" and collect the proceeds for my benefit "after deducting its fees, charges and expenses."

3. That it had on May 26, 1983 received a Notice of Levy which was made "pursuant to an illegal and fraudulent deficiency assessment."

4. That I had notified Simon & Schuster that said "Notice of Levy was illegal, fraudulent and unconstitutional as applied to [me]" and that Simon & Schuster, "agreed to hold all funds due [me] in an interest bearing account and not release the funds to the Internal Revenue Service without a court order."

5. That I had "relied upon such agreement to [my] detriment."

6. That despite such an agreement, S & S had "on or about December 22, 1983 released $34,974.00" to the IRS and "thereafter released a further sum of approximately $99,000."

7. That the money owed to me was released without prior notice to me and without my "permission or consent and without a court order."

8. That the actions of S & S constituted "a fraud practiced upon the plaintiff."

9. The actions of S & S constituted "a breach of its agreement with the plaintiff."

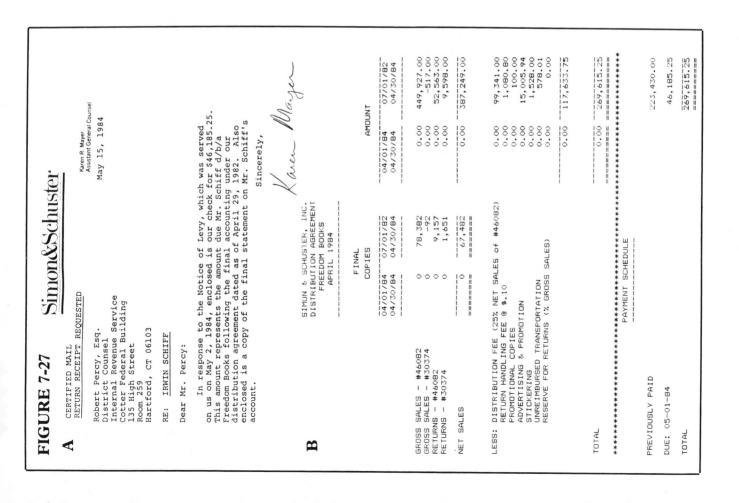

FIGURE 7-27

Simon & Schuster

A

CERTIFIED MAIL
RETURN RECEIPT REQUESTED

Karen R Mayer
Assistant General Counsel

May 15, 1984

Robert Percy, Esq.
District Counsel
Internal Revenue Service
Cotter Federal Building
135 High Street
Room 259
Hartford, CT 06103

RE: IRWIN SCHIFF

Dear Mr. Percy:

In response to the Notice of Levy, which was served on us on May 2, 1984, enclosed is our check for $46,185.25. This amount represents the amount due Mr. Schiff d/b/a Freedom Books following the final accounting under our distribution agreement dated as of April 29, 1982. Also enclosed is a copy of the final statement on Mr. Schiff's account.

Sincerely,

Karen Mayer

B

SIMON & SCHUSTER, INC.
DISTRIBUTION AGREEMENT
FREEDOM BOOKS
APRIL 1984

	FINAL COPIES		AMOUNT	
	04/01/84 07/01/82		04/01/84 07/01/82	
	04/30/84 04/30/84		04/30/84 04/30/84	
GROSS SALES - #46082	0	78,382	0.00	449,927.00
GROSS SALES - #30374	0	-92	0.00	-517.00
RETURNS - #46082	0	9,157	0.00	52,563.00
RETURNS - #30374	0	1,651	0.00	9,598.00
NET SALES	0	67,482	0.00	387,249.00
LESS: DISTRIBUTION FEE (25% NET SALES of #46082)			0.00	99,341.00
RETURN HANDLING FEE @ $.10			0.00	1,080.80
PROMOTIONAL COPIES			0.00	100.00
ADVERTISING & PROMOTION			0.00	15,005.94
STICKERING			0.00	1,528.00
UNREIMBURSED TRANSPORTATION			0.00	578.01
RESERVE FOR RETURNS (% GROSS SALES)			0.00	0.00
			0.00	117,633.75
TOTAL			0.00	269,615.25

PAYMENT SCHEDULE

PREVIOUSLY PAID	223,430.00
DUE: 05-01-84	46,185.25
TOTAL	269,615.25

Other issues, such as conspiracy to deprive me of certain constitutional rights was incorporated by reference. Unfortunately my attorney omitted raising one of the most important issues of all, that as of the day the initial Notice was received, the monies due me had actually been transferred to another party. He also neglected to clearly point out that all of the money subsequently turned over represented after acquired property, which S & S was not required to turn over on any basis.

S & S RESPONDS

On May 1, 1984 the law firm of Proskauer Rose Goetz & Mendelsohn representing S & S filed a Motion to Dismiss my lawsuit on the following grounds. It stated in its Memorandum of Law that:

"Nothing more substantial is alleged in the complaint than that [S&S] complied with an [IRS] levy. Since by law [S&S] was both compelled to honor the levy and discharged from liability to the delinquent taxpayer plaintiff, the complaint is absolutely barred."

The Memorandum then went on to set forth what were alleged to be the "FACTS," in this case, which can be summarized as follows:

1. "Plaintiff is a zealous tax protester, who in his campaign to have the Federal income tax declared unconstitutional, has long been engaged in protracted battle with the IRS. For many years he has apparently not filed tax returns. As described by Judge Gurfein in an opinion reversing, on an evidentiary ground, his 1979 conviction for income tax evasion, plaintiff is "an extremist who reserved the right to interpret the decision of the Supreme Court as he read them from the layman's point of view." *United States* v. *Schiff*, 612 F.2d 73, 75 (2d Cir. 1979).

   "In 1980, plaintiff was again found guilty of income tax evasion, *United States* v. *Schiff*, 647 F2d 163 (2nd Cir.) cert. denied, 454, U.S. 935 (1981). His subsequent attempt to sue the government counsel responsible for his prosecution failed, and attorney fees were awarded to the defendants. *Schiff* v. *United States*, Civil No-81-316 (d. Conn. 11/9/81) Burns, J.)

   "Undeterred by criminal conviction and adverse judicial determination, plaintiff continues his active defiance of the tax laws. In June, 1983, his complaint seeking to enjoin the IRS from collecting taxes assessed against him for 1976, 1977 and 1978 was dismissed. *Schiff* v. *United States*, Civil B-83-289 (D.

Conn. 6/27/83) (Burns, J.). The same assessment disputed in that action is the underlying subject of this complaint.

2. That in April 1982 I contracted with S & S to distribute my book pursuant to an agreement in which S & S was "obligated" to distribute the book and to deliver the proceeds to [me], after deducting its own fees, charges, and expenses."

3. That on May 26, 1983 the IRS "served on Simon & Schuster a *Notice of Levy*...(and)...beginning on December 22, 1983, Simon & Schuster complied with the levy." [emphasis added]

4. I had brought a law suit seeking $10 million in damages from four federal defendants and S & S.

5. That I had charged the four federal defendants with violating my constitutional rights by "seeking to enforce the income tax" improperly and unconstitutionally and sought to deprive me of certain other constitutional rights.

6. That I had charged that S & S "conspired with federal defendants to deprive [me of my] constitutional rights, breached a purported agreement not to honor the levy without a court order, and had defrauded me.

7. That in dismissing the federal defendants I had left S & S alone "to uphold the constitutionality of the federal income tax" as well as compelling it to justify "its own *compliance with the levy*." [emphasis added.]

It is clear that Proskauer Rose Goetz & Mendelsohn's introductory statement was entirely false, but I don't hold this against them. They were entitled to seek to win their case any way they could. And if this required misstating the law and the facts and hoodwinking their opponents and the court; well, that's what they were being paid to do. But this merely underscores what the public is up against. The government's illegal use of Notices of Levy permits, encourages, induces, and allows high powered and highly paid law firms to misstate both the facts and the law (before a sympathetic court) to the detriment and injury of members of the public who don't have or can't afford comparable counsel.

Turning specifically to its misstatements, it is clear that since the government pretends that a Notice of Levy and a "levy" are one and the same, Proskauer pretended the same thing! As you know, S & S never "complied" with any "levy," since no Notice of Seizure was ever given or used.

Nothing was "seized." S & S told the government everything it wanted to know and mailed it a stream of checks covering the funds it wanted.

The federal government didn't have to do anything more exhausting than slip three notices into three envelopes. So, S & S never "complied" with any "levy." Accordingly, their was nothing in the law that discharged it from "liability."

So, S & S was not "absolutely barred" from "liability" as was falsely claiming in that opening paragraph. The fact that S & S was not "compelled to honor the levy" is clear from all the correspondence between them and the IRS. In addition, since every penny it turned over to the IRS represented after acquired property, they were not "compelled" in any manner, shape or form to "honor the levy." So much for the accuracy of Proskauer's opening statement.

Now let's turn to the alleged "FACTS" it presented (I have numbered my comments to correspond to their above counterparts).

1. Proskauer's rendition of my previous battles with the IRS was obviously designed to remind the court that I had not been exactly a good boy when it came to federal income taxes, and that this should be considered—regardless of whether or not this had anything to do with the case and/or the law at hand. In seeking to influence the court in this manner, Proskauer made a number of false and hypocritical observations. For one thing, as of that date, I had never been found guilty of tax evasion. With respect to the claim that I was waging a "campaign to have the Federal income tax declared unconstitutional," I never waged such "campaign"—since my whole approach to the income tax is that it is *voluntary;* so why should I want (or need) to have such a "law" declared unconstitutional? But if I were so "engaged," certainly Proskauer's client, when it agreed to distribute a book entitled *How Anyone Can Stop Paying Income Taxes,* had joined me in that battle and received $100,000 for its trouble!

But, note further that in Proskauer's grand peroration of my court battles there is also a suggestion that I was involved in or sought to involve others in violations of tax law. What is so ironic about this is that before Simon & Schuster agreed to distribute my book, Al Reuben, then S & S's sales manager, told me that it would have to pass legal scrutiny. For all I know, besides submitting to its own own legal department, S & S might have also sought the opinion of outside counsel—which could have been this same Proskauer firm! In any case, I was told two weeks later, that the book had passed legal muster! For Proskauer to have taken this tack, when S & S had taken great pains to assure itself of the book's legal accuracy (and made $100,000

in doing so), took a lot of chutzpa. But what did they have to lose—they had no truthful defense, so lies and fraudulent claims were the only things at their disposal.

Another thing that should not be overlooked, is that even though S & S sold 67,482 copies of my book, not one copy, to my knowledge, was ever returned by someone claiming that the book did not deliver what the title promised. And when I terminated my contract, S & S would have been happy to have continued distributing the book!

Suppose someone sought to market a book entitled *How Anyone Can Flap Their Arms and Fly,* or *Eat As Much Food As You Want, And Lose Weight.* Don't you think such books would be returned to the book stores if they couldn't deliver on those promises? And, don't you think that reputable book stores and book chains would immediately stop stocking such books? But those titles are *no less probable* than mine which incredibly proclaimed that *Anyone Can Stop Paying Income Taxes!* Yet, to my knowledge, I never heard of one copy being returned because the book didn't deliver on its promise—and book stores and book chains kept reordering that book for years!

So, all of the claims and innuendos contained in those three paragraphs, besides being irrelevant, were false and hypercritical as well.

2. Here Proskauer admits that under our contract (which the government induced S & S to breach) S & S was "obliged...to deliver the proceeds" of my book to me, after "deducting its own fees, charges and expenses." Article 1, Sect. 10, Clause 6 of the Constitution specifically bars the States from passing any "law impairing the obligations of contracts." Obviously, the Founding Fathers recognized the sanctity of contracts, and didn't intend for the federal government to "impair such obligations" either; so they gave the federal government **no power to do so!** And, powers not given to the federal government (pursuant to the Ninth and Tenth Amendments and the rights "reserved" there under) **it doesn't have!**

Thus the federal government has no authority to interfere with such contract "obligations" **which the issuance of Notices of Levy to the public permits it to do.** Of course, the law itself isn't unconstitutional on this ground, because the *law itself doesn't give the government any such power!* What *is* unconstitutional is the Regulation that extended the law, and *the law's unconstitutional enforcement by the courts.*

3. Proskauer admits here that on May 26, S & S was "served [with] a Notice of Levy." So why didn't it simply say that S & S "complied with the Notice of Levy"? Because it was seeking the protection that the law allegedly provides

only with respect to levies, but not to Notices of Levy. So Proskauer resorted to some verbal sleight of hand to slip S & S out of one category and into the other.

6. We never claimed that S & S was liable because it complied with a "levy." We clearly claimed it was liable because *it complied with a "Notice of Levy" which it was under no obligation to honor.* So here again Proskauer fraudulently (but in the interest of its client)[12] misstates the nature of my complaint.

7. And finally Proskauer grandiosely claims that S & S was left with the awesome responsibility of "uphold(ing) the constitutionality of the federal income tax" for which the court was obviously expected (and invited) to lend it a helping hand. (It did) In addition, S & S reminded the court that the government's ability to use Notices of Levy in this manner, was also at risk. This was Proskauer's not so subtle way of reminding the court that if it allowed this matter to go to a jury trial (which was my right), the federal government might well lose its ability to continue embezzling money with Notices of Levy.

To support these arguments Proskauer simply made additional false statements and/or cited cases that either did not apply or were themselves violative of applicable statutes. Typical were the following. "The person in possession of property upon which a levy has been made has only two defenses etc., etc." and "There can be no dispute that Simon & Schuster was bound to comply with the levy." First of all no "levy had been made" and S & S had already been assured by the IRS that they didn't have to turn over any property until the matter was decided by a court. So, all such allegedly supporting statements by Proskauer were merely shams. As far as S & S' agreement not to turn over property without a court order was concerned, Proskauer said, "Supposing...such an agreement was made...the purported agreement is contrary to law and therefore is clearly unenforceable." Such a claim was nonsense. Such an agreement was not "contrary to law" as the IRS' Legal Reference Guide makes clear, and it had been accepted by the IRS. Proskauer also sought to make the point that if I did not owe any taxes, I could always sue the government for a refund—which, of course, I proceeded to do. But, the difference is, I can't collect substantial damages for breach of contract against the government, which a jury might have awarded me against Simon & Schuster.

S & S Appeals To The Courts

But, the real reason that Proskauer believed that it could get away with all of its irrelevant and false claims is reflected in this representation to the court:

"If plaintiff's complaint states a claim upon which relief can be granted, it would follow that every recipient of a levy would be exposed to litigation for honoring the levy...There is no allegation in Mr. Schiff's complaint that could not be made by any and every taxpayer. To uphold this complaint would thus pose a serious danger to the effective [i.e. illegal] enforcement of the tax laws."

While my suit obviously involved numerous elements that would not have been available to "every taxpayer," still this was Proskauer's way of telling the court "damn the facts, if you don't find for us on this Motion to Dismiss, you will be endangering the government's continued ability to extort income taxes!" Obviously Proskauer found a sympathetic ear in court.

While significant material was omitted by my attorney in his initial complaint (while also obscuring the most important issues with relatively unimportant ones) these omissions were largely corrected in his Response to S & S's Motion to Dismiss and in a Supplement thereto. And, while my attorney could have focused far more effectively on the issues he did raise, he still raised enough of them to have at least gotten me before a jury.

In response to the Motion to Dismiss, we now raised or expanded on the following issues (as well as raising some others);

1. That S & S's General Counsel had notified the IRS (paragraph 5, Figure 7-17 letter of November 28) that as of the date of the Notice, only $12,980 "was due and owing." While this representation was somewhat inaccurate (since earlier Mr. Gigante had notified S & S that no money was owed to me and if any money was so owed as of that date, it was owed to Howy Murzin, and not to me), this representation makes the point that all monies turned over by S & S **in excess of this amount, had to represent after acquired property,** which was not subject to the initial Notice.

2. That I had notified S & S that the attempted seizure of my funds by the IRS was (as you know it to be) "illegal and improper," and on the basis of conversations between Karen Mayer and the IRS, I had been assured by S & S that they would "await a court order prior to turning over" any funds and that I had relied on this promise.

3. That on Janury 18, 1984 S & S "issued a schedule of amounts to be due to the Plaintiff in the future [but S & S] was under no obligation to issue such a schedule." [While this was true, my attorney should

have made the added point, that such disclosures violated my rights under Code Section 7602 and related sections].

4. That the above actions of S & S constituted "a breach of the confidential relationship which existed, that payments would be deferred until" a court order was issued. [Such disclosures by S & S represented a breach of confidentiality even if the other promise was not made.]

5. Such payments by S & S "before a judicial determination...denied [me] the benefits of [my] contractual expectations and [my] right to due process of law."

6. That had S & S really believed that they had a duty to turn over any money pursuant to a Notice of Levy they would have done so "immediately after service...and in the absence of a Court order." They therefore assumed the risks of such "questionable acts...[and]...the risk of liability to the plaintiff."

7. That S & S had turned over property in violation of the prohibition against a continuous levy—accepted only by section 6331(e)(1) which provides for an exception only for wages.

8. That "A Notice of Levy is Not a Levy," and appropriate case law was cited and Forms 668-A and 668-B were submitted as an exhibit to the court to make this point even clearer.

9. That "no levy could have been made because no Notice of Seizure was even given"; and case law and Section 6335(a) were specifically quoted to establish this point.

10. That "Treasury Regulation 301.6331-1(a)(1) that allows for the seizure of property based solely upon a mere Notice of Levy" conflicted with the "plain language of the statute," while regulations "are only valid to the extent that they harmonize" with such language.

11. That "since no levy on the plaintiff's property could have arisen from a Notice of Levy [S & S] cannot be held harmless for its actions."

12. That pursuant to our contract S & S "became an agent of "plaintiff" and extensive case law was presented showing that S & S breached such fiduciary duties as: "An agent is not permitted to assume two distinct and opposite characters in the same transaction—

acting for himself and pretending to act for his principal," *Canpagna* v. *U.S.*, 474 F. Supp. 573 and *Strong* v. *Strong*, 36 A 2d 410.

13. S & S "had a right...recognized by the IRS (see Holmberg letter) not to turn over the money until a court order...It voluntarily relinquished that right for no apparent reason and commenced a course of conduct of cooperation and assistance with the IRS to the detriment of the plaintiff, its principal."

14. That Section 332 of the Legal Reference Guide for Revenue Officers (as quoted to, and submitted in court) clearly provides for a court determination when a Notice of Levy is not "honored". This should have certainly put the court on notice that court determinations of the issues involved, where Notices of Levy are used, are provided for in the IRS' own manuals. And additional case law was submitted to the court to support this view.

JUSTICE DENIED

On October 30, 1984 the Honorable Warren W. Edginton, a United States District Court Judge sitting in Bridgeport, Connecticut, granted S & S Motion and dismissed my law suit! Honorable Judge Edginton would not even let me into court to litigage any of the issues I raised! How could he do this, and why? His three line reason is appended to the bottom of S & S' motion—Figure 7-29. Note his reason! Since Simon & Schuster "has already paid levy, it has no further obligation to the plaintiff." That's it! No hearing! No jury trial! No nothing! How does that grab you? And all the while you thought that America was no banana republic! He claimed that his authority for this outrageous decision was the "case law" represented by *United States* v. *Augspurger*, 508 F. Supp. 327. If you check this case, you will discover that it involved a lower court decision concerning the legality of penalties that were added to an amount sought to be collected by "levy"—actually Notices of Levy.

It seems that the IRS had erroneously paid Charles H. Augspurger a tax refund of $61,080.62 prior to his death which it subsequently tried to collect from Mrs. Augspurter, the executrix of her husband's estate. All facts in this case were not presented in this decision, since two other decisions had preceded it.[13] Another defendant in the case was the investment banking firm of Loeb, Rhoades & Co. from whom the IRS was also seeking restitution, plus penalties. I assume that Loeb, Rhoades & Co. had acted as a trustee of estate assets and apparently both they and Mrs. Augspurger had refused to honor Notices of Levy which the United States subsequently sought to *reduce to judgment* by bringing a court action! As for Mrs. Augspurger, the court stated, "Plaintiff's motion for judgment, as against Augspurger, is unopposed by such defendant and accordingly will be granted." "Loeb's argument," as to why they refused to respond to the "levy" involved "two distinct components." "One is that the first and largest of the three penalty assessments against Augspurger that form the basis of plaintiff's levy against Loeb had been abated and that Loeb's liability is therefore limited to the sum of the two later assessments, or $41,773, plus interest." The other "component" involved the legality of the added penalty itself.

Thus the Augspurger case, on which Judge Edginton relied, had absolutely nothing to do with my case. That case involved the failure of *recipients* to honor Notices of Levy on the basis that *the underlying assessments were invalid*. It would be comparable only if S & S refused to honor the Notices because it challenged the underlying assessments and the government brought a court action to force it to do so. Augspurger had absolutely nothing to do with the absolute right of one private party to sue another for breach of contract!

In addition, **this very case alone proves that a Notice of Levy has to be reduced to judgment in order to be legally enforceable**—since that's precisely why the litigants in *Augspurger* were in court! Thus S & S' Motion to Dismiss this action on the grounds they raised, was totally baseless—as *Augspurger* itself proves! And, though the funds involved here were only 30% of those involved in my case, and the issues far fewer and less complex, it generated three court hearings and three published opinions—while my case generated **no hearings at all** and a three line dismissal! How's that for "Equal protection under the law"?

What the court ruled in *Augspurger* was as follows:

> The small number of decisions in which this issue has been raised consistently support this position by denying a person obliged to turn over funds under a tax lien the opportunity to argue that there was no legal basis for the imposition of the lien. The only defenses available to such person are that he did not have custody or control of property or rights belonging to the assessed taxpayer or that he had **"reasonable grounds" for refusing the levy.** (Numerous citings omitted and emphasis added.)

As you can see, the only issue addressed by *Augspurger* was whether a party "obliged to turn over property" could refuse to do so by claiming "that there was no legal basis" for the lien itself. In such a case the court, relying on "a small number of cases," said no. However, it then went on to add that there were defenses available to those who had **"reasonable grounds for refusing"** to comply with the Notice. (Note also how the court erroneously treated "levy" and "Notice of Levy" as one in the same). So, if one claims that one has "reasonable grounds" for "refusing" to comply with a "levy" (i.e. Notice of Levy) *Augspurger* stands for the proposition that one need not comply! And certainly S & S didn't have to comply! So, in granting a Motion for Dismissal, Judge Edginton relied on a case **that clearly established my right to go forward!**

Let me show you how one can be fooled by what one assumes words say rather than what they actually say. I had always assumed that what Judge Edginton had ruled was that since S & S was "required" to turn over the funds they had statutory protection and could not be sued for doing so. I believed that because (1) that was the basis of S & S' claim, and (2) that would have been the only legal or logical basis for granting it. It was not until I reread Edginton's "decision" in preparation for this chapter, did I realize that's not what he ruled at all! He didn't say S & S was absolved from liability because it was so "required." He only ruled that since Simon & Schuster had "already paid" a levy it had "no *further* obligation" to me. But I wasn't suing S & S in connection with any "further obligations." I was suing them on the basis that they had reneged and breached a "prior" obligation which caused me financial loss! What had any of S & S' "further obligations" to do with my lawsuit? Nothing! Such an erroneous claim had obviously been contrived by the court so as to *give the appearance* that the court was granting S & S' motion on the basis claimed—**when such was not the case at all!**

I had always assumed that the basic fraud in Edginton's three line "decision" was his claim that S & S "paid a levy" when he knew otherwise. But now I realize that the greater fraud was in his claim that only because Simon & Schuster had "already paid" the levy, the suit was being dismissed. What had the fact that it had "already paid" the levy have to do with dismissing my law suit, if in doing so S & S violated contractual obligations, their fiduciary duties owed to me as my agent, the law (as contained in Code Section 6331(b) and (c)), and their additional assurances given me that they would not turn over any money to the IRS without a court order? What are breach of contract suits for anyway? Presumably, Judge Edginton would have dismissed my lawsuit against S & S **regardless of anything S & S might have done**—so long as S & S had "already paid" the money to someone else! In your wildest dreams, could you have ever imagined that federal court decisions could rest on such fatuous logic?

So, in dismissing my law suit for breach of contract because the funds were "already paid," Judge Edginton not only threw out the window the very case on which he relied, but also out the window went: the "due process clause" of the Constitution; the laws as contained in Code Sections 6331(a), 6331(b), 6331(c), 6502(b); all laws governing agency and contracts; and, of course, all common sense. And this, mind you, is the same judge that's hearing my current refund suit against the government.

MY APPEAL

I don't want to continue beating a dead horse (since I believe you already have the picture) but I think the public should have a realistic picture of the hypocrisy and duplicity that extends even into the upper reaches of the federal judiciary. I believe it is important to review what happened when I appealed Edginton's decision. In my appeal to the Second Circuit, I could only raise issues that were raised in my initial complaint. With this in mind, these were the main issues I raised.[14]

1. The property surrendered was not property upon which a levy had been made.

2. No levy can arise from a mere Notice of Levy.

3. Assuming "arguendo" that a levy was made, successive levies were required to reach the property taken.

4. The IRS and Simon & Schuster acknowledged that a court order was required to obtain enforcement of the "levy."

Summarizing my proof with respect to (1) above, I included as exhibits the Notice of Seizure (shown in Figure 7-11) and page 58 from the *Legal Reference Guide For Revenue Officers* (Figure 7-9). The Notice of Seizure coupled with my quote of the entire Section 6502(b) (Figure 7-10) *proved that, by law, no levy had been made.* As I stated "Since no notice of seizure was given—no levy could have been made." What could be plainer or simpler than that? I also quoted Section 334.4 of the Guide in which the IRS admits that: "Service of notice of levy...is ineffective to reduce the property to possession." Quoting further from my appeal I pointed out to the Second Circuit that:

> The Internal Revenue did not comply with any of the requirements for a levy. To conclude then, that there was levy, is to engage in whimsical fantasy with a total disregard for the law...The Defendant is not a person who surrendered property upon which a levy was made and, therefore, does not lawfully enjoy the protection afforded by U.S.C. 6332(d).

In connection with point 2 (though there might be some overlapping with point 1) I quoted the entire Section

6331(a) and pointed out that the law specifically provided that Notices of Levy could only apply to the accrued wages and salary of federal employees, and that the application of elementary principles of statutory construction precluded the court from extending the law to any other property. So, there is no question that the Second Circuit now knew—if it didn't know it before—that *by law,* Notices of Levy only applied to the accrued wages and salaries of federal employees and *to nothing else!*

In connection with point 3 above, I quoted from Code Setions 6331(c) and (d)(1) as well as other sources to prove that after acquired property (requiring successive notices) had been involved. Summarizing my claim on this issue I stated:

> This section (6331(c)) requires successive levies to reach property not reached by a prior levy. Even the Levy and Notice of Levy forms...prove that successive levies are required as they state "all property...now in your possession and all money...owing from you to this taxpayer are levied upon."...Therefore, any money not in the third parties possession or that subsequently became owing was not attached by the levy and *a successive levy was required.*

> In spite of this requirement, Defendant continued to turn Plaintiff's property over to the Internal Revenue Service even though it...became owing, after demands were made by the serving of the notice of levy."

To support my claim under point 4 above, I included as exhibits the letters shown in Figures 7-19 through 7-25, in conjunction with which I quoted Section 334.2 of the *Guide* which states that, "In the event the Final Demand is not responded to, a suit will ordinarily be required to reach the property." My conclusion was summarized as follows:

> The above communications and reference materials show that the Defendant had a clear and accurate understanding of the law and in fact had an agreement with the Internal Revenue Service that a court order would be required before turning over Plaintiff's property. Rather than wait for a court order...they turned Plaintiff's property over to the Internal Revenue Service in spite of their obligation to the Plaintiff not to do so."

S & S's ANSWER

Simon and Schuster's Brief in Opposition revolved around two claims:

1. It claimed that its "compliance with a facially valid

notice of levy...exonerates it from liability...pursuant to 26 U.S.C. 6332(d)," and

2. The "plaintiff is precluded from raising on this appeal a claim not presented to the district court regarding property that came into Simon & Schuster's possession after it received a notice of levy."

To support its first claim, S & S simply restated all of the false arguments with which you are already familiar. For example, in stating that "Simon & Schuster was obligated to honor the notice of levy," they conveniently overlooked the letter they got from the IRS which clearly established it had no such obligation. S & S also noted in their Brief that Schiff:

> By spinning out his tangled distinctions between a levy...and a notice of levy...and his challenges to revenue regulations...Mr. Schiff would embroil Simon and Schuster in his own farfetched disputes with the IRS, and would force Simon & Schuster to undertake the burden of determining, at its peril, whether the IRS employed the proper forms to accomplish the levy.

First of all, these "distinctions" weren't *mine* and they weren't "tangled." They are clear and were derived from the law itself and from the IRS' own Guide for Revenue Officers. Secondly, Simon & Schuster did not have to determine anything "at its peril" since it could have simply awaited a court order as it had agreed to do. And thirdly, my argument didn't simply invoke the use of "proper forms," but concerned *two different kinds of summary procedures—* **one granting legal immunity, and another that didn't.** So all of Simon & Schuster's arguments were pure rubbish.

With respect to Simon & Schuster's agreement not to turn over funds to the IRS, its Brief noted that Schiff:

> Alleged merely that Simon & Schuster agreed not to release his funds to the IRS without a court order, implying that a contract was made between himself and Simon & Schuster. Not only would such an agreement to frustrate the IRS have been illegal...but Schiff alleged neither consideration to support the agreement nor compensable damage as a result of its supposed breach."

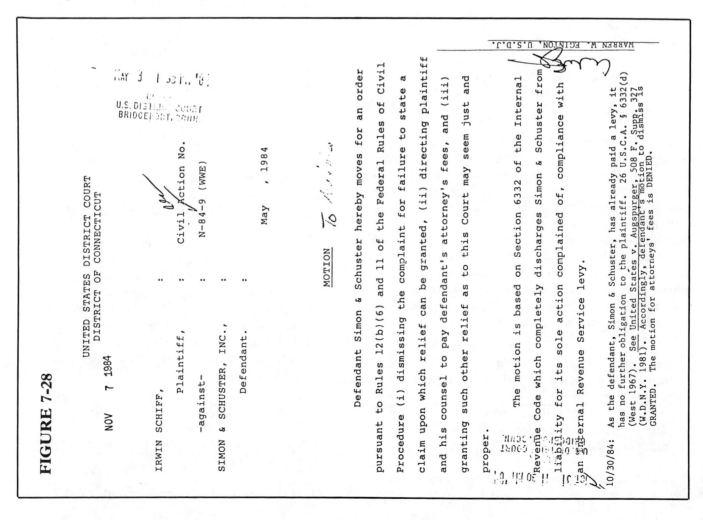

FIGURE 7-28

For one thing such an agreement (contract) was not illegal as the IRS letter of October 6, *The Guide for Revenue Officers* and *Augspurger* make clear. In addition, such an agreement is essential if recipients of such Notices want to avoid the "burden" and the "peril" to which Proskauer referred. As to the "consideration," this (as well as other arguments) was answered in my Reply Brief, while the "compensable damages" was what the jury was supposed to determine!

Since Simon & Schuster could not refute that a continuous levy had been used (and after acquired property handed over) it simply pretended that this argument had never been raised before.

> Mr. Schiff claims for the first time on this appeal that Simon & Schuster wrongfully turned over to the IRS funds owed to him that came into possession after the notice of levy was first issued...The point therefore is not before this court and should be disregarded.

While I will admit that I could have raised this issue more forcefully, it was nevertheless raised, as explained in my Reply Brief. **So this fundamental issue was never even addressed by Simon & Schuster in its Brief in Opposition!**

THE GOVERNMENT IS INVITED IN!

The Second Circuit also invited the United States Department of Justice to submit a brief in support of Simon & Schuster! The government's 19 page brief which was submitted by Glenn A. Archer, Jr., the Assistant Attorney General, also carried the names of four other members of the Justice Department: Michael L. Paup, William S. Estabrook and John A. Dudeck, Jr. from the Tax Division, and Alan H. Nevas, United States Attorney for Connecticut. The Justice Department's 19 page brief is simply (as you know it had to be) a conglomeration of lies, half-truths and fraudulent statements.[15]

What is amusing, is that the government sought to buttress its arguments by using as its authority (no less than three times!) Professor Saltzman's book, *IRS Practices and Procedure.*

Oral Argument

Oral argument was heard on June 5, 1985 before Chief Justice Wilfred Feinberg, and Circuit Court Judges Jon Newman and Thomas Meskill. Standing before this three judge panel, I held up a notice of seizure and pointed out that since it was never used in my case, **no levy, by law, could have been made.** I pointed this out in a manner that

those three judges could not fail to comprehend. "Unless there is a Notice of Seizure," I said and "there was no Notice of Seizure, there was no levy." I also read directly from the law itself (Section 6331(a) where a Notice of Levy was only made applicable to the accrued wages and salary of government employees and I also read directly from the *Guide for Revenue Officers.* I pointed out that the government never "seized" anything from S & S, that "Simon and Schuster would tell them when the money was due and then mail the check." I pointed out that if the government could legally get money from third parties that easily, why couldn't it just "use the telephone"?

While one only has ten minutes to argue on appeal, my presentation was further cut short by Judge Newman who wanted to know if I had paid a fine imposed upon me by the Second Circuit for filing an alleged "frivolous appeal" in connection with a previous appeal of a Tax Court decision. I hadn't, so the court asked that I give them a written explanation as to why, by the next day.[16]

But Judge Feinberg did ask a few good questions of Simon & Schuster's attorney on the issue of my "agreement" with S & S not to turn over any money to the IRS without a court order. "Ms. Schrag," he asked, "how could the district court judge decide the question of whether or not there was an agreement on a motion to dismiss, based on the pleadings?" He wouldn't of course, but Ms. Schrag's answer was that it was "Our position that there was no such agreement. However,...even if there were such an agreement," she said, "Section 6332 supersedes it."

HOW COURT DECISIONS ARE FABRICATED

The Second Circuit's two page decision is shown in Figure 7-29. As you can see, Judge Newman, who wrote the decision, misrepresented the issues he chose to address, and those he couldn't misrepresent **he simply ignored!** This is what happens when judges work from predetermined conclusions—they work backwards, eliminating and distorting as they go. Readers of this decision would hardly know of the distortions it contained or the issues it refused to address. Yet this is how "case law" is made!

Because Judge Newman's decision is so insidiously fraudulent, it deserves a little analysis. First of all note how Judge Newman pretends (picking up on Simon & Schuster's similar distortion, at Notes A and K) that the only issue I raised with respect to the Notice of Levy is that apparently the IRS *had used the wrong form!*—that "it had honored an improperly perfected levy" (note A), that I contended that because "the IRS, by using a "Notice of Levy" form rather than a 'Levy' form, did not properly

FIGURE 7-29

SCHIFF v. SIMON & SCHUSTER, INC.
Cite as 780 F.2d 210 (2nd Cir. 1985)

211

Irwin Schiff, Hamden, Conn., pro se.

Minna Schrag, New York City (Ronald S. Rauchberg, Proskauer, Rose, Goetz & Mendelsohn, New York City, on the brief), for defendant-appellee.

(Alan H. Nevas, U.S. Atty., New Haven, Conn., Glenn L. Archer, Jr., Asst. Atty. Gen., Michael L. Paul, William S. Estabrook, John A. Dudeck, Jr., Tax Div., Dept. of Justice, Washington, D.C., filed a brief for the U.S. as amicus curiae.)

Before FEINBERG, Chief Judge, MESKILL and NEWMAN, Circuit Judges.

JON O. NEWMAN, Circuit Judge:

This is an appeal in a somewhat ironic lawsuit. Some years ago Irwin Schiff, the appellant, wrote a book entitled *How Anyone Can Stop Paying Income Taxes.* Simon & Schuster, the appellee, decided to distribute the book, apparently giving more consideration to the book's potential for profit than to its message. The book produced royalties for its author. The Internal Revenue Service sought to levy upon those royalties to collect taxes owed by Schiff. Simon & Schuster honored the levy. Schiff then brought this suit against Simon & Schuster, claiming that it had [A] honored an improperly perfected levy and was liable to him for the sums paid to the IRS. Some might say that Schiff was taking a chapter from his own book. Others might say that Simon & Schuster should have judged this book by its cover. The District Court said that Schiff's legal position had no merit. We say the District Court was correct, and we therefore affirm.

This case is a minor skirmish in Schiff's ongoing—and losing—battle against the IRS. Schiff has not filed tax returns since 1973; he has been convicted of income tax [B] evasion and has sought without success to enjoin the IRS from collecting taxes assessed against him for tax years 1976,

1977, and 1978. In 1979, this Court described Schiff as "an extremist who reserve[s] the right to interpret the decisions of the Supreme Court as he read[s] them from his layman's point of view regardless of and oblivious to the interpretations of the judiciary." *United States v. Schiff,* 612 F.2d 73, 75 (2d Cir.1979).

Under the terms of the contract with Schiff, Simon & Schuster was to distribute the book and deliver the proceeds to him after deducting its own fees, charges and expenses. On May 26, 1983, the IRS [C] served a notice of levy and an attested copy of a federal tax lien on Simon & Schuster for $197,044.19 in taxes due and owing by Schiff for the years 1976 through 1978. After an exchange of correspondence and the issuance of a second notice of levy on [D] December 2, 1983, Simon & Schuster paid the IRS $34,974, and subsequently an additional $99,000 from appellant's share of his book's sale proceeds. On January 4, 1984, Schiff instituted this action, seeking damages from Simon & Schuster, the Commissioner of Internal Revenue, the Secretary of the Treasury, and two IRS officials. He claimed that by honoring the notices of [E] levy, Simon & Schuster had committed fraud and breach of contract, and that Simon & Schuster had conspired with the federal government to deprive him of his constitutional rights. On April 6, 1984, appellant voluntarily dismissed his action against the federal defendants by stipulation. Subsequently, the District Court for the District of Connecticut (Warren W. Eginton, Judge) dismissed appellant's complaint against Simon & Schuster for failure to state a claim and then denied appellant's motion to amend the judgment. This appeal followed.[1]

DISCUSSION

The Internal Revenue Code requires that [F] "any person in possession of (or obligated

[1] The appeal was previously dismissed without prejudice for appellant's failure to pay double costs and damages previously imposed by this Court as a sanction for a frivolous appeal in an earlier case. *Schiff v. Simon & Schuster, Inc.,*

with respect to) property or rights to property subject to levy upon which a levy has been made shall, upon demand of the Secretary or his delegate, surrender such property or rights (or discharge such obligation) [G] to the Secretary or his delegate...." 26 U.S.C. § 6332(a). Failure or refusal to surrender to the IRS property subject to levy creates personal liability for the amount not surrendered, plus costs and interest. *Id.* § 6332(c)(1). Compliance with the obligation to honor the levy extinguishes liability to the claimant of the property. *Id.* § 6332(d).

[H] [1, 2] Only two circumstances justify non-compliance with a levy: Either the person levied upon is not in possession of the property or the property is subject to a [I] prior judicial attachment or execution. *United States v. Sterling National Bank & Trust Co,* 494 F.2d 919, 921 (2d Cir. 1974). Appellant does not contend that either of these circumstances existed in this case. The fact that appellant disputes the validity of the underlying tax assessment does not alter Simon & Schuster's [J] obligation to honor the levy, *see United States v. Augspurger,* 508 F.Supp. 327, 328-29 (W.D.N.Y.1981).

[3] Appellant contends that the IRS, by using a "Notice of Levy" form rather than a "Levy" form, did not properly make a [K] levy upon his property. Therefore, Schiff asserts, Simon & Schuster was entitled to disregard the notice of levy and was even barred from complying with its demands. This argument is absolutely meritless. Appellant ignores 26 U.S.C. § 6331(b), which states that "[t]he term 'levy' ... includes [L] the power of distraint and seizure *by any means*" (emphasis added). It is well established that a "[l]evy on property in the hands of a third party is made by serving a notice of levy on the third party." M Saltzman, *IRS Practice and Procedure* [M] ¶14.15 at 14-70 (1981). The Treasury Regulations expressly provide that a "[l]evy may be made by serving a *notice of levy* on any person in possession of, or obligated with respect to, property or rights of property subject to levy...." 26 C.F.R. § 301.- [N]

6331-1(a)(1) (emphasis added). Because these regulations have long been in effect without substantial change, they are "deemed to have received congressional approval and have the effect of law." *Helvering v. Winmill,* 305 U.S. 79, 83, 59 S.Ct. 45, 83 L.Ed. 52 (1938) (footnote omitted). Contrary to appellant's claims, the regulations are neither unreasonable nor plainly inconsistent with the terms of the statute; they must therefore be sustained. *Commissioner v. South Texas Lumber Co,* 333 U.S. 496, 501, 68 S.Ct. 695, 698, 92 L.Ed. 831 (1948).

[O] Without exception the case law supports the use of a notice of levy. *E.g., United States v. National Bank of Commerce,* — U.S. —, 105 S.Ct. 2919, 2924, 86 L.Ed.2d 565 (1985) ("In the situation where a taxpayer's property is held by another, a notice of levy upon the custodian is customarily served pursuant to section 6332(a). This notice gives the IRS the right to all property levied upon...."); *Phelps v. United States,* 421 U.S. 330, 335, 95 S.Ct. 1728, 1732, 44 L.Ed.2d 201 (1975) ("[t]he notice of levy and demand served on the assignee were an authorized means of collecting the taxes ...."); *St. Louis Union Trust Co. v. United States,* 617 F.2d 1293, 1302 (8th Cir.1980) ("[t]he usual and recognized means of distraint and seizure of property is a notice of levy"); *United States v. Sterling National Bank & Trust Co., supra,* 494 F.2d at 920 (IRS levied on bank account by serving notice of levy on bank). In sum, there is nothing to call into question the validity of either the notice of levy or Simon & Schuster's compliance with it.

We have considered all of appellant's remaining claims and find them to be equally without merit. The judgment of the District Court is affirmed.

765 F.2d 61 (2d Cir.1985) (per curiam). Upon Schiff's payment of the $2,758.40 owed to the Internal Revenue Service as an appellate sanction, the appeal was reinstated, and the views of the Government were invited.

make a levy upon his property," (note K).

This, of course, is not what I contended at all—**and Judge Newman knew it!** I never claimed that the "levy" was "improperly perfected"—I claimed that *NO LEVY HAD BEEN MADE AT ALL!* And if no levy were made, then Judge Newman's entire decision goes right *down the drain* since it is entirely predicated on the specious claim that a "levy" was made—and therefore Simon and Schuster was entitled to the protection afforded by Section 6332(a) (**Note H**). Note that Judge Newman is seeking to establish his contrived claim, even has the nerve to quote (at note L) that a levy "...includes the power of distraint and seizure by any means." And while Judge Newman added emphasis to "by any means," my money was not seized "by any means." **It was not "seized" at all.** My copy of *Webster's New World Dictionary* defines "seize" as: "to take forcible legal possession of; confiscate; to take forcibly and quickly; grab; to take hold of suddenly or forcibly, etc., etc." So whom is Judge Newman trying to kid? The government didn't "seize" one penny from Simon & Schuster. As I mentioned earler, Simon & Schuster simply mailed them the money in an envelope—and even paid the postage! So how can anyone claim (as did Judge Newman) that such funds were "seized"?!

At note B, Judge Newman claims that I had been convicted of tax evasion. As if this issue was relevant to the issues presented here. In addition, Judge Newman's observation that I had "sought without success to enjoin the IRS from collecting taxes assessed against him for the years 1976, 1977, 1978" was due to the arbitrary operation of the Anti-Injunction Statute[17] and the phony tax assessment provided by the government at that time.

At notes C and D, Judge Newman acknowledges that a Notice of Levy was served on May 26, 1983 and another one on December 2, 1983[18] and that $133,974 was turned over. Obviously the bulk of these funds had to represent "after acquired property" **which became payable to me between those two dates!** In addition, since Newman insists that the funds were "seized", why did it take the IRS over six months to "seize" them? But, note that while the issue of after acquired property is implicit in the material covered in Notes C and D (though hardly anybody reading this decision would be aware of this)—Newman *totally avoids addressing this issue* in his decision! **Yet it was fundamental to my complaint and in my argument opposing dismissal!**

At note E, Judge Newman mentions my claim that Simon & Schuster had committed fraud and breach of contract—yet nowhere in his decision does he address this issue. His claim (at notes F and G) that the Internal Revenue Code requires that "any person in possession of...property...on which a levy has been made shall upon demand...surrender such property" he knew was sheer poppycock. First of all, no "levy had been made" and his claim is belied by the letter that the IRS sent to Simon & Schuster on August 6, 1983—a copy of which he had. And if Simon & Schuster was requried to turn over the property, why did it take them six months to do so? Obviously, they could have held off indefinitely. My mistake was that I didn't immediately sue Simon & Schuster to get a court determination while they still had the money.

At note I, Newman states that there are only two circumstances that justify non-compliance with a levy. This, however, overlooks *Augspurger* (which he then had the nerve to cite) which held that one can refuse to honor a levy as long as one had "reasonable grounds" to do so.

A Straw Man, Raised

Newman's claim (at note J) that "plaintiff dispustse the validity of the underlying tax assessment does not alter Simon & Schuster's obligation to honor the levy" was a claim so distorted as to constitute outright fabrication. This allegation was actually directed at the government defendants who were initially included in my law suit, but later dropped. In my initial complaint this charge was merely incorporated by reference (along with some other allegations) in my charges against Simon & Schuster but it never really figured in my actual claim against Simon & Schuster. My claim against them had nothing to do with the "underlying tax assessment"—but with S & S's violation of contractual and fiduciary obligation and in turning over after acquired property. So here Newman stresses a claim I never really made while he totally ignores two others I made!

At note N, Newman quotes the Regulation, that he knows is void—(since it illegally extended the law)*and ignores the law itself!*—that I dwelt on in my briefs and that I emphatically stressed (without challenge) at oral argument. He states that "because these regulations have long been in effect without substantial change, they are 'deemed to have received approval and have the effect of law'." That claim is utter nonsense since no regulation, that absolutely **changes the law** as that Regulation does, can have "the effect of law." Besides, the Supreme Court has held (but the name of the case escapes me) that, "The repetition of a wrong does not create a right."

Court Decisions Based
On Law Books, Not Law

Notice that at note M, Judge Newman uses Professor Saltzman as his authority. So while I, a *pro se* litigant, rely on the law and IRS manuals, the Circuit Court Judge closes his eyes to both and bases his decision on private, personal opinions. **Now you know that something has to be wrong in any legal system that practices this kind of nonsense!**

And finally, at note O, Newman states that "Without exception, the case law supports the use of a Notice of Levy." Naturally, since the "case law" he relied on would be just as unlawful as his decision—**which would now become "case law" for others!** If "the case law supports" *this* decision, you, dear reader, know that the law itself *does not!* Someone once said that the public should never see how two things are made—sausage and laws. Maybe to this we should add—and federal court decisions.

THE ILLEGALITY OF THE DISMISSAL

And, finally, I should put the dismissal of my law suit into its proper legal perspective, which lay readers might have some difficulty doing. First of all, while I might have produced a better complaint—the complaint is not the be all and end all of a law suit. It merely alleges in a general way the injury requiring legal redress. All of the facts and specifics are developed in pre trial discovery and at trial. For example, Rule 8(a) of the Federal Rules of Civil Procedure only requires that in instituting a law suit for damages:

A pleading which sets forth a claim for relief...shall contain (1) a short and plain statement of the grounds upon which the court's jurisdiction depends...(2) a short and plain statement of the claim showing that the pleader is entitled to relief, and (3) a demand for the judgment for the relief the pleader seeks.

This, my complaint did. So, to have dismissed it without giving me the opportunity to develop my claim through pre trial discovery and a trial, was simply to deny me the use of the courts in violation of the Sixth Amendment. The court's authority to grant a dismissal is further put into perspective by the following observation by Chief Justice Burger in *Sheuer* v. *Rhodes* 416 U.S. 232.

When a federal court reviews the sufficiency of a complaint before the reception of any evidence either by affidavit or admission, its task is necessarily a limited one. The issue is not whether a plaintiff will ultimately prevail, **but whether the claimant is entitled to offer evidence to support the claims.**

Indeed it may appear on the face of the pleading that a recovery **is very remote** and unlikely but that is not the test. Moreover, it is well established that, in **passing on a motion to dismiss,** whether on the grounds of lack of jurisdiction over the subject matter or for failure to state a cause of action, **the allegations of the complaint should be construed favorable to the pleader.** (emphasis added)

So, it is clear that there was no basis in either law or fact for the judges involved to have denied me access to the court. They did so simply to prevent me from proving my case—which I certainly would have done—so as to protect the federal government's extortionary tax activities. In this connection all of the judges involved were merely co-conspirators along with Simon & Schuster and the IRS in extorting over $200,000 from me. And, of course, all of the judges involved in this dismissal have sent people to jail for stealing a whole lot less.

It should now be clear to you that the federal judiciary has absolutely no interest in enforcing the "laws" as they apply to income taxes. It should also be clear that the federal government has absolutely no right to intrude into the contractual obligations and relationships that exist between members of the public, which the serving of Notices of Levy (as opposed to making its own seizures) allows them to do. It should also be clear that the serving of a Notice of Levy on Simon & Schuster terminated a business relationship that up until that time was both amicable and profitable and caused both parties to expend time and money on litigation that the government had no right generating—and which, of course, the law itself does not even authorize.

In addition, it will become increasingly clear that the IRS imposes income taxes and especially penalties in total violation of the law. When direct taxes were first imposed, tax collectors (who were independent and contracted by the federal government) could be sued individually if they sought to extract taxes not legally owed. So, this obviously acted as a check to arbitrary and capricious tax claims. But now the public, as a practical matter, is denied the right to sue IRS agents, so these highwaymen are free to prey upon the public in any manner they choose. And while the Code does provide punitive provision for such activity (Code Sections 7214(1), (2), and (7), getting the U.S. Department of Justice to enforce these provisions is a feat comparable to squaring a circle.

Without getting into a discussion here as to how the government's summary seizure powers were judicially carved out as an exception to the due process clause of the Constitution, it obviously can no longer be tolerated by the public—a public, that is, that has any common sense.

All those who claim to believe in constitutional rights, limited government and the free enterprise system must bring as much pressure on Congress as possible to eliminate Section 6331. It should be perfectly obvious, that for "We the People" to permit a statute to exist that gives the federal establishment the power to "seize" (from us!) property "by any means" (i.e. without hearings and court orders) and then expect federal judges (who are part of that establishment) to see to it that such a power is lawfully exercised, makes about as much sense as entrusting the controls of a Greyhound bus to a nine year old.

NOTES TO CHAPTER 7

1. The recently passed "Taxpayers' Bill of Rights," I thought, might offer the public some help, but now I don't think so. Taxpayers, of course, already have a Bill of Rights—its in the Constitution. But that's the last place Congress would ever look. There might, however, be some aspects of the the Bill that could be explored and employed to some advantage. I will look into it when I finish this book. Those wishing to be notified when that happens can send a stamped, self-addressed envelope to Freedom Books.

2. However, I suspect that the main reason why the courts are able to ignore the IRS' failure to send out Form 17 is that, since the public is totally unaware of its existence and importance, it is never brought up in litigation! However, I will raise this issue in my pending civil law suit, and I should get a summary judgment just on this failure alone. However this assumes an honest court, so such an assumption may not be realistic.

3. If anyone reading this book happens to come across such a reference, I would appreciate having it. Please send it to me in care of Freedom Books, P.O. Box 5303, Hamden, CT 06518.

4. By statute (Section 6334) some items are excluded from levy, such as: the first $1,500 of a person's personal property, $1,000 in the tools of one's trade and school books. Who said the federal government has no heart?

5. The two documents shown in Figures 7-5 and 7-6 were served on my sister in connection with an IRS attempt to seize her automobile, which had been given to her by my son. Since it was never actually seized by the IRS, a notice of seizure was never issued.

6. The use of guns were illegally employed here. See Figure 7-12.

7. Actually a Notice of Levy is also mentioned in Section 6332(b), in connection with "life insurance and endowment contracts." One could, therefore, argue that a Notice of Levy can only be used with respect to such proceeds and to the wages and salaries of government employees, since these are the only two items to which the statute makes Notices applicable. But its inclusion here makes no sense and obviously conflicts with the Notice's original purpose. It was, no doubt, simply added to Section 6332 to give the added appearance of legitimacy to that application. But since this reference does not actually appear in Section 6331 itself—it probably does not technically fall within the law covering seizures, and so is probably just another of the government's dirty tricks—which I leave to others to analyze.

8. Lt. Col. (Ret) Albert J. Bushong from Rochester, New York flew a fighter plane for his country in Korea. It rewarded him by sending him to jail for one year for failing to file an income tax return that both he and the government knew wasn't required. In addition, over the last three years an appreciative government has been taking out of Al's Air Force retirement pension, approximately $1,500 for income taxes, penalties and interest that Al also doesn't owe. When Al told me about this a few months ago, I asked him if he had gotten a Notice of Levy *each and every month that the funds were taken.* He told me, no. Well the government has been using a continuous levy on *payments which weren't wages!* The government, pursuant to section 6331(e), can only use a continuous levy "on salary and wages"—and a retirement pension is neither of these! So I told Al to file a claim for refund on this basis. If it is denied by the IRS, he will then sue the government for recovery in a federal district court or in the U.S. Court of Claims. He should have no trouble winning this one—since what the government did is an out and out violation of law. **And all other veterans who have had this experience shouldn't have any trouble recovering their funds on this basis either!***

9. One might argue that technically this section does not expand the law, because this passage is made applicable only to property "subject to levy." And since none of the property listed is *actually* "subject to levy" the regulation doesn't really expand the law! While such Talmudic reasoning is technically correct, this is just the kind of argument the courts easily dismiss as "frivolous." Besides,

if only one court got away with saying it was lawful, it would immediately become precedent for any court to say the same thing—while the specific language of the regulation would now become moot.

10. While I eventually came to recognize this principle, had I thoroughly understood it from the moment the Notice of Levy was served, I believe the ultimate episode involving Simon & Schuster might have been averted.

11. This is why third parties (especially fiduciaries) cannot be put in this kind of perilous and compromising legal position by the government. The reason that Notices of Levy cannot apply to after acquired property even according to the Treasury's illegal Regulation, (except as to salaries, see Section 6331(e)[1]) is because the government has fraudulently sought to transform a Notice of Levy into an actual levy. Since a levy means "seizure by any means" property can't be seized twice. In other words, once Greb seized D. Linquent's car (and its contents) this property could not be seized again. It would require another seizure (levy) to seize additional property. Applying this same logic to a bank "seizure"; once Greb "seized" the $169.73, he would require a new Notice to "seize" again.

The reason that the law *appears* to provide an exception for "salaries and wages" is because the Notice was meant only to apply to wages—those belonging to government employees. Once the government notifies an employee (by way of a Notice of Levy) that it intends to apply their future wages to paying off the alleged tax debt owed the government (their employer), the government obviously does not need to do this each and every week. Such a Notice (or letter) would logically apply "until the liability out of which such levy arose is satisfied" just as Section 6331(e)(1) says. So once the real purpose of a Notice of Levy is understood, Section 6331(e)(1) will be seen as not really providing any exception to the general rule that a levy cannot be continuous. However, the very fact that there appears to be an exception in the law proves that Notices of Levy cannot apply to other than government employees. **Since, if the government could, by law, get the after acquired wages of those other than its own employees, then there would be no earthly reason why the same principle shouldn't apply to all other forms of after acquired property.** The only basis on which the apparent exception of making a "levy on salary or wages...continuous from the date such levy is first made" (as stated in Section 6331(e)(91)) when all other levies can't be, is because such Notices can only legally and logically apply to the salaries of government employees, as provided by Section 6331(a). This apparent exception in the law is no more of an "exception" than if an employer, in notifying one of its employees that "all of your future wages will be

applied to your debt with the company," also added in the same letter, "This will be the only notice you get until your debt is repaid."

So this apparent exception to the statutory prohibition against continuous levies, proves (if, indeed, further proof is needed) that the government has been fraudulently using Notices of Levy to extort and trick third parties into illegally turning over to the government money belonging to others. But in resorting to such trickery and extortion, is the government breaking any laws? The answer is no. The government, remember, wrote into the law its right to seize property "by any means." So the government apparently feels it has a legal right to get its money by extortion, bribery, mail and wire fraud, under false pretenses and in ways that are generally not available to the rest of us. So, as you can see, the only real distinction between the federal government and the Mafia is that the government really has a license to steal, the Mafia doesn't. However, while the law might protect federal thugs who "seize" property illegally, it provides no such protection to third parties who are taken in by, or submit to such trickery and/or intimidation to the detriment of others.

12. Since the very word "lawyer" comes from the Latin word to "twist"—Prosakauer here is merely doing a lot of lawyering.

13. The decision itself stated "The confused and confusion background to this suit is set forth sufficiently in my two prior Memorandums and Orders herein and familiarity therewith is assumed." These prior decisions were footnoted as being 452 F. Supp. 659 (D.C. March 20, 1978) and 477 F. Supp. 94 (D.C., Sept. 13, 1979)

14. While I handled the appeal myself—*pro se*, I am indebted to an attorney friend of mine, Dick Viti, of Atlanta, Georgia, who actually drafted all of the pleadings in connection with this appeal.

15. It simply was not practical for me to rehash their Brief—since my comments would only be repititious. However for those who might want this Brief as well as all of the supporting Briefs that went into this appeal, i.e. my Brief, S & S's Answer, my Reply, The Justice Department's Brief, my Reply and the transcript of Oral Argument, send $15.00 plus $3.00 for postage and handling to Freedom Books.

16. Ultimately the Second Circuit ruled in *Schiff* v. *Simon & Schuster, Inc.* 766 F.2d 61 (1985) that it wouldn't consider my appeal unless I paid the $2,758.40 penalty. So, I paid it to get a ruling on this appeal. My previous appeal, of course, was not "frivolous" at all. But even if it were, it

should have been the attorney who filed it that should have been fined—not me. Remember, in order to practice law one has to be licensed and admitted to the bar. In so doing, one actually becomes an "officer of the court." So, if an "officer of the court" submits a frivolous appeal, it should be he who is fined, not the client. How can a lay member of the public recognize that an appeal is frivolous when the court's own "officer" doesn't? And, when the "officer of the court" charged the client for submitting it!

17. See pages 346-349, 363, 393-395, and 399 of *The Great Income Tax Hoax*.

18. My lawsuit was instituted on January 5, 1984, before all of the monies had been turned over to the IRS, so those sent after that date were not mentioned in my suit. This is unfortunate since (I should have amended my complaint to include those payments) the violations that occurred with respect to the last three payments are clear cut violations of the prohibition against the use of a continuous levy.

---

*When William M. Bierman of Sebering, Florida, read this, he contacted me, because the government was illegally doing this to him. In a series of cogent letters prompted by this reference, Mr. Bierman was able to extract the following, from Lewis I. Baurer, Director, Office of Planning and Management, Internal Revenue Service, in a letter to him dated November 6, 1991:

"Pension benefits of the federal government are subject to common law rights of offset, which allows credits to be applied to debits when both exist between two parties (the taxpayer and the party). [However, this is not true in this case.] However, as a policy matter, the Service decided that it will not undertake to place a continuous offset on retirement benefits."

Because of this issue being raised in **The Federal Mafia**, and the tenacious persistence of William M. Bierman, millions of dollars in veteran's pensions will no longer be stolen in the future as they have been in the past. And, obviously, if the process were ever legal, the Service would not have needed to "decide" to stop doing it.

IMPORTANT...IMPORTANT...

IMMEDIATELY, get IRS Form 911, "Application for Taxpayer Assistance Order (ATAO) to Relieve Hardship," so you will have it ready **in case the IRS threatens you with seizure action.** This is a form that is supposed to be reviewed by the Taxpayer Ombudsman, a position created by the Taxpayers Bill of Rights. Follow the instructions that appear on the reverse side of the form. The form states that the IRS "will acknowledge your request within one week of receiving it," and that, "while we are reviewing your application, **we will take no further enforcement action.**"

As far as the description of the problem is concerned, the seizures will be based upon a lien filed by the IRS in which the IRS claims that taxes "have been assessed...demand for payment of this liability has been made." Though you can not raise the issue of "liability" on a Form 911, you can claim that the amount you allegedly owe was **never** assessed and that you **never** got the "demand for payment" claimed. This should keep the IRS busy for a while trying to produce all of the assessment documents that it does not have, and also trying to produce the "notice and demand" (Form 17) that it never sent you.

While this is going on, file a law suit in state court to remove the lien that was filed against you in your local township to support the seizures. This is a law suit to "quiet title" (also, refer to page 213). Your law suit (complaint) need not be more than two or three pages. Simply allege that the allegations in the lien are false: No taxes were ever lawfully assessed, no demand for payment was ever made, and you have no liability for the taxes claimed.

You can attach to your complaint an affidavit swearing to these averments, but only do so if you are familiar with all of the material in this book. The above will only apply to those who filed *no tax returns for the years at issue.* If you filed returns for the years at issue, you will have to make adjustments in these averments, based on your actions and what you learned from this book.

I have put together a packet of material consisting of a sample three-page letter to be sent to third parties (including a suggested affidavit and exhibits, taken from this book) which should convince them that they do not have to honor notices of levy. Contact Freedom Books (203-281-6791) for details. However, there are many third parties who, out of fear of the IRS, **will refuse to be convinced**, and may have to be sued. If the amount involved is under $2,000, you can sue them in small claims court. In any case, my packet will be helpful in providing a basis for that suit, and to help you put it together.

— CHAPTER 8 —

HOW TO STOP PAYING INCOME TAXES

"The history of liberty is the history of the limitation of governmental power, not the increase of it."
—Woodrow Wilson

Since you know that no Code section makes you liable for income taxes, you know you have no more of a legal obligation to pay that tax than you have to pay wagering and (direct) alcohol and tobacco taxes. In addition, you also know that before you could even owe an income tax, it would have to be assessed and a notice, (Form 17A) sent to you demanding payment. You also know that without your sending in a tax return, the government doesn't even have the authority to assess you, let alone estimate or bill you for the amount of income taxes you didn't pay! So what's the problem? Of course, if you want to *voluntarily* pay the tax—go right ahead. But if you don't want to *volunteer*—what then?

Overlooking the lawless responses the government is capable of making,[1] how can Americans stop paying a tax for which they have no legal liability? The fact that I should even have to ask such a question is itself a commentary on the general level of consciousness of the American public. In *How Anyone Can Stop Paying Income Taxes,* I addressed this question (page 61) as follows:

If you are self-employed, retired, or simply living on dividends, interest, rent, alimony, etc., it is easy to stop paying income taxes. Just stop! On the basis of the material in the first four chapters of this book, you should know that you do not have to file an estimated tax return or pay quarterly tax estimates and also that as long as you have not been officially assessed or notified by the government that you owe any taxes, you don't have to pay the government a penny.

While this is still true today, a new obstacle was created since those words were written which, I believe, was caused in large measure by the very success of those words which showed multitudes of Americans how they could legally stop paying income tax. In 1983 the federal mafia introduced a new extortionary device—"backup withholding"—to which I will return later in this chapter.

Obviously, no one is required to pay income taxes or file estimated or 1040 returns with respect to a tax for which no one is liable. So, for those who are self-employed or retired, stopping the payment of income tax is easy. All those people have to do is just stop. Wage earners, on the other hand, believe that they are required to have income taxes deducted from their paychecks. Most don't know that the law allows them to stop such withholding. Let's turn to that.

HOW TO STOP YOUR EMPLOYER FROM WITHHOLDING TAXES FROM YOUR PAY

Section 3402(n) (Figure 8-1) is the statute that permits you to stop your employer from withholding taxes from your pay. Notice that the section provides that:

Notwithstanding any other provision of this section, an employer shall not be required to deduct and withhold any tax under this chapter ...if there is in effect...a withholding exemption certificate...certifying that the employee...

(1) incurred no liability...for the preceding taxable year, and
(2) anticipates that he will incur no liability for income tax...for his current year.

So the law provides that your employer is not required to withhold income taxes from your pay as long as you supply him with a statement that you were not "liable" for income tax last year or this year. Based upon your current understanding of the law, do you think you could supply him with such a statement? I would also point out, that even if you paid the tax last year it was not because you had an income tax liability. You paid "voluntarily" (actually you probably paid it out of either fear or ignorance) without "owing" the tax or having any "liability" for doing so. **You can't incur a "liability" that doesn't exist.**

The W-4

The "exemption certificate" which supposedly allows employees to stop withholding is the Form W-4, which employees fill out when first hired. Until a few years ago, that form was rather simple. Figure 8-2 shows the form used in 1982 when *How Anyone Can Stop Paying Income Taxes* was published. Figure 8-3 is the front of the form in use today. Note the special instructions which are now included to discourage the claiming of "exempt." Note especially the claim that "You may not claim exempt status, if you can be claimed as a dependent of another person." **There is no such provision in the law!** In addition, what can something that *someone else might claim* have to do with what *I have a right to do under the law?*[2] As far as the other provisions of that paragraph are concerned, as explained earlier, no one receives any "income" that is taxable within the meaning of the law. So, *if you understand this,* one can claim "exempt" on the new form as easily as one could on the old one. The government simply tried to make the proccess more confusing in order to discourage people from doing it. But also note, that completing the "Personal Allowances Worksheet" only applies to those "who are not exempt."!

FIGURE 8-1 — Internal Revenue Code Section 3402(n)

> **(n) Employees incurring no income tax liability.**—Notwithstanding any other provision of this section, an employer shall not be required to deduct and withhold any tax under this chapter upon a payment of wages to an employee if there is in effect with respect to such payment a withholding exemption certificate (in such form and containing such other information as the Secretary may prescribe) furnished to the employer by the employee certifying that the employee—
>
> (1) incurred no liability for income tax imposed under subtitle A for his preceding taxable year, and
>
> (2) anticipates that he will incur no liability for income tax imposed under subtitle A for his current taxable year.
>
> The Secretary shall by regulations provide for the coordination of the provisions of this subsection with the provisions of subsection (f).

Note further that the W-4 actually changes the wording in the statute—when there clearly was no need for it. The law says nothing about tax "refunds," and it speaks of a tax "liability", not "owing" the tax. There can be no doubt that the W-4 was worded to conflict with the law in order to frustrate its lawful application. In any case, employees who understand the income tax "law" can still claim "exempt" on the new W-4. Since they know they didn't have an income tax "liability," they could not have "owed" income taxes for either year. And, since the tax was collected illegally[3] on the basis of fraud, fear and intimidation, all employees certainly had a "right" to a full refund— regardless of whether or not the federal mafia recognizes that "right."

One's ability to claim exempt on a W-4 is perfectly consistent with the voluntary, self-assessment nature of the tax. If you couldn't claim exempt but were compelled to have taxes taken from your wages then the income tax would not be "voluntary," but compulsory. This is why the student syllabus (Figure 1-3) correctly informed students that this was the form on which employees "tell their employers how much to withhold." Of course, the government, in practice, disregards the law in this respect, along with everything else it disregards.

Employees who claim exempt may have employers who needlessly send their W-4s to the IRS in response to some non-compelling IRS directive. In all likelihood, such employees will receive a form from the IRS entitled "Questionnaire To Determine Exemption From Withholding." The form is obviously illegal since it asks whether or not one filed a return the previous year and then inquires about one's previous years income. Since the government regards non filing a crime, the form, in effect, asks recipients to incriminate themselves. The form also asks about receipt of "income." Thus it seeks to mislead the public into making representations about an "income" it never received. But the form really reveals its fraudulent character because of the question it doesn't ask! Since the form is sent to people who have claimed that they had no income tax liability, why doesn't the form ask, "Why do you claim you have no income tax liability?" The government doesn't ask that question because it's afraid of the answer it could get, which could be—"Because the law does not establish any such liability." So the government doesn't even ask the one question that is relevant to the exemption claim!

When you get your Questionnaire, you will have to decide how to answer it. Since you will be dealing with a criminal government that acts in arbitrary and unpredictable ways,

FIGURE 8-2

FIGURE 8-3

1988 Form W-4

Department of the Treasury
Internal Revenue Service

Purpose. You must complete Form W-4 so that your employer can withhold the correct amount of Federal income tax from your pay.

Exemption From Withholding. To be exempt, you must have owed no Federal income tax last year **and** must not expect to owe any this year. You may not claim exempt status if you can be claimed as a dependent of another person, have any nonwage income, and expect your total income to be more than $500. If exempt, only complete the certificate at the bottom of this page.

Basic Instructions. Employees who are not exempt should complete the Personal Allowances Worksheet. Additional worksheets are provided on page 2 for employees to adjust their withholding allowances based on itemized deductions, adjustments to income, or two-earner/two-job situations. For accuracy, complete all worksheets that apply to your situation. The worksheets on this form are designed to help you figure the number of withholding allowances you are entitled to claim. However, you may claim fewer allowances than this.

Head of Household. Generally, you may claim head of household filing status on your tax return only if you are unmarried and pay more than 50% of the costs of keeping up a home for yourself and your dependent(s) or other qualifying individuals.

Nonwage Income. If you have a large amount of nonwage income, from sources such as interest or dividends, you should consider making estimated tax payments using Form 1040-ES. Otherwise, you may find that you owe additional tax at the end of the year.

Two-Earner/Two-Jobs. If you have a working spouse or more than one job, figure the total number of allowances you are entitled to claim on all jobs using worksheets from only one Form W-4. This total should be divided among all jobs. Your withholding will usually be most accurate when all allowances are claimed on the W-4 filed for the highest paying job and zero allowances are claimed for the others.

Advance Earned Income Credit. If you are eligible for this credit, you can receive it added to your paycheck throughout the year. For details, obtain Form W-5 from your employer.

Check Your Withholding. After your W-4 takes effect, you can use **Publication 919,** Is My Withholding Correct for 1988?, to see how the dollar amount you are having withheld compares to your estimated total annual tax. Call 1-800-424-3676 (in Hawaii and Alaska, check your local telephone directory) to obtain this publication.

Personal Allowances Worksheet

A Enter "1" for **yourself** if no one else can claim you as a dependent . . . . . A ______

B Enter "1" if:
1. You are single and have only one job; or
2. You are married, have only one job, and your spouse does not work; or
3. Your wages from a second job or your spouse's wages (or the total of both) are $2,500 or less.

. . . . . B ______

C Enter "1" for your **spouse.** But, you may choose to enter "0" if you are married and have either a working spouse or more than one job (this may help you avoid having too little tax withheld) . . . . . C ______

D Enter number of **dependents** (other than your spouse or yourself) whom you will claim on your tax return . . . D ______

E Enter "1" if you will file as a **head of household** on your tax return (see conditions under "Head of Household," above) . . E ______

F Enter "1" if you have at least $1,500 of **child or dependent care expenses** for which you plan to claim a credit . . . . F ______

G Add lines A through F and enter total here . . . . . ▶ G ______

For accuracy, do all worksheets that apply.
- If you plan to **itemize or claim adjustments to income** and want to reduce your withholding, turn to the Deductions and Adjustments Worksheet on page 2.
- If you are **single** and have **more than one job** and your combined earnings from all jobs exceed $25,000 OR if you are **married** and have a **working spouse or more than one job,** and the combined earnings from all jobs exceed $40,000, then turn to the Two-Earner/Two-Job Worksheet on page 2 if you want to avoid having too little tax withheld.
- If **neither** of the above situations applies to you, **stop here** and enter the number from line G on line 4 of Form W-4 below.

Cut here and give the certificate to your employer. Keep the top portion for your records.

Form **W-4** — Department of the Treasury, Internal Revenue Service

Employee's Withholding Allowance Certificate

▶ **For Privacy Act and Paperwork Reduction Act Notice, see reverse.**

OMB No. 1545-0010 — **1988**

1 Type or print your first name and middle initial — Last name — 2 Your social security number

Home address (number and street or rural route)

City or town, state, and ZIP code

3 Marital Status: ☐ Single ☐ Married ☐ Married, but withhold at higher Single rate.
Note: *If married, but legally separated, or spouse is a nonresident alien, check the Single box.*

4 Total number of allowances you are claiming (from line G above or from the Worksheets on back if they apply) . . . 4

5 Additional amount, if any, you want deducted from each pay . . . . . 5 $

6 I claim exemption from withholding because (check boxes below that apply):

a ☐ Last year I did not owe any Federal income tax and had a right to a full refund of **ALL** income tax withheld, **AND**

b ☐ This year I do not expect to owe any Federal income tax and expect to have a right to a full refund of **ALL** income tax withheld.

c If both **a** and **b** apply and you satisfy the additional conditions outlined above under "Exemption From Withholding," enter the year effective and "EXEMPT" here. Do not complete lines 4 and 5 above . . . ▶ Year 19

7 Are you a full-time student? (**Note:** *Full-time students are **not** automatically exempt.*) ☐ Yes ☐ No

Under penalties of perjury, I certify that I am entitled to the number of withholding allowances claimed on this certificate or, if claiming exemption from withholding, that I am entitled to claim the exempt status.

Employee's signature ▶ **Date ▶** , 198

8 Employer's name and address **(Employer: Complete 8, 9, and 10 only if sending to IRS)** — 9 Office code — 10 Employer identification number

---

Form W-4 (1988) Page **2**

Deductions and Adjustments Worksheet

Note: *Use this worksheet only if you plan to itemize deductions or claim adjustments to income on your 1988 tax return.*

1 Enter an estimate of your 1988 itemized deductions. These include: qualifying home mortgage interest, 40% of personal interest, charitable contributions, state and local taxes (but not sales taxes), medical expenses in excess of 7.5% of your income, and miscellaneous deductions (most miscellaneous deductions are now deductible only in excess of 2% of your income) . . . . . 1 $______

2 Enter:
- $5,000 if married filing jointly or qualifying widow(er)
- $4,400 if head of household
- $3,000 if single
- $2,500 if married filing separately

. . . . . 2 $______

3 **Subtract** line 2 from line 1. If line 2 is greater than line 1, enter zero . . . . . 3 $______

4 Enter an estimate of your 1988 adjustments to income. These include alimony paid and deductible IRA contributions . . . . . 4 $______

5 **Add** lines 3 and 4 and enter the total . . . . . 5 $______

6 Enter an estimate of your 1988 nonwage income (such as dividends or interest income) . . . . . 6 $______

7 **Subtract** line 6 from line 5. Enter the result, but not less than zero . . . . . 7 $______

8 **Divide** the amount on line 7 by $2,000 and enter the result here. Drop any fraction . . . . . 8 ______

9 Enter the number from Personal Allowances Worksheet, line G, on page 1 . . . . . 9 ______

10 **Add** lines 8 and 9 and enter the total here. If you plan to use the Two-Earner/Two-Job Worksheet, also enter the total on line 1, below. Otherwise, **stop here** and enter this total on Form W-4, line 4 on page 1 . . . . 10 ______

Two-Earner/Two-Job Worksheet

Note: *Use this worksheet only if the instructions at line G on page 1 direct you here.*

1 Enter the number from line G on page 1 (or from line 10 above if you used the Deductions and Adjustments Worksheet) . . . . . 1 ______

2 Find the number in **Table 1** below that applies to the **LOWEST** paying job and enter it here . . . . . 2 ______

3 If line 1 is **GREATER THAN OR EQUAL TO** line 2, subtract line 2 from line 1. Enter the result here (if zero, enter "0") and on Form W-4, line 4, on page 1. **DO NOT** use the rest of this worksheet . . . . . 3 ______

Note: *If line 1 is **LESS THAN** line 2, enter "0" on Form W-4, line 4, on page 1. Complete lines 4–9 to calculate the additional dollar withholding necessary to avoid a year-end tax bill.*

4 Enter the number from line 2 of this worksheet . . . . . 4 ______

5 Enter the number from line 1 of this worksheet . . . . . 5 ______

6 **Subtract** line 5 from line 4 . . . . . 6 ______

7 Find the amount in **Table 2** below that applies to the **HIGHEST** paying job and enter it here . . . . . 7 $______

8 **Multiply** line 7 by line 6 and enter the result here. This is the additional annual withholding amount needed. 8 $______

9 **Divide** line 8 by the number of pay periods each year. (For example, divide by 26 if you are paid every other week.) Enter the result here and on Form W-4, line 5, page 1. This is the additional amount to be withheld from each paycheck . . . . . 9 $______

Table 1: Two-Earner/Two-Job Worksheet

Married Filing Jointly		All Others	
If wages from **LOWEST** paying job are—	Enter on line 2 above	If wages from **LOWEST** paying job are—	Enter on line 2 above
0 - $4,000	0	0 - $4,000	0
4,001 - 8,000	1	4,001 - 8,000	1
8,001 - 18,000	2	8,001 - 13,000	2
18,001 - 21,000	3	13,001 - 15,000	3
21,001 - 23,000	4	15,001 - 19,000	4
23,001 - 25,000	5	19,001 and over	5
25,001 - 27,000	6		
27,001 - 32,000	7		
32,001 - 38,000	8		
38,001 - 42,000	9		
42,001 and over	10		

Table 2: Two-Earner/Two-Job Worksheet

Married Filing Jointly		All Others	
If wages from **HIGHEST** paying job are—	Enter on line 7 above	If wages from **HIGHEST** paying job are—	Enter on line 7 above
0 - $40,000	$300	0 - $23,000	$300
40,001 - 80,000	550	23,001 - 48,000	550
80,001 and over	650	48,001 and over	650

Privacy Act and Paperwork Reduction Act Notice.—We ask for this information to carry out the Internal Revenue laws of the United States. We may give the information to the Department of Justice for civil or criminal litigation and to cities, states, and the District of Columbia for use in administering their tax laws. You are required to give this information to your employer.

☆U.S. Government Printing Office: 1987—183-053 23-0916750

you will have to respond based upon that understanding, in conjunction with the knowledge you acquired through this book. It would also be helpful if you were familiar with the more in-depth treatment of certain aspects of this subject as covered in *The Great Income Tax Hoax*. You might return the questionnaire with the comment that since you are not liable for income taxes *as you have already indicated on your signed and sworn to W-4*, none of the questions are applicable to you, and if the IRS doesn't believe your sworn W-4, then, **"Why don't you charge me with perjury?"**

There is nothing in the law that says you have to explain why you are "exempt" to the IRS. Suppose the government sent you a questionnaire asking why you weren't filing wagering or tobacco tax returns. Do you think that you would have to answer it, and spend 25 cents of your own money doing it? Since a W-4 is signed under penalties of perjury, if the government thought your claim was false, its only legitimate recourse would be to charge you with perjury—which you have enough knowledge to refute. But instead of doing that (since it knows it will generally lose in such prosecutions), the federal mafia finds it easier and more lucrative to simply intimidate spineless employers into stealing the wages of their own employees for its benefit— regardless of their sworn and unrefuted statements!

So, you may find that even though you correctly respond to the IRS's inquiry, you might still be fined $500.00 for filing an "incorrect W-4." Your employer might be "directed" to disregard your W-4 and to withhold even more taxes than would otherwise be the case. Your employer might also be "directed" to take both the fine and the larger tax payments (that you also don't owe) out of your pay. AND THE OVERWHELMING MAJORITY OF AMERICAN EMPLOYERS WILL DO JUST THAT! In addition, your government is now using W-4s upon which individuals have validly claimed "exempt" as evidence of **an affirmative act of tax evasion** and prosecutes and imprisons people accordingly! All of this is happening because the American public (with a magnificent assist from the media) has allowed this nation to degenerate into a neo-fascist state where neither law nor the Constitution holds much interest for either the government or its courts.

INTIMIDATING EMPLOYERS

IRS audits are costly and disruptive even if the IRS finds nothing wrong. So employers seeking to discourage them are easily intimidated by the IRS, and send "exempt" W-4s to the IRS even though there is no law requiring them to do so. If the IRS wants information on an employee, it has to issue an IRS "summons" to secure that information pursuant to Code Section 7602 (see the following chapter). If the IRS could get information without having to issue a Section 7602 summons, then there would be no need for the IRS to ever have to issue one—and, indeed, there would be no need for Section 7602 altogether.

The only information an employer has to disclose (since he elected to withhold) is the amount of taxes withheld, but he certainly is not required to submit an employee's W-4 to the IRS without first getting an IRS summons or subpoena.

But even assuming that an employer is required to submit an employee's W-4, he certainly is not required to honor a letter—even a signed one—"directing" him to *disregard* his employee's sworn W-4 statement with respect to his tax liability! **The law, in fact, directs him to do otherwise.** The fact that the overwhelming majority of American employers obey these unsigned IRS letters, provides the clearest proof that this nation as a whole no longer has any regard for constitutional rights—and that our legal profession consists largely of incompetents.

As covered in detail in *The Great Income Tax Hoax* (pp 389-393) lawyers for state and city government and large American corporations have told me time and again that they have to obey these benign IRS letters because "we have to do what the IRS tells us." If this were true, this would mean that the wages of American workers belong to the government—not to the workers. And if the government can require employers to turn over large portions of an employee's salary without a court order (or even a Notice of Levy!), why couldn't the government, with equal logic, order employers to turn over the employee's automobile (parked in the corporate parking lot) or his lunch pail or the contents of his wallet. Yet incredibly, this is what American lawyers now tell employers *they are required to do!*

Any employer who gets such a letter can throw it right into the trash can where it belongs. However, if you are an employer and want proof of that, then write the following letter to the IRS if you receive one.

Dear Mr. IRS Man,

I received your unsigned letter informing me to disregard my employees signed and sworn W-4 statement (and his attached affidavit), which you claim is "false." Accordingly, I request that you answer the following questions with respect to your letter.

1. What is the name or names of the individual or individuals who determined that my employee's W-4 statement was "incorrect"?

2. What is the basis upon which it was determined that the W-4 statement is "incorrect"?

3. Am I required by law to disregard my employee's W-4 and his affidavit simply because the IRS "directed" me to do so?

4. If your answer to question 3 above is yes, please provide the Code Section that requires me to do so.

5. What are the penalties that I might be subject to if I do not follow your "directive"?

6. What is the Code Section that establishes and enumerates such penalties?

Until I receive satisfactory answers to these six questions, I will continue to honor my employee's W-4 and his affidavit as I am authorized to do by Code Section 3402(n).

The IRS will not even bother answering that letter But if it does, I would appreciate receiving a copy.

W-4s Should Be Signed "Under Duress"

It is clear that no employee signs a W-4 voluntarily. This being the case, employees should indicate this right on the form. The reason for this is that since the government now claims that filing an allegedly incorrect W-4 *constitutes an affirmative act of tax evasion*—one puts oneself in jeopardy just by filling one out. **Understanding this, one wonders why any employee would risk doing so.** (The same argument, of course, applies to filling out an income tax return.) Thus, when you fill out a W-4, you should *take steps to prevent the government from using it against you.* In order for the government to do that, it would have to claim that you filed it voluntarily. The government can't (legally) compel you to submit a document (in this case, just to work), and then use it against you![4]

So, you should write after your signature: "involuntarily submitted in order to get paid" or "signed and submitted under duress." Confirmation of this will be found on the

---

FIGURE 8-4

AFFIDAVIT

(Establishing my "exempt" status with respect to Federal income taxes pursuant to 26 USC 3402[n])

TO: _____   DATE: _____
      (employer's name)

This is my sworn affidavit, submitted pursuant to Section 3402(n) of the Internal Revenue Code (reproduced below), certifying that:
   1. I incurred no liability for income tax imposed under subtitle A for the preceeding taxable year;
   2. I anticipate I will incur no liability for income tax imposed under subtitle A for the current taxable year; and
   3. I had a right to a full refund of any and all amounts withheld for both years.
   You can see by checking my statement against the law itself that I have fulfilled all the requirements contained in the law. The law makes it perfectly clear that "not withstanding any other provision of this section..." (i.e. Section 3402[n]) that you "...shall not be required to deduct and withhold any tax..." from my wages if I provide you with the certified statement contained in this affidavit. Let me further point out that under law (Section 3402[n]) I am not required to provide you or the IRS with any other document or statement because this affidavit fulfills all the requirements contained in the law.
   Let me further remind you that no mimeographed letter or alleged regulation can abrogate or supercede my sworn statement and the clear language and intent of the law as shown below.

INTERNAL REVENUE CODE SECTION 3402(n)

"(n) Employees incurring no income tax liability.
   Not withstanding any other provision of this section, an employer shall not be required to deduct and withhold any tax under this chapter upon a payment of wages to an employee if there is in effect with respect to such payment a withholding exemption certificate (in such form and containing such other information as the Secretary may prescribe) furnished to the employer by the employee certifying that the employee-
   (1) incurred no liability for income tax imposed under subtitle A for his preceding taxable year, and
   (2) anticipates that he will incur no liability for income tax imposed under subtitle A for his current taxable year.
The Secretary shall by regulations provide for the coordination of the provisions of this subsection with the provisions of subsection (f)." *(emphasis added)*

NAME: _____
SIGNATURE: _____

NOTARY: _____
MY COMMISSION EXPIRES: _____

back of the form, in the Privacy Act Notice. It specifically states that, "You are required to give this information to your employer." If you are "required" to give it, then you didn't give it voluntarily. Then, if you are ever charged with tax evasion on the basis of filing an allegedly incorrect W-4, you should be able to keep the government from using it against you at trial on the grounds that *it was not voluntarily made.* You will now have a statement to that effect on the front and confirmation of it on the back. You will also argue that unless you filed one, you would not have been hired—let alone paid.

In addition, employees should submit the affidavit shown in Figure 8-4. This affidavit conforms exactly to the wording of the law (since the government's W-4 does not) and since it reproduces the law itself, it should help convince employers that as long as they have such a statement from an employee, the law completely absolves them from any liability with respect to that employee's withholding taxes. **How much more proof would they need?**

AND NOW FOR THE BIG SURPRISE! WITHHOLDING TAXES ARE NOT EVEN INCOME TAXES!

Would you believe that American wage earners are paying a tax **that they don't even know exists?** Incredibly, the federal government has conned the American public into believing that it is an "income" tax that is being withheld from the salaries of American workers—when, in reality, American workers have been made subject (and are paying) a totally different (and illegal) tax—a "wage" tax![5]

The World War II "Victory Tax"

The hitherto unknown wage tax came about as a result of World War II. From the inception of the current income tax in 1913 and until 1942, income taxes were not due until March 15th of the following year, when it became payable in a lump sum or in three installments. When you think about it, how could a tax on income earned during any given year become due and payable before that year ended? One would not know how much one earned until the year was over. Any taxes paid prior to the end of the year represented **MONEY THAT COULD HAVE BEEN INVESTED *AND LOST* BEFORE THE YEAR ENDED** and so would not have been fully taxable as income for that year! The income tax, remember, is *a tax on income earned for the year,* not a tax on the income earned during any given *day, week or month.* So, what right would the government have to tax one's income before one's complete net income for the full year could be determined? None whatsoever! However, during the Second World War the government wanted to make sure it collected income taxes from a new class of taxpayers that had never paid it before—the working class. (Prior to WW

II only the affluent paid income taxes). The government realized that the average worker would spend his wages as he received them, and would never set aside enough to pay the tax the following year—either in a lump sum or in three installments. So the tax had to be taken from him as he got paid, **or the government in many cases would never see it.**

However, **on what basis could the government demand money in advance—before it was legally due—which was March 15 of the following year?** None, whatsoever. So the government apparently devised a scheme to make the withholding tax look like an income tax while it *actually adopted another form of taxation* which, though illegal, the government could get away with as long as its illegality *were not challenged in the courts on this basis.* If the new tax were successfully disguised, nobody would challenge it, since no one would even know it existed![6] Remember, if the income tax of 1894 had never been challenged (and subsequently declared unconstitutional) the government could also have collected that tax—even though it, too, was unconstitutional! Somebody *first has to challenge its unconstitutionality.*

PROOF THAT WITHHOLDING TAXES ARE NOT INCOME TAXES

Chapter 3 of the Code is entitled "WITHHOLDING OF TAX ON NONRESIDENT ALIENS AND FOREIGN CORPORATIONS" and falls within Subtitle A. And, if income taxes were being withheld from Americans, it too would have fallen within Subtitle A. Section 1441(d) of Chapter 3 states that "the collection of the tax (was) imposed by Section 871(a)"—a section that also falls within Subtitle A. But wage withholding for Americans *is not contained in Subtitle A* as is withholding from non-resident aliens and foreign corporations—*but is in Subtitle C,* along with other forms of "Employment Taxes." In addition, it provides that the tax withheld is "imposed" pursuant to *that* subtitle and **not pursuant to Subtitle A, the title which imposes income taxes!**

A Misleading and Fraudulent Caption

The new "wage" tax (i.e. "withholding") was established in Code Sections 3402(a) and 3402(d) as shown in Figure 8-5 where it appears under the misleading caption of "Income tax collected at source." But, if you read the law itself (concerning which the caption need have no relationship) you will see that "income" taxes are not being withheld at all, but that **a new "employment tax" was created.**

The paragraph states that:

Every employer making payment of wages shall

deduct and withhold *upon such wages a tax* determined in accordance with...

Unlike Section 1441, no mention of "income" tax appears anywhere in Section 3402 and the section is worded entirely different from Section 1441. All this section says is that "a tax" shall be deducted and withheld from such "wages." It says nothing about it being an "income tax" that is withheld.

But two other Code sections (6413(a) and (b) Figure 8-6) prove that such "withheld" taxes are not income taxes at all. Note that both Sections 6413(a) and (b) speak of taxes *"imposed"* by several other sections AND SECTION 3402! **But income taxes are imposed in Section 1 of the Code. So, if what is being withheld from your wages was "imposed" by Section 3402, then what is being withheld is certainly not income taxes!**

But the illusion as to what is really happening is further punctured by Code Section 3402(d) which states in relevant part that:

> If the employer...fails to deduct and withhold the tax...and thereafter the **tax against which such tax may be credited is paid,** the tax so required to be deducted and withheld shall not be collected from the employer..."

So what is actually happening is that the "wage tax" can be taken as a *credit* against the income tax due on April 15th. Instead of an income tax being withheld (which would be unlawful since that tax would be withheld before it was assessed and before it could be statutorily due)—wages were (illegally) taxed as they were paid, and workers were allowed to take this as a **credit against income taxes which supposedly would fall due later**—after returns were filed and the tax assessed. The illusion was complete since in practice it worked out the same, and **a misleading caption was placed on Code Section 3402 to disguise the whole illegal scam!**

WITHHOLDING—FROM SOURCES OTHER THAN WAGES

Before *How Anyone Can Stop Paying Income Taxes* came out, self employed and retired individuals were not faced with the prospect of having income taxes involuntarily and illegally taken from dividends and bank interest, as they are today. As a result of a variety of withholding techniques (from sources other than wages) it is now practically (though not totally) impossible to open a bank or brokerage account without having to give a Social Security number. While the government claims that this is to prevent under-reporting of dividend, interest, and other types of income, I believe that

---

FIGURE 8-5

§ 3102. Income tax collected at source

(a) Requirement of withholding

(1) In general

Except as otherwise provided in this section, every <u>employer making payment of wages shall deduct and withhold upon such wages a tax determined</u> in accordance with tables or computational procedures prescribed by the Secretary. Any tables or procedures prescribed under this paragraph shall—

(A) apply with respect to the amount of wages paid during such periods as the Secretary may prescribe, and

(B) be in such form, and provide for such amounts to be deducted and withheld, as the Secretary determines to be most appropriate to carry out the purposes of this chapter and to reflect the provisions of chapter 1 applicable to such periods.

(d) Tax paid by recipient

If the employer, in violation of the provisions of this chapter, fails to deduct and withhold the tax under this chapter, and <u>thereafter the tax against which such tax may be credited is paid,</u> the tax so required to be deducted and withheld shall not be collected from the employer; but this subsection shall in no case relieve the employer from liability for any penalties or additions to the tax otherwise applicable in respect of such failure to deduct and withhold.

---

an equally important reason is to enable the government to trace those who may not be filing. The government can also find out where your assets are so they can be more easily "seized" with Notices of Levy. Even though the bank and brokerage people who ask for your Social Security number may be convinced that "the law requires us to get it," you know from Figure 2-11 that this simply is not true. If there were such a law, the Social Security Administration would not claim that "Such use is (not) required...by law." This alone *proves* that "backup withholding" rests on fraud. Banks even ask for Social Security numbers when people open checking accounts on which **no interest will be paid** and so no need exists for this information. But as one bank official told me, "We've become snitches for the IRS." But the bank's and brokerage firm's reason for allegedly having to get your Social Security number is based on three false assumptions:

1. that individuals are required to file and pay income taxes;

2. that individuals are required to disclose their Social Security numbers to private organizations, and

3. that all interest and dividend payments **are actually wages received from an employer.**

So let's see how these false and fraudulent assumptions are woven into the law.

For Starters:
Make the "Law" Incomprehensible"

The provisions of withholding from sources other than wages are strewn across no less than 16 different Code sections (3402-3406, 3501-3510, and 6109 inclusively) and involve more than 320 subsections and subsubsub-subsections. As a result, no member of the public can possibly figure it all out without spending numerous hours trying to do so. Consequently they have to believe almost anything told to them by the government or the payor. As a result, it is also impossible for me to realistically cover all aspects of such withholding, but I will cover enough of it to convince you that it's all based on fraud. However, the "law" provides what might be considered "liability" traps for those who allegedly "must" withhold. So, such organizations and persons are advised to check out the "law" for themselves, though I will present enough of it to convince anyone that legally, no one is really required to take any notice of it.

What The Law Appears To Provide

The withholding provisions for dividends and interest are different from those covering pensions and gambling winnings, and no doubt, affect far more people. These provisions seem to suggest (Section 3406(a) Fig. 8-7) that payors of interest and dividends are required to deduct 20% for income tax purposes if:

1. the payee fails to furnish his TIN to the payor[7],
2. the Secretary notifies the payor that the payee supplied him with an incorrect TIN number,
3. the Secretary notifies the payor that backup withholding should be commenced because the payee failed to properly report interest and dividends,
4. the payor failed to certify that he is not subject to withholding.

Proof that "backup withholding" is a fraud can be seen from the opening paragraph of the Code Section 6109 as shown in Figure 8-8. This is the Section identified in the Privacy Act Notice (Figure 8-9 Note F) of Form W-9 which is supplied by the IRS to payors for the purpose of securing Social Security numbers, though many payors now create their own forms.

Did you recognize why this section cannot apply to income taxes? Did you notice that "income taxes" is not mentioned in the section? I will address the one apparent exception in Section 6109(1)(4) in a moment. This section is not in Subtitle A and there is no cross-reference making it applicable to that subtitle; the reason for that will soon be apparent.

FIGURE 8-6

§ 6113. Special rules applicable to certain employment taxes

(a) Adjustment of tax

(1) General rule

If more than the correct amount of tax imposed by section 3101, 3111, 3201, 3221, or 3402 is paid with respect to any payment of remuneration, proper adjustments, with respect to both the tax and the amount to be deducted, shall be made, without interest, in such manner and at such times as the Secretary may by regulations prescribe.

(2) United States as employer

For purposes of this subsection, in the case of remuneration received from the United States or a wholly-owned instrumentality thereof during any calendar year, each head of a Federal agency or instrumentality who makes a return pursuant to section 3122 and each agent, designated by the head of a Federal agency or instrumentality, who makes a return pursuant to such section shall be deemed a separate employer.

(3) Guam or American Samoa as employer

For purposes of this subsection, in the case of remuneration received during any calendar year from the Government of Guam, the Government of American Samoa, a political subdivision of either, or any instrumentality of any one or more of the foregoing which is wholly owned thereby, the Governor of Guam, the Governor of American Samoa, and each agent designated by either who makes a return pursuant to section 3125 shall be deemed a separate employer.

(4) District of Columbia as employer

For purposes of this subsection, in the case of remuneration received during any calendar year from the District of Columbia or any instrumentality which is wholly owned thereby, the Mayor of the District of Columbia and each agent designated by him who makes a return pursuant to section 3125 shall be deemed a separate employer.

(b) Overpayments of certain employment taxes

If more than the correct amount of tax imposed by section 3101, 3111, 3201, 3221, or 3402 is paid or deducted with respect to any payment of remuneration and the overpayment cannot be adjusted under subsection (a) of this section, the amount of the overpayment shall be refunded in such manner and at such times (subject to the statute of limitations properly applicable thereto) as the Secretary may by regulations prescribe.

(5) States and political subdivisions as employer

For purposes of this subsection, in the case of remuneration received from a State or any political subdivision thereof (or any instrumentality of any one or more of the foregoing which is wholly owned thereby) during any calendar year, each head of an agency or instrumentality, and each agent designated by either, who makes a return pursuant to section 3125 shall be deemed a separate employer.

As you can see from Sections 6109(a) and (a)(1), these sections only apply to persons "required by regulations proscribed by the Secretary," with respect to "Any person required under the authority of this title to make a return, statement, or other document..." Since no one is "required" either by any "regulation(s) proscribed by the Seccretary" or the Code itself "to make a return..." in connection with income taxes—**this section and any Code section based on it—can not apply to income taxes!** Further proof of this is found in the fact that "backup withholding" is not even tied to the income tax imposed in Subtitle A but to the "wage" tax imposed in Subtitle C. Therefore, since backup withholding is based on a provision of the law *having nothing to do with making returns, statements or lists,* why was this language used? It was done to mislead the public into believing that such withholding is related to the income tax when, in fact, it isn't. To complete the illusion the term "income tax" was slipped into subsubsection (a)(4); but, as you can see, its use there is related to those who *prepare tax returns,* and does not relate to *taxpayers* themselves.

CAMELS, BEING DUCKS, CAN FLY

In order to create a legal basis for all forms of "backup withholding," the government makes a claim no more rational than the one stated above. Would you believe that the basis for all such withholding (from gambling winnings to stock dividends) is that **such payments are really wages** received from one's employer? No, I'm not kidding, I'm serious. As you can sec, Section 3406(h)(10) (Figure 8-10) provides (with respect to "reportable" interest, dividend and "other reportable payments") that:

Payments which are subject to withholding under this section shall be treated **as if they were wages paid by an employer to an employee** (and the amounts deducted and withheld under this section shall be treated as if deducted and withheld **under Section 3402).**

A similar assumption will be found in: Code Section 3402(o)(1) with respect to payments for supplemental unemployment, annuity and sick pay benefits; Section 3402(q)(7) with respect to gambling winnings; Section 3402(r)(2) with respect to some types of stock distributions (though this section was repealed in 1986); and Section 3405(a)(1) with respect to pensions, annuities and certain deferred income and nonperiodic distributions. Ask yourself, why did the government have to assume that all of these distributions were *wages* when they obviously *are not?* **Why couldn't the government have simply provided for such withholding without having to make such an ASININE AND FALSE ASSUMPTION?** You should know the answer to that. If what were being withheld were income taxes, the government would run into the same

---

FIGURE 8-7

§ 3406. Backup withholding

(a) Requirement to deduct and withhold

(1) In general

In the case of any reportable payment, if—
(A) the payee fails to furnish his TIN to the payor in the manner required,
(B) the Secretary notifies the payor that the TIN furnished by the payee is incorrect,
(C) there has been a notified payee underreporting described in subsection (c), or
(D) there has been a payee certification failure described in subsection (d),

then the payor shall deduct and withhold from such payment a tax equal to 20 percent of such payment.

(2) Subparagraphs (C) and (D) of paragraph (1) apply only to interest and dividend payments

Subparagraphs (C) and (D) of paragraph (1) shall apply only to reportable interest or dividend payments.

FIGURE 8-8

§ 6109. Identifying numbers

(a) Supplying of identifying numbers

When required by regulations prescribed by the Secretary:

(1) Inclusion in returns

Any person required under the authority of this title to make a return, statement, or other document shall include in such return, statement, or other document such identifying number as may be prescribed for securing proper identification of such person.

(2) Furnishing number to other persons

Any person with respect to whom a return, statement, or other document is required under the authority of this title to be made by another person shall furnish to such other person such identifying number as may be prescribed for securing his proper identification.

(3) Furnishing number of another person

Any person required under the authority of this title to make a return, statement, or other document with respect to another person shall request from such other person, and shall include in any such return, statement, or other document, such identifying number as may be prescribed for securing proper identification of such other person.

(4) Furnishing identifying number of income tax return preparer

Any return or claim for refund prepared by an income tax return preparer shall bear such identifying number for securing proper identification of such preparer, his employer, or both, as may be prescribed. For purposes of this paragraph, the terms "return" and "claim for refund" have the respective meanings given to such terms by section 6696(e).

For purposes of this subsection, the identifying number of an individual (or his estate) shall be such individual's social security account number.

FIGURE 8-9

Form **W-9**
(Rev. December 1987)
Department of the Treasury
Internal Revenue Service

Request for Taxpayer Identification Number and Certification

Give this form to the requester. Do NOT send to IRS.

Please print or type

Name (If joint names, list first and circle the name of the person or entity whose number you enter in Part I below. **See instructions if your name has changed.**)

Address

City, state, and ZIP code

List account number(s) here (optional) ▶

Part I Taxpayer Identification Number

Enter your taxpayer identification number in the appropriate box. For individuals and sole proprietors, this is your social security number. For other entities, it is your employer identification number. If you do not have a number, see *How To Obtain a TIN*, below.

Note: *If the account is in more than one name, see the chart on page 2 for guidelines on whose number to enter.*

Social security number

OR

Employer identification number

Part II For Payees Exempt From Backup Withholding (See Instructions)

Requester's name and address (optional)

Certification.—Under penalties of perjury, I certify that:

(1) The number shown on this form is my correct taxpayer identification number (or I am waiting for a number to be issued to me), **and**

(2) I am not subject to backup withholding either because I have not been notified by the Internal Revenue Service (IRS) that I am subject to backup withholding as a result of a failure to report all interest or dividends, or the IRS has notified me that I am no longer subject to backup withholding (does not apply to real estate transactions, mortgage interest paid, the acquisition or abandonment of secured property, contributions to an individual retirement arrangement (IRA), and payments other than interest and dividends).

Certification Instructions.—You must cross out item (2) above if you have been notified by IRS that you are currently subject to backup withholding because of underreporting interest or dividends on your tax return. (Also see *Signing the Certification* under *Specific Instructions*, later.)

Please Sign Here **Signature ▶** **Date ▶**

Instructions

(Section references are to the Internal Revenue Code.)

A **Purpose of Form.**—A person who is required to file an information return with IRS must obtain your correct taxpayer identification number (TIN) to report income paid to you, real estate transactions, mortgage interest you paid, the acquisition or abandonment of secured property, or contributions you made to an individual retirement arrangement (IRA). Use Form W-9 to furnish your correct TIN to the requester (the person asking you to furnish your TIN), and, when applicable, (1) to certify that the TIN you are furnishing is correct, (2) to certify that you are not subject to backup withholding, and (3) to claim exemption from backup withholding if you are an exempt payee. Furnishing your correct TIN and making the appropriate certifications will prevent certain payments from being subject to the 20% backup withholding.

Note: *If a requester gives you a form other than a W-9 to request your TIN, you must use the requester's form.*

How To Obtain a TIN.—If you do not have a TIN, you should apply for one immediately. To apply for the number, obtain **Form SS-5,** Application for a Social Security Number Card (for individuals), or **Form SS-4,** Application for Employer Identification Number (for businesses and all other entities), at your local office of the Social Security Administration or the Internal Revenue Service. Complete and file the appropriate form according to its instructions.

To complete Form W-9 if you do not have a TIN, write "Applied For" in the space for the TIN in Part I, sign and date the form, and give it to the requester. For payments that could be subject to backup withholding, you will then have 60 days to obtain a TIN and furnish it to the requester.

During the 60-day period, the payments you receive will not be subject to the 20% backup withholding, unless you make a withdrawal. However, if the requester does not receive your TIN from you within 60 days, backup withholding, if applicable, will begin and continue until you furnish your TIN to the requester.

Note: *Writing "Applied For" on the form means that you have already applied for a TIN* ***OR*** *that you intend to apply for one in the near future.*

As soon as you receive your TIN, complete another Form W-9, include your new TIN, sign and date the form, and give it to the requester.

What Is Backup Withholding?—Persons making certain payments to you are required to withhold and pay to IRS 20% of such payments under certain conditions. This is called "backup withholding." Payments that could be subject to backup withholding include interest, dividends, broker and barter exchange transactions, rents, royalties, nonemployee compensation, and certain payments from fishing boat operators, but do not include real estate transactions.

If you give the requester your correct TIN, make the appropriate certifications, and report all your taxable interest and dividends on your tax return, your payments will not be subject to backup withholding. Payments you receive will be subject to backup withholding if:

(1) You do not furnish your TIN to the requester, or

(2) IRS notifies the requester that you furnished an incorrect TIN, or

(3) You are notified by IRS that you are subject to backup withholding because you failed to report all your interest and dividends on your tax return (for interest and dividend accounts only), or

(4) You fail to certify to the requester that you are not subject to backup withholding under (3) above (for interest and dividend accounts opened after 1983 only), or

(5) You fail to certify your TIN. This applies only to interest, dividend, broker, or barter exchange accounts opened after 1983, or broker accounts considered inactive in 1983.

For other payments, you are subject to backup withholding only if (1) or (2) above applies.

B Certain payees and payments are exempt from backup withholding and information reporting. See *Payees and Payments Exempt From Backup Withholding*, below, and *Exempt Payees and Payments* under *Specific Instructions*, on page 2, if you are an exempt payee.

Payees and Payments Exempt From Backup Withholding.—The following lists payees that are exempt from backup withholding and information reporting. For interest and dividends, all listed payees are exempt except item (9). For broker transactions, payees listed in (1) through (13), and a person registered under the Investment Advisers Act of 1940 who regularly acts as a broker are exempt. Payments subject to reporting under sections 6041 and 6041A are generally exempt from backup withholding only if made to payees described in items (1) through (7), except that a corporation that provides medical and health care services or bills and collects payments for such services is not exempt from backup withholding or information reporting. Only payees described in items (2) through (6) are exempt from backup withholding for barter exchange transactions, patronage dividends, and payments by certain fishing boat operators.

(1) A corporation.

(2) An organization exempt from tax under section 501(a), or an individual retirement plan (IRA), or a custodial account under 403(b)(7).

(3) The United States or any agency or instrumentality thereof.

11

Form **W-9** (Rev. 12-87)

Form W-9 (Rev. 12-87) Page **2**

(4) A state, the District of Columbia, a possession of the United States, or any political subdivision or instrumentality thereof.

(5) A foreign government or a political subdivision, agency or instrumentality thereof.

(6) An international organization or any agency or instrumentality thereof.

(7) A foreign central bank of issue.

(8) A dealer in securities or commodities required to register in the U.S. or a possession of the U.S.

(9) A futures commission merchant registered with the Commodity Futures Trading Commission.

(10) A real estate investment trust.

(11) An entity registered at all times during the tax year under the Investment Company Act of 1940.

(12) A common trust fund operated by a bank under section 584(a).

(13) A financial institution.

(14) A middleman known in the investment community as a nominee or listed in the most recent publication of the American Society of Corporate Secretaries, Inc., Nominee List.

(15) A trust exempt from tax under section 664 or described in section 4947.

Payments of **dividends** and **patronage dividends** generally not subject to backup withholding also include the following:

- Payments to nonresident aliens subject to withholding under section 1441.
- Payments to partnerships not engaged in a trade or business in the U.S. and that have at least one nonresident partner.
- Payments of patronage dividends not paid in money.
- Payments made by certain foreign organizations.

Payments of **interest** generally not subject to backup withholding include the following:

- Payments of interest on obligations issued by individuals. **Note:** *You may be subject to backup withholding if this interest is $600 or more and is paid in the course of the payer's trade or business and you have not provided your correct TIN to the payer.*
- Payments of tax-exempt interest (including exempt-interest dividends under section 852).
- Payments described in section 6049(b)(5) to nonresident aliens.
- Payments on tax-free covenant bonds under section 1451.
- Payments made by certain foreign organizations.
- Mortgage interest paid by you.

Payments that are not subject to information reporting are also not subject to backup withholding. For details, see sections 6041, 6041A(a), 6042, 6044, 6045, 6049, 6050A, and 6050N, and the regulations under such sections.

Penalties

C **Failure To Furnish TIN.**—If you fail to furnish your correct TIN to a requester, you are subject to a penalty of $50 for each such failure unless your failure is due to reasonable cause and not to willful neglect.

Failure To Include Certain Items on Your Tax Return.—If you fail to properly include on your tax return certain items reported to IRS, such failure will be treated as being due to negligence, and you will be subject to a penalty of 5% on any part of an underpayment of tax attributable to that failure unless there is clear and convincing evidence to the contrary.

D **Civil Penalty for False Information With Respect to Withholding.**—If you make a false statement with no reasonable basis that results in no imposition of backup withholding, you are subject to a penalty of $500.

E **Criminal Penalty for Falsifying Information.**—Willfully falsifying certifications or affirmations may subject you to criminal penalties including fines and/or imprisonment.

Specific Instructions

Name.—If you are an individual, generally provide the name shown on your social security card. However, if you have changed your last name, for instance, due to marriage, without informing the Social Security Administration of the name change, you may enter your first name and both the last name shown on your social security card and your new last name.

Signing the Certification.—

(1) Interest, Dividend, and Barter Exchange Accounts Opened Before 1984 and Broker Accounts That Were Considered Active During 1983.—You are not required to sign the certification; however, you may do so. You are required to provide your correct TIN.

(2) Interest, Dividend, Broker and Barter Exchange Accounts Opened After 1983 and Broker Accounts That Were Considered Inactive During 1983.—You must sign the certification or backup withholding will apply. If you are subject to backup withholding and you are merely providing your correct TIN to the requester, you must cross out item (2) in the certification before signing the form.

(3) Real Estate Transactions.—You must sign the certification. You may cross out item (2) of the certification if you wish.

(4) Other Payments.—You are required to furnish your correct TIN, but you are not required to sign the certification unless you have been notified of an incorrect TIN. Other payments include payments made in the course of the requester's trade or business for rents, royalties, goods (other than bills for merchandise), medical and health care services, payments to a nonemployee for services (including attorney and accounting fees), and payments to certain fishing boat crew members.

(5) Mortgage Interest Paid by You, Acquisition or Abandonment of Secured Property, or IRA Contributions.—You are required to furnish your correct TIN, but you are not required to sign the certification.

(6) Exempt Payees and Payments.—If you are exempt from backup withholding, you should complete this form to avoid possible erroneous backup withholding. Enter your correct TIN in Part I, write "EXEMPT" in the block in Part II, cross out item (2) of the certification, sign and date the form. If you are a nonresident alien or foreign entity not subject to backup withholding, give the requester a completed **Form W-8,** Certificate of Foreign Status.

(7) TIN "Applied For."—Follow the instructions under *How To Obtain a TIN*, earlier, sign and date this form.

Signature.—For a joint account, only the person whose TIN is shown in Part I should sign the form.

F **Privacy Act Notice.**—Section 6109 requires you to furnish your correct taxpayer identification number (TIN) to persons who must file information returns with IRS to report interest, dividends, and certain other income paid to you, mortgage interest you paid, the acquisition or abandonment of secured property, or contributions you made to an individual retirement arrangement (IRA). IRS uses the numbers for identification purposes and to help verify the accuracy of your tax return. You must provide your TIN whether or not you are required to file a tax return. Payers must generally withhold 20% of taxable interest, dividend, and certain other payments to a payee who does not furnish a TIN to a payer. Certain penalties may also apply.

What Name and Number To Give the Requester

For this type of account:	Give the name and SOCIAL SECURITY number of:
1. Individual	The individual
2. Two or more individuals (joint account)	The actual owner of the account or, if combined funds, the first individual on the account[1]
3. Custodian account of a minor (Uniform Gift to Minors Act)	The minor[2]
4. a. The usual revocable savings trust (grantor is also trustee)	The grantor-trustee[1]
b. So-called trust account that is not a legal or valid trust under state law	The actual owner[1]
5. Sole proprietorship	The owner[3]

For this type of account:	Give the name and EMPLOYER IDENTIFICATION number of:
6. A valid trust, estate, or pension trust	Legal entity (Do not furnish the identification number of the personal representative or trustee unless the legal entity itself is not designated in the account title.)[4]
7. Corporate	The corporation
8. Association, club, religious, charitable, educational, or other tax-exempt organization	The organization
9. Partnership	The partnership
10. A broker or registered nominee	The broker or nominee
11. Account with the Department of Agriculture in the name of a public entity (such as a state or local government, school district, or prison) that receives agricultural program payments	The public entity

[1] List first and circle the name of the person whose number you furnish.
[2] Circle the minor's name and furnish the minor's social security number.
[3] Show the name of the owner.
[4] List first and circle the name of the legal trust, estate, or pension trust.

Note: *If no name is circled when there is more than one name, the number will be considered to be that of the first name listed.*

12

problem it faced with respect to wage withholding. They solved *that* problem by illegally *creating (and hiding)* a "wage" tax. Since the government was successful in fooling the public with that one, it evidently felt that it could now chance pulling off an even greater scam. So they now **applied the illegal wage tax to things that weren't even wages!** If the government can claim gambling winnings and stock distributions are wages, why can't it claim that 7-Up is bourbon and chocolate kisses are cigars and tax them accordingly? **Apparently there is no end to the amount of wool the government is capable of pulling over the eyes of the American public.**

STOPPING SUCH ILLEGAL WITHHOLDING

Putting a stop to such illegal withholding depends on the real nature of the distribution since the "law" treats them differently. But if all distributions are regarded as "wages," how can such differences apply? Thus the law is unconstitutional (and thus void) for another reason: it lacks uniformity. For example, to stop withholding from pensions, annuities and deferred income all one has to do is "elect to have (withholding) not apply" (pursuant to Code Section 3405(a)(2)). **That's all there is to it!** And one can make the same election with respect to non-periodic distributions pursuant to Code Section 3405(b)(3)(A). But I have come across individuals who were having taxes taken out of their annuity payments, who didn't know they could stop it that easily. God only knows how many annuitants are currently unknowingly having taxes withheld.

Gambling Winnings

The law with respect to gambling withholding is illegal for a variety of reasons, since apart from everything else, it is not uniform, not only with respect to other types of withholding but even within its own category. For example, under Section 3402(p)(2) winnings from state-conducted lotteries are subject to withholding if the amount exceeds $5,000 while for jai alai, dog and horse tracks, withholding is authorized if the amount won exceeds $1,000 and is 300 times the amount wagered. Winnings from slot machines, bingo and keno, on the other hand, are exempt from withholding altogether. And while the law with respect to all other types of withholding provides some mechanism whereby the payee can stop it, I can't find a similar provision with respect to gambling winnings. So such discrimination has to be illegal!

In addition, I believe that some race tracks might be withholding even when there is no need for it. Such withholding should not occur unless the amount won exceeds 300 times the wager. This would eliminate withholding from *all regular races,* since I don't believe any

FIGURE 8-10

(10) Coordination with other sections

For purposes of section 31, this chapter (other than section 3402(n)), and so much of subtitle F (other than section 7205) as relates to this chapter, <u>payments which are subject to withholding under this section shall be treated as if they were wages paid by an employer to an employee</u> (and amounts deducted and withheld under this section shall be treated as if deducted and withheld under <u>section 3402</u>).

horse ever goes off at 300 to 1. This would leave withholding to things like the daily double or a trifecta. I mention this only because I seem to recall people telling me that their winnings had been made subject to withholding even though I don't recall being told that their win involved anything so dramatic as the daily double or a trifecta.

But the withholding of gambling winnings is ridiculous (and obviously illegal) even if the proper amount is withheld. Let's assume an individual goes to the track with $1,000 and bets it all on the first race and wins $30,000: $5,800 would be withheld. Now let's assume that he bets on the remaining races and loses all of them including the $24,200 he got from that first race. So he borrows bus fare and goes home slightly depressed, having **lost $1,000** for the day—**yet he paid $5,800 in taxes!** Does that make sense to anybody?

PREVENTING WITHHOLDING ON INTEREST AND DIVIDENDS

As explained previously, Section 3406(d)(1) provides for payee certification that "payee is not subject to withholding under Subsection (a)(1)(C)." All payees can certify to this on the following basis.

1. They are not liable for income taxes.
2. Since interest and dividends are **not wages,** such receipts cannot (on the basis of law, fact, and common sense) be subject to a "wage" tax, **regardless of what Section 3406(h)(10) says.** Such a provision is obviously void because it is patently absurd and **contrary to fact.**
3. If, on the other hand, interest and dividends *are wages,* then payees are authorized to claim exempt pursuant to Section 3402(n).

As you can see from the above, no one can really be required to submit to withholding on interest and dividend income. So what's the problem? The problem is that when you deal with the federal government you're dealing with the mafia, of whom most banks and brokerage firms (having licenes to protect and who are themselves afraid of

IRS audits) are afraid. They are more afraid of the IRS than in keeping you as a client. So you face a problem. How you choose to deal with it depends on a number of variables. Assuming that you are self-employed and not filing tax returns, and the IRS has not bothered you: obviously, if you give your Social Security number to a bank or brokerage firm, this may help the government figure out that you're not filing. This might facilitate IRS harassment.

If you are only opening up a checking account and can persuade the bank (as I was able to do by using Figure 2-11) that you are not required to give them your Social Security number you will suffer no consequences since nothing will be withheld anyway. If, on the other hand, the account is interest-bearing and you don't give the bank your Social Security number, it will probably deduct 20% of the interest and send it to the government. Since the bank won't have your Social Security number I'm not sure how the government accurately credits this receipt. Undoubtedly its computers can track people either by name or by number. If you don't file for a refund you will obviously lose what was deducted (unless you plan to file for a refund and then sue later in a district court). Again, however, this might call attention to the fact that you haven't been filing, and increase the probabiity of IRS harassment. So, if it's a savings account you want, you will be better off with one in Canada. Canadian banks won't ask for your Social Security number, and while they will withhold 15% for Canadian

FIGURE 8-11

AFFIDAVIT

To Establish My Exemption From Backup Withholding

Since backup withholding is predicated on the assumption that interest/dividends or   are wages paid by an employer to an employee section 3402(n) is applicable.

INTERNAL REVENUE CODE SECTION 3402(n)

(n) Employees incurring no income tax liability.—Notwithstanding any other provision of this section, an employer <u>shall not be required to deduct and withhold any tax</u> under this chapter upon a payment of wages to an employee if there is in effect with respect to such payment a withholding exemption certificate (in such form and containing such other information as the Secretary may prescribe) furnished to the employer by the employee certifying that the employee—

(1) incurred no liability for income tax imposed under subtitle A for his preceding taxable year, and

(2) anticipates that he will incur no liability for income tax imposed under subtitle A for his current taxable year.

The Secretary shall by regulations provide for the coordination of the provisions of this subsection with the provisions of subsection (f).

Pursuant to Section 3402(n), this is to certify that I incurred no liability for income tax imposed under subtitle A last year, and I will incure no liability for income tax this year either. Thus I am also exempt from backup withholding pursuant to this section.

Account No. _____   _____

State of _____

County of _____

Before me, the undersigned, a notary public within and for the said county and State, personally appeared and swore to the truthfullness of the above representations.
Witness my hand and notarial seal this   day of   1989

My Commission expires   _____
                                        Notary Public

taxes, you will still be out less than if the same amount were deposited in an American bank and you would not have alerted the IRS. If you can't open up a U.S. checking account without disclosing your Social Security number, you might consider a Canadian bank for that too. You can keep your account in dollars, mail in your deposits, and write checks just as you would on any American account. I am told Canadian banks only respond to orders from Canadian courts. So, obviously, they will not turn over money pursuant to an IRS Notice of Levy. This feature alone makes them preferable to American banks. For details you might write to the Bank of Montreal, P.O. Box 1, Toronto, Canada M5X-1A1.

However, though the Bank of Montreal won't have your Social Security number, it's still a bank, and the U.S. has a tax treaty with Canada. I don't minimize the IRS' ability to get information from any regular North American bank. In addition, there may be some restrictions with respect to the transfer of funds to a foreign bank, so you would want to check that out. The U.S. has now embarked on a program to impose on Americans the types of currency controls that Mjalmar Horece Greeley Schacht (his mother was a Danish-American), Hitler's Minister of Economics, designed for Nazi Germany in 1934.

An alternative to commercial banking is afforded as a service of the National Commodity and Barter Association (NCBA) located at 8000 E. Girard Ave., Suite 215, Denver, Colorado 80231. Their telephone number is 303-337-9617. The NCBA is not a bank, is not incorporated, is not a member of the Federal Reserve, does not loan out funds, does not engage in fractional reserve shenanigans, and is not subject to banking regulations. Among other things, NCBA offers services along lines that you will find helpful. You can keep your funds in silver coins or in U.S. currency (non-redeemable Federal reserve notes) more accurately referred to by the Exchange and its members as "FRNS." They will not ask you for your Social Security number and your constitutionally protected right to privacy will be respected. The NCBA offers various types of services for its members, so you might call or write to them for details.

CLAIMING "EXEMPT" WITH RESPECT TO INTEREST AND DIVIDENDS

As referred to in 3406(a)(1)(D) (Figure 8-7), there is such a thing with respect to "backup withholding" as "payee certification failure." This is as close as this statute gets to Section 3402(n). Actually (as explained later) since backup withholding is based on interest and dividends **being wages** subject to tax under Section 3402, then the provisions of Section 3402(n) should apply, and one should be permitted to claim "exempt" simultaneously with opening up the account. However Section 3406 allows such

"certification" only when the government invokes provision (c) of Section 3406. That is when the Secretary notifies the banks to commence withholding because of alleged "under-reporting," even though you provided your Social Security number in accordance with provision (a). Only then are payees presumably authorized to claim that they are not subject to withholding. However this provision apparently doesn't apply if you fail to give your Social Security number to the bank, pursuant to provision (a). In that case, there doesn't seem to be a provision for "payee certification...that such payee is not subject to withholding." Despite this omission you should still be able to claim "exempt" since you know that the law does not require (nor could it) for such withholding. Therefore, I have created an all purpose Affidavit (Figure 8-11) that you might try using even when you open an account. The success you might enjoy will depend on your own powers of persuasion, how much the bank or brokerage firm wants your business, its willingness to examine the facts, and how fearful they are of the IRS. It might be helpful if you provide them with this chapter to read. Other procedures you might adopt are covered elsewhere in this book.[8]

Before leaving this subject, it might be helpful to briefly examine Form W-9 just to gain additional insight into the extent of the fraud the government practices in connection with "backup withholding."

1. At note A, the form uses the word "must" and not "required" for reasons you already know.
2. The use of the word "required" (Note B) here is false. Nothing in the law says that anyone is "required" to do so.
3. A "reasonable cause" (C) is that you are not liable for the tax, had no "income" within the meaning of the law, and bank interest and stock dividends and trading profits are not "wages" that can be **lawfully taxed as such.**
4. You will not be making a "false statement" (Note D) and not one without a "reasonable basis" for all the reasons stated above.
5. Note E explains why you should claim on any statement in connection with backup withholding that it is not being supplied voluntarily. You were *forced* to make any "certifications or affirmations" to prevent payors from illegaly turning over your money to the government. Remember, if the government gets any of your dividends or interest through the backup withholding ruse—and you do not file regularly—you will have to file a refund claim and then sue to get it back. In filing such a claim you will have to admit to not having filed a tax return. Such an admission may expose you to criminal charges (pursuant to Code Section 7203 for willfully failing to file). However, you can seek to frustrate that effort by again indicating that your claim for a refund was not made voluntarily but in response to the government's illegal confiscation of your money. It's either that or filing a return to get the money back or trying

to prevent the illegal confiscation of your funds before it occurs.

6. The government's claim at Note F is false. Nowhere in Section 6109 is anyone "required" to furnish their "correct identification number" as is verified by Figures 2-11 and 8-6.

It is certainly a sad commentary on the state of affairs in America when anyone of average intelligence can figure out that they are not subject to a "law," but still have to spend time, money and energy seeking ways to avoid it. That's the price we now must all pay for permitting the federal mafia to get away with murder.[9]

NOTES TO CHAPTER 8

1. Unfortunately, some people who were persuaded by *How Anyone Can Stop Paying Income Taxes* that they could legally stop paying income taxes (they could) went to jail. How many, I don't know. But they and their families paid a terrible price because of what they learned. Not that any of it was wrong; on the contrary—it didn't go far enough. And though the book carried the same warning that appears in this one, and cautioned about the corruption of our courts, it is still painful to contemplate the degree of suffering that some experienced because of the information I provided. I also thought I had included material that would prevent what happened to myself (I wrote of my having gone to jail for not filing) and others from happening to them. So, I must again warn you regarding the use of this information. There is no question that **it is all correct.** Paying and filing income taxes are, by law, voluntary. The law, as you will now discover, also provides you with a means for stopping the withholding of that tax; which, by any legitimate standard, you have a perfect right to do. But, by doing so, you run the risk of going to jail! That's just how it is in Amerika! So, you have to consider whether or not it's worth the risk. As I write this, (June 6, 1989) the pictures of what has happened in China are still vividly in mind—especially the ones showing a student stopping a column of tanks with nothing but courage. This book should have convinced you that the freedoms Americans *think* they possess are largely *illusory.* We may, indeed, be freer than others in this world, but we are certainly not as free as Americans once were and not as free as our Constitution supposedly guarantees. We are losing more of our freedom (along with our former economic superiority) each day. The question is, what risks and steps can and should Americans prudently take to recapture that freedom? Should Americans simply cave in to the kind of government tyranny that is fully documented in this book?

2. What might appear to be an exception to this is the provision found in many divorce decrees that the one paying alimony gets to deduct it, while the one receiving it must declare it. Such an arrangement, however, is based on mutual consent. However, suppose the one receiving the alimony believed it was taxable at the time the agreement was made, but now discovers that they are not "liable" for the tax. Are they necessarily still bound by that agreement?

3. Apart from employees being given a fraudulent Privacy Act Notice and being intimidated into paying the tax by the publicity given to the criminal prosecutions of those who failed to file, employees had no "income" within the meaning of the law. In addition, the income tax is not imposed pursuant to any of the taxing clauses of the constitution. So on these bases, all employees had "a *right* to a full refund"—even though they might not have claimed one.

4. However, the government does just that when it prosecutes people for income tax evasion. It claims that returns are *required* to be filed, then uses those same returns against those who do, *to gain their convictions!*

5. The current "wage" tax is illegal on various grounds— and should be *constitutionally challenged by somebody on this basis.* The wage tax amounts to an unapportioned direct tax on the main type of property owned by America's working class—their labor. Even if one wanted to argue (albeit incorrectly) that the 16th Amendment gave the government the right to tax income without apportionment, it certainly did not give it the right to tax labor without apportionment. But, in addition, how could the federal government (either legally or equitably) put a direct tax on labor without putting an *equal direct tax on capital?*

6. Apparently in 1943, the government believed that it was better to create an illegal tax rather than to graft illegal provisions onto an existing one. However such concerns don't seem to bother the government today.

7. Note that the "law" here only speaks on one's TIN (Taxpayer Identification Number) and not one's Social Security number. Do you want to speculate why? My original Social Security card carried the inscription "Not To Be Used For Identification." This inscription no longer appears on cards issued today. The reason it was once there was to placate those who opposed the bill on the grounds that such numbers would become I.D.s—which was never the Act's purpose. It probably would have been defeated if this were proposed or even suggested.

8. In addition, it should be noted that the law covering notification to commence backup withholding applies only to "underreporting." It is crystal clear that this can only apply in cases where *a return is filed and such interest is not reported.* By "law" and logic it cannot apply when returns are not filed—since no "self-assessment" took place! However, I am sure the IRS will apply the "law" to situations when no returns are filed (and thus no "underreporting" occurs) and the courts will, no doubt, reject any argument addressed to the "laws" proper application as "frivolous.'

9. It came to my attention after I had finished writing this chapter, that most (if not all) of America's major stock brokerage firms are withholding proceeds from the sale of stock—when Social Security numbers are not supplied—in total violation of the provisions of back-up withholding. What these firms are doing is deducting **20% from all stock sales,** even though such withholding is not required by law—even if we assume that back-up withholding is otherwise legitimate. For example: suppose you invest $10,000 with one of America's major brokerage firms and three months later you sell the stock, through the same broker, for $10,000. If you haven't supplied the brokerage firm with your Social Security number, it will withhold $2,000 and send it to the government. Then suppose they invest the remaining $8,000 for you in another stock, and three months later you again sell it for what you paid, or $8,000. This time they will deduct and send $1,600 to the government. So now the government has $3,600 of your money and **you still haven't earned a quarter!** But suppose you only got $5,000 on your first trade—what happens then? In that case, American brokerage firms would still send $1,000 to the government, **even though you lost $5,000 on the sale!** Can you believe this! So I called the legal department of one of America's largest brokerage firms—and they confirmed it! I was told, "Look, we don't like it either. It costs us money. But we're obligated to follow the law." When I asked the firm's lawyer what law (Code Section) "required" them to deduct 20 percent out of every sale (if I did not give them my Social Security number), he would only say, "It's somewhere in the 6,000 sections, but there are pages and pages of regulations on this. And, there is nothing we can do about it. It's the law." All of that was nonsense, of course, since there is no law that requires it. And the only way to stop this is for a number of people to buy, say $1,000 of stock, not give the firm their Social Security number, sell the stock, and if they withhold $200, sue them in small claims courts for the $200. After enough brokerage firms lose these suits, maybe they'll stop this practice. What the law "says" is that in the event of the failure of the payee to furnish his TIN to the payor, the payor has to deduct (theoretically, of course) 20 percent of "any reportable interest or dividend payment" or "any other *reportable payment.*" Now it's one thing for a

brokerage firm to claim that interest or dividends are "reportable," since the law *specifically identifies them,* and assuming one files, they generally are. But the law says nothing about withholding **anything** from the *mere sale of stock.* It only refers to "other reportable payments." But the only sales that are theoretically "reportable" are those that result in gains! Wash sales are not "reportable payments," and certainly a stock loss is not a "reportable payment"! **No one is "required" to deduct stock loses from their income taxes.** They are *supposedly* required to report stock gains, *because they are theoretically taxable—losses and wash sales are* **not taxable on any basis!**

So why do brokerage firms withhold in such cases? They do it because they can get away with it, and because the law is not really enforceable as written. Since firms have no way of knowing whether any given sale results in a reportable gain—they deduct 20% from **all sales!** In our first example, the firms own records would disclose that there was no "reportable payment." But suppose the stock were purchased from another broker. In that case the selling broker would not know (without spending time and money to find out) whether the stock sold was initially purchased for $5,000, $10,000 or $15,000. So it deducts the 20% **regardless of whether or not there is a "reportable payment."** But that's the government's problem or the brokers problem—**not the payee's problem.** The most the law "says" that can be deducted is 20 percent of the "reportable payment." If one sells a stock for a loss, there is no "reportable payment." So what does this mean? It means that Americans are now having payments deducted from stock sales that the law doesn't even authorize—simply because it is expedient for the brokerage community to do it that way! Well I suggest that the public make it more costly for them **to do it that way!** The fact that since there is really no cost effective way to withhold taxes from stock sales, means that such sales should not be subject to withholding—for this and other reasons! What this policy also means is that Americans who want to trade stock are **forced** (actually *blackmailed*) into revealing their Social Security number, **even though there is no law** that requires it! Why should a seller of stock (who doesn't want his stock broker to know his Social Security number) lose 20% of a sale (when no law requires that either!), simply because brokerage firms can't economically collect what they *think* the law "requires" *in any other way?*

Of course, when you speak to those in charge at these firms they tell you, "We're only following the law. You'll get it back when you file your return." Well, you know that's *not* the law. Why should the government be able to hold your money, interest free? Why should you have to file a return in order to get it back? Maybe you don't want to file! If Americans don't want to give their Social Security numbers to stock brokers, they are forced to deal with foreign brokers!

— CHAPTER 9 —
AVOIDING IRS AUDITS & SUMMONSES

*"An individual taxpayer may refuse to exhibit
his/her books and records for examination...
under the Fifth Amendment...and Fourth Amendment."*
—IRS Handbook for Special Agents

If anything strikes terror into the heart of the average American, it's the prospect of an IRS audit. Audits can involve substantial legal and accounting expenses and divert precious time away from business and personal affairs. But what is ironic about this is that there is no law that says anyone is required to be audited.

This is fully substantiated (as was formerly mentioned) in paragraphs 342.12 of the IRS's own *Handbook for Special Agents* (Figure 2-9). Paragraph 342.12 explains that in refusing to be audited one should have clear proof that one has done so on constitutional grounds. As shown in this paragraph, on at least three occasions federal judges (though this has happened many more times) have instructed juries that "in the absence of such claims, it is not error for a court to charge the jury that it may consider the refusal to produce books and records, in determining willfulness." This provides added insight into the integrity of the federal judiciary and the nonsensical and contrived basis on which many Americans are now sent to jail.

Since it is perfectly clear that no one is legally required to be audited (there is no law that requires it and the Constitution forbids it), why should juries be instructed, *on any basis,* that such a refusal can be considered "in determining (criminal) willfulness." Sometimes the basis (constitutional or otherwise) as to why a defendant refused to be audited is not, for various reasons, fully developed at trial—since it may not seem that significant to the defendant or his lawyer. This happened to me where such an instruction was given. In each of the three cases cited above, the defendants could have gone to jail simply because they refused to be audited! Remember, **no law required them to be audited anyway!** The reason is that none of the defendants could have been convicted **unless the jury found "willfulness" proven beyond a reasonable doubt.** If this were the the *only* basis (or a significant element) for such a finding, these defendants could have been found guilty *on this basis alone*—**regardless of anything else they might have been charged with.** If the prosecution could not have proven willfulness *on any*

other basis, they all would have gone free! **So this is irrefutable proof that not only are Americans now being sent to jail for having done nothing illegal, they might also go to jail for simply claiming a constitutional right that was not clearly revealed at trial!**

The reason one does not have to submit to an IRS audit or even turn over one's books or records in response to a more compelling IRS summons is that if one were required to do either, the IRS could not use the information it gathered to determine possible criminal culpability or to assess *civil fines and penalties.* If the IRS could do neither with audit information, then there would be no point in their conducting audits or issuing summonses! This is made additionally clear by section 342.15 (see Chapter 2, Figure 2-9) of the IRS *Handbook.* Nicola was indicted for income tax evasion and "objected for the first time" at his trial to an IRS agent's testimony, which included information received from Nicola at an audit. However, when Nicola attempted to prevent this information from being used against him, look what the judge said.

> "But he did not refuse to supply the information required. Did he waive his privilege? ...it was necessary for him to claim immunity before the government agent and *refuse to produce his books.* After the government had gotten possession of the information *with his consent* it was too late for him then to claim constitutional immunity." (emphasis added)

So here the court admonishes Nicola for not having asserted his constitutional rights *at the audit,* **by refusing to produce his books** and give information. Note that the court states that Nicola gave the information "with his consent"—i.e. voluntarily. Of course many Americans believe that they are "required" to do so (from a practical standpoint they are, as will be explained shortly), so to claim that it was done with Nicola's consent is purely speculative and probably false. Nicola probably did not even realize that he had a right not to turn over the incriminating information and then was probably convicted because of it.

Additional Proof That
Income Tax Returns Are Not "Required"

Of course, everything that sections 342.12 and 342.15 say about IRS audits applies **with equal force** to income tax returns—since all information on those can *also* be used against you! So, if you can *refuse to be audited* on constitutional grounds, why can't you *refuse to file a return on those very same grounds?*[1] And, as a matter of fact, in 1927 the Fourth Circuit Court of Appeal said just that in *Sullivan v. U.S.*, 15 F.23 809 (see Reply Brief, Appendix). Note the final line in section 342.12 concerning a court's refusal to hold someone in contempt for not producing "his/her books and records," on the grounds that such a "disclosure...would provide a starting point for a tax evasion case." The real "starting point" for a tax evasion case, however, is the **filing of a return—so why wouldn't the same reasoning apply there?**

And, as was already pointed out in Chapter 2, if you surrender your Fifth Amendment right *by filing*—you are subsequently compelled to surrender your Fourth Amendment right *as well!* So the *only way* you can retain *both of the constitutional rights which the IRS handbook admits you have*—without risking financial punishment—is by **not filing!**

THE FRAUDULENT
IRS SUMMONS (SUBPOENA)

If an individual or business refuses to be audited, the IRS generally responds by issuing an IRS Summons—often ominously entitled "Collection Summons." These summonses might just as well be called subpoenas, (and in many court cases they are) since they operate essentially in the same manner. By law, they have absolutely nothing to do with income taxes (as you might have guessed) but, nevertheless, the IRS uses them to gather information from both taxpayers and third parties alike, for that purpose. Despite the fact that an IRS summons BY LAW cannot apply to income taxes, there have been at least a dozen Supreme Court decisions involving them and hundreds if not thousands of cases at the appellate and district court levels. As a result, the American public has been bilked out of untold millions (if not billions) in fraudulent legal fees, as well as having had to absorb needless and incalculable economic costs in both time and money.

THE LEGAL BASIS
FOR AN IRS SUMMONS

The IRS' ability to inquire into an individual's affairs with respect to taxes is contained in Chapter 78 of Subtitle E which is entitled "Discovery of Liability and Enforcement of Title." It should be obvious that this Chapter does not apply to income taxes for two reasons. First, it does not appear in Subtitle A and there is no cross reference from that title making this Chapter applicable to it. Secondly, since the Chapter concerns the "Discovery of (Tax) Liability," it cannot apply to income taxes, since *there is no such tax "liability."*

The Need For a Tax "Liability"

Sections 7601 and 7602 (Figure 9-1) clearly establishes that without the existence of a potential tax "liability," the IRS has no authority to issue a summons, and since no such "liability" exists with respect to income taxes, the IRS has no authority to issue summonses in connection with income taxes. **What can be plainer or simpler than that?** Note that Section 7601 only authorizes the IRS to "inquire after

---

FIGURE 9-1

Code Section 7601
Sec. 7601. Canvass of districts for taxable persons and objects.

(a) General rule.
The Secretary shall, to the extent he deems it practicable, cause officers or employees of the Treasury Department to proceed, from time to time, through each internal revenue district and inquire after and concerning all persons therein who may be liable to pay any internal revenue tax, and all persons owing or having the care and management of any object with respect to which any tax is imposed.

(b) Penalties.
For penalties applicable to forcible obstruction or hindrance of Treasury officers or employees in the performance of their duties, see section 7212.

Code Section 7602
Sec. 7602. Examination of books and witnesses.

(a) Authority to summon, etc.
For the purpose of ascertaining the correctness of any return, making a return where none has been made, determining the liability of any person for any internal revenue tax or the liability at law or in equity of any transferree or fiduciary of any person in respect of any internal revenue tax, or collecting any such liability, the Secretary is authorized—
(1) To examine any books, papers, records, or other data which may be relevant or material to such inquiry;
(2) To summon the person liable for tax or required to perform the act, or any officer or employee of such person, or any person having possession, custody, or care of books of account containing entries relating to the business of the person liable for the tax or required to perform the act, or any other person the Secretary may deem proper, to appear before the Secretary at a time and place named in the summons and to produce such books, papers, records, or other data, and to give such testimony, under oath, as may be relevant or material to such inquiry; and
(3) To take such testimony of the person concerned under oath, as may be relevant or material to such inquiry.

and concerning all persons therein *who may be liable to pay any internal revenue tax.''* Therefore the IRS has no authority to inquire "after" anyone who does not have a potential tax liability. And though further on the section speaks of "persons owning or having the care and management of any objects with respect to which any tax is imposed," the existence of a possible tax "liability" with respect to the person inquired about must, obviously, exist.

Section 7602, however, is the crucial section and clearly reveals the fraud that has been perpetrated on the American public, since it reveals that *the IRS never* had the authority to issue summonses or *inquire into the affairs of people in connection with income taxes.* (This is how the section appeared until 1983. We will cover the additions shortly.) It also reveals why no employer, bank, brokerage firms, etc., etc., is required to reveal anything to the IRS ABOUT ANYBODY without first getting a Section 7602 summons. Since Section 7602 is presumably the law that authorizes the IRS to pry into the private and business affairs of Americans (thus interfering with contractual and privacy rights) this is the law that the IRS *must follow* when it **wants to do such prying.** The IRS can't merely *ask* third parties for information concerning other Americans. It must get it by way of a Section 7602 summons! If the IRS can compel such information without having to issue a summons, **then what purpose does Section 7602 serve?**

As you can see, the first paragraph of Section 7602 uses the word "liability" no less than three times! Without the existence of a potential tax "liability," the section **is not even applicable,** *so obviously it has no applicability to income taxes!* This is further confirmed by Section (2), though Section (1) deserves some comment. This latter section can be misleading since it deals with what IRS agents are "authorized" to do, but *imposes no obligation on the public.* It "authorizes" IRS agents to "examine any books, papers, records, etc., etc.," but *only if one chooses to voluntarily give his records to the agent.* Just because IRS agents are "authorized" to "examine" such documents does not mean that anyone is legally obligated to supply the agents with the documents they are "authorized" to "examine." All IRS agents are "authorized" to use telephones and have lunch, but that does not mean that anyone is obligated to let them use *their* phone or *feed* them!

But Section 7602(a)(2) is the crucial provision. Note that IRS agents are only authorized to issue summonses with respect to persons:

liable for the tax or *required to perform the act,* or any officer or employee of such person, or any person having possession...(of material)...relating to the business or person *liable* for the tax or *required to perform the act.*

As you can see, this section gives the IRS no subpoena power in connection with income taxes or any other specific tax. It only authorizes agents to subpoena records with respect to some tax "liability" or some "act" that is "required" to be "performed." Obviously any such subpoena should identify the Code section establishing the "liability" or the "act" required to be performed. However, **no such references will ever appear in any summons involving income taxes.** Can you guess why?

There are, as you already know, numerous Code sections dealing with various tax "liabilities." You can be sure that when summonses are issued in connection with those taxes, *the section creating the tax liability will be identified.* In addition, there are numerous sections requiring persons to perform certain acts with respect to other taxes. As you already know, sections 5741 and 5555(a) require tobacco manufacturers and liquor dealers to keep records (thus they are required to perform some "act"), so summonses *can be* issued with respect to those "acts." Now you have concrete confirmation of the claim found in the third paragraph of this book when I said that the government tricked the American public "into believing that those enforcement provisions of the Code that apply to other, non-voluntary taxes (such as alcohol and tobacco taxes), also apply to income taxes when in fact, they do not." Here you can see one dramatic example of that technique.

COMPOUNDING THE FRAUD

Proving that there are no limits to the unconstitutional lengths to which the government can *now* go (without any objection from the nation's legal establishment) in the collection of income taxes, the government, in 1983, added

FIGURE 9-2   **Code Section 7602**
(a portion of the 1983 Additions)
(b) Purpose may include inquiry into offense.
The purposes for which the Secretary may take any action described in paragraph (1), (2), or (3) of subsection (a) include the purpose of inquiring into any offense connected with the administration or enforcement of the internal revenue laws.
(c) No administrative summons when there is justice department referral.
(1) **Limitation of authority.** No summons may be issued under this title, and the Secretary may not begin any action under section 7604 to enforce any summons, with respect to any person if a Justice Department referral is in effect with respect to such person.
(2) **Justice department referral in effect.** For purposes of this subsection—
(A) In general. A Justice Department referral is in effect with respect to any person if—
(i) the Secretary has recommended to the Attorney General a grand jury investigation of, or the criminal prosecution of, such person for any offense connected with the administration or enforcement of the internal revenue laws.

sections (b) and (c) to section 7602 (Figure 9-2). Note that section (b) apparently authorizes IRS agents to issue summonses to investigate "*any* (alleged) offense" in connection with internal revenue laws. Presumably this includes *criminal* as well as *civil* infractions and thus would give every IRS agent greater subpoena powers than that possessed by federal grand juries! The reason is that federal grand juries need *probable cause* before they can issue subpoenas—but IRS agents don't! All IRS audits, which summonses are designed to augment, are necessarily "fishing expeditions." They are intended to allow the IRS to verify the accuracy of tax returns. Before starting such a "fishing expedition" IRS agents haven't the vaguest idea if the return being audited is correct or not—or on what basis it might not be correct. *It undertakes its audit to find these things out!*

So section 7602(b) would now seem to authorize similar fishing expeditions (lacking probable cause) to determine criminal culpability—powers that even federal grand juries *don't have!* And if IRS employees can be given such broad subpoena power, why can't such power be given to federal employees in other departments and agencies? They, too, could be given intimidating titles such as "agents" or "officers." Then, government could do away with cumbersome grand jury investigations altogether, and use grand juries merely to review the material gathered by the subpoena powers possessed by legions of federal employees!

In addition, if section (b) gives IRS agents such broad authority to inquire "into *any* offense" in connection with internal revenue laws, then what purposes do the limitations and restrictions contained in section (a) serve? None whatsoever! **So why wasn't that section simply eliminated from the Code?** Also, taken by itself, section (b) would appear to give IRS agents the power to subpoena *anything* and *anybody,* just as long as they could relate it to "*any* offense connected with. . .internal revenue laws." How many people would recognize that this apparently limitless subpoena power, **was still restrained by the restriction in section 7601** that any such subpoena must relate to the potential "liabilty" of the person inquired "after"? Even if such an obvious limitation were raised in court, federal judges would now be in position to dismiss it as being an argument "without merit" or "frivolous" or, as is often the case, to simply ignore it altogether.

Supposedly, the limitation on the IRS' authority to issue subpoenas for the purpose of conducting "fishing expeditions" with respect to criminal culpability is contained in section (c). This provides that they cannot be issued once a Justice Department *referral* is in effect. That is, a subpoena can't be issued once the IRS *recommends* to the Justice Department that a grand jury investigation or criminal prosecution of the taxpayer be undertaken. So, all IRS agents have to do to serve as one-man grand juries (but with greater subpoena power) is to *hold off* making any such

recommendations until they have *finished* their fishing expeditions! But can section 7602 summonses *really* be used in this manner?

Some Case Law on the Subject

In 1934 the Second Circuit Court of Appeals (in *Rasquin* vs. *Muccini* 72 F.2d 688) rejected an attempt by the IRS to summon the records of John M. Phillips from the executor of his estate. Phillips, who died in 1928, had filed no returns for the years 1922 to 1926. In barring the use of an IRS summons in that case, the panel (which included the noted jurist Mr. Learned Hand) ruled that:

> Neither of the statutes under which the summonses were expressly issued gives any such power to the collector. . .this section only gives power to require the attandance of witnesses and taking of testimony under oath "for the purpose of ascertaining the correctness of any return or for the purpose of making a return when none has been made.★★★" It does not give the collector authority to summon witnesses and compel them to testify **in aid of the collection of taxes.** (Emphasis added.)

Does this sound as if IRS agents had subpoena powers under section 7206 to investigate **any and all** possible offenses "connected with. . .internal revenue laws"? Historically, the courts have held that "Section 7602 authorizes the examination of taxpayer's records to determine "the 'correctness' of an income tax return," (*Boren* v. *Tucker* 239 F2d 767) and "whether (an) inspection sought 'might have thrown light upon' the correctness of the taxpayer's returns." (*Foster* v. *U.S.*, 265 F.2d 183, 187). In *Boren* the court went even further and added that it is "Against public policy for the Judicial branch of the Government to lend its support to the use of an *unrestricted* administrative subpoena power." *This, of course, is exactly what 7602(b) is now* **(illegally) designed to provide!**

In its most influential decision on the subject of 7602 summonses, the Supreme Court in *Reisman* v. *Caplin,* 375 U.S. 440 (at page 449) stated:

> Furthermore, we hold that in any of these procedures before either the district judge or the United States Commissioner, the witness may challenge the summons on any appropriate ground. This would include, as the circuits have held, the defenses that the material is sought for the **improper purpose of obtaining evidence for use in a criminal prosecution.** (Emphasis added.)

So the Supreme Court held that it was "improper" to use 7602 summonses to obtain evidence for use in a criminal prosecution. But apparently that's okay today, just so long as no "referral" has been made!

It must be obvious that giving individual IRS agents greater subpoena powers than that possessed by federal grand juries must be unconstitutional. It is important to note that, taken *together,* sections 7601 and 7602 don't do that—but in *practice* (when viewed *separately*) they certainly do!

But even the definitive *Mertens* isn't conceding that the 1983 additions to the Code *enlarged* the IRS's subpoena power. In discussing these powers in its 1989 edition (at paragraph 47.77), *Mertens* listed its authority under section 7602 as follows: (1) To "ascertain the correctness of any return," (2) to "make a return where none has been filed," (3) to "determine the liability of any person paying an internal revenue tax," (4) to "determine the liability at law or equity" or any transferee or fiduciary or any person with respect to any internal revenue tax, and (5) to "collect any internal revenue tax liability."

So *Mertens* is still generally sticking to the limitations contained in 7602(a), and is not conceding that the IRS now has the authority to subpoena records in connection with *"any offense* connected with. . .the internal revenue laws," and, I suggest, you do the same!

PROTECTING YOURSELF AND FIGHTING BACK

Since you already know that the federal government is only out to rob you (through lies and intimidation) when it comes to income taxes, your cooperating with the government merely amounts to your cooperating with a burglar. It's like holding his ladder or flashlight, leading him to your safe, providing him with its combination, pointing out the drawer where you keep your good silver and giving him a jump start so he can make his getaway.

As you already know, there is no law that says you have to submit to an audit. If the IRS wants to see your books and records it has to summon them pursuant to section 7602. Since it doesn't really like to do this, it will seek out ways to intimidate you into providing your records without having to subpoena them. But if you have already filed you are forced to submit (or see your deductions disallowed) and thus there is very little you can do about it. So you might as well consent to be audited—especially if you can support all of your deductions. However, that does not mean that you have to give in to every disallowance or that you have to be a pussy cat. I can also appreciate that in this situation (since the auditing agent can make arbitrary decisions about what is deductible) you want to stay on his good side. But certain

people get raked over the coals every year, and they might want to take a different approach. If you're one of those people who generate a lot of deductible receipts, which, for your own convenience, you keep in an orderly manner, there is no law that says you have to provide them to the IRS in the same fashion. You could bring all of your receipts to the audit in a big, brown paper bag, or maybe even two bags. If the IRS agent wants proof of a deduction, you might simply hand him one of the bags and tell him he can find the receipt in there. Offer to leave the bags with him, so he can sort them out for himself while assuring him that he will find receipts for all deductions. If he tells you that you have to provide them in any particular fashion, ask him to show you the law that says so. There isn't any!

IF YOU HAVEN'T FILED

If you haven't filed, then **under no circumstances** should you submit or **even** voluntarily **talk to any IRS agent with respect to any year for which you haven't filed.** (See Chapter 11) When I say don't talk, I mean DON'T TALK! Anything you say to IRS agents can be used against you. But more importantly, they will lie to grand juries, in court, and in documents that they might have to complete to assess fraud penalties *concerning what* you *might* have said! So you're better off not giving them an opportunity to even *claim* they spoke to you. I learned this the hard way. Remember if you haven't filed, the government may want to (illegally) prosecute you and/or to (illegally) assess fraud penalties against you. Remember also it can use statements of IRS agents for this purpose. But those who don't file can take a far more resolute stand than those who do file, since THEY CANNOT BE LEGALLY ASSESSED OR REASSESSED. Since they will not have paid "voluntarily", the IRS will be required to send them "notices and demands"—which they can't do! So non-filers are in a much better position to sue for refunds than are filers. (See Chapter 10.) The object of non-filers is merely to begin compiling a documented record they can show to any jury, that will disprove that they acted "willfully," should the government decide to prosecute them for a nonexistent tax "crime." You can do this by showing the steps you took to cooperate with the IRS and its failure to respond in kind. For example, if you get any kind of letter from the IRS concerning your alleged "tax liability," you can respond with a letter such as this one:

Dear Mr. IRS Man:

I received your letter (put in form number) of (date) and cannot answer it in the manner requested, because it lacks the information that makes a reply possible.

For one thing, you state that I may be charged a penalty for failing "to file a *required* tax form or to provide tax information"; however, you fail to identify the Internal

Revenue Code section that contains this *requirement,* so it is impossible for me to know if I am "required to file" or "not required to file."

In addition, you forgot to identify the Code section that might make me *liable* for the tax in question. Therefore, in order for me to be able to answer your questions, please identify for me the following:

1. The Code section establishing the filing "requirement" referred to;

2. The Code section stating who is *liable* for the tax in question.

Without this information it is impossible to answer your letter. When you supply me with the requested information, I will be in a position to answer your questions, and will do so immediately.

The IRS cannot answer such a letter and never does. They may simply ignore it and press on. However, I have known people who have sent such a letter and have never heard from the IRS again. But the principles and wording embodied in that letter can be adapted to various written requests received from the IRS. In *How Anyone Can Stop Paying Income Taxes,* concerning IRS audits, I wrote:

> In my Untax Seminars...I explain how citizens can deal with this type of IRS intimidation (intimidating people into believing they were required to produce their books and records in response to a mere letter request) and perhaps employ a little reverse intimidation of their own. One procedure, for example, is to telephone the IRS agent on the day before the scheduled audit (preferably late-afternoon) and simply break the appointment. Any number of good excuses should suggest themselves. That thousands of Americans are, indeed, adopting this policy became clear on June 10, 1981, when Roscoe L. Egger, the current IRS Commissioner, stated at a congressional hearing on the problems that the IRS was having with growing national tax rebellion:

> "...processing tax protester cases is much more difficult than other cases. . .Tax protesters often have strongly resisted our efforts to obtain information through frequent cancellation and rescheduling of interview appointments; failure to keep scheduled appointments; demanding that all questions and communications be made in writing; and withholding of records that were specifically identified and requested by the examiners, thus necessitating the issuance and court enforcement of summonses to obtain any taxpayer and third party records.

At my last "trial" this was used against me—even though it had nothing to do with the "crimes" I had been accused of committing. The prosecutor told the jury that I advised people to lie to IRS agents and make appointments and then break them. Of course he neglected to tell the jury that I also advised them that, according to the law, income taxes had to be assessed and notices sent to those who allegedly owed the tax and that the IRS sought to extort the tax without doing either—and that they had to fight fire with fire. If you think about it, "lying" to the IRS is really no different than "lying" to a stick-up man. If you are accosted by one who demands all your money and you tell him you don't have any—even though you have a $100 bill secreted in the heal of your left shoe—is that lying?

But I really never told people to actually lie to the IRS except once when I got carried away at a seminar which several IRS agents were taping. But, I corrected that shortly thereafter by pointing out that the government can charge people criminally (under section 101 of the U.S. Criminal Code) for giving false information to the government. Of course, if this provision were ever applied against the government, most of Congress, the IRS, the Department of Justice, and the federal judiciary would be behind bars.

But in those years we had far less information than we have today and so had to adopt certain tactics to make up for this lack of knowledge. We know so much more today that such measures are no longer necessary.

The point is that by refusing to submit to informal IRS requests, the IRS will be forced to use a 7602 summons if it really wants to see your books and records.

HANDLING AN IRS SUMMONS

Now you know that such a summons does not even apply to income taxes and you also know that pursuant to section 342.12 of the *Handbook for Special Agents* you're under no obligation to turn over your books and records pursuant to such a summons, so you should actually welcome the opportunity it affords you to strike a blow at the two headed, fire-breathing IRS monster and get some money out of it at the same time. Remember, all you are required to do is show up with your books and records (if you have any)—but you "may decline to submit them for inspection on constitutional grounds." So what's to worry?

Conducting Your "Investigation"

As you can see from *U.S.* v. *Roundtree,* 420 F2d 845 (1969) (Figure 9-3), one who receives an IRS summons "is entitled to *investigate*" its purpose. You might begin your "investigation" (after submitting your claim for witness fees, as explained later) by showing the IRS agent the excerpt from *Roundtree* which establishes your right to conduct your "investigation." You should begin your investigation by requiring the agent to identify himself. You want his name, rank and serial number. You have to know exactly whom you are dealing with and whether or not he is authorized to conduct such an interview. In getting this information, ask the agent for his home address. IRS agents are instructed *never* to give this out and you will not get it. However he will tell you that he will give you his office address, but that's not good enough. The reason is (and you should explain this to him) that during the course of the summons interview he might *violate* one or more of your constitutional rights and provide you with a basis for *suing him.* So you need to know his home address so you can *serve him* with the necessary papers. For example, when I sued several employees of the Connecticut State Tax Department, I served them at their office. However, Judge Ellen Burns, a Connecticut District Court Judge, dismissed

---

FIGURE 9-3
U.S. v. *Roundtree,* 420 F.2d 845 (1969)

But we cannot agree with the court's granting of the Government's motion to quash the taxpayer's attempted deposition of the agent in charge of this case. The Government argued that because it had instituted "a summary proceeding in aid of an administrative investigation rather than a plenary action", the district court should exercise its discretion under Fed.R.Civ.P. 81(a)(3) to deny all discovery, and now seeks to justify that denial on appeal. We have been careful to avoid ruling "that discovery would always be improper in cases of this nature", 400 F.2d at 212 n. 12. We conclude that the taxpayer is entitled to investigate the IRS's purpose where such purpose has been put in issue and may affect the legality of the summons.[15] Rule 26(b) instructs us that a party is entitled to examine a deponent on "any matter, not privileged, which is relevant to the subject matter involved in the pending action". The district court has authority to curtail the deposition if it is conducted unreasonably. Fed.R.Civ.P. 30(d); United States v. Howard, 3 Cir.1966, 360 F.2d 373, 381. But if the taxpayer succeeds in producing evidence that would repel a motion for summary judgment under Rule 54, the district court should allow him to proceed to trial.

---

my suit against them, ruling that I could not serve them at their offices. Also when I wanted to subpoena several IRS agents in connection with a recent hearing, I discovered that when agents leave the employ of the IRS or change offices, the IRS will not give out any information as to their whereabouts, which makes subpoenaing them difficult. That is also why in all court matters involving IRS witnesses, you should insist that they identify themselves by giving their home addresses and not just their office addresses, as is their practice.

But getting back to your summons interview, the agent will refuse to give you his home address, which, I believe, should provide you with a lawful basis for not proceeding any further. However, since there are important issues you have to cover, you are not prepared to leave. But raising this issue will allow you to immediately turn the tables on your would-be inquisitor. So after raising the issue, arguing about it, and failing to get the information requested, you might say, "Look, I believe that I would be well within my rights if I left right now. I don't believe that I have to submit to a summons interview without getting this information. As far as I'm concerned I've complied with the summons. I'm here with my books and records but you are unwilling to provide me with the information I need to complete my investigation. But, since I want to be cooperative with the IRS, I'll stay and continue." I should have mentioned earlier that you should have brought a tape recorder and one witness to record all of this. Also, all relevant records should have been brought in a sealed box clearly labeled "Personal Records and Other Secret Stuff."

Now To The Question of "Liability" and/or The "Acts" You Are "Required" to Perform

Continue your "investigation" by inquiring into the tax for which you are allegedly "liable" and/or the "act" you are allegedly "required" to perform. If an older summons (those used prior to January 1, 1983) was used, it will state near the top "With respect to the tax liability of," and then your name. Those issued now generally say, "With respect to," and then your name. However, reference to a tax liability will be included further on. Of course, it won't *identify the Code section establishing the alleged liability* so that's what you want to "investigate." "Precisely what kind of a tax liability are you inquiring about? Your summons didn't say, nor is any Code section identified. Does this have to do with wagering taxes? Tobacco taxes? Or what?" Now you wait for an answer. If he says income taxes, you ask, "What Code section establishes an income tax liability?" At this point you should be prepared to produce copies of those Code sections that appear in Figures 3-2 and 3-3. It would be more effective if you had an Internal Revenue Code with you, with the relevant Code sections tabbed and highlighted for easy reference.[2] If you don't have a Code, you can find one in any law library and you can photo copy the appropriate Code sections. You will be able to produce Code sections showing that, while section 7602 might be applicable to others, it certainly is not applicable to you, and the Agent wil not be able to make a contrary showing.

You might go over section 7602 with the agent and say, "What Code section requires me to perform an act to which your summons can apply?" When the IRS agent can't find either a "liability" or an "act" to support his summons, you can become very indignant. "You mean you issued this summons without having any statutory basis for doing so? Get your supervisor out here. What's his name?" As you can see, you will be in a position to be just as forceful as you want. Since the IRS attempted to intimidate you with its summons, you might enjoy reversing the role. But you cannot let them mislead you with Code sections that simply will not apply.

They will be unable to produce any section to support the issuance of the summons[3] and, you have to be knowledgeable and forceful enough not to be misled by any Code section they might produce.[4]

The Two "Magical Questions"

At some appropriate point you will want to pose your two "magical questions." And you should do this before you allow the agent to terminate the interview—for a reason that will soon be clear. These two questions should be asked precisely as they are written below. So memorize them before going to the interview. The first question is...

If I turn over these books and records to you, could the government use any of the information contained in them against me?

You already know the answer to that, **but you want to hear it from the agent.** Don't let him divert or distract you from getting a specific answer to this question. You will need the correct answer so you can ask your next question. If he says "I don't know," then you respond by saying, "Then go find out," or possibly, "Then let's get your supervisor in here, maybe he'll know the answer." If he says that he won't get him or answer the question on his own, then you respond by saying that you aren't going to turn over any records until somebody answers that question for you. However, you really should have no trouble getting a "yes" answer to that question. This will set the stage for your next question, which should be...

Am I legally required to give the government any information that it can use against me?

You already know the answer (and will have a copy of Figure 2-9 for back-up support) but you want the answer to come from the agent. Naturally, the answer he must give you is, "no." So, at that point, the agent would have told you that you are not required to give him your books and records.[5] You should clearly reinforce this by saying, "You are perfectly right. I'm not turning over my books and records because I'm exercising my constitutional rights under the Fourth and Fifth Amendments." Make sure to get that clearly on your tape recording. After making that statement, you can pick up your books and records and leave. You would have fully complied with the summons.

The reason that you want the agent to **specifically tell you that you are not required to give him your books and records** is to strengthen your position in case he decides to use the court to enforce his summons.

AND DON'T FORGET THE MONEY!

Another advantage of waiting for a summons rather than responding to an audit *invitation,* is that those who are summoned are entitled to witness and mileage fees! This is provided for in Code section 7610 (Figure 9-4). Note that section (a) provides for "fees and mileage to persons who are summoned." The limitation in section (b)(1) only applies to the costs of producing documents (as provided for in section (a)(2)), not to the witness and mileage allowances provided for in section (a)(1). Few people summoned ever apply for such reimbursement, and IRS agents will even deny that such a reimbursement provision exists. Don't let them fool you. You are entitled to at least $30 as a witness fee and 20¢ per mile!

FIGURE 9-4 [Sec. 7610]
SEC. 7610. FEES AND COSTS FOR WITNESSES.
(a) IN GENERAL. The Secretary shall by regulations establish the rates and conditions under which payment may be made of—
(1) fees and mileage to persons who are summoned to appear before the Secretary, and
(2) reimbursement for such costs that are reasonably necessary which have been directly incurred in searching for, reproducing, or transporting books, papers, or other data required to be produced by summons.
(b) EXCEPTIONS. No payment may be made under paragrah (2) of subsection (a) if—
(1) the person with respect to whose liability the summons is issued has a proprietary interest in the books, papers, records, or other data required to be produced, or
(2) the person summoned is the person with respect to whose liability the summons is issued or an officer, employee, agent, accountant, or attorney of such person who, at the time the summons is served, is acting as such.
(c) SUMMONS TO WHICH SECTION APPLIES. This section applies with respect to any summons authorized under section 6420(e)(2), 6421(f)(2), 6427(j)(2), or 7602.

After receiving an IRS summons, immediately call the agent and tell him to have Form 1157 ready for you at the interview. This is the form on which claims are made for witness and mileage fees. He might not have heard of it. He might claim that you are not entitled to reimbursement. Tell him that you are, and insist that he have the form for you. Be sure to complete it before doing anything else at the interview. While you won't give the IRS any documents or information in connection with its summons, at least you can still make the IRS pay *something* for putting you through the inconvenience.

ENFORCING AN IRS SUMMONS

Unlike an IRS request for an audit, the issuance of an IRS summons carries legal force (actually illegal force) which has to be reckoned with. If one does not comply with an IRS summons, section 7604 of the Code allows the agent to seek court help to compel compliance. Thus, unless you comply with the IRS's summons you could find yourself in front of a federal judge who, in many cases, doesn't care about the law. He can jail you for contempt pursuant to section 7210 and also fine you $1,000 and/or imprison you for up to one year if you refuse to turn over your books and records pursuant to section 7602—as he "interprets" it!

Therefore you want to be able to prove that you complied with the original summons if the agent decides to seek the court's help. If you asked the two "magical questions" correctly, you will have proof that you not only complied with the summons, but that the agent even **told you that you didn't have to give him your books and records**—and that you did not do so for **the constitutional reasons that you both agreed applied.** And remember, you also have the backup authority as contained in Figure 2-9 which you should be prepared to read to the court. You can also raise some of the same issues you raised with the agent—such as which Code section makes you "liable" for the tax or requires you to perform any act. You can also direct those two "magical questions" to the bench, and see how the court responds. All in all you will be loaded for bear in any such court proceeding.

In case the court should disregard both law and reason and order you to turn over your records, you say, "In other words, your honor, you are ordering me to turn over my books and records and unless I do you will hold me in contempt?" He will have to answer yes to that. So, get a transcript of the proceeding and you will have proof that your records were not turned over voluntarily but were compelled under threat of contempt. On this basis, you should have no trouble getting all of this information suppressed, if the government ever tries to use it against you.

THIRD PARTY SUMMONSES

In cases where individuals refuse to surrender their books and records and successfully assert their constitutional rights, the government will seek to get records and information from third parties who, regardless of the merits of the summons, may consider that their best interest lies in cooperating with the IRS. Though banks are the favored source for such information, the IRS will seek out information from other sources such as customers, employers (including one's own corporation) and accountants. Banks will supply the IRS with copies of bank statements and cancelled checks, from which the IRS will (illegally) estimate non-existent income tax "liabilities." It will also use this material as evidence in court against those it seeks to prosecute for nonexistent tax "crimes" and to determine civil fines and penalties. If it weren't for my bank records, the government couldn't have (illegally) prosecuted me twice for tax "crimes," nor seized (illegally) over $250,000 of my property. You might consider this when you think about using American banks—if you are unwilling to take the steps (as will be explained later) to prevent this. The government can even get your records and working papers from your own accountant. If an attorney, on the other hand, prepares your taxes, your records I believe, will be protected on the basis of client-lawyer privilege. No such protection, however, extends to records in the hands of your accountant. For this reason you might insist that he keep them—including his working papers—at your office and only take possession of them when he works on them. You might also get him to agree to return all of your records (including his working papers) if your relationship terminates. If he won't agree to this, you might consider getting an accountant who will. You might even consider having a contract containing such a clause, and if he ever turns over records to the IRS (or a grand jury) because of his having retained records in violation of that clause, you could, I believe, sue him for any damages that resulted from his breaching that aspect of your contract.[6]

If the IRS can't utilize bank records, to construct a "bank deposit" return, it may try to (illegally) concoct a "net worth" return. This is when the IRS seeks to estimate annual income from the annual increase of one's assets. Naturally, both types of IRS-generated "returns" are illegal, since nowhere in the Code is the IRS authorized to *estimate* one's income **on any basis** when an individual refuses to voluntarily "self-assess" himself.

In addition (as you already know) since a 7602 summons can't even apply to income taxes, all of the summonses described above are illegally issued to third parties. The question is, what can you do about it?

QUASHING THIRD PARTY SUMMONSES

Prior to January 1, 1983, when the IRS sent a third party a summons, you could simply call up that party and demand that he not turn anything over to the IRS—and even threaten him if he did. You could tell him, in no uncertain terms, that by turning over your records, he would be violating fiduciary and contractual obligations. You could tell him that, since the summons was not a court order, he was not obligated to obey it and you would no longer do business with him if he did. In addition, you would sue him for any damages that would result. Based upon such reasons many third parties **would refuse to turn over the requested records,** which would then force the IRS to initiate a court proceeding against the third party to get them. At such a hearing the taxpayer had a right to intervene and cross examine the IRS agent who issued the summons and compel him to identify the code section establishing the "liability" or "act" to which his summons allegedly applied. Naturally, based on such a confrontation, the **government could not prevail.** So guess what? **The federal mafia changed the rules!**

Putting An Impossible Burden On Private Citizens

Starting on January 1, 1983 the government decided to make it far more difficult (if not impossible) and much more expensive for private citizens to try to interfere with its illegal use of third party summonses. The government put the burden of initiating any such legal action *on private citizens*—in a manner that few could carry. If a taxpayer now wants to intervene[7] to prevent the IRS from getting third party records and testimony, he must now—*at his own expense*—initiate his own court action! He is now told he has to file a motion in district court (with copies to all third parties) asking the court to quash the summons and he has 20 days from the date of the mailing of such notice to him in which to do it! The IRS must send him, by registered or certified mail, a copy of the summons at least 23 days in advance of the hearing. But, as you can see, the average taxpayer would have little time to figure out how to utilize court procedures to quash an IRS summons in federal court. If, among other things, he was out of town or for some reason the mail was delayed, the hearing will already have taken place, after which all of his objections will be ruled moot. But, even if he does get a copy of the summons in time, the average taxpayer wouldn't be able to figure out how to quash it, nor be willing to incure the expense involved, especially if he feels that his amateurish efforts will prove futile. If he seeks the help of a lawyer, most will want about $2,500 to initiate an action in federal court, but, in any case, the fee would be no less than $500—usually demanded in advance.[8]

When the IRS sends taxpayers their copies of such summonses, an apparently helpful government (!) also sends along four pages of instructions on how taxpayers can go about quashing the summonses.[9] They are told in the opening paragraph:

Enclosed is a copy of a summons served by the IRS to examine records or to request testimony relating to records which have been made or kept of your business transactions or affairs by the person summonsed. If you object to the summons, *you are permitted to file a lawsuit* (That's really big of them don't you think?) in *the United States District Court in the form of a petition to quash the summons in order to contest the merits of the summons.*

It then goes on to say:

1. You must file your petition to quash in the United States District Court for the district where the person summonsed resides or is found.

Authors comment: Even if he lives in another state, say 3,000 miles away, you are supposed to file your suit and contest it there!

2. You must file your petition within 20 days from the date of this notice and *pay a filing fee as may be required by the clerk of the court.*

Comment: That fee will usually be about $85.00 for every summons sought to be quashed. And the IRS could send out a half dozen (or more) summonses—and all around the country!

3. You must comply with the Federal Rules of Civil Procedure and local rules of the United States District Court. To assist you, Federal Rules of Civil Procedure 4(a), 4(b), 4(c), 4(d): (4), 7(a), 8(a), 8(e), 10, and 11 are reprinted for you.

Comment: Thus taxpayers are given approximately two weeks to learn how to use The Federal Rules of Civil Procedure (as well as the rules that apply in their local district court—which are not given to him) to quash an IRS summons in federal court.

4. You must also, *within 20 days from the date of this notice,* send a copy of your petition to quash certified or registered mail to (a) the person summonsed, and (b) the Internal Revenue Service at the address shown on the summons to the attention of the Internal Revenue Service officer before whom the summonsed person is to appear.

Comment: Obviously, since the summons is sent 23 days before the scheduled hearing, and if the taxpayer responds by mail on the 19th or 20th day, no court would have time to rule on the merits of the Motion. And, if the summonsed party turned the records over to the IRS before the court could rule, the court would ultimately rule the matter moot—regardless of the merits of the motion! The federal mafia doesn't miss a trick![10]

5. A copy of your petition to quash must also be served on (a) the United States Attorney for the district where your petition is filed, and (b) the Attorney General of the United States Department of Justice, Washington, D.C. 20530, pursuant to Federal Rules of Civil Procedure 4(c) and 4(d): (4).

6. You must also comply with the service of process requirements contained in Rule 4 of the Federal Rules of Civil Procedure. The United States District Court Clerk's Office has preprinted forms for this purpose.

Taxpayers are further informed, among other things, to "State the basis for the court's jurisdiction," and to support their "request for relief by a sworn affidavit." As you can see, the government is not at all squeamish about placing all sorts of financial and procedural barriers to block interference with its illegal use of third party summonses.

PREPARING YOUR AFFIDAVIT AND MOTION TO QUASH

A Sample Motion to Quash a third party summons is shown in Figure 9-5. Naturally you will remove all references that don't apply to your case. You will also need to attach a short affidavit to your motion. This need only contain three averments;

1. That I am over 18 years of age and understand the obligations of an oath.
2. That no section of the Internal Revenue Code of 1954, as amended, makes me "liable" for any federal tax.
3. That no section of the Internal Revenue Code of 1954, as amended, requires me to perform any act with respect to any federal tax.

NATURALLY, you should not file such a motion and affidavit unless you are thoroughly convinced that all of these statements are true. To remove all doubt refer to the Internal Revenue Code itself and/or seek legal advice from a competent professional.

In response to your motion and affidavit, the government will have to file an answer and the IRS agent issuing the summons will have to allege the contrary in a contesting affidavit—which I don't see how he can do, without committing perjury. If you do get a hearing, which, under the law (but which, as you already know, often does not count for much in federal court) you are entitled, you should have fun cross-examining the IRS agent on his affidavit. Based upon what you have learned, you should have no qualms about subjecting yourself to similar cross-examination. The government will not be able to produce any Code section that either makes you liable for income taxes or requires you to perform any act with respect to it. Any Code section it produces will simply be misleading, and I assume you now know enough to be able to handle it.

On the basis of the law then, you should be able to quash all third party summonses related to your alleged income tax "liability."

ANOTHER EXAMPLE OF "DUE PROCESS"

On March 19, 1984, two Connecticut banks received IRS summonses in connection with my bank records which said:

You are summonsed and required to appear before Thomas Cingo, an officer of the Internal Revenue Service to give testimony and to bring with you and to produce for examination, books, records, papers, and other data relating to the tax liabilty or the collection of the tax liability or for the purpose of inquiring **into any offense** connected with the administration or enforcement of the internal revenue laws concerning the person identified above for the periods shown.

The periods shown were from January 1 through December 31, 1979. The summonses said that they were "Issued under authority of the Internal Revenue Code"—but no Code section was cited! However, instructions for quashing a 7602 summons were attached to the copies I received. **Now the summonses were illegal on their very face** because they asked for records and testimony regarding **"any offense** connected with the administration or enforcement of the internal revenue laws." Based upon Section 7601 and the legal history of these summonses, IRS agents simply do not have such broad summonsing authority. "Any offense" obviously includes criminal offenses—but potential criminal offenses **are not encompassed by Section 7602** nor (as you shall also see) are they encompassed by the Code itself! The Internal Revenue Code is purely a civil Code and can only be **legally used to determine civil liabilities** and civil infractions. **It cannot be used to investigate possible criminal violations of law—which the term "any offense" obviously includes.** In order for the government to investigate possible *criminal* violations, it needs **a grand**

FIGURE 9-5

UNITED STATES DISTRICT COURT
DISTRICT OF CONNECTICUT

IMA FREEMAN,

   Petitioner,

vs.   Date:

UNITED STATES,

   Respondent.

PETITION TO QUASH INTERNAL REVENUE SERVICE SUMMONS

Petitioner, Ima Freeman, hereby alleges as follows:

1. This is a proceeding brought under the authority of Section 7609(b)(2) of the Internal Revenue Code of 1954, as amended, to judicially quash the enforcement of an Internal Revenue Summons

2. Greb DeMonay, is employed as a Regular Agent in the office of the District Director of the State of Connecticut located at 777 Demonic Ave., Sleezport, Connecticut 07777.

3. Agent Greb DeMonay is conducting an investigation, the purpose of which is to secure information and the production of books and records of Petitioner with regard to Petitioner's alleged income tax liability for the taxable years 1988, 1986, 1885, 1984 and 1983.

4. Pursuant to said investigation, Agent Greb DeMonay issued a summons purportedly in accordance with Section 7602 of the Internal Revenue Code and caused it to be served upon The Freedomville National Bank & Trust Co. summoning it to produce the confidential books, papers and records of Petitioner.

5. The said Agent Greb DeMonay sent notice of said summons to Petitioner and Petitioner has, within the 20th day from the date of such notice, to commence an action to quash said summons.

6. Said summons was erroneously issued by Agent Greb DeMonay, since said Section 7602 does not apply, in any way, to petitioner or to his agents, debtors or fiduciaries for the following reasons:

a. With respect to Section 7602(a)(1). While this provision authorizes Internal Revenue Service personnel to "examine any books papers, records, or other data"; the provision itself imposes no legal obligation upon petitioner, his agents, debtors or fiduciaries to furnish the material that IRS agents may be "authorized" to examine.

b. With respect to section 7602(a)(2). This provision only authorizes the IRS to summon persons "liable for tax or required to perform the act" or other persons having records related to these conditions. Since petitioner is not a person "liable" for any federal tax nor "required to perform any act" with respect to any federal tax. he does not fall within this provision of Code Section 7602(a)(2).

c. With respect to provision 7602(a)(3). Since this provision only authorizes the IRS to "take testimony" that may be "relevant" to sections (a)(1) and (a)(2) and since neither of these sections, as explained above, applies to either petitioner or his agents, debtors or fiduciaries, section 7602(a)(3) also, does not apply to Petitioner or his agents, debtors or fiduciaries.

d. Thus no provision of section 7602, as explained above, applies to Petitioner his agents, debtors or fiduciaries.

e. The action of the Respondent by his agents, in seeking to enforce a 7602 summons which does not apply to Petitioner, his agents, debtors, and fiduciaries is, therefore, unlawful and amounts to an abuse of process.

7. My affidavit attesting to the above is attached and marked Exhibit B.

WHEREFORE, Petitioner respectfully requests:

1. That this court enter an order quashing the enforcement of the attached summons;

2. That this court enter an order requiring Respondent to pay all costs incurred by petitioner in seeking to quash its unlawful summons.

3. That this court grant such other relief as it deems proper.

Dated at Freedomville, Connecticut, this 1st day of June, 1989

                                    Ima Freeman, Petitioner

                                    711 Victory Drive
                                    Freedomville, Connecticut.

Page 2

jury subpoena and those can only be issued by a grand jury pursuant to a *showing of probable cause*. **The use of such a sweeping summons** by IRS agents (who were referred to as "officers," to obviously give their summonses greater intimidating power) was **clearly a violation of law—for which there can be no argument!**

On April 6, 1984 I moved to quash both summonses. Since they were raised while I was traveling around the country, the motions were submitted for me by a Connecticut attorney. Because a grand jury investigation of me was then in progress, and, given the all-encompassing language of these summonses (which was far broader than what had been authorized by section 7602 up until approximately a year before), we charged that the "purpose of the summons is to accumulate evidence for a criminal prosecution of the petitioner." In addition to this claim (and the claims incorporated in paragraph 6, as shown in Figure 9-5, we also claimed that the enforcement of the summonses would be illegal and contrary to law because "Section 7602(b)...is unconstitutional as it applies to the Petitioner in that its provisions are overly broad, vague and unenforceable." We also claimed that the section is "violative of Petitioner's constitutional rights...deprives (him) of his rights to privacy, and due process of law and the right to be free from unreasonable searches as guaranteed by the Fourth and Fifth Amendments to the Constitution." And finally we claimed that the IRS sought to enforce the summons in violation of "the authority vested in it pursuant to Section 7602 of the Internal Revenue Code." In addition to the relief requested, as shown in Figure 9-5, we also asked, "That the Court enter an order. . .declaring Section 7602 of the Internal Revenue Code unconstitutionally vague and unenforceable." The reason I specifically mention this is so that you will have a better understanding of the differences between the motion I filed and the one suggested in Figure 9-5. This will also give you a more accurate basis for judging the actions taken by the U.S. Department of Justice, and the court in my case, and for evaluating your prospects.

Since section 7602(b) had only recently been adopted, its constitutionality had not, to my knowledge, been challenged, which, for all the reasons cited, I thought I should do. Maybe for the purposes of defeating my own particular summons, I should have left that issue out. But I certainly had a right—if not a duty—to raise it.

But by raising this broader issue, I provided both the Justice Department and the Court with an opportunity to completely avoid addressing the basic issues covered in paragraph 6 of Figure 9-5. Had I not raised the larger issues, I would have forced the government and the court to concentrate on the first issues, which they could not (I don't think) have misstated or gotten around.

For example, in his seven-page Answer to my Motion, Peter Sklarew, trial attorney for the Tax Division of the U.S. Department of Justice, focused almost entirely on the fact that the information allegedly sought was not to determine criminal culpability but "to determine the taxpayer's correct income tax liabilities for 1979, the year under examination, and to prepare a federal income tax return for the taxpayer for that year if it is determined that the filing of such a return was required by law." However, Mr. Sklarew never identified the law that established that alleged "liability" or the alleged filing "requirement." Obviously, Mr. Sklarew knew better,[11] but he also knew that he could get away with lying with impunity in his response. To my knowledge, Mr. Sklarew is still with the Justice Department misstating both fact and law (in violation of Rule 11[12]) for the benefit of Uncle Sam.

I had, of course, given the government a sworn affidavit that I had no "tax liability" for the year at issue. If Mr. Sklarew believed I had a "tax liability" for that year why didn't he charge me with perjury? With respect to his claim that the informaton was sought so the government could prepare a tax return—that too, was a lie! Though the government got my bank records, it never—to this day— ever prepared a tax return from the information it obtained. Figure 3-5(D) contains the 1979 tax return which the IRS prepared for me. It's blank! So how was the information which the government obtained used to prepare that tax return? This was merely another of the many lies strung together by Mr. Sklarew in his answer to the court.

Mr. Sklarew also had the nerve to charge in his response that, "The petitions to quash were brought by Irwin A. Schiff in bad faith for the purposes of harassing the government and interfering with the administration of the federal tax system." But I swore that I had no "tax liability" and that I was not required to "perform any act." If this were true (and Mr. Sklarew made no attempt to refute these claims), how could my motions have been brought in "bad faith"? And if my claims were true, it is clear that I filed them not to "harass the government," but to prevent the government from harassing me! This is just the kind of legal balderdash one gets in responses from the U.S. Department of Justice. Mr. Sklarew also asked that the court "Order that petitioner's counsel pay the United States its attorney's fees and costs" and that the "proceedings in these actions not be scheduled until respondent's motion for summary relief and attorney's fees, which will be filed shortly, is determined by the court." In other words, the Justice Department wanted the court to award it costs and attorney's fees *before* any hearing (where parties could cross-examine each other concerning their respective claims) ever took place!

Prior to receiving the government's response, I had received a call from my attorney who told me that he had received a letter and a phone call from Mr. Sklarew threatening him that unless we withdrew our motions, **he would seek punitive damages against my lawyer!** This, of course, was nothing but **old-fashioned blackmail!** When my lawyer told me this, I immediately called Mr. Sklarew and, with a witness listening in on an extension, the following conversation took place.

"Mr. Sklarew, this is Irwin Schiff. Did you threaten my attorney with money damages unless he withdrew my Motions to Quash?

"Yes, I did. The motions were totally without merit," (or words to that effect).

"But, Mr. Sklarew, they are *my* motions, not *his,* and I *forbid* him to withdraw them. So how can you seek penalties from him?"

"The law gives me that right," (or words to that effect).

"I'll tell you what Mr. Sklarew. I'll agree to withdraw my motions right now. All you have to do is tell me the Code section that makes me liable for income taxes. So why don't you get a Code, and we can dispose of this right now."

Sklarew apparently got a Code and returned to the phone and said...

"Code section 1 creates the liability."

"Mr. Sklarew, I'm surprised at you. Where does the word 'liability' appear in that section? That section merely imposes the tax, but doesn't say who is liable for it. You'll have to do better than that."

Pause...

"It's Section 61."

"You must think you're talking to a dummy? I'm looking at section 61 right now. The word 'liability' doesn't even appear in that section. However, I also have in front of me Code section 5005(a), and it clearly says 'The distiller or importer of distilled spirits shall be liable for the taxes imposed.' Can't you find a section like that for income taxes? Unless you can, section 7602 can't apply."

"Section 7602 can apply whether you're liable for the tax or not."

"Oh really Mr. Sklarew. Do you *really* believe that?"

"Yes, I do."

"Well, you stick to that story, and I'll see you in court."

Since I had a witness that would testify to Sklarew's claim that the government could legally summons my records (pursuant to Code section 7602) even if I didn't have an income tax liability, I couldn't wait to face Mr. Sklarew in court. But I was to be denied that pleasure, because Judge Edginton (the same judge who wouldn't let me into court to sue Simon & Schuster) **dismissed my motions to quash without giving me any hearing at all!**

Figure 9-6 is a letter my attorney received from D. Patrick Mullarkey of the United States Justice Department around this time. Note how Mr. Mullarkey's letter focuses on only

one of the approximately seven or eight issues we raised in those motions to quash and threatens sanctions against my lawyer if our motions weren't withdrawn **because of that one issue.** Obviously, the mighty U.S. Department of Justice was fearful of having to meet us in a courtroom where we would have an opportunity to cross-examine the **agent who issued the summons. And with the help of a very protective federal judge, it didn't have to.**

But it is clear that the U.S. Department of Justice wasn't really concerned about the issue it focused on, but on the other issues we raised which weren't mentioned either in that letter or the court's decision. Note too, that there were not less than five government lawyers (including the Assistant Attorney General) who were advised of this blackmail effort.

In his decision Judge Edgington stated that "The respondent (the government) has met its burden of establishing a prima facia case...by its filing of an affidavit by the agent seeking enforcement." **I also filed an affidavit!—which refuted the agent's affidavit, but the honorable Judge Eginton makes no mention of that!** Judge Eginton made sure I was denied the opportunity to cross-examine that agent on his affidavit—to prove it was false! **Talk about the government getting to play with a stacked deck!**

In his ruling, Judge Eginton merely directs his attention to the broader issues we raised, such as citing the Tax Equity and Fiscal Responsibility Act of 1982 and the district court case of *Godwin* v. *United States,* 564 F. Supp. 1209 as holding that "a summons may be issued for a criminal purpose as long as there was no Department of Justice referral." That is exactly what I was challenging as being unconstitutional! In his ruling Judge Edginton disregarded the Supreme Court decision of *Reisman* v. *Caplan* (supra). The following will show har far the courts go in allowing the IRS to abuse its summons power.

Judge Eginton proceeds to attack my claim that section 7602(b) is unconstitutional in the following manner:

Petitioner asserts that 26 U.S.C. Sec. 7602(b) is unconstitutional in that it is overly broad, vague and unenforceable. This argument is also without merit. Section 7602(b) clearly defines the scope of an administrative summons. [This statement is obviously false. Pursuant to that section, its scope is boundless.] It puts the taxpayer on notice that an administrative summons may be used for the purposes enumerated in sections 7602(a)(1), 7602(a)(2), 7602(a)(3).

Well, if that were true then why was section 7602(b) ever adopted? And couldn't the public figure out "the scope" of

FIGURE 9-6

U.S. Department of Justice

Tax Division

GLA:DPM:PSklarew:lac
5-14-4879 8457024
5-14-4876 8456689

Washington, D.C. 20530

May 31, 1984

EXPRESS MAIL

Re: Schiff v. United States, Civil Nos. N84-242 and
N84-243 (USDC Conn.)

Dear Mr.

This is to confirm a telephone conversation between trial
attorney Peter Sklarew of this office and yourself. As indicated
by Mr. Sklarew, because the petitions to quash in the above-named
case raise only defenses that have been squarely and uniformly
rejected by numerous courts, the United States will move for
attorneys fees against both you and your client, pursuant to
recently amended Rule 11 of the Federal Rules of Civil Procedure
if it remains necessary for the United States to file a response
and a motion for summary enforcement of the summonses. If you and
your client will concede this case, Mr. Sklarew will draft a
stipulation and agreed enforcement order. However, inasmuch as
the United States' response is due on June 11, 1984, we request
that you call Mr. Sklarew by Wednesday, June 6, and indicate
whether or not you plan to press ahead with this case.

Concerning your indication to Mr. Sklarew that you are aware
of persons who have been called to testify before a grand jury
regarding criminal tax liabilities of Mr. Schiff, Mr. Sklarew has
made appropriate inquiries to both the United States Attorney's
office and the Internal Revenue Service and has reconfirmed that
no Justice Department referral as defined in 26 U.S.C. Section
7602(c)(2) is in effect with respect to Irwin A. Schiff for the
1979 tax year. (Please note that Section 7602(c)(3) provides
that each taxable period is treated separately.) We assure you
that, if we are forced to move for enforcement of the summonses
in an adversarial posture, we are prepared to attest to these
facts by affidavit or sworn declaration.

We hope this case can be resolved with a minimum of expense
so that it will not be necessary to move for attorney's fees, and
look forward to your reply in this regard. Mr. Sklarew's
telephone number is 202-724-6560.

Sincerely yours,

GLENN L. ARCHER, JR.
Assistant Attorney General
Tax Division

By: *D Patrick Mullarkey*

D. PATRICK MULLARKEY
Chief, Civil Trial Section
Northern Region

cc: Frank H. Santoro
     Michael Hartmere
     Assistant U.S. Attorneys
     New Haven, Connecticut

the summons from those "enumerated" sections he refers to? The public had done that for over 50 years! Why the sudden need to have them "clearly defined" now? Obviously, **that was not the purpose of section 7602(b) at all,** as any rational person should be able to figure out. It was adopted to furnish the IRS with an apparent (and more illegal) authority for using **broader and more comprehensive language** in its summonses than had **hitherto been possible. Such language would not have been possible before January 1, 1983.** To buttress his decision, rendered on October 18, 1984 (or some six months after I had filed my motions) Judge Eginton cited *Reed* v. *United States,* 54 AFTR 2d 84-5336.

The *Reed* decision was rendered on May 20, 1984 or approximately one month after I had filed my motions. I was totally unaware of that decision until it surfaced in Judge Edginton's decision. It is clear from the *Reed* decision that Richard and Julia Reed raised substantially the same issues I raised in my motions. They are identified in the decision as "tax protesters" who, characteristically, were handling this matter *pro se,* that is without the help of professional counsel. Since I had published a suggested motion to quash containing all of these elements in the December 1983 (Vol. 1 No. 6) issue of *The Schiff Report,* I have no doubt that the Reeds filed a replica of that motion. This being the case, the Reeds had to have included in their

motion the issues contained in paragraph 6 of Figure 9-5. However, no mention of these issues is contained (let alone dealt with) in that decision. But, at least, the Reeds got a court hearing, which I never did. But the *Reed* decision is a phony, since like mine, it did not deal with all of the issues that the Reeds must have raised.[13]

But if Judge Eginton was so sure of his conclusions, why did he deny me a hearing where those conclusions could be *debated* in open court and where I could confront the IRS agent on his affidavit? I wasn't granted a hearing because Judge Eginton knew that in such a confrontation the government would lose! **So he denied me a hearing, guaranteed by law, to protect the government.**

As far as all my other claims (as covered in Figure 9-5) were concerned, Judge Eginton dispatched them all with one trenchant observation, "The remaining grounds asserted by the petitioner are without merit and unsupported by law." **And all the while, I thought I had the law on my side!!**

Judge Eginton denied my motions to quash without even granting me a hearing, and then fined my attorney $1,749.50 for violating Rule 11!

Again, *welcome to Amerika!*

NOTES TO CHAPTER 9

1. The judge could have made the *exact* same ruling (and comment) when and if Nicola objected to the introduction of his tax return. In that instance, the judge, similarly, would have overruled the objection on the grounds that it was filed "with his consent," (i.e. "voluntarily"). However, the judge probably would not have added (as he did here) that Nicola *should have refused to file* for the same reason that applied to his books and records; because, in all likelihood, *this judge had probably sent people to jail for making that very claim!*

2. If you don't have an Internal Revenue Code you can order one from Freedom Books for $37.00.

3. If they try citing the broad powers of section 7602(b), you show them where that power is *limited* by the restrictions imposed by section 7601.

4. You really have no need to fear this. IRS agents generally have little knowledge of the Internal Revenue Code and even profess ignorance of it, and have never, to my knowledge, even sought to produce a Code section to prove

anything. What you will undoubtedly discover is that you know more about income taxes than its whole office put together, and you will leave with that euphoric feeling. This has been reported to me time and time again.

5. Corporate and other types of books and records which might be in your custody and control are not covered by the Fifth Amendment. You can only use the two "magical questions" in connection with *your own* books and records. However, if you don't have the records, you don't have to produce them and *you can take the Fifth* as to what might have happened to them!

6. The government might seek to hold such contracts (designed to protect one's constitutional right to privacy from illegal government seizure and intrusion) void as being against public policy. But one cannot be sure, so it might be worth a try. Naturally such an argument must be tailored to meet the practical needs of your accountant. Obviously accountants retain records they no longer need; however, if yours needs them, you'll have them.

7. Actually, under the law, third parties can still refuse to turn over the records for all of the reasons covered and force the IRS to bring court action, even if a motion to quah is not initiated! At such a hearing, I believe, taxpayers can still intervene in the same manner as they could before. Third parties could also cross-examine IRS agents in the manner suggested and easily defeat the summons. Most third parties, however, have neither the time nor inclination to do this. And, because of their own tax vulnerability, they profess to "having to do what the IRS says." This is another example (along with Notices of Levy) of how the Gestapo principle works. As a result of the new law, however, I believe that unless a taxpayer submits a motion to quash, there is little he can now do to stop the illegal turning over of his records to the IRS.

8. Since traditional lawyers won't raise the right issues (the ones we covered), their efforts will fail, so most taxpayers will end up throwing away their money.

9. The IRS may be terminating this practice, or agents may simply fail to send out the material. I heard from someone who received copies of three IRS summonses that had been sent out regarding him, but he did not receive any information from the IRS as to how to quash them.

10. Suppose that, in that case, the taxpayer could sue the third party for any resulting damages. This entails more legal expenses which most private parties can ill afford. This represents another example of how federal tax policy generates ill will, clashes and legal controversey between private citizens in the conduct of their own private affairs—

11. As a member of the Justice Department, Mr. Sklarew had to know how the Justice Department uses Code sections 6103(h) and (i) in criminal prosecutions. He had to know that, under no circumstances, could I have been "required" to file an income tax return. If he couldn't figure that out, he never should have been allowed to graduate from law school.

12. Rule 11 of the Federal Rules of Civil Procedure provides that those signing pleadings or motions of any kind believe, to the best of their knowledge, that the arguments made are "well grounded in fact and warranted by existing law or (have) a good faith argument for the extension, modification, or reversal of existing law," and are not made to "harass or to cause unnecessary delay or needless increase in the cost of litigation." For violations of these provisions the court may impose sanctions on the party who signed the pleading or the represented party (or both) which may include an order to pay the other party the amount of the reasonable expenses incurred.

13. **IMPORTANT:** An additional issue that can be raised in connection with the issuance of any summons is that the person issuing the summons was *never delegated to do so by the Secretary!* In all such confrontations, one should demand that the agent involved *produce the "Delegation Order"* authorizing him to subpoena (summons) you or any other third party. Without such a "Delegation Order," the subpoena is void!

Addendum to Chapter 9

On May 22, 1990, after this chapter had long since been completed, I received copies of summonses that IRS Revenue Agent Robert Netcoh had sent to three Connecticut banks, asking for records related to my accounts for the years 1983-1989. Since these summonses were dated May 11, 1990, this only left me with nine days to quash them. To make matters worse, I was already under pressure to meet a filing deadline in connection with my appeal of Judge Eginton's decision in my recovery suit—but I got it out in time. In the process, I discovered additional ways for attacking 7602 summonses. In developing this material, I also discovered, to my surprise, that Eginton's earlier dismissal of my motion to quash had been published, *Schiff* v. *United States*, 628 F. Supp. 9. However, few lay people who read it will realize that none of it is based on *any* court-room testimony or argument. This, again, demonstrates that "case law" can be based on *nothing* but the prejudicial and biased sentiments of the man writing the decision. Yet these published decisions, **unsupported by any testimony or court room argument** became influential "case law" upon which other decisions rest!

It is important, when filing your motion to quash, to include the issue regarding the absence of a delegation order. It should be included as paragrah 6(f) as follows: "Since Agent Grebb DeMonay was never delegated by the Secretary to summon anybody with respect to the alleged 'tax liability' referred to in the summons, this court is without jurisdiction to enforce it."

In addition, I learned that the IRS never sends out "attested" copies as *required* by Code Section 7603—**thus making all IRS summonses illegal and void just on this basis alone!** An attested copy is one that contains a certification that it is a true and correct copy of the original summons retained by the agent. (For a fuller explanation of this, see Rule 44 of the *Federal Rules of Civil Procedure*.) Therefore, include this in your motion as follows: "Since Grebb DeMonay did not furnish to the Freedomville National Bank & Trust Co. an 'attested copy' of the summons, as require by Code Section 7603, said summons is illegal an void."*

Also, if you have some basis for contending that the summons was issued to harass you (which will be true of all 7602 summonses, but you might have some specific, additional grounds), allege this as well, since this will provide a basis for insuring a hearing and/or discovery—if the summons is not quashed for lack of a delegation order and attestation. I stated in my motion that the "Summons was issued by Agent Netcoh in order to harass petitioner in

various ways having nothing to do with any 'tax liability'."

In addition, include with your motion discovery requests for admissions, interrogatories and documents. Ask the government to admit that the summons did not identify the nature of the "tax liability" referred to in the summons, nor the Code section in which it appears. Also ask them to admit that the summoning agent was never delegated by the Secretary to summon anybody in connection with the "tax liability" referred to, and that the summons sent was not an "attested copy." By way of interrogatories, I asked: "In referring to an unspecified and alleged 'tax liability,' does this refer to the tobacco tax liability contained in Section 5703 (yes or no)?" I fashioned three similar interrogatories using the alcohol, foreign insurers, and wagering tax liabilities contained in sections 5005, 4374, and 4401(c). Since I *must* get a "No" answer to each of those, I followed them up with: "If the 'tax liability' referred to in the summons is not the 'liability' referred to and identified in Sections 5703, 5005, 4374, or 4401(c), then in what Code section is it referred to and identified?" I also asked if the "tax liability" referred to was payable by stamp or on the basis of a return, and if by return, the Code section that states that such a tax liability "shall be paid on the basis of a return." I also asked whether Revenue Agent Netcoh had ever discussed the sending of these summonses with certain individuals and government departments and agencies, and whether or not a Justice Department "referral"—as provided for in 7602(c)—was in effect. I requested copies of the following documents: the delegation order, if it were claimed that Netcoh had been duly delegated; the Code sections creating and identifying the "tax liability" referred to, and the section providing that such a liability "shall be paid on the basis of a return"; a copy of the assessment, if it were claimed that one was made; and copies of all letters, memorandum and memos of telephone conversations between Netcoh and all individuals wherein the sending of these summonses was discussed. This last request was made to enable me to **meet my burden** of proving that the summonses were issued for the illegal purpose of harassing me.

In order to foreclose any possibility of the court not granting me either the hearing or discovery, I reminded the court of two things: it was my burden to show that the summonses were issued for an improper purpose, and that I had a right to discovery. I sought to do both in paragraphs 4 and 5 of my motion, as follows:

4. Since petitioner has the burden of showing that the summons was issued for an improper purpose (see

U.S. v. *Zack,* 521 F.2d. 1366; *U.S.* v. *Kis,* 658 F.2d 526; *U.S.* v. *Fisher,* 500 F.2d 1366, and *U.S.* v. *Roundtree,* 420 F.2d 845) and that the enforcement of the summons is an abuse of the court's process (*U.S.* v. *Roundtree,* supra, and *U.S.* v. *Prichard,* 438 F.2d 969), petitioner cannot meet his burden unless the court allows petitioner to cross-examine Revenue Agent Netcoh...or compel the government to respond to the discovery requests attached.

5. The Federal Rules of Civil Procedure [discovery] apply to proceedings for the enforcement of an administrative summons. See *U.S.* v. *Powell,* 379 U.S. 48, 58 n. 18; *U.S.* v. *Salter,* 432 F.2d 697,700; *U.S.* v.*Roundtree,* 420 F.2d 845, 851; *U.S.* v.*Nunally,*

278 F. Supp. 843; and *U.S.* v. *Cortese,* 614 F.2d 914.

If you have the time and really want to put the summoning agent through the wringer, depose him. This is clearly provided for within your right of discovery. (See *Roundtree,* Fig. 9-3.)

In any case, I was notified on June 25, 1990 that the matter had been assigned **to Judge Dorsey!** It will be interesting to see what develops.

*I am indebted to Billie Murdock of Salt Lake City, Utah for her research on delegation orders, and to Bob Minarik of Rochester, Indiana for his research on "attestation."

- UPDATE TO SECOND EDITION -

Well, "Judge" Dorsey did it again! He awarded the government a summary judgment. And in so doing, he violated all law by: (1) illegally granting the government a protective order so it wouldn't have to answer even a minuscule amount of discovery material; (2) refusing to hold a hearing; and (3) resolving all disputed issues of fact in favor of the government. I really have to work on getting him impeached; I certainly have enough evidence for it.

Fortunately, the government forgot to summon one of the banks I used during this period, so it issued another summons—which gave me another opportunity to file another motion to quash. This time I got a different judge, but the government moved again for a summary judgment, based on the principle of collateral estoppel. In my earlier motion to Judge Dorsey, I had raised the issue that the summonses were not attested copies; however, I never produced copies for the court. I merely raised the issue and anticipated proving it through discovery or at the hearing. Judge Dorsey, however, ignored this issue entirely. In the second case, though, I asked the bank to fax me a copy of the summons it received—and sure enough—it was not an attested copy. In this case, I supplied the court with a copy of the defective

summons and cited *Mimick* v. *United States,* 91-1 USTC 50,700, a case decided in January, 1991. In *Mimick,* a district court quashed an IRS summons because the summons served on the bank was not an attested copy. Therefore, based on *Mimick* and my supplying the court with a copy of the summons, which was also not an attested copy, I can't see how Connecticut District Court Judge Ellen Burns can fail to quash the summons. My response to the government's motion for a summary judgment was filed over two months ago (at this writing) and Judge Burns has yet to rule.

For more information on this (and some new information that I did not raise in either of the above actions), see the added material in the "Addendum to Second Edition," which begins on page 259. In any case, try to get a copy of the summons sent to the third party. If there is no attestation endorsement on it, it is a defective summons. In addition, given our current fax capability, it is my hope that I can supply you with sample motions to quash (and also include discovery questions for the government) - which should enable you, especially in light of the new material covered in the Addendum, to quash third party summonses. Contact Freedom Books (203-281-6791) for details.

— CHAPTER 10 —
SUING THE GOVERNMENT
AND AN UNEXPECTED INTERRUPTION

"Power tends to corrupt, and absolute power corrupts absolutely."
—Lord Acton

It is exactly 9:30 a.m., Sunday, August 7, 1989, and I am finally able to return to this book. Yesterday afternoon I Express-Mailed to the United States Court of Claims, in Washington, D.C, legal papers due there tomorrow. After devoting four weeks of intensive work on two very important legal briefs, as well as other very pressing legal matters, I breathed a sigh of relief and treated myself to a leisurely dinner at one of our better neighborhood restaurants. I then returned to my studio apartment and began sorting and refiling all of the papers and documents that had piled up everywhere. With the decks now cleared (and the apartment tidied up a bit), I am finally able to begin inputting material into my Toshiba lap-top computer, from which the final few chapters of this book will emerge.

Hopefully I have delivered all of the information as promised in the introduction. Now I will provide you with additional information to prove that *there are no laws* making anything connected with either the payment or non-payment of income tax a crime. These facts will prove that all criminal tax prosecutions, as well as civil penalties in connection with income taxes, are not authorized by law. You will see that in all such prosecutions, the real criminals are not those being prosecuted, but those prosecuting. After presenting this material, I will provide you with methods for protecting yourself. I will show you how and on what basis you can sue the government for what might have been extorted from you, and provide more information concerning how federal courts and the U.S. Justice Department really operate. You probably have some idea of this already, however, their actual operation is still far worse than what I have been able to convey so far. This nation, I fear, will never be able to return to its proper destiny until the public at large begins to figure out how and why the integrity of America's legal system went awry.

I began writing this book in September, 1988, approximately three weeks after I was ransomed out of federal incarceration by a family member. I had served 20 months of federal confinement on trumped-up charges of income tax evasion. I was framed by the U.S. prosecutor and the presiding judge, in a manner equal to that of anything the old West or the Soviet Union had to offer. At this point I've been at this book for almost one year. My initial hope was to have it completed by April, 1989, but I was forced to revise my expectations and shoot for September, 1989. Now it is clear that I will not even meet that target date.

A LITTLE LITIGATION

The reason my writing has taken so long to complete (apart from the fact that the book is longer and far more complex than I had envisioned), is that I have a good deal of personal litigation to contend with. At the same time, I have had to deal with Judge Peter C. Dorsey's illegal interference in my parole. These lawsuits caused many time-comsuming delays and distracting anxieties. For example, while writing this book, I have been engaged in the following litigations:

(1) Suing the government in Federal District Court for all of the funds it illegally seized from me for the years 1976, 1977, and 1978. (See Reply Brief in the Appendix),

(2) Suing the government in the United States Court of Claims for all the money it illegally seized from me for 1975;

(3) Litigating a fraudulent "deficiency" in Tax Court for 1979;

(4) Helping my two sons (ages 23 and 25) litigate a matter in Tax Court due to IRS claims that monies allegedly due from me for the tax year 1974 are now owed by them, because I transferred my home to my sons;

(5) Seeking to vacate my illegal conditions of probation pursuant to a Rule 35 motion before the same judge who imposed them. Judge Dorsey denied my motion, so I appealed to the Second Circuit Court, which sustained his decision. On May 26, 1989, I filed a motion for a rehearing *en banc*, (see Appendix), which is still pending at this date.

(6) In continuation of my efforts to get my conviction overturned pursuant to a Rule 2255 habeas corpus action (which I initiated while still imprisoned), I had a "hearing" before Judge Dorsey on December 11, 1988. He rejected my petition—which I shall cover in some detail later on. Had I been an axe-murderer, he probably would have reversed it based on the evidence I presented!;

(7) In addition, Judge Dorsey forced me to consume considerable time fighting his illegal intrusion in my parole status—where I am under the supervision of the Parole Commission and not a Connecticut District Court. He initiated (in league with the Department of Justice) a comprehensive investigation of my financial affairs ostensibly to determine my *current* ability to pay the $27,406

in court costs he had imposed on me. In order to press this investigation, the Justice Department, Judge Dorsey, and my parole supervisor (along with the Parole Commission) had to pretend—illegally—that I am currently on probation, *not parole!* The real purpose of this investigation, however, was to give the Department of Justice some basis for developing a perjury case against me, since I had testified under oath and had previously given the government sworn affidavits regarding my financial affairs. Obviously the Justice Department and Dorsey hoped to find inconsistencies that might lead to perjury charges. Remember, those charges would not need to be legitimate— any contrived basis would do! The time I would then have to devote in fighting them (even if I proved myself innocent!) would severely interfere with my ability to finish this book. And, obviously, for reasons which will soon become apparent, Judge Dorsey and the government *hope* this book will never see the light of day.

In addition to these federal matters, I am litigating the following matters in State Court:

(1) A malpractice suit against John R. Williams, the lawyer who represented me in my last conviction;

(2) A negligence lawsuit against Alan Ufland and the financial conglomerate, Investor's Diversified Services (IDS). In this case, Ufland was IDS' local branch manager who facetiously (but with devastating effects) wrote the words "tax evader" as my occupation on a money market fund application I had aplied for on behalf of Irwin Schiff, Inc. This he had done on *his own initiative.* The government introduced this application at my trial as proof that *even I* **considered myself a tax evader**—the very charge the government had to prove! At trial, Ufland had neither the honesty nor the courage to admit simply that he had entered these words as a lark, apparently not believing that they would have any real significance. Both of our offices were in the same building, so Ufland was well aware of my reputation (and prior conviction) for not filing tax returns, and "tax evader" was apparently his pea-brain understanding of what my activities amounted to.

Certainly I would never have stated that I was a "tax evader," since such a claim would have mocked everything that I had ever written on or spoken of on the subject of federal income taxes. Furthermore, how could "tax evader" be anybody's *occupation?* Besides, Ufland knew I was running an insurance agency and a publishing company right in his own building. Nonetheless, Ufland permitted the Court (and to a lesser degree the prosecutor) to lead him by the nose in claiming that though **he could not recall the interview, I had undoubtedly given him this information "in the normal course" of doing business!** The reason that Ufland did not remember the

interview is that **it never happened!**

Since it was a corporate application with little information required, I merely signed the application with only the corporate named filled in, and turned it in to the front office at IDS—without even seeing Ufland. Judge Dorsey took over his examination from Michael Hartmere, the prosecutor, because he apparently felt that Hartmere was not eliciting Ufland's testimony in a believable enough *or damaging enough manner.* Dorsey literally had to put the words "in the normal course" of business right in Ufland's mouth, to convince the jury that even though Ufland couldn't recall the interview, it surely must have happened, and that he surely must have gotten this confession from me!

It certainly *was not* "in the normal course" of business, to obtain, for example, even a "birth date", let alone the "occupation" of a corporate applicant. The IDS front office had apparently mistaken the application for a personal one, because it took information from prior applications of mine on file. However, you may be sure there is no insurance or mutual fund salesman alive who would not recall an interview in which the applicant gave as his "occupation"— not an occupation—*but an admission of criminal culpability!* Had it ever happened, Ufland would have been relating the incident at mutual fund conventions and sales meetings for years on end. One can picture the interview as Ufland would have us believe occurred:

"What is your occupation, Mr. Schiff?" (though he would have called me Irwin.)

"I'm a tax evader."

"Oh, a tax evader—okay. I haven't had one of those before. I'll just fill that right in here in the space provided..." and so he nonchalantly fills it in...without a word...question...or comment! Is that believable?

Yet that was Ufland's testimony! Also the entry appeared *below* my signature. On this basis alone, its suspect and prejudicial character far outweighed any probative value it might have. In addition, an applicant's occupation is usually the type of information a mutual fund salesman fills in based upon his own knowledge. He generally fills in that information *after* he closes the sale and the applicant has left the interview. It is a question that is hardly ever asked— especially if there are prior applications on file and the salesman knows the client.

Despite all of this, Dorsey allowed this obviously fraudulent "confession" to be introduced at trial so that it could be used against me. And Michael Hartmere, the "mafia's" prosecuting attorney, lovingly focused on it in his final summation to the jury.[1]

On June 12, 1989, Connecticut Superior Court Judge Beverly J. Hodgson granted the defendant's motion for "summary judgment" in the Ufland case, on the grounds that my suit was barred by the statute of limitations because the application was dated 1980 and I didn't bring suit until 1987. However, as I pointed out to the court, the application did not *surface* until my trial in October, 1985 and I brought suit within two years of first learning of it—and within two years of my suffering the damages caused by it. This, I believe, satisfies Connecticut law. Therefore I am convinced that Judge Hodgson's decision went against both the law and the facts, and I have notified the Connecticut Supreme Court of my intention to appeal.

(3) The lawyer who represented me in connection with the Simon and Schuster matter sued me for $10,200 he claims I still owe him for that case and others. As a result of his initiating that lawsuit, I have countersued for substantial damages in regard to that and other matters.

The bulk of all of the above litigation provided me with most of the information for this book—which you will now be able to use in litigating your own lawsuits against the government.

The brief that I dispatched yesterday to the U.S. Court of Claims was entitled, "Plaintiff's Answer To Defendant's Reply To Plaintiff's Response To Defendant's Motion For Summary Judgment and Response to Plaintiff's Motion For Summary Judgment." Undoubtedly many will find that a little confusing, so let me explain it. In this action, I am the plaintiff and the United States is the defendant, and I am suing the government for the $8,000 plus interest that it took from me in 1983 (pursuant to notices of levy) for taxes, penalties and interest allegedly due for 1975. (See my Form 4340 in Figure 10-1.) I began this lawsuit on January 11, 1989, and the brief I mailed yesterday replies to the earlier motions for summary judgments filed by both the government and myself.

SUMMARY JUDGMENTS

Normally when one sues another party, one anticipates a trial where the issues are resolved by either a judge or jury, based upon evidence and testimony given under oath. However, if one party believes that they have secured enough information from the other party by way of pre-trial discovery, or because of some defect in jurisdiction, one can move for a summary judgment. That is, a party moves the court to decide in its favor without a trial, on the grounds that it has provided the court with enough information to prove its case, thereby a trial would be superfluous. I have developed such a position in connection with all three of my current civil lawsuits against the federal government!

FIGURE 10-1

Certificate of Assessments and Payments

Name of Taxpayer	Address (Number, street, city, and state)	EIN or SSN	
Irwin A. Schiff	144 Shepards Knoll, Hamden, CT 06514	047-16-2491N	1040

Date (a)	Explanation of Transactions (b)	Assessment (Abatement) (c)	Credit (Credit Reversal) (d)	Balance (e)	DLN or Account Number (f)	23C Date (g)	Period Ending (h)
04-20-83	Additional Tax Assessed	3,226.39			06647-111-20001	04-20-83	7512
	Fraud Penalty	1,613.20					
	Failure to Pay Tax Penalty	139.68					
	Restricted Interest	3,138.24					
05-17-84	Payment		6,927.08				
03-25-85	Payment		1,380.69				
05-15-86	Restricted Interest	190.26		.00			
04-20-84	First Notice						

I certify that the foregoing transcript of the taxpayer named above in respect to the taxes specified is a true and complete transcript for the period stated, and all assessments, penalties, interests, abatements, credits, refunds, and advance or unidentified payment relating thereto as disclosed by the records of this office as of the date of this certification are shown therein.

Signature of Director (required for certification) SUPERVISOR PAYMENT & CERT. UNIT	Location INTERNAL REVENUE SERVICE CENTER NORTH ATLANTIC REGION, ANDOVER, MA 01812	Date 03-24-88

Form **4340** (Rev. 7-90)   PS/gd

After I instituted my lawsuit, and after a status conference in which both counsel for the government and I explained our respective positions (I testified via telephone from New York), Appeals Court Judge, John P. Weise ordered both the government and me to file motions for summary judgment. First the government was required to file its motion; I then had 30 days to file a reply and to make a similar motion of my own. The government in turn had 30 days in which to reply to mine, and finally, I had 14 days in which to answer the government's reply to my response to their motion, and to respond to their reply to mine. I hope that's all clear! In any case, all of that obviously took time away from writing—and that was not the only litigation I had to attend to this month. Approximately one week before, I had filed a comparable brief in District Court in connection with my much bigger lawsuit to recover over $200,000 (now probably over $400,000 with interest) that the government seized from me for the years 1976, 1977, and 1978.

*   *   *   *   *   *   *

It is now Saturday morning, August 12, 1989, or some seven days since I wrote the above. I am no longer sitting in front of my delightful Toshiba lap-top. I am using a portable prison Olivetti! On Tuesday morning, August 8, at approximately 10:30 a.m., I was illegally arrested, "violated,"[2] and reincarcerated. Apparently the federal mafia did not want me to make public those briefs that I had just filed, and so it decided to lock me up as fast as it could in order to prevent them from being made public—at least for this tax season! They, of course, know that I am writing this book, but they don't know how comprehensive nor how advanced it is. Surprise!

My violation occurred during my regular reporting session with my "parole-probation" officer, Patrick F. Walsh; (I will shortly explain the reason for this illegal title). These monthly meetings usually take about an hour, during which time I hand in a written report covering my activities for the month. This discloses: how many days I worked, how much money I earned, how much money might have been given or loaned to me by others, my total current indebtedness, whether I moved or changed jobs, and whether or not I have been arrested. After about 15 minutes into the interview, two U.S. marshalls came into the room and proceeded to arrest me. I was being "violated," and without further ado, my hands were handcuffed behind me. When I asked on what grounds I was being violated, I was told that I had not paid my income taxes for the years 1980, 1981, and 1982—(those were the *same charges for which I had been originally incarcerated!*)—and that I had associated with a known felon, or words to that effect. (See news story, Figure 10-2.) For reasons that will soon become apparent, I realized that these two charges were contrived, since paying

income taxes was not even a condition of my parole—and I hadn't associated (to my knowledge) with any felon.

Within minutes I was shown the document (Figure 10-3) containing the official charges, and saw to my surprise that the "felon" was Fred White (a fictitious name), a New Haven *attorney!* I had contacted Fred shortly after being paroled, concerning the possibility of his testifying as a witness at my forthcoming habeas corpus (Rule 2255) hearing. Fred had prepared a trust instrument for me which the U.S. prosecutor had fraudulently but effectively used against me at my trial.[3] I wanted Fred's testimony concerning that instrument, and also his expert testimony regarding some other related matters. The 2255 hearing (getting its name from Section 2255 of the United States Code of Civil Procedure) is for the purpose of vacating one's sentence—so this was a pretty important hearing. At this time I was living in Forest Hills, New York. When I commuted to New Haven to prepare for this hearing, and to file numerous motions in connections with it, Fred's convenient, downtown office was one of the first places I visited. Fred agreed to be a witness for me, both with respect to the trust instruments and in other areas I outlined. Since Fred had not testified at my trial, he was unaware of how this trust had been used against me. I had to familiarize him with this and also explain the other reasons for which I wanted his testimony. Fred also allowed me to use his copy machine to prepare the motions I needed to file with the U.S. Attorney and at the U.S. courthouse, both of which were only half a block from his office. When I would drop by Fred's office to advise him about the status of my hearing (its date was changed twice), I could count on using his copy machine to prepare the motions I was continually filing in connection with this hearing.

During this period, Fred never told me that he had pleaded guilty to failure to file a tax return, which is only a misdemeanor. I didn't even realize that Fred was having problems with the IRS until the IRS (illegally) closed his office a few months later. I understood that this was in connection with an enforcement of an alleged civil tax "liability." The IRS had similarly "seized" property from me, but while they had never closed my office, I was well aware that this was not an uncommon practice. It never dawned on me, however, that Fred had been involved with criminal tax charges. The lawyer that I ultimately retained to handle my 2255 hearing decided to confine the limited time we had to areas other than those for which I wanted Fred's testimony. Since I was using another expert witness, my attorney also felt that Fred's testimony might detract from his. Thus, Fred's testimony was never used.

In any case, I couldn't help thinking that if they arrested me for seeing Fred, how could they avoid arresting Fred for seeing me?! On Wednesday, August 8, 1989, I was able to

FIGURE 10-2

Back in jail, Schiff accused of not paying income taxes

By Ben Boulton
Register Staff

Nationally known tax protester Irwin Schiff, author of "How Anyone Can Stop Paying Taxes," was arrested Tuesday and is back in jail for parole violations that include not paying taxes, a probation official said.

Schiff, formerly of Hamden, was sentenced in U.S. District Court in Hartford in 1985 to three years in prison and fined $30,000 for evading taxes for 1980, 1981 and 1982. He was released on parole Aug. 8, 1988, after serving about 20 months of the sentence at a federal prison in Pennsylvania.

Parole conditions required Schiff not to break the law and not to associate with known felons, said Phil Bigger, federal probation supervisor in Brooklyn, N.Y.

Schiff, 61, allegedly violated those terms by not paying the approximately $49,000 he still owes in personal income taxes from 1980 through 1982, Bigger said. Schiff also was accused Tuesday of associating with a known felon. Bigger would not name the felon.

Schiff was arrested at a Brooklyn federal probation office on a warrant issued by the U.S. Parole Commission. He moved to New York last year, soon after his release from prison.

Schiff has maintained that the federal income tax is voluntary and self-assessed and that the methods the government uses to collect taxes is unconstitutional.

He is being held at the Metropolitan Correctional Center in Manhattan and he could not be reached for comment Tuesday. He will have no opportunity to post bond and is not likely to be released soon, Bigger said.

Irwin Schiff
1985 photograph

Within the next few days a probation officer will conduct a hearing to determine whether the Parole Commission had "probable cause" to issue the warrant, Bigger said. Such cause would exist if Schiff has not paid the taxes he owes, he said.

Assuming probable cause is found, the commission will conduct a parole revocation hearing within 90 days, according to

Turn to Schiff, Page 4

Continued from Page 3

Bigger. Schiff cannot be released on bond while the hearing is pending.

If the commission revokes Schiff's parole, he would be sent to prison to complete some or all of the remainder of his parole, which expires Dec. 16, Bigger said.

"At some point he will run out of time," Bigger said, meaning that once the parole expires, Schiff cannot be returned to jail for violating parole stemming from the 1985 conviction.

Schiff also was convicted in 1980 on two counts of failing to file personal income tax returns for 1974 and 1975. He served six months in prison and paid a $10,000 fine on those charges.

Books Schiff has written include "The Great Income Tax Hoax" and "The Tax Rebel's Guide to the Constitution of the United States and the Declaration of Independence."

He also has lectured on tax resistance, but is barred from doing so under conditions of parole.

Schiff formerly ran an insurance agency in Hamden.

---

contact Sue Gallant, the proprietor of Box Stop, a Hamden, Connecticut firm that is handling my book orders and providing me with telephone answering services. She informed me of the story that had appeared in the *New Haven Register,* reporting that I had been arrested for not paying income taxes and for "associating with a known felon." It is significant to note that initially the Parole Commission "would not name the felon." The reason that they refused to do so was that Fred was *not* a felon, because failure to file a tax return is a misdemeanor—not a felony! Apparently the Parole Commission believed that it could get away with this false accusation. The following day I was able to reach Ben Boulton, the reporter, and explain to him that the alleged "felon" was none other than "Fred White," with whom Ben was familiar. I also mentioned to Ben that I hoped he wouldn't include Fred's name, since I didn't want to generate any additional unfavorable publicity for him. I explained that I was telling him this so that he would know the nature of the non-"felon", with whom I was accused of "associating." This would prove that all the charges were contrived. In a follow-up story that appeared in *The Register* the next day (Figure 10-4), the Parole Commission now confirmed that the "felon" was indeed Fred White, "who was convicted in 1986 of failing to file an income tax return." However, since failure to file is not a felony, I had *not* associated with a "felon" after all, as the Parole Commission had initially released to the press!

During this time I had also contacted Mike Maco, a reporter with the *Bridgeport Post*. I gave him an account of

what had happened and why. Though the *Post* had not carried the original story, I suggested to Mike that he cover the story because the *Post* is located across the street from the Federal Court House in Bridgeport, where most of my explosive briefs had been recently filed. I suggested to Mike that he might read them—and then it would be obvious *why* I had been "*violated.*" However, I don't know how the *Post* treated the story.

In contacting Mike the day after the story broke in the *Register* which identified Fred as the "felon," Mike said, "Don't you know what just happened?" "No," I replied. "They just arrested Fred White," he incredulously informed me, "and he's in jail, too." Undoubtedly when Fred's name unexpectedly surfaced, the powers that be realized that they would have to arrest him in order not to appear *inconsistent* and *prejudiced* in arresting me! However, since Fred never served any time in jail, they are obviously charging him with a violation of probation, not a violation of parole. In any case, *that's U.S. "justice" in action.*

It is also important to note that I hadn't seen Fred since November of 1988—or some nine months prior to my arrest. The authorities knew that I had met with him long before August 8, 1989, since I had routinely reported this to my parole officer during my reporting sessions. If seeing Fred were *really* a violation of my parole conditions, I would have been violated long before August 8, 1989. The ridiculousness in all of this is to consider why not associating with felons is a general condition of both parole and

FIGURE 10-3

U. S. DEPARTMENT OF JUSTICE
UNITED STATES PAROLE COMMISION

WARRANT APPLICATION

ISSUING REGION NORTHEAST		**Date**	August 2, 1989
Case Of SCHIFF, Irwin		**Reg. No.**	08537-014
Race W	**Birth Date** 2/23/28	**FBI No.**	370 216T6
(Sentence) Began 12/28/86	**District From** Connecticut		

Original Offense Failure to File Income Tax Returns
Sentence Length/Type 3 years, RA   **Released** 8/8/88
District To E/NY   **Transferred To**   **M.R.**   **Parole** X
Violation Date 8/88   **Termination Date** 12/16/89

You shall, unless you have been convicted of a new offense, be given a preliminary interview by an official designated by a Regional Commissioner to determine if there is probable cause to believe that you have violated the conditions of your release, and if so, whether to release you or hold you for a revocation hearing.

At your preliminary interview and any subsequent revocation hearing you may present documentary evidence and voluntary witnesses on your behalf, and, if you deny the charge(s) against you, you may request the presence of those who have given information upon which the charges are based. Such witnesses will be made available for questioning unless good cause is found for their non-appearance.

You may be represented by an attorney or other representative of your choice, or, if you are unable to pay for counsel, an attorney will be provided by the U.S. District Court if you fill out and promptly return a Form CJA-22 to a U.S. Probation Officer.

If, after a revocation hearing, you are found to have violated the conditions of your release the Commission may: (1) restore you to supervision, and, if appropriate, (a) reprimand you; (b) modify your conditions of supervision; or (c) refer you to a residential community treatment center for the remainder of your sentence; or (2) revoke your parole or mandatory release, in which case the Commission will also decide when to consider you for further release.

If you have been convicted of a new offense (committed while on parole) which is punishable by a term of imprisonment, you will not receive sentence credit for the time you spent on parole. If the Commission finds that you absconded or otherwise refused to submit to parole supervision, the Commission may order that you not receive credit toward service of your sentence for that amount of time. (If your original sentence was imposed for violation of the District of Columbia Criminal Code, you will not receive credit for time spent on parole regardless of whether or not you have been convicted of a crime.)

A special parole term violator whose parole is revoked shall receive no credit for time spent on parole.
CHARGES:

1.   (a) FAILURE TO FILE FEDERAL TAX RETURNS
     (b) FAILURE TO PAY TAXES
On or about 10/25/85, in U.S. District Court, District of Connecticut, subject was convicted of income tax evasion for the years of 1980, 1981 and 1982. Since his release on parole, subject has failed to file tax returns or pay taxes for 1980, 1981 and 1982. Information contained in letter dated 6/28/89 by USPO Walsh.
I ADMIT [   ] or DENY [   ] the above charge(s).

2.   ASSOCIATION WITH A PERSON HAVING A CRIMINAL RECORD:
From 8/88 through 11/88, Subject associated with   , a person with a record of prior criminal convictions, as evidenced by their conviction in U.S. District Court, District of Connecticut dated September, 1986. Information contained in letter dated 6/28/89 by USPO Walsh.
I ADMIT ( ) OR DENY ( ) THE ABOVE CHARGES

Date Warrant Issued   August 2, 1989
District To Which Sent   E/NY
Date Warrant Req. Recv'd 7/5/89   Warrant Recommended By: `
Preliminary Interview Required: YES [X] NO [   ]   KATHLEEN A. PANNER, Hearing Examiner
KAP:tls   #1   U.S. Parole Commission
( ) Commission   ( ) Inmate   ( ) Institution   ( ) USPO   ( ) Interviewing Officer   ( ) Chron

PAROLE FORM H-20
Rev. 6/87

FIGURE 10-4

Parole violations 'fabricated,' Schiff claims

By Ben Boulton
Register Staff

Tax rebel Irwin Schiff charged Wednesday that the government "fabricated" parole violations to retaliate against him for working on a new book and for pressing a claim that the government owes him more than $300,000.

Schiff, a former Hamden resident who wrote "How Anyone Can Stop Paying Taxes," was arrested Tuesday on charges that he violated parole stemming from a 1985 conviction for income tax evasion.

In a hurried telephone interview from the Metropolitan Correctional Center in New York, Schiff said government officials are aware of embarrassing information he intends to include in an upcoming book

and that his arrest was an attempt to stifle him.

He also said "I blew them (the government) apart" in legal motions seeking return of money he said the Internal Revenue Service illegally seized from his publisher in 1974.

Assistant U.S. Attorney Peter Jongbloed, who is representing the government in Schiff matters, would not comment on the charges. Jongbloed said his office had nothing to do with the U.S. Parole Commission's attempt to revoke Schiff's parole.

Phil Bigger, supervisor of federal probation in Brooklyn, N.Y., confirmed Wednesday that the Parole Commission acted independently of other federal agencies in seeking the parole revocation.

Schiff, 61, was sentenced in U.S. District

Court in Hartford in 1985 to three years in prison for evading taxes for 1980, 1981 and 1982. He was released on parole Aug. 8, 1988, after serving about 20 months.

Parole conditions require Schiff to pay the back taxes he owes and to avoid associating with people with criminal records or with people who advocate violating tax laws, Bigger said.

Schiff allegedly broke those terms by not paying the approximately $49,000 he still owes in personal income tax from 1980 through 1982, Bigger said. Schiff also is accused of associating with a New Haven lawyer who was convicted in 1986 of failure to file an income tax return.

Turn to Schiff, Page 6

Schiff: Tax rebel fights back

Continued from Page 3

Schiff denied that parole conditions require him to pay the back taxes, but he conceded that the IRS has been seeking the payments. He also said that he didn't know ___ had a criminal record. ___ couldn't be reached for comment.

Schiff will remain in custody without bond at least until a revocation hearing, which may not occur for another 60 to 90 days, Bigger said. If the parole commission prevails, Schiff will be returned to prison to serve some or all of the remainder of his parole, which expires Dec. 16.

---

probation. The authorities are obviously trying to prevent felons from conspiring to commit other crimes. Assuming, however, that the authorities knew that the only subjects that felons would talk about would be the weather, religion, politics, and poetry, would there be any reason for prohibiting such benign contacts? It is only because the authorities cannot be sure that these are the only things that felons might talk about—that they prohibit all contact. Now does anyone think that Fred and I plotted to evade taxes or fail to file tax returns together?

As far as the second charge is concerned, at no time did my parole officer *ever mention* anything about my paying $49,000 in back taxes for the years 1980, 1981 and 1982. As a matter of fact, until I saw that figure in *The New Haven Register*, I hadn't the faintest idea what the government claimed I owed for those years, since they had *never sent me a deficiency notice!* In addition, if the Parole Commission were really serious about my paying these taxes, wouldn't my parole officer have brought up the subject of my making some payment towards this amount and/or asked me something about my association with Fred White—*before* "*violating*" me? He never did.

With all the overcrowding in federal jails, with federal law enforcement personnel stretched to the limit because of the national drug problem, and with the federal government plagued with enormous deficits, Fred and I sit in jail, for the reasons indicated. Would that make sense to anyone if it weren't for the REAL REASON I was violated?

AN UNPLANNED DIGRESSION

The American public has an unrealistic picture of our legal system because some violent criminals have had their convictions set aside on what might appear to be minor

technicalities. For example, in the famous Miranda case, Miranda confessed to murder. Yet, because he had not been properly advised of his right to remain silent, his conviction based on that confession, was thrown out. (Because I am now writing from the confines of jail, I cannot conveniently check all my facts, which may cause some minor inaccuracies). I am sure that you are also familiar with other instances where people, who were apparently guilty of heinous crimes, are released for what appears to be minor infractions of due process—such as illegally obtained evidence or confessions. From such instances, the public has gained the impression that the American legal system bends over backwards to protect the rights of individuals caught in the criminal justice system. What the public overlooks, however, is that in all such cases, the individuals involved usually do not represent a threat to the *government*, only to other members of society! In such cases the legal system can afford to be magnanimous. But let the individual in question be a threat to the government (such as a so-called "tax protester")—**and due process goes right out the window!** Tax protesters get no more due process than would *anyone* threatening the government in *any* other totalitarian state. The only difference is that in America, the appearance of justice is hypocritically maintained (since the public and the media generally don't know the difference) and the punishment is not generally as severe or as *final*.

THE LEGAL MASQUERADE

Those who had a hand in my prosecution and incarceration—from the IRS agents who were rehearsed in perjurious testimony, the U.S. prosecutor who rehearsed them, and the presiding judge who manipulated the proceedings, to the appellate judges who sustained my conviction—all knew that they were participating in a conspiracy to send an innocent man to jail. If any of them had sought to visit such injuries on another as private citizens, they all would have risked being sent to prison. As protected government witnesses, and as above-the-law federal prosecutors and judges, however, they each knew that they could get away with it. In order to understand completely the unlawful nature of my current situation, you have to be more familiar with the terms of my original sentence. I received three years incarceration on count one, and three years incarceration on counts two and three, to be served concurrently. Incarceration was suspended on the latter two counts, and for them I was placed on probation, which was to begin after I finished my sentence on count one. All three counts involved charges of tax evasion for the years 1980, 1981, and 1982. A fourth count involved my failure to file a corporate tax return for 1980. On that count I was given a one-year jail sentence to be served concurrently with the three years I would serve on count one. I was also fined $7,500 on each count, or $30,000 in all plus a fine of $27,406 in costs. In addition, numerous special conditions (of which you are already aware) were made a part of my probation.

That last amount was indeed ironic. Remember (from Chapter 6) that I had offered to plead guilty *immediately* in order to save the government and myself the costs of my prosecution, if either the government or the court would merely produce the statute that made me liable for the taxes at issue—but they refused to do so. **Now they would impose on me the costs that I had offered to save them!** But the cost of my trial was far greater than $27,406. As far as my $30,000 fine is concerned, most of the time the non-payment of such fines does not affect one's right to be paroled. In my case, however, Judge Dorsey made my fine *committed*—which meant that I couldn't be paroled unless it was paid (see Figure 10-5). As a result of the legal expenses of my trial and appeal, and because of some disastrous investments, I was dead broke when I entered jail on December 16, 1986. However, since prison officials now put illegal pressure[4] on inmates to pay their fines, whether or not they are committed, I was paying about $10.00 per month toward my committed fine.

Actually my sister was mailing in the payments for me. When I was granted parole after serving 18 months, I believed that this installment arrangement would suffice until I got back on my financial feet. After all, I had already

given a sworn affidavit to the government, revealing all of my assets and liabilities which clearly showed that I did not have the $30,000 to pay them. As a matter of fact, that statement showed that I was actually deep in debt. When it came time for my parole, however, the institution would not let me out unless I paid the $30,000! **Who said America has no debtor prisons?** I remained in prison almost *another two months* until a family member *ransomed me out!* Based upon the terms of my parole, I knew I would have 18 months to finish my book, the proceeds from which would get me out of debt and allow me to pay back the money I borrowed to get out of jail. I also believed that I would have 18 months of relative freedom in which to more effectively pursue my efforts to reverse my conviction and/or eliminate these odious conditions of probation, based upon the actions I had already initiated. It is obvious that I could not have accepted parole if it also meant paying $27,406 in court costs (which the government tried to collect from me after my release), paying $49,000 of back income taxes that they now claim I owe (but for which I have never received a deficiency notice—let alone a demand for payment!), and also contend with those treacherous conditions of probation. My current incarceration is proof that the federal government's signature on an agreement isn't worth the paper it's written on—which you should already know from America's five-cent dollar. The government said to me, "We will let you out on parole if you pay us $30,000." They didn't say a word about my parole being contingent on my paying them another dime—especially when I didn't have it.

After *borrowing* and giving them the sum *demanded*, they take my money and then deny me parole because I allegedly owe the $49,000 for which I was *originally incarcerated!* Thus our government doesn't even have the integrity of the ordinary kidnapper who might at least release his captive upon receipt of the ransom demanded!

THE IRS REARS ITS UGLY HEAD

Within a few days of being paroled, I received a letter (Figure 10-6) from the IRS, which is perfectly clear: if I didn't make immediate arrangements to pay my 1980, 1981, and 1982 income taxes, I would be reincarcerated. While Mr. Leeker did not come right out and say that, his letter is skillfully worded to convey just that impression. Since his letter was *deliberately extortionary,* there would seem to be no reason why he should be treated any differently by the Justice Departent than any run-of-the-mill, would-be extortionist. For one thing, since I was released to parole, *not probation,* this Special Condition did not apply! For another thing, this Special Condition makes no claim that it applies to income taxes, Leeker automatically assumes (and wants me to believe) *that it does!* While stating that the issue involves a *civil* matter, he, nevertheless, threatens me with *criminal* punishment; and, of course, the "liability" he

FIGURE 10-6

Internal Revenue Service
District Director

Department of the Treasury
Group 1214 - 4th Floor
936 Silas Deane Hwy.
Wethersfield, Ct. 06109

Person to Contact: C. Leeker

Telephone Number: 258-2045

Refer Reply To: E:II:1214:CAL

Date: August 10, 1988

Mr. Irwin A. Schiff
68-38 Yellowstone Blvd.
Forest Hills, New York 11375

Dear Mr. Schiff:

As we have advised you in the past, this office is responsible for resolving the civil aspects of your federal income tax liability for the years ending December 31, 1980, 1981 and 1982. Further, the Special Conditions of Probation require that you "remain current insofar as all legally required tax payments with reasonable and good faith compliance and shall file all returns required by tax laws."

I have indicated to you in the past that this office expects you to comply with these conditions within one month of your release. Since you were released from Loretto FCI on August 8, 1988 I would anticipate receipt of the returns for each of these years on or before September 8, 1988.

If you wish, you can contact me at the above telephone number or address.

Very truly yours,

CRAIG A. LEEKER
Group Manager

FIGURE 10-5

U.S. Department of Justice
United States Parole Commission
Chevy Chase, Maryland 20815

Certificate of Parole

PROVIDED THE COMMITTED FINE IS PAID OR OTHERWISE DISCHARGED ACCORDING TO LAW

Know all Men by these Presents: It having been made to appear to the United States Parole Commission

that   IRWIN A. SCHIFF   , Register No.   08537-014   , a prisoner in

the   FCI LORETTO   is eligible to be PAROLED, and in that said prisoner substantially observed the rules of the institution, and in the opinion of the Commission said prisoner's release would not depreciate the seriousness of this offense or promote disrespect for the law, and would not jeopardize the public welfare, it is ORDERED by the said United States Parole Commission that said prisoner be PAROLED on

JUNE 16   , 19 88 ; until   DECEMBER 16   , 19 89 , and that said prisoner is to remain within the limits of

EASTERN DISTRICT/NEW YORK

Given under the hands and the seal of the United States Parole Commission this   12TH   day of   MAY   , nineteen hundred and   88   .

UNITED STATES PAROLE COMMISSION.

By MARYANNE DANIEL, SOCIAL SCIENCE TECHNICIAN

Initial Risk Category: 10

Advisor   CHIEF U.S. PROBATION OFFICER, E/NY

Probation Officer

I have read, or had read to me, the conditions of release printed on the reverse of this certificate and received a copy thereof. I fully understand them and know that if I violate any, I may be recommitted. I also understand that special conditions may be added or modifications of any condition may be made by the Parole Commission upon notice required by law.

Irwin A. Schiff
WITNESSED   Case Manager   8/5/88
(Title)   (Date)

08537-014
(Register Number)

UNITED STATES PAROLE COMMISSION:
The above-named person was released on the 8th day of August, 19 88 with 495 days remaining to be served.

Deborah J. Shandor, Inmate Systems Manager
FOR: ROBERT J. BARNCASTLE, Warden

PAROLE FORM H-4
SEP 30

1. Inmate Copy

speaks of doesn't even exist! This is another example of how the federal mafia seeks to extort income taxes from the public.

As you saw from my en banc petition, the courts have ruled that all criminal fines, penalties, and reparations imposed by the federal court must relate to the specific "offense for which the conviction was had." This means that the only taxes that Judge Dorsey might theoretically require me to pay, as a condition of probation, were income taxes related to 1980, 1981, and 1982—the years for which my conviction "was had."[5] Then why didn't Judge Dorsey simply make the payment of these taxes a condition of probation? Why did he employ such broad language so as to encompass all kinds of taxes and for *any* year, thus making the condition illegal (but not *apparently* so!) as a matter of law? Apart from his assuming that the condition might not be challenged on this basis (he and other judges have been getting away with this for years) and that the Second Circuit would sustain it, even though it was illegal, he simply did not want to impose a condition *that was clearly illegal on its face*. He knew that filing and paying income taxes are based on voluntary compliance (even though he might instruct juries otherwise), yet he simply could not get himself to specifically order the payment of a voluntary tax under pain of imprisonment. Instead, he fashioned a broad condition that had the appearance of legality, but which could be applied arbitrarily to achieve the same result.

I sent Leeker a four-page reply to his letter, explaining that: (1) I was on parole and not on probation, so this condition did not apply to me; (2) the Condition did not mention income taxes if that were the tax he was alluding to; and (3) I was "current" in so far as all federal taxes were concerned, and if he would send me proof of any 23C assessment demand made upon me (by way of a Form 17A) which remained unpaid, "I would pay such outstanding liabilities immediately." *To this day neither Leeker nor anyone else at the IRS has ever answered that letter!*

THE RELUCTANT EX-PROSECUTOR

On September 28, 1988 my son, Andy, and I drove to Waterbury, Connecticut for the purpose of subpoenaing Michael Hartmere. I wanted his testimony at my 2255 hearing, since he was responsible for developing all of the perjurious testimony the government used in indicting and convicting me. In the interim, however, he had managed to become a juvenile court judge in Waterbury, so we drove there to serve him. We arrived at his court around 1:00 p.m., and Andy went in, hoping to be able to find an opportunity to hand him his subpoena. Due to visiting restrictions, however, he was unable to do so. We decided to wait until court closed and try to serve Hartmere when he went to his car, which he parked in a garage adjoining the court.

However, departing court employees noticed Andy and me waiting outside the court. Andy had apparently drawn attention to himself when he sought to serve Hartmere earlier, and these employees alerted Hartmere that we were waiting for him. When Hartmere finally emerged from juvenile court around 5:15 p.m., he was flanked by a uniformed cop and (as we later learned) a probation officer. When my son peacefully approached this trio with the subpoena clearly unfurled in his outstretched hand, and told Hartmere he had a federal subpoena for him, Hartmere reacted as if my son were holding up a cross, and he was the vampire. "Get away from me," Hartmere shrieked, raising his hands, "or I'll have you arrested." The probation officer now sought to block Andy's approach by placing himself between him and Hartmere, while the cop chimed in with, "If you know what's good for you, you'll do what the judge says." This violent reaction from these minions of the law, intimidated Andy from serving the subpoena, so immediately following this incident we paid a visit to Waterbury police headquarters and lodged a complaint against the cop for obstructing justice. Is this the way you would expect a Connecticut State judge and a former U.S. prosecutor (who himself had subpoenaed hundreds of people) to react when someone tried to subpoena *him*?

The next day my parole officer suddenly informed me that my far harsher conditions of probation had been in effect "since your release from prison on August 8, 1988." (See Figure 10-7.) That's strange, why hadn't anybody mentioned this *before*? Obviously no mere parole officer had the authority to change overnight the terms of my parole. However, since a parole officer can exercise considerable arbitrary power over you, one doesn't want to antagonize him by not doing what he says, even when you know it's not part of your parole. I had a book to write and important litigation to press ahead with, so I did not want to get bogged down contesting parole restrictions that Walsh was clearly fabricating. From the notation appearing at the bottom of Walsh's letter, it is apparent that Hartmere had persuaded Peter Jongbloed, an Assistant U.S. Attorney in the New Haven office, and his former underling to intercede with Walsh in illegally restricting my parole activities in ways not covered in my parole agreement.

Approximately two weeks later, at my next reporting session, Walsh handed me a document entitled "Conditions of Probation" that he wanted me to accept and sign. This document claimed that I was on probation—not on parole. I objected to the switch and refused to sign the document. Overlooking for the moment that Walsh's claim was ridiculous, why should I have objected if Walsh wanted to claim that I went straight to probation from prison (thus eliminating 14 months of parole)? The reason is that my conditions of probation contained those odious provisions discussed earlier, which were absent from my conditions of

FIGURE 10-7

UNITED STATES DISTRICT COURT
EASTERN DISTRICT OF NEW YORK
PROBATION OFFICE

RALPH K. KISTNER
CHIEF PROBATION OFFICER

STEPHEN J. RACKMILL
DEPUTY CHIEF PROBATION OFFICER

Brooklyn, New York
September 29, 1988

75 CLINTON STREET, ROOM 412
BROOKLYN 11201-4201
718-330-2626

U.S. COURTHOUSE
UNIONDALE AVENUE AT HEMPSTEAD TURNPIKE
UNIONDALE 11553
516-485-7140

U.S. COURTHOUSE
300 RABRO DRIVE
HAUPPAUGE 11788
516-582-1105

Mr. Irwin Schiff
144 Shepherds Knoll Drive
Hamden, Connecticut 06514

Dear Mr. Schiff:

As per our telephone conversation on this date, you are hereby
advised that your conditions of probation, as directed by the
court at the time of sentencing, have been in effect since your
release from prison on August 8, 1988. A copy of those special
conditions are attached.

In view of the above you are hereby advised that the permission
which was previously granted, is rescinded and you are <u>not</u> to
attend the fund raising dinner in Yonkers, New York on October 7,
1988.

In addition, you are not to attempt to visit or meet <u>with Judge
Hartmere.</u>

See you in my office on Tuesday, October 11, 1988 at 9:00 A.M.

Very truly yours,

RALPH K. KISTNER
Chief U.S. Probation Officer

PATRICK F. WALSH
U.S. Probation Officer

PFW:ag

cc: AUSA Jongbloed
    U.S. Probation
    New Haven, Conn.

FIGURE 10-8

Name __IRWIN A. SCHIFF_____ Register Number ____08537-014____

To: United States Parole Commission

It is recommended that the Parole Commission modify the conditions of release of the above-named person by the addition or
revision set forth below. By copy of this proposal, NOTICE is hereby given to the releasee, who may object or comment to the
Commission within ten days after he receives this NOTICE. If the Commission approves the proposed modification it shall
become effective not later than twenty-one days following the ten-day period referred to above.

(1) Parolee shall remain current insofar as all legally required tax payments
    with reasonable and good faith compliance and shall file all returns
    required by tax laws.

(2) Parolee shall not associate or maintain any relationship with any group
    that advocates non compliance with or violation of tax laws.

(3) Parolee shall not participate in or promote any meeting sponsored or
    promoted by groups or individuals formed or brought together, such as
    seminars, media events or any other forum for the purpose of promoting
    or advocating non compliance with or violation of tax laws.

__E. D. N. Y.__   __11-10-88__   __Patrick F. Walsh__
(District)   (Date)   (Probation Officer)

To be Completed by Releasee:

_____ I hereby waive the ten-day waiting period and agree to the proposed modification of conditions.
(Initials)

_____ I object to the proposed modifications of conditions and my reasons are stated on the reverse side of this form.
(Initials)

__11/10/88__   _____
(Date)   (Releasee)

parole. Moreover, their arbitrary enforcement would be in the hands of Judge Dorsey, not the Parole Commission, and since I believed that Dorsey would be more prone to disregard the law than would mere bureaucrats, I thought I had more to fear from Judge Dorsey than from the Parole Commission. Based on other factors that I still do not fully understand, if you are violated while on probation, you can be re-sentenced by the judge, and such a prospect held risks which I did not want to face. The point is, I expected I would have 14 months while on parole (under conditions more benign than were my conditions of probation) in which to either vacate my conviction completely or revoke my conditions of probation and simultaneously write my book (which I believe would also vindicate me) *before* I had to face those conditions of probation. Failing to do any of the above, I believed I would have time to seek the opinion of a specialist in post-conviction law before accepting probation (under those conditions). So when I refused to accept his claim that I was on probation (and not parole), Walsh announced he would propose adding these conditions to my conditions of *parole*—which I also had a right to contest. The fact that he would be proposing them to the Parole Commission was itself proof that I was on parole—not probation—as he had just contended!

As you can see from Figure 10-8, I objected to Walsh's conditions when they were proposed. I also had 20 days to contest them in writing, which I did in a 15-page memorandum to the Parole Commission. In that memorandum I pointed out that under the law, the Parole Commission had no authority to impose the vague conditions that Walsh had proposed. If the Parole Commission was to accept Walsh's recommendation, it would so advise me in a "notice of action," but it never did. I was eventually informed by Walsh that his proposed conditions were never adopted by the Commission. Thus, no condition involving either the filing or paying of income taxes was ever added to my conditions of parole—**and these, you remember, were two of the "conditions" for which I was violated.**

Despite all of the above, which clearly indicates I was on parole and *not* on probation, Walsh, the U.S. Attorney's Office, and Judge Dorsey continued to pretend that I *was* on probation. On March 3, 1989, Raymond M. Hassett, Special Assistant to the U.S. Attorney of the State of Connecticut, filed a motion with Judge Dorsey that I be examined as a "civil judgment debtor" with respect to the $27,406.98 of court costs that had also been imposed on me. (See Figure 10-9) In moving for that hearing, Hassett contended that such a payment was a "special condition of probation" and that I was "presently on probation" and thus Dorsey had the authority to compel such payment. Although this representation was patently false, Judge Dorsey readily agreed to it. As you can see, Dorsey granted

the government's motion in only four days (including mail time) BEFORE EVEN GIVING ME A CHANCE TO RESPOND! Hassett and Dorsey were now involved together in a criminal conspiracy to see if they could either get me violated on some basis or create a situation out of which a charge or perjury might emerge.

On March 11, 1989, I filed an 11-page motion for reconsideration in which I pointed out the following:

(1) There would be "serious violations" of my Fifth Amendment Rights if I consented to testify at such a hearing.

(2) The Court had granted the government's motion without giving me a chance to be heard or to seek the advice of counsel.

(3) The government's motion was "fraudulent on its face" because I was on *parole* and *not probation*—and I supplied the Court with numerous documents attesting to this.

(4) I had accepted parole on the basis that I pay a $30,000 committed fine, and that my release to parole was not contingent upon my paying another dime to the government.[6]

(5) If one were to assume that I were released on probation on August 8, 1988, that would mean that on that date I completed my sentence on Count One and "commenced" serving two "concurrent" sentences on Counts Two and Three. "It is clear that neither the Parole Commission nor the U.S. Attorney, nor the Court has the authority to reduce *in this manner* the defendant's sentence on Count One from 36 months to 19 months, 22 days—nor his total six-year sentence under Counts One, Two and Three from 72 months to 55 months and 22 days."

I also pointed out to Dorsey why he had no authority to change my sentence in this manner; that court documents would reveal that I had no money to pay these costs; and that I was not even working at the time, but rather was engaged in extensive *pro se* litigation to (1) recover substantial amounts of money owed to me by the government, (2) to reverse my conviction and (3) to illuminate my conditions of probation.

In a five-page reply dated March 25, 1989, attorney Hassett said, among other things, the following:

While it is true that the defendant is on parole as to Count One, he simultaneously remained on a three-year probation as to Count Two, which commenced immediately upon his release from custody. Since the

FIGURE 10-9

UNITED STATES **FILED** COURT

DISTRICT **MAR 6 2 AM '89** CONNECTICUT

UNITED STATES OF AMERICA,
                  Plaintiff,   U:S. DISTI...
                                      NEW HAVEN CONN

            v.   : CRIMINAL NO. N-85-20 PCD

IRWIN A. SCHIFF,   : MARCH 3, 1989
                  Defendant.   :

MOTION FOR CIVIL EXAMINATION OF
JUDGMENT DEBTOR

The Plaintiff in the above-entitled action represents:

1.   That subsequent to a jury conviction, on December 18, 1985, the defendant, Irwin A. Schiff, was sentenced to three (3) years imprisonment and fined $30,000 stand-committed.

2.   That a special condition of probation specified by the sentencing Court requires the defendant to pay the costs of prosecution.

3.   That the government's request for a bill of costs in the amount of $27,405.98, was granted on November 5, 1986.

4.   That the defendant erroneously paid a total of $30,200 toward the stand-committed fine resulting in a $200 overpayment.

5.   On February 14, 1989, the Court ordered the $200.00 overpayment, referenced in paragraph 4 above, to be forwarded to the office of the United States Attorney as a partial payment for the bill of costs imposed upon the defendant.

6.   That the defendant has been released from incarceration and is presently on probation.

7.   There remains due and owing to the United States of America costs of prosecution in the amount of $27,205.98.

3/7/89: The motion for examination is granted and this matter is referred to Magistrate Margolis for a hearing on the debtor's ability to pay, including the entry of such discovery orders as she deems appropriate, the Magistrate having previously presided at a similar hearing involving the debtor. SO ORDERED.

Peter C. Dorsey, U.S.D.J.

defense unquestionably has a dual status, it is apparent that the special conditions of probation are immediately applicable.

All of that was pure nonsense, since it would mean that I was *concurrently* serving out Counts One, Two and Three—even though my sentence specifically provided that only Counts Two and Three *were to be served* **concurrently.** This was pointed out to Dorsey in my Answer. I also filed a motion to dismiss the hearing for lack of jurisdiction (for which I supplied ample grounds), a second motion for a 30-day continuance to acquire local counsel, and a third "Motion Requesting Grant of Immunity." All three motions were denied. In denying my motion to dismiss, Judge Dorsey stated, "Moreover, even if [the costs were] considered to be a condition of probation as defendant contends, his probation (and thus all conditions of same) become effective on release from physical custody." This, however, was a total fabrication as my "Warrant Application" of August 2, 1989 (Figure 10-3) was to subsequently prove.[7]

Judge Dorsey obviously realized that based on my Rule 2255 and Rule 35 motions, which I had already submitted to him, that I had gathered enough evidence of malfeasance on his part to warrant his removal from the bench, if not to **justify his indictment** on a variety of grounds. At this point, Judge Dorsey seemed clearly determined to put me back in jail in order to prevent the disclosures in this book from coming to light.

In early April I also filed a 15-page "Petition for Writ of Prohibition," together with a seven-page affidavit in which I asked the Second Circuit Court of Appeals to order:

"The Honorable Peter C. Dorsey...to vacate his granting of the government's motion for Civil Examination of Judgement Debtor...and that he be further enjoined from interfering with petitioner's parole supervision over which he has no jurisdiction but into which he has forced his intimidating presence. Since Petitioner is currently on parole with respect to Count One, pursuant to a Judgement and Commitment Order issued December 18, 1985, he is under the jurisdiction and supervision of the U.S. Parole Commission and is not under the jurisdiction and/or supervision of any Connecticut District Court, which now illegally seeks to exercise such jurisdiction."

While I gave the Second Circuit ample documentation and case law to prove all of the above (and my petition went unanswered by Judge Dorsey), the Second Circuit simply denied my petition *without reason* on May 5, 1989. So much for the Second Circuit exercising any supervision over the

lawless acts committed by district judges under its control.

Failing to quash the hearing, I now faced the prospect of complying with Magistrate Margolis's order of March 3, 1989 (Figure 10-10) or be "held in contempt" and arrested.

If the purpose of this hearing were merely to determine my ability to pay that fine, why should it have been necessary for me to provide the government with "a list of all individuals or entitites, real or fictitious, who have received money, property, or gratuitous transfer in excess of $100 [from me] in the last ten (10) years"—which would have predated my alleged "debt" by some six years?!

The government claimed that Dorsey had jurisdiction pursuant to Connecticut law (since there is no federal statute that authorized it) involving civil judgement debtors. Can you imagine a legitimate court threatening to arrest a private debtor if he did not immediately disclose such comprehensive information to a private judgement creditor? Such information could only be solicited by a creditor, pursuant to normal discovery procedures. That would involve taking a deposition or submitting interrogatories following a motion for installment payments. The debtor could then make standard objections to which the creditor might then seek the court's help to compel disclosure *over those objections*. In this case, however, the court sought to **immediately compel disclosure under threat of *arrest!*** And this, mind you, was taking place under a *civil* statute!

Since I had previously testified under oath and had also given the government a sworn affidavit as to what my assets and liabilities were, I knew that the government's (and Dorsey's) real purpose was merely to create a pretext for violating me or to gather information out of which perjury charges could be manufactured if my present testimony deviated in the *slightest* from any prior testimony. For this reason, I was uncertain how to proceed in order to avoid the trap that Dorsey and Hartmere were trying to lay for me. Remember, the government did not need actual evidence of perjury—they just needed a pretext for fabricating the charges—just as they had fabricated my charges of tax evasion. Furthermore, even if I were to prove my innocence the time and effort involved to do this would divert valuable time, effort, and money away from my other suits and completing this book. Based on all of these considerations, I responded to Magistrate Margolis's order by writing to Attorney Hassett on May 2, 1989 as follows:

(1) I reminded Attorney Hassett that Judge Dorsey in denying my Motion for Immunity, stated that "I could raise my claims of privilege at the time of examination. Obviously, this must apply with equal force to the documents and information I was ordered

FIGURE 10-10

UNITED STATES DISTRICT COURT

DISTRICT OF CONNECTICUT

                                        FILED
                                        MAR 13 1989
                                        U.S. ...

UNITED STATES OF AMERICA,   :
          Plaintiff,   :
                                 :   CRIM
     v.   :   CIVIL NO. N-85-20 PCD
                                 :   MARCH 3, 1989
IRWIN A. SCHIFF,   :
          Defendant.   :

O R D E R

Plaintiff having filed a motion to examine judgment debtor and for a hearing on defendant's ability to pay the judgment rendered against defendant, it is hereby:

ORDERED that the defendant, IRWIN A. SCHIFF, appear before U.S. Magistrate Margolis in ~~Court~~ Room Number 435 at U.S. Court House, Bridgeport, Connecticut on the 26th day of April , 1989, at 10:00 o'clock in the a. m., and then and there be examined under oath concerning his assets and his ability to pay the judgment. The Court may make such orders at the hearing or thereafter that it determines to be reasonably calculated to facilitate payment of the judgment. It is further

ORDERED that defendant provide counsel for the Government, five (5) days prior to the aforementioned hearing, all the following documents:

(1) defendant's completed income tax returns filed for he last five (5) years;

(2) a completed financial statement to assist the Court's evaluation of defendant's ability to pay;

(3) a complete and comprehensive list of any and all bank accounts used by the defendant for the past five (5) years, including but not limited to: (a) the location where each account was opened, (b) the precise account number, (c) the highest and lowest balance maintained in the respective account, (d) the balance presently in each account.

(4) a complete and thorough list specifying each and every trust in which the defendant has or has had a legal, equitable, or fiduciary interest for the past ten (10) years.

(5) a complete and thorough list detailing all properties legally or equitably owned in part or in full, in the past ten years.

(6) a list of all individuals or entities real or fictituous, who have received money, property, or gratiutous transfers in excess of $100.00 from the defendant in the last ten (10) years.

Each and everyone of the aforementioned documents must be received at the office of the United States Attorney, 915 Lafayette Blvd., Bridgeport, CT 06604, c/o Special Assistant United States Attorney, Raymond M. Hassett, no later than (5) five days prior to the scheduled hearing.

The defendant is further advised that his failure to timely provide, counsel for the government with the documents noted above, failure to appear before the Court at the aforementioned time and place as ordered above may subject him to being held in contempt of Court and having a capias issued for his arrest.

Dated this 13th day of March, 1989.

                                        J.G.W.
                                        U.S. Magistrate

to furnish."

(2) Therefore, with respect to paragraphs 1, 3, 4, 5, and 6 of the court's order, I took the Fifth and pointed out to Hassett that the disclosure of any such information "could be used against [me] by both the Justice Department and the IRS."

(3) In compliance with paragraph 2 of Magistrate Margolis's order, I furnished the government with a statement disclosing I had approximately $62,000 of debts and $846.00 in a few bank accounts.

Despite the clear-cut illegality of the hearing, Magistrate Margolis conducted it with reasonable fairness.

Not content with only my testimony on the subject of my finances, the government next subpoenaed Sue Gallant, an owner of the firm that provides answering services for me and fulfills book orders. She was ordered by Stanley A. Twardy, Jr., the U.S. Attorney, and by the court, to submit to examination and to:

...bring with her and produce...any and all copies or originals of contracts, memorandum, reports, notations, documents, correspondence, literature, papers, notes, rough drafts, notebooks, work pads, messages, telegrams, mail-grams, tape recordings, transcripts, records, pamphlets, books, letters, inventories, releases, agreements, receipts and other recorded data in the control or custody of the deponent, Suzanne Gallant, or Box Stop, In., which relates in any manner or form to the interaction between the deponent Suzanne Gallant or Box Stop, Inc., or their agents and the defendant, Irwin Schiff, or his agents.

All of this, again, was for the alleged purpose of determining whether I was *currently able to pay the U.S. government approximately $27,200 pursuant to Connecticut civil law!* If you believe that, I have a bridge I'd like to sell you!

Finally on June 10, 1989, the government submitted a one-page motion to the court for an "Order of Installment Payments" which, according to Connecticut law, had to be done *before* this whole process could have started. The government (as my "judgement creditor") despite its having submitted both Sue and myself to examination, offered no suggestion as to how much I should be ordered to pay, but moved the "...court [to] order the defendant to immediately commence making monthly installment payments in an amount to be determined by the court."

On July 31, 1989 (or eight days before I was violated), I

replied with a four-page answer in which I explained why I was in in no financial position to make any payments and, furthermore, that since I was under the jurisdiction of the Parole Commission the court was "without jurisdiction to order such payments at this time." I also pointed out to the court that all of my time was currently spent in *pro se* litigation and in writing my book (activities which were not revenue producing), but that I was "optimistic in that [I would] ultimately prevail in one or more of [these] lawsuits." I further pointed out that I believed that I could reverse my conviction "on the basis of [my] 2255 appeal to the Second Circuit which will eliminate these court costs completely." And lastly, I stated in paragraph 15:

Even if all of this litigation fails, defendant antici- pates he will earn more than enough from his next book to pay everybody off, including the government.

As of this date and after the taking of all that time and testimony, Judge Dorsey still has not ruled on the government's motion for a court order regarding those installment payments!

It is clear, therefore, that those hearings were not conducted for the purpose claimed, and you also know another reason why I was violated. The government and Judge Dorsey knew I was nearing completion of this book and both wanted (for good reason) to thwart its publication. Violating me on trumped up charges seemed as good a way as any to do just that.

MY $400,000 TAX REFUND SUIT

Another governmental concern with the publication of this book are the revelations stemming from this case. My reply brief, reproduced in full in the Appendix, really needs no further comment from me. At the risk of sounding immodest, my brief completely demolishes the government's case, while also revealing why the U.S. Department of Justice should be called, more appropriately, the U.S. Department of *Injustice.* I sent that brief to the government only a few weeks prior to my violation, and while it covers many Code sections and Treasury regulations with which you are now familiar, it focuses on one which I have not yet covered.

Section 6501(c)(3)

Would you believe that this tiny, three- and a quarter-line Code section is the very statute that practically all of the IRS' illegal assessment procedures are designed to circumvent? I discovered this Code section during my last imprisonment, and stopped the government cold with it in Tax Court. I used it again here. The sub-section, located in

Section 6501, is entitled "Limitations on assessment and collection," and states:

> (3) **No return:** In case of failure to file a return, the tax may be assessed, or a proceeding in court may be begun without assessment, at any time.

What this section means is, *if you do not file an income tax return, the government must* **sue you in a district court and win,** *before it can start to collect any income taxes from you.* This is because it cannot assess you unless you do file, so Secton 6501(c)(3) gives the government **no other recourse but to sue!** This tiny statute clearly establishes that the government only has *two choices* when there is a "failure to file." It must collect the tax either by:

> (1) making an assessment—which it can't do unless you file, or by

> (2) "a proceeding in court...without assessment."

If the government chooses (1) above, it could collect the tax (illegally, of course) by utilizing Code Section 6331; while if it chooses (2) and wins, it could collect the tax (somewhat more legally) pursuant to a judgment and court order. However, what Section 6501(c)(3) *bars* the government from doing, is to try collecting the tax *before doing either!* Yet, this is *exactly* what the government has been doing! Thus Section 6501(c)(3) clearly establishes that all such governmental activities are illegal, and that all Treasury and IRS employees (from the Secretary on down), federal judges and Justice Department attorneys who have been participating in this practice *are nothing but a pack of law breakers*—in case you had any lingering doubts.

The main reason why the government does not want to bring suit (apart from finding it easier to steal than to sue) is that, if it brought suit, it would have the burden of proof. This is why the government has arranged that the burden of proof (as in refund and Tax Court suits) falls on *you* and *not them.* In the former instance, you would be able to move for dismissal on the ground that no section of the Code made you "liable" for the taxes claimed. To successfully defend against such a motion, the government would be compelled to produce the statute that made you "liable" for the tax— **which it could not do! So to avoid being placed in this position, the government forces you to sue them!** (A plaintiff can't bring suit, and then ask the court to dismiss the suit *he brought!*) Only defendants can move for dismissal, as the government has done to me on several occasions. True, I moved for dismissal on my Tax Court suit, but I had unusual grounds for doing so. I also claimed I had been duped and coerced by the government into bringing that suit **based on a fraudulent deficiency notice,** and because the government threatened to begin

confiscating my property if I didn't file a Tax Court petition within 90 days.

It is specifically to get around Section 6501(c)(3) that the government criminally fabricates tax returns, deficiency notices, Forms 4340, and notices of demand.

The Hartman and Harrison Decisions

I have already treated, to some degree, the perverse *Hartman* decision. My Reply Brief, however, throws the fraudulence of this decision into even bolder relief. Nevertheless the government and the courts widely use this decision to buttress briefs and to support decisions. My brief also explains the fraud involved in the *Harrison* decision. That decision was based on a false premise, and the *Hartman* decision was based on **a total perversion** of what *Harrison* held. And this is how "case law" is made—one fraudulent decision resting on another fraudulent decision—and there must be hundreds if not thousands of fraudulent decisions all resting on these two!

Chief Judge Karlton and the Fuller Decision

Not all federal judges are judges in name only, and Chief Judge Karlton of the Eastern District of California appears to be an exception. As covered in my reply brief, he threw out a $500 penalty that the government had levied on an innocent taxpayer, and in doing so, explained why he was not going to follow the logic of a dozen courts *that went the other way!* That took real judicial courage and integrity, qualities often hard to find on the federal bench. The appeal court judges who reversed Karlton proved that they weren't fit to carry his gavel. But in reversing his decision, the appellate court revealed the utter absurdity of the entire income tax system, and proved my earlier contention that no legitimate court could fail to find our tax laws "void for vagueness." If our tax "laws" are admittedly based on "self-assessment," how is it possible that a *Chief* Judge in the federal court system, after *specifically* researching the meaning of "self-assessment" *still* did not know what it meant? If that doesn't *prove* that the whole income tax system is one gigantic fraud, then what would?

The Sullivan decision

In my reply brief, I also discuss the *Sullivan* case which is covered in much greater detail in *How Anyone Can Stop Paying Income Taxes.* It is a case that appellate and district courts have been misrepresenting for over 50 years. Had Oliver Wendell Holmes not written a basically fraudulent opinion upholding Sullivan's conviction (after it was reversed by the Fourth Circuit Court of Appeals), the income tax would have been history long ago. Yet while his decision was basically fraudulent, it still *permitted*

Americans to file income tax returns containing *no information*. Measured by today's standards, his decision was a liberal one. However, the unquestionable unconstitutionality of any alleged filing requirement is thoroughly dealt with in the appellate decision *he reversed!* Unfortunately, **America no longer has appellate courts like that today!**

MY TAX COURT CASE

Just prior to my being incarcerated in December, 1986, I filed a petition with Tax Court, contesting the Deficiency Notice that the IRS had sent me with respect to my alleged 1979 income tax "liability." If you do not contest such a notice within 90 days, the IRS will begin confiscating your property by unlawfully applying Section 6331. I petitioned the Tax Court to forestall such unlawful confiscations—even though there was not much left to confiscate.

It is important for those *who have not filed tax returns* to request copies of their assessments (pursuant to section 6203) immediately after receiving a Deficiency Notice! This will show, as did my 1979 Form 4340 (Figure 5-9F), that some kind of "return" was filed and that an alleged 23(c) "Zero" assessment was made. **Both claims, as you already know, will be fraudulent.**

Once you get a Deficiency Notice, the courts, the IRS, and the Justice Department enforce the "law" as if you now have only two court choices.[8] You must either:

(1) Petition Tax Court for a "redetermination" of your "deficiency," or
(2) Pay the amount claimed and sue the government in district court for a refund.

What you do depends on several variables.[9] If there were a relatively small amount of money involved, I would have formerly advised you to simply let the government illegally confiscate it by its use of Section 6331. When you eventually sue for a refund, you will be in a stronger position because the IRS will not have sent you a Form 17A (pursuant to Treasury Decisions 1995) prior to such seizures. *Thus you will be able to use this failure against the government.* But if you pay the amount "voluntarily," you will forfeit this argument. If the amount involved is substantial, and any such confiscation might put you out of business or cause unacceptable deprivation, you obviously should not take that approach. I believe that generally our courts will be of absolutely no help in the face of threatened IRS seizures, regardless of how arbitrary and excessive the government's demands might be. However, this is what I believed *before* I discovered section 6501(c)(3) and the other material presented in this book. If you effectively incorporate all of this material in a request for a restraining order (which **I did**

not do when I moved for one in 1983), the courts might have no choice but to grant it! The fact that you can now use Code section 6501(c)(3) against the IRS and all of the Code sections and regulations dealing with "original" vs. "supplemental" assessments (which I also did not know about in 1983), should make your request *far more difficult for a court to reject than was mine*—even given the "anti-injunction" statute, Code section 7421. (For an explanation of this statute, see *The Great Income Tax Hoax*, pages 346-352.)[10] Based on all of the information contained in this book, there is no reason why any good lawyer should not be able to draft a formidable request for a restraining order for people who have never "self-assessed"! The only problem might be the cost. My lawyer charged me over $5,000 in 1983. After I complete this book, I should be able to develop a far better one, along with a supporting brief, for a lot less money.

In all cases, you will want to go for a restraining order during that 90-day period. And only if that attempt fails will you go to Tax Court or allow the IRS to seize your money by not going to Tax Court.

*　*　*　*　*　*　*　*　*　*

DEAR READER:

As I write these very words, it is 8:30 a.m., Saturday, August 26, 1989. I am still locked up in the Federal Correctional Institute at Otisville, New York. I have not, as yet, had my preliminary "violation" hearing, and I don't know how long they will hold me. Since I am now separated from my records and research material, I cannot be as thorough as I had intended with the remaining material. Even completing the final editing of all chapters will now be more difficult and time consuming. It is impossible for my loyal friend and neighbor to dig out of my extensive and somewhat confusing filing system all of the documentation I needed to use in connection with these concluding chapters. I apologize for this. Those interested in specific documents, however, will be able to get them from Freedom Books at prices which will generally reflect only the cost of copying, plus any postage and handling charges involved.

*　*　*　*　*　*　*　*　*　*

THE LEGAL RATIONALIZATION FOR 6331 SEIZURES

I mentioned earlier that I would explain the "legal" basis for 6331 seizures, which any semi-conscious American should recognize as being unconstitutional for all of the reasons stated in Chapter 11. How can the government get away with 6331 seizures? It all began during the Civil War[11] when the federal government was desperately short of money. (This was before it decided to merely start printing "money" at will.) It sought measures to expedite the collection of taxes. As in all wars, civil rights sometimes go right out the window (as 150,000 Americans of Japanese ancestry discovered during World War II). So, the government passed laws allowing itself to seize property in payment of taxes, based on tax collectors' claims that such amounts were owed. The legality of such seizures was maintained on the premise that as long as the taxpayer had the right to *sue later* for a refund—"due process" was preserved.[12] While such reasoning might have applied *during a war* in which the nation was fighting for its very life, such reasoning certainly has no place in peacetime America—*especially in light of how we know the IRS actually operates!* So the actual legality of section 6331 seizures should be judged on the following:

(1) While the Constitution may provide for the suspension of habeas corpus during wartime, such an argument vanishes during peacetime. Our government was created to *protect rights*—not to violate them—**and not simply to collect taxes.** But this is something that federal courts have forgotten long ago. (A specific admission of this by the courts themselves is included in pages 288-290 of *The Great Income Tax Hoax.*)

(2) Federal tax collectors during the Civil War could be held personally liable if they collected taxes which were not really owed. Moreover, they did not have the power to arbitrarily assess fraud penalties and phoney interest charges. Thus they were unlikely to seize property in payment of taxes which were not really owing. This restraint *no longer applies today*, as my reply brief clearly demonstrates. The federal government has, since the Civil War, adopted measures making it virtually impossible to sue IRS personnel *who knowingly engage in seizing property in payment of taxes, penalties and interest which are not* owed! How they do this and how they are protected in their thievery has already been amptly documented in this book.

(3) The claim that the theoretical right to sue for refund after payment or seizure (which the government even now seeks to deprive me of) provides the "due process" envisioned in the Constitution is utter nonsense. In many cases, after paying the sums demanded, the taxpayer has little left over to hire a lawyer to effectively sue for a refund. In addition, merely paying the amount demanded can put you out of business—*because of the penalties and interest charges alone!* Even if you ultimately prevail, *you only get back the money you paid (plus interest), but no compensation for the loss of your business, and the accompanying anguish and other deprivations.* Besides, it could take you years to recover! Furthermore, suing the government can itself be a tricky business in which a taxpayer can be foreclosed on a number of procedural technicalities. **The government has nothing to lose and everything to gain by making illegal and arbitrary demands and/or seizures!**

(4) In having to sue the government in *its own courts* before judges whose very salaries are derived from the funds stolen from you and me (and who have years of fraudulent "case law" to draw upon and protect them), the fight appears to be largely hopeless, even with an air-tight case.

(5) While federal judges do have the authority to intervene and prevent arbitrary and capricious "assessments" and seizures, they rarely do. If necessary, they justify these failures by falsely claiming a lack of jurisdiction.

For all of the above reasons—and others—the claim that "due process," as enshrined in the Constitution, is preserved as long as Americans can later bring suit to recover, is a claim that can only be made by either fools or charlatans![13]

Getting Back to Tax Court..

Suing in Tax Court is like being forced to play poker with a stacked deck—only *you* don't know it's stacked. Eighty-five percent of all Tax Court "judges" were former tax attorneys for either the Justice Department or the IRS. Most of their adult lives have been spent misrepresenting the "law" for the benefit of the government. So how can you get a fair hearing before such judges? You can't! Tax Court isn't really a court at all—though most of the judicial system pretends that it is. In reality and pursuant to actual law, Tax Court is merely another bureaucratic agency that masquerades as a court. Around 1928, I believe, the Board of Tax Appeal (a strictly bureaucratic agency) was miraculously transformed into a "court," and ordinary bureaucrats suddenly became "judges." While all federal judges are appointed for life under the Constitution, Tax Court judges are appointed for a term of years (seven, as I recall)—so they are, by definition, *not federal judges.*

In any case, a suit in Tax Court is unlike a suit conducted in a district court. To begin with, you cannot get a jury trial in Tax Court. Furthermore, discovery procedures are more informal in Tax Court, which was probably designed to simplify procedures—yet it often complicates them. Before you can make formal discovery demands, you must first make them informally. In my experience, the IRS didn't provide the information when I requested it informally, so I merely had to request it *again*, formally. Additionally, in district court you will not have a judge whose whole adult life has been spent misrepresenting tax "law." And while many district court judges may not be any better, there is always a chance that you will get the exception to this rule. There are no exceptions (to my knowledge) in Tax Court. All things being equal, you will be better off suing for a refund in district court, rather than going to Tax Court. If you lose in Tax Court you can appeal to the appropriate appellate court or to the U.S. Court of Claims. If you lose in district court, you can also appeal to the approriate appellate court. Overlooking any possible Supreme Court appeals, theoretically you get two bites of the apple—but so-called "tax protestors" will be happy to learn that *I have discovered how to get a third bite!*

In the final analysis, if you do not want the IRS to begin seizing your property after it sends you a Deficiency Notice, you must submit a petition to Tax Court (if you fail to get a restraining order) contesting the proposed deficiency within 90 days. The IRS will then be restrained from seizing any property as long as your Tax Court suit is pending.

By requesting copies of your assessments, (as previously recommended) you will have documented proof that no assessments were made *prior to your Deficiency Notice being sent.* Also, as soon as you commence your Tax Court (or district court) suit, you should also request copies of your assessments for all the years in contention from opposing counsel (as part of discovery)[14]

If you have not filed returns, you will have to be told by opposing counsel that no assessments against you were ever made. I was told this by opposing counsel even though I already had a 4340 that claimed a prior "zero" 23C assessment was made! Once I discovered section 6501(c)(3), however, I realized the clear cut subterfuge being perpetrated, and moved for a dismissal of my Tax Court suit, on grounds that the Tax Court lacked jurisdiction. I subsequently had a "hearing" on this motion *over a year ago in Washington, D.C. While my motion was denied, I still have not heard from that court or the IRS on that suit!*

MY 1979 TAX COURT SUIT

When I discovered the above material, I should have moved for a summary judgment instead of moving for dismissal as I did. At that time, however, I did not know much about the use of summary judgments. Though my initial motion for dismissal went unanswered—and therefore unopposed—by the government, it was nevertheless, summarily denied by the court *without any reason being given.* So, I filed an even longer Motion for Reconsideration. That, too, went unanswered by the government, and that, too, was denied by the Tax Court *without opinion.* While still incarcerated in Loretto, Pennsylvania, I was (accidentally, I now believe) granted a court hearing on that motion and another motion I had filed to compel disclosure. The hearing was scheduled to take place in Washington, D.C. in August, 1988, during the second week following my release from F.C.I. Loretto. Tax Court rules provide that a memorandum of the arguments you intend to raise can be submitted to the Court and to the opposing side. I therefore called opposing counsel and asked

them if they were going to file such a memorandum, since I would then get a copy. I also notified them that I would do so, and they would get their copy in a few days. I was curious to see on what grounds the government would oppose my motion, since it had so far not done so. I was informed by the government that it would file a memorandum and that I would also get my copy in a few days. However, the government **never submitted any such memorandum!** Consequently, by the time I appeared in Tax Court, I had already submitted to the government and to the Court *three* separate documents, explaining why Tax Court *had no jurisdiction* to hear the matter—**and the government had submitted nothing in reply!**[15]

When the Tax Court judge finally appeared on the bench and before the government or myself had uttered a word—either in support or opposition of my Motion to Dismiss—the judge said:

"Mr. Schiff, as far as your Motion to Dismiss is concerned, the Second Circuit has already ruled that your arguments are frivolous, so your motion is denied."

THAT WAS IT! I couldn't believe my ears. I had come all the way to Washington for this? (The other motion was unimportant, and I would not have made the trip for that alone.) This was supposed to be a "hearing," but the judge denied my motion without "hearing" one word in opposition. I reminded the court that I had flown in from New York at considerable expense for a "hearing," but no "hearing" was taking place! Incredulous, I adamantly insisted on a "hearing." Opposing counsel still had not uttered one word! Finally the judge angrily announced that if I did not desist, he would ask opposing counsel for a Motion for Summary Judgment, which he would grant. I then had to shut up or lose the case right then and there![16]

Not surprisingly, the Second Circuit had never ruled on these arguments before, **since I had never made them!** The court's claim that it did so was a total fabrication. Yet, while my motion was denied, I have not heard *one word* from the Tax Court or the government since! As long as the case sits there, the IRS cannot confiscate my property in payment of my alleged 1979 taxes.

The reason I have not heard from Tax Court is that they know I raised arguments which they simply cannot refute. The Tax Court also realizes that the issues I raised in my Motion to Dismiss go right to the heart of how that Court has been illegally acquiring jurisdiction over non-filers, and that if I ultimately lost my trial, it would be forced to write an opinion addressing those arguments, which so far it has avoided. By ruling against me, it would also force the Second Circuit to write an opinion addressing these arguments, since I would obviously appeal any adverse Tax Court decision. However, both the Tax Court and the Second Circuit would have difficulty getting around the issues presented in my Motion to Dismiss (despite all of their expertise in writing fraudulent opinions). To avoid both possibilities, the Tax Court appears willing to forget the whole matter, which is undoubtedly why I haven't heard from either it or the government for over 20 months. In the meantime, while busy with other matters, I haven't pressed the issue and have been just as content to let the case sit there!

THE THIRD BITE

As stated earlier, I once believed (as do most others) that as a practical matter, you could only expect two court hearings in connection with any one taxable year: an initial hearing in either Tax or District Court, and an appeal from either decision. While you could further appeal to the Supreme Court, it is unlikely that it would hear the matter. It should be noted however, that all of the litigation in Tax Court would involve the correctness of an alleged "deficiency," and not whether the deficiency would *later* be lawfully assessed and collected.

When, during my last incarceration, I saw with even greater clarity than before, why the collection of my 1974 and 1975 income taxes had been illegal, I believed I had made the discovery too late. Why I believed this, requires an understanding of how you go about suing the government.

SUING THE GOVERNMENT

Suing the United States usually takes an act of Congress, but there are exceptions—and suits to recover taxes erroneously and illegally collected is one of them. The specific statutes covering this are 28 U.S.C. 7422 and 28 U.S.C. 1346(a)(1). However, before you can sue, you must first file for a refund with the IRS, pursuant to section 7422(a). If you do not, you cannot sue. In addition, unless you *pay the entire amount at issue before you file a refund*—regardless of how excessive the claim may be—you cannot sue. The lunacy and inequity of such a requirement is apparent in the following illustration.

Suppose the IRS claims that you owe the government $1,000,000 (and you can see from my reply brief how "legal" such a claim might be), you first would have to pay the one million before you could file or sue for a refund! Suppose, however, that the IRS had already seized $300,000 toward that amount, but cannot find any more assets to take because you have nothing left—even though they believe you have more stashed away! It could be that because of business adversity, bad investments and other factors, you are now broke. How do you pay the remaining

$700,000 so that you can sue to recover the $300,000 already seized illegally? You can't! So you cannot get any of that money back even though all of it was illegally taken. (This is precisely my situation with respect to the $18,000 the government illegally took from me for 1974). It would make no difference if that amount were $10,000, $50,000, or $700,000. While this bar against suing is not 100 percent absolute, in practice it is. District courts will almost never deviate from this principle. Therefore, since individuals in this situation have "no recourse at law," they should have access to the court's "equity" jurisdiction. Federal courts, however, refuse to exercise equity jurisdiction on these situations. In addition, requests for refund (as allegedly required by section 6511) have to be made within two years of payment. If you discover that your money was illegally seized after two years have passed, you are automatically barred from recovery![17] Lastly, you have to give the IRS six months to reject your claim before you can bring suit.

Another provision you must take into consideration is that you cannot raise issues in your lawsuit that you did not raise in your refund claim. In my case, while the government had seized enough money to pay all my alleged tax "liabilities" for 1975 (thus allowing me to sue), I had one small problem: all of the funds were taken prior to the two-year rule. Consequently, I was prevented by Section 7422 from seeking a refund. But wait ... my Form 4340 (Figure 10-1) showed a $190.26 interest credit within these last two years! You can see from the entries on my Form 4340 that the actual seizures (i.e., "payments") were made on 5/17/1984 and 3/25/1985, but a credit was recorded on 5/15/1986. Code Section 7422(d) states that, "The credit of an overpayment.., shall ... be deemed to be a payment ... at the time such credit is allowed." SAVED BY THE BELL! The Justice Department, however, is now trying to claim, **contrary to law,** that Section 7422(d) **does not apply!** There is really no end to their deceit.

What undoubtedly occurred is that the IRS had confiscated $190.26 more than what I allegedly owed; therefore, my account showed a credit balance. Instead of refunding the difference to me when they discovered their mistake, or applying it to another year, **they decided to steal another $190.26** by simply plugging in a contrived interest penalty to neatly *balance out the account!*

Since section 7422(d) clearly states that I made my final "payment" within the last two years, I immediately filed for a refund on March 29, 1986. And, after six months, I filed suit in the U.S. Court of Claims—*even though I had already litigated that taxable year in Tax Court and the Second Circuit Court of Appeals.* **So this became my third bite at the apple.**

MY REFUND SUIT IN THE
U.S. COURT OF CLAIMS

What did I see in my 1974 and 1975 4340's that showed I had an open and shut case against the government? My 4340s reveal that the government had no tax returns for those years—not even "dummies" prepared for me. So how could the IRS have assessed the "deficiency" even if the Tax Court determined one existed? Without the IRS having any tax returns for those years, there is *no way* that the government could have legally assessed anything, including a deficiency. In addition, the funds were seized without the IRS ever having made a lawful demand, by sending me a Form 17A as required by Treasury Decision 1995. So, I sued the government (after the "deficiency" had been judicially determined in Tax Court and affirmed by the Second Circuit) on the basis that it had collected the alleged "deficiency" in violation of no less than 10 statutes: Code sections 6020(b), 6201, 6203, 6204, 6215, 6861, 6303, 6321, 6322, and 6331, and their supporting regulations. The government's obligation to restore these funds to me (plus interest) cannot even be seriously argued. If the U.S. Court of Claims can rule against me on this, it will have to throw the whole Internal Revenue Code out the window. I doubt the U.S. Court of Claims will stoop to that.[18]

GETTING *YOUR* THIRD BITE

Actually obtaining this third bite will be relatively easy for those who file no returns. Moreover, your third bite should substantially increase the workload of the U.S. Court of Claims as long as the government keeps insisting on stealing money in this fashion. If you do not file a return, **there is no way the IRS can legally assess you for any taxes** (and now you know how they have been going about it), nor can the IRS ever make a lawful demand before confiscating the litigated "deficiency." So you will always be able to sue the government on the basis that they violated the above listed Code sections, *even after fully litigating the amount of the deficiency in Tax Court and in a court of appeal.*

THE GOVERNMENT'S DEFENSES

In response to my complaint, the government raised only two affirmative defenses: (1) Since the amount at issue had already been litigated in Tax Court and the Appellate Court, the Court of Claims, pursuant to section 6512, was without jurisdiction to hear the suit, and (2) my suit was barred by the two-year rule of section 6511. While both claims are false, the first one is actually laughable!

I pointed out in my initial Reply to the government's Answer that the question of how the "deficiency" would be collected (either legally or illegally) was *never raised* by me in any previous lawsuit, so how could it be barred by section

6512? This, however, did not stop the government from repeating the claim in their motion for summary judgment. In my reply, I pointed out the facetiousness of this claim by listing all the Code sections the government had violated in collecting the "deficiency." I argued that what the government was claiming was that once a "deficiency" had been determined (and affirmed on appeal), a taxpayer couldn't sue the government even if it collected that deficiency at the point of a gun! Therefore, such a claim was absurd.

Verification of my reasoning came later (which I then incorporated into a subsequent brief), when I discovered that section 6512(a)(3) contained a *specific exception* regarding funds that had been "collected ... upon the making of levy." Since all the funds at issue had been collected by levy, section 6512 did *not* bar my suit *after all*, as the Justice Department had contended. The Justice Department had merely *lied again*—as usual!

My suit in the U.S. Court of Claims was completed in relatively short order. I filed suit in January, 1989 and filed my cross-motion for summary judgment on August 5th, or four days before I was violated. Though the court is located in Washington, D.C., it proved to be an easy court in which to conduct litigation. Furthermore, the Court seems to be giving me the fairest hearing I have ever received in any federal court—which is really not saying much; however, the real test will come when it issues its ruling.

SUING IN FEDERAL COURT

If you did not file a tax return, and the IRS has taken enough of your money to satisfy its total tax claim (and assuming your request for a restraining order was denied), you can sue for a refund (and a jury trial) in district court—on several grounds. But first, remember—you must file a claim for refund. The IRS form for this purpose is Form 843 (Figure 10-11) Notice that while the form lists a number of federal taxes for which it can be used, income taxes is *not* one of them! As a matter of fact, that form specifically states that it is *not* to be used for income taxes, and the reverse side says the same thing. Note that the word "overpayment" is *always* used in connection with income tax refunds. Why do you suppose the public is told it cannot seek a refund on Form 843, but must file "amended" income tax returns for this purpose?

As you can see from the wording on the lower portion of the form, it can be used for claims involving taxes allegedly "illegally, erroneously, or excessively collected." Since the government knows full well that under the law it can only collect income taxes on the basis of voluntary payments, it does not want to authorize income tax refunds on claim forms that even suggest that such taxes could have been

FIGURE 10-11

Form **843**
(Rev. December 1983)
Department of the Treasury

RL (7)

Claim

▶ See Instructions on back.

OMB No. 1545-0024

If your claim is for an overpayment of income taxes, do NOT use this form (see Instructions)

Please type or print

Name of taxpayer or purchaser of stamps

Number and street

City or town, State, and ZIP code

Fill in applicable items—Use attachments if necessary

1 Your social security number

2 Employer identification number

3 Internal Revenue Service Center where return (if any) was filed

4 Name and address shown on return, if different from above

5 Period—prepare separate form for each tax period
From _____, 19 ___, to _____, 19 ___

6 Amount to be refunded or abated
$

7 Dates of payment

8 Type of tax
☐ Employment ☐ Estate ☐ Excise ☐ Gift ☐ Stamp

9 Kind of return filed
☐ 706 ☐ 709 ☐ 720 ☐ 940 ☐ 941 ☐ 990-PF ☐ 4720 ☐ Other (specify) ▶

10 If this claim involves refund of excise taxes on gasoline, special fuels or lubricating oil, please indicate your tax year for income tax purposes

11 Explain why you believe this claim should be allowed and show computation of tax refund or abatement.

Under penalties of perjury, I declare that I have examined this claim, including accompanying schedules and statements, and to the best of my knowledge and belief it is true, correct, and complete.

Signed _____ Dated _____, 19 ___

For Internal Revenue Service Use Only
☐ Refund of taxes illegally, erroneously, or excessively collected
☐ Refund of amount paid for stamps unused, or used in error or excess
☐ Abatement of tax assessed (not applicable to estate or gift taxes)

For Paperwork Reduction Act Notice, see Instructions on back.

Director's Stamp
(Date received)

Form **843** (Rev. 12-83)

RL (8)

Form 843 (Rev. 12-83)   Page 2

Instructions

Paperwork Reduction Act Notice.— We ask for this information to carry out the Internal Revenue laws of the United States. We need it to ensure that taxpayers are complying with these laws and to allow us to figure and collect the right amount of tax. You are required to give us this information.

You can use this form to claim a refund of certain taxes you overpaid or an abatement of those you have been overassessed. For example, you can use it for overpayments of employment taxes or excise taxes.

Do **not** use this form to make a claim for overpayment of income tax. Individuals who filed Form 1040, 1040A, or 1040EZ must use Form 1040X, Amended U.S. Individual Income Tax Return, to claim an overpayment. Corporations who filed Form 1120 must use Form 1120X, Amended U.S. Corporation Income Tax

Return, to claim an overpayment. Other income tax filers should file a claim on the appropriate amended tax return. (Follow the instructions on the appropriate form for filing an amended return.)

Your agent may make a claim for you. In this case, the original or a copy of the power of attorney must be attached to the claim.

If you are filing the claim as a legal representative for a decedent whose return you filed, attach to the claim a statement that you filed the return and are still acting as the representative. If you did not file the decedent's return, attach to the claim certified copies of letters testamentary, letters of administration, or similar evidence to show your authority.

If a corporation is making the claim, the person authorized to act in its

behalf must sign the claim and show title.

Completing the Return.—Fill in all applicable items on the front of this form. Be sure to check the appropriate box in item 8 to show the type of tax. Also check the appropriate box in item 9 to show the kind of return that was filed.

In item 11 specify in detail the reasons for filing the claim. You must also show your computation of the tax refund or abatement.

Where to File.—File your claim with the Internal Revenue Service Center where you filed your return.

If your claim is for alcohol and tobacco taxes, see the regulations on the particular tax to determine whether you should file with the Regional Director, Bureau of Alcohol, Tobacco and Firearms.

For Internal Revenue Service Use Only

Transcript of Claimant's Account

(Complete only for miscellaneous excise taxes and alcohol, tobacco, and certain other excise taxes imposed under subtitles D and E, Internal Revenue Code.)

The following is a transcript of the record of this office covering the liability that is the subject of this claim.

A—Assessed Taxes

Tax Period and Class of Tax (a)	Document Locator No. (b)	Reference and Date (c)	Amount Assessed (d)	Date or Sched No. (e)	Amount (f)	AB (g)	CR (g)	Remarks (h)

Paid, Abated, or Credited

B—Purchase of Stamps

To Whom Sold or Issued (i)	Kind (j)	Number (k)	Denomination (l)	Date of Sale (m)	Amount (n)	Document Locator No. (o)	Period Commencing (p)	Remarks
						If Special Tax Stamp, State		

Prepared by (Initials)   Date   Office

☆ U.S. Government Printing Office: 1984—421-108/262

Form **843** (Rev. 12-83)

collected in any other way. Think about it: how can an "overpayment" be anything but voluntary? However, property *seized* pursuant to section 6331 can hardly be termed "overpayments." Yet, the government wants the public to pretend they are—and seek refunds on that basis! In addition, since the government also knows that all income taxes had to have been collected (legally), pursuant to tax returns filed by taxpayers, they force those seeking refunds to "amend the returns" they allegedly filed—even if they didn't file any! These are the lengths to which our despicable government will go to extend, maintain, and perpetuate the fiction that it collects income taxes pursuant to law! **Don't let them get away with it!** Prepare your own refund claim using Form 843 as a guide, but caption it "REQUEST FOR FUNDS ILLEGALLY COLLECTED." Then, using Form 843 as a guide, supply the government with all of the information called for on Form 843.

ISSUES TO RAISE IN YOUR CLAIM

If the government took your property by distraint and you never filed, i.e. "self-assessed," you can seek a refund (in paragraph 11) on the following basis.

(1) No lawful assessments were made;

(2) No demand for payment prior to seizure of the funds at issue was ever made;

(3) No lawful lien against the funds at issue ever arose;

(4) The funds were taken in violation of the "due process" and taxing clauses of the Constitution.

You could also claim that you were not "liable" for the taxes for which the funds at issue had been seized.

If after six months you hear nothing from the IRS, or if the IRS rejects your claim sooner, you can institute a lawsuit in federal court on the same grounds used in your refund claim. If you would like a copy of my refund suit and an initial set of sample discovery material (requests for documents, interrogatories, and admissions), please write to Freedom Books and enclose a self-addrsesed, stamped envelope, with $15.00, and specify this information.

As I write this it is September 1, 1989. The government will apparently try to keep me locked up until my parole terminates on December 16, 1989 at which time they will try to figure out a way to violate me *immediately* at the start of my probation. By doing so they intend to keep me continually incarcerated in order to prevent me from finishing this book and bringing its message to the American public. Hopefully you will help me frustrate their plans.

NOTES TO CHAPTER 10

1. For those wanting to see the actual examination of Ufland by Judge Dorsey and his assumption of the prosecutor's role, simply send a self-addressed, stamped envelope to Freedom Books, requesting Judge Dorsey's Examination (if these transcript pages are missing from the Appendix in this book).

2. I was paroled from federal incarceration on August 8, 1988 (after serving 20 months of a 36-month sentence), pursuant to certain conditions of parole. When you are "violated," you are accused of violating one or more of those conditions, and if you cannot refute those charges, you can be returned to confinement to finish the balance of your sentence *or more.*

3. Some years before my trial, "Fred" had prepared for me the Schiff Family Spray Trust, which would actually become funded and operational only at my death. I was divorced with two minor children, so I created the trust primarily for their benefit. However, I invested the trustees with broad discretionary powers to use the money unequally for their benefit (depending upon actual need and other

considerations) or to benefit other members of my family (sisters, nephews, or nieces) who might have a more critical need. Sometime later, I made revocable assignments of property to the trust. This meant I assigned assets to the trust (bank accounts, royalties, my home and my businesses), but reserved the right to revoke all such "assignments" and to use all such property *exclusively for my own benefit.* Basically in these circumstances, **you continue to treat the property in exactly the same way as if no "assignments" were made**—and the law and your creditors treat the property the same way. Specifically, all such property is still fully included in your estate for estate tax purposes, all income from the property is still treated as taxable to you, no gift taxes are paid when the "assignments" are made, and the property is readily attachable by your creditors. The prime reason for using these trusts is that your property passes immediately to the trust at your death (for the benefit of your heirs) *without going through probate* (thus saving what could be years of probate delays) and all probate costs. However, by making such "assignments," one in no way interferes with the claims of one's creditors who can attach such property in exactly the same manner as they could before. The government at my trial fraudulently represented that in making these "assignments," **I had sought to place assets beyond the reach of the IRS or to "cloud their title."** Such a claim was *utter nonsense*, but in raising this issue (over defense objections), Judge Dorsey instructed the jury that I had **actually transferred the property to a trust!** Any semi-conscious lawyer would know that such a claim **was ridiculous but that is what Judge Dorsey told the jury!** In addition, since I had only been charged with concealing income (to evade taxes)—**not concealing assets**—the introduction of this issue was not only *fraudulent* but would also serve to confuse the jury (which was obviously Judge Dorsey's intention) as to what I had *actually* been charged with.

4. Prison officials illegally pressure inmates by denying furloughs to inmates who would otherwise qualify for them, or by denying them "preferred housing." That is, instead of getting a two-man room, they have to live in a dorm. In a recent Bureau of Prison publication, it was reported that a warden in a southern facility was awarded a cash bonus of $3,000 because of his success in persuading prisoners to pay their fines. But, you'd better believe he didn't persuade them with logic.

5. Actually, even the payment of such taxes *cannot* legally be made a condition of probation. The government, remember, imposes both civil and criminal penalties in connection with income taxes. Therefore, once it imposes criminal penalties on you for any given year, any subsequent punishment must be civil in nature—or else the government would be punishing you criminally, twice for the same crime. This obviously occurs if you are sent *back* to jail for not paying the same taxes for which you were *originally* incarcerated!

6. I later discovered that under the terms of my parole, Walsh could require me to make payments toward my court costs—*based upon my ability to pay*—however, Walsh had never raised this issue. If Walsh had the authority to press for such payments, why did the Justice Department and Dorsey get into the act? The reason is that Walsh had no authority *to order a court hearing* which could expose me to perjury charges—but Dorsey did!

7. All of the documents eventually supplied to me by the Parole Commission in connection with my revocation hearing in October, 1989, *all* claimed that I was on parole. There was absolutely no mention in any of them that I was on probation or had "dual status," proving that all such claims by Hassett and Judge Dorsey regarding my being on probation were **all total fabrications.**

8. Before availing yourself of either court, you have the right to request that the disputed amount be considered by the Appeals Office, which is your last administrative remedy. You should request such a hearing before paying the IRS a dime more. At that hearing, raise the issues you have learned thus far, and be sure to tape the interview.

9. There are really too many variables in connection with this complex issue for me to advise you on the single best course of action. All I can hope to do, within the limitations of this book, is to explain as best I can the legal ramifications of each course, as I understand them, and you will have to decide what is the best course for you to follow.

10. In a nutshell, Section 7421 appears to bar federal courts from enjoining the collection of income taxes and was adopted during the Civil War. It really is a vicious statute since while the courts have ample authority to circumvent this general rule, they pretend they do not, and so use this statute as an excuse for allowing the government to plunder at will.

11. As extensively covered in *The Great Income Tax Hoax*, (and to a lesser degree in *The Biggest Con*), Americans have lost every war from the Civil War on. (Vietnam was not the first war we lost.) During the Civil War and every war thereafter, the federal government assumed "emergency" wartime powers and/or passed laws to enable itself to fight that war. These wartime measures and newly created powers (generally in the areas of money and taxation) remained largely intact after each war was over and served to unconstitutionally enlarge the federal government's peacetime powers. These war-related measures substantially reduced an American's economic freedom while also substantially reducing the standard of living that the nation would otherwise have enjoyed.

12. However, in my current refund suit, even this fiction was not preserved, since Judge Edginton ruled I was not entitled to any such "hearing"! See Epilogue and Appendix.

13. For further confirmation of this, see the results of both my refund suits as covered in the Epilogue.

14. After completing this book, I will try and prepare a sample Tax Court petition which all non-filers might use. I cannot do this for filers, because each one of those returns wil be different. Also, I plan to make available for non-filers, an initial set of discovery material (such as a request for documents, interrogatories and admissions) which could be presented to opposing counsel. The government's answers should enable you to immediately move for a summary judgment. I am also planning on providing follow-up discovery assistance as needed. In any case, this book has

already provided enough information to enable you to handle discovery on your own.

15. If my petition were dismissed for lack of jurisdiction, the IRS could not confiscate any of my property in payment of what it claimed I owed for 1979. In order for the IRS to do so, it would first have to send me a Deficiency Notice which would have given the Tax Court the jurisdiction to hear the matter. If that Court had to dismiss my petition for *lack of jurisdiction,* it would mean that the IRS had *not* done so!

16. If time permits, I will include in the Appendix the transcript pages from this "hearing" in which this colloquy occurred. If they are missing, just send $1.50 in postage and a self-addressed envelope to Freedom Books and they will be sent to you.

17. Actually, Section 6511, which all courts apply to income taxes (the two-year rule), *does not even apply to that tax!* The section only applies "in respect of which tax the taxpayer is *required* to file a return." Since, as you know, income tax returns are not "required," this section cannot apply to income taxes! The Justice Department, however, is even now trying to use this section against me in my current lawsuit in the U.S. Court of Claims—which I effectively refuted in an extensive answer in my Reply Brief (see Appendix).

18. IT DID! (See Epilogue).

— Addendum to Chapter 10 —

Having done more research (and rethinking) in connection with the two appeals I filed as a result of the Eginton and Weise decisions (see Epilogue), I have concluded that refund claims, subject to two-year statute of limitations, and the need to pay the entire amount at issue before filing a claim, only applies to funds *voluntarily* paid—even under protest, and not property *deprived* pursuant to Code section 6331. Notice I said "property deprived," which includes funds extorted from third parties, since such property is not "paid" or "collected" within the meaning of those terms. In your lawsuit, you will charge that your property (call it property even if only money is involved) was "illegally *deprived* pursuant to the due process and taxing clauses of the Constitution."

I was misled by 28 U.S.C. 1346(a)(1) into thinking that it, and Section 7422 of the Internal Revenue Code, applied to property *deprived* pursuant to Section 6331. I now realize that these sections only apply to funds *voluntarily* paid—which is why you don't want to pay *anything, voluntarily,* to the IRS. 28 U.S.C. 1491 gives the U.S. Court of Claims jurisdiction to hear lawsuits "Against the United States founded either upon the Constitution, or any Act of Congress, or any regulation of an executive department..." So, if you had property deprived by the IRS during the last *six years* and you *never* filed a return or *received* a Form 17A prior to seizure, you can bring suit, in my judgment, in the U.S. Court of Claims pursuant to this statute without filing a refund claim, and regardless of the total amount the IRS claims you owe. If the amount of your lawsuit is under $10,000, (including your claim for interest) and you would like a local jury trial, you can *also* file suit in a local district court under 28 U.S.C. 1346(a)(2)—*not* (a)(1), as I had been misled to believe. The provisions of 1446(a)(2) are comparable to those in 1491, only you are limited in district court to $10,000, and both statutes are subject to a more liberal six-year statute of limitations: the former by 28 U.S.C. 2401, and the latter by Section 2501.

Since your lawsuit will be based on your claim that the IRS *deprived* you of property in *violation* of the Constitution, acts of Congress, Treasury regulations and a Treasury decision, your lawsuit will fall squarely into either section. If you did not file a return for the year or years in question, you can charge in your lawsuit that your property was *deprived* in violation of the taxing and due process clauses of the Constitution; Internal Revenue Code Sections 6201, 6203, 6204, 6303, 6321, 6322, 6331, 6501(c)(3); Treasury Regulations 301.6201-1, 301.6203-1, 301.6204-1, 601.103(a) and (b); and Treasury Decision 1995.

The two briefs I filed in connection with my Claims Court appeal (an original and a reply brief) will be helpful in providing you with more legal support for your lawsuits. As I write this Addendum, June 16, 1990, I am still a federal prisoner in Morgantown, West Virginia, and am awaiting the government's reply to the appeal I filed in the Second Circuit in connection with the Eginton decision. I am currently working on my reply brief to the government's answer to the appeal I filed with the U.S. Court of Appeals for the Federal Circuit in connection with the Wiese decision. In connection with that appeal, the government's 22-page reply was totally fraudulent—as one would expect. In any case, all of these briefs and decisions will be available to you.

IMPORTANT: In addition to the above, you can file lawsuits to **REMOVE ALL IRS LIENS** from both real estate and personal property by invoking Sections 28 U.S.C. 2409 or 2410. Removing liens from your personal property will prevent the IRS from issuing and/or enforcing notices of levy. You will now have enough information to fashion powerful lawsuits to **quiet title** as provided for in those statutes. **HAPPY HUNTING!**

— CHAPTER 11 —
GETTING FRAMED IN FEDERAL COURT AND TECHNIQUES FOR FIGHTING BACK

*"They that can give up essential liberty to obtain
a little temporary safety deserve neither liberty nor safety."*
—Ben Franklin, 1759

One thing that I have not nailed down as definitively as I might is the fact that there are no laws making "crimes" of income tax offenses, and in addition, that federal courts were never given jurisdiction *to even prosecute for such "crimes."* This means that all those who have been so prosecuted, were prosecuted (and perhaps convicted) illegally! Actually, you should have been able to figure this out from what transpired at my "arraignment" and the fact that no one can have an income tax "liability." In order to even be subject to such charges, one, by law, would have to have been "liable" for the tax. But what you should really find mind-blowing is the extent to which the federal judiciary has been involved in conducting illegal trials—for which they had no jurisdiction! And if this can happen in connection with income taxes—in what other areas is this also happening?!

There are various ways of proving the above. For one thing, if you check the index of the Internal Revenue Code, you will not find an entry dealing with such things as "liability," "failure to file or pay," or "penalties" in connection with income taxes. However, you will find such entries in connection with such other taxes as: alcohol, gasoline, occupational, petroleum products, tobacco, wagering, and withholding taxes. In addition, there is no mention of any income tax crime in the U.S. Criminal Code (Title 18)—though various crimes in connection with numerous other federal taxes are specifically provided for in that title. But more important than this is the simple fact that federal district courts were never given jurisdiction to prosecute anyone in connection with income tax crimes—pursuant to the Internal Revenue Code itself!

Before a district court can prosecute anyone for anything, two things have to happen. First, Congress must make a specific act (or omission) a crime, and secondly, it must give the courts "jurisdiction" (i.e. authority) to prosecute that crime. (Since I have covered this subject more fully in prior books, I will not explore it elaborately here.) In the case of income taxes, Congress has done neither. It never made failure to file income tax returns, or income tax evasion, crimes. Nor did it give federal courts jurisdiction to prosecute anyone for such offenses.

As you already know from the discussion that took place at my "arraignment" between Magistrate Eagan and myself, neither Eagan nor Michael Hartmere could identify any Code section which gave the Court jurisdiction to prosecute me criminally for allegedly violating Sections 7201 and 7203 of the Internal Revenue Code. The Code section that confers general jurisdiction on district courts to hear matters related to the Code is Section 7402(f) which is entitled, "General jurisdiction." This entire three line section reads as follows:

For general jurisdiction of the district courts of United States *in civil actions* involving internal revenue, see Section 1340 of Title 28 of the United States Code. (emphasis added)

Thus it is plain that district courts were only given jurisdiction to hear "civil actions"—not criminal ones—as far as the Internal Revenue Code is concerned. And even for "civil actions," the Code refers to the jurisdiction contained in Section 1340 of Title 28, the United States Code of Civil Procedures. This alone proves that all trials involving alleged *criminal violations* of Code Sections 7201 (tax evasion) and 7203 (failure to file) were all illegal, and that federal judges never had jurisdiction to conduct them. When I raised this very issue in a pre-trial motion to dismiss the charges (though the motion went in through my lawyer), the government responded by claiming that jurisdiction was conferred in Section 3231 of Title 18, which grants district courts jurisdiction "over all crimes against the United States." The government's claim was nothing less than prosecutorial fraud, and Dorsey's acceptance of it—judicial fraud.

For one thing, failure to file income tax returns and income tax evasion are never mentioned *anywhere* (either in the Internal Revenue Code or the Criminal Code) as being "crimes against the United States." Secondly, the legislative history of Section 3231 will reveal that its reference only applies to "crimes" defined in Title 18. Thirdly, if that section really conferred criminal jurisdiction on district courts, it, *obviously,* would have been specifically cited in Section 7402, as Section 1349 of Title 28 was cited.

And fourthly, if this were the statute that conferred jurisdiction on the court, why wasn't it mentioned in my indictment? Can the government *really* charge one criminally for allegedly violating one title, but later claim that it acquired jurisdiction to prosecute from *another* title never before mentioned? In addition, why didn't the government and/or Magistrate Eagan cite this section at my "arraignment" when the issue was raised, and where the merits of the government's claim could be argued in open court? If that statute really did give the court jurisdiction, it would have been cited either in Code Section 7402 or within Sections 7201 and 7203, as is done, for example, in Code Section 5557(a) which ends by saying, "Section 3041 of Title 18 of the United States Code is hereby made applicable in the enforcement of this subtitle." Since no such reference to Title 18 appears anywhere in the Code with respect to income taxes, no such connection as alleged by the government and accepted by the court is possible!

Michael Hartmere's claim, and Judge Dorsey's acceptance of it amounted to nothing less than a criminal conspiracy on their part to conduct a criminal trial that both of them knew was illegal!

Suing Federal Judges Personally

Apart from proving that all income tax prosecutions have been illegal, what else does a judge's lack of jurisdiction mean? Among other things, it means that all such convictions can be overturned on this basis regardless of how many appeals might have been made (and lost) on other grounds. It also means that the presiding judge can *be sued personally!* While judges can not be generally sued, regardless of how many trial errors they commit, then can be sued if they conduct a trial over which *they have no jurisdiction!* The problem with suing judges is that most so-called "tax protesters" (who, in some cases, have the knowledge) generally don't have the cash. To sue a judge on this basis requires high powered legal talent (willing!) to do it. You have already seen the ease with which federal courts can dismiss civil law suits they don't like. You can imagine how they might handle such a lawsuit against one of their own! But certainly Leona Helmsley, who was just convicted on tax evasion, and Victor Pozner, the Miami billionaire, who was illegally convicted of tax evasion a few years ago, possess the financial means to not only overturn their illegal convictions on a variety of grounds, but also to sue the presiding judges personally. Only a few days ago Leona was convicted on 33 counts of conspiring to defraud the U.S. Government, mail fraud, and the filing of false returns. (This is how the "Justice" Department gets *three charges* from the filing of *one, allegedly false return!*) But in reality, it was the United States Government who had conspired *to con and defraud her!* For one thing, she had no "income" that could even be taxable within the meaning of the Code. For another, she could not have been subject to a tax that

was not imposed, pursuant to any of the taxing clauses of the Constitution. (See my Reply Brief in the Appendix.) And for another thing, since I believe that a good deal of her "income" came from real estate—such "income" would have had to be taxed on the basis of apportionment in any case (pursuant to the *Pollock* decision). This factor would have been an even greater consideration in the Pozner prosecution, since I believe the bulk of his income came from real estate and therefore could not have been taxed except on the basis of *apportionment*.[1]

Also, as of this moment, the Internal Revenue Service is seeking to collect about one billion dollars in taxes, interest, and penalties from Bunker Hunt. Despite his millions (or what's left of them), he does not know that *he doesn't owe the government a dime!* As a result, he will probably make some kind of a deal (based upon the ignorance of his lawyers) to pay them a good portion of it!

HOW LEONA'S LAWYERS COULD HAVE PREVENTED HER PROSECUTION!

In order for Leona Helmsley to be convicted of all of the tax crimes with which she was charged—and indeed for the government to have any case at all—the government would need to introduce her tax returns *so that they could be used against her!* All that her high-priced attorneys would have had to do to keep those returns out (thus stopping the trial dead in its tracks), was to have objected to their admittance on the grounds that Leona "was *required* to file them, and since she did not file them *voluntarily*, they amounted to compelled testimony and 'confessions' which could not, therefore, be used against her." The only way that those returns could have been admitted (if this objection were raised) is if the court ruled that they were filed "voluntarily." At this point her attorney could have simply responded, "But your honor, didn't Code Section 6012 (handing the bench a copy of the Section) require her to file?" In addition, her attorney would have offered the bench a copy of that page from the Justice Department's Prosecuting Manual which claims (and cites case law) that income tax returns are "required" to be filed! In addition to that, her attorney should have had in his hand a copy of the Second Circuit's decision in *U.S. v. Irwin Schiff*, 612 F.2d 73 (as well as numerous other Second Circuit decisions that held the same thing), in which the Second Circuit, in upholding my conviction for failing to file returns for 1974 and 1975 stated, that unless "individuals file returns from which a tax can be computed" they go to jail! So on this basis, how could the court in Leona's case have ruled that she filed "voluntarily?" Her attorney could even have argued (and it could have been true!), that "The defendant knew that Irwin Schiff went to prison for not filing tax returns, and therefore she filed so as not to go to prison herself!" Using all of these arguments and such supporting material, there is no way that the government could have gotten her allegedly false returns "in." And without them, the trial would have collapsed. Actually her trial should have been aborted at the arraignment. But then how much money could her attorneys have charged? With a protracted trial and numerous appeals, her legal bills will now probably run into the millions! From such "trials," the legal fraternity reaps a financial bonanza, so why should they abort or collapse them?

GETTING IT BOTH WAYS

What the government has been doing is sending people to jail for not filing, on the grounds that filing is required. Then, in order to use tax returns against those charged with income tax and related crimes, it claims that *filing is not required!* **The "mafia" has been getting it both ways!**

But the reports of Leona's charges are actually unclear. If she were charged with ordinary tax evasion (violating Section 7201 of the Internal Revenue Code), the court would not have had jurisdiction. If, on the other hand, she was charged with violating provisions of Title 18 (the U.S. Criminal Code), the Court would have had jurisdiction, though in none of those sections would the words "income taxes" have appeared. If the government doesn't want to take any jurisdictional chances (and if the prosecutor knows what he is doing), instead of charging one with income tax evasion under the Internal Revenue Code, he will charge one with giving the government "false information" in violation of Section 1001 of the Criminal Code. In charging Leona with seeking to "defraud the government," perhaps in violation of some provision of Title 18, it would appear that this is what they might have tried to do. In any case, to prosecute her on any of these charges, they would have had to get her returns "in"—returns *that her attorneys could have easily kept out!*

On occasion when tax lawyers and Internal Revenue public relations people are confronted with the fact that tax returns can be used against those who file, they will make the untrue and irrelevant observation that the government will only use such information "if it is false!" What is totally spurious about this claim is that there have been numerous individuals whom juries have acquitted of evasion charges—which shows that the information the government claimed was false, actually was not. So it is not true that the government will use only "false information" from returns to prosecute people of tax evasion. This is *proof* that the government can even use *truthful* information from *your* return to prosecute you for tax evasion! Two celebrities that were recently prosecuted for tax evasion were Don King, the fight promoter, and Jerry Lee Lewis, the singer. Though both were found not guilty, what did their prosecutions cost them in time, money and aggravation? In

addition to tax evasion charges, the government can also charge you with mail fraud, even if you send in a truthful return. What they claim, of course, has nothing to do with the actual truth of the claim. Based on all of these risks, why would anyone want to file income tax returns?

If you are determined to pay your "fair share" (so congressional and bureaucratic influence peddlers can use your money to subsidize various pressure groups and individuals with political connections), why not simply figure out what your taxes are and send the government a check? Why send them a document that can be used against you in so many ways? At the very least, if you file a return, you should write on it that "This is not being filed voluntarily, but is being filed as required by Code Section 6012 so that I will not be prosecuted pursuant to Code Section 7203." But would you believe that some people who have done this (as recommended in *The Great Income Tax Hoax*) were actually fined $500? That is, however, a cheap price to pay (and you can bring a lawsuit to fight the fine which, when you think about it, is totally outrageous!) for knowing that your return can never be used against you. Thus you could never be charged with tax evasion—at least on the basis of your having filed a false return. You could even *lower* your "fair share" by the amount of the anticipated $500 fine, and since your return can't be used against you, you will still come out even!

REPORTING ILLEGAL INCOME

One of the most ridiculous things that the American public has come to accept (proving that the American public has little understanding of constitutional safeguards or what being an American is all about) is the alleged requirement that even those engaged in illegal activities must report their illegal income. I address this issue, not out of any regard or sympathy for those directly concerned, but merely to illustrate the absurdities that the American public— including our highly touted media—is capable of accepting. It also underscores the monumental hypocrisy in our criminal justice system. On one hand, we require law enforcement people to read people their rights upon arrest, while at the same time requiring people to report illegal income. *How can one report illegal income without incriminating oneself?* It can't be done! But in totally ignoring obvious constitutional rights with respect to one segment of society (admittedly a reprehensible one) we simply make it easier for the government and the courts to ignore *all sorts* of constitutional rights with *respect to the rest of us!*

Requiring those engaged in illegal activities to report their illegal income is tantamount to Congress passing a law requiring all those who commit crimes to report them, or else they'll be committing another crime! If one is caught for having committed a crime (but did not report it), one is charged with two crimes! Does anyone believe—given the Fifth Amendment—that such a law could stand up? Does anyone believe that any country (even one without a Bill of Rights) would ever pass such a law? *Yet, in fact, America has.* Our courts, perhaps (given their complexion) might even hold such a law constitutional. The media is now increasingly reporting that those arrested for one crime or another (drugs and espionage come immediately to mind) are also being charged with tax evasion—for not reporting the illegal income earned. How can the government get away with this, given the Fifth Amendment? Well, the courts have concocted the ridiculous theory (based on subverting and misstating the *Sullivan* decision) that as long as you aren't required to divulge the "source" of your income—only the amount—one does not incriminate oneself. Those earning money illegally are supposed to report it as "miscellaneous" income, and presumably on a "net" basis. Such an assumption is, of course, absurd (and legally impossible) for a variety of reasons. Suppose an American serviceman working at a secret military installation is also selling secrets to a foreign power who paid him $100,000 per year for his troubles. What is he supposed to do? Does he report $15,000 of wages and $100,000 as "miscellaneous" income on his 1040? Is there anyone in their right mind who believes that the FBI and/or Army or Navy intelligence wouldn't be on him in a minute and that he would not be arrested in short order?

Suppose a $20,000 a year bank employee embezzled $200,000 from the bank. If he reports the $200,000 as miscellaneous income but doesn't reveal the source, will he really not have incriminated himself? Does a drug dealer show on a Schedule C such normal and necessary expenses (I would imagine) as payments to assassins, bribes to politicians and law enforcement personnel, the cost of airplanes, trucks, speedboats and weapons, as well as the wages of his "employees?" Should he deduct, withhold and report all of the various payroll taxes? And would he send his hired assassins an IRS Form 1090 to cover what he paid them for rubbing someone out—with copies sent to the IRS? If people earning illegal income are not required to report it on a Schedule C, but simply as miscellaneous net income, then why can't legitimate business owners do the same thing? How can people engaged in breaking the law be treated, for tax purposes, better than people who don't? And even if these criminals reported their illegal income as "miscellaneous," wouldn't they still be subject to audits like the rest of us? Suppose the IRS went over the books of a drug dealer and determined that he under-reported the "net" amount of his illegal "miscellaneous" income. Would the IRS simply charge him with tax evasion and overlook the fact that his income came from the business of drug dealing? The whole thing is ridiculous and merely proves

that *Alice in Wonderland* isn't fiction. **America is living it!**

While incarcerated, I met people who not only pleaded guilty to various crimes, but (on the advice of counsel) also pleaded guilty to tax evasion—a crime they never committed. In order to be found guilty of tax evasion, the government has to prove that you under-reported your income for *the specific purpose of evading taxes!* Obviously, those who don't report illegal income do so to avoid revealing *that they committed a crime.* Invariably all of the prisoners I spoke to who pleaded guilty to tax evasion told me that they would have loved to have been able to report their illegal income, so they could spend the money openly instead of having to hide it. But by reporting it, they would have incriminated themselves with respect to the crimes they committed to get it.

THE "MAFIA" WANTS ITS CUT

I came across a government study of approximately 250 pages which was devoted to estimating how much revenue the government loses because of people who avoid paying taxes on income derived from crime and related activities. The study covered and estimated the government's loss from every type of crime imaginable—from burglaries and stick-ups to mail fraud, hijacking, airline and train pilferage, gambling, drugs, and prostitution. In that latter section, which took about 40 pages, the government actually analyzed the world's oldest profession in terms of those that worked as ordinary street walkers, in massage parlors, and the "higher class" call girls. The study attempted to estimate how many tricks each one of them might turn and the average price per trick. From this the study postulated the total revenue prostitution generated and what the government loses **because it doesn't get reported.** True to its mafia character, **the federal government believes that it is entitled to a cut from everyone's action—even your neighborhood mugger, pimp and hooker.**

WHERE ARE OUR PRIORITIES?

While the public is not appalled by the government's claim on illegal income, they are appalled by the fact that some school kids might not get to recite the Pledge of Allegiance, or that somebody burned the American flag. Talk about values getting screwed up.

With respect to the Pledge, the words could just as well be changed to "I pledge blah, blah, blah, to the blah-be-de-blah, blah, etc., for all that the public really understands about it. "And to the Republic for which it stands..." what Republic? The American Republic vanished years ago. How many Americans really know the difference between a democratic republic—which is what we are supposed to be—and a democracy and/or the neo-facist state that we have become. It was a republic that our Founding Fathers sought—through a brilliantly fashioned Constitution—to create, while sparing us the injustices they associated with democracies. (For a greater elaboration of this subject, see *The Great Income Tax Hoax.*) As for "Liberty and Justice for All," how much "liberty" do working Americans now have when the government takes as much as 50 percent of their productivity and then requires them to report every financial transaction? Serfs had more liberty! As for "Justice," I am writing these very words from jail while the government knows I am not guilty of any crime. I know of hundreds of others who were or are in the same boat. Who is kidding whom? By compelling millions of impressionable school children to recite the Pledge of Allegiance, we only perpetuate the fiction that these values still exist in America and that America is the same country today that existed when the Pledge was written. **Why do we mislead our children in this fashion?**

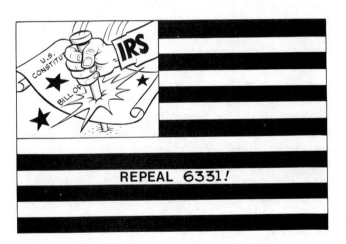

As far as the flag is concerned, I suggest that real patriots take their flags and respectfully put them away in moth balls. To fly Old Glory over the land that America has become, I suggest, is to show disrespect for that flag. I suggest that truly knowledgeable and understanding Americans will now fly another flag, which I will dub The New Reality. Instead of its stripes being red and white, they would appropriately be black and white. I would replace the field of stars with a framed replica of a scrolled Constitution—with a stake driven through its heart. Yes, it is that flag, The New Reality, that Americans should fly—at least until Code Section 6331 is repealed.

While I have already referred to certain aspects of my last trial, I feel that I should cover more of it to give you a better idea of what transpires in American courts even today. The public undoubtedly associates all trials (especially those in lofty federal courts) as careful and conscientious efforts to arrive at true and just verdicts. The public hardly associates

trials in federal courts with those often depicted in melodramatic westerns; where the judge is beholdin' to the local cattle baron, whose grip on the town is threatened by the defendant. Nor does the public associate such trials with those often depicted as taking place in the deep South with roughly the same cast of characters—but with different accents. But such trials (also with different accents) do take place in federal courts—as my trial and those of many others prove! Take the case of Kevin Roulee, that took place in upstate New York in 1988. Kevin's hardhitting articles attacking the illegal enforcement of the income tax appeared regularly in the local press, until the "mafia" decided to frame him in order to silence him. In that case, the U.S. prosecutor, Craig Benedict, succeeded in preventing Kevin from being represented by an attorney of his choice; an attorney who had successfully beaten Benedict in several "tax protester" prosecutions before. In order not to have to face Kevin's lawyer, this spineless and coniving federal prosecutor petitioned the court to have Kevin's attorney disqualified on the grounds that he had an alleged drinking and drug history. *As if Benedict were really concerned about the quality of Kevin's representation,* Kevin told the court, "I am only asking that he be allowed to represent me, not marry my sister." But Judge Neal denied Kevin—who now sits in federal prision—the counsel of his choice (even though the lawyer was a member in good standing of his local, out of state bar association) on these grounds. "Justice for all?" Horsefeathers!

Getting back to my case, however, I was charged in the indictment of failing to file tax returns, failing to pay taxes, and concealing income—all for the alleged purpose of "evading and defeating" income taxes for 1980, 1981, and 1982. These charges allegedly constituted a felony pursuant to Code Section 7201. In addition, I was charged with one count of failing to file a corporate return for 1980; an alleged misdemeanor pursuant to Section 7203. All of these charges were erroneous—as a matter of law—on a variety of grounds. Four of these grounds are as follows:

1. There is no mention of income taxes in any of the Code Sections I allegedly violated;

2. There is no cross-reference in subtitle A making these punitive sections, which are contained in subtitle F, applicable to that subtitle;

3. Since neither I nor my corporation was "liable" for any such tax, I could not be guilty of evading or not filing anything in connection with it; and

4. Congress had never made either offense a crime, nor had it given any court jurisdiction to criminally prosecute anyone for allegedly violating these Code sections.

While I could cite other reasons (including the fact that I had earned no "income" that was taxable or the fact that the Internal Revenue Code had never been enacted into positive law) as to why my prosecution was illegal as a matter of law, these four reasons *alone* conclusively establish that my "trial" was as illegal as any that had ever been staged in Nazi Germany or the Soviet Union under Stalin. While my trial was a farce to begin with, Judge Dorsey's rulings and conduct simply expanded it to ludicrous proportions. Dorsey knew right from the outset that I was not guilty of any crime and that he had no jurisdiction to even conduct the trial. This is clear from what transpired at my "arraignment" and from my pre-trial motion offering to immediately plead guilty, if I could be guilty of the crimes purely as a matter of law; overlooking all other pre-trial motions that he denied without hearings of any kind. He, of course, began orchestrating the charade from the "arraignment" by arranging for it to be conducted before Magistrate Eagan, who could claim to not having the jurisdiction to addresss the issues Dorsey knew I would surely raise. He then proceeded to deny me a bill of particulars; fabricated decisions to pre-trial motions;sought to discredit my own witnesses and denied me others whose testimony would be damaging to the government's case, while leading government witnesses so that their testimony would appear credible and most damaging. Neither time nor space will enable me to do justice to his egregious conduct, but I should provide more details with respect to *some* of it.

A BILL OF PARTICULARS

A bill of particulars is an explanation of the charges that are often generally made in the indictment, so that the defendant will know with greater clarity, what he is accused of doing. I was accused of "concealing" income in order to "evade and defeat" the income tax for the years in question. However, my indictment did not specify in what manner I sought to do this. Merely accusing me of "concealing" income was tantamount to accusing me of committing murder without telling me who I allegedly murdered or when and how I allegedly did it. In addition, my indictment accused me of seeking to "evade and defeat" taxes "owed" as well as failing to file returns that were "required" by "law." However, the indictment did not identify the "law" that made me "liable" for the tax or that "required" me to file those returns. So in my bill of particulars, I asked the government (among other things) to identify the manner in which I sought to "conceal" and to identify the Code sections that "required" me to file, and that established my alleged "liability." But the government refused to answer these questions on the specious grounds that doing so would require them to reveal "their theory of the case." And the court sustained their objection even though there is

extensive case law holding that bills of particulars should be granted, especially in income tax evasion cases. The government sought to bolster its spurious claim by stating that, since it made available to the defense all of the documents it intended to use at trial, it was required to do no more. Apart from the fact that there were hundreds of documents involved, none provided *any clue* as to how they might be used to indicate "concealment."[2]

In addition to everything else, I had deposited during these very years approximately $50,000 in cash to my bank accounts (something that those seeking to "conceal" their income don't do), so I was totally incapable of giving my lawyer any clue as to what the government might contend at trial as the basis for its "concealment" claim.

Concerning this subject, my lawyer eventually said, "Well, I guess we will just have to find that out at trial!" What made this statement by an experienced criminal trial lawyer so absurd (as I would later discover when doing research on criminal procedure) is that one is not supposed to be "surprised" at criminal trials in this manner.

My lawyer would never have presumed to defend a murderer or even a jay walker on this basis—without knowing before he set foot into the courtroom who his client was supposed to have murdered and when and how he was supposed to have done it. And if defending a jaywalker, he would have to know before he set foot in the court room where and when the jaywalking allegedly took place. Yet my lawyer—an otherwise experienced criminal trial lawyer—believed he could defend me on these counts of tax evasion without having the faintest idea how the government would contend I went about "concealing" before he walked into the courtroom.

THE "AFFIRMATIVE ACT" OF EVASION

In order to be guilty of tax evasion, one must be found guilty of committing an "affirmative act" of evasion. Not filing returns and/or not paying the tax are "Omissions" and only (allegedly) punishable as misdemeanors under Code Section 7203. In order to be guilty of a felony, one must *do something*—rather than merely have *failed to do something!* If one files a false return, that in itself is an affirmative act—also perjurious—presumably designed to mislead the government concerning what you "owed." But suppose you don't file a return. What, then, is the "affirmative act?" This very question was addressed in 1943 in the granddaddy case of *U.S. vs. Spies*, 317 U.S. 492, which involved the prosecution for tax evasion of an accused on the basis that he had failed to file and failed to pay the taxes allegedly due. In reversing *Spies'* conviction, the Supreme Court held that such conduct only constituted misdemeanors under Code Section 7201. The government, the court said, had to prove something more than this—an "affirmative act"—in order to find Spies guilty of the *felony* of tax evasion. The court then gave examples of such "affirmative acts" as: keeping a double set of books, destroying records and concealing income and assets for the purposes of evading taxes. Interestingly enough, Spies had allegedly sought to do just that, by depositing income to the bank accounts of relatives and/or in the names of fictitious persons. However, since the government had not accused him of this, his conviction was reversed. The "affirmative act" charged in my case was "concealment" of income, and this is what the government had to prove in order for me to be found guilty of tax evasion.

The fact that the indictment also accused me of failing to file and failure to pay (technically known as "lesser included offenses") could only serve to confuse the jury as to what they had to find me guilty of in order to find me guilty of tax evasion. In order to INSURE that the jury would be thoroughly confused on this issue, Judge Dorsey repeatedly instructed them (without objection from my lawyer) that the indictment had accused me of COMMITTING TAX EVASION "THREE WAYS." *This instruction was totally false* since the indictment had only accused me of seeking to evade taxes *one way:* by "concealing" income. But based on Judge Dorsey's totally erroneous instruction, the jury had every right to believe that I would be guilty of tax evasion even if the government only proved me guilty of evading taxes one way—by not filing tax returns. You can also see reference to this erroneous "three way" claim repeated in the appellate decision—so even the Second Circuit committed the same error as was committed by the trial court!

In any event, the government's entire case was built on the following six claims:

1. I used foreign bank accounts to conceal my income;

2. I transferred assets to a trust to put those assets beyond the reach of the IRS and/or to "cloud their title."

3. I admitted on a mutual fund application that I was, in deed, a "tax evader."

4. I had not filed or paid income taxes for the years 1980, 1981 and 1982.

5. I had written books and lectured extensively allegedly encouraging people to break the law by not filing and paying income taxes.

6. I had used non-reproducible pens in writing out checks.

Obviously issues 4 and 5, as you already know, had absolutely nothing to do with tax evasion. However, while I was not charged with number 5 above, considerable irrelevant evidence of this alleged activity was allowed into the trial, and—as will be more fully explained later—could have been the very reason I was convicted of tax evasion. IN addition, it was my alleged activity in this regard that influenced my sentencing by Judge Dorsey—even though it was not the "crime" for which I had been convicted! In addition, my use of non-reproducible pens had absolutely nothing to do with "concealment" of income. If anything, they could only have "concealed" expenditures—thus *increasing* my taxable income. The use of such pens was done to protect my privacy, since banks will (illegally) turn over all evidence of such *private expenditures* to the IRS. any case, all my *deposits* were not made by non-reproducible pens, so there was no "concealment" of "income" by their use! This is merely an example of how nothing but pure hot air was used to convict me. Since the government had no case, it would even make a big issue over my use of these pens on *expenditures* as to how I tried to "conceal" my "income"!

In addition, since I had not divested myself of any property, claim number "2" was totally specious, though it occupied a significant portion of the "trial." Besides being specious, it was totally irrelevant, since I had not been charged with "concealing" assets, only "concealing" income.

Once again the introduction of this issue could only confuse the jury (as Judge Dorsey intended it to) as to exactly what the government had to prove in order for me to be guilty of the crime alleged. So, issue number "1" was the *only relevant issue* to the charge of tax evasion. Every other issue which the court allowed the jury to consider was either false or irrelevant.

FABRICATING A PROSECUTION

The government's entire case of concealment rested on a blatant fraud; that I had concealed approximately $6,000 in foreign banks—a claim that the prosecutor and the judge knew was TOTALLY false! In addition, the government knew that during the same period, I had deposited over $50,000 *in cash* to my Connecticut accounts. Over this same period, the government admitted that over $1,000,000 had passed through my hands. The amount allegedly concealed represented a *miniscule* percentage of what I could have "concealed," if that had been my intention. My attorney's total failure to expose a fraud upon which the government's case rested (or even point it out to the appellate court), was comparable to a lawyer failing to bring a jury's attention to an affidavit he had from the Vatican certifying that his client was actually having lunch with three Cardinals and the Pope at the very time the prosecution contended he committed the crime!

MY "FOREIGN BANK ACCOUNTS"

In 1980 I made a modest investment in an off-shore mutual fund. ITEK (which later turned out to be a scam) allegedly invested in precious metals and currencies and employed trading techniques not available to American funds—such as short selling. One could also keep one's account in various currencies enabling one to also profit if the currency one selected appreciated against the dollar. However, the account had to be opened with the same currency in which it was to be kept. So having elected to keep my account in Swiss francs, I purchased 10,000 Swiss francs from my local bank (at a cost of just under $6,000), which then sent its own check payable to ITEK to its Geneva bank. Approximately one year later I liquidated 90 percent of the investment and ITEK sent me a check for approximately $5,500 drawn on a Cayman Island bank, which I deposited in my local bank. My bank cleared it through a Boston bank, and after absorbing about $25 in collection charges, the net amount was credited to my Hamden account. Complete records of these transactions existed in no fewer than three New England banks. Now is there anybody who will claim that there was anything "concealed" about these transactions, or that they involved "dealings with foreign banks?" When the government introduced these checks at trial, through representatives of two banks (I had apparently changed banks in the interim), both government witnesses testified on cross-examination that there **was nothing concealed about either transaction!**

PERJURY: IT DOESN'T APPLY TO EVERYONE

While I have met fellow prisoners serving time for perjury, none of them had been prosecution witnesses. Only defense witnesses get prosecuted for perjury, especially if their testimony seriously prejudices the government's case. Government witnesses are never prosecuted for perjury no matter how prejudicial their testimony might have been to the defendant. Think about it. Would prosecutors accuse their own witnesses of perjury and thereby risk reversing convictions for which they labored so long to secure? I'm sure it has happened, but its probability is comparable to being struck by lightning. Indeed in many cases (and certainly in mine), it is the prosecutor who *engineers the perjury.* Consequently, prosecution witnesses, unlike defense witnesses, can lie profusely and with ease while on the witness stand. In addition, since witnesses can't even be sued civilly—even if a defendant can prove that their perjurious testimony led to their conviction—prosecution witnesses have nothing to lose (and often much to gain) by committing perjury for the benefit of the government. This is especially true of IRS agents; five of whom testified

against me, and they were the government's *only hostile witnesses!*

MISLEADING THE GRAND JURY

The government had for about 18 months tried to indict me, and finally succeeded with a second grand jury. On March 13, 1985 (after being somewhat quiet for 10 months while writing my new book), I released *The Great Income Tax Hoax,* which exposed (in a manner somewhat different than here) the income tax for the scam it is. Within three weeks, I had major television and radio appearances in Cincinatti, Detroit, Philadelphia, Baltimore, New York, and Boston, and was focusing a great deal of attention on the book. Therefore the "mafia" decided that it had better stop the truth from getting out. Two "hit men," Ted Wethje, an IRS agent and Michael Hartmere, a U.S. prosecutor, were directed to produce an *immediate indictment*—regardless of how many falsehoods they had to contrive to do it. This team successfully completed its assignment on April 3, 1985. I cannot quote verbatim, but among the many lies told to the grand jury was that Freedom Books was a "tax protest organization!" In addition, Wethje told the grand jury that I was "required" to file, but didn't, 'in order to evade taxes that I knew I owed. Since Wethje was familiar with my books and *The Schiff Report* (I had sent copies to Hartmere to present to the grand jury) he and Hartmere both knew that such testimony was false. Wethje also mislead the grand jury as to what actually occurred when he and another agent came to my home one morning and said they would like to ask me some questions. Like a fool, I let them in!

Wethje asked me if I had filed returns for 1980, 1981 and 1982. I placed an Internal Revenue Code on the table in front of them (as their own transcript shows) and asked them to show me what Code section required me to file. Neither of them would. And during the course of the interview, I would ask them this question *no less than eight times*—and with the same results. I even said, "As far as I know, I have filed all tax returns I am required to file," but "I don't want to break any laws, so I "would appreciate your showing me the law that requires me to file." It was only in that context—when it was clear to all concerned that neither they nor I believed that I was required to file—that I admitted to not filing. However, this is something that one should never tell an IRS agent. I might have said, in that context, that "I·didn't file because we both know that I'm not required to file and you can tell that to the Commissioner." What this liar told the grand jury was totally out of context—as their own transcript, which the grand jury never saw, clearly establishes. In telling the grand jury that I had admitted to not filing, Wethje left out the fact that I also claimed that *I was not required to file.* Wethje also failed to tell the grand jury that I had placed an Internal Revenue Code before him and his colleague and asked them *repeatedly* to show me the the law that required me to file—and that they had refused to do so! In relating our conversation to the grand jury, Wethje made it appear that I simply refused to file for no other reason than to *evade taxes*. Since the first chapter of my book, *How Anyone Can Stop Paying Income Taxes* is also entitled, "Surprise the Income Tax is Voluntary," and contains many of the same documentation that appears in the first chapter of this book, both Wethje and Hartmere knew that I sincerely believed I was not required to file for a number of valid legal reasons—**not because I sought to evade taxes.** Wethje's entire testimony on this issue was a tissue of lies, as he and Michael Hartmere both knew.[3]

As far as the two checks were concerned, Wethje misrepresented them to the grand jury in several ways, two of them being: (1) that they involved transactions with foreign banks, and (2) Swiss and Cayman Island banking laws prevented the IRS from "determining their taxability". THAT WAS THE GOVERNMENT'S WHOLE CONCEALMENT CASE! Not only did Wethje testify falsely concerning my alleged "bank accounts," he also lied about the government's inability to "determine their taxability." Since the outgoing one was a disbursement, it could not be taxable on *any* basis. And since the incoming check was deposited into *my bank account*, the IRS could claim that it was *fully taxable*, and put on me the burden of proving otherwise—the IRS does this all the time! It is standard IRS operating procedure! The two checks presented absolutely no problem to the IRS, as far as their "taxability" was concerned. This is one of the other areas for which I wanted "Fred White's" testimony at my 2255 hearing. As a tax lawyer, he would have exposed Wethje's claim as being a total fabrication; that based upon his knowledge and experience, the government would have had no trouble determining the "taxability" of those checks.

In addition, the outgoing check was sent in 1980, and since it constituted a *disbursement* (**not an item of "income"**) **it could not constitute evidence of "concealment" of "income" for 1980! True, the incoming check was received in 1981, but does one really conceal income by depositing it to one's bank account? In addition, the incoming check constituted** *a return of capital* and wasn't income at all! In 1982 no foreign checks were sent or received! So for that year, the government's entire foreign check ploy was not even applicable! Thus the *only possible* year that the "concealment" claim might have applied was 1981. But the government used it to indict me for *three years*.[4] The government was allowed to get away with this *triple scam* at my trial because my lawyer was totally asleep at the switch. I assume that the main reason was his inability to get a bill of particulars. Therefore, he was totally unaware of the "foreign bank account" scam until it was sprung at him at trial; though it wouldn't have taken much for him to expose it even then, since I had time to explain it to him. Obviously though, we would have been able to deal with it more effectively, had he known about it before the trial began.

Apart from all of the above, Agent Wethje, the government's sole witness on this as well as Michael Hartmere, both knew that I had been merely dealing with a benign mutual fund and not with "foreign banks." This was clearly shown at trial when Wethje, during cross-examination, disclosed that he was familiar with "Capramax," ITEK's management company. He referred to the "Capramax transaction" and stated that Capramax was "in the process of some type of liquidation." That revealed that the government *had* traced my bank's check (which had been made payable to ITEK), to its management company. Thus, Hartmere and company knew all along that I was dealing with a mutual fund when they falsely represented to the grand jury (and my jury at the trial) that I was "dealing with foreign banks." The government relied on its ability to mislead both juries based on its awareness that the public invariably associates the words "Swiss" and "Cayman Island banking" with "concealment" and tax evasion. I can hear Wethje saying to Hartmere, "Do you think we can get away with it," and Hartmere replying, "What have we got to lose?" This totally fraudulent foreign banking claim (because of my lawyer's unconscionable failure to even raise the issue on appeal) next found its way into the Second Circuit's sustaining decision, where it was also used against me. In its opinion, the Second Circuit stated, "The government sought to prove Schiff's evasive intent...through...evidence of his dealings with banks in Switzerland and the Cayman Islands," (at page 110), and that, "There was ample evidence to support a finding that he concealed or attempted to conceal his income," (page 115).

As you already know, there were no "dealings" with such banks, while the issue of "concealment" (as you will soon discover) was *totally charged out* of the case by Judge Dorsey, and therefore had nothing to do with my conviction—as the Second Circuit knew! It had no business even mentioning this subject in its opinion.

EXCULPATORY EVIDENCE

Few Americans really understand that the function of grand juries is to protect the public from the prosecutorial zeal of governments—especially when they want to prosecute citizens for political reasons—which is what my prosecution was all about. This is borne out by Dorsey's revealing sentencing speech. Before individuals can be put to trial, the government is supposed to first convince a grand jury that there is "probable cause" to believe that the accused *could have* committed the crime. The grand jury does not have to be totally persuaded, as does the petit jury; it arrives at its verdict on the basis of a majority vote. In the case of a petit jury, a guilty verdict must be unanimous. Presumable, U.S. attorneys who provide grand juries with the evidence of criminal culpability, have no particular axe to grind. And, presumably, they are bound by their oath "not to gain a conviction, but to see justice done," which is another meaningless oath attached to our legal system. To enable grand juries to arrive at true and just verdicts, prosecutors are supposed to reveal to them, in addition to incriminating information, other information tending to negate guilt. If such exculpatory information, in the possession of the prosecutor, is not revealed to the grand jury, then the grand jury's proceeding amounts to a charade and mockery. An example of just one devastating piece of such exculpatory evidence in my case, which was known to Hartmere, *but concealed from the grand jury*, was the fact that I had converted some $25,000 in cash (from seminars I conducted around the country) to cashier's checks, which I then deposited to my Hamden, Connecticut bank accounts. This established bank documentation for "income" that otherwise could have easily been concealed. I had also deposited *another* $25,000 in cold, hard cash received from seminars closer by—once *again creating a bank record of "income"* which could have easily been concealed if that were my intention.

While Michael Hartmere and his IRS puppet were conning the grand jury into believing that I had "concealed" $6,000 in non-existent bank accounts abroad, I was actually creating bank records of *10 times that amount of cash income* which I could have easily "concealed" in the good old U.S. of A.—*if I were at all interested in doing so.*

I had sent Hartmere considerable material to present to the grand jury. This included copies of my books; *Schiff Reports;* an affidavit attesting to the fact that I had never been assessed for any of the years at issue; that I had no "liability" for the tax; and that I had earned no "income" that was taxable under the Internal Revenue Code. In addition, I wrote Hartmere *and* the grand jury asking for permission to testify, *which I was never allowed to do.*

Most grand jury targets seldom want to testify even if they are invited. For one thing, their testimony can be used against them if they are later indicted. For another, they testify before the grand jury without benefit of a protective counsel, so they can be asked questions that might not be permitted in an actual court room. While it is not mandatory that a target who requests to testify be permitted to do so, he should have that absolute right. What earthly reason would a prosecutor have for denying such a request? If a target is really guilty of the crime alleged, his testimony, given without benefit of counsel, would only make it easier for the prosecutor to convict him later! The only possible reason for denying a target access to the grand jury is that he might prevent an indictment from being handed down. This is why all targets should have *an absolute right to testify* if they request it. U.S prosecutors simply cannot be trusted to objectively present all exculpatory evidence (or *any*

evidence for that matter), especially when the "mafia" wants an indictment for political reasons. (For more on grand juries, see *The Great Income Tax Hoax).* Not only did I write letters to both Hartmere and the grand jury asking to be called, I also made the request personally, as the grand jury was convening for one of its sessions. I told them that I would be waiting outside for their call. I waited until long after they left, since they left by a rear entrance, and I was never called.

One of the defense witnesses that Judge Dorsey would not permit to testify was a Mrs. Dorothy Lewis of Old Saybrook, Connecticut. She had been the secretary of a prior grand jury that had refused to induct me. I had written individual letters to a few members of the grand jury, stating my innocence of any wrong doing and that Michael Hartmere was solely interested in framing me. When that letter was discussed, there was some apparent interest in calling me. At this point, Michael Hartmere (exhibiting some annoyance at the discussion) informed the grand jury that there was no need to call me, and that he would write me accordingly. Such a letter would have been illegal, and Hartmere knew it. Any such letter would have had to come from Mrs. Lewis, the grand jury's secretary. The grand jury is part of the judicial branch of government, while Hartmere serves in the executive. Any such overt action by Hartmere in the direct affairs of the grand jury would be an obvious violation by him of the separation of powers doctrine. Hartmere, of course, knowing this, never sent me that letter. His representation to the grand jury that he would do so, however, was simply a ploy to cut off any further discussion of the subject.

The reason that Michael Hartmere did not want me in the grand jury with him is that in this situation he would have no federal judge to hide behind. He was also aware that some individuals prevented indictments from being handed down by confronting prosecutors before grand juries. I sent the grand jury a letter, contained in a *Schiff Report,* from just such a person. I had received a letter from Lee Mele, then of Franklin Lakes, New Jersey, informing me that on February 10, 1982 in an appearance before a grand jury in Newark, New Jersey, he had prevented his own indictment. He stated, "The information I derived from your latest book, *How Anyone Can Stop Paying Income Taxes* was responsible for the grand jury returning a verdict in my favor...I can't thank you enough for having written this book." No non-filer, and even filers, with an average intelligence and speaking ability (but having a grasp of what is in this book) should have any trouble routing any federal prosecutor who tries to endict him before a grand jury. At trial, it is only a judge's ability to misstate the law (which a prosecutor shouldn't be able to do, as long as the target goes into the grand jury room armed with this book!) and prejudice the trial in other ways that win convictions for the government, not the prosecutorial skills of U.S. attorneys.

GETTING AWAY WITH
WORSE THAN PERJURY

While I discussed perjury, I never raised the question of why it should be a crime. The only reason can be that the giving of false testimony can produce a *false legal result;* causing an innocent person to be found guilty, or a guilty person innocent. If the false testimony in no way altered the final result, the perjuror might still face the possibility of going to jail, even though his testimony caused no legal harm. Granted that the giving of false testimony is morally and ethically wrong, but its actual invidiousness is in its ability to produce a *false legal result, not in its mere giving.* But suppose a judge *deliberately produces a false legal result* by deliberately misquoting applicable law or ignoring it altogether. HOW IS THIS ANY DIFFERENT FROM PERJURY COMMITTED BY A WITNESS UNDER OATH? As a matter of fact, it's worse! False testimony might not produce a false legal result, but the *deliberate* falsification of law on the part of the judge ALWAYS WILL! In this book you will find numerous examples of just that—committed by the same people who send *others* to jail for committing perjury!

DELIBERATE MISSTATEMENTS
OF LAW BY JUDGE DORSEY

Based on our suspicion that there was a deliberate withholding of exculpatory evidence from the grand jury, my attorney filed a pre-trial motion either to get transcripts of grand jury proceedings, or to move for dismissal of the charges on this ground. In denying our motion on this issue, Judge Dorsey claimed that the Second Circuit had ruled in *U.S. v. Ciambrone*, 601 F2d 616 that federal prosecutors were not obligated "to furnish" exculpatory information to the grand jury unless they were "requested to do so by the grand jury itself." When I read that in Judge Dorsey's decision, it didn't make any sense to me for two reasons:

1. How would grand jurors know what kind of exculpatory material the prosecutor had, or of its very existence, and
2. How would the defense know that the grand jury didn't ask for it without seeing the transcripts in question?

Since my attorney, who has a reputation of being a first rate criminal lawyer, accepted Judge Dorsey's ruling with what appeared to be an understanding shrug of the shoulders, who was I to argue? It was not until I was in prison doing research for my habeas corpus petition that I discovered how Judge Dorsey had deliberately *falsified* the Second Circuit's holding in *Ciambrone!* What *Ciambrone* actually held was as follows:

The prosecutor's right to exercise some discretion and selectivity in the presentation of evidence to a grand jury does not entitle him to mislead it or engage in fundamentally unfair tactics before it. The prosecutor for instance, may not obtain an indictment on the basis of evidence known to him to be perjurious...(and)...where a prosecutor is aware of any substantial evidence negating guilt he should, in the interest of justice, make it known to the grand jury, at least where it reasonably can be expected to lead to the jury not to indict.

Thus my indictment was secured in total violation of *Ciambrone*. It was secured on the sole testimony of Ted Wethje, which, as Hartmere knew, was perjurious throughout. Hartmere also kept from the jury the fact that I had converted $50,000 of cash receipts to bank deposits. Would the grand jury had indicted me of "concealment" if they had known that I had deposited far more cash to my domestic accounts than what Hartmere claimed I sought to "conceal" abroad? Hartmere knew that I had written to the IRS about my assessments for the years in question, and that I had been told that no assessments had been made. So both Hartmere and Wethje, having read my books, knew that I couldn't *possibly* believe I owed taxes for years in which I was told that *no assessments had been made.* But they didn't tell that to the grand jury either. Nor did they accurately report my conversation with Wethje and his partner, which would have demonstrated my belief (also reflected in my books) that I believed that filing was *voluntary.* There is no question that I was framed by Wethje and Hartmere, in clear violation of *Ciambrone.* Further, in *Ciambrone,* Judge Friendly, in a dissenting opinion, added more insight regarding how prosecutors should act before grand juries:

Before the grand jury, the prosecutor has the dual role of pressing for an indictment and of being the grand jury's advisor. In case of conflict, the later duty must take precedence. (citings omitted)

And further, Judge Friendly said:

The ex parte [one sided] character of grand jury proceedings makes it peculiarly important for a federal prosecutor to remember that in the familiar phrase, the interest of the United States, "in a criminal prosecution is not that it shall win a case, but that justice shall be done"...And while "A prosecutor is not presently obligated to *search for* and submit to a grand jury evidence favorable to the defense or negating guilt, *when it is not requested by the grand jury."* The corollary is that when a grand juror requests advice, the prosecutor may not fence with him, but must respond fully and fairly. (Quoting from *Berger* v. *U.S.,* 295 US 78, 88 an *U.S.* v. *Cox,* 342 F2d 167, 189-90 (emphasis added).

Further, Judge Friendly observed that, "By refusing to indict, the grand jury has the unchallengable power to defend the innocent from government oppression by unjust prosecution."

So what Judge Dorsey did in order to deny our motion was to flagrantly *misquote* and *misapply* the *Ciambrone* decision. While *Ciambrone* clearly called for the dismissal of my indictment based on the outrageous withholding of exculpatory material (let alone providing a basis for, at least, reviewing transcript material), Dorsey totally perverted the decision so he could avoid rendering a decision favorable to the defense. He did this by simply substituting the words "to furnish" where the decision had used the words "to search for." There is no doubt that *Ciambrone* stands for the proposition that prosecutors are bound to turn over exculpatory material in their possession whether grand juries ask for it or not—but they don't have to "search for" such materials unless requested to do so. In this manner, Dorsey falsified the *Ciambrone* decision in order to make a decision favorable to the government. This is how federal judges, with apparently no twinge of conscience, falsify case law to enable them to contrive false decisions.

Dorsey's deliberate falsification of *Ciambrone* was child's play, compared to what he would pull towards the end of the trial.

JURY INSTRUCTIONS

I have already explained that in order to be found guilty of tax evasion, I had to be found guilty of committing an "affirmative act" of evasion—and the "act" selected in my case was "concealment" of income. I have also explained that by charging me with *three* separate offenses (two "omissions" and one "act") the jury could easily be confused (and they were) as to what they had to find proven in order to convict me of tax evasion. Somewhere in the second half of my trial, my lawyer asked me if I wanted a "lessor included offense" charge[5] since he had been asked that by the court.

If I had said yes, the Judge would have instructed the jury that it could find me guilty of one or both of the lessor included offenses instead of finding me guilty of the greater crime of tax evasion. However, I believed that the jury would find me guilty of the lessor included offenses (since it was admitted that I had not filed or paid taxes for the years in question) because I knew that Judge Dorsey would also misstate the law on "willfulness."[6]

Because I rejected the "lessor included offense" charge, the jury now had to find me guilty of tax evasion ("concealment") or acquit me of this and the lessor included

offenses. The fact that Judge Dorsey specifically inquired about a "lessor included offense" charge, proves that he deliberately mislead the jury when he instructed them that I had been accused of committing tax evasion "three ways"— a claim also made by the Second Circuit in its affirming decision. In any case, Dorsey presented these three separate "offenses" (two minor and one major offense) to the jury in two different ways. At times they were presented as being three distinct "ways" in which I had sought to commit tax evasion, while at other times, they were presented as being "three elements" of the same "crime." Both representations were false and could only confuse the jury concerning what the trial was all about, and so the jury never knew (and, I must admit, neither did I nor my lawyer) what the government had to prove in order to find me guilty of tax evasion. But focusing for the moment on merely one of those two false representations, the one in which the Court presented them as being *elements* of the same crime, then obviously *all* of those elements had to be proven before I could be found guilty of tax evasion. And up until his duplicious and scurelous supplemental instruction, that is exactly what Judge Dorsey had told the jury. The following, for example, represents four of perhaps a dozen or so instructions on the same theme that Dorsey had, from time to time, given to the jury.[7]

1. If the Government has not proven the case against him *in all respects* beyond a reasonable doubt, then *he is entitled to your verdict of acquittal of the charges.* (Transcript page 87)

2. In a prosecution of a criminal charge, the Government has the burden of *proving every element of the charge* beyond a reasonable doubt. (Transcript page 85)

3. As I previously indicated to you, the Government has the burden of proving *each element* of the charges against Mr. Schiff beyond a reasonable doubt... If the government *fails to prove that he violated the statute by failing to prove any one of the three elements* as to any of the three charges, THEN THE DEFENDANT MUST BE ACQUITTED. (Transcript page 98)

4. If (the government) *fails to prove each element* of a charge beyond a reasonable doubt, *you must acquit the defendant of that charge.* (page 30 of the jury charge as numbered in the appeal exhibits to the Supreme Court).

(Emphasis added throughout)

There is no doubt that the charge of "concealment" had to be proven even if we *incorrectly* assume that it was merely *one element* of the "crime"; though contrary to Dorsey's instruction, it wasn't merely *an element*. It constituted the entire crime assuming that it could also be proven that the "concealment" was done "willfully" for the purpose of evading taxes that were "due and owing." (And since I had never been assessed for tax for those years [as both the court and the prosecutor knew] the taxes weren't even "due and owing").

PREPARING THE JURY CHARGE

The court prepares its "jury charge" from "proposed jury instructions", submitted to it by both the prosecution and the defense. One of the proposed instructions that my attorney should have submitted, is that the jury be instructed that it had to find "concealment" of income proven beyond a reasonable doubt—or it had to acquit me of the charge of tax evasion. This would have been as fundamental as requesting, in a murder trial, that the jury be instructed that it had to find that the defendant actually killed the victim, before it could find him guilty of murder in any degree. But *amazingly* my attorney *never asked for such an instruction*—so it was never given! Instead, my attorney asked for an instruction that the government would have to prove that I had sought to evade taxes "in some manner" *undescribed* and *unspecified!* CONSEQUENTLY JUDGE DORSEY NEVER INSTRUCTED THE JURY THAT IT HAD TO FIND ME GUILTY OF THE CRIME FOR WHICH I HAD BEEN CHARGED! He got around it, because of the negligence of my attorney and by giving the jury a conglomeration of nonsense as to what it had to find proven in order to convict me; which would be pointless to analyze further.[8]

"DEFEATING" THE TAX

Within five minutes of being sent out, pursuant to an "Allen" charge, the jury sent Dorsey a very interesting question.[9] It had noted that I had been accused of seeking to "evade and defeat" the tax, so it wanted to know what was the difference between the two. In the discussion that followed, it was discovered that neither Judge Dorsey, nor Michael Hartmere, nor my attorney knew the difference! Dorsey decided to instruct the jury that they both meant the same thing, and that it could *disregard* any possible distinction between them! (Since I do not have the trial transcript here in jail, I can't be certain of Dorsey's specific words). However, in my case, not making a distinction would be crucial, since one might believe that my efforts to expose the illegal manner in which income taxes were extracted was the equivalent of attempting to "defeat" the tax! While in most tax prosecutions, such an accusation would have little significance, in my case it did! However, using one's First Amendment rights to criticize or expose the income tax is hardly what is meant by "defeating" the tax within the meaning of Section 7201. Because the court

made no effort to explain what "defeating" the tax meant, given the type of "evidence" the court had allowed into the trial, and given the remarks of the prosecutor with respect to my alleged "tax protest" activities, along with the court's supplemental charge, I could have been convicted of income tax evasion simply because some jurors believed that in writing books and giving lectures antagonistic to the income tax, I HAD ATTEMPTED TO "DEFEAT" THE TAX!

AN INTERESTING ARRAIGNMENT QUESTION!

The jury's question and total inability of a judge and two lawyers to answer it, provides an interesting arraignment issue—one which I never thought to raise! Those charged with tax evasion are also simulaneously charged with seeking to "defeat" the tax—unless the government discontinues the charge based on these disclosures! Since these two accusations are stated in the *conjunctive*, both *have to be pleaded to* and *both accusations proven*. But how can one intelligently plead to "defeating" the tax (as distinguished from attempting to evade it) unless one knows what that means? Its meaning would have to be explained by the judge or magistrate who conducts the arraignment. It is my belief that in such instances the court will not be able to distinguish between the two if asked to do so. If the court merely says that they mean the same thing, then the accused might properly ask that the redundant accusation be stricken from the indictment! But the court can't do that, since that would amount to amending the indictment. Yet, if the court cannot explain what it means (as distinguished from "evading" the tax), then how can one plead to the charge? I can't see how the arraignment could continue without the accusation being either *distinguished* or *expunged!*

A CRIMINAL JURY INSTRUCTION

If I were to tell you that a U.S. district court judge, in responding to a jury question as to what it had to find proven in order to convict a defendant, replied, "Find him guilty of anything you like"—how many people would believe it? And if I were then to ask, "But *suppose* that it *really happened*, would you then believe that a U.S. court of appeals would sustain such an instruction as proper?" Just how many people would believe that? BUT THAT'S **EXACTLY WHAT HAPPENED IN MY CASE, AND HERE IS THE PROOF.**

Fortunately for me, someone on the jury noticed that while the indictment accused me of "concealing" income, Judge Dorsey had never charged them that this had to be proven. So within minutes of its previous question, the jury asked another, as follows:

While concealing income appears in the indictment in

connection with the first three counts, it does not appear in your charge to the jury. Is it necessary to prove this item beyond a reasonable doubt when reaching our verdict?

Obviously the answer to the jury's question was "yes"—for a variety of reasons. First of all, as Judge Dorsey had already explained at least a dozen times, the government had to prove "all elements of the crime" and certainly "concealment" was one of them. Not only was it an "element," it constituted the entire crime of tax evasion, assuming it could further be shown as having been done "willfully." Without finding "concealment" proven, I could only be found guilty of the "lessor included" offenses. How much time should it have taken Judge Dorsey to answer the question? **What actually happened, however, should at the very least, get both Judge Dorsey and now Judge Hartmere removed from their respective benches—if not get them indicted for violations of oath of office and/or obstruction of justice.**

Immediately upon reading the jury's question, Judge Dorsey stated, "The jury is quite correct. That phrase is not, does not actually appear in the charge, and *there has been no exception to the charge in that respect.*" So now Dorsey knew (because of a perceptive jury—not because of my lawyer) that he never told the grand jury it had to find me guilty of committing the crime charged by the grand jury in its indictment! How could any verdict be valid on *any* basis? At the same time, Dorsey put my lawyer on notice that any error made by the court was my lawyer's fault for not objecting to the charge, either when it was proposed or immediately after it was given. This was not entirely true. While my attorney was grossly negligent in not seeing to it that the court charged the jury on "concealment," it amounted to plain error that the court itself had not even done so. Error of this magnitude should have been caught by the court regardless of the gross negligence and incompetence of my own lawyer. After all, Judge Dorsey is supposed to know something about law, too!

In the courtroom discussion that followed, Michael Hartmere immediately argued that "concealment" did not have to be proven because, "It was only one of the ways Schiff had been charged with evasion," (quotes mine). This was a claim that he was shortly to repeat. Both statements were lies, but quite in keeping with Hartmere's basic character. In a pre-trial memorandum (which I came across while preparing for my 2255 hearing), Hartmere told Judge Dorsey that pursuant to the *Spies* decision, the government had to "prove the affirmative act of concealment charged in the indictment." Yet he now argued to the court that it did not have to be proven! And this scoundrel currently sits as a Connecticut Superior Court judge! (If I get out of jail before this book goes to press, you will find this memorandum in the Appendix. If it is not there and you would like a copy of

it, simply send a stamped, self-addressed envelope to Freedom Books requesting "Documented proof that Judge Michael Hartmere is an unconscionable liar.")

There can be no doubt that, based on that memorandum, and everything else they ever learned in law school, both Hartmere and Dorsey knew that the jury had to find "concealment" proven beyond a reasonable doubt before it could convict me of tax evasion.

My attorney, of course, kept insisting (though ineffectively) that "concealment" had to be proven because, "It was an essential element of the crime." He failed to point out, however, that without "concealment" *there wasn't even a crime of tax evasion* and that without it proven, I would only be convicted of the "lessor included offenses"—an instruction we had rejected. In addition, my attorney failed to mention why such an instruction would violate the *Spies* decision as well as other Supreme Court and Second Circuit decisions. Had he raised these objections, there is no question that the Court never could have gotten away with charging "concealment" *out of the case!* What Dorsey did, in legal terms, is known as "amending the indictment," an act which every federal judge knows is illegal. Reducing Judge Dorsey's answer to bare minimum, I have reproduced the following, which was taken right from the Second Circuit's sustaining decision. There can be no question that everyone was fully aware of Dorsey's absurd and illegal answer to the jury's question. Among other things, Dorsey said:

> In the indictment there are three ways in which the government has made the charge that there was a willful attempt in some manner to evade or defeat the tax. What you must be concerned with is whether the government has proven to your satisfaction beyond a reasonable doubt each of the three elements as I have charged them to you. Therefore, the answer to your question *is not really either yes or no* in the sense of the evasion, and the only act of evading that you find proven was by the concealing or attempting to conceal, then the answer is yes. But if you find that *some other manner* which is the third element of the proof necessary is something, and this again *is for you to decide* if it happens to be the case, is an act *or omission* other than concealment, but which nonetheless constitutes a willful attempt on the part of the defendant to evade or defeat the tax, *then the answer to the question is no.* (Emphasis added.)

Remember, that quotation, (along with four or five pages of additional instruction) was in response to a simple question, "Did concealment have to be proven, yes or no?"! Obviously, the jury couldn't be sure of what Dorsey actually said—and neither was Dorsey or the Second Circuit. The bottom line impression they would have received is "No, it doesn't have to be proven as long as you find anything else proven. What? I don't know, but I'll leave it up to you!"

I have already spent considerable time analyzing the issues in this case, and I certainly don't need to spend anymore regarding this absurd instruction. Simply for the fun of it, though, and in the words of Elizabeth Barrett (or was it Robert Browning?) let us "count the ways."

1. What, for example, does "But if you find some other manner in which the third element of the proof necessary is something, and this is for you to decide if it happens to be the case," really mean?

2. The indictment did not charge me with committing evasion "three ways," as Dorsey again, for the upteenth time, told the jury.

3. How could Dorsey even have referred to the possible proof of "each of the three elements as I have charged them to you," when he just got through admitting that *he had completely failed to charge them on the third element?!*

4. How can the answer be "yes or no," as to whether the jury has to find the accused guilty of the act alleged?!

5. If the jury can find "some other manner" proven—what other "manner" would that be? The only "manner" charged in the indictment was "concealment" of income. How could Dorsey instruct the jury that it was free to convict me of "some other manner?"

6. How can individual jurors—on their own—decide what "act or omission other than concealment" constitutes an act to "evade or defeat" the tax within the meaning of Code Section 7201? Can they, on their own, decide that one who allegedly encourages people not to pay income taxes is guilty of seeking to "defeat" the tax within the meaning of Code Section 7201? *According to Dorsey, they are!*

7. If the jury can find me guilty of some "act or *omission*" in lieu of the affirmative act charged in the indictment, then it can also find me guilty of tax evasion based on *omissions alone!* This is directly contrary to the *Spies* decision and also the Supreme Court's decision in *Sansone*, 380 U.S. 343, and *every appellate decision on this issue.*

In essence, Dorsey told the jury that if it didn't find me guilty of the crime charged in the indictment, then it was free to *convict me of anything else!* **AND THIS MAN STILL SITS ON THE FEDERAL BENCH!**

THE SECOND CIRCUIT CONFIRMS MY CONVICTION

It is really unnecessary to spend much time commenting on the Second Circuit's decision sustaining my conviction, since it must be obvious that any appellate court that could sustain Dorsey's supplemental instruction is capable of sustaining *anything.* Suffice it to say, that Circuit Court Judge, Thomas J. Meskill (a former Connecticut governor) who wrote the decision and Circuit Court Judge Amalya Kearse, and District Court Judge Charles M. Metzner (sitting by designation) who made up the appellate panel, all had to know that I was never convicted of the crime they sustained. If they couldn't figure that out, they had no business graduating law school, let alone sitting on a federal bench. Apart from such an observation being simply self-evident, here is some legal evidence to support it.

In the Second Circuit's own case of *Alessi v. U.S.*, 593 F.2d 476 (1979), that court set aside Alessi's confession to income tax evasion because, as the court held:

The indictment would hardly convey to a layman that the phrase "by concealing and attempting to conceal from all proper officers of the United States his true and correct taxable income" required the Government *to prove concealment* by something more than failing to file an income tax return.

If the Second Circuit knew that in 1979, how come they didn't know it in 1986? And more recently in *U.S. v. Nelson*, 791 F.2d 336 (1986), The Fifth Circuit set aside a conviction because it held that the trial court, by not instructing the jury that Nelson, in order to be found guilty of tax evasion, had to be found guilty of an affirmative act, violated both *Spies* and *Sansone*. Specifically the court said:

The instruction allows the jury to convict the defendant without finding "some willful *commission in addition* to the willful omissions" proscribed by the misdemeanor statute of failing to file a return. Thus, the trial court erred. Further, the error cannot be deemed harmless, and defendant Nelson's conviction on Count II must be reversed. (emphasis added)

That's simple enough. If the Fifth Circuit can understand it, why can't the Second Circuit?

In a two-page article entitled, "Is Affirmative Misconduct Necessary For Tax Evasion?" which appeared in the February 1987 issue of the *Journal of Taxation*, tax lawyer Elliot Silverman wrote:

The Second Circuit's decision in *Schiff*, 801 F2d 108 (1986)... raises some serious questions. Indeed...

the circuit's opinion seems to be in direct conflict with a principle that practitioners have thought, until now, to have been settled law for over 40 years—that mere *inaction* (i.e., not filing a return or paying tax) is not sufficient to constitute the felony of tax evasion unless accompanied by some affirmative misconduct.

Commenting on Dorsey's supplemental instruction, Mr. Silverman wrote:

> The defendant requested the district court to answer the question "yes": the Government requested that the question be answered "no." The district judge instead gave a long (and, in the author's view, rather confusing) answer, to the effect that proof that there was an attempt to evade the tax "in some manner" would be sufficient, even if this "manner" were some "act or omission other than concealment."

> The answer was clearly wrong, because it permitted the jury to find that mere inaction...was sufficient to convict the defendant of the felony of tax evasion, even if it found that he had *not* committed any affirmative acts (such as attempting to conceal his income). This result flatly contradicts the Supreme Court's oft-cited, unanimous decision in *Spies*, 317 U.S. 492 (1943), never questioned since it was handed down.

Since Mr. Silverman had no trouble at all figuring out that Dorsey's supplemental instruction was "clearly wrong," that it "contradicted" *Spies* and "conflicted" with 40 years of "settled law," how could Judges Meskill, Kearse, and Metzner not have noticed it?

In order to justify its lawless decision, the Second Circuit felt it had to include another observation that merely reveals its knowledge that its decision was falacious. On page 115, Judge Meskill observes that, "There was ample evidence to support a finding that he concealed or attempted to conceal his income." But "concealment," as Judge Meskill had to know, *was charged out of the case!* So what difference did it make if such evidence was "ample" or not? I was not convicted until Judge Dorsey, as Judge Meskill *must have known,* told the jury that it did not have to find "concealment" proven. Besides, if the evidence was "ample," why did Judge Dorsey charge it out of the case? It is clear that while Judge Meskill took "concealment" out of the case in order to sustain Dorsey's supplemental instruction, he later felt compelled to put it back in *to justify the conviction!* The fact that he could do both without doing violence to his legal or ethical sensibilities is another indication of what "case law" can be made of.

All of the judges who had a hand in the destruction of my two businesses, plunging me into depression, causing me to

be held captive for months (at this point, 24 months), compelling the payment of $30,000 so I could be ransomed from confinement (and who are now seeking to extort another $79,000), and who are responsible for my having to spend (so far) $60,000 in defense costs—all knew I was innocent. What would happen to individuals who engaged in such activities if they were not federal judges?

A Useless Appeal To The Supreme Court

On the presumption, I suppose, that it is better late than never, my attorney finally raised the right issue when he appealed my conviction to the Supreme Court. This being that the trial court's supplemental instruction violated the *Spies* rule and permitted me to be convicted of income tax evasion based upon omissions alone. Unfortunately for me, my attorney's awakening came a little late. The Supreme Court declined to hear my appeal, probably for the following reasons, as contained in the Government's Brief in Opposition:

> At the outset, we note this contention—that the challenged instruction suggested to the jury that evidence of petitioner's failure to file a return or his failure to pay income taxes would constitute a sufficient basis to convict for attempted tax evasion— *is raised for the first time in this court. Petitioner did not raise this objection in the trial court, nor did he raise it in the court of appeal. Accordingly, the claim should not be considered.* (citings omitted)

> In any event, petitioner's contention is without merit. Because petitioner *did not timely object* to the charge on this ground, *thereby giving the trial court the opportunity to rectify the alleged error.* (emphasis added)

Thus the government argued that the Supreme Court should not hear my appeal because my attorney had not objected to the errors of which he now complained.

This made it *at least the third time* that the negligence and ineffectiveness of my attorney was specifically mentioned. It was, as you know, noted by Judge Dorsey immediately following the jury's question, and it was even mentioned by the Second Circuit in its affirming decision, when it dismissed my lawyer's claim that Dorsey's use of the "in some manner" language constituted reversible error. The Second Circuit was able to reject what otherwise would have been a valid claim, by pointing out that, "The (trial) court had used similar language *many times* in its oral and written charges *without objection.*" (Emphasis added.) So at each level of the trial and appeal process my attorney's ineffectiveness was duly noted by either the government or the court.

ATTACKING ONE'S SENTENCE AND CONVICTION "COLLATERALLY"

One can still attack one's sentence and conviction by way of Rule 35 and 2255 motions, even after all direct appeals fail. The former attacks the legality of the sentence, while the latter attacks the constitutionality of the conviction. After I saw the *totally worthless*, less than two-page Rule 35 motion submitted by my attorney, I received the court's permission to supplement it with a motion of my own. Together with my reply brief, this came to about 75 pages, not counting numerous exhibits. It clearly establishes that my sentence and special conditions of probation were illegally imposed.

That appeal was rejected by both Dorsey (to whom it had to be directed) and the Second Circuit, again casting aside all law and reason, sustained his decision on appeal. My petition for a rehearing *en banc* on its decision is still (as of this writing) pending. If it is denied, I will have to appeal to the Supreme Court—and, at this point, I could use some legal help.

A Habeas Corpus Attack

A habeas corpus petition has to allege violations of constitutional rights. My petition was based on: violations of my Sixth Amendment right to a fair trial, since my conviction was derived directly from Judge Dorsey's total misstatement of the law and because of the ineffectiveness of my attorney; and violation of my Fifth Amendment right to be tried on the basis of a valid indictment. All lawyers are "officers of the court," and if one's lawyer is ineffective, it is the court's fault for appointing ineffective officers. It is clear that my indictment was secured on the basis of prosecutorial fraud, by testimony that the prosecutor knew was perjurious and by his withholding of exculpatory information. Because of this, the indictment was patently invalid, and the trial court had no jurisdiction to conduct a trial on this basis alone. Ineffective counsel is a particularly popular and powerful 2255 argument, and many a conviction has been overturned on this issue alone. I certainly had no trouble establishing this issue in my case. The definitive case on this is *Strickland* v. *Washington,* 466 U.S. 688, and the failures of my attorney easily meet every test established in that decision.

MY 2255 HEARING

To prove the fact that my indictment and conviction were based upon perjurious testimony and the ineffectiveness of my attorney in not exposing it, I was able to get as a witness at that hearing, the IRS agent-auditor, John Lynch, who was also the government's summation witness at my trial. As mentioned earlier, the fact that I had deposited to my Hamden bank account more than four times as much cash as the government claimed I was concealing abroad presented a little problem for Michael Hartmere, the government's erstwhile prosecutor. Getting this fact by the grand jury was no problem for Hartmere. He simply wouldn't mention it. But how do you get this fact by the petit jury? This obviously presented some difficulty.[11] Hartmere's criminal mind, however, proved equal to the task. Together with the IRS witnesses, who routinely provide perjurious testimony as a routine part of their job, Hartmere devised a scheme involving "re-deposits of cash." In this manner, Hartmere believed he could slip this devastating piece of evidence past the defense without the defense even being aware of what was happening. Regardless of whatever else I might say of Michael Hartmere, I must admit that his plan was brilliant and it worked like a charm! I only wonder how many other convictions he has secured on the basis of equally dishonest tactics. I can only imagine the euphoria and hilarity that existed in the prosecution's camp when they saw how *perfectly* their prosecutorial scam had worked!

Hartmere began greasing the skids for his scheme prior to getting to the troublesome cash deposits. In going over checks and deposits (immediately prior to the cash deposits), Hartmere showed Lynch a $10,000 government check which represented the matured value of a Treasury Bill I had purchased. He asked Lynch how the government had treated the check, and Lynch responded by saying, "Since we could not determine its taxability, we eliminated it from Schiff's taxable income." I could not understand Lynch's claim that the IRS couldn't determine its "taxability," since that could easily be determined. (It was the difference between what I had paid for the bill and what I had received for it!) I leaned over to my lawyer and said, "How could they not know its 'taxability' when they also have the check with which it was purchased?" His answer was that, "They're not charging you with evading any taxes in connection with that check, so why are you concerned about it?" He answered with annoyance that I had distracted him from listening to Lynch's testimony.

This is exactly the *reaction* that Michael Hartmere had counted on! By claiming that the IRS could not determine the "taxability" of the check (when by IRS standards it was easily determinable), he had appeared to be needlessly—if not perhaps gratuitously—attempting to reduce the amount that the government would claim that I sought to evade! What was the *defense* supposed to do? Should it jump up and insist that the interest portion of that check was taxable and therefore I must have sought to evade even more taxes than the government claimed? Lynch proceeded to do the same with several other checks, including an obvious dividend check from Agnico-Eagle, a Canadian gold mine. When Lynch said that he couldn't determine the taxability of that check, I again whispered to my lawyer, "But that's a dividend, how could they *not know* its 'taxability'?'' Again, what were we supposed to do—look a gift horse in the mouth? The answer, I now know is yes—especially when the "gift" comes from the United States Department of Justice! Now that the trap was set, Hartmere sprang it. "And did you come across some *re-deposits* of cash?" said Hartmere, leading his witness. "Yes," said Lynch, and he proceeded to explain that, "Under the theory that they represented re-deposits of cash, checks that had been reduced to cash and re-deposited, we elimiated them from Schiff's taxable income to avoid any possibility of duplication." "And was that for Schiff's benefit?" asked Hartmere. "That was for Schiff's benefit," replied Lynch. So now the jury was additionally led to believe that the government was being scrupulously fair, when what Hartmere was actually doing was slipping the cash deposits right by the jury and the defense. Now Lynch began to monotonously intone some six figures which the government would not claim constituted "taxable income," so they would never be mentioned again, either by the prosecution *or the defense.*

It was not until I reviewed my trial transcript while being held as a federal prisoner, did I really focus on this aspect of Lynch's testimony. When I reviewed it and totaled the six figures that he had innocently intoned, I discovered that they came to $25,000! Why would the government not seek to attribute as taxable income $25,000, when I had seen them claim as income *any receipt* that went into one's bank acount? And, why would they have "theorized" that I would waste my time cashing numerous small checks and then redeposit the proceeds? It was also plain that even if I had done what the government claimed, there still couldn't have been any duplication of deposits. Had I cashed the checks as they were received, they would not have been "deposited" initially—but merely cashed. If I then deposited the cash received from those checks, it would only have been ONE deposit! There couldn't be any "re-deposits." So why shouldn't the government have included these deposits as taxable income? And why did Hartmere concoct such a ridiculous theory about re-deposits? It was then that I realized what had happened. The $25,000 represented ordinary cash deposits which Hartmere did not want the jury to know I had made. He contrived the nonsense about re-deposits which he knew were ordinary cash deposits, in order to slip it by the jury and the defense. He anticipated that the defense would not be alert and perceptive enough to object to the government's contention that I had *evaded less taxes than what the evidence clearly pointed to!* And to insure that the defense would be *thoroughly confused* as to what he was up to, he even eliminated from my taxable income *check receipts that were clearly taxable!* He realized that without using this cash and check income, the government could still claim that I had sought to evade about $50,000 in taxes, and so he didn't

need the taxes on an additional $25,000 of income to convict me of evasion. Yet in eliminating this $25,000, he would rob the defense of a devastating piece of exculpable evidence that alone would have knocked the government's concealment claim into a cocked hat.[12] One must, however, give the devil his due. As a daring and imaginative prosecutorial ploy, Hartmere's plan was brilliant and its execution perfect. He risked (as you will soon see) total exposure with his IRS witness getting caught of committing perjury on a variety of grounds. But he relied on the sheer audacity of the ruse combined with his understanding that my attorney appeared not to know what was going on, in order to pull it off. In addition, since the government's case was obviously built on nothing but hot air, Hartmere felt he had nothing to lose. Proving that while Hartmere may be a scoundrel, he is certainly a resourceful one.

In addition to all of the above, I uncovered two documents that prove conclusively that IRS agent Lynch committed perjury at my trial, while Hartmere in leading him, was guilty of subordination of perjury. One such document was the transcript of an interview that took place between my bookkeeper, Lynch, and Wethje, when these two IRS agents paid a visit to her home to question her regarding my activities and those of Freedom Books. The transcript shows that Lynch specifically asked her if I had made any "re-deposits of cash," and she responded with a very firm, "No." The other document, the transcript of her testimony before the grand jury, shows that when Hartmere asked her the very *same question,* he got *the very same negative answer!* So there is no question, that apart from everything else, both Hartmere and Lynch had received direct assurances from my own bookkeeper that there were no "re-deposits of cash" as they had both fraudulently conspired to have my jury believe!

At my 2255 hearing, Lynch was asked by my attorney, Jeff Dickstein, what evidence he had to support his trial "theory" that I had made "re-deposits" of cash, rather than having made mere "deposits" of cash. He replied that he had *no evidence.* When he was asked to reconcile his claim at trial that I had made "re-deposits" with such lack of evidence, and when, in addition, he had been told by my bookkeeper that no such "re-deposits" were made, he could not do so. When Lynch could offer no evidentiary basis for his "re-deposit" theory, or explain why the government had eliminated $25,000 of cash receipts from my taxable income, Judge Dorsey thought it was time to offer the government some help. From the bench he offered the following suggestions:

(1) Since the deposits were cash, their "source was unknown," so, presumably, the government might disregard them, and

(2) He theorized that perhaps the government thought I had simply withdrawn too much cash from my accounts and had "re-deposited" the overage! Dorsey's first theory was, of course, absurd, since that would mean that in constructing the taxable income of any retail operation the government would eliminate all cash receipts because their "sources" were unknown. In addition, the government would still have referred to such entries as "deposits" and not "re-deposits." While Dorsey's second reason simply disregarded the statements of my bookkeeper that no such "re-deposits" had been made, this latter suggestion prompted the defense to ask the government to produce its worksheets on which my cash deposits and withdrawals were recorded. When they were examined, it was clear that there was no correlation between the cash withdrawals and re-deposits as Dorsey had suggested. The cash deposits were in large sums and made during the period from January to April—when I put on my seminars. The withdrawals were much smaller and rather uniform—reflecting normal cash withdrawals to meet normal operating needs. It was apparent that Dorsey's gratuitous suggestions were cut from the same cloth as was the government's original "re-deposit" *theory.*

An expert witness, attorney William Cohan, testified that my attorney's failure to impeach Lynch's testimony concerning a devastating piece of exculpatory evidence, was an example of ineffective representation. Consequently, the jury was never presented with this information, even though the attorney had the documents to do so. In addition, Cohan testified that my attorney's failure in not requesting that the jury be instructed that it had to find "concealment" (the act I had been charged with committing) proven beyond a reasonable doubt, was, in and of itself, establishment by the defense of ineffective counsel. He also testified that for my attorney not to have objected to the court's failure to charge on concealment following the main charge, also constituted ineffective counsel; but not to have done so for the reason given by my attorney was an admission that he was not even familiar with the *rudiments of trial procedure,* clearly demonstrating a totally unacceptable level of legal represen-

tation at a criminal trial! In addition, Cohan testified that my attorney's failure to raise *Spies* as well as other cases immediately prior to the court's giving of its fatal supplemental charge, and not to have raised this issue on appeal (as was noted by the government in its Brief in Opposition to the Supreme Court) were clear examples of representation that fell far below the level which any defendant had a right to expect, and that these failures met every test of ineffective counsel as established by the Supreme Court in *Strickland,* and even more recently in *Kimmelman* v. *Morrison,* 477 U.S. 365.

My expert witness also testified that Dorsey's supplemental instruction was **dead wrong**, for all the reasons you already know, and further supported his own assessment with the similar one made by Elliot Silverman in his well researched and scholarly article that had appeared in the *Journal of Taxation.*

The Government did not put on an expert of its own to refute this testimony, nor did it seek to challenge this testimony *in any appreciable way.* Certainly neither the Government nor Dorsey challenged, *in any way* his claim that Dorsey's supplemental instruction—which led directly to my conviction—**was dead wrong.** During this portion of his testimony, Dorsey did not make a peep!

The supposed winner of a 2255 contest is the one that presents the greater "preponderance of evidence." In this case, I not only furnished the "preponderance of evidence," I furnished virtually *all of it.* For all intents and purposes, **the Government presented nothing in opposition.** How could it? Despite this, Dorsey denied my 2255 claim and insisted that his suplemental instruction had been *legally correct;* that my attorney's representation had not been ineffective; and that Lynch's testimony had not been perjurious, consequently tht no exculpatory material had been withheld from either the petit or grand jury.

This should give you some idea of how the federal government "wins" tax trials, related appeals, and other motions in federal "courts."

NOTES TO CHAPTER 11

1. Real estate income enjoys a particular place in federal taxation. The first direct taxes imposed by the federal government were on real estate. And since those taxes were apportioned, *we have a precedent for the apportionment of all real estate taxes*—which would include the *income from real estate,* as the Superior Court, in *Pollock,* held. But this aspect of real estate income is totally unknown within the real estate community! The history of **federal real estate taxes** (which were levied on four separate occasions) is extensively covered in *The Great Income Tax Hoax.*

2. For example, even if I noticed the IDS application as I went through the three boxes that were filled with documents, radio, TV and seminar tapes, it all appeared irrelevant. What connection, for example, would I think that a corporate application for a mutual fund might have to do with the charges against me, except possibly to indicate I was making money on which a tax was allegedly due? I would never have noticed (even if I gave the document a second glance) the words "tax evader," almost illegibly inserted at the bottom of the application, which, in addition, was only faintly discernible on a practically illegible, darkened photo copy. Who would have thought as I briefly noted this benign corporate application that I was looking at a significant piece of the government's case? Nor would I have realized when I looked at two checks which were evidence of the purchase and liquidation of a mutual fund that I was looking at the government's entire case of "concealment"! I had been assigned the job of sifting through these documents by my lawyer who wanted me to pick out those documents that I believed were relevant to the charges. **I couldn't find any!** All that they showed was that I had earned some money and had generated business and personal expenses. There was nothing in the government's entire file that would have indicated how I sought to "conceal" my income or on what basis the government would seek to prove its claim at trial! So the government, protected by Judge Dorsey, never had to identify in what manner I sought to "conceal" my income (or the laws that allegedly "required" me to file and which made me "liable" for the tax)—so I had no opportunity, prior to trial, to prepare any direct defense to what the government would contend at the trial. This is not the way a criminal trial is *supposed* to work.

3. For a copy of the IRS transcript of that home interview and Wethje's account of it as told to the grand jury, send a self-addressed, double-stamped, standard size envelope to Freedom Books, and request "Documents Showing How IRS agent Ted Wethje misled the Grand Jury."

4. All of this was fully explained to Judge Dorsey in my Rule 35 and 2255 motions. Copies of both motions, the government responses, and Dorsey's ruling are available to you. Despite this obvious showing of prosecutorial fraud

and perjury on the part of Wethje (in addition to other issues), Dorsey denied both motions.

5. Before retiring to reach its verdict, the judge "charges the jury." Presumably in its charge he explains: the law, how the jury should evaluate and apply the evidence and what it has to find proven in order to convict the defendant. In charges related to the alleged "crime" of willful failure to file income tax returns, it must now be obvious that *all federal judges misstate the "law."* If they didn't, *no one would ever have been convicted of this non crime!* (Again, compare what federal judges do in such instances to the crime of perjury!) Without going into detail, I would venture to say that federal judges misstate the law *in every income tax trial!* In addition, they will instruct juries that they are bound to accept "the law" as given them by the court, and that they are not to take into consideration such things as: the potential sentence, or their feelings regarding the law in question. Such instructions, *too,* are lies. American jurors can take into consideration ANYTHING THEY WISH IN DECLARING SOMEONE NOT GUILTY. And if they think that the potential sentence is too severe or that the applicable law is too harsh, vague, caprecious, or just plain screwy, they can vote *not guilty* regardless of what the judge says on the matter. This is known as "jury nullification," and allows American jurors *to vote their own conscience* regardless of what the judge tells them. This principle goes all the way back to when jury trials were held even before the Supreme Court. And in *Georgia v. Brailsford,* John Jay, America's first Chief Justice who presided over numerous sessions of the Constitutional Convention, so instructed a jury before that court. (For more on jury nullification, see *The Great Income Tax Hoax.*) **However, if a federal judge knows that a potential juror understands his rights as a juror, he will dismiss him from jury duty!** This is merely one way in which federal judges **stack juries in favor of the government.** If you are a potential juror, don't let the judge know that you are familiar with "jury nullification" and if you get to be a juror in a tax case, just vote not guilty—simply on the basis that you already know that the law will be falsely stated and applied.

6. Unlike other crimes, all so-called tax crimes have to be committed "willfully"; that is, with the defendant's belief that the law *required* him to act in the prescribed manner, and that he didn't have any basis *for not doing so.* In other words, it is not a crime to fail to file or evade taxes, it is only an alleged crime to do so "willfully." However, in such cases (especially if the defendant is considered a "tax protestor) courts not only misstate the law with respect to filing, they also misstate the meaning of "willfulness," and generally instruct jurors that it means something done "purposefully" and "deliberately" as opposed to

"accidentally." This is a complete perversion of what "willfully" really means as used in tax statutes. There are other ways of misleading jurors regarding the meaning of "willfulness," and Judge Dorsey used all of them!

7. I reminded Judge Dorsey of these instructions by quoting about a dozen of them verbatim in my Rule 35 and 2255 motions, and pointing out how all of them contradicted his supplemental instruction. But Dorsey was unmoved. Yet, if Dorsey's supplemental instruction was correct, then these instructions were incorrect. However, if these instructions were correct, then Dorsey's final instruction to the jury (which was the direct cause of my conviction) was incorrect! You try figuring out how Dorsey could have given both these instructions *and* his final supplemental one!

8. Those wishing copies of Judge Dorsey's some 75 pages of jury instruction, including the jury's questions, and courtroom discussions leading to Dorsey's supplemental instruction, send $4.00 and $2.00 to cover postage and handling, together with a self-addressed, standard size envelope to Freedom Books.

9. The "Allen" charge (sometimes known as the "dynamite" charge or the "shotgun" instruction) is used to coax verdicts out of deadlocked juries. Dorsey did this by giving jurors reasons why his having to call a mistrial would be unfortunate. "Another trial," he said, "will be unnecessarily costly for both the government and the defendant. The next jury, in all probability, will not be anymore informed than is this one...etc, etc., etc," while urging jurors to be persuaded by the views of others. In some federal jurisdictions, I understand, "dynamite" charges are never used, while in others they lead to automatic reversals (if convictions result) if the charge is objected to—which it was in my case. In some states (California, for example), the "Allen" charge is banned altogether. A "dynamite" charge is given to benefit the government, since a "hung jury" is practically a win for the defendant, because he goes free and stays free if the government decides not to retry him. In any case, the government will throw in the sponge after two or three hung juries. In addition, the defense is in a better position to win

the next trial, since it is now familiar with the government's case. Had Judge Dorsey done what justice required (which would have been to have declared a mistrial on the three evasion counts when the jury, after three days of deliberation, announced itself deadlocked) the government never would have been able to convict me of tax evasion. In addition, the government would not have been able to convict me if I had taken the stand in my own defense. Why I allowed my attorney to persuade me not to do so has caused me many sleepless nights since that "trial."

10. My rule 35 and 2255 briefs, together with the Government's replies, answers, my reply briefs, hearing testimony, and the courts rulings, probably come to over 250 pages of material, not counting exhibits. It is all available to those requesting parts or all of it, but I really don't know exactly how much material there is. In any case, it will add for more detail (if that is considered necessary) to the issues I have covered, plus provide extensive, additional proof of the lying nature of Justice Department attorneys.

11. Because Hartmere was prosecuting me pursuant to what is known as the "bank account" theory of the case, he had to go over all of my bank deposits and expenditures at trial—which were introduced and explained through Lynch. Consequently, Lynch's testimony was very lengthy, tedious and boring, making it ideally suited to slip something this devious and diabolic past the defense and the jury.

12. Another example of how Hartmere would capitalize on the jury's failure to know that I had deposited $25,000 of outright cash occurred at final summation. My attorney had sought to argue that since I had converted $25,000 of cash receipts to cashier's checks which I then deposited, showed that I was not engaged in concealing income. Hartmere countered the argument by claiming that this only indicated that I was reluctant to travel around the country with large amounts of cash, not that I was honest. He, of course, could not make this claim in connection with the $25,000 in cash that I had also deposited outright! So when he made this argument to the jury—along with all of his others—*he knew that this argument, too, was a lie!*

— CHAPTER 12 —

AMERICA: GOING DOWN THE ECONOMIC DRAIN

I have accumulated many magazine and newspaper articles, and other economic data that I intended to use in this part of the book. Due to my imprisonment, however, I am forced to treat the topic in a far more general and condensed manner than I had hoped. What all this material points to is that America is no longer the world's preeminent industrial and financial nation. In fact, we are far from it—we are now the world's largest debtor. This data also reveals that while the standards of living in most other industrialized nations are rising, America's standard of living is falling.

This is something that any semi-conscious American should be able to conclude just by walking around with his eyes open, without supporting data from me. However, many Americans still perceive America in terms of its former greatness; when the manufactured goods that once flowed in abundance from our factories were regarded as the world's best, and when Americans enjoyed a standard of living second to none. Today, however, these factories are closed. Meanwhile, thousands of American servicemen are being discharged in Germany and *staying there*, because Germany's standard of living is now higher than our own! Yet not that long ago, when I was stationed there in 1950, Germans were still picking up cigarette butts from the gutter that American G.I.'s had thrown away. Most Americans also refuse to grasp the amazing significance that Japan, a nation with a mere fraction of our resources, *has now become richer than the United States!* Thirty years ago Americans would have regarded the likelihood of that happening as equivalent to a Martian takeover by 1989!

America's slide from riches to rags should be apparent from a variety of circumstances, all of which contradict the nation's historic economic and financial experience. Unfortunately, most Americans view these recent developments as unrelated aberrations. They are, however, all manifestations of the same syndrome—the **economic destruction** that has been brought about by an **ever expanding government, fueled by its ability to illegally extract income taxes.** Let us briefly touch upon some of these symptoms that not only contradict all of our earlier economic experiences, but also run contrary to what is happening in most other industrialized nations.

(1) **The rising tide of homelessness in America.** This phenomenon, which has reached the flood stage, did not happen even when millions of penniless immigrants were pouring into America at the turn of the century. Nor did it occur *even* in the depths of the "depression."

(2) **America's horrendous $150 billion trade deficit.** This massive turnaround in America's former position as the world's leading industrial nation is indicative that the average American now *consumes* more than he *produces*. America is foolishly seeking to paper over this disparity by selling off its real estate and businesses, and by going deeper into national debt. But what happens when we have no more businesses to sell and the world refuses to give us more credit?

(3) **The $150 billion savings and loan loss.** This banking loss is five times greater than what the nation experienced during our "terrible" depression, and which created the "need" for more federal control over our banking system and FDIC "insurance." However, during the period 1928-1932, actual bank losses only amounted to $1.7 billion, and even adjusting for our .05¢ dollar, would only make the comparable loss $35 billion—or one-fourth of what the nation has *currently sustained!*

In addition, Americans have been conned into believing that their bank deposits are actually "insured" by the government. In reality, the government does not have a dime in any such insurance. All "premiums" paid in for this "insurance" are spent by the government as fast as they come in. The government then gives itself I.O.U.'s (which it calls government bonds—but which are nothing more than journal entries) for the "premiums" it now spends, and claims that these "bonds" (journal entries) represent trust fund "assets." The only way these so-called "bonds" can be used to pay off defaulted debts would be for the government to tax the public *again* to get the money to redeem the "bonds" it claims it holds! In reality, any major banking default (which is inevitable) or "run," could only be met by the government **revving up its presses!** The government will, therefore, "pay off" on its promises all right: the only question is **WHAT WILL THAT MONEY BE WORTH?**

(4) **The ever increasing percentage of women in America's work force is, itself, proof of the nation's falling standard of living.** Now that it has become virtually impossible for the average American husband to support his family on his *after tax* income, increasing numbers of women are compelled to seek work outside the home. Instead of honestly attributing this phenomenon to America's deteriorating economic situation, and candidly facing the host of other social problems this condition is causing (such as those stemming from the increased lack of juvenile supervision), know-nothing social critics and government economists attribute this trend to women's lib and the simple desire of American families to acquire luxuries. Granted, there are large numbers of women who prefer working to staying at home, but there are far more who would prefer to stay at home if they had the choice—especially those who have small children. Yet 50 percent of such mothers now *have to work.* Consequently, we hear cries about America's lack of daycare centers, when the cry

should be, why should America need day care centers at all? Why didn't we need them 40 years ago? Because 40 years ago the average American housewife didn't have to work to help meet the mortgage payments, car payments, insurance, clothing, electric, and food bills.

In 1948, for example, an American worker could buy a new home in Levittown, New York for $7,800. The same house today probably costs $175,000. When it was purchased in 1948 (for a few hundred dollars down and a 4 percent mortgage), mortgage payments, taxes and insurance probably didn't total $75.00 per month. These expenses today (assuming the buyer could raise the $25,000 down payment) would probably be upwards of $2,000 a month. So, while one working parent could have easily afforded that house in 1948, how many could do so today? In many cases, home ownership is even beyond the reach of two hard-working parents. I hear the trend in California is for two families to buy a home and share the kitchen and living room. Yet for years, government economists have been telling us that all our economic indicators are going up!

(5) **The increasing ownership by foreign nationals of substantial segments of the American economy.** As American assets flow with accelerating speed into foreign hands, American politicians assure us that this is merely indicative of the "confidence" that foreign "investors" have in the American economy. Horsefeathers.

What we are witnessing (and they say that Nero fiddled while Rome burned!) is a massive transfer of American wealth to foreign hands. This represents a **dramatic turnaround** in the relationship that has existed between Americans and the rest of the world for most of the 20th Century. As far as it being indicative of foreign "confidence" in the American economy, foreigners have always had confidence in the American economy (and to a far greater extent *before* rather than now!) so why didn't all of this foreign buying occur before? The reason is that not until about 1980 did foreigners generally become rich enough (and Americans poor enough, by comparison) to **outbid Americans for our own assets!**

As it now stands, about 10 percent of all Americans who work in factories do so in foreign-owned factories; while 20 percent of the prime real estate in New York City is foreign

owned, along with 20 percent of Washington, D.C., 30 percent of Dallas, 45 percent of Los Angeles, and virtually all of Hawaii. Four of the top six "American" tire companies are now foreign owned along with CBS Records and Columbia Pictures. I suppose that not until Japanese businessmen buy the Empire State Building, the World Trade Center, and IBM will Americans wake up as to what is happening.

Unfortunately, the time factor and my imprisonment prevented me from covering this subject more fully. I was prepared to treat it also in terms of America's deteriorating infrastructure, the projected costs of cleaning up our toxic wastes, and repairing the nation's crumbling highways, and the drug problem. The nation's tragic drug situation is also directly related to deteriorating economic conditions **brought about by government.** The federal government will never solve this problem because it is its **principal cause!**[1]

I also believe that the coming 1992 integration of the European Common Market and the increasing wealth and prosperity it will generate there, coupled with Europe's declining need for American military protection, (as the communist world disintegrates), will cause it to no longer humor us by accepting America's irredeemable paper "dollars" as a reserve currency. You can be sure that a wealthier and financially more powerful Europe will want a *respectable* reserve currency,[2] and will no doubt develop one of its own. When that occurs, America will be expected to pay for its imports in either goods or a convertible currency, just like everybody else. At which point, I expect, the United States economy will go into a free fall that will, by comparison, make our immediate economic history look like raging prosperity.

It is clear that America's changing fortune is the direct result of the 1943 imposition of withholding taxes as a "temporary" World War II "Victory" tax. Prior to that time, the superiority of the American standard of living and productive power relative to the rest of the world **was overwhelming.** Today, it is non-existant! Tragically, most Americans are not even aware of this change in the nation's fortunes, why it happened, and the direction in which America is now heading. **America better wake up fast,** before it's too late—IF IT'S NOT TOO LATE ALREADY!

NOTES TO CHAPTER 12

1. How the federal government is directly responsible for America's falling standard of living is covered **IN DEPTH** in my first book, *The Biggest Con: How the Goverment Is Fleecing You,* and in a cartoon book (so even a child of 10 can understand it) entitled, *How An Economy Grows and Why It Doesn't,* and I recommend both books to you. In addition, various phases of how the income tax has contributed to America's falling standard of living (and how the tax can be replaced) has been covered in one form or another in all of my previous books on taxes, which I also recommend to you.

2. All talk about a "resurging" and "strengthening" dollar is like talking about a midget "resurging" and "strengthening" against Mike Tyson. The real strength of a currency is shown by its internal interest rates and what a government has to pay to borrow money. Interest rates in Germany and Japan are about one-third of what they are here; thirty or forty years ago it was *the other way around.* During the 1930s, for example, the United States Government could borrow money for one-half a percent and *lower.* Now it must pay twelve times that amount. If interest rates were ever lowered here to what they are in Germany and Japan, American prices would go through the roof and the dollar would become practically worthless— thus finally bringing its realistic market value in line with its intrinsic (and illegal) character.

When interest rates were *lower* in America than *anyplace* else in the world, American manufacturers enjoyed a *substantial comparative advantage* in their capital costs—so they could afford to pay American workers *higher wages* **and still be competitive.** Now that American manufacturers *must pay higher interest rates* than manufacturers in most other industrialized nations, **they must pay lower wages—to stay competitive—or go out of business!** So this is yet another way by which an irresponsible government *has forced a lower standard of living* on this nation. It has been Congress's *willingness* to use inflation to finance its continuing *deficits* that has *driven up interest rates—***which must now drive down wages.**

— EPILOGUE —

"The power to tax involves the power to destroy."

—Chief Justice John Marshall
McCulloch v. Maryland, **(1819)**

As I begin re-writing this Epilogue, it is December 9, 1989, and I have been illegally incarcerated for four months. Because I believed that the material already covered in this book warranted immediate release, even if it was not flawlessly presented, I had reserved "press time" to have it printed by November 1, 1989. As you can see, I am way behind schedule. My original version of the Epilogue, completed in October, has mysteriously been "lost."[1] In addition to re-writing it from the notes and rough drafts I still have, I will also bring you up to date on my civil litigation and current incarceration. People have been calling my answering service daily to seek the help I can no longer provide. This book, even if less complete than I would have preferred, should be able to supply that help and provide considerable help to others being illegally harassed and pressured by the IRS or getting zapped in our courts.

The "mafia" has kept me locked up for as long as it could, and I am now waiting to be released. I fear, however, that this same "mafia" will immediately seek to illegally reincarcerate me for allegedly violating conditions of probation, just as they have illegally incarcerated me for allegedly violating conditions of my parole (even though they still contend that I have been serving probation and parole simultaneously).

Figure E-1 is a copy of a certified letter I received today from Robert A. Pisker of the IRS. Note that it threatens to use the non-payment of my 1980, 1981 and 1982 income taxes (an admittedly "civil matter") as a basis for violating me while on probation. This would then make the *third* time the government would have used the non-payment of these taxes as the basis for incarcerating me (See my reply, Figure E-2). Remember, such charges would not have to be legal,

---

FIGURE E-1

```
Internal Revenue Service          Department of the Treasury
District Director                 Group 1214 - 4th Floor
                                  936 Silas Deane Hwy.
                                  Wethersfield, CT  06109


                                  Person to Contact: Robert G. Pisker

Federal Correctional Institution  Telephone Number: 258-2045
Morgantown, West Virginia  26505
                                  Date:  November 28, 1989
Attention: Mr. Irwin A. Schiff
           #08537-014


Dear Mr. Schiff:

As we have advised you in the past, this office is responsible for resolving
the civil aspects of your Federal Income Tax matters for years ending December
31, 1980, 1981, and 1982.  Your Judgement and Probation/Commitment Order dated
December 18, 1985 included Special Conditions Of Probation which state in part
that you "shall remain current insofar as all legally required tax payments
with reasonable and good faith compliance and shall file all returns required
by the tax laws".

Various records in our possession indicate that your Federal Income Tax and
Penalty liabilities are $57,850.00, $13,683.00, and $118,558.00, for the years
1980, 1981, and 1982, respectively.  We expect that you will make
arrangements to pay these liabilities, and file Returns in accordance with the
above referenced Probation Conditions.  Also, we have no record of any Federal
Income Tax Returns filed by you for years 1983 through 1988; these returns
should be filed as well.

You may file returns or make payments for each of the years 1980 through 1988
by mailing them to my attention at the above address.  Also, please contact
me at the telephone number or address shown above if you would like to
discuss these matters further.


                         Sincerely,


                         ROBERT G PISKER
                         Group Manager
```

FIGURE E-2

IRWIN A. SCHIFF
08537-014
MORGANTOWN, W.V. 26507-9003

December 9, 1989

Robert G. Pisker, Group Manager
Internal Revenue Service
Group 1214 - 4th Floor
936 Silas Deane Hwy.
Wethersfield, Ct. 06109

Dear Mr. Pisker:

I am writing this in response to your letter of November 28, 1989, which was received here on December 8, 1989. Although your letter clearly identifies the issues involved as being "civil" in nature, you, nevertheless, clearly threaten me with imprisonment (presumably as a probation violation), if I supposedly fail to attend to the "Civil aspects of [my] Federal Income Tax matters for years ending December 31, 1979, 1980, 1981 and 1982." Therefore, despite the clearly extortionary character of your letter (and for reasons that will soon be apparent), I shall address all of the issues you raise, so there will be no doubt as to its criminal intent and character.

First of all, your letter needlessly warns me concerning some apparently new conditions of which I should supposedly be made aware -- namely conditions of probation. This is to inform you that I was "released to probation" on August 8, 1988 -- see Asst. U.S. Attorney Raymond M. Hasset's motion for installment payments of my court costs dated March 3, 1988 and Judge Dorsey's ruling of April 7, 1989 in which he stated that my "Probation (and thus all conditions of same) became effective on [my] release from physical custody." This is further confirmed by the attached letter from the Parole Commission stating that my "Parole and probation [have been] running concurrently." (Emphasis added) So what purpose is your letter intended to serve?

In addition, I was incarcerated for 20 months for allegedly failing to file returns and pay income taxes for the years 1980-1983, and was released to probation for allegedly committing that "crime" on August 8, 1988. However a year later, on Agust 8, 1989 I was incarcerated for a second time for allegedly committing the same offense. This second imprisonment was predicated on the basis that I had presumably committed the "crime" again --but this time as a parole violation. This occurred even though I had been assured by Judge Dorsey and Asst. U.S. Attorney Hasset that I was on probation, not parole! Now you threaten me with imprisonment for a third time for allegedly committing the same offense -- as an alleged probation violation! So, subjecting me to double jeopardy was not quite enough -- you mean to inflict triple jeopardy!!! Just how many times can the Federal government imprison someone for allegedly committing the same offense?

In addition, you state that, "Various records in our possession indicate that your Federal Income Tax and Penalty liabilities ..." total some 189 thousand dollars for the years 1980-1982. Why is it that none of the "various records" to which you refer have ever been sent to me? I have never even received a Deficiency Notice for any of these years, let alone a notice and demand for payment! Suffice it to say that the alleged "liabilities" are totally erroneous, so I would appreciate your sending me a valid Deficiency Notice so that I can file my petition to Tax Court and litigate the issue in the proper legal forum.

- 2 -

Since you apparently occupy a postion of some authority at the IRS, how could you not know that I had no legal obligation to pay any of the amounts to which your letter refers, until the Tax Court had an opportunity to rule on the matter? For your further edification I recommend you read the court's ruling of September 6, 1989 (Schiff v. U.S.A., Civil No. N-86-354 (WWE)) in which Judge Eginton ruled that I have "The right to petition Tax Court and contest the Commissioner's determination prior to the payment of any taxes." (Emphasis added). Therefore, based upon this Connecticut District Court ruling alone (though its substance should have been known to you) -- your letter is extortionary on its very face.

The last year for which the Commissioner has sent me a Deficiency Notice was 1979, and that year is currently under litigation in Tax Court. So instead of seeking to extort funds from me (which I don't have anyway) by threatening me with imprisonment for the non-payment of alleged civil tax liabilities which have never been judicially determined by any court of competent jurisdiction, I suggest that you and your colleagues at the IRS get busy and prepare and send to me valid Deficiency Notices for any year which you claim I have outstanding tax "liabilities" -- I will then take it from there.

In addition, while I don't even regard income tax returns as falling within the conditions of my Judgment and Commitment Order (since such returns are not "legally required," and if you think otherwise, I would appreciate your quoting for me the Code section that says so), I have, nevertheless, filed within the last 30 days income tax returns for the years 1980 through 1988. These returns correctly show my tax "liabilities" for those years, and I suggest that you check around the office and find them.

And further, since your letter refers to my alleged tax "liabilities," you failed to cite the Code section in which such "liabilities" are presumably established - therefore, I am requesting that you do so by return mail.

And, in conclusion, since I doubt that you acted alone in sending me an extortionary letter under color of law, I am sending a copy of your letter to the Attorney General for investigation of possible violations of 26 U.S.C. 7214(a)(1) and (2) and Sections 241 and 242 of the U.S. Criminal Code.

Yours truly,

Irwin A. Schiff

CC Mr. Richard Thornburg, Attorney General
    United States of America
    Main Justice Building
    10th Street & Constitution Ave., N.W.
    Washington, D.C. 20530

* This is not intended to imply that the Internal Revenue Code establishes an income tax "liability" even after a Tax Court ruling.

or even rational, since whom do I have to complain to? Once the "mafia" closes ranks, it can hold you for as long as it wants, and for whatever reason it wants to. This being the case, I am going to have to complete this Epilogue in a hurried fashion and may have to leave some material for later editions. Before I turn to my civil litigation, let me bring you up to date on what has transpired as a result of my alleged parole violations.

After being arrested on August 8, 1989, I was supposed to have a preliminary hearing within 30 days for the purpose of determining whether or not there was a "probable cause" for my arrest. If none were found, the Code of Federal Regulations (CFR 28-2.48(d)(1)) provides that, "A decision to release the parolee shall be implemented without delay." If "probable cause" is found, a final revocation hearing is held within 90 days. It is also important to understand that an alleged parole violator is not even required to be incarcerated while his alleged violations are being investigated, if "In the opinion of the Regional Commissioner, incarceration ... is not warranted by the frequency or seriousness of the alleged violations, the parolee is not likely to fail to appear for revocation proceedings, and the parolee does not constitute a danger to himself and others." (CFR 28-2.44-02). In addition, Section 2.44-03(b) recommends that "The warrant application be limited to *convictions* and to administrative charges if, sustained, indicate a *substantial infraction* of the conditions of release," (emphasis added). Thus, on the basis of these criteria alone, there was no reason to arrest *or* incarcerate me before the charges against me were proven!

The problem with preliminary hearings, however, is that they are conducted by other probation officers. In other words, Probation Officer "A" conducts the hearings of those who Probation Officer "B" violates, while Probation Officer "B" conducts the hearings of those who Probation Officer "A" violates. This being the case, what is the likelihood of either "A" or "B" *not* finding "probable cause" for each other's violations? In any event, I wanted Probation Officer Walsh's presence and testimony at my hearing, but was told that he was on vacation and would not be available until after Labor Day, and I would have to waive my right to a 30-day hearing if I wanted him there. (In retrospect, I now realize that should not have been necessary). So, in order to insure Walsh's appearance, I waived my right to a 30-day preliminary hearing.

At the hearing I had an opportunity to read the four-page memorandum signed by Walsh (but submitted by Ralph K. Kistner, Chief U.S. Probation Officer, and approved by James M. Fox, Supervising U.S. Probation Officer) which, allegedly, had served as the basis for my arrest and incarceration. The memorandum was a rambling collection of lies and fraudulent representation, which simply does not merit the time and space necessary to include here, nor would such an analysis serve any useful purpose. Suffice it to say that it revealed Walsh to be a reprobate rogue, with as much business being a probation officer as he would have being a brain surgeon. It also reveals that Supervisory Probation Officers Kistner and Fox will apparently approve anything put in front of them. So much, therefore, for the checks and balances supposedly built into the parole and probation systems.

I had engaged a law firm specializing in post-conviction law to represent me in this matter. An attorney from the firm had an oportunity to question Walsh, concerning his prior claims that my conditions of probation were in effect. Under his questions, a formerly cocky Walsh now squirmed and faltered as he sought to explain, in a voice that was barely audible, that my conditions of probation "really would not go into effect" until I had finished my parole— thus admitting that all of his previous claims were outright lies.

In any case, I did not get the formal results of Wilson's findings (his report to the Parole Commission) until four weeks later. Wilson refused to send his report directly to my attorney, thus further hampering our ability to deal with it. Wilson announced at the conclusion of my preliminary hearing that he would *not* find "probable cause" on the charges involving Fred White, but would find "probable cause" on the others. This of course, was after it had been clearly pointed out to him that: (1) filing and paying income taxes *were not even* conditions of my parole, and (2) violating me on these grounds would itself violate the Fifth Amendment prohibition against double jeopardy, since I had already gone to jail for these "offenses." Wilson, however, had obviously been instructed to find probable cause on *something,* so he did.

Between my arrest on August 8 and my preliminary hearing on September 21, 1989, I was bussed back and forth between the Metropolitan Correctional Center (MCC) in Manhattan and the Federal Correctional Institute (FCI) in Otisville, New York, *four times* before finally being bussed to FCI Morgantown with a one-week layover at K-Dorm in Lewisburg Penitentiary.

"DIESEL THERAPY" OR THE "MERRY-GO-ROUND"

Federal prisoners are generally moved from one correctional facility to another by prison bus, though the Bureau of Prisons occasionally uses airplanes which, I understand, the Government took from drug dealers. Occasionally for short trips, automobiles or vans are used, but most transfers are made by bus. The buses have barred windows and caged interiors in which prisoners sit, shackled hand and foot, with hands further shackled to chains girding their waists.

You discover you are being transferred when told by a correctional officer (CO), "You have 15 minutes to get your stuff (consisting largely of personal grooming articles, gym clothes, a radio, books, letters and legal files) over to R&D." At R&D (Receiving and Discharge), CO's put it into cardboard boxes and generally give you a receipt, accounting for each item. Prisoners then seal the boxes with tape and write their name, inmate number and ultimate destination on each side of the box with a black marking pen. The property is then sent by certified mail to that destination, or in some cases, it might accompany you on the bus, if the trip is direct, which is unlikely.

Before leaving the institution, inmates turn in all of their institutional clothing, and after a thorough body search, they will be issued a light pair of khaki pants, a tee shirt and a pair of blue and white slipper-like sneakers to travel in. At the next institution, which might only be a temporary one along the way, the shackles are removed and traveling clothes will be turned in. After another body search they will get into a brown jumpsuit which they select from a shelf, bin, or a pile on the floor. They are then fingerprinted, photographed and given two short interviews. One covers their medical history and the other is designed to see whether they might be in any danger from other inmates in that institution, because they might have testified against someone, or because they might have been a former cop, prosecutor or judge who might have had something to do with putting someone in there.

Inmates are then usually given a box breakfast and/or lunch to replace any meals they might miss while traveling. The breakfasts will generally consist of a box of corn flakes, a container of milk, a hard boiled egg or two, and maybe an orange. Lunches will *always* consist of two sandwiches— one cheese and one bologna, a container of milk, two sugar cookies, and maybe an apple.

While each step in the processing procedure takes only a few minutes, inmates spend endless hours just sitting in "bull pens" waiting to get through it. For example: in going from MCC New York to FCI Otisville, New York, I was awakened at 2 a.m. to begin processing, even though I had turned in all my property five hours earlier. We did not leave New York, however, until 5 a.m., and even though we arrived at Otisville about 7 a.m., we did not finish processing until 3 p.m. With the exception of the two hour bus ride and 20 minutes of actual processing time, 36 prisoners and I spent most of those extra 13 hours standing or lying on the floor of the various "bull pens" we were shuttled in and out of. To avoid the boredom of waiting, prisoners lucky enough to be able to do so, would sleep. Since there was never enough bench space in the various "bull pens" we were kept in, prisoners would try to sleep on the floor, using sneakers and empty milk containers as pillows. In one 6x9-foot "bull pen" there was not even enough space to accomodate those who wanted to sleep on the floor, so they took turns lying, sitting or standing.

Prisoners are not generally sent directly to their final destination, but go from one penal institution to another until they finally arrive where they are supposed to. They will wait at those interim institutions as "holdovers" until enough prisoners are assembled to warrant sending a bus to *another* institution along the way. In this manner, prisoners can wait weeks or even months before being moved further on toward their final destination. On this basis it can take a prisoner six months or more to finally arrive at his assigned institution. When he finally does arrive there, he might be assigned somewhere else and so starts the merry-go-round again.

"Holdovers" are not integrated into the general population of inmates. Most federal prisoners, other than those in the highest security levels, have a fair degree of relative freedom and opportunity for movement, even taking into consideration the differences that exist among higher level institutions. In most federal institutions, for example, prisoners generally work a five-day week which starts at 7:30 a.m. and ends about 4 p.m. They might work in landscaping, at the motor pool, in food service, construction, laundry, work as electricians, carpenters, plumbers, teachers, orderlies, or as production workers in prison industries. Besides providing prisoners with an opportunity to earn money to send to their families or spend in prison commissaries, it offers the opportunity to learn skills, to socialize, and for many, to avoid boredom. Prisoners will be excused from work to attend such daytime classes as English, math, typing, computer, drafting, welding, and such other courses as might be available. In their off hours (usually until 8 or 9 p.m.), prisoners can work out in the gym or in the "yard," participate in intramural sports, pursue hobbies such as leathercraft, pottery, painting, or attend various self-help groups. They can also pursue litigation in the law library, attend religious services in the chapel and have visitors. *None* of these activities are available to "holdovers." For one thing, "holdovers" have no personal property, including legal files and address books, which have all been sent to their *final* destination. Their access to a telephone is also sharply reduced, and without phone and address books, they can only call or write those whose numbers and addresses they have memorized. Prison phones do not have access to telephone information services.

Because a prisoner is not given advance notice of when he is being moved or where he is going, suddenly his family and attorney will stop hearing from him. This lack of advance information, we are told, is to prevent any possibility that others will attempt to free a prisoner while he is in transit and outside of institutional enclosures.

The point is that the federal government, in many cases, deliberately transfers prisoners to distant locations as a form of punishment, and to encourage certain prisoners to "cooperate" in providing the government with information it wants. It is also used to substantially reduce a prisoner's ability to pursue litigation and contact the media. Since this form of third degree and incommunicado, also known as "diesel therapy" is abused by the Bureau of Prisons, its ability to administer this form of punishment should be drastically curtailed. And, to the ACLU: Where were you on this?

MY REVOCATION HEARINGS— AND HOW THE PAROLE COMMISSION DISREGARDED THEM

I arrived at FCI Morgantown on Friday, October 27, 1989. Because my prison file had not yet arrived, I was put in "administrative detention," i.e., solitary confinement, and was not released into "population" until Monday, October 30. I spent the weekend locked up, frustrated because I had looked forward to having the weekend to prepare for my forthcoming hearing, work on this book, and make some phone calls. I also discovered, upon my release from solitary, that my three boxes of personal property sent from FCI Otisville had not yet arrived. Among other things, they contained my complete file on my violation and a number of supporting documents that I needed to support my testimony at the hearing. Fortunately I had sent some of this material to my attorney. Had I not engaged one, I would have walked into the hearing devoid of any supporting documents.

My revocation hearing was held on November 1, 1989, two days after my release from solitary, by Hearing Examiners William Tenney and James Rogers. After a discussion of the charges and my reply, the panel asked us to leave the room so they could consider their decision. When we returned, we were informed that the panel had concluded that I had *not* violated the terms of my parole and that it would recommend my *immediate release*. The proof for this was so overwhelming, that short of standing law and logic completely on their heads, no other decision was possible. The panel reminded us, however, that the final word rested with the Regional Commissioner, Mr. Daniel Lopez, who would have 21 days to notify us of his decision. A week or so later, I asked Mary Lou Lindquist, my case manager at Morgantown (who had attended the hearing),

how long it normally took to get released following a recommendation for "immediate release." Mary Lou replied, "I don't know. In the three years I have been attending revocation hearings, I have never seen anything like this happen before." What she meant was, that by the time an alleged violation reaches the revocation hearing stage, the only issues that normally remain to be resolved are how much "street time" might be forfeited and how many additional months of jail time the examiners would recommend. Mary Lou had never seen what amounted to a dismissal of the original charges, and recommendation for immediate release at the revocation hearing level.

Basically, the Parole Panel's finding meant that there was no legal basis for my arrest and for the 85 days I had already spent incarcerated. Obviously the civil liability implications of this would not be lost on the Commissioner. I had to wait 28 days before getting his 21 day Notice of Action. When it finally came from the Northeast Regional Commissioner, this is what it said:

Void hearing of November 1, 1989 and remand to institution for rehearing on December 7, 1989...

A back dated supplemental warrant accompanied the Notice, which supposedly furnished a basis for my continued incarceration, because the hearing panel's decision had demonstrated that there never was any. The supplemental warrant stated:

On or about 12/18/85...subject was ordered to pay the cost of prosecution regarding his conviction of 10/25/85...the costs assessed were $27,405.98. Since his release on parole on 8/8/88, subject has willfully refused to pay the Court-imposed obligation. Information contained in letter dated 6/28/89 by USPO Walsh.

CAN YOU BELIEVE IT! Overlooking the fact that there is nothing in the law or in the regulations which grant the Commissioner with authority to "void" revocation hearings he doesn't like, I was being violated for not paying costs which had been under continuous litigation since March 3, 1989, (See Raymond Hasset's Motion for Civil Examination, Figure 10-9, Chapter 10) and which, as of the date of my arrest, was *still* unresolved! It was only after I had received the Supplemental Warrant, that I discovered that on August 28, 1989 (just three weeks after my arrest), Magistrate Margolis had ruled on the government's motion for installment payments. She had ordered me to make monthly payments of $323.88, with the first installment not becoming due until Sept. 11, 1989. In preparation for my second revocation hearing, my attorney called Judge Dorsey's chambers to inquire about the status of that litigation and was told of Magistrate Margolis's decision and order. Because it had been sent to my New York address, I had never been aware of it. Magistrate Margolis's decision itself reveals the utter speciousness of Commissioner Lopez's accusation. Based upon a full blown court investigation, it had already been judicially determined that I did not possess the funds to pay what Commissioner Lopez now accused me of "willfully refusing" to pay! In addition, why should I have paid *anything* before the court had an opportunity to rule?

ZERO INCOME RETURNS

Despite all of the above, something good actually came out of that hearing! During the course of it, one of the examiners commented on the fact that he believed I had been violated *for the wrong years!* Since I had already been punished for failing to file and pay for the years cited in the warrant (he even commented on the double jeopardy character of the warrant!), he thought that I should have been violated for some *other* year and proceeded to question me on whether or not I had filed for 1983 and 1984! However, my lawyer quickly pointed out that he had no authority to question me about those years, so he stopped that line of questioning. However, because of his questioning, it became clear that if I were to beat these charges, the Parole Commission might quickly violate me for those years! It was my attorney's view that if I did not file for those years, I would be exposing myself to additional parole violations as well as probation violations and he urged me to file for all of those years as quickly as possible. This I did, and so was able to write in my leter to Robert G. Pisker (Figure E-2) that I had filed all of my returns for the years 1980 through 1988. In filing them, however, I only showed "0.00" (zero) income, "0.00" (zero) expenses, and "0.00" (zero) taxes due. In every other way I provided the government with the usual information, such as my address, social security number, excemptions, deductions, etc. Along with these returns (which I had to create, since I didn't have official ones for any of those years), I included two attachments. One was a statement which pointed out that I was filing each return upon the advise of my attorney to avoid possible future incarceration. This clearly established that these returns were *not* filed voluntarily.

Secondly, I appended to each return, Figure 3-7 (Chapter 3), which shows all four "dummy returns" which were treated as lawful returns by the IRS and Judge Eginton, and explained that if those unsigned blank "dummies" were valid returns, than certainly mine—signed under penalty of perjury and containing information from which a tax could be computed—were too. Filing such "zero income returns" would apear to have the following advantages over not filing at all:

(1) You can't be charged with failing to file a return. (At least, I wouldn't think so, but anything is possible in federal court.) When individuals filed Fifth Amendment returns, they were charged with "failure to file," because the courts ruled (erroneously) that they hadn't filed a return "from

which a tax could be computed." (This, of course, would clearly establish "dummy returns" as being invalid—but who said the federal courts had to be consistent?) But a "zero income return" contains information from which a tax *can* be computed—the tax being zero.

(2) With respect to the risk (since you sign the return under penalty of perjury) of being charged with tax evasion or swearing falsely on the return; for one thing, you would *not* have sworn falsely because no one earns "income" within the meaning of our tax laws. "Income" for the purpose of federal income taxes *means* a corporate profit. This was already explained in earlier chapters, but a more detailed explanation is provided in *The Great Income Tax Hoax,* and I would hope that anyone doing this would be totally familiar with this concept. Even if the government should try to use the statement and document against you, you should be able to prevent it, since you will be able to show that the return was *not* submitted voluntarily—but was filed so as to protect you from possible criminal prosecution. Attached to your return you should append a statement along the following lines:

> While I do not believe that the law requires me to file an income tax return, I have filed one anyway, out of fear that if I did not, the U.S. Department of Justice would prosecute me for failing to file an income tax return for the year _____ pursuant to 26 U.S.C. 7203, or charge me with income tax evasion for that year, pursuant to 7201, or charge me with violating some statute that I do not even know about. Thus, this return is *not being filed voluntarily.*

I believe that this statement, attached to your "zero income return" would prevent the government from ever being able to use the document against you. But again, this assumes that the "mafia" obeys the law. So, "you pays your money, and you takes your chances."

(3) A "zero income return" will shorten the statute of limitations for the year in question. When you file a return, the government has only three years (absent proof of fraud) to contest it. When you don't file at all, they have six years. That was why I had a shorter statute of limitation for 1976 (as opposed to the years 1977 and 1978) even though I filed a Fifth Amendment return.

(4) While I formerly believed that by filing a "zero income return" one would have self-assessed, thus enabling the IRS to legally (using that term loosely) make supplemental assessments; I have now concluded that this is not so. The IRS can not lawfully assess a zero, and I doubt that it could ever produce a Form 23C showing a zero assessment. Section 6203 only provides the Secretary with authority "for recording the liability of the taxpayer." Even if there were such a thing as an income tax "liablity," a zero would not be "recording" it. That would only be the "recording" of an *absence* of liability!

For more information on "zero income returns," see Figure A-9, pages 274, 275.

MY SECOND REVOCATION "HEARING"

Normally, parole hearings are conducted according to fixed schedules at each penal institution, with examiners staying a week or so, in order to hear parole matters affecting many inmates. In this case the hearing examiners were coming to Morgantown *just for me!* Instead of having two examiners, this time only William Tenney made the trip. Since the Parole Commission (on instruction from above) had already determined what the verdict would be, why pay the travel expenses for two examiners? Following the same procedures used at my first hearing, my attorney and I were asked to leave the room while Tenney contemplated his decision. When we returned he informed us that he found me guilty as charged in the supplemental warrant, but, "Since this is only a technical violation, you will not lose any street time," and "you will still be eligible for immediate release," (or words to that effect).[2]

Although Tenney pointed out that while I would still be eligible for "immediate release," he reminded me once again that the "final decision" would have to come from the Regional Commissioner and that he could take "twenty-one days to respond." Since there was no lawful way that the Commissioner could take away enough street time to hold me for even another day, and overlooking why Tenney's guilty finding was contrary to *both* the law and the facts, my attorney reminded him that I had already been incarcerated for over a month since my first revocation hearing and there should be no reason why the Commissioner had to take *another* 21 days to order my immediate release. Tenney agreed, and said that he would try to have Morgantown contacted the next day.

TENNEY'S FINDING: ILLEGAL ON ITS FACE

Unfolding events were to prove that my arrest, incarceration, and the hearings themselves had been even more illegal than I had suspected or have written about so far. I will, therefore, cover them more fully, so as to eliminate *any* possible doubt that America, indeed, has *criminals implementing its criminal justice system.*

The law governing how hearing officers are to judge the evidence presented at revocation hearings is covered in 28 CFR 2.50-01, which states as follows:

> A primary illustration of the difference between a criminal trial and a revocation hearing is that in a criminal trial, a conviction may be obtained only if the Government proves its case beyond a reasonable doubt. In a revocation hearing, the panel need only find that a violation is shown by a preponderance of the evidence [18 U.S.C. 4214(d)]. This simply means that the weight of all the evidence before the panel must be toward showing a violation.

Thus it is clear that in finding that I had "willfully refused" to pay $27,405.98 of courts costs, William Tenney had broken the law (as it is contained above), which he, of course, had been instructed to do by his superiors at the Parole Commission, who had also been told by their superiors in the Justice Department to do the same.

There was, of course, no evidence presented at that "hearing" that I had "willfully refused" to pay $27,405.98 of court costs as Tenney ruled, while *all* of the evidence (and not just a preponderance of it) pointed the other way! To be legally culpable of "willfully refusing" to pay the amount charged in the supplemental warrant ($27,405.98), Tenney would have had to have evidence of the following with respect to that amount:

(1) That I had the ability and means to pay it;
(2) That I believed I had a duty to pay it, and
(3) That I had no justifiable excuse for not paying it.[4]

UPDATE, Second Edition: After the first edition of this book was printed, I discovered that William Tenney had actually reported to the Parole Commission that he did not find "willfulness" present. Thus, his report actually established that no violation had occurred.[3]

For example: We provided documents showing that I did not have the money to pay even a *fraction* of the amount claimed, let alone the entire amount. These included sworn financial documents that I had prepared while I was still incarcerated, and which were designed to show that I couldn't pay the $30,000 committed fine; my monthly parole reports, which showed that I was some $50,000 in debt and not even earning enough to cover my current living expenses; the recent decisions of *two* federal courts allowing me to preceed in *forma pauperis* on two appeals; and Magistrate Margolis's recent decision in which she had determined, based upon the court's examination of the facts that I could pay only a tiny fraction of the court costs.

In contrast to this, Tenney could not produce a single document to sustain a belief that I had the ability and means to pay the amount claimed, without which there was not even a basis for suggesting that "willfulness" existed. But we didn't stop there. I also produced documents that clearly revealed that I didn't even *believe* I had a duty to pay these costs as a condition of parole. One such document was a letter I had sent to Kathleen Pinner (and she was the one who *signed* my warrant application!) in which I stated that:

(1) "There was no provision that my parole was also contingent upon my paying the costs of my prosecution," and

(2) "Even in Patrick L. Walsh's recommended modification of the terms of my parole ... no recommendation was made that payment of $27,205.88 of the costs of prosecution be added as a condition of my parole."

This is the letter that drew her response (as shown in Figure E-3). Note that she doesn't correct my false impression by informing me that the payment of these costs is a condition of my parole, but claims that my "parole and probation" are running "concurrently," thereby seeking to justify the court's investigation of my ability to pay these costs as a condition of probation! So why should I have believed that the payment of these costs was a condition of parole and not a condition of probation? And because a federal court was already investigating my ability to pay these costs, I certainly had a perfectly justifiable excuse for not paying them, until the court rendered its decision—which, as of the time of my violation it had not done! If there ever was a showing of a *lack* of "willfulness," this was it!

What, therefore, was Tenney's basis for ruling that I had "willfully refused" to pay these court costs? It rested solely on a claim of Patrick J. Walsh that was contained in the following paragraph of his letter to the Commissioner of 6/28/89, in which he wrote:

On May 11, 1988 Schiff filed a habeas action. On December 7, 1988 a hearing was held and his request was denied on May 15, 1989. On April 13, 1989, Schiff was directed by his parole officer to begin payment of all taxes owed and all court costs. He denied that he owed any taxes and refused to pay court costs.

It is clear that this paragraph is pure fiction. For one thing, Walsh wouldn't have asked me to pay something that he knew the court was investigating. Secondly, if he had asked me to pay these costs, I would have obviously told him what I told the court—that I was unable to pay them. I wouldn't have simply "refused"! And if Walsh could mention the court activity with regard to my "habeas action," why wouldn't he have mentioned court activity involving these courts costs of which he was aware? Apart from the fact that Walsh's claim is an obvious fabrication,

FIGURE E-3

U.S. Department of Justice
United States Parole Commission

2nd & Chestnut Streets
Custom House, 7th Floor
Philadelphia, Pennsylvania 19106

April 5, 1989

Irwin Schiff
68-38 Yellowstone Blvd., Apt A-53
Forrest Hills, NY 11375

Dear Mr. Schiff:

Reference is made to your letter dated March 9, 1989 and received March 13, 1989.

Basically, you appear to be contesting the fact that you are under parole and probation supervision. Please be advised that you were paroled on June 16, 1988 until December 16, 1989. According to my conversation with US Probation Walsh, you are also under a probationary term of 36 months. The parole and probation are running concurrently. Neither the Court or the Parole Commission has "tampered or changed the term of your sentence" which you alleged in your letter. Apparently, neither the court, US Attorney nor the Parole Commission are confused on this issue but rather it appears as though your understanding is not clear. As I have noted above, you are under concurrent parole and probation jurisdiction and you are encouraged to abide by the conditions of both probation and parole so as not to warrant any parole violation action by either the Commission or the courts.

Sincerely,

Linda M. Stokes for

KATHLEEN A. PINNER
HEARING EXAMINER

KAP/cdw

even if it were true it still would not establish "willfullness" because Walsh gives *no indication* where the money would come from to pay these costs, despite the fact that I had been submitting financial statements to him *every* month! Against all of the evidence, and in total violation of the law (as specifically contained in 18 U.S.C. 4214(d)), Tenney found me guilty of "willfully refusing" to pay $27,405.98 of court costs.[4] Talk about a kangaroo hearing!

Immediately after my second revocation hearing on December 5, 1989, I became somewhat optimistic about being released, believing that the "mafia" had exhausted all the time they could with their mickey-mouse charges. I had also put off writing this new, updated Epilogue, hoping against hope that my original version might be found. I really didn't relish the idea of having to totally rewrite and retype it. When I still had not received any word by December 13, I started to suspect that they might, indeed, be trying to take away all of my street time, so that I might not have the opportunity to attend to all of my appeals or complete this Epilogue from the outside.

Friday, December 15, 1989 was the last day that this institution could release me prior to my having completed my full three-year sentence. Actually my term was up on Saturday, but they didn't normally release inmates on that day. By Sunday, I would be here illegally. On Friday morning I inquired at the records office if I was going to be released, since my term was up, and to my knowledge there were no detainers that would interfere with my being released. As of that date neither I nor the institution had received any notice that the Parole Commission had confiscated all of my street time, which was the only basis upon which the institution could hold me. This was confirmed that morning by Linda Eade, who is in charge of releasing inmates. She told me that she had not as yet been notified by the Parole Commission that my street time had been taken from me. When I asked her on what basis the institution was holding me, she said, pursuant to the supplemental warrant. She did say, however, that the Parole Commission was apparently going to take away my street time, otherwise she would have been notified to release me. Later that afternoon I checked with my Case Manager, Mike Zenk, as to what was going on. He told me that the institution still had not received any word, and the last thing he had heard was that my file was in Washington—which meant that the decision to release or hold me was not being decided by the Regional Commissioner in Philadelphia, but at a higher level. This was later confirmed by my lawyer who was also making calls trying to determine my status. He was also of the opinion that they had decided to take my street time (as illegal as that would be) since there would be no other way they could hold me. He also confirmed that he couldn't get any information from Philadelphia because, "Your file is now in Washington."

That evening, Friday, December 15, 1989, I was working in the law library on this Epilogue when I came across Section 2.48 entitled "Supplemental Warrant Application." I don't know why I had not noticed this section before, but it *proved* that my supplemental warrant was *totally illegal!* Subparagraph (a)(1) of that section provides as follows:

When *new violations are brought to the attention of the Regional Commissioner,* a supplemental warrant application may be issued at any time prior to the normal expiration of supervision.

Subparagraph (c) provides that:

Additional charges which come *to light* during the preliminary interview may be used, and a supplemental warrant application should be issued *if time permits.* [Emphasis added throughout.]

These provisions, along with a few others, make it clear that a supplemental warrant can only be used to raise *new charges that come to light* after the original warrant is issued ("if time permits"!) so that they can be addressed *along with the original charges* at the *same* revocation hearing!

This section makes makes it crystal clear that a revocation hearing can *not* be based solely upon a supplemental warrant as was my second "hearing." Logically, it couldn't work any other way as the following example illustrates. Suppose the Commissioner was aware of four alleged violations at the time he issues the original warrant, but only charges two violations and holds two "in reserve." If the parolee beats the two violations at his revocation hearing, the Commissioner could now charge him (in a supplemental warrant) with *one* of the violations being held "in reserve," and now conducts a second revocation hearing. If the parolee beats that charge too, the Commissioner then issues *another* supplemental warrant charging the fourth alleged violation. Assuming that the Commissioner had enough "stored" violations, he could conceivably keep the parolee incarcerated for life! But, it gets worse.

My supplemental warrant was not issued on the basis of "new violations," but was based on an alleged violation that was known to the Commissioner *before* the original warrant was issued. This is *admitted* in the warrant itself, which specifically states that it is based on "information contained in letter dated 8/28/89 by USPO Walsh"! So the alleged violation was *known* to the Commissioner more than a month before the original warrant was issued! Thus, not only couldn't my revocation hearing be held on the basis of that supplemental warrant, but the supplemental warrant **itself was illegal** and *could not have been issued according to the law as contained in 28 CFR 2.48!*

I was, therefore, a little perplexed by the fact that my attorney had overlooked these factors and had *actually allowed* my second revocation hearing to take place. The very least he could have done, it seemed to me, was to specifically raise these issues and provisions *immediately* at the start of that second hearing—but he failed to do so.[6]

Since I made these discoveries at about 7 p.m. on Friday evening, I prepared a memorandum for the warden containing this information and delivered it to the officer on duty at 10 a.m. on Saturday morning, December 16, 1989, so that the warden would be clearly on notice *before* his illegal detention of me would begin.

I was able to speak to Warden Cox on the following Monday morning in the inmate dining room. Yes, he had received my memorandum, but was not prepared to do anything about it, and suggested that I might meet with him the next morning at 7 a.m. The next morning he was brief, and informed me that he would do nothing until he received word from the Parole Commission to release me. So that was it.

That evening I realized that I would have to file a 2241 Habeas Corpus petition to get out. This is somewhat comparable to a 2245, except it is addressed to the local federal court rather than to the trial court because it does not involve a trial issue.

Upon further reading of 26 CFR, in preparation for my 2241, I made other startling discoveries which revealed that *everything* about my parole revocation *had been illegal,* and further, that if my attorney had been effective, *I would have been released immediately following my preliminary hearing that had been conducted in September.*

WHY *ALL* OF MY PAROLE REVOCATION CHARGES WERE ILLEGAL!

28 CFR Sections 2.40-08 and 2.40-15 reveal the **utter illegality** of **all** of the charges brought against me in *both* warrants. Not only were these charges outrageously false as a *matter of fact,* they were **totally illegal as a matter of law!**

For example, with respect to the charge involving Fred White: It is not enough to say that probable cause was not found by Probation Officer Wilson and this charge dismissed because, based on Section 2.40-08, it could *not even have been legally made!* And that fact had also escaped my attorney who had me believing that Wilson had given me some kind of a break by dismissing this charge simply because Fred White was not a felon. My attorney pointed out that my condition of parole did not make this distinction, but only referred to persons with "criminal

records," not necessarily felons. So he believed there was *at least* some *legal* exposure, even if the facts themselves clearly vindicated me. However, I now found out that there was **not even a legal exposure,** since Section 2.40-08 states that:

> For the purpose of this provision, the term "criminal record" refers to a conviction for a felony or any other offense for which a term of imprisonment exceeding one year was, or could have been, imposed.

Thus, pursuant to law, I could not have been legally violated because of my "association" with Fred White— regardless of the facts—since he had never been convicted of a felony or "offense for which a term of imprisonment exceeding one year was, or could have been, imposed"! In addition, this section further provides that:

> Unless it is clear that the parolee...knows that an associate has a criminal record...a warrant or summons charging a violation of this condition ordinarily should not be issued unless the releasee has first been given a warning by his Probation Officer that the associate in question has a criminal record and that further association would be a violation of the release condition.

Before I could have been arrested (or even summoned) for allegedly associating with Fred White, it would first have to be established that I knew of Fred's criminal record, and had been *warned by Walsh not to associate with him!*

Not *one* of these conditions was present in my case, as every probation officer, supervisor, and reviewer who was involved in my arrest and incarceration, including the commissioner who signed the warrant, had to know!

It Was Lawfully Impossible For Me To Be Violated For Not Paying Either Taxes or Court Costs

Both warrants illegally accused me of not paying taxes and court costs. The first paragraph of Section 2.40-15 titled "Satisfaction of Court Orders [Including the Payment of Fines, Restitution Orders, Court Costs and Assessments, and Court Ordered Child Support or Alimony Payments]," states as follows:

> When a parolee is subject to an outstanding fine, restitution order, court costs and assessments, court ordered child support or alimony payment, and is unable to pay the obligation in one sum, the following procedures apply:

Note that there is no mention here of *taxes.* The reason is obvious. All of the listed items have to do with *court imposed obligations,* and *taxes are imposed by statute.* Obviously, the payment of taxes can *not* be a condition of either parole or probation! However, the courts disregard this distinction along with everything else they disregard. Even if we *assume* that the payment of taxes *can* be a condition of parole, the following conditions would have to be satisfied *before* I could have been violated for allegedly failing to pay them—or my court costs for that matter. The following are complete and direct quotes from 26 CFR Section 2.40-18.

(a) The U.S. Probation Officer will meet with the parolee to develop a written plan for the payment of fine, restitution order, etc. The plan will include, among other things, a payment schedule and the amount to be paid at each installment. It will include also the following clause: "This plan, and the obligations described herein, are part of the conditions of my parole." The parolee will supply all financial information and records necessary to the development of the plan and will sign the plan, along with the U.S. Probation Officer. A copy of the signed plan will be forwarded to the U.S. Parole Commission.

(b) As to the payment schedule and the amounts to be paid at each installment, the plan will include any relevant court ordered installment payment schedule. If no such installment payment schedule exists, one will be developed that takes into acount, among other things, the amount of the fine [restitution order, etc.], any interest and penalties due as well as the parolee's employment status, earning ability, financial resources, and the economic burden that the payment of the obligation will impose on the parolee or his dependents. While feasible, the installment payment term for fines and restitution orders should not exceed two years.

(d) If the parolee refuses to accept the terms of the plan in general, refuses to accept the installment payment schedule, and/or refuses to sign the plan, the U.S. Parole Commission will be notified. The U.S. Parole Commission will then resolve any outstanding disputes as to terms and installment payments schedules, completing the plan as necessary and making the terms and schedules contained therein themselves as a special parole condition.

(e) Any changes to or modifications of the plan will be reduced to written form and signed by the parolee and the U.S. Probation Officer. A copy of the signed change or modification will be forwarded to the U.S. Parole Commission.

(f) If the parolee does not make diligent effort to make the payments according to the schedule in the plan, the U.S. Probation Officer will report such failure to the U.S. Parole Commission as a violation of the conditions of parole.

Before I could have been legally violated for allegedly not paying either my taxes or those court costs, *all* of the above procedures would have to have been followed—**BUT NOT *ONE* OF THEM WAS!**

At my preliminary hearing, my attorney asked Walsh if he had ever worked out a payment schedule with me for the payment of those taxes based on my income and expenses, and Walsh said that he had not. This is confirmed in Probation Officer Wilson's "Summary Report of Preliminary Interview," which he furnished to the Regional Commissioner. In it Wilson states:

U.S. Probation Officer Walsh recalled directing the subject to pay his taxes, but acknowledged that he was unaware of the amount owed by the parolee and had initiated no payment schedule.

Thus, pursuant to the above regulations (the law in this case!), not only could I *not* have been violated for non payment of either taxes or court costs, but all of those who took part in my arrest and incarceration in violation of Section 2.40-18 should be criminally prosecuted pursuant to a variety of laws for having done so.

While my lawyer had questioned Walsh about his failure to develop a payment schedule, he did so primarily to establish that Walsh had never discussed payment of these taxes with me at all. Since, if he had, he would have certainly discussed some kind of payment schedule with me. By admitting that he had not, Walsh was obviously admitting to lying about ever discussing the payment of these taxes with me. In this case, however, Wilson was apparently free to believe otherwise, and rule accordingly. Had my lawyer produced Section 2.40-18 following Walsh's admission, Wilson would have had no choice but to dismiss this charge, since, by law, the development of a payment schedule was a *condition precedent to any* parole violation for non payment. There is no question, that had my lawyer produced this section at a preliminary hearing, I would have been released in September, *and this book would have already been in the hands of the public!*

On December 21, in connection with a motion for a continuance that I was submitting to the Second Circuit Court of Appeal, I stopped at the records office to get a copy of the supplemental warrant. I had apparently misplaced my own copy, and I wanted one to attach to the motion. I discovered, however, that the records office *had no such warrant* in my file, yet I was *now* informed by Mr. Lancaster (Ms. Eade being on vacation) that I was being held pursuant to the *original* warrant. It then occured to me that the institution had never received a copy of my supplemental warrant because it had no need of it. It had been issued merely to me as *notice* of the additional charge that would be brought up at my revocation hearing—a hearing that had already taken place! Therefore, the supplemental warrant never had any legal significance—it was born dead. Ms Eade had merely been misled (when she made telephone inquiries to the Parole Commission to find out about my release status on December 15, 1989) by the Parole Commission into thinking that Morgantown could hold me on it until the Regional Commissioner made up his mind concerning the results of my (illegal) second revocation "hearing."

When I realized this, even though I had already filed my 2241 with the United States District Court of the Northern District of West Virginia, I decided to give Warden Cox another chance to release me without having to pursue further court litigation. At 7:30 a.m. on December 26, 1989 I handed him my Second Notice, bringing all of the above to his attention. This should have further revealed to him the utter illegality of my continued detention at his hands.

Later that morning I chanced to meet him on the institution grounds, and asked him if he had received any further word on my status. He said that he had not, but believed that the Parole Commissioner would be taking away my street time. Under these circumstances, he would continue to hold me. He also advised me that the only thing I might do was to file a 2241, which I had already done. Later on, when I returned to my unit, I found in my mail a copy of the order that had been sent to him by the District Court of Northern West Virginia, asking him to show cause

within twenty days as to why he was holding me.

It is clear that the "mafia" has now held me for no less than five months on *totally illegal charges and procedures!* But this will really not be anything new. It did the same thing in connection with the twenty months of incarceration I served on my original sentence, to say nothing of the fines I paid and time I spent on parole. These five months will represent more jail time than I spent in connection with my first 1979 conviction, when I was sentenced to six months, and served four months and eight days, with time off for good behavior. At this writing, the time I have already spent incarcerated in connection with this *totally illegal* parole violation is the equivalent of a seven-month jail sentence!

FLASH: As I was walking out the door of my unit to photo-copy some of these manuscript pages, I was handed my second Notice of Action by my case manager. Would you believe that Daniel L. Lopez, the Regional Commissioner, stripped me of *all* my street time for not paying those court costs?! And in doing so, he cites as a basis "USPO's letter dated 6/28/89," in which USP Walsh claims to have "directed" me to pay those costs on April 13, 1989. If I murdered ten people, they couldn't have taken away more street time! In addition, the Commissioner's Notice of Action is dated December 19, 1989, or three days after his jurisdiction terminated! Now does anyone have any lingering doubt that the Commissioner, along with all the others with whom he conspired in sending out that Notice of Action, belongs behind bars?

MY REFUND SUIT IN THE U.S. COURT OF CLAIMS

On October 4, 1989, oral argument was heard before Judge John P. Wiese in Washington, D.C. on the motions for summary judgment that had been submitted in that case. My "appearance" was made via telephone from FCI Otisville, New York, where I was then incarcerated. The next day (October 5, 1989) Judge Wiese, in a five-page decision, ruled that since I hadn't made any payments within two years of seeking a refund, my claim was barred by the two-year rule contained in Code Section 7422.

In his ruling[7] Judge Wiese does not even *mention* Subsection 7422(d), which, of course, formed the statutory basis for my suit and which his ruling *totally ignored.*

Anyone reading his decision would have no idea of the existence of that subsection, let alone my extensive reliance on it in all of my briefs and at oral argument. His conspicuous failure to even mention Subsection 7422(d) and explain why my reliance on it was ill advised proves conclusively that Judge Wiese *knew he was breaking the law* (as contained in Subsection 7422(d)) when he dismissed my law suit against the United Staes. This is another example of the lawlessness that goes into federal judicial decisions and the lawlessness in federal "case law." This hardly represents the only error in Wiese's decision—but why go any further?

I notified the U.S. Court of Appeals for the Federal Circuit that I am appealing Judge Wiese's decision and requested (pursuant to an Affidavit) that I be permitted to do so in forma pauperis, which was granted. My informal brief was due December 15, 1989, but it was impossible for me to meet that deadline, so I requested a 30 day continuance until January 15, 1990. Even if it is granted, however, I will not now have the necessary time to do it right. When I moved for the continuance (December 1, 1989), I thought I might be getting out in a matter of days, so I could work on it. In any case, I should have no trouble reversing Wiese's decision at the appellate level. If I do not, I would relish presenting the issues involved in this case to the Supreme Court. I would present them with a real sticky wicket. The problem is that all of these appeals are extremely difficult to do within the confines of prison walls, and I don't have the money to hire competent outside counsel—which is another reason why the scoundrels are holding me.

MY $500,000 SUIT FOR REFUND IN DISTRICT COURT

On September 6, 1989, Judge Warren W. Eginton did the legally impossible. He granted the government a summary judgment (see his 12-page ruling in the Appendix) on its summary seizure of my property, including the award of civil fraud penalties—based on *unsigned* documents! Now if that does not CONVINCE YOU THAT FEDERAL JUDGES ARE JUDGES IN NAME ONLY—NOTHING WILL!

There should be no need for me to analyze Eginton's ruling, since he merely repeated every fallacious argument made by the government, and despite the fact that my Reply Brief had already torn them all to shreds. One has to wonder if Eginton even bothered to read my Brief. I did not get his ruling until September 15, and on September 20 I filed a 20-page Motion to Reconsider, which I supplemented on October 6. Commenting generally on his ruling, I said:

> Your ruling indicates that America has come back *more than full circle,* since even George the III would not have the temerity to seize the property of his colonial subjects in the manner in which the Federal Government has seized mine—apparently with this court's blessing. I only regret that I am not sufficiently gifted in either intellect or in my command of the English language to respond to your breathtaking ruling in the manner it deserves.

I also pointed out that since his ruling accused me of "failing to provide evidence," that:

> I produced evidence that the original assessments were never made, that the 1986 assessments were time barred and a Treasury Decision and a Form 17A that proved that the interest assessments were totally fraudulent...(that apparently)...''evidence'' is simply

wasted on this court.

Judge Eginton's ruling shatters the fiction that summary seizures of property by the government are constitutional because individuals *have* a post-seizure remedy—you have *no* post-seizure remedy if a court thinks you have an air-tight case *against the government!* How many more reasons do you need for demanding that your congressman and senators repeal Section 6331? There are some Americans who want to make a congressman's position on abortion the sole issue for deciding whether he should be voted in or out. If anything, a congressman's or senator's position on 6331 should be made such an issue. Any congressman or senator who, in light of Judge Wiese and Edginton's decisions, would continue to allow the government to "seize property by any means" simply does not deserve to be in office. There should be *no compromise* on this.

Note how Eginton goes about perverting "case law" as represented in *Dixon.* Pursuant to *Dixon,* Forms 4340 are only "presumptive proof" if "no evidence to counter this presumption" is presented. This was fully covered in my Reply Brief, but totally disregarded in Eginton's ruling Anyone reading his decision would assume that (1) he correctly quoted *Dixon,* and (2) I had submitted no evidence rebutting the presumption it refers to—but, both assumptions would be wrong! Yet, Eginton's ruling will now serve as "case law" for others—especially in Connecticut. In addition, note how Eginton relies on *Hartman,* (page 4 of the 12-page ruling in the Appendix) a decision totally discredited in my Reply Brief and one which, it is clear, even the government does not believe.

Note, too, that Judge Eginton's claim that it is my "contention" that [my] income cannot constitutionally be taxed" is *nothing but a bold-faced lie!* My "contention," as Eginton well knew, was *not* that my income couldn't be "constitutionally taxed," but that it must be taxed *either* on the basis of apportionment, *or* as a uniform "duty, impost or excise." However, Eginton (as well as the government) wouldn't touch this argument with the proverbial "ten foot pole," so they both lied to avoid having to address it! Obviously, neither could refute it, *so they made no effort to do so!*

Notice too, that Eginton couches all of his statements and arguments in language most favorable to the government and which would throw anyone reading his decision (who was unfamiliar with the facts) completely off the track. He states, for example, that: I challenged "the procedures used by the IRS in determining the existence of a deficiency" (page 3); that I argue that "the tax assessments are incorrect" (page 7); that I merely made "conclusory denials" (page 8); and that my claim with respect to the "demand" issue was my mere asserting that the IRS "should have used a different form." I am sure that you will recognize that these representations are sheer nonsense. I didn't challenge the deficiency "procedures" used by the IRS—I *proved that they didn't follow any*. I didn't argue that the assessments were "incorrect"—I *proved that none were made, nor could have been made under the law*. I didn't claim that the "demand" should have been made on a "different form"—I proved that, *since no demand was ever made* pursuant to Treasury Decision 1995, *no lien* could have arisen pursuant to which summary seizures of my property could have been made **as a matter of law!**

Note, also, the deception in connection with my 1976 income taxes. Eginton begins by saying "plaintiff's argument that the assessment made against him for ... 1976 is barred by the statute of limitations must fail as a matter of law." How many, reading this decision, would know that I supplied the court with a government document that made *precisely the same claim?* So, it wasn't merely "my argument" at all! And as for "my argument" failing "as a matter of law"—the exact opposite is true, as is clearly proven in my Reply Brief. Eginton even admits that, "absent fraud," the statute of limitations barred the collection of my 1976 taxes. However, the government *never proved* fraud for that year! Eginton's further claim that I did not file "a proper return" for that year is irrelevant, since he already admitted that the return had to be "fraudulent"— *not* improper! Here Eginton admits to being *an accessory after the fact* in the embezzlement of my money—yet this man sends people to prison for stealing far lesser amounts!

Earlier in this book I questioned whom it was that actually determined the civil fraud penalties that IRS agents collected without court orders, and suggested that, perhaps, it was their cleaning ladies. In my case, as I'm sure you will find in *all* cases, they were *not determined by anyone*— even a cleaning lady would be an improvement! The documents assessing them, as Eginton well knew, were *not signed by anyone*. Thus, Eginton knew that the over $50,000 the government seized from me for this penalty was no more legal than any monies ever taken by John Dillinger at the point of a gun. That will give you a rough idea of the level of hypocrisy that exists on the federal bench. One wonders how Eginton can impose jail sentences on thieves, extortionists and embezzlers with a straight face, much less with a clear conscience.

But, even if the documents were signed, no affirmative acts of evasion are listed on them. This is confirmed by the "persuasive evidence" that Eginton claims (page 11, paragraph two) was indicative of the fraud I allegedly committed. Not *one* affirmative act of tax fraud is contained in that paragraph. Eginton claims that he can find civil fraud (for specific years, no less!) on the basis that I am, *in general,*

an allegedly "intelligent person with broad knowledge of tax law" and, because I "appeared on television discussing the same"! Since when do these things constitute tax fraud— even if proven to be true? The funny part is that the statement is not even true for the years at issue, 1976, 1977 and 1978, when I certainly did not have "broad knowledge of tax law." Most of what I now know, I learned subsequent to 1979. Up until then, I don't think I had ever looked into an Internal Revenue Code. My approach to income taxes prior to 1979 was largely based upon constitutional arguments and what was then known as the "money argument." While this is really immaterial, I mention it only to demonstrate the mind-blowing enormity of the nonsense upon which Eginton's decision was based.

Eginton's Finding of Civil Fraud

Eginton should be impeached (if not indicted on a variety of criminal charges) just on this holding alone! He knows, as well as he knows his own name, that the government is required to prove *civil* tax fraud just as it is required to prove *criminal* tax fraud. In this instance, Eginton is willing to allow the government to escape its burden of proof so as to insure its being able to keep the $500,000 (including accumulated interest) that it now owes me. As I pointed out to Eginton in my Motion to Reconsider, this would make him an "accessory after the fact." Can you imagine how a jury would react to such an overt showing of governmental fraud? Is it any wonder, therefore, that Eginton was determined to prevent me from bringing such matters to the attention of a jury?!

In connection with Eginton's decree that I committed tax fraud for the years 1976, 1977 and 1978 (on the basis of no evidence or testimony), I asked him:

One wonders why this court even bothers holding criminal trials. Why doesn't the court simply read the indictment or information and decide accordingly?

Note that on page 10 Eginton admits that "the government bears the burden of proving fraud by clear and convincing evidence." Well, to whom does the government have to prove it? I asked him in connection with his admission that it was my "burden of going forward" and of "ultimate...persuasion" (page 7):

If I have the burden of "going forward" and of "persuasion," how can you legally keep me from "going forward" and "persuading" a jury, as is my right? Who am I to persuade—a federal judge who apparently knows he is being paid from funds stolen from the plaintiff?

Since Eginton admits that the government has to prove

fraud on the basis of "evidence," doesn't he know what that word means? Apparently not! I sought to enlighten him with its definition, as contained in *Black's Law Dictionary*, to wit, evidence is:

> Any species of proof, or probative matter, *legally presented at the trial of an issue,* by the *act of the parties* and through *the medium of witnesses,* records, documents, exhibits, concrete objects, etc., etc., etc., for the purpose of inducing beliefs in the minds of the court or jury as to their contention. *Taylor* vs. *Howard,* 111 R.I. 527, 304 A.2d 891, 893 (emphasis added).

"Thus," I told Eginton, "it is clear that this court has determined plaintiff's guilt, with respect to his having committed fraud for 1976, 1977 and 1978, on the basis of *no evidence, whatsoever*—and that its ruling on this issue *alone* is a fraud and a sham!"

To make doubly certain that Eginton was fully cognizant of his folly on this particular area (which pretty much reflects his decision as a whole), I quoted extensively from case law on this issue, including the following cogent observation from the Second Circuit's own case of *Paddock* vs *United States,* a case cited (but not quoted) in my Reply Brief: "He who alleges fraud must prove it." (At page 567 of *Paddock*.) Contrary to all case law, Eginton would allow more *allegations* of fraud to be the *legal equivalent of fraud itself.*

In addition, the admission by Eginton that he was sustaining fraud on the basis of *"prior action involving plaintiff"* (last paragraph, page 11) is such an overtly asinine claim as to make further comment on this issue unnecessary.

How Objective Could Eginton Be?

Now, in addition to everything else, I also pointed out to Eginton that:

> This court has no business taking it upon itself to be the arbiter of all the issues in this case, because *this court is not a neutral and disinterested party.* Since this court dismissed plaintiff's law suit against *Simon & Schuster,* 780 F.2d 210, on the grounds that S&S was required to turn over the money because plaintiff owed it to the government, if plaintiff proved to a jury (or proved, as a matter of law, as he has already done) that he didn't owe the money, this would establish that this court's dismissal in the case was erroneous. To avoid getting egg all over its face, this court apparently decided to throw out: all case law, all reason, all fairness, and even judicial ethics in deciding a case in which the court has a substantial personal interest.

CASE LAW AND "DUMMY RETURNS"

Eginton's explanation of how the Commissioner, presumably, is authorized to use "dummy returns" will not be found in any statute, nor in any Treasury Department Regulation, *but is based solely on Eginton's lawless imagination.* This is how federal judges not only create "case law" that is unrelated to anything passed by Congress, but actually *vitiates* laws it *does* pass. His explanation directly contradicts Treasury Regulation 601.103(b) which explains how deficiencies are supposed to be determined and assessed. This regulation makes it perfectly clear that the income tax is based on "self-assessment" and that all deficiencies must be based on returns *filed by taxpayers.* There is nothing in Regulation 601.103(b) that remotely suggests that deficiencies can be determined in the manner described by Eginton, or that the Commissioner is legally empowered to assume that individuals who file *no* returns can be presumed to have self-assessed themselves with a "zero" liability on the income tax returns *they didn't file!* I addressed this aspect of Eginton's Ruling as follows:

> In claiming that the IRS can make assessments on the basis of "dummy returns," this court has *tossed out the window* the following Code Sections and Treasury Regulations: Section 6020, 6201, 6204, and 6211 and Regulations 301.6201-1, 301.6204-1 and 601.103(b).

> To claim, as the court did (page 5), that "By proceeding in this manner," the IRS is able to grant all "taxpayers the same procedural rights, even those taxpayers who fail or refuse to file returns," is for the court to fail to recognize that *the procedural requirements* (which the court euphemistically calls "rights") *between filers and non-filers are different,* and *BY LAW are not "the same."* Admittedly, the income tax is based on "self-assessment," so the law does not provide the "same procedures" for those who voluntarily "self-assess" and those who do not. By allegedly "proceeding in the (same) manner," (when the law requires different "manners"), simply allows the IRS to disregard *all law!* All tax assessments as this court undoubtedly knows, must come from either "returns" or "lists." The "administrative" use of "dummy returns" is designed—as was pointed out by plaintiff—to circumvent Code Section 6501(c)(3)— which your Ruling fails to even mention! Section 6501(c)(3) specifically provides that when returns are not made (without which no assessments can be made)—the IRS is *required* to *sue* the citizen for any taxes allegedly owed. So while this court cites inappropriate and meaningless case law, *it totally ignores the statutes themselves!* Thus the creation of fraudulent "dummy returns" is not designed, as the court falsely contends, to "extend rights,"—but to

DENY THEM!

Judge Eginton's ruling should convince you that federal court decisions can be contrary to *all* facts and *all* law. In this case, the public will know the law and the facts, and can see right through his ruling. But suppose it *didn't* know the law or the facts—what then? In that case, it could be totally fooled. The question then becomes: to what extent is the public fooled by similar rulings produced by other courts? Maybe, at this point, we should throw out *all* case law and insist that court decisions be based *solely* on what the statutes say. And if our judges can't figure out the law from the statutes, maybe the statutes, too, should be thrown out for being "void for vagueness." Why should citizens be subject to the kind of "law" represented by Eginton's ruling?

How About This!

As luck would have it, within days of receiving Eginton's ruling, a friend sent me the Treasury Department publication *Handbook on Determining Statute of Limitations*, Document No. 7081 (3-86), which had some very interesting things to say about "dummy returns." The publication contained a number of questions and answers designed to familiarize appeals officers with how to apply this statute in various situations. One of the questions was as follows:

A case file contains a "dummy return," Form 1040, for calendar year 1980. When does the statute of limitations expire?

The Treasury Department's answer was as follows:

A "dummy return" is simply a copy of taxpayer's copy of a return filed. It is not a "substitute for return." Therefore, simply apply regular statute of limitations rules. If the return is timely filed, then the statute of limitations expires on 4/15/84.

You can stop rubbing your eyes in disbelief, because that is exactly the answer given in the *Handbook*. Let's analyze it.

1. Why would the IRS ever want "a copy of the taxpayer's copy" of the return he presumably filed? Since it presumably had the original return the taxpayer filed, why wouldn't it simply make a copy of the *original* if it needed another copy of the filed return. Why would it ever *need*, or ever *want* a "copy of the taxpayer's copy?"

2. How does the IRS get "a copy of the taxpayer's copy" anyway? Suppose the taxpayer refuses to give the IRS "a copy of [his] copy." Suppose he never kept a copy? Wouldn't this mean that in these circumstances, no

"dummy return" could ever exist? Apparently so—since in these instances the IRS obviously couldn't get "a copy of taxpayer's copy of a return filed."

3. In my case, admittedly, there were no "returns filed." So where did my "dummies" come from? Does this mean that on top of everything else, even my "dummy returns" were "dummies"? There is no question about it. I had "dummy, dummy returns"!

4. Since the Treasury Department clearly states that a "dummy return" is not a "substitute for return," how could the IRS have labeled my "dummy returns" "substitute for return"?

There can be no doubt that *every* representation made by the IRS, the Justice Department and Judge Eginton concerning my alleged "dummy returns" was (in case you still have any doubts) *totally false*. On the other hand, the Treasury Department's description of a "dummy return" is so absurd that one must logically ask, why would the Department have come up with such a screw-ball definition?

As I explained earlier, the Treasury Department is very careful, in official publications, never to make claims that are obviously *illegal*. The government leaves that up to its invulnerable judiciary.

In its *Handbook*, however, the Treasury Department was *forced* to publically and officially acknowledge "dummy returns"—something that it *knew* that no law nor Treasury Regulation even authorizes. Therefore, it knew that it had to come up with a public description that was so benign that no one could possibly attribute to "dummy returns" any legal significance whatsoever. They were, the Department would publically proclaim, merely *copies* of *copies* of returns *already filed!* Who, therefore, could possibly take such documents seriously, or attribute to them—as Eginton did—any legal significance whatsoever? Judge Eginton's entire discourse on the legal significance of dummy returns can be seen to have merely been a figment of his own vivid imagination (supported by some case law of other judges with equally vivid imaginations)!

If the Treasury Department were ever confronted with Judge Eginton's description and use of dummy returns, it might respond as follows:

"What do you want from us? We never made that claim, and we have no control over what federal judges say. As far as this Department is concerned, our official position, as reflected in Treasury Document 7081 (3-86), is that a dummy return is nothing but a copy of a return filed by a taxpayer. We clearly never claimed that it is a substitute for a taxpayer's return or that assessments can be made from them. If Judge Eginton or any other federal judge wants to make that claim, that is their business. We have no authority over the judiciary, so take the matter up with them— but leave *us* out of it!

On October 6, 1989, I filed an "Amended Motion to Reconsider" based upon my discovery of this Treasury Document and asked Eginton to:

Take judicial notice of the attached document and judicial notice that all of the court's references to the alleged legal acceptability of "dummy returns" serving as an alleged basis for assessments is, itself, *contradicted by this officially published IRS document.* And, thus, any ruling based upon the alleged validity of such documents *must be erroneous.*

After pointing out to the court several of the observations I made above, I stated, among other things, that:

Since the entries on the "dummy returns" filed in this case and the entries on the Forms 4340 submitted by the government claim to be "Substitute for Returns", their claimed status is clearly contradicted by the Treasury Department itself! Document 7081 specifically says that a "dummy return" is *not* a "substitute for return." So, how can the Justice Department and this court claim otherwise?

Thus, this court's claim (page 5 of its ruling) that the plaintiff's claim that the instant assessments could not be lawfully based on the instant "dummy returns"—the only returns admittedly held by the defendant—"must fail as a matter of law", is utterly without foundation and is, itself, *repudiated by the Treasury Department itself!*

It is also clear from Document 7081 (3-86) that this court cannot take it upon itself to disregard clearly stated Treasury Department representations regarding *its own internal documents* and attribute to them legal qualities that *even the Treasury Department does not claim and which, indeed, are even repudiated by that Department.*

Based upon the above, *it is perfectly clear* that this court has as much legal right to claim that all of the "assessments" in this case could have been legally made on the basis of "dummy returns" as it would have in claiming that these assessments could have been made on the basis of a *Chinese laundry ticket!*

Though this official Treasury Department document **totally demolishes the entire foundation** upon which

Judge Eginton's ruling was based, he remained unmoved. Now you have irrefutable proof that in America "laws" (i.e., case law) can be based on nothing more than **pure, unadulterated judicial b--- s---!**

WOULD YOU BELIEVE, A PEARL?

Who would have believed that somewhere in Judge Eginton's ruling there is actually *something* salvageable! Notice that after Eginton develops his little theory as to how the IRS can assess taxes even when individuals file no returns, he goes on to state (page 5) that this procedure gives individuals "the right to petition Tax Court and contest the Commissioner's determination *prior to the payment of any taxes*"!

Here, Eginton clearly admits (and rightly so) that I didn't have to pay any taxes for any of the years for which I now sit in jail, because I was never sent a Deficiency Notice for those years which would have allowed me to go to Tax Court "prior to the payment" of those taxes! I am in jail because the Parole Commission (i.e., the government) says I haven't paid the taxes that Eginton says I never had to pay, anyway! Of course, this is exactly what I argued (among other things) in my Rule 35 and in my *en banc* petition to the Second Circuit—but, here, I have a Connecticut District Court judge saying the same thing!

On October 10, 1989, based upon Judge Eginton's ruling, I filed a supplement to my pending *en banc* petition and requested that the Second Circuit order my immediate release. I argued to the court that by its "sustaining a condition of probation requiring me to 'remain current in so far as all legal tax payments' it was irreconcilable with Judge Eginton's ruling"; and, further, his ruling makes "crystal clear the illegality of my current incarceration" while also making "crystal clear how a condition of probation, sanctioned by this court, is capable of being capriciously applied, since it was illegally used to incarcerate me as a condition of parole."

I also pointed out that I had already been criminally punished in several ways and that I had "*earned* a modification of my criminal punishment (parole) based upon my guidelines, conduct as a prisoner, and because *I had paid a committed fine!*" And, since I was now back in prison for the same crime for which I was convicted, I was clearly being criminally punished *twice for the same offense.* In addition, I pointed out to the court that since I had been convicted of criminal tax fraud, the IRS was now free to impose *civil fraud penalties* on me, which "I am collaterally estopped from contesting" because I had already been convicted of criminal tax fraud for those years. Since Judge Dorsey had apparently determined that I was incapable of even paying those court costs, how could I pay $50,000 in taxes? Therefore, and on top of everything else, "I have been incarcerated for debt." I then asked the court, "I wonder how things work in totalitarian countries where citizens are not protected by a constitution?"

I closed my motion by asking:

"Will it be the position of the Second Circuit that the federal government can punish citizens within its jurisdiction THREE TIMES for committing the SAME OFFENSE—twice criminally and once civilly. And if so, is one to assume that double jeopardy laws no longer have any application in this circuit?"

And by suggesting that:

It would be a wise use of the limited judicial time available for the Second Circuit to order my immediate release from an obviously illegal and unconstitutional imprisonment so as to avoid the appearance that the Second Circuit is insensitive to overt violations of law and the abuse of constitutional rights within its jurisdiction.

Based on all of the above, it should now be clear to you that Americans are no longer protected by a constitution. The Dorseys and Egintons have seen to that. It is also clear to me that the release of this book is probably my only hope of getting out of jail in the immediate future, and is, I am sure, my only real hope of ever getting a lawless and vengeful government off my back. Obviously I am innocent of any wrongdoing, but this has not stopped the government from imprisoning me for over 24 months *before*, six months *now* (as of this writing), and for as many more months as they will try to get away with in the future. I am not the only one the government has done this to, but I am probably the only one that you have read about! My only hope is that this book will make a broad and significant public impact and elicit some kind of public outcry. It may also be that only this kind of public reaction will help those many other innocent Americans who are also locked up in numerous penal institutions and those now being hounded to pay taxes, penalties and interest they do not owe and cannot afford. The only reason that the federal judiciary breaks the law as *extensively* as it does, is that it believes the law is sufficiently complicated, and the public sufficiently gullible that it would never catch on as to what is really going on. They also believe that the only segment of society capable of exposing them—the lawyers—can be counted on *not* to do so! However, now that *you know* the truth—hopefully *you will do something about it!*

One good way to get started is to get a copy of this book to your local newspaper (and to any other media source you can think of) and see to it that the charges in it are addressed and publicized. Hopefully, you will do the same in connection with your congressmen and senators. It is also important that a special effort be made to involve members of the House and Senate Judiciary Committees, since these committees are specifically charged with overseeing our legal system. By now it must be perfectly clear to you that, at least when it comes to federal income taxes, THE UNITED STATES DOESN'T HAVE ANY!

It is to be expected that congressmen and senators will not be enthusiastic about getting involved in an issue that proves that the U.S. Government has, for years, been collecting income taxes illegally and has been unlawfully putting people in jail. But they should be dragged, kicking and screaming if necessary, to this issue no matter how reluctant they are to face it. This book will provide them with all the facts they need to know, so don't be put off by excuses that the problem is too complicated or too difficult. I believe that this is the most important issue facing the nation, and the root of all of its economic and social problems. This book proves that the federal government breaks the law on a massive scale and it can easily be shown that it is this criminal growth of government that is resonsible for America's falling standard of living and declining position in the world's economic and financial affairs. What else could be causing both conditions? What are your congressmen and senators going to do about it? What are *you* going to do about it?

It is now May 25, 1990, as this book goes to press. I am still being illegally held prisoner in Morgantown, West Virginia. Robert E. Maxwell, Chief Judge for the Northern District of West Virginia (which sits in Elkins) is determined to make a mockery of the constitutional right of habeas corpus and the laws pursuant to which it is to be implemented. For example: Section 2243 of the Code of Judicial Procedure provides that the government answer a habeas corpus petition "within *three* days" from the court's order, "unless for good cause additional time, not exceeding *twenty* days is allowed." This is to be followed by a hearing not more than *five* days after that "unless for good cause additional time is allowed." Judge Maxwell gave the government the full 20 days to respond, even though no additional for "good cause" was shown or requested. Then, on top of that, and over my objection, he gave the government another twenty days—or *forty* days in all—just to tell the court why it was holding me. The obscenity of such a forty day allowance becomes clear when you realize that each inmate's prison file contains the paperwork that instantly reveals why he is being held, and if an institution can not immediately tell a court why it is holding someone, then that individual should be released!

On January 31, 1990 the government filed its answer with the court, but no hearing, where I would have an opportunity to demolish the government's answer, was scheduled and no party had requested "additional time." Instead, I was forced to waste more time composing a 35-page reply (submitted on February 12, 1990), which specifically detailed how the Parole Commission violated no fewer than nine Justice Department regulations (most of which you already know), two statutes (Sections 4209(b) and 4214 of the Criminal Code) and the constitutional prohibition that no person shall be placed "twice in jeopardy...for the same offense." In addition, since the government's reply was obviously false and evasive, I requested that Rule 11 sanctions be imposed against William A. Kolibash and Lisa A. Grimes, the government attorneys who prepared its response.

When it eventually became apparent (from this and other court inaction) that the court was simply going to ignore my habeas corpus rights, I notified it on March 2, 1990 that I wished to take the pauper's oath provided in Section 3569 of the U.S. Criminal Code. This statute allows those imprisoned for debt (as I am) to submit to examination, take an oath, and "be released without further imprisonment."

On March 6 and again on March 14, I received two fraudulent responses from the court (actually from Magistrate David L. Core) as to why the court was illegally refusing to examine me on my indigency claim and why they would not allow me to take the oath provided by law. I then realized that further entreaties to this court were futile.

On March 26, 1990, I filed a petition with the Fourth Circuit Court of Appeals in Richmond, VA, asking it to appoint a panel to conduct one or the other hearing as required by law, because "It is clear...that the Honorable Chief Judge Robert E. Maxwell has absolutely no intention of obeying the law as contained in the above two statutes; therefore, a panel selected by this court is essential to insure the public is afforded their statutorial and constitutional rights within this Circuit."

The lawless actions of Judge Maxwell (whom, I understand, is normally a fair and considerate judge), simply confirm that when it comes to federal income taxes, America has no laws, no courts, and, with a few exceptions, no judges.

NOTES TO THE EPILOGUE

1. After my second revocation hearing, I optimistically awaited for what I thought would be my "immediate" release. I had other legal work to attend to which needed my immediate attention, but which I had let slide in anticipation of being able to do it from the outside where I would have access to my computer and most of my records. I also began to update the original Epilogue that I had completed in Otisville, but which still had not arrived in Morgantown since I had been moved. I completed it on October 19, 1989 and was ready to mail it out for printing production to begin the next day, after I had a chance to photo-copy it. However, before I could do that, I was informed that I was being shipped out, and was given approximately 15 minutes to get ready. Believing that I was going back to MCC, New York (and that my personal property would accompany me on the bus), I had no qualms about packing the Epilogue with my other property. After eight weeks at Morgantown, however, two boxes of my personal property (including the box containing the completed Epilogue) **still had not arrived!** I have been told that they were "lost" in transit and my counselor has been trying to locate them. The two boxes were sent by certified mail from Otisville, about 200 miles away, and had my name and prison number written on each side of the box.

How could they have been "lost"? The original Epilogue contained everything that is now contained in this re-written version, with the exception of events that have since occurred. Thus the "mafia" now has an even better idea of what this book will contain (and I wanted to surprise them!). Undoubtedly the "mafia" is trying to hold me for as long as possible in order to prevent this book from being released— but I intend to disappoint them.

2. "Street time" is the period a parolee spends on parole, though in the eyes of the law he is still regarded as serving his time as if he were incarcerated. Consequently, a parolee is subject to numerous restrictions and reporting requirements and experiences a considerable loss of personal liberty. Despite this, he can still lose his street time, even over minor matters, and be made to do it *again*—only this time, incarcerated. There is no question that this kind of *double punishment* violates the spirit, if not the letter, of the double jeopardy clause of the Fifth Amendment. I wish I had time to describe examples that illustrate how this practice is viciously and callously abused. In addition, the added expense of having to house erroneously incarcerated parolees, plus the welfare costs of supporting families who were formerly being supported by productive citizens, must

be enormous! I know of one case where such a parolee ran up thousands of dollars of hospital expenses which now had to be borne by the taxpayers. And while the parole system has been abolished for those currently convicted, there will still be thousands of currently incarcerated federal prisoners who will be subject to it, which is why the laws that allow the Parole Commission to confiscate street time must be revised. There is simply no question that the U.S. Parole Commission can not be trusted to exercise either restraint, compassion or intelligence in exercising this power.

In order for Tenney and the Parole Commission to find a way to keep me incarcerated for even another day, they would have to be able to confiscate over eight months of street time, since I had now spent twenty-four months incarcerated on a thirty-six month sentence. And, taking into consideration my "good time," I only had to do twenty-seven months and twenty-two days to complete my sentence. Since parole counts towards your sentence, (and I had spent twelve months on parole) I was already eight months past my "max out" date—as the term is known in prison parlance. Therefore, the Parole Commission would have to confiscate eight months of street time in order to get me before my "max out" date to hold me for another day. However, there is simply no lawful basis upon which the Commission could do that. It could only take away *all* of my street time if I had been convicted of a crime. It could take away *some* of my street time from the time I failed to obey a valid order of my parole officer (See 26 CFR 2.52(c)(1) and (2).) Since the former condition obviously didn't apply, the only street time it could take away would have to be based on Walsh's claim that he had "directed" me to pay those court costs on April 13, 1989, and I "refused." However, even if the Parole Commission confiscated *all* of my street time from that date forward, I would *still* have twenty-four months of incarceration and over eight months of parole time to apply toward my twenty-seven month, twenty-two day "max out" date. Thus the "mafia" would still have no basis to hold me for another day. All of this, remember, is purely theoretical, because Tenney had informed me that since my violation was "technical," I would not lose *any* street time.

3. Through discovery requests, in connection with my initiating a habeas corpus action, I obtained a copy of William Tenney's report to the Parole Commission. On page three of that report he states that, though "This examiner finds that Subject is in violation of parole as charged because he did not pay court costs . . . this examiner does not make a finding that Subject *willfully refused to comply.*" (emphasis added.) Since Mr. Tenney did not find "willfulness" present, *no violation was possible.* Tenney's actual finding was known to William

Kolibash, U.S. Attorey for the Northern District of West Virginia, and Lisa Ann Grinmes, Ass't. U.S. Attorney, both of whom represented the government in opposing my habeas corpus petition, and also to Robert E. Maxwell, Chief Judge of West Virginia, before whom my petition was heard. **The fact that these three kept me incarcerated for seven months AFTER HAVING PROOF that NO VIOLATION HAD OCCURRED, gives you some idea of the type of criminals that sit on the federal bench and work as attorneys for the U.S. Department of Justice.**

4. The issue here is not whether I had refused to pay even a *lessor* mount, but that I had refused, and was being held for not paying the *entire* amount. Proof that Walsh had never discussed paying these costs with me is that no lesser amount is indicated in his letter. Had Walsh ever asked me to pay anything toward these costs, it would have been for a lesser amount. Since Walsh obviously knew that I had no accumulated funds and was not gainfully employed, he would have asked me to pay some token amount, such as $10 per month. And it would have been for not paying this lesser amount that he had ordered me to pay, that I might have "refused"—not for failing to pay the entire amount!

5. Actually, even my revocation hearing of November 1, 1989 was *illegal on entirely other grounds!* Pursuant to Section 2.49 of the Code of Federal Regulations, I was entitled to, and should have received a *local* revocation hearing within *sixty days* of my arrest "reasonably near the place of the alleged violation(s) or arrest," since I had fulfilled all of the requirements of the section from which that quote was taken—Section 2.49. In addition, a revocation hearing has to be held "within 90 days of the execution of the warrant" (28 CFR 2.49-02). Because my second revocation "hearing" was held 114 days after the execution of the warrant, it was also *totally illegal* just on this ground! In addition, 28 CFR 2.52-01(e) provides that: "In *all* cases, the possibility of forfeiture must be discussed with the prisoner at the time of review...and the possible *period* which may be forfeited *must be discussed at that time*"! Since this was not done *either,* my current incarceration is also illegal *on this ground alone!* Thus we see demonstrated, time and time again, that law means nothing to the federal mafia.

6. For a copy of this decision, send $2.00 and a stamped, self-addressed envelope to Freedom Books, requesting Judge Wiese's decision. For a copy of my appeal brief and decision, send $10 to Freedom Books.

ADDENDUM TO SECOND EDITION

This update to the Second Edition was begun in the latter part of June, 1991, and will be published in January, 1992—about 18 months after the completion of the First Edition. I will bring you up to date on the litigation that was pending when the first edition went to press, and also provide you with some additional, helpful information—some of which is of **EXTREME URGENCY!**

MY $500,000 REFUND SUIT

Incredibly, not only did the Second Circuit affirm Judge Eginton's decision granting the government a summary judgment following its summary "seizure" of my property, *Schiff* v. *U.S.*, 919 F.2d 830, but it fined me double costs and $5,000 for filing what it termed was a "frivolous appeal." However, if ever an appeal was justified, this one was. So how much more evidence does one need regarding the criminal nature of the Second Circuit Court of Appeal?

I opened my oral argument to its appellate panel, consisting of Judges Wilfred Feinberg, Roger J. Miner, and William H. Timbers, as follows:

Good morning your Honors, this is truly an historic occasion. I do believe this is the first time in American legal history that an appellant has attempted to reverse a decision in which he was found guilty of committing civil tax fraud without the trial court receiving one iota of evidence or testimony on the issue.

I believe, also, that this is the first time an appellant has ever sought to overturn a decision in which a District Court ruled that the U.S. Government can seize private property without ever holding hearings—let alone the trial called for by law—concerning whether: the taxes claimed were actually owed, the penalties imposed were legally justified, and whether the property was seized according to law. If the Second Circuit can affirm such a decision, then the Second Circuit, consistent with such a holding, should also declare America a fascist state and end the illusion that, as far as income taxes are concerned, America is a nation governed by law and a Constitution.

All of the funds at issue...were seized, expropriated, deprived...without one hearing ever being held. If this represents American justice in action, one is hard pressed to distinguish it from what might have been practiced by Atilla the Hun or Genghis Kahn—the U.S. Constitution and all of our fancy law schools and courthouses notwithstanding.

And I closed my ten-minute argument as follows:

18 USC 241 makes it a crime for two or more persons to conspire to deprive any American of any right or privilege secured to him by the Constitution or laws of the United States. So if this panel were ever to rule that the appellant can be deprived of property in payment of a tax that is not imposed pursuant to any of the taxing clauses of the Constitution, and also can be deprived of property in violation of such Code Sections as 6201, 6303, 6321, 6322, and 6331, as well as numerous others as cited by appellant in his briefs, than this panel will be guilty of having violated 18 USC 241 and thus guilty of a crime far more serious than many for which all of you, as judges, have sent others to prison.

There is no question that if I could get Judges Eginton, Feinberg, Timbers, and Miner before a federal grand jury, I could get them all indicted for violating 18 USC 241 and other statutes—with their ultimate convictions presenting no particular problem. The problem is that since federal judges know that U.S. prosecutors will never charge them **with the courtroom crimes they commit** (since they commit them in favor of the government), they commit them without any trepidation. This is why the federal judiciary probably represents the greatest single body of unindicted law breakers in the country.

I filed a petition for certiorari to the Supreme Court (docket number 90-8119) on May 20, 1991. If the Supreme Court does not reverse this decision, you will know that the Supreme Court is just as culpable as the Second Circuit.

By the time this second edition is published, the Supreme Court will have decided whether or not to grant certiorari. If it does, the Second Circuit's decision will be overturned and a lethal blow will have been delivered against the income tax—which is why the Supreme Court may not hear the case. On the other hand, because the Court cannot help but recognize the blatant lawlessness of the Second Circuit's decision (while recognizing that the lay public will also see it too), it may feel compelled to hear it, or risk exposure for the praetorian court it really is. I contacted most of the wire services, major newspapers and newspaper syndicates in the hope that they would be interested in my pending petition, but to no avail. I also contacted the ACLU to see if it would submit an *amicus curiae* brief, but they never even answered my letters or returned my phone calls. Apparently the right not to be deprived of property without due process of law is not one of the rights the ACLU believes to be important. Unbelievably, I wrote most of the above on the morning of June 26, 1991, and that afternoon I received a letter from the Supreme Court informing me that my petition for a writ of certiorari was turned down on June 24, 1991.

Because I added that petition to this edition, I must apologize to you for any nausea you may experience whenever you see reference to the Supreme Court's alleged commitment to the Constitution. In any case, now that **I have exhausted all of my legal remedies**, WHAT CAN I DO *NOW* TO GET BACK THE MONEY THE UNITED STATES TOOK FROM ME *IN VIOLATION OF ALL LAW*? Obviously, the United States cannot be permitted to keep this money. If justice can not be found in our courts, I have to look elsewhere.

I will be contacting both of my New York senators and my representative to introduce a bill in Congress which requires the government to reimburse me for the money, plus interest, it took (i.e. *stole*) from me **without giving me any hearings whatsoever!** I hope I can count on your help in this effort, because if the government can do this to me, it can do it to you. I would appreciate your contacting your own senators and congressmen to help line up support for such a bill. This would also show Congress that the public is aware of what occurred in my case, and is outraged by it. For obvious reasons, members of Congress will not be enthusiastic about helping me get my money back. But if you press the issue, what can they say? Can they justify—on any basis—that the government is keeping my money that they took in this manner? If the government can get away with this, then the Constitution is dead and America has become little better than a fascist state. How can anyone argue the point?

MY TAX COURT CASE

Since my last comments on Tax Court, I found out a lot more about that "court" and discovered it to be an even greater fraud than I had suspected. The seeds for that fraud were sown on October 21, 1942, when the U.S. Congress—while the nation was distracted by World War II—passed a bill declaring that the United States Board of Tax Appeals "should be known" as the Tax Court of the United States, but "with the same powers, tenure, and jurisdiction as had formerly been provided for the United States Board of Tax Appeals." Can Congress change a bureaucratic agency into a "court" by simply giving it another name, but without changing any of its powers, duties or jurisdiction? The answer, of course, is no. Why would the government want to fool the public in this manner? Obviously, to intimidate and

mislead it for a number of reasons. For one thing, the public, by believing that it was "in court" when it was merely before a governmental agency, could be more easily conned into thinking it was getting the "due process" of law it associates with the courts, and is provided for in the Constitution. In addition, the public would be less apt to understand the extremely *narrow* jurisdiction that the Board of Tax Appeal really had, if it were called a "Court" rather than a "Board." The public would also hold a "Court" in higher esteem than a "Board," and could be more easily intimidated. In addition, federal courts would be able to cite Tax Court decisions (in their own decisions) if the public believed that those "decisions" came from a legitimate court, rather than a government agency. An important ingredient in the government's overall INCOME TAX SCAM was to *dupe the public into thinking that a government agency was actually a court of law.*

In any case, I had a Tax Court "trial" in connection with my alleged 1979 deficiency on November 27, 1990. (Remember, this case started in May of 1986—some five years ago.) My "trial" and the testimony and cross-examination of IRS Agent Thomas Cingo, the government's key witness, along with the comments and conduct of Judge Charles E. Clapp, II, who conducted the "trial," and the post trial briefs filed by the government and myself, should convince anyone of the kangaroo character of that "Court."

All of Thomas Cingo's testimony was based on his initial claim that he had "investigated" my 1979 return prior to his determining my alleged 1979 deficiency. This claim had to be made by him because pursuant to Treasury Regulation 601.104(a), a "deficiency" can only be determined after "a return is selected for examination." Without claiming that he had "investigated" (i.e. examined) my 1979 tax return, there could not be any "deficiency" for the Tax Court to "redetermine"—which is the only jurisdiction it has.[1] The first question put to Mr. Cingo by the government was, did he investigate my 1979 tax return. His answer was, yes. However, on cross-examination he admitted that no 1979 return was filed by either myself or the government. Obviously, his claim—under oath—was perjurious. The following is a brief excerpt from my post trial brief where I focused on this particular issue.

When I cross-examined Mr. Cingo, I asked him, "In my case, you had no return?" (last line, page 171 of Trial Transc.) Mr. Cingo answered, (first line, page 172) "Correct." *Obviously*, Mr. Cingo's opening answer to Mr. Best's initial question was perjurious. Based upon his later admission on cross-examination that he had no 1979 tax return of mine to *investigate*, his only truthful answer to Mr. Best's OPENING QUESTION, which was, "In your ca-

FIGURE A-1

Part I – Referral Information

13. Describe specific statements or actions taken by the taxpayer indicating intent to defraud or evade, include statements made during the interview(s) which were false, misleading or contradicted by further investigation *(attach statement if necessary)*.

Agent was instructed by CID, Review and District Counsel not to make any direct contact with the taxpayer, unless permission was secured in advance.

14. What was the taxpayer's explanation or defense given in response to examiner's request for explanation of discrepancies which are the basis of this referral *(attach statement if necessary)*.

No contact made. T/P's position matter of public record.

15. What was the preparer's explanation or defense given in response to examiner's request for explanation of discrepancies which are the basis of this referral *(attach statement if necessary)*.

N/A

16a. Name and address of person(s) preparing return(s)

N/A

16b. Name and address of representative

N/A

16b. EIN of person(s) preparing return(s)

N/A

16d. Have the proposed adjustment(s) been discussed with the taxpayer or representative?
☐ Yes *(explain)* ☒ No

d. DIF Score

17. Source of return
a. District Office Code: 0 6
b. Source Code: 4 4
c. Activity Code: 0 6
e. AIMS Project Code: N/A

18. Total time charged through referral date *(in hours)*: 6 8

Attach copies of –
(i) First two pages of tax returns and supporting income and expense schedules;
(ii) Altered documents.

19. Initiator's –
a. Name
Last Name: d i N G O | First Name: T H O M A S
b. Grade: 1 2 | c. Group No.: 2 0 5
d. Signature
e. Telephone No.: 645-2084
f. Date M D Y: 04 16 85

Telephone Number: 695-2003

Signature of Group Manager
Date: 4/22/85

Signature of Branch Chief
Date: 5/2/85

Signature of Chief, Examination Division
Date: 5/7/85

Part II – For Criminal Investigation Division Use Only

20. Civil fraud
☐ a. Concur
☐ b. Reclassify
Criminal fraud
☐ c. Declined
☐ d. Accepted *(Case level)*

Special Agent assigned to case
Last Name | First Name | Grade

Signature of Chief, Criminal Investigation Division
MAY 8 1985

21. Reason for declination of criminal referral
☐ a. Deceased taxpayer
☐ b. Age/health/education
☐ c. Small criminal tax liability
☐ d. Lack of pattern
☐ e. Dual prosecution
☐ f. Voluntary disclosure
☐ g. Lack of intent
☐ h. Civil closing before referral
☐ i. Technical adjustment
☐ k. Accounting error
☐ k. Preparer's error
☐ l. Documentation not available

If box 20c is checked, attach CI Closing Report or Memorandum of Declination

Form 2797 (Rev. 11-83)

FIGURE A-2

Part I – Referral Information – Continued

13. Describe specific statements or actions taken by the taxpayer indicating intent to defraud or evade, include statements made during the interview(s) when were false, misleading or contradicted by further investigation *(attach statement if necessary)*.

SEE ATTACHMENT C

14. What was the taxpayer's explanation or defense given in response to examiner's request for explanation of discrepancies which are the basis of this referral *(attach statement if necessary)*.

CONSTITUTIONAL GROUNDS

15. What was the preparer's explanation or defense given in response to examiner's request for explanation of discrepancies which are the basis of this referral *(attach statement if necessary)*.

NO PREPARER INVOLVED.

16a. Name and address of person(s) preparing return(s)

N/A

16c. Name and address of representative

N/A

16b. EIN of person(s) preparing return(s)

N/A

16d. Have the proposed adjustment(s) been discussed with the taxpayer or representative?
☐ Yes *(explain)* ☒ No

d. DIF Score

17. Source of return
a. District Office: 0 6
b. Source Code
c. TPI Class: 1 0

18. Total time charged through referral date *(in hours)*: SEE EXHIBIT # 5

Attach copies of –
(i) First two pages of tax returns and supporting income and expense schedules;
(ii) Altered documents.

19. Initiator's –
a. Name
b. Grade: 1 2 | c. Group No.
d. Signature
e. Telephone No. | f. Date

Telephone Number
Signature of Group Manager | Date

Signature of Branch Chief | Date

Signature of Chief, Examination Division | Date

Part II – For Criminal Investigation Division Use Only

20. Civil fraud
☐ a. Concur
☐ b. Reclassify
Criminal fraud
☐ c. Declined
☐ d. Accepted *(Case level)*

Special Agent assigned to case
Grade

Signature of Chief, Criminal Investigation Division

21. Reason for declination of criminal referral
☐ a. Deceased taxpayer
☐ b. Age/health/education
☐ c. Small criminal tax liability
☐ d. Lack of pattern
☐ e. Dual prosecution
☐ f. Voluntary disclosure
☐ g. Lack of intent
☐ h. Civil closing before referral
☐ i. Technical adjustment
☐ j. Accounting error
☐ k. Preparer's error
☐ l. Documentation not available

If box 20c is checked, attach CI Closing Report or Memorandum of Declination

Form 2797 (Rev. 9-8)

pacity as Revenue Agent, did you investigate the (1979) income tax return of Petitioner, Irwin Schiff?"... should have been, "No, I did not," and not, "yes (I did)." Therefore, all the rest of Mr. Cingo's testimony is IRRELEVANT because it ADMITTEDLY rests on a false and fraudulent foundation: that he "investigated" a return when he *admittedly did not*. Therefore, all of his testimony that followed can not be given any weight or credence by this court! Obviously, as I have already stated, had he given a truthful answer to Mr. Best's opening foundation question, no further testimony from him concerning my alleged "deficiency" would have been legally possible.

The Court even sought to protect Mr. Cingo later on when I again asked him (at page 18): "Did you select my return for examination?" The court immediately responded (not even waiting for Cingo to answer or the Government to object), "Look, you argue that with me. I'm not—not going to—." After an objection by Mr. Best, the court continued, "It's not appropriate questions for Mr. Cingo, and I'm not going to let you ask them AND I'M NOT GOING TO LET HIM ANSWER." The Court was determined not to let Mr. Cingo testify on cross-examination that he never examined "my return," because the Court realized that such an admission (which he had, nonetheless, already made!) would render all his testimony that he had determined a deficiency, inadmissible.

On cross-examination, and despite Judge Clapp's attempt to prevent him from testifying on this issue, he admitted that he determined my "total" tax liability - *not* a deficiency. And since the Tax Court's jurisdiction is limited to only "redetermining a deficiency," it had no jurisdiction to determine my "total" income tax liability.

Though $22,000 in fraud penalties were imposed on me, the document imposing the penalty (see Figure A-1) contained no allegation that I had committed any act of tax fraud in 1979. All it said was that the IRS made "no contact" with me, and based on that, three IRS agents charged me with having committed tax fraud. Based on this evidence, there is no fair minded person who would not agree that these three should be prosecuted for attempted extortion and for violating a number of other laws.[2] While knowing full well that no fraud had been committed, however, they also knew that their extortionary efforts would be protected by their partners in crime on the federal bench and at the U.S. Department of Justice. As proof of this, Judge Clapp would not even allow me to examine Cingo concerning the basis of the government's fraud claim. And, the government's lawyer would never question him on it during his direct

testimony. The trial transcript reveals the following dialogue between Judge Clapp and myself.

JUDGE CLAPP: What are you driving at?

SCHIFF: I'm trying to determine if he determined civil fraud according to the way civil fraud is supposed to be determined.

JUDGE CLAPP: Well, what difference does it make how he determined it?   * * * * * *

SCHIFF: I want to know on what basis he determined I committed tax fraud.

JUDGE CLAPP: What difference does it make?

SCHIFF: Are you familiar with the Spies case?

JUDGE CLAPP: I don't care what basis he made it on. It doesn't make a bit of difference. He made that determination and we are here reviewing that determination, and that is the point of his proceeding. How Mr. Cingo arrived at it and whether he was right or wrong - he may have done it by shooting darts at a dart board. I don't care.

Tax Court judges don't care how IRS agents determine fraud penalties. As far as they are concerned, they can do it by "shooting darts at a dart board." However, if I had let 90 days go by without petitioning Tax Court, IRS goon squads could start seizing $22,000 of my property *based on nothing more than their dart throwing ability*. And, Americans are having billions of dollars in penalties extracted from them *on this very basis!*

No matter how often I pressed the court, it simply would not identify any section of the code that established the tax liability it claimed I owed.

Though final briefs were submitted on April 10, 1991, as of this writing I have not yet received the Tax Court's decision.

I believe that the Trial Memorandums submitted, the two briefs filed by the Government and myself, together with the relevant transcript pages are so revealing and would be so helpful to those who are forced to go to Tax Court, that I intend to publish all this material (in manual form) when I get the Tax Court's final decision. For now, beginning on the following page, I have included some excerpts taken from my Reply Brief filed on April 10, 1991.

F
WITH RESPECT TO THE GOVERNMENT'S PROPOSAL THAT THE COURT IMPOSE $25,000 IN PUNITIVE DAMAGES ON PETITIONER FOR INSTITUTING THIS ACTION

If additional evidence is needed to PROVE CONCLUSIVELY THAT THE IRS IS A CRIMINAL ORGANIZATION, then its attempt to extort an additional $25,000 in damages from petitioner, for having instituted this action, is ALL OF THE PROOF THAT ANYONE SHOULD NEED!

I have already blown away all of the Government's arguments it raised to support its diabolic proposal (page 28 of its brief) when I responded to its "Points Relied Upon." However, the proposition that one petitioning Tax Court from a Deficiency Notice containing civil fraud penalties—which by law, the IRS must prove—should be subject to additional penalties for compelling the IRS to prove the fraud alleged, is such a heinous proposal that it must be more fully addressed.

When I received the Commissioner's invalid and fraudulent Deficiency Notice, I only had two options. I could either pay the Government the $68,147.71 the IRS claimed I owed, and sue for a refund in district court, or I could petition the Tax Court. Since I did not have $68,147.71, the first option was closed to me. However, if I did not petition Tax Court within 90 days, the IRS could begin confiscating whatever meager assets of mine they could find, in the same *illegal manner* as covered in Chapter 7 of Exh. 9. [Author's note: I submitted a copy of *The Federal Mafia* as my Exhibit #9.] So to prevent IRS highwaymen from illegally seizing whatever assets I had left (following their illegal seizures of most of my property, see Chapter 7 of Exh. 9), I had NO CHOICE but to petition Tax Court for at least THREE REASONS:

1. To prevent the lawless seizure of my property 90 days from the date of my alleged Deficiency Notice;
2. To create the legal forum in which the IRS would have to prove the fraud alleged, on the basis of "clear and convincing evidence," and to
3. Get discovery, so I could establish that, at the very least, its $22,100 civil fraud claim was erroneous.

The fact that I have clearly proved (especially through discovery) that the IRS' fraud claim was TOTALLY BASELESS, and overlooking all other considerations, the mere EXISTENCE of *a civil fraud penalty* in a Deficiency Notice is JUSTIFICATION ENOUGH for ANYONE to petition Tax Court ON *ANY* BASIS - if for no other reason than to compel the IRS to prove the fraud alleged. Clearly what the IRS is attempting to do here is develop a precedent (if it has not done so already) whereby the threat of ADDITIONAL PUNITIVE DAMAGES will dissuade some, against whom fraud penalties have been imposed, from petitioning the Tax Court, thus eliminating, in those cases, the need for the IRS to prove the fraud alleged - as it is required to do by Section 7454(a).

AND IF THIS DOES NOT PROVE THAT THE IRS IS NOTHING BUT A CRIMINAL GANG, THEN WHAT MORE PROOF *IS* NEEDED?

But in addition, the fact that the Government would even make such a proposal to this court is further proof that respondent is convinced that the U.S. Tax Court is TOTALLY DEVOID OF JUDICIAL INTEGRITY, since if the Government thought otherwise, *it never would have made such a diabolic proposal to the court.*

G
THE CONSEQUENCES OF THE U.S. TAX COURT BEING A COURT IN NAME ONLY

It is clear that Judge Charles E. Clapp II took umbrage on my pointing out that the U.S. Tax Court is not really a court (transcript pages 6, 7, 49, 124, 125). On page 124, Judge Clapp even suggests that by my reminding him of this, I was attempting to "insult" the court, and "not doing (myself) any good." (transcript page 125). But how could I "insult" the court by reminding it of its true, legal nature? When on October 21, 1942 Congress declared that the United States Board of Tax Appeals "should be known" as the Tax Court of the United States but "with the same powers, tenure, and jurisdiction as had formerly been provided for the United States Board of Tax Appeals," this name change COULD NOT HAVE POSSIBLY changed the real nature of that agency. Obviously, if the U.S. Tax Court is a court, though it has no greater "powers, tenure and jurisdiction" THAN HAD THE BOARD OF TAX APPEALS, *then that bureaucratic agency WAS ALSO A COURT!*

Tax Court judges apparently do not like to be reminded of this, since this might inhibit them from rendering judgments and opinions on legal issues which are outside the scope of their jurisdiction—as Judge Hamblin did in *Schiff* v. *Commissioner,* supra. The danger to petitioners in not knowing that the U.S. Tax Court is not a real court is that petitioners will argue issues before that "court" which the court has no jurisdiction to consider, and so, such arguments will not help their case. BUT THEY WILL KNOT KNOW THIS, SINCE THE "COURT" WILL NOT INFORM THEM OF IT.

Thus, they will make wasted arguments and have false expectations - which is exactly what happened to me the first time I went to Tax Court. So, I want to put this "court" on notice - THAT IT IS NOT GOING TO FOOL ME *THIS TIME!*

QUASHING IRS' BANK SUMMONS

On July 19, 1991, I received a 13-page ruling of Ellen B. Burns, Chief Judge of the District of Connecticut granting the government's request for the summary judgment, as discussed on page 187. In doing so, Judge Burns:

1. denied me a hearing,
2. denied me discovery,
3. resolved all controverted issues of fact in favor of the government, in violation of the principle upon which summary judgments are supposed to be granted.

On the issue of attestation, and contrary to the decision in *Mimick* v. *United States*, 91-1 U.S.T.C. 50,700, Judge Burns said:

1. That I had no "standing to address this issue," and it could only be raised by the bank,
2. "The word 'attested' is not defined" in the Code, and
3. That she is "not compelled to adopt the unnecessarily restricted interpretation of a Nebraska District Court."

In claiming that I had no standing to address this issue, though no such problem was raised in *Mimick,* she said:

> Under the statute "[T]he notice...will not be permitted to assert as defenses the enforcement issues which only affect the interests of the third-party recordkeeper." S. Rep. No. 938 Cong. 2d Sess. 370-71 (1976), reprinted in 1976 U.S. Code Cong. & A News, 2897, 3800. Defenses belonging to the third-party record-keeper include "the defense that the third-party recordkeeper was not properly served."

The above is an example AS TO WHY "JUSTICE" IN AMERICA IS REALLY A JOKE. In this case, I had both *the statute and case law* on my side - BUT IT WAS NOT ENOUGH. *Judge Burns still managed to find for the government!* She did so by citing some material that allegedly has a bearing on this issue. Therefore, to understand what the "law" is in America, the public is expected not only to know what the statutes say, what the case law is, but is also expected to be familiar with the type of obscure source material cited by Judge Burns. HOW RIDICULOUS CAN THE SITUATION GET?

I really have no time now (Judge Dorsey is trying to put me in jail - read on) to check the applicability of the sources she cites, but obviously no bank is really interested in resisting a IRS summons, so they will not raise any objection to turning over people's records. In effect, Judge Burns' ruling nullifies the attestation provision as contained in the law.

If this is an objection that a bank could have raised BUT DID NOT, (and the public has no standing to raise it), then obviously the public should be able to sue any bank who does not raise this objection, but turns over records based upon an improperly executed summons.

As far as attestation not being defined in the Code - it certainly is defined in *Black's Law Dictionary*. Based on that definition, the summons sent to the bank violated Section 7603. In deciding against me on this issue, Judge Burns further stated that I had only submitted "a copy of the front side of the summons" not the back sides, so presumably the attestation clause might have been there. However, it should have been up to the government to make that argument in a reply brief and/or to supply the back side with the attestation clause, but it never did. Incidentally, all of these arguments were raised by Judge Burns *on behalf of the government* - the government never raised them at all. With this kind of legal help, the government can win these cases just with paralegals. It doesn't have to spend good money on lawyers.

Judge Burns' refusal to follow the *Mimick* decision illustrates that federal judges can pick and choose those

FIGURE A-3

DEPARTMENT OF THE TREASURY
WASHINGTON

June 28, 1991

RE: Treasury Order 150-10

Mr. Irwin A. Schiff
404 E. 55th Sreet
Suite 8-H
New York, NY 10022

Dear Mr. Schiff:

Thank you for your letter of May 24, 1991, to the Department of the Treasury regarding Treasury Order 150-10.

Treasury Order 150-37, "Commissioner of the Internal Revenue Delegated Responsibility for Internal Revenue Laws," dated April 22, 1982, has been renumbered 150-10. A certified copy of the Treasury Order 150-10, which is a valid and current Order, is enclosed.

The annual indexes published by the Federal Register do not indicate publication of this Order. The records maintained by the Office of Management Support Systems, which manages the Treasury Orders and Directives System, do not indicate whether this Order had been filed with the Federal Register in 1982. However, this Order would not have to be published in the Federal Register because there is no legal requirement to publish internal delegation Orders in the Federal Register.

Delegation of authority orders authorizing Internal Revenue Service employees to perform specific duties or activities need not be published in the Federal Register. See United States v. McCall, SCR No. 89-15 (N. D. Ind., January 4, 1990) or Hogg v. United States, 428 F 2d 274 (6th Cir. 1970), cert. denied 401 U.S. 910 (1971). When Treasury Orders are published in the Federal Register, this is generally done for the convenience of the public rather than pursuant to any legal requirement.

The Department of the Treasury's view is that current Treasury Order 150-10 delegates responsibility, and all necessary authority, to the Commissioner of the Internal Revenue Service to administer and enforce Internal Revenue laws. Sections 7801 and 7802 of the Internal Revenue Code expressly provide authority for this delegation.

Sincerely,

Robert T. Harper

Robert T. Harper
Director, Office of Management
Support Systems

Enclosure

court cases (outside their own circuits) they want to follow and those they do not. How nonsensical can a legal system be! If this is the case, how can Americans really know what the "law" is.

I do not have the luxury of time or space to address Judge Burns' claim that the government's failure to publish Treasury Order 150-10 is irrelevant. Suffice it to say that federal judges can contrive legal reasons to support any decision they want to make.

In attempting to refute my claim that the agent involved had no delegated authority to summon my bank records, the government contended that his authority was Delegation Order No. 4, published in the *Federal Register* on January 25, 1989. If you read that Delegation Order you will see that it claims to derive its authority from Treasury Order No. 150-10. Therefore, if Delegation Order No. 150-10 is without "legal effect and general applicability," so would Delegation Order No. 4. *According to the law* (44 USC 1505 and 5 USC 552) orders which are not published are without "general applicability and legal effect" as far as the public is concerned.

Figure A-3 contains a letter I recently received from Robert T. Harper of the Department of the Treasury which confirms that Treasury Order 150-10 was never published in the *Federal Register*. If it were, *he would know about it!* However, Mr. Harper obviously realized why I was seeking such confirmation, so he thought he would try and confuse me about it. Notice he states that, "There is no legal requirement to publish internal delegation orders in the *Federal Register*." That is true. If the Secretary wanted to delegate authority to certain Treasury Department employees to make coffee for the office, that delegation order would not have to be published in the *Federal Register*. Technically there is "no legal requirement" that internal delegation orders have to be published, but if they are not, they are "without general applicability and legal effect," as far as the public is concerned. *At least, that is supposed to be the law!* But, like in *Alice in Wonderland*, the "law" in America is anything that federal judges say it is.

IMPORTANT: Only within the past several weeks I was provided with **OFFICIAL PROOF** that Section 7602 (the section providing for IRS summonses) does not even *apply* to income taxes, but only to alcohol, tobacco products and firearms—thus giving further proof that Judge Burns' decision was totally contrived. Everything that I have already written about Section 7602 proves that it does not apply to income taxes, but now I'm talking about additional, drop-dead proof.

As you know the IRS does not enforce the collection of income taxes based upon the laws themselves. But, like all government agencies, it supposedly enforces the

law based upon the regulations written to implement the law. These regulations are contained in volumes known as Codes of Federal Regulations. If you want to find the implementing regulations for any law, you can check a volume (that will be found in most law libraries) entitled *Index to Code of Federal Regulations*. If you look under 26 USC (1954 I.R.C.) in that volume, at Section 7602, you will see that you are referred to "27 Parts 170,296." The "27" refers to the Code of Federal Regulations (cited as CFR) number 27, which is entitled "Alcohol, Tobacco Products and Firearms." Since the implementing regulations for Code Section 7602 are contained in the CFR dealing with alcohol, tobacco products and firearms—but not in CFR 26, which deals with the Internal Revenue code in general—you now have added proof of what I wrote on page 170 of this book: "By law (IRS summonses) have absolutely nothing to do with income taxes." I did not raise this issue in my motion discussed above (I did not know about it then), but it, ALONE, should be enough to quash any 7602 summonses issued in connection with income taxes.

THE CHEEK DECISION, OR HAPPY DAYS ARE HERE AGAIN!

On January 8, 1991, the Supreme Court, in *Cheek* v. *U.S.*, (111 S. Ct. 604) came down with a decision that was front page news in papers around the country. In this decision, the Supreme Court reversed the conviction of John L. Cheek who had been convicted of tax evasion and failure to file. At his trial, Mr. Cheek correctly argued that his wages were not income. In reversing his conviction, that court said:

> It was error for the court to instruct the jury that petitioner's asserted beliefs that wages are not income and that he was not a taxpayer within the meaning of the Internal Revenue Code should not be considered by the jury in determining whether Cheek had acted willfully.

In handing down its ruling, the Supreme Court (citing such cases as *U.S.* v. *Murdock,* 290 US 389; *U.S.* v. *Pomponio,* 429 US 10; and *U.S.* v. *Bishop,* 412 US 346) stated what any court should have known: "Taken together, *Bishop* and *Pomponio* conclusively establish that the standard for the statutory willfulness requirement is the 'voluntary, intentional violation of a known legal duty'." In other words, "willfulness" is not based upon what a defendant *should have believed,* but what he *actually believed.* However, as I stated on page 233, footnote 6, "Courts not only misstate the law with respect to filing, they also misstate the meaning of 'willfulness'."

If John Cheek did not have the $55,000 that the filing of his two appeals cost, he would have gone to jail simply because his judge mislead the jury regarding the meaning of "willfulness." Do you think that all of those appellate judges who upheld those incorrect guilty verdicts did not know what they were doing? Do you really think that they needed the Supreme Court in the *Cheek* decision to tell them the legal meaning of "willfulness"? What they never expected (and, frankly, neither did I) is that the Supreme Court would some day hear the issue!

Courts are now reversing decisions where similar instructions were given—which occurred at both of my trials! The *Cheek* decision alone proves on just this ONE issue that **I was never lawfully convicted of ANY crime!**

For example, at my last trial Judge Dorsey instructed the jury that:

> In determining whether a Defendant acting knowingly and willfully, you may consider, as well, whether the Defendant deliberately closed his eyes to what otherwise would have been obvious to him. A finding beyond a reasonable doubt of a conscious purpose to avoid enlightenment would permit an inference of knowledge.

> Stated another way, a defendant's knowledge of a fact may be inferred from willful blindness to the existence of that fact. You may consider whether or not the Defendant displayed a deliberate indifference or refusal to be informed in this regard. It is entirely up to you as to whether you find any deliberate closing of the eyes, and the inferences which may be drawn from any such evidence.

Cheek says such an instruction was **dead wrong,** and violated every Supreme Court decision bearing on the meaning of "willfulness"—as Judge Dorsey **was told by my attorney both before and after he gave the instruction.** In addition to all of his other crimes, Judge Dorsey **knowingly misled the jury** on the meaning of "willfulness."

Dorsey's erroneous jury instruction was also cited in my appeal to the Second Circuit (an issue which I had also raised when I appealed my first conviction) but the Second Circuit ignored it. I also raised the issue in two appeals to the Supreme Court, which, in both cases, refused to hear it. An issue the Supreme Court **twice refused to address in** *my* **case,** they heard in *Cheek*—and reversed accordingly.

THE IMPORTANCE OF THE *CHEEK* DECISION

Based on the *Cheek* decision, federal judges will not be able to mislead juries on the issue of "willfulness" as easily in the future. **According to the *Cheek* decision, if you sincerely believe the information in this book and act accordingly, you can not be found guilty of failure to file and/or tax evasion.** However, you should still be prepared to put on an intelligent defense if the federal mafia decides—illegally—to prosecute you. To help you do that, I have prepared an 18-page Trial Memorandum that explains how I believe such a defense should be handled - including, how I might be utilized as a defense witness for you.

Incidentally, all those convicted of tax crimes pursuant to a jury instruction as used against John Cheek and myself (which would include practically all "tax protestors") should be able to get their convictions reversed, and they should institute court actions to do so.

Without speculating as to why the Supreme Court heard Cheek, but not others who raised the same issue, we can all be grateful to him for pursuing his case and prevailing. However, it is also clear from that decision that the Supreme Court knows that no one is required to file income tax returns and that wages are not income (as Cheek claimed), but wrote its decision so as to mislead the public into thinking the Supreme Court believes otherwise.

If you read the decision, you will see that the Court continually refers to a "duty" to file, not a "legal requirement" to do so. The difference should be obvious. In the event of war, all able bodied men might have a "duty" to volunteer, but there is no "legal requirement" that they do so. Since the Supreme Court knows that no such "requirement" exists in the law, it employed the word "duty" so as to mislead the public without actually misstating the law. Also, in two places in its decision, it talks about "whether the defendant knew of the duty *purportedly* imposed..." (emphasis added). In both places the Court was referring to the "duty" of filing a tax return. If the Court believed that such a "duty" existed, would it have used the disclaimer "purportedly"? (Read the sentences with "purportedly" left out.)

In trying to give the impression that John Cheek's professed belief that wages are not income was incorrect, the Supreme Court listed *numerous* sources that allegedly "made it plain that wages should be returned as income." What does "returned as income" really mean? Why didn't the Supreme Court say, "reported as income"? Also, the general public would not know that the Court's use of "should"—in this instance—was the legal equivalent of "may." In addition, if wages really had to be reported, the Supreme Court would not have listed the many sources it did. It would have said instead, that Cheek's belief that wages are not income is clearly contrary to Section 61 (or some other Code section) that requires the reporting of wages as income. The failure by the Supreme Court to use such clear cut language **was no accident!**

The Supreme Court, in allegedly explaining Cheek's other options, stated that he "was free to pay the tax that the law purported to require, file for a refund and if denied, present his claims of invalidity, constitutional or otherwise, to the courts," or "**without paying the tax**, he could have challenged claims of tax deficiencies in the Tax Court." (emphasis added)

You should now know that both of these alleged options as suggested by the Court *are specious*. For one thing, if he paid the tax, there is no guarantee he would get the "hearing" referred to by the Supreme Court. I DID NOT GET ONE, SO WHAT GUARANTEE DID CHEEK HAVE THAT HE WOULD GET ONE? Secondly, how could he go to Tax Court when he had not filed a return. There was no "deficiency" to consider? Cheek could not raise the wage issue in Tax "Court" because that agency has no jurisdiction to even consider such a question. If Cheek did raise it, the Tax Court would simply dismiss the claim as frivolous and perhaps impose an additional $5,000 penalty on him for having raised a "frivolous" issue. In discussing these alleged "options,"

the Supreme Court was engaging in double talk. But, because of the complexity of the "law", the Court WAS FULLY CONFIDENT that it could get away with it.

What the law actually required of Cheek was that **he had to do nothing**. If the government believed he owed an income tax, they were required then, pursuant to 6501(c)(3), to <u>sue him</u> for what it claimed Cheek owed. Instead of doing that, however, the government filed criminal charges against him. If he did not have the $52,000 to cover the cost of his appeals, he would have gone to jail. **SO MUCH, THEREFORE, FOR THE HONESTY OF THE SUPREME COURT.** In any case, thank God for its *Cheek* decision.

ADDITIONAL PROOF THAT ALL INCOME TAX PROSECUTIONS ARE ILLEGAL

Figure A-4 is a letter that I recently received from Senator Joseph R. Biden, Jr. Chairman of the Senate Judiciary Committee. It verifies that all felonies are in Title 18, The U.S. Criminal Code. The only exception noted by Biden was "certain drug offenses... encom-

---

FIGURE A-4

JOSEPH R. BIDEN, JR., DELAWARE, CHAIRMAN

EDWARD M. KENNEDY, MASSACHUSETTS
HOWARD M. METZENBAUM, OHIO
DENNIS DeCONCINI, ARIZONA
PATRICK J. LEAHY, VERMONT
HOWELL HEFLIN, ALABAMA
PAUL SIMON, ILLINOIS
HERBERT KOHL, WISCONSIN

STROM THURMOND, SOUTH CAROLINA
ORRIN G. HATCH, UTAH
ALAN K. SIMPSON, WYOMING
CHARLES E. GRASSLEY, IOWA
ARLEN SPECTER, PENNSYLVANIA
HANK BROWN, COLORADO

RONALD A KLAIN, CHIEF COUNSEL
JEFFREY J PECK, STAFF DIRECTOR
TERRY L. WOOTEN, MINORITY CHIEF COUNSEL
AND STAFF DIRECTOR

United States Senate

COMMITTEE ON THE JUDICIARY
WASHINGTON, DC 20510–6275

March 21, 1991

Mr. Irwin A. Schiff
404 East 55th Street, Suite 8-H
New York, New York 10022

Dear Mr. Schiff:

Thank you for your letter regarding the Senate Judiciary Committee's report on the Criminal Code Reform Act of 1981.

I appreciate your interest in this matter. The effort to consolidate all felonies into Title 18 of the U.S. Code was generally achieved. However, one exception is that there are provisions for certain drug offenses, which were included in the Crime Control Act of 1990, that are encompassed in Title 21 of the U.S. Code.

Again, thank you for your letter. I hope this information is helpful. Please feel free to contact me if I may be of assistance in other matters.

Sincerely,

Joe Biden

Joseph R. Biden, Jr.
Chairman

passed in Title 21." Notice that he makes no claim that there are any offenses "encompassed" in Title 26 (i.e. the Internal Revenue Code). Also, in Figure A-5, I have reproduced Section 1329 of Title 8, which deals with immigration and nationality. Note that this section provides district courts with both "civil and criminal" jurisdiction. As I pointed out on page 214, the comparable jurisdictional section in the Internal Revenue Code (Title 26) Section 7402(f) only provides federal courts with *civil* jurisdiction, and contains no mention of criminal jurisdiction. Apart from everything else in this book, Figures A-4 and A-5, taken together with pages 214 and 215, clearly establish that John Cheek, Pete Rose, I, and **thousands of other Americans have been illegally prosecuted, fined, and imprisoned by federal judges who never had jurisdiction to do so.** That will give you a rough idea of the kind of criminality that exists on the federal bench and within the U.S. Department of Justice. It also reveals the incompetence and culpability of practically the entire U.S. legal establishment that allowed these prosecutions to take place.

IMPORTANT: CONTACT YOUR SENATORS, CONGRESSMEN, AND OTHERS!

In response to Senator Biden's letter to me of March 21, 1991, I sent him a six page letter on April 27, 1991, supported by about 100 pages of exhibits, in which I pointed out to him that federal courts were:

1. allowing the federal government to NOW seize private property without holding hearings *of any kind,* in total disregard of relevant statutes, a significant body of case law, and the United States Constitution;

2. claiming that the IRS can assess income taxes without having any tax returns at all, in violation of every statute and regulation on the issue;

3. granting the government summary judgments (without holding hearings and/or allowing for any discovery) when private citizens attempted to quash IRS summonses, pursuant to Section 7609.

I pointed out that federal courts have nullified Section 7609 even after a citizen performed all the complicated and expensive procedures imposed by that statute. In my letter I stated:

Prior to "TEFRA" (passed in 1982), the United States was required to institute an action to compel court enforcement of IRS summonses, which allegedly placed a "heavy burden" on the Government. So Congress shifted this "heavy burden" to the shoulders of the already overtaxed and overburdened public by enacting IR Code Section 7609(h). This placed the financial and procedural burden

---

FIGURE A-5

IMMIGRATION AND NATIONALITY   **8 USCS § 1329**

§ 1329. Jurisdiction of district courts

The district courts of the United States shall have jurisdiction of all causes, civil and criminal, arising under any of the provisions of this title. It shall be the duty of the United States attorney of the proper district to prosecute every such suit when brought by the United States. Notwithstanding any other law, such prosecutions or suits may be instituted at any place in the United States at which the violation may occur or at which the person charged with a violation under section 275 or 276 [8 USCS § 1325 or 1326] may be apprehended. No suit or proceeding for a violation of any of the provisions of this title shall be settled, compromised, or discontinued without the consent of the court in which it is pending and any such settlement, compromise, or discontinuance shall be entered of record with the reasons therefor.

---

on the public for initiating court actions to prevent enforcement of illegal IRS summonses (while removing both burdens from the Government). However, this was not supposed to AFFECT THE SUBSTANTIVE LAW: that is change the Government's burden of proving that the summonses in question were issued for a lawful purpose. BUT THAT IS NOT THE WAY THE COURTS "ENFORCE" SECTION 7609(h). When a private citizen goes to the trouble and expense of initiating a Court action in conformity with Section 7609(h), the Government often moves for summary judgments on the basis of self-serving affidavits completed by IRS agents (for which they do not have to be cross-examined) – AND THEY GET IT! Not only did Congress put a heavy legal and financial burden on the public by establishing Section 7609(h), IN MANY CASES IT REMOVED THE GOVERNMENT'S ENTIRE BURDEN OF HAVING TO ESTABLISH THAT THE SUMMONSES WERE ISSUED FOR A LAWFUL PURPOSE. PRESUMABLY THIS WAS NOT CONGRESS' INTENT, YET THIS IS HOW THE COURTS NOW ENFORCE SECTION 7609(h). Therefore, the U.S. Congress must now rectify this situation by either repealing Section 7609(h) and requiring the Government to again initiate court actions as before, OR pass legislation denying summary judgments to the Government in 7609(h) actions. IT WOULD BE THE HEIGHT OF LEGISLATIVE HYPOCRISY IF CONGRESS WERE TO ALLOW THE GOVERNMENT TO HAVE IT BOTH WAYS! In addition, since Congress has passed a law preventing the courts from "restraining the assessment or collection of any tax" (Section 7421), why can't it pass a law preventing the Government from getting summary judgments in connection with 7609(h) actions?

And, finally getting back to your letter of March 21, 1991, in which you state that all felonies have been "consolidated" into Title 18 with the exception of some drug offenses "encompassed in Title 21," this, of course, was in line with the purpose of the Senate Judiciary Committee's report on the Criminal Reform Act of 1981 as stated in its report of 11/30/1981 (S. 1630) that "Present statutory criminal law...unnecessarily burdens the responsibility of assuring every man of knowing what he may do and what he may not do"; since presumably criminal laws scattered throughout various Titles create "a hodgepodge of conflicting, contradictory, and imprecise laws with little relevance to each other or to the state of criminal law as a whole," (at pages 3 & 4). And further the Report stated (at page 7), "*All* Federal *felonies, many of which are presently codified outside Title 18, will be integrated into the Code.*" This being the case, how can Federal courts, as they now do, allow criminal trials to take place for alleged *criminal violations* of the Internal Revenue Code? This practice would appear to be not only in conflict with:

1. your letter of March 21, 1991,
2. the Criminal Code Reform Act of 1981,
3. the Committee's Report of 12/22/1981 (S. 1630), but in further conflict with the fact that:
4. Congress has never seen fit to "codify" any IR Code felony, since it never enacted the IR Code into positive law,
5. nor did it ever give district courts anything but civil jurisdiction (as provided in Section 7402(f) in connection with alleged IR Code violations.

In view of all of the above, how can Federal Courts, as they now do, conduct criminal, felony trials for alleged income tax "crimes" (allegedly violations of Code Sections 7201) when no such "crimes" appear in Title 18, NOR ARE EVEN PROVIDED FOR IN THE INTERNAL REVENUE CODE ITSELF? (There are no penalties mentioned anywhere in the IR Code in connection with income taxes, though sections such as 4414, 4484, 4998, 5148, 5601, 5560, 5604, and 5681 provide for, or cross-reference to, penalties in connection with other taxes—but no such penalty provisions or cross-references appear *anywhere* in the IR Code in connection with income taxes!)

This being the case, how could I have been criminally prosecuted in 1985 for a crime known as income tax evasion, when no such crime appears in either Title 18 nor in the IR Code itself? However, when I raised all of the above issues at my "arraignment" and in pre trial motions, they were simply ignored by the court. In addition, even if there were such a thing as tax evasion, Connecticut District Court Judge Peter C. Dorsey instructed my jury that it could convict me of that "crime" even if the Government did not prove the act of evasion I

was charged with committing! And this instruction was sustained by the Second Circuit on appeal! (See article [Exhibit G] from the Feb., 1987 issue of *The Journal of Taxation* confirming this fact.) But this was only part of the Federal frame up. Three IRS agents gave perjurious testimony under the direction of the U.S. Attorney - which can be easily verified. This kind of conduct is also NOT UNCOMMON AT TAX "TRIALS."

Thus I gave Senator Biden proof of the many injustices now taking place in federal courts, of which you are now aware, and I closed my letter by saying:

In view of the above, I am requesting that you hold hearings on this matter and allow myself and others who have experienced the Nazi-like administration of American "justice" to testify on this issue. *This is not a judicial matter but a congressional one.* The judiciary is ignoring the laws passed by Congress and blatantly, arrogantly, and illegally making up its own laws (by enforcing, as law, their own lawless decisions) - in violation of Article 1, Section 1 of the United States Constitution. AND THIS CONGRESS MUST STOP.

I stand ready to give considerable testimony on this issue, based on my considerable knowledge of our tax laws, their historic underpinnings and my considerable experience as a victim of the Federal court system.

On May 24, 1991, I sent him another letter with a copy of my petition to the Supreme Court. As of this date, Senator Biden has not responded to either letter. It is important that you contact your own senators and those on the Committee and ask what action they are taking to correct the situation *covered in my letters* of those dates. The U.S. Congress must be made to take responsibility for the LAWLESSNESS WHICH IS NOW TAKING PLACE IN FEDERAL COURTS AND FOR WHICH I HAVE GIVEN THEM AMPLE EVIDENCE.

JUDGE DORSEY IS TRYING TO HAVE ME RE-INCARCERATED!

Various events have occurred over the last 120 days which forced me to write and then rewrite this section. When I first wrote it (in the latter part of July, 1991), I explained how I might be back in jail because of Judge Dorsey's attempt to have me reincarcerated by instigating false charges that I violated my probation conditions. Dorsey scheduled a probable cause hearing for July 31, 1991. On July 28, 1991 I wrote:

I am trying to finish this Second Edition just in case Judge Dorsey terminates my probation and I find myself

FIGURE A-6

United States District Court

DISTRICT OF CONNECTICUT

U.S.A. vs. Irwin A. Schiff   Docket No. N-85-20 (PCD)

Supplemental Petition on Probation and Supervised Release

COMES NOW   Carmelo Medina   PROBATION OFFICER OF THE COURT presenting an official report upon the conduct and attitude of probationer Irwin A. Schiff who was placed on probation by the Honorable Peter C. Dorsey, U.S. District Court Judge sitting in the court at Hartford, CT, on the 26th day of December, 19 85, and imposed the general terms and conditions thereofore adopted by the court and also imposed special conditions and terms as follows: Violation of Title 26, U.S. Code, Section 7201 (Income Tax Evasion) as charged in Counts 1, 2 and 3 of the Indictment and Title 26, U.S. Code, Section 7203 (Failure to File Corporate Returns) as charged in Count 4 of the Indictment.

Committed to the custody of the Attorney General or his authorized representative for imprisonment for a period of three (3) years imprisonment on Count 1; Three (3) years imprisonment on Count 2; execution of sentence of imprisonment is suspended forthwith and the defendant is placed on probation for a period of three (3) years to commence upon release from custody on Count 1. Sentence of imprisonment on Count 2 to run consecutively to sentence imposed on Count 1;
(See page 2 - attached)

RESPECTFULLY PRESENTING PETITION FOR ACTION OF COURT FOR CAUSE AS FOLLOWS:

This Petition supplements the Probation Form 12 filed on April 23, 1991.

Based on the information provided by the Assistant U.S. Attorney's Office and the Internal Revenue Service, Mr. Schiff has not adhered to Special Condition No. 3, "The defendant shall remain current insofar as all legally required tax payments with reasonable and good faith compliance and shall file all returns required by tax laws." Copies of individual tax returns Form 1040 for the years 1980-1981-and 1982 attached.

PRAYING THAT THE COURT WILL ORDER that this form serve as a Summons to be issued by Certified mail/return receipt requested, for Mr. Schiff, ordering him to appear before the Court at Hartford, CT on ___ at ___ to show cause why his probation should not be revoked.

ORDER OF COURT   Respectfully,

Considered and ordered this ___ day of ___, 19___ and ordered filed and made a part of the records in the above case.

_____
U.S. District Judge

United States District Court

District of Connecticut

U.S.A. vs. Irwin A. Schiff   Docket No. N-85-20

Petition for Probation Action

COMES NOW   Carmelo Medina   PROBATION OFFICER OF THE COURT presenting an official report upon the conduct and attitude of probationer Irwin A. Schiff who was placed on probation by the Honorable Peter C. Dorsey, U.S. District Court Judge sitting in the court at Hartford, CT, on the 26th day of December, 1985, and imposed the general terms and conditions of probation theretofore adopted by the court and also imposed special conditions and terms as follows:

Violation of Title 26, United States Code, Section 7201 (Income Tax Evasion) as charged in Counts 1, 2, and 3 of the Indictment and Title 26, United States Code, Section 7203 (Failure to File Corporate Returns) as charged in Count 4 of the Indictment.

Committed to the custody of the Attorney General or his authorized representative for imprisonment for a period of three (3) years imprisonment on Count One; Three years imprisonment on Count Two; execution of sentence of imprisonment is suspended forthwith and the defendant is placed on probation for a period of
(See page 2 - attached)

RESPECTFULLY PRESENTING PETITION FOR ACTION OF COURT FOR CAUSE AS FOLLOWS:

On July 20, 1990 Mr. Schiff was advised by Revenue Agent Robert Netcoh that the Income Tax Returns which he filed for the years 1983 through 1988 are not valid returns. (Copy of letter attached).
On August 24, 1990 Mr. Schiff responded to the revenue agent claiming these were valid returns. (Copy of letter attached).
On October 2, 1990 Joseph Long, IRS Attorney responded to Mr. Schiff's letter advising that the IRS had determined that the returns for 1983 through 1988 do not qualify as tax returns under the Internal Revenue Code.
On October 13, 1990 Mr. Schiff responded to the letter of Joseph Long, Esq. Mr. Schiff claims the returns to be valid. Based on the above the probationer has violated Special Condition No. 3, "Defendant shall remain current insofar as all legally required tax payments with reasonable and good faith compliance and shall file all returns required by tax laws."

PRAYING THAT THE COURT WILL ORDER a summons to be issued requiring the probationer to appear before the Court to show cause why his probation should not be revoked. A certified copy of this document, delivered personally to the probationer, shall serve as the summons.

ORDER OF COURT   Respectfully,

Considered and ordered this ___ day of ___, 19___ and ordered filed and made a part of the records in the above case.

_____
U.S. District Judge

back in Jail on July 31. With only seven days left to serve, Judge Dorsey could revoke my probation, if he claims he finds the charges proven, and order that I do the whole three years AGAIN - only this time I would be incarcerated. He would not have to credit me (based upon his jaundiced reading of the law) with *any* portion of the three years I have already spent on probation.

If this does occur, you will know just how illegal such an action was (and you will have **additional proof** of the criminality that exists on the federal bench and in the Justice Department).

My only protection, therefore, would have to come from the public, who, knowing the facts, might do something to secure my release. I have included enough material so that the public, being fully informed, might come to my aid.

The documents contriving these charges are shown in Figure A-6. The first one was signed by Judge Dorsey on April 23 and the second was signed by him on July 3. Both are false for a number of reasons. For one thing, Mr. Medina states "under oath," that both "official report(s)" are based "upon the conduct and attitude of Irwin A. Schiff." Since Mr. Medina never met me before he prepared his first "report," how could he swear to any such thing? It is obvious that his first "report" was based on a false oath. And, though Mr. Medina did meet me by the time he signed the second petition, it also rests on a false oath as the following will clearly prove.

Mr. Medina's first petition merely claims that on July 20, 1990, I was "advised by Revenue Agent Robert Netcoh that the income tax returns (I filed) for the three years 1983 through 1986 were not valid" and that on October 2, 1990, I was advised of the same thing by Joseph Long (the same gentleman who could not identify any Code section that made me "liable" for income taxes--see page 96). Note that neither petition charges me with disobeying an instruction of a probation officer, or of committing a crime—the only two items I could be in violation of—according to the terms of my probation (see Figure A-7). On May 31, 1991 (prior to the Supplemental Petition being filed), in a 27-page Motion To Dismiss the Petition, I addressed this issue as follows:

It is clear from 18 USC 3655 that it is *only* probation officers, *not* federal employees in general, who are authorized to "furnish to each probationer under his supervision" guidance and supervision. It is clear from this and other provisions of 3655, as well as my "Conditions of Probation and Supervised Release" that I am only required to take probation "instruction" and "supervision" from the probation officer (appointed pursuant to 18 USC 3654) assigned to me. As far as I knew, that was Mr. Walsh, not Mr. Netcoh nor Mr. Long.

My "Conditions of Probation and Supervised Release" provided that I shall "follow the instruction of the probation officer," and do not require me to "follow the instructions" or advice of every Tom, Dick, and Harry who attempt to advise me regarding whether I am, or am not, conforming to the conditions of my probation. In addition, the Probation Department is a part of the judicial branch of government, while the IRS is part of the executive branch. To claim, therefore, as Mr. Medina's "Petition for Probation Action" does, that I was obliged to accept probation supervision from members of both branches of government at the same time, would, in this case, constitute an illegal violation of the separation of powers doctrine.

What Mr. Medina's petition does not mention is that the letters sent to me by Mr. Netcoh and Mr. Long were also sent to Mr. Walsh, my probation supervisor, who is attached to the Brooklyn probation office, and were part of a series of letters and phone calls by IRS and Justice Department personnel designed to persuade and/or intimidate him into violating me - but he never did.

Typical of these is the one sent to him by Mr. Netcoh on February 25, 1991 (see Figure A-8). It is clear from that letter that Mr. Netcoh was getting extremely frustrated at being unable to convince Mr. Walsh that I was in violation of the terms of my probation, since I had, correctly, convinced him that I was not. Four months prior to this letter, on 10/22/1990, Mr. Netcoh had written to Mr. Walsh as follows: "The Internal Revenue Service will be contacting you to ask for a meeting to request you to consider revoking Mr. Schiff's probation." But that letter, like all of his other letters, was ignored by Mr. Walsh, who **never advised me that I had to file any returns other than those I had filed, nor that I had to pay any income taxes** for any of the years cited in those petitions.

Thus, the artifice employed by Judge Dorsey is obvious. Since my actual probation supervisor was not going to violate me on the grounds contained in Mr. Medina's petitions, Judge Dorsey got a Connecticut probation officer to (illegally) make those charges in order that I could be brought before him to rule that I was guilty of the violations claimed. Judge Dorsey had *already* framed me on charges of income tax evasion, and now felt *entitled* to frame me on these charges, too.

On August 24, 1990, as noted in Mr. Medina's petition, and while I was still incarcerated, I sent a five-page letter to Robert Netcoh (with copies to Judge Dorsey and my probation supervisor, Mr. Walsh) in which I told him that:

1. He had neither the authority nor expertise to make the claims he did;

FIGURE A-8

Internal Revenue Service
District Director

Department of the Treasury
936 Silas Deane Highway
(4th floor, E:1215 rjn)
Wethersfield, CT 06109

Telephone Number: (AC 203) 258-2039

Date: 2/25/91

Patrick Walsh, Parole Officer
U.S. Probation Office
75 Clinton Street
Brooklyn, N.Y 11201

RE: Irwin Schiff

Dear Mr. Walsh:

Enclosed is a television VHS Video tape of the Cable News Network Program "Sonya Live" aired on November 8, 1990. It is a fifteen minute exchange between Mr. Schiff and Donald Alexander, former Commissioner of the Internal Revenue Service. Mr. Schiff states that filing of income tax returns and providing information to the IRS is voluntary. He states that he had filed returns with zeros so the IRS can't put him back in prison.

It has been six months since Mr. Schiff has been out on probation. He was notified numerous times of his return filing requirements. His statements on this program and his previous letters to me, which I have provided your with copies, clearly shows he has no intention of filing returns.

Mr. Schiff has been convicted twice for not filing returns. The Court instructed Mr. Schiff to file returns as a Special Conditions of his Probation. He is blatantly disobeying the Courts instructions.

Mr. Walsh it is know time to consider revoking Mr. Schiff Probation for not complying with the Special Conditions of his Probation that he remain current insofar as all legally required tax payments with reasonable and good faith compliance and file all returns required by the tax laws.

Mr. Walsh. I have made this request several times before when I provided you with other evidence of Mr. Schiff refusal to comply with the Courts instructions. Please call me so that I may know what action you plan on taking with regard to my request.

Enclosed is Notice 129 which explains the Disclosure Limitations relating to the information I have provided you in regards to Mr. Schiff's filing of his income tax returns.

Cordially,

Robert Netcoh
Revenue Agent

cc: Mr. Irwin Schiff

FIGURE A-7

PROB 7A
(Rev. 6/88)

Conditions of Probation and Supervised Release

UNITED STATES DISTRICT COURT

FOR THE

DISTRICT OF CONNECTICUT

Name Irwin A. Schiff   Docket No. N-85-20(PCD)

Address 68-38 Yellowstone Blvd., Forest Hills, New York 11375

Under the terms of your sentence, you have been placed on probation/supervised release (strike one)

by the Honorable Peter C. Dorsey   , United States District Judge for

the District of Connecticut   . Your term of supervision is for a period of three (3) **,

commencing August 8, 1988

CONDITIONS

It is the order of the Court that you shall comply with the following conditions:

(1) You shall not commit another Federal, state, or local crime;

(2) You shall not leave the judicial district without the permission of the court or probation officer;

(3) You shall report to the probation officer as directed by the court or probation officer, and shall submit a truthful and complete written report within the first five days of each month;

(4) You shall answer truthfully all inquiries by the probation officer and follow the instructions of the probation officer;

(5) You shall support your dependents and meet other family responsibilities;

(6) You shall work regularly at a lawful occupation unless excused by the probation officer for schooling, training, or other acceptable reasons;

(7) You shall notify the probation officer within seventy-two hours of any change in residence or employment;

(8) You shall refrain from excessive use of alcohol and shall not purchase, possess, use, distribute, or administer any narcotic or other controlled substance, or any paraphernalia related to such substances, except as prescribed by a physician;

(9) You shall not frequent places where controlled substances are illegally sold, used, distributed, or administered;

(10) You shall not associate with any persons engaged in criminal activity, and shall not associate with any person convicted of a felony unless granted permission to do so by the probation officer;

(11) You shall permit a probation officer to visit you at any time at home or elsewhere, and shall permit confiscation of any contraband observed in plain view by the probation officer;

2. The returns I filed fell within the *Long* and *Kimball* decisions (see page 244 and Figure A-9);

3. If my probation officer doubted the returns I filed were valid, he could report that to the court and I would **amend them in any manner so as to make them acceptable to the court;**

4. If he believed I swore falsely on the returns I filed, he should report that to the Department of Justice so they could file criminal charges against me for violating Sections 7201 and 7203 of the Internal Revenue and/or Section 1001 of the U.S. Criminal Code;

5. As I had already told Robert Pisker if Netcoh believed my "zero" figures were wrong, he should send me Deficiency Notices and I would see him in Tax Court - but I could not owe any taxes until the matter was litigated either in Tax Court or some other court;

6. In any case, I had no records to prepare income tax returns along the lines he thought necessary, nor the money to pay any taxes even if I owed them;

7. In discussing my tax returns with such third parties as Mr. Walsh, he had left himself open to prosecution pursuant to Section 7213 of the IR Code.

Mr. Long's response of October 2 (as referred in Mr. Medina's petition) was principally to assure me that IRS Agent "Robert Netcoh had not violated any provision of federal law." Along with this, Mr. Long also stated that the documents I filed did "not qualify as tax returns under the Internal Revenue Code," and I challenged that claim on a variety of grounds including the fact that, according to the Supreme Court in *Merchant's Loan & Trust Company* (see page 42), I had no income for any of the years in question. In addition, I advised him that while the improvised returns I filed while a federal prisoner in F.C.I. Morgantown were valid, I was, nevertheless, **refiling** for all of those years **using official IRS 1040's.** On October 13, 1991, (and subsequent to the dates of any letters referred to in Mr. Medina's report) **I filed amended tax returns** for all the years 1980-1990, along the lines shown in Figure A-9.

In reality, Mr. Medina's petition was triggered by my agreeing to be a defense witness in a trial that was to take place in Rockford, Illinois. On April 17, 1991, I notified my probation supervisor, Mr. Walsh, that I needed travel permission to go to Rockford on April 23 to testify. Since I had not anticipated any problem getting such permission, I had not bothered being formally subpoenaed. Two days later, however, I was informed by Mr. Walsh that permission had been denied. When I asked why, he said that according to my conditions of probation I could not "participate in a media event." How giving testimony

at a criminal trial is participating in a "media event," I don't know, but I immediately called the attorney, and he faxed a subpoena to me. I notified Mr. Walsh that I had been subpoenaed and requested travel permission to honor it. That was on Friday afternoon, and Mr. Walsh told me that he would check with Judge Dorsey, and that I should call him on Monday, April 22, for an answer. When I called on Monday, he was not in, and I was told to call the New Haven Probation Office. There I was told by a Mr. Visokay that he would check with Judge Dorsey and get back to me the next day. He called back that same day, however, and said that permission had been granted, but that I should call him as soon as I returned from Rockford. I did not get back from Rockford until Monday evening, April 29, and called the New Haven office the next day. I was now connected with Mr. Medina, who informed me that he was recommending to the Court that I was in violation of the terms of my probation. When I asked him on what basis, he told me that I had not filed tax returns as required. When I told him that was not true, that I had not only filed once, but that I had filed *twice,* he was unmoved. When I asked him why my probation supervisor had not charged me with such a violation, he told me that he had been told as much by Mr. Walsh, but, in any case, *he* was now my probation supervisor. He then told me that I was to report to the New Haven Probation Office that Friday. I then called Mr. Walsh and asked him if he had told Mr. Medina that I had not filed tax returns for the years in question. He told me he had not, and that all he had said was, that since he was not a lawyer he did not know if they were or were not tax returns.

It is clear from this that when either Mr. Medina or Mr. Visokay spoke to Judge Dorsey on Monday, April 22, 1991 about my travel permission, they were told by him to violate me. Judge Dorsey was, obviously, concerned that I would shorty be off probation and free to travel and promote a book that proved he was unfit to be a federal judge. Clearly, without such an instruction from the court itself, no probation officer would, *on their own initiative,* seek to violate someone *who was not under their own probation supervision*—let alone do so **without even interviewing the probationer in question!** There can be no doubt that it was on the instructions of Judge Dorsey on April 22 that Mr. Medina fabricated the charges that Judge Dorsey signed on April 23.

When I met with Mr. Medina that Friday, I was given the Petition for Probation Action, to which were attached the letters referred to, plus portions of the improvised returns I had filed from F.C.I. Morgantown. When I asked Mr. Medina how he could swear that his report was based on my "conduct and attitude" even though he had never spoken to me in his life, he was nonplused. When I asked him why the returns I filed on October 17, 1990 were missing from his report, he said he was

FIGURE A-9

Form 1040 Department of the Treasury—Internal Revenue Service
U.S. Individual Income Tax Return 1982

For the year January 1–December 31, 1982, or other tax year beginning _____, 1982, ending _____, 19___ OMB No. 1545-0074

Your first name and initial (if joint return, also give spouse's name and initial) Last name
Irwin A. Schiff

Present home address (Number and street, including apartment number, or rural route)
444 E. 52d St. Apt. 8-H

City, town or post office, State and ZIP code
New York, N.Y. 10022

Your social security number 097-16-249_
Spouse's social security no.
Your occupation Writer
Spouse's occupation

Presidential Election Campaign Do you want $1 to go to this fund? ... Yes [ ] No [ ]
If joint return, does your spouse want $1 to go to this fund? ... Yes [ ] No [ ]
Note: Checking "Yes" will not increase your tax or reduce your refund.

For Privacy Act and Paperwork Reduction Act Notice, see Instructions.

Filing Status (Check only one box.)
1 Single
2 Married filing joint return (even if only one had income)
3 Married filing separate return. Enter spouse's social security no. above and full name here ▶
4 Head of household (with qualifying person). (See page 6 of Instructions.) If the qualifying person is your unmarried child but not your dependent, enter child's name ▶
5 Qualifying widow(er) with dependent child (Year spouse died ▶ 19___). (See page 6 of Instructions.)

Exemptions (Always check the box labeled Yourself. Check other boxes if they apply.)
6a Yourself [ ] 65 or over [ ] Blind
b Spouse [ ] 65 or over [ ] Blind
c First names of your dependent children who lived with you ▶
d Other dependents:
e Total number of exemptions claimed 1

Income (Please attach Copy B of your Forms W-2 here. If you do not have a W-2, see page 5 of Instructions.)
7 Wages, salaries, tips, etc. 7 $0 00
8 Interest income (attach Schedule B if over $400 or you have any All-Savers interest) 8
9a Dividends (attach Schedule B if over $400) .... 9a 9% Exclusion 9c $0 00
c Subtract line 9b from line 9a ....
10 Refunds of State and local income taxes (do not enter an amount unless you deducted those taxes in an earlier year—see page 9 of Instructions) 10
11 Alimony received 11
12 Business income or (loss) (attach Schedule C) 12 $0 00
13 Capital gain or (loss) (attach Schedule D) 13
14 40% capital gain distributions not reported on line 13 (See page 9 of Instructions) 14
15 Supplemental gains or (losses) (attach Form 4797) 15
16 Other pensions and annuities. Total received 16
17a Fully taxable pensions, IRA distributions, and annuities not reported on line 17 17a
b Taxable amount, if any, from worksheet on page 10 of Instructions 17b
18 Rents, royalties, partnerships, estates, trusts, etc. (attach Schedule E) 18
19 Farm income or (loss) (attach Schedule F) 19
20a Unemployment compensation (insurance). Total received 20a
b Taxable amount, if any, from worksheet on page 10 of Instructions 20b
21 Other income (state nature and source—see page 11 of Instructions) ▶ 21
22 Total income. Add amounts in column for lines 7 through 21 ▶ 22 $0 00

Adjustments to Income (See Instructions on page 11)
23 Moving expense (attach Form 3903 or 3903F) 23
24 Employee business expenses (attach Form 2106) 24
25 Payments to an IRA. You must enter code from page ___ 25
26 Payments to a Keogh (H.R. 10) retirement plan 26
27 Penalty on early withdrawal of savings 27
28 Alimony paid 28
29 Deduction for a married couple when both work (attach Schedule W) 29
30 Disability income exclusion (attach Form 2440) 30
31 Total adjustments. Add lines 23 through 30 31

Adjusted Gross Income
32 Adjusted gross income. Subtract line 31 from line 22. If this line is less than $10,000, see "Earned Income Credit" (line 62) on page 15 of Instructions. If you want IRS to figure your tax, see page 3 of Instructions. ▶ 32 $0 00

(19)

Page 2

Form 1040 (1982)

33 Amount from line 32 (adjusted gross income) 33 $0 00
34a If you itemize, complete Schedule A (Form 1040) and enter the amount from Schedule A, line 30. Also see page 12 of the Instructions.
Caution: If you have unearned income and can be claimed as a dependent on your parent's return, check here ▶ [ ] and see page 12 of the Instructions. Also see page 12 of the Instructions if:
  • You are married filing a separate return and your spouse itemizes deductions, OR
  • You file Form 4563, OR • You are a dual-status alien.
34b If you do not itemize, complete the worksheet on page 13. Then enter the allowable part of your charitable contributions here ▶ 34b
35 Subtract line 34a or 34b, whichever applies, from line 33 .... 35 1,000 00
36 Multiply $1,000 by the total number of exemptions claimed on Form 1040, line 6e 36 1,000 00
37 Taxable income. Subtract line 36 from line 35 37
38 Tax. Enter tax here and check if from [ ] Tax Table, [ ] Tax Rate Schedule X, Y, or Z, or [ ] Schedule G 38
39 Additional Taxes. (See page 13 of Instructions.) Enter here and check if from [ ] Form 4970, [ ] Form 4972, [ ] Form 5544, or [ ] section 72 penalty taxes 39
40 Total. Add lines 38 and 39 ▶ 40 $1,000 00
41 Credit for the elderly (attach Schedules R&RP) 41
42 Foreign tax credit (attach Form 1116) 42
43 Investment credit (attach Form 3468) 43
44 Partial credit for political contributions 44
45 Credit for child and dependent care expenses (attach Form 2441) 45
46 Jobs credit (attach Form 5884) 46
47 Residential energy credit (attach Form 5695) 47
48 Other credits—see page 14 48
49 Total credits. Add lines 41 through 48 ▶ 49 $0 00
50 Balance. Subtract line 49 from line 40 and enter difference (but not less than zero) ▶ 50 $0 00
51 Self-employment tax (attach Schedule SE) 51
52 Minimum tax (attach Form 4625) 52
53 Alternative minimum tax (attach Form 6251) 53
54 Tax from recapture of investment credit (attach Form 4255) 54
55 Social security (FICA) tax on tip income not reported to employer (attach Form 4137) 55
56 Uncollected employee FICA and RRTA tax on tips (from Form W-2) 56
57 Tax on an IRA (attach Form 5329) 57
58 Advance earned income credit (EIC) payments received (from Form W-2) 58
59 Total tax. Add lines 50 through 58 ▶ 59 $0 00
60 Total Federal income tax withheld 60
61 1982 estimated tax payments and amount applied from 1981 return 61
62 Earned income credit. If line 33 is under $10,000, see page 15 of Instructions 62
63 Amount paid with Form 4868 63
64 Excess FICA and RRTA tax withheld (two or more employers) 64
65 Credit for Federal tax on special fuels and oils (attach Form 4136) 65
66 Regulated Investment Company credit (attach Form 2439) 66
67 Total. Add lines 60 through 66 ▶ 67 $0 00
68 If line 67 is larger than line 59, enter amount OVERPAID 68
69 Amount of line 68 to be REFUNDED TO YOU ▶ 69
70 Amount of line 68 to be applied to your 1983 estimated tax ... ▶ 70
71 If line 59 is larger than line 67, enter AMOUNT YOU OWE. Attach check or money order for full amount payable to Internal Revenue Service. Write your social security number and "1982 Form 1040" on it. ▶ $ 71 $0 00
(Check ▶ [ ] if Form 2210 (2210F) is attached. See page 16 of Instructions.) ▶ $

Under penalties of perjury, I declare that I have examined this return, including accompanying schedules and statements, and to the best of my knowledge and belief, it is true, correct, and complete. Declaration of preparer (other than taxpayer) is based on all information of which preparer has any knowledge.

Your signature _____ Date 10/13/1982
Spouse's signature (if filing jointly, BOTH must sign)

Preparer's signature _____ Date _____ Check if self-employed [ ] Preparer's social security no.
Firm's name (or yours, if self-employed) and address _____ E.I. No. _____ ZIP code _____

FIGURE A-9 (CONTINUED)

To: The Internal Revenue Service:

This statement is being submitted as part of my 1990 income tax return, and is an integral part of that return.

Even though I know that no section of the Internal Revenue Code:

1. establishes an income tax "liability," as, for example, Code Sections 4401, 5005, and 5703 do with respect to other taxes;

2. provides that income taxes "have to be paid on the basis of a return" – as, for example, Code Sections 4374, 4401(c), 5061(a) 5703(b) provide with respect to other taxes;

I am filing anyway, because I have been twice prosecuted for the non-existent crime of allegedly failing to file income tax returns as allegedly required by Code Sections 7201 and 7203 of the Internal Revenue Code.

Therefore, this return is not being filed voluntarily but is being filed so as to prevent my illegal prosecution for allegedly failing to file an income tax return for the year 1990.

It should be noted that the courts have ruled that "A (1040) form with `zeros' inserted in the spaces provided...qualified as a return.'" See U.S. v. Long, 618 F.2d 74 (9th Cir. 1980; U.S. v. Kimbal, No. 87-1392 D.C. No. Cr.-86-0017-ECR (9th Cir. filed 2/26/1990); and U.S. v. Moore, 627 F.2d 830 (7th Cir).

It should also be noted that I had "zero" income according to the Supreme Court's definition of income (Note 1), since in Merchant's Loan & Trust Company v. Smietanka, 255 U.S. 509 (1921, at pages 518 & 518) the Court held that "The word (income) must be given the same meaning in all of the Income Tax Acts of Congress that was given to it in the Corporation Excise Tax Act (of 1909)" Therefore, since I had no "income" in 1990 that would have been taxable under the Corporation Excise Tax Act of 1909, I can only swear to having "zero" income in 1990. Obviously, knowing the above, if I were to swear to having received any other amount of "income", I would BE SWEARING FALSELY and thus would be GUILTY OF COMMITTING PERJURY.

Note 1. The word "income" is not defined in the Internal Revenue Code, U.S. v. Ballard, 535 F.2d 400, 404, but, as stated above, it can only be a derivative of corporate activity. The Supreme Court has held this numerous times. "Whatever difficulty may be about a precise and scientific definition of `income' it imports, as used here...the idea of *gain or increase arising from corporate activities,"* Doyle v. Mitchell, 247 U.S. 179 (1918). "Certainly the term `income' has no broader meaning in the 1913 Act than in that of 1909 (See Straton's Independence v. Howbert, 231 U.S. 399, 416, 417), and ...*we assume that there is no difference in its meaning as used in the two acts,"* Southern Pacific Co. v. John Z. Lowe, Jr., 247 U.S. 330, 335 (1918).

PLEASE TAKE NOTE

For those who want to file this kind of a return, the sixth paragraph shown on my page 3 should be amended, as follows:

"I am filing anyway, because I have heard that people are illegally prosecuted for the non-existent crime of allegedly failing to file income tax returns as allegedly required by Code Sections 7201 and 7203 of the Internal Revenue Code. Therefore, this return is not being filed voluntarily but is being filed to prevent my illegal prosecution for allegedly failing to file an income tax return for the year 1990."

IMPORTANT!

The author believes that the filing of this type of a return will satisfy the (illegal) filing requirement generally imposed as a condition of parole and probation.

unaware of them. I asked him how could he claim, therefore, that his petition was based upon my "conduct and attitude," and he had no answer for that either. I then asked him if he had read the *Kimball* and *Long* decisions which were mentioned in my letters. He said he had not. I showed him those decisions and asked him to read where they held that tax returns that reported "zero" income and "zero" taxes due still qualified as returns. I then asked him, "Based on these decisions, how can you claim that I did not file tax returns for those years?" He answered, "Well, you have a good point; just show those cases to the judge and you have nothing to worry about."

I pointed out to him that he should have considered that before he violated me, and what he was saying was tantamount to telling someone about to be falsely indicted, "Look, don't worry, just show these cases to the jury and they won't convict you."

I pointed out to him that **I had plenty of experience being unjustly convicted in federal tribunals**, so I had little confidence in the assurances he now gave me. I also told him that I had been framed by Judge Dorsey before, and that I had no doubt it would happen again, and that what he had just said proved that he did not *now* believe that I had violated the terms of my probation.

I asked him, "Why should I have to appear before Judge Dorsey on *any* basis?" Mr. Medina answered that, since the charges were already filed, there was nothing he could do about it.

Shortly thereafter I met with Mr. Visokay, supervisor of the New Haven Office, and told him I needed to have counsel appointed for my forthcoming hearing because I did not have the funds to hire one on my own. He gave me a financial affidavit to complete and told me to give it to Judge Dorsey. He assured me that, "He will simply take your affidavit and dismiss the hearing until counsel is appointed. He won't conduct any hearing if you don't have a lawyer."

Before describing that "hearing" which took place on May 31, and my subsequent attempt to get Judge Dorsey to recuse himself, I want to quote further from my Motion to Dismiss the charges, since it not only reveals why the charges are utterly specious, but also provides some **new information** regarding OMB numbers that you can use in various situations, and which will be particularly helpful to those who, like myself, (illegally) had the filing of income tax returns and the paying of income taxes made a condition of probation. (In order to conserve space, this extended quotation has not been indented, but is in a different type style.)

DID THE TERMS OF MY PROBATION REQUIRE ME TO FILE INCOME TAX RETURNS?

The answer to this question is NO. First of all, my conditions of probation do not even mention income tax returns. It merely says, "shall file all returns required by law." Are income tax returns one of the returns "required by law"? IR Code Section 4374 (related to taxes "imposed on each policy of insurance") states that such taxes, "shall be paid on the basis of a return." Section 5703(b) states, with respect to tobacco taxes "imposed by Section 5701" that "Such taxes shall be paid on the basis of a return." Section 5061 states that, "The taxes on distilled spirits, wines and beer shall be collected on the basis of a return." Thus, by the conditions of my probation I was required to file, for example, insurance, liquor and tobacco tax returns if I were "liable" for such taxes. And, if I were liable for such taxes and did not file the required returns, I suppose I would have violated the conditions of my probation. But **I can not find *any* Code section that requires *me* to** "pay income taxes on the basis of a return." Obviously, this condition can not apply to income taxes since no Code section requires me to "pay income taxes on the basis of a return."

In discussing this with Mr. Walsh, I handed him an Internal Revenue Code and asked him, in connection with his duties under Sec. 3655, to identify for me the "returns required by tax laws" which the conditions of my probation require me to file. He handed the Code right back to me and said, "How should I know, I'm no lawyer," or words to that effect. Thus, Mr. Walsh did not know what returns were "required by tax laws" or what I was required, by the terms of my probation, to file. Thus he could not "instruct (me) regarding this (condition)" as required by law (paragraph 1, Section 3655). However, in his letter of July 20, 1990, Mr. Netcoh refers to sections 6011 and 6012 "and the regulations" as somehow creating a civil requirement for filing. This is not what the Official IRS Privacy Act Notice says—which I have attached as Exhibit S. This is my—and the public's—**Official Notice** as to what conditions have to be present to determine whether or not one is required to file, and not what individual IRS employees have to say about the matter. Now, the official IRS Privacy Act Notice **does not say** that Sections 6011 or 6012 "require" the filing of income taxes. The Privacy Act Notice states that these sections (along with 6001) say, "you must file a return (unspecified) for any tax (unspecified) you are *liable* for." So, these sections only apply to such as: wagering taxes - "liability" created in Section 5005; tobacco taxes - "liability" created in Section 5703. But these sections can not apply to income taxes because THERE IS NO CODE SECTION THAT CREATES AN INCOME TAX "LIABILITY." Contrary to what Mr. Netcoh claimed in his letter, the official IRS Privacy Act Notice informs the public that these sections do not **require** the filing of income tax returns. In addition, the IRS Privacy Act Notice gives the public a Miranda warning that all information on a tax return can be turned over to the Department of Justice and used against them [see page 30]. So, clearly, there can be no law requiring Americans to supply such information to the Justice Department. [Other applications of the Privacy Act Notice are omitted.]

Also, 44 USC 3512 states that "No person shall be subject to any penalty for failing to maintain or provide information to any agency if the information collection request... does not display a current control number assigned by the Director," and the public is allowed to rely on these published OMB numbers to determine if the form and consequently the Code section to which they apply, applies to them. These OMB numbers are displayed in 26 CFR 602.101 (Exhibit U). As the court is aware, income taxes are imposed in Section 1 of the Internal Revenue Code. However, the only OMB number assigned to that section (the first entry in 602.101) is OMB number 1545-0067. Now, the document with that OMB number is Form 2555 "Foreign Earned Income" attached as Exhibit V. Since I did not have any foreign income and since there is no other government form assigned to reporting the taxes imposed in Section 1 of the Code, there can be no government form that I am required to complete in connection with the income tax imposed in Code Section 1..."

My motion then went on to prove that even though the conditions of my probation did not require it, I still filed valid income tax returns for all the years in question, and that I would have amended those returns *in any manner acceptable to the court* if I had been told to do so by my probation supervisor.

WAS I, BY THE TERMS OF MY PROBATION, REQUIRED TO PAY INCOME TAXES?

The answer to this question is NO. My 3rd Condition of probation simply required me to "remain current in so far as all legally required tax payments with reasonable good faith compliance." It is clear from the letters I received from Mr. Pisker and Mr. Netcoh that they both sought to intimidate me into thinking that the terms of my probation required me to *voluntarily* pay income taxes for each of the years subsequent to 1980. However, it is clear that the only taxes that can be made payable "as a condition of probation (are)... all taxes and penalties lawfully determined to be due and collectible." *U.S.* v. *Taylor*, 305 F.2d 183 [other citings omitted]. In addition, Judge Eginton ruled in *Schiff* v. *U.S.* [as did the Supreme Court in *Cheek*] that one has a "Right to petition Tax Court **prior to the payment of any taxes.**" Thus, it is clear that since the Commissioner has not contested the amount of taxes I showed on the returns I filed, the Commissioner ACCEPTED MY FIGURES AS CORRECT! Also note that the Deficiency Notices I received from the IRS *even for years when I filed no tax returns* [See Figure 5-1] all stated that I could "contest this

deficiency in court **before making payment**." Since the last Deficiency Notice I received from the IRS was for **1979**, no "legally required tax payment" as stated in my Special Conditions can be *due for any year subsequent to 1979.* Yet, even for 1979 there can be no tax "due." I had a Tax Court trial on November 27, 1990 involving the $68,000 in taxes and penalties the IRS claims I owe for 1979 and no decision, as yet, has been handed down. Obviously no taxes can even be considered to be "legally required", even for 1979! But even if the Tax Court ruled I owed taxes for 1979, I could not pay it because I am broke. Therefore, even for that year I would still be in "good faith compliance," since the taxes would not be "collectible" pursuant to *U.S.* v. *Taylor.*

It is clear from all of the above that I could not have possibly violated any of the conditions of my probation, as charged.

Now with regard to the hearing that was held on May 31. The first thing Judge Dorsey wanted to know was, where was my lawyer. I told him that I didn't have the money to hire one, and requested that he appoint counsel for me. I had completed a financial affidavit given to me by the probation office for that purpose. Judge Dorsey ignored all of that as if I had just talked to the wall, and proceeded to lecture me on the seriousness of the charges, and that I had enough experience to know that I needed a lawyer to defend against them. I told him I realized that, but I did not know a lawyer who would work for nothing, and that I still owed over $10,000 in past legal bills. For reasons which I do not now fully understand (but which will become clearer tome when I eventually see the hearing transcript), I agreed to go forward with the hearing, without counsel. I foolishly, as I recall, agreed to do so for three reasons: (1) I had been led to believe by Judge Dorsey that this was only a probable cause hearing, and that I would have appointed counsel at a final, revocation hearing if probable cause were found; (2) I believed there was no way that even Judge Dorsey could find probable cause, given that my second set of tax returns were never even considered by Mr. Medina and were missing from his report; and (3) I felt that I might just as well try and get this whole thing over with, if I could. I should have known that Peter C. Dorsey is not to be trusted *on any basis.*

The very first thing the government did was to move to introduce my missing tax returns. To say I objected "strongly" would be to put it mildly. I told the court that it was their absence that had induced me to go forward without an attorney and what the government was attempting to do was "tantamount to amending an indictment." When it appeared that the Court was going to let them in anyway, I said, "I know you are doing something illegal, but I don't know why, so obviously I can not proceed without counsel." And I now refused to go further without an attorney. At this point the "hearing" stopped, and Judge Dorsey now turned to examining my affidavit, which clearly showed I was still heavily in debt and did not have the means to hire a lawyer. Judge Dorsey felt compelled to remind me several times that "If this affidavit is not 100 percent accurate" I would be laying myself open to charges of perjury. And I stated, just as often, that the affidavit was "substantially correct," since no one can be sure precisely what his assets, liabilities, income and expenses were at any given moment. The hearing ended shortly thereafter with Judge Dorsey telling me that he would appoint counsel who could get a transcript of the "hearing" that had just transpired. He also instructed Peter Jongbloed, the government's counsel, to answer the motion I had just filed. At which time, Mr. Jongbloed reminded the court that, "There is a time factor involved here," meaning that my probation would soon terminate. To which Judge Dorsey replied, "I am aware of that."

THE SUPPLEMENTAL PETITION

Following the hearing, I waited to be notified of the attorney who was to be appointed for me. Instead, on August 6, I received Mr. Medina's Supplemental Charge, which states that "information" was "provided by the Assistant U.S. Attorney's Office and the Internal Revenue Service" that I had not "adhered to Special Condition No. 3., etc., etc." and attached to it were my tax returns that were missing from his first Petition. The totally specious character of this second Petition will be readily apparent to every probation officer in the country. For one thing, we are not told who the people were who supplied the "information." Were they secretaries at those offices? Secondly, there is no claim that any of this information was ever communicated to me, so how could this relate, in any way, to my conditions of probation? This Supplemental Petition was even more fraudulent than the original, since it did not even allege that I was told anything by anybody. After receiving it, I filed a motion that it, too, be dismissed.

On July 7, either by inadvertence or design, I received a ruling that Judge Dorsey had made on June 3—or more than a month before I received it—that rejected my request for appointment of counsel. Neither space nor time will allow me to analyze this portion of his ruling. Suffice it to say that he either **lied about or ignored** everything contained in my affidavit. Besides, the extent of Judge Dorsey's deceit can be more easily demonstrated by the following claims contained in that ruling. For example, he writes:

As a probable cause hearing was in process when the defendant requested counsel and the government completed its presentation of evidence

on the issue of probable cause, defendant shall, on or before June 14, 1991, be permitted to supplement his pending motion, or challenge the government's documentary proof, or make any offer of proof on his own behalf in support of a request for any further hearing on the issue of probable cause.

Further, Judge Dorsey would say, "It should be noted that, at least initially, the defendant expressed an intent to represent himself at the hearing." If this were true, why would I have gone to the hearing with a financial affidavit *already prepared*? And as for the government "completing its presentation of evidence," not one word of testimony was taken, nor was one witness called. So how could the government have "completed its presentation of evidence"? In point of fact, the government did not even *begin* to present its case. It is apparent that Judge Dorsey feels no compulsion to tell the truth *at any time—yet this is what sits on the federal bench in Hartford, Connecticut.*

It is clear that as of June 3, Judge Dorsey knew that he did not have time to appoint counsel for me and still get those hearings in before my probation terminated. Another reason why he would not want to appoint counsel (which the law says I am *required* to have—if I face incarceration as a result of an adverse ruling—is that he really couldn't face any member of the bar who looked at the government's case. Any lawyer would be appalled by what he saw, and would not understand on what basis Judge Dorsey would even hear the matter. Saving himself from this kind of embarrassment was another reason for his having to fabricate a basis for not appointing counsel.

The blatant fabrication in Judge Dorsey's Ruling of June 3 (which arrived too late, I believe by design, for me to request the hearing offered), and his refusal to appoint counsel indicted to me that he was prepared to do *anything* to find me guilty. Therefore, on July 18, pursuant to 28 USC 144, I filed an 8-page affidavit (supported by a 50-page brief and 50 pages of exhibits) asking him to recuse (remove) himself from this case. Section 144 provides that "Whenever a party...files a timely and sufficient affidavit that the judge before whom the matter is pending has a personal bias or prejudice either against him or in favor of the adverse party, such judge shall proceed no further, but another judge shall be assigned to hear such proceeding." According to 46 A Jur 2d, 215, "If the affidavit is legally sufficient, it compels the retirement of the judge from the case, without passing on the truth or falsity of the facts affirmed." Since my affidavit was "legally sufficient," *by law* Judge Dorsey **had to recuse himself!** My affidavit accused him of extensive personal bias and for having a personal reason for wanting me incarcerated. "I have written and published a book," my affidavit stated, "that provides extensive documentation [of which Dorsey was aware] as to why he is unfit to be a federal judge; therefore, he wants to violate and incarcerate me, so that I will not be at liberty to promote and sell such a book." In addition, my affidavit accused him of subornation of perjury with respect to the generation of the charges, and of anti-Semitism.[3]

On July 19 I filed a formal complaint with the U.S. Attorney, charging him with subornation of perjury in connection with the false oaths made by Mr. Medina.

In addition to all of the above, on July 27 a Connecticut sheriff served Judge Dorsey with a lawsuit in which I sued him for civil damages in connection with (among other things) conducting my previous trial without criminal jurisdiction and for having illegally generated the current charges against me.

Yet, as far as I know, he still intends to preside at my forthcoming hearing. Can you believe it?

And while I believe that Rule 32.1 of the Federal Rules of Criminal Procedure which provides that "A hearing and **assistance of counsel are required** before the terms or conditions of probation or supervised release can be modified..." (emphasis added) would preclude him from changing my current status from "supervised release" to "incarceration" and/or extending my probation beyond the three year period (now set to terminate August 8), I can not be sure. Since Judge Dorsey is CAPABLE OF ANYTHING, and since he believes that the Second Circuit will back anything he does to me, he may do it anyway. If he does, I hope that you, having all of these facts, will join with others to pressure Congress and the President to GET ME OUT! I want to thank you now for all of your help.

POST HEARING COMMENTARY

How about that, I'm still free! Had I gone in, the book would have ended with the last paragraph. Let me now bring you up to date.

My "hearing" was a total farce and anyone who reads the transcript (which will be made available) will be convinced that Judge Dorsey should not be allowed to judge a dog fight, much less an action in a court of law. He would not allow me to cross-examine Mr. Netcoh on his understanding of the meaning of income, where the Code made me liable for taxes, where it says I had to pay such taxes, on the basis of a return, and on the relevance of the OMB numbers. Mr. Netcoh even claimed he did not know what OMB numbers were. In addition, the government, through Mr. Netcoh, introduced an unsigned schedule which reputed to show that I allegedly owed over $225,000 in taxes for the years 1980-1989. However, for the years 1980-1982, the schedule made a

distinction between "Income for civil purposes" and "Income for criminal purposes." These distinctions were totally spurious, since no such distinction exists in the law. The government made it here because it had previously understated what it believed my income was (see pages 230-231). So, this is how they now sought to get around it. Judge Dorsey would not allow me to cross-examine Mr. Netcoh on where the law made such distinctions. Instead, Judge Dorsey put his own, asinine explanation into Netcoh's mouth, and said to me, "Now, go on to something else." But where Judge Dorsey blatantly obstructed justice was when Mr. Medina was on the stand. Judge Dorsey would not allow me to cross-examine him on what was said when he presented me with the charges. What I wanted to elicit from him was his admission that he had told me that if I just showed those cases to the judge, "I'd be okay," which would have demonstrated that, at that time, even *he* did not believe I had violated the terms of my probation. **But Judge Dorsey would not allow me to cross-examine concerning this conversation!** He ruled that it was irrelevant and insisted that I "move on." When I tried to press ahead with this line of questions, Judge Dorsey threatened to hold me in contempt if I did not "move on." Mr. Medina also testified that it was Peter Jongbloed, the government's counsel, who told him (as referred to in the Supplemental Petition) that I was in violation of the conditions of my probation. Since he was now prosecuting me, this admission is fraught with illegality.

The first witness I called was Dr. Frank DePino, an optometrist from New Haven who was with me when I met Medina. He was going to testify as to what Medina said, which would have proven Medina's testimony perjurious, if he denied saying it. **JUDGE DORSEY WOULD NOT LET HIM TESTIFY, AND EXCUSED HIM AS A WITNESS.** What more can I say?

I took the stand and testified that the conditions of my probation did not require me to file income tax returns or pay the tax; that despite this, I filed accurate and lawful returns for all the years in question, that I had no income for any of the years at issue and, therefore, owed no taxes for any of those years, and that even if I did, I had no money to pay such taxes. (Based on the Supplemental Petition, the government claimed that, in addition to not filing, I also failed to pay taxes for those years; however, it offered no evidence that I had any money with which to pay any portion of the taxes claimed.) Obviously, I offered *irrefutable* statutory, case law and documentary proof for all of my claims. When I finished my testimony, I eagerly awaited Mr. Jongbloed's cross-examination. You can imagine my disappointment, therefore, when following the completion of my testimony, Mr. Jongbloed called out, "No questions."

The hearings ended on August 1, with Judge Dorsey

claiming to have found "probable cause." He could have, with equal logic, found "probable cause" that I shot Kennedy and kidnapped the Lindburgh baby. In any case, he ordered the government and myself to file statements by August 23, 1991, and September 13, respectively.

At the outset of the hearing, I filed a motion asking that my original conviction be vacated since I had been convicted pursuant to Judge Dorsey's "closing of the eyes" instruction, which the Supreme Court in *Cheek* clearly branded was illegal. He denied the motion for lack of jurisdiction. However, on August 23, I filed two petitions for writs of coram nobis (pursuant to 28 USC 1651) asking that both of my previous tax convictions be vacated, since identical "closing of the eyes" instructions were used in both cases, and convictions are now being reversed on even lessor deviations from the meaning of "willfulness." I can not see how my convictions can not be reversed—let alone how I can be imprisoned *again* for these alleged probation violations. Anything is possible in the Second Circuit.

I also discovered that, even after one completes his probation, and for two years thereafter, he can still be charged with having violated the terms of his probation. Apparently Judge Dorsey can rule that I violated the terms of my probation, even after August 8, when my probation will, officially, be completed.

On August 24, 1991, I received the "Government's Memorandum Concerning Schiff's Probation Violation." In it, Peter Jongbloed acknowledges that, "On June 16, 1988, Schiff was released on parole [it was really August 8] ... and also began serving the three-year probation period." This means, that based upon the government's miscalculation, I completed my three years of probation on June 16, 1991. Despite this, the government claimed *twice*, that I am "currently on probation" despite the fact that it did not dispute the case law I cited that established that the year I spent in jail for that parole violation still counted as time spent on probation.

In essence, Mr. Jongbloed did not attempt to challenge, let alone seek to refute, any of the claims and issues I raised. If he could have done so, he would have tried it when he had me under oath on the witness stand. I tried to put him on the stand (based on Mr. Medina's testimony) but he objected violently, and Judge Dorsey dutifully protected him from what would have been, for him, a novel experience—having to tell the truth in court. Obviously, his Memorandum was nothing but a tissue of lies and irrelevancies. What else do government lawyers have to go on in income tax cases?

I will now turn to preparing my Reply Brief and we will see what happens. Meanwhile, be sure to subscribe to the Schiff Audio Report. I hope to see you at the tax workshops I am planning to conduct around the country. And, consider this: the average Russian now has less to fear from his government than we have to fear from ours. How does that hit you? Peace.

NOTES TO ADDENDUM

1. Since the Tax Court's jurisdiction only extends to "redetermining deficiencies," by what logic can this be extended to include determining whether or not anyone committed an act of civil tax fraud—carrying substantial, additional financial penalties? This should only be the function of regular courts of law, and, I submit, only decided by juries. In a normal Tax Court case (where a petitioner has "self-assessed" himself with an income tax, and does not challenge its underlying premises), there are generally no facts in dispute, only the application of the "law" to those facts. However, whether a person "willfully" committed tax fraud is *not based on any admitted set of facts*. This is a *question of fact* involving such issues as one's state of mind, intent, etc., concerning which no federal bureaucrat, *acting alone*, should be allowed to judge—especially one who is not even a legitimate judge! How can anyone who might find themselves in Tax Court because they challenge various aspects of the law's enforcement, get an impartial "trial" on these issues, and the issue of "fraud" from a judge

who not only makes his living from the scam, but is **an important part of it.** How ridiculous can a situation be? Yes, this is what passes for "justice" in America!

2. This Fraud Referral Report was, at least, signed! The Fraud Referral Reports that were used to impose and extract the $50,000 in fraud penalties (held to have been legitimate by the Second Circuit), are shown in Figure A-2. Apart from alleging no act of fraud, **they were not even signed!** Here you have irrefutable proof of the kind of criminal extortion being practiced by the IRS and **protected by the courts.**

3. At the hearing of May 31, in response to a question I had asked, Judge Dorsey replied, "Don't give me any of your rabbinic answers." To me and a Christian friend of mine in attendance, the tone with which the remark was delivered, conveyed overtones of anti-Semitism. My friend provided me with an affidavit to that effect, which I attached to my own affidavit.

REVISED APPENDIX, SECOND EDITION

Due to the amount of new material that has been added to this Second Edition Appendix, certain documents that were included in the original appendix have been eliminated. They are: the letter sent to the author from Glenn Archer and D. Patrick Mullarkey of the U.S. Department of Justice, the author's Petion For a Rehearing *En Banc*, the author's Reply Brief to the government's request for a summary judgment in connection with its imposition of fraud penalties and its summary seizure of over $200,000 of the author's property, and Judge Eginton's Ruling of September 6, 1989 granting that summary judgment.

Editor's Note: The following "Editor's Note" appeared in the original edition of this book:

Editor's Note: As this book goes to press (July 25, 1990), Mr. Schiff is still incarcerated. Readers who would like copies of any documents referred to, that are not already included within the book's contents, may send for them after September 1, 1990. Please direct any inquiries or orders to:

FREEDOM BOOKS
60 Skiff Street, Suite 300
Hamden, CT 06517
(203) 281-6791

Unfortunately, the same situation may exist today! The facts are as follows:

On Wednesday, November 20, 1991, a U.S. marshall served a federal subpoena on the author, Irwin Schiff, ordering him to appear in Houston, Texas, on Monday, November 25, to be a defense witness at a trial. After making plane and hotel reservations, Mr. Schiff contacted most of the Houston media and notified them that he would be available to be interviewed concerning the illegality of that trial and the illegality of the lien placed on the home of Wanda and Jack Biggers (see dedication). The Houston media responded favorably and all asked the author to contact them when he arrived. One of the television stations suggested that they would seek permission to get a camera in the court room. When the Houston media began contacting the court for trial details, the federal mafia, not wanting this kind of publicity, responded in the following manner.

On Friday, November 22, 1991, Carmelo Medina telephoned Mr. Schiff to allegedly "remind" him that he had a hearing before Judge Dorsey in Hartford, on Monday, November 25. This was strange, because Mr. Medina had never before "reminded" the author of any hearing. In addition, Mr. Schiff had not spoken to Mr. Medina since August 7, 1991, which was the day the author completed his three years of probation, so there was no reason for his phone call. He obviously made it because (as the following will show) no written notice of any kind had been sent to Mr. Schiff, so a ruse had to be devised to notify him. *(Continued on page 282)*

When Mr. Schiff explained to Mr. Medina that he had not received any notice of such a hearing, Mr. Medina stated that the notice was sent to the author's current address some two weeks before. When Mr. Schiff further explained that he had been subpoenaed for a trial on that very day, Mr. Medina stated that the author's appearance in Hartford took precedence; however, he could not offer any information concerning the specific nature of the hearing.

Mr. Schiff then called Judge Dorsey's chambers and explained to his law clerk that he had just been notified of the hearing by phone, but that since he had not received any prior written notice, he was obviously not prepared to deal with it. In addition, he informed the law clerk that he had been subpoenaed to appear in Houston on that very day. Judge Dorsey's law clerk responded matter-of-factly: "Well, in that case, the hearing will have to be postponed. Let me check with Judge Dorsey," The tone of her voice indicated that she fully expected the judge to change the hearing date. When she returned to the phone, however, she said that Judge Dorsey, expected him at the hearing in Hartford. She also stated that a notice had been sent to the author's current address some two weeks before. When Mr. Schiff asked her to fax him a copy of the order, or to read it to him over the phone so that he would at least know what the hearing was about, she offered reasons why she could not do that.

On November 25, 1991, the date of the hearing, Mr. Schiff attempted to check the docket sheet in Hartford. He was informed that it was kept in New Haven. Later in the day, Mr. Schiff, accompanied by a friend, Joseph Letscher visited the New Haven office. They discovered that the last entry on the docket sheet was for 11/5/1991, and nothing was recorded with respect to any order asking Mr. Schiff to appear for a hearing on 11/25/91. The author got a certified copy of the docket sheet and then asked Alice Montz, the clerk in charge of such matters, if she had any paperwork from Judge Dorsey that had not been docketed. She told Mr. Schiff and Mr. Letscher that she did not. They then asked her how long she kept orders and other material received from Judge Dorsey before it was added to the docket, and she stated that it was done the same day it was received, or certainly within a day or two. Mr. Schiff also discovered that because the docket sheets were kept in New Haven, (along with the current addresses of all interested parties) all notices and orders in connection with this case were also sent out of New Haven—not Hartford—so **neither Mr. Medina nor Judge Dorsey's law clerk knew for sure where the alleged order was sent.** In any case, on the following day Ms. Montz informed the author that while his correct, current address was shown on the docket sheet, his old, incorrect address was still in the computer and, therefore, the notice was sent to the wrong address because "a new clerk was on duty that day." She then told Mr. Schiff that she would advise Judge Dorsey of this. It still did not explain, however, why the alleged order had never been docketed. Even if it had been sent to the wrong address, the post office would have forwarded it to the author. **Clearly, no such notice was ever sent to Mr. Schiff.**

The "hearing" was a joke, as have been all of the "hearings" conducted by Judge Dorsey. Again, disregarding all facts and all law, Judge Dorsey ruled that Mr. Schiff had violated the terms of his probation and ordered him to serve a two year sentence beginning on January 17, 1992. Had Mr. Schiff not filed those petitions for *corum nobis* (see page 280), Judge Dorsey would have immediately ordered him locked up! Because, at the "hearing," the government submitted its answer to one of those petitions, Judge Dorsey gave Mr. Schiff 30 days to respond, and then allowed time for rendering his decision. Based upon the *Cheek* case, the author's underlying conviction **must be vacated.** However, this assumes that we are dealing with an honest judge, which is, obviously, not the case here.

Mr. Schiff plans to file an immediate habeas corpus because Judge Dorsey's decision is so illegal on many grounds. For one thing, the author **never had a revocation hearing** pursuant to Rule 32.1 of the Rules of Criminal Procedure, which is a prerequisite for any probation revocation. When Mr. Schiff moved that Judge Dorsey recuse himself from this action, he accused him of seeking to conduct a revocation hearing without having first conducted a probable cause hearing, In seeking to refute this charge, Judge Dorsey responded in his "ORDER RE MOTION TO RECUSE" as follows:

> Defendant's assertion that he is being denied a probable cause hearing is blatantly false. He has been noticed for a **probable cause hearing** on July 31, 1991. (emphasis added)

Mr. Schiff had initially believed that Judge Dorsey was attempting to hold a revocation hearing; however, this statement clearly establishes that the hearing held on July 31, 1991, was a probable cause—not a revocation—hearing. Judge Dorsey even announced, at the end of that hearing, that he found "probable cause" (see page 280).

Thus a revocation hearing had to be held following that hearing, pursuant to the following provisions of Rule 32.1(a)(2), and the author "given":

(A) written notice of the alleged violation;
(B) disclosure of the evidence against the person;

(C) an opportunity to appear and to present evidence in the person's own behalf;

(D) the opportunity to question adverse witnesses; and

(E) notice of the person's right to be represented by counsel.

The only hearing following the probable cause hearing of August 31 was the hearing of November 25. At that "hearing," the government called no witnesses, and refused to allow Mr. Schiff to call either Mr. Netcoh or Mr. Medina to the witness stand. The author was not notified of his "right to be represented by counsel," and Judge Dorsey completely ignored Mr. Schiff's objection that he was being forced to proceed without counsel. Initially, he was not even aware of the purpose for the hearing. When Peter Jongbloed, the government prosecutor, first appeared in the courtroom, Mr. Schiff asked him what the hearing was about. Mr. Jongbloed answered, "I don't know."

After the hearing got underway, it became clear that this was not to be a "hearing" at all, but an alleged forum where the author could allegedly make a statement as to why his probation (which he had already fully completed) should not be revoked. When Mr. Schiff realized this and pointed out to the court that there could be no revocation without a revocation hearing, Judge Dorsey said, "You already had a revocation hearing," (or words to that effect) which the record will show (*United States v. Irwin A. Schiff*, Criminal No. N-85-20 (PCD)) **IS A TOTAL FABRICATION.**

At the probable cause hearing of July 31, the government introduced an unsigned, nonsensical schedule purporting to show that Mr. Schiff owed some $232,000 in taxes for the years 1980-1989. In order not to give Judge Dorsey *any* basis for revoking his probation, he filed returns for the *third time* and reported as his taxes the full amounts shown by the government on its totally fraudulent schedule. With those returns, Mr. Schiff attached statements declaring that while he believed that his actual tax liabilities were "zero" as he had previously reported, he was filing new returns showing his acceptance of the government's figures—"so I will not be found to be in violation of the terms of my probation and sent to jail," he stated. It should be obvious why such a declaration rendered each of those returns null and void and useless for any lawful purpose.

On September 5, 1991, however, the IRS filed tax liens against Mr. Schiff for all of the taxes *he reported on those returns*—over $230,000 in IRS liens—therefore admitting that the author filed valid (for their illegal purposes) returns during the period of his probation! (The "zero" returns Mr. Schiff had previously filed were no less

"valid.") Therefore, in addition to other issues, the author will raise in a Motion for Reconsideration and in his petition for habeas corpus, the following:

The government and this court are estopped from claiming that I did not file valid tax returns during this period—since the IRS accepted the returns I filed during my probationary period and acted upon them to my detriment. The court, therefore, can not hold, **also to my detriment**, that I **did not** file tax returns while on probation. It cannot allow the government to use the returns I filed while on probation to my detriment; while, at the same time, claim that I did not file tax returns **during this period.** Such a holding would be **contrary to fact and all logic, equity and reason** and so can not be lawful pursuant to the legal maxim, *Nihil quod est contra rationem est licitum.* (Nothing is lawful that is contrary to reason.)

It is clear that the government does not want Mr. Schiff discussing taxes and this book around the country during the 1991 tax season. Because of the publicity the author can focus on the government's illegal collection of income taxes, (as shown by the response of the Houston media) they have decided to incarcerate him. They know that, regardless of how illegal this is, the courts can dawdle with any habeas corpus he might file, and keep him illegally locked up for a long time—as they did in connection with his parole violation.

Once again, welcome to Amerika!

NOTE:

Because of the circumstances under which each edition of **The Federal Mafia** was published, we were not able to include a comprehensive index.

If you would like to receive an index (when completed) which will include page references for all of the Internal Revenue sections and court decisions referred to, simply send one dollar and a stamped, self-addressed envelope to:

Freedom Books, Order Dept.
P. O. Box 5326
Evansville, IN 47716
(812) 477-8628

MEMORANDUM IN SUPPORT OF MOTION TO DISMISS

COUNTS 1, 2 and 3

SINCE THE INTERNAL REVENUE CODE DOES NOT MAKE THE DEFENDANT LIABLE FOR INCOME TAXES

I

ISSUES PRESENTED

The Internal Revenue Code of 1954 (unlawfully referred to as "26 U.S.C." in the indictment) contains no provisions:

(A) establishing a "liability" for any such alleged "tax,"

(B) establishing any legal requirements or duty that such an alleged "tax" is required to be paid,

(C) authorizing the government to *assess* any such "tax" when neither a tax return nor a list is filed by the taxpayer,

(D) authorizing the government to *estimate* such a "tax" when neither a return nor a list is filed by the taxpayer.

II

DEFENDANT WILLING TO PLEAD GUILTY

If the government will produce any Code sections which (1) make the defendant and Irwin Schiff, Inc. "liable" for an income tax, (2) which states that such a tax is "required" to be paid, and (3) the section of law that authorizes the government to "estimate" such a tax when neither "returns nor lists are made" as provided for in Code Section 6201(a)(1), then the defendant will immediately plead guilty to counts 1, 2 and 3 of the indictment and will thus save the State and himself the expense of further court appearances and a criminal trial on all counts. If the government cannot produce such code sections, then all counts must be immediately dismissed as a matter of law.

POINTS AND AUTHORITIES

I

THE INTERNAL REVENUE CODE OF 1954 (UNLAWFULLY REFERRED TO BY THE GOVERNMENT AS "U.S.C. 26") PROVIDES NO LIABILITY FOR A

FEDERAL INCOME TAX AND ESTABLISHES NO REQUIREMENT THAT ' SUCH AN ALLEGED "TAX" BE PAID.

Before any tax is due and payable, the law has to clearly provide for such a tax and clearly establish a lawful duty on the part of a citizen that such a tax is required by law to be paid.

"Keeping in mind the well settled rule, that the citizen is exempt from taxation, unless the same is imposed by clear and unequivocal language, and that where the construction of a tax is doubtful, the doubt is to be resolved in favor of those upon whom the tax is sought to be laid." *Spreckles Sugar Refining Co. v. McClain* 192 US 397, 416.

Section 4401 of the Internal Revenue Code provides (with respect to internal revenue taxes on wagering) that:

"Each person who is engaged in the business of accepting wagers shall be *liable* for and shall *pay* the tax..."

Section 5005 (a) of the Internal Revenue Code provides (with respect to internal revenue taxes on distilled spirits) that:

"The distiller or importer of distilled spirits shall be *liable for the taxes imposed thereon by section 5001(a)(1)*."

Section 5703(a)(1) of the Internal Revenue Code provides (with respect to internal revenue taxes on tobacco products) that:

"The manufacturer or importer of tobacco products and cigarette papers and tubes shall be liable for the taxes imposed thereon by section 5701."

As is clearly shown by these three code sections, the mere imposition of a tax does not, of itself, create any liability on the part of a citizen with respect to the payment of, or the conforming to, any of the provisions connected with that tax.

Obviously, the Code imposes wagering, liquor and tobacco taxes but the defendant can not be guilty of evading such taxes merely because they are "imposed" because the Code does not make him liable for such taxes.

Similarly, the Internal Revenue Code does not make the defendant "liable" for the payment of any income tax simply because it is "imposed" in the Code. Nowhere does the Code state that "anyone having income is liable for and shall pay the income tax imposed in section 1 of the Internal Revenue Code."

Since no section of the Internal Revenue Code of 1954 makes the defendant "liable" for the income "tax" imposed in Section 1, and since the Code contains no provision that "requires" the payment of such a "tax", the defendant could not, as a matter of law, be guilty of evading a tax which, by law, he was not liable for or required, by law, to pay.

Section 6201 of the Internal Revenue Code provides in relevant part that:

"The Secretary is authorized and required to make the...assessments of all taxes... imposed by this title."

Section 6203 provides that:

"The assessment shall be made by recording the liability of the taxpayer in the office of the Secretary...(and) Upon request of the taxpayer, the Secretary shall furnish the taxpayer a copy of the record of the assessment."

In addition, section 6303 of the Code entitled "Notice and demand for tax" provides in relevant part, that the Secretary shall:

"...within 60 days, after the making of an assessment of a tax pursuant to section 6203, give notice to each person liable for the unpaid tax, stating the amount and demanding payment thereof. Such notice shall be left at the dwelling or usual place of business of such person, or shall be sent by mail to such person's last known address."

Attached and marked "Exhibit A" is a letter the defendant received from James E. Quinn, the District Director of the IRS, dated October 11, 1984, in which he states that: "In respect to the years 1979 through 1984, our records do not reflect any assessments."

Thus as late as October 11, 1984 it is clear that the defendant could not possibly have owed and/or sought to evade any Federal income taxes that he could have legally owed for the years covered by counts 1-3 of the indictment; yet, the U.S. Department of Justice contacted everyone that the defendant did business with and inferred to them that the defendant was evading income taxes for those years.

It is instructive to note that the letter the defendant received from the District Director, informing him that he owed no income taxes for the years 1979-1984, was received in response to a request made by the defendant under provisions of the Privacy Act, U.S.C. 552a in which the defendant agreed to pay as much as $10.00 for a copy of his assessment.

The defendant's Privacy Act request was made only after the IRS had ignored numerous requests of the defendant that he be furnished copies of his assessment for those years as the Secretary was obligated to furnish to him free of charge, as is specifically provided for in section 6303.

It is therefore obvious that the defendant was not trying to evade the payment of any tax; but, on the contrary, the defendant was literally pestering the Secretary for copies of his tax assessments which the Secretary was *evading* furnishing to him. Eventually, of course, the defendant was notified by the Director that no assessments had been made for the years charged in counts 1-3.

In addition, the defendant to this day has never received from the government any notice of any income taxes due for the years 1980, 1981, and 1982 pursuant to sections 6201, 6203 and 6303 as provided for in the Internal Revenue Code of 1954.

As the Supreme Court pointed out in *Bull v. U.S.* 295 US247, 259:

II

THE INTERNAL REVENUE CODE DOES NOT EVEN AUTHORIZE THE GOVERNMENT TO EITHER ASSESS OR ESTIMATE INCOME "TAXES" WHEN THE TAXPAYER HAS NOT HIMSELF VOLUNTARILY SUBMITTED A "RETURN OR LIST."

Code section 6201(a) authorizes the Secretary to assess all taxes "imposed by this title...which have not been duly paid by stamp at the time and in the manner provided by law."

So the only taxes that the Secretary can assess on his own are those taxes payable by stamp which have not been paid "in the manner provided by law." With respect to taxes paid on the basis of a return, section 6201(a)(1) only authorizes the Secretary to assess such taxes "as to which returns or lists are made..." Since the defendant did not make any "returns or lists" for the years covered in the indictments, the government has no authority to even assess "taxes" for the years shown.

THE GOVERNMENT IS NOT EVEN AUTHORIZED BY LAW TO ESTIMATE THE AMOUNT OF INCOME TAX THE DEFENDANT ALLEGEDLY "OWES."

Section 6201(a) of the Internal Revenue Code states in relevant part:

"Whenever any article upon which a tax is required to be paid by means of a stamp is sold or removed for sale...without the use of a proper stamp, it shall be the duty of the Secretary...to *estimate* the amount of tax which has been omitted to be paid and to make assessment therefore upon the person or persons...liable for such tax."

Nowhere in Chapter 63 (the chapter containing section 6201) does the Code similarly state that the Secretary is authorized:

"to *estimate* the amount that has been omitted to be shown and paid when a return or list is *not* filed and to make assessment therefore upon the persons liable for such tax."

Thus, nowhere in the Code is the government authorized to even *estimate* income taxes allegedly due from the defendant since he has not supplied the government with either "returns or lists" for the years covered in the indictments.

Thus the government's estimate of the alleged amount of the defendant's taxable income as shown in the indictments is not even authorized by law and was illegal.

III

THE GOVERNMENT FOLLOWED NONE OF THE PROCEDURES PROVIDED FOR IN THE INTERNAL REVENUE CODE WITH RESPECT TO THE ASSESSMENT AND DEMAND FOR SAID INCOME TAXES.

"A tax is an exaction by the sovereign, and necessarily the sovereign has an enforceable claim against every one within the taxable class for the amount lawfully due from him. The statute prescribes the rule of taxation. Some machinery must be provided for applying the rule to the facts in each taxpayer's case, in order to ascertain the amount due. The chosen instrumentality for the purpose is an administrative agency whose action is called an assessment. The assessment may be a valuation of property subject to taxation, which valuation is to be multiplied by the statutory rate to ascertain the amount of tax. Or it may include the calculation and fix the amount of tax payable, and assessments of federal estate and *income taxes are of this type. Once the tax is assessed, the taxpayer will owe the sovereign the amount when the date fixed by law for payment arrives.*"

Since the defendant had never been assessed for any taxes for the years 1980, 1981, 1982 he could not have owed any taxes for those years and hence could not be guilty of tax evasion as a matter of law.

"Criminal liability for income tax evasion depends on showing that the taxpayer was under civil liability to pay tax and that his civil liability was clear." *Ingram v. U.S.* 360 US 672.

"In order to convict a defendant of tax evasion, the government must prove that he actually owed some taxes in excess of the amount stated on his return." *U.S. v. Kelner*, C.A.W. Va., 1982, 675 F2d 602.

"Essential elements of crime of income tax evasion were: (1) additional substantial tax due and owing, (2) attempt by defendant to evade or defeat same, and (3) willfulness of attempt." *U.S. v. Pawlak*, D.C.N.Y. 1972, 352 F. Supp. 794.

"A defendant in a tax evasion case is entitled to show that no money was owing to the government in the prosecution year." *U.S. v. Wilkins*, C.A. Va. 1967, 385 F.2d 465.

"A defendant cannot be convicted of income tax evasion unless it is shown that additional tax is actually due, even though fraudulent concealment of income is established." *Holt v. U.S.*, C.A. Cal. 272 F.2d 272.

The defendant obviously therefore (since he owed no taxes for the years covered in the indictment) could not be guilty of tax evasion as a matter of law.
It is therefore clear that (in addition to the above) the defendant can not, as a matter of law, be guilty of income tax evasion because of:

(1) The absence of any provision in the Internal Revenue Code of 1954 making the defendant *liable for* or *requiring him to pay* the income "tax" imposed in Section 1.

(2) The absence of any provision in the Internal Revenue Code that allows the government to *assess* or even *estimate* any tax *paid by return* when "returns or lists" are not made as was illegally and fraudulently charged in the indictment.

(3) The explicit provisions of Code sections 6201, 6203 and 6303 which require that all internal revenue taxes be assessed, recorded, and demanded of taxpayers (before they can be owed); none of which was done with respect to the taxes allegedly "owed" and "evaded" by the defendant.

(4) The letter received by the defendant from District Director James E. Quinn on October 11, 1984 informing him that no income taxes had been assessed against him for the years covered in the indictment.

(5) The clear holding by the Supreme Court in *Bull v. U.S.*, supra, that no income taxes can be "owed" until such taxes have been assessed.

(6) In addition I attach (and mark as Exhibit B) a case right on point in which the Supreme Court of S. Carolina reversed James Goodman's conviction because he did not owe a tax since he had not been assessed.

It is obvious from all of the above that the defendant did not "owe" any income taxes, as a matter of law, as was falsely charged in the indictment. And since the defendant did not "owe" any income taxes for the years 1980, 1981 and 1982, as a matter of law, and since the Internal Revenue Code of 1954 contains no provision making the defendant "liable" for the tax or establishing any requirement that such a "tax" be paid, the defendant could not, as a matter of law, have evaded any "tax" for which he had not been made "liable", and thus he could not, as a matter of law, fall within the provisions of "26 U.S.C., 7201" (as was illegally cited in the indictment) and thus, the defendant demands that said indictments against him be dismissed with prejudice.

Respectfully submitted,
Irwin A. Schiff
pro se

IN THE

SUPREME COURT OF THE UNITED STATES

DECEMBER TERM, 1991

APPLICATION NO. A-781

(CERT. NO. 90-8119)

IRWIN A. SCHIFF,

Petitioner,

UNTIED STATES OF AMERICA,

Respondent.

PETITION FOR A WRIT OF CERTIORARI TO

THE UNITED STATES COURT OF APPEALS

FOR THE SECOND CIRCUIT

IRWIN A. SCHIFF
Petitioner, Pro Se

QUESTIONS PRESENTED

1. Can Federal courts deny jury trials to individuals who have their property seized to satisfy alleged tax deficiencies and penalties, but who later sue, seeking recovery, on the grounds that 1. no taxes were "due and owing"; 2. the penalties were unjustified; and 3. in any case, the IRS carried out the seizures in violation of law? The Second Circuit, in denying petitioner a trial on just such

issues, refused to follow Phillips v. Commissioner, 283 U.S. 589, 597-599 and Laing v. United States, 423 U.S. 161, at pages 197 & 198, (and every decision ever handed down on governmental seizures) and in so doing, also declared the Due Process clause of the United States Constitution dead in the Second Circuit - and it can only be resuscitated for the inhabitants of the Second Circuit by the Supreme Court reversing this decision.

2. Are Federal courts free to award summary judgments to the United States in connection with its exaction of civil fraud penalties, in actions brought to contest such charges and such exactions - as occurred in this caSe? And in awarding such summary judgments, are Federal courts free to ignore the holdings of the Supreme Court in Spies v. U.S. 317 U.S. 317, and Sansone v. U.S. 380 U.S. 343, that tax fraud is to be based on proof that the person so charged committed affirmative acts designed to evade a tax believed to be "due and owing" - elements which were never even alleged here, much less ever proven?

3. Can Federal courts enforce, by distraint, the payment of a Federal tax which, admittedly, does not fall in to any one of the three taxing clauses of the United States Constitution - in violation of Polloch v. Farmer's Loan and Trust, 157 U.S. 428 and Brushaber v. Union Pacific R.R. 240 U.S. 1 - as the Second Circuit has ruled here?

4. Are Federal courts free to ignore the law and hold - as the Second Circuit has done in this case - that income taxes do not have to be assessed from either returns or lists, even though Section 6201(a)(1) of the Internal Revenue Code clearly states that taxes. not paid by stamp, shall be assessed from "returns or list (which) dare made." And. are not. Federal courts that hold that income taxes need not be assessed from returns voluntarily filed and/or

information voluntarily given, violating the "self-assessment" nature of the tax as held in Flora v. U.S., 262 U.S. 145, 176 and Laing v. U.S., 423 U.S. 161, 191?

5. Are Federal courts free - as the Second Circuit has done here - to enforce payment, by distraint, of taxes for which Congress never made petitioner liable?

6. Are Federal courts free to claim - as the Second Circuit has done here - that parties who do not go to Tax Court are barred from seeking recovery, of funds paid, in district courts? And does this not violate the specific holding in Laing v. United States, supra, at page 197-198, that such parties are so entitled? Therefore, unlike other Circuits, inhabitants here can not be assured of being able to sue for the recovery of taxes (even if paid under duress) in district court, unless this decision is overturned.

7. Are Federal courts free - as the Second Circuit has done here - to award summary judgments by deciding all issues of law and fact - in favor of the party moving for summary judgment? And if this decision is allowed to stand, will not litigants in the Second Circuit be at the mercy of Federal judges who could, as occurred here, award summary judgments in a total arbitrary and capricious manner?

8. Are Federal appellate judges to be allowed to impose punitive fines and sanctions on appellants who file justifiable appeals but raise issues that appellate judges would prefer not to deal with and/or because such judges have a personal bias against appellant? It is perfectly clear from the above "Questions Presented" that petitioner's appeal was justified on any one of a number of grounds. Despite this, the Second Circuit imposed double costs and a $5,000 fine on petitioner. If these sanctions are not lifted by the Supreme Court then it will have acquiesced to a chilling of a

citizen's right to use the appeals process and it will also, in the process, have participated in an abridgment of an American's rights under the First, Fifth, Seventh, and Eighth Amendments to the United States Constitution.

* * * * * * * * *

> > > NOTICE FROM PUBLISHER < < <

IN THE INTEREST OF ECONOMY, THE TABLE OF CONTENTS, TABLE OF AUTHORITIES (I.E. COURT CASES, TREASURY REGULATIONS, ETC. ETC.) AND SUPPORTING EXHIBITS HAVE NOT BEEN INCLUDED. ALSO THE PETITION PRESENTED HERE IS SINGLE SPACED, THOUGH IT WAS DOUBLE SPACED WHEN SUBMITTED TO THE SUPREME COURT. THE CITATIONS OF THE DECISIONS APPEALED FROM ARE AS FOLLOWS: THE TRIAL COURT'S DECISION (WHICH WAS REPRODUCED IN THE FIRST EDITION OF THIS BOOK) IS, DISTRICT OF CONNECTICUT, CIVIL NO. N-86-354(WWE), SEPTEMBER 6, 1989 (I DON'T KNOW IF IT HAS SINCE BEEN PUBLISHED) AND THE APPELLATE DECISION IS SCHIFF V. THE UNITED STATES, 919 FED 2D. 830 (2ND 1990). READ BOTH DECISIONS IF YOU ARE STILL UNCONVINCED THAT FEDERAL JUDGES - KNOWINGLY - WRITE DECISIONS THAT HAVE NO RELATIONSHIP TO EITHER THE LAW OR THE FACTS!

PETITION FOR A WRIT OF CERTIORARI
TO THE UNITED STATES COURT OF APPEALS
FOR THE SECOND CIRCUIT

Petitioner, Irwin A. Schiff, respectfully prays that a writ of certiorari issue to review the judgment and opinion of the United States Court of Appeals for the Second Circuit entered in the above-entitled cause on November 21, 1990 with a denial of a petitioner's motion for reconsideration entered on January 4, 1991.

I.

OPINION BELOW

The memorandum opinion of the Court of Appeals is attached as Exhibit A, its denial of petitioner's motion for reconsideration attached as Exhibit B, and the Connecticut District Court's opinion is attached as Exhibit C.

II.

JURISDICTION

The opinion of the Court of Appeals for the Second Circuit of the United States Court was filed on November 21, 1990 and its denial of petitioner's motion for reconsideration was filed on January 4, 1991. The jurisdiction of this Court is invoked pursuant to 62 Stat. 928, 28 U.S.C. 1254(1).

III.

CONSTITUTIONAL PROVISIONS INVOLVED
==================================

ARTICLE 1. SECTION 1 of the United States Constitution provides that:

Congress shall make all laws......

ARTICLE 1, SECT. 2, CLAUSE 3, of the United States Constitution provides in relevant part:

Representative and direct taxes shall be apportioned among the several states which may be included within this Union, according to their numbers....

ARTICLE 1, SECT. 8, CLAUSE 1, of the United States Constitution provides in relevant part:

The Congress shall have the power To lay and collected taxes, duties, imposts and excises...but all duties, imposts and excises shall be uniform throughout the United States.

ARTICLE 1, SECT. 9, CLAUSE 4, of the United States Constitution provides:

No capitation, or other direct, tax shall be laid unless in proportion to the census or enumeration herein directed to be taken.

THE FOURTH AMENDMENT OF THE UNITED STATES CONSTITUTION

provides in relevant part:

The right of the people to be secure in their persons, houses, papers, and effects against unreasonable...seizures, shall not be violated...

THE FIFTH AMENDMENT OF THE UNITED STATES CONSTITUTION provides in relevant part:

No person shall...be deprived of...property without due process of law

THE SEVENTH AMENDMENT OF THE UNITED STATES CONSTITUTION provides in relevant part that:

In Suit at common law . . .the right of trial by jury shall be preserved.

THE EIGHTH AMENDMENT OF THE UNITED STATES CONSTITUTION provides in relevant part:

Excessive bail shall not be required, nor excessive fines imposed, nor cruel and unusual punishments inflicted.

IV.

STATEMENT OF FACTS

During the period 5/25/83 through 5/17/84 the Internal Revenue Service deprived petitioner of approximately $212,000 of property - in violation of numerous provisions of the Internal Revenue Code, Treasury Department regulations, Treasury Decision 1995 and the United States Constitution

The property deprived by distraint was money owed to petitioner by Simon & Schuster, but which it was persuaded to turn over to the United States without benefit of a court order, based solely on its receipt of notices of levy which were issued in violation of numerous provisions of Section 6331 of the Internal Revenue Code. It turned over the funds even after receiving assurances from the IRS that it did not have to do so without a court order (See letter from IRS to this effect (attached as Exhibit D). Assurances that the publisher would not turn over the funds at issue without a court order is confirmed in letters sent to the IRS and to petitioner by Simon & Schuster as shown by Exhibits E & F. However, in violation of this agreement and these assurances, Simon and Schuster began turning over to the United States all of the funds at issue after petitioner, relying on this promise, cancelled his distribution agreement with that firm. It is also clear from Simon and Schuster's letters to respondent dated November 28, 1983, December 12, 1983, December 30, 1983, January 18, 1984, and May 15, 1984 (attached as Exhibits G, H, I, J) that all of the funds at issue were turned over to the United States in violation of:

1. its promise not to turn over any funds without a court order.

2. a fiduciary obligation owed to petitioner not to provide financial data to respondent concerning petitioner unless

A-6

compelled to do so in accordance with Section 7602. and

3. Code Sections 6331(b) and (c), since these transfers clearly represented transfers of "after acquired property" in violation of these sections. (Note 1)

When petitioner had previously sought to obtain a temporary order restraining the IRS from seizing his property, as it threatened to do in a "FINAL NOTICE," pending a hearing on the merits of the Government's claim - a Connecticut district court ruled (Schiff v. United States, N-81-316 Conn. 1983), that the Anti-Injunction statute prevented such relief and that petitioner's only legal recourse was to pay the taxes and penalties sought, and sue for a refund.

When petitioner requested the IRS restore to him the funds it had illegally induced/and or intimidated Simon and Shuster into turning over to it, it refused to do so; whereupon petitioner instituted a lawsuit in a United States district court for their recovery - which two prior federal courts had ruled was his "only legal recourse."

Petitioner's complaint was captioned "Complaint to Recover Illegal Tax Collection" (exhibit K) though it should have been captioned "Complaint To Recover Property Illegally Deprived" since these funds were "collected" only in the sense that Jessie James "collected" funds. Petitioner's complaint alleged that all of the funds at issue were "collected"

1. Without any "tax liability" ever being "identified by any Government official."

2. "In violation of the Due Process and taxing clauses of the U.S. Constitution,

3. "Without any lawful assessment," having been made, and that.

4. The IRS seized a portion of the property at issue to satisfy civil fraud penalties - which the Government had the burden of proving - BUT NEVER DID!.

In its Answer of December 12, 1986, the United States denied the first three allegations, but admitted the fourth.

During an extended period of discovery (conducted largely by petitioner while a federal prisoner) the United States produced documents or admitted to the following - most of which is supported and sworn to in Petitioner's Affidavit (hereinafter referred to as Pet. Aff.) which was provided to the trial court with petitioner's Motion for Summary Judgement, and is attached here as Exhibit L, or is contained in the decisions of either the trial or appellate courts.

1. In response to an interrogatory asking the United States to identify the taxing clause or clauses in the United States Constitution pursuant to which it had imposed the income tax on petitioner, it responded by claiming that it had imposed the tax on him pursuant to ALL THREE (!) of the Constitution's taxing clauses and the 16th Amendment (Pet. Aff. pars. 25 & 26).

2. Admitted it bore the burden of proving the civil fraud alleged, for which it had deprived petitioner of approximately

$50,000 of the funds at issue.. (Def. Aff. par. 27)

3. Produced a document (Form 895) which admitted that the funds deprived with respect to 1976 had become time barred by the Statute of limitation as of 4/15/1980 or some three years prior to their being actual deprived. (Def. Aff. par 5)

4. Admitted that it had deprived petitioner of all of the funds at issue without first sending petitioner the statutory notice and demand (as required by Sections 6303, 6321 and 6331) but sent. instead. identified in Treasury Decision 1995 (IRS Form 17) which made no demand whatsoever for the funds at issue. (Pet. Aff. pars. 21 & 22)

5. Neither the Government, trial or the appellate courts could produce or identify any document or Treasury Regulation that identified Form 3552 as being the "notice and demand" called for by statute, nor provide any proof that Treasury Decision 1995 had been repealed, or that Form 17 had been legally replaced by Form 3552.

6. Claimed to have made the assessments in the instant case "pursuant to the provisions of 26 USC 6201 in conjunction with 26 USC 6213(c)." (Pet. Aff. par. 11)

7. However, the Government could produce no proof, such as a copy of a Summary Record of Assessment (Form 23C), to support its claim that it made "zero." original assessments against petitioner on 12/27/82 for each of the years at issue as certified to by respondent on petitioner's Forms 4340 (Exhibits 4, 5, and 6 of the "United States' Statement of Material Facts." attached as petitioner's Exhibit M), and which were, in any case, contradicted by letters petitioner's received from the IRS itself (Exhibits N & O) that no assessments on that date were ever made (Pet. Aff. pars 11, 12, 13, 14, and 15.)

8. In addition, respondent could produce no "supporting records" for its claimed 12/27/82 assessment as required by CFR 301.6203-1. (Def. Aff. pars. 16, 17, and 18)

9. When respondent produced the Fraud Referral Reports, (IRS Form 2797) the documents pursuant to which the fraud penalties had been imposed, attached as Exhibits P, contained no claim that petitioner had committed any affirmative act of tax fraud for any of the years shown (only that petitioner had failed to file), and the documents themselves WERE NOT EVEN SIGNED! - even though the documents and the IRS "Procedure Manual," CALLED FOR NO LESS THAN THREE SIGNATURES! (Pet. Aff. par 28)

10. In response to discovery requests, respondent could not identify any affirmative act of tax evasion that petitioner allegedly committed for any of the years at issue, that fell within the meaning of Spies v. U.S., 317 US 492 or Sansone v.U.S., 380 US 343. (Pet. Aff. par. 37)

11. Respondent admitted during discovery that failure to file does not constitute civil tax fraud (Pet. Aff. par. 39) -though this was the only allegation contained in petitioner's Fraud Referral Report - thereby ADMITTING that all of the funds at issue taken to satisfy the fraud penalties. WERE TAKEN ILLEGALLY.

12. During discovery, respondent twice claimed to have assessed the taxes at issue from returns prepared pursuant to IR Code Section

6020(b). (Pet. Aff., par. 8)

13. However, when petitioner proved in his Motion for Summary judgment (attached Exhibit Q, pages 10-16) that this claim was false – since blank, unsigned "returns" (shown as Exhibit 2 in petitioner's Exhibit M) do not qualify as returns within the meaning of Section 6020(b), thus establishing that all the alleged assessments were fraudulent – respondent changed its claim, and NOW CLAIMED to have prepared "dummy returns." (See respondents Motion for Summary Judgment and the trial court's decision, Exhibit C, pages 4 & 5)

14. All of the above was pointed out to the Second Circuit in pages 30 through 34 of petitioner's opening brief, which THOROUGHLY DISCREDITED the trial court's claim that the assessments at issue could have been made from "dummy returns" AS CONTENDED IN THE TRIAL COURT'S DECISION.

15. Having thus TOTALLY DISCREDITED (especially in the light of Treasury Document No. 7081 (3-86), Exhibit B, petitioner's opening appeal brief) the prior claim of both the Government and the trial court that assessments could be made from "dummy returns," the Government in its reply brief NOW CHANGED ITS CLAIM AGAIN –and now claimed it could make assessments WITHOUT HAVING ANY RETURNS AT ALL, which claim was adopted by the Second Circuit in its decision, Exhibit A.

16. In addition to all of the above, the United States could not identify, during discovery, any Code Section that made petitioner "liable" for the taxes alleged (Petitioner's Affidavit pars. 34, 35, and 36) – and no such Code section WAS EVER IDENTIFIED by either the trial or appellate courts in EITHER DECISION!

17. And in addition, since petitioner irrefutably proved in his briefs that the assessments and deprivations at issue WERE DONE IN VIOLATION OF CODE SECTION 6501(c)(3) – this argument was NEVER EVEN ADDRESSED (let alone refuted) by either court in either decision.

18. In view of the above paragraph's 1, 2, 3, 4, 5, 6, 7, 8, 9, 10, 11, 12, 16, and 17, petitioner moved for a summary judgment – there being nothing left for a jury to decide, since petitioner had established (as a matter of law) that the Government had deprived petitioner of all of the funds at issue:

a. in violation of all three taxing clauses of the Constitution (The government's claim that it had imposed the income tax pursuant to all three taxing clauses of the Constitution was an obvious admission that it had imposed the tax pursuant to none of those clauses),

b. without making any lawful assessments,

c. without making a lawful demand on petitioner prior to the deprivation of the property at issue,

d. without having any basis – either factual or legal – for the fraud penalty,

e. in violation of the statute of limitations, and

f. without being able to identify any Code section making petitioner "liable" for the taxes alleged.

In short petitioner, when discovery was completed, had established – beyond any reasonable doubt – that all of the funds at issue had been deprived in violation of NO LESS then the following statutes, Treasury regulations and Treasury decisions (overlooking the violations of the Constitution) – Code Sections: 61, 6001, 6011, 6020(b), 6201, 6203, 6204, 6303, 6321, 6322, 6331, 6501(c)(3); Treasury regulations 601.103(a) & (b), 601.104(a), 301.6201-1(1), 301.6203-1, 301.6204-1 and Treasury Decision 1995. Therefore, he moved for a summary judgement, since he had proven, as a matter of law, all of the relative issues charged in his complaint. However, instead of granting, petitioner a summary judgment as all of the above facts warranted, the trial court, and as affirmed by the Second Circuit, in violation of ALL law and in violation of ALL legal precedent awarded the Government a summary judgment in connection with A SUMMARY SEIZURE OF PROPERTY INCLUDING CHARGES OF CIVIL FRAUD, thereby changing the character of the American Republic if this decision is allowed to stand.

VI.

REASONS FOR GRANTING WRIT

In upholding the trial court's granting the Government a summary judgment with respect to summary "seizures" of property (taken by distraint allegedly pursuant to IR Code Section 6331) and in connection with Government allegations that petitioner committed civil tax fraud (within the meaning of Code Sections 6653(b) and 7454(a)) for all the years at issue, the Second Circuit Court of Appeal disregarded...

1. The United States Constitution.

2. The Internal Revenue Code.

3. All court precedent (including its own) bearing on governmental "seizures" of property.

4. The lawful basis pursuant to which summary judgments can be granted, and

in doing all of the above, the Second Circuit held that despite the United States Constitution and our professed commitment to "due process of law," in the final analysis, the Untied States can NOW deprive citizens of property in a manner not unlike how Atilla the Hun might have done it:

A

CAN THE UNTIED STATES DEPRIVE PEOPLE OF PROPERTY WITHOUT EVER HOLDING PRE SEIZURE OR POST SEIZURE HEARINGS?

To hold, as the Second Circuit Court of Appeal has done in this case, that the United States can take citizen property by distraint without EVER HAVING TO PROVE IN ANY COURT OF LAW THE VALIDITY OF ITS CLAIM is so incredible an assertion, that one would imagine that it would not be necessary for petitioner to have to proceed ANY FURTHER THEN THIS to get this decision reversed. Does this pro se petitioner REALLY have to cite case law to the Supreme Court and SERIOUSLY ARGUE to it that any such proposition is RIDICULOUS ON ITS VERY FACE – and that it flies in the face of ALL law ALL tradition and EACH AND EVERY

DOCUMENT, going back to the Magna Carta, associated with the creation of this Nation? However, as petitioner wrote in his opening brief to the Second Circuit (page 9):

One would think it would hardly be necessary for a pro se. Federal prisoner to have to point out to a United States Appellate Court, that the claim that the Federal government can constitutionally deprive a person of property without the need of having either a pre deprivation or post depriva- tion hearing is repugnant to all Federal case law, the U.S. Constitution and every concept of a civilized society. Yet this is precisely what the Honorable Warren G. Eginton be- lieves, as reflected in his decision of September 6, 1989.

Then, after citing for the court the Due Process clause of the Constitution and quoting the definition of "due process" from *Black's Law Dictionary*, I pointed out to the Appellate court that:

One would think that it would not be necessary for appellant to proceed any further, since this 15 line quotation from *Black's* — proves that all of the property at issue was deprived in violation of the Due Process clause of the Constitution, because appellant has never been "HEARD" in any court of law on any of the issues of law or fact in connection with the deprivation of his instant property! In addition, NO EVIDENCE of any kind (as defined in *Black's Law Dictionary*, see page 13 of appellant's Motion to Reconsider) with respect to the legitimacy of the government's claim WAS NEVER RECEIVED BY ANY COURT! Despite this, the Honorable Warren G. Eginton thinks that the deprivation of appellant's property under these circumstances CAN BE FINALIZED within the meaning of the Due Process clause of the Constitution and in harmony with American jurisprudence. In addition, every fact or liability at issue was "conclusively presumed" against appellant and for the Government: the depriver of the property. Thus based solely on this 15 line quote from *Black's Law Dictionary*, it would appear impossible that any legitimate legal tribunal could sustain Judge Eginton's ruling. However, not wanting to entrust the success of my appeal to a mere 15 line quotation from *Black's* (though, in this case, it would appear sufficient) appellant will press ahead and seek, in this case, to kill an ant with a howitzer —recognizing that based on *Black's* definition, *Blacks's* has already _proven_ my case for me!

However, not only was *Black's* definition not sufficient (as it should have been) to get the Second Circuit to reverse the trial court's decision, neither were petitioner's opening brief, reply brief, oral argument (attached as Exhibit R), and his Motion for Reconsideration (all of which are incorporated in this petition by reference). These only resulted in petitioner being fined double costs and $5,000 and being prevented from having a habeas corpus appeal being heard. (Note 2.)

In any case, the appellate court's claim that the Federal government can deprive people of property without ever giving them either a pre seizure or post seizure hearing FLIES IN THE FACE of the following Supreme Court decisions - all of which were pointed out to Second Circuit in number of petitioner's underlying briefs): Fuentes v. Shevin, 407 U.S. 67; Joint Anti-Fascist Committee v. McGrath, 341 U.S.123, 170-172; THE DEFINITIVE CASE of Phillips v. Commissioner, 283 U.S. 589, which is right on point: Stanley v. Illinois, 405

U.S. 645; Bodie v. Connecticut, 401 U.S. 371, 378; Coe v. Armour Fertilizer Works, 273 U.S. 413, 424; Mathews v. Eldridge, 424 U.S. 319; Wolf v. McDonnell 418 U.S. 539, 557-558; Dent v. West Virginia, 129 U.S. 114, 124-125; Armstrong v. Manzo, 380 U.S. 545, 552; and Gannis v. Ordean, 234 U.S. In addition, the court's decision is directly contrary to its own decisions in; Kalb v. U.S. 505 F2d 506 (1974), and Lee v. Thornton 538 F2d 27 (1976), which were also cited by appellant in his underlying briefs.

B

CAN THE UNITED STATES IMPOSE,
AND THEN EXTRACT BY DESTRAINT, CIVIL FRAUD PENALTIES,
AND NEVER HAVE TO PROVE THE FRAUD ALLEGED,
EVEN WHEN A LAW SUIT IS BROUGHT CONTESTING THE ALLEGATIONS?

This, too, is such a ludicrous proposition (though it is NOW the "law" in the Second Circuit, as contrasted to what the law is IN ALL THE OTHER CIRCUITS), that one would think it would not have to be seriously argued to be reversed. As stated on page 53 of petition's Answer to the Government's motion for summary judgment (attached hereto as Exhibit R and incorporated herin by reference):

Since the elements of civil tax fraud are exactly the same as for criminal tax fraud (deferring only in the degree of the Government's burden) the U.S. Department of Justice has as much right asking for a summary judgement to allegations of civil fraud as it would asking for a summary conviction to an indictment alleging criminal violations of 7201 (i.e. tax evasion), or to an information alleging violations of Section 7203...AND THE DEFENDANT KNOWS THIS FULL WELL! The Government has not only already admitted to its burden....(Plaintiff's Affidavit par 27) but it even admits this in its instant Reply!

Therefore, if the Government can extract civil fraud penalties WITHOUT A TRIAL (even when challenged in a court suit to prove the fraud alleged), why can't it ALSO extract penalties for criminal tax fraud WITHOUT A TRIAL? One makes about as much sense as the other.

Could the Government charge a person with criminal tax fraud (tax evasion) and then sentence him to prison without a trial, on the grounds that he had been convicted of the same offense before, and had "obviously" done it again? However, this is exactly what Judges Feinberg, Timbers and Miner are contending here. The sole basis for their claiming that Petitioner committed tax fraud for all of the years at issue is that:

1. "He was convicted of willfully failing to file tax returns for the years 1974 and 1975." (and other years not mentioned here), and

2. "Schiff's background makes it inconceivable that he was unaware of his obligation to file returns and pay taxes. In light of Schiff's repeated attempts to evade his obligation to pay income taxes, we hold that summary judgment was justified on the issue of whether civil fraud penalties were properly assessed because of his failure to file returns for the years 1976-1978." (at page 433)

I defy the Supreme Court to find a more injudicious assertion in the entire annals of American jurisprudence —while many Americans have gone to jail for perjury for providing false testimony that undoubtedly had less of a legal impact then the FALSEHOODS being contended here.

For one thing, Judges Feinberg, Timbers, and Miner KNOW that they can not sustain a finding of civil tax fraud on the basis claimed – of "omissions" alone and without a court trial, and in this case, a jury determination. Secondly they also knew, on the basis of extensive material contained in SIX OF PETITIONER'S UNDERLYING BRIEFS, that because petitioner WAS FULLY AWARE THAT:

1. the income tax is not imposed pursuant to any of the Constitution's three taxing clauses or the Sixteenth Amendment (pages 18-30 of petitioner's appeal brief)

2. Sections 6103(h) & (i) provide that all return information can be used against those who file (see page 13, Exhibit W)

3. no law makes petitioner "liable" for income taxes. (See paragraph 17, this brief, under "Statement of Facts," and page 49 of petitioner's appeal brief.)

4. no law requires petitioner "to pay" income taxes.

5. he received no "income" that could possibly fall within the meaning of "income" as defined by the Supreme Court in Merchant's Loan and Trust Company v. Smietanka, 255 U.S. 509, 518,519, (as cited and quoted on page 34, Exhibit Q.

6. in any case, he could not possibly "owe" anything unless the Government won a law suit brought against him pursuant to Code Section 6501(c)(3) –

it is "inconceivable" that Schiff believed he had ANY OBLIGATION to either file returns and pay taxes – and not the other way around as the Second Circuit contended.

And thirdly, since the Second Circuit knew that the alleged fraud allegations were VOID AS A MATTER OF LAW (since the Referral Reports were DEVOID OF THE THREE SIGNATURES REQUIRED BY LAW) – it is inconceivable that it did not know that its claim that "the fraud penalties were properly assessed" was WITHOUT MERIT just on this basis ALONE!

In any case, apart from the Second Circuit's decision FLYING IN THE FACE of Spies and Sansone because it basis a fraud claim on OMISSIONS ALONE, and apart from its decision FLYING IN THE FACE of the IRS Procedures Manual (as quoted and discussed in pages 29-33 of Exhibit Q), its additional claim that fraud penalties need not be proven on the basis of "clear and convincing evidence" even in law suits brought to contest the allegations. FLIES IN THE FACE OF THE LAW (Code Section 7454(a)) ITSELF and EVERY case in EVERY CIRCUIT (including the Second Circuit) bearing on this question. As noted at page 35 of petitioner's opening brief to the trial court (Exhibit Q):

As far as the courts are concerned, civil fraud as contemplated by section 6653(b):

Is the intentional commission of an act or acts for the specific purpose of evading a tax believed to be owing. See Webb v. Commissioner, 394 F2d 366 (21 AFTRA 2d 1150] (5th Cir. 1968) T.C. Memo. 1966-8 (66.081 P-H Memo T.C.]; McGee v. Commissioner, 61 T.C. 249 (1973), aff. 519 F.2d 1121 (36 Aftra 2d 75-5888] 5th Cir 1975], cert denied 424 U.S. 967 (1976). *** The burden of proof rests on respondent, and he must meet that burden with clear and convincing evidence. (citings omitted)
John B. Kotmair Jr. 86.73 P-H TC

(The finding of fraud in this case was also directly contrary to Kotmair Jr., as cited above and as fully developed in petitioner's opening brief to the trial court.)

And as pointed out at on page 19 of petitioners Motion for Reconsideration, the Second Circuit's instant claim that courts do not have to prove fraud in suits brought to contest the allegation FLIES IN THE FACE of such Second Circuit decisions as: Paddock v. U.S. 280 F2d 563 (2d Cir 1960); Leberman v. John Blair & Co., 880 F2d 1555, 1560 (2d Cir 19800; Patrick v. LeFevre 745 F2d 153, 159 (2d Cir. 1984), and the Second Circuit case of United States v. Prince, 348 F2d. 746 (2d 1965) WHICH IS RIGHT ON POINT! Commenting on Prince in his Motion for Reconsideration, petitioner noted (Exhibit B, page 20), that:

In this case (one in which the taxpayer voluntarily paid the taxes alleged and in which he signed a Form 870 Ad Agreement, entitled "Offer of Waiver of Restrictions on Assessments and Collection of Deficiency in Tax and of Acceptance of Over assessment ," so that the seizure of property was not an issue, as it is in the instant case) the court sustained a lower court's granting of a summary judgment to the government in connection with the taxes allegedly owed, but reversed and "remanded for TRIAL as to the fraud penalties and interest thereon." (emphasis added) In rejecting the lower court's granting of a summary judgment as to the fraud penalties, the Second Circuit stated on page 748:

"The situation differs, however, as to the portion of the judgment reflecting the fraud penalties and interest thereon. The assessment of fraud penalties concededly carries no presumption of validity, the burden of proof on this issue resting on the Government both under the Code, 26 U.S.C. 7454 and the cases Paddock v. United States, 280 F.2d 563 (2 Cir 1960); Clark v. C.I.R. 266 F. 698 (9 Cir. 1959)."

So, as petitioner pointed out, this shows that, in this case, the Second Circuit is, at least consistent, since in rendering judgment. "The Second Circuit not only ignores the U.S. Constitution, all relevant Internal Revenue Statutes, all relevant Treasury Regulations, a Treasury Department decision - but also ALL OF ITS OWN CASE LAW!

It is therefore obvious, that since:

1. no allegations exist that petitioner committed any affirmative act of tax fraud for any of the years at issue.

Page 11

2. the Fraud Referral Reports were not signed.

3. the fraud alleged was never proven on the basis of "clear and convincing evidence." in any court of law.

the Second Circuit's finding of civil fraud is, in this case, TOTALLY WITHOUT MERIT.

C.

WITH RESPECT TO THE SECOND CIRCUIT'S HANDLING OF THE ISSUE INVOLVING THE TAXING CLAUSES OF THE CONSTITUTION

The meritless nature of the Second Circuit's decision is further revealed in its response to this issue - an issue which was extensively covered in all of petitioner's underlying briefs. (pages 25-28, Exhibit Q; pages 41--48 of Exhibit S); pages 18-30 of petitioner's opening Appeal Brief; pages 27-33 of petitioner's Reply Brief; and pages 7 through 9 of his Motion for Reconsideration. Exhibit B. Despite all of this, the Second Circuit (as did the trial court) contrived to avoid addressing this FUNDAMENTAL CONSTITUTIONAL ISSUE with a two line response which deliberately misrepresented the issue and the few cases cited.

Since this issue was extensively developed in all of the underlying briefs as mentioned and cited above, it is unnecessary for me to develop the argument in full detail here. Suffice it to say that:

1. The United States can not ignore the argument, as it has done here.

The two great subdivisions embracing the complete and perfect delegation of the power to tax and the TWO CORRELATED LIMITATIONS AS TO SUCH POWER (as) aptly stated by Chief Justice Fuller in *Pollock v. Farmer's Loan & Trust Company*, supra: at page 557. "In the matter of taxation, the Constitution recognizes the two great classes of direct and indirect taxes, and lays down two rules by which THEIR IMPOSITION MUST BE GOVERNED: The rule of apportionment as to direct taxes, and the rule of uniformity as to duties, imposts and excises."

2. In addition, the 16th Amendment "Conferred no new power of taxation" on the Federal government, *Stanton v. Baltic Mining Co.*, 240 US 103,122; and so its taxing power "Must (still) be construed in connection with the taxing clauses of the ORIGINAL CONSTITUTION and the effect attributable to them BEFORE THE AMENDMENT WAS ADOPTED" (emphasis added). *Eisner v. Macomber*, 252 US 189, 205 (1929).

3. It is also clear from 1. above and the following quote from page 19 of that decision, that "The Amendment contains nothing repudiating or challenging the ruling in the Pollock case." - so THE RULING IN POLLOCK STILL STANDS - which is that "income" taxes, NOT IMPOSED as excises "relieved ...from a consideration of the source" ARE UNCONSTITUTIONAL *if not apportioned!*

Page 12

4. Clearly, therefore, the 16th Amendment gave the Federal government no power to impose taxes on "sources" of income such as: wages, dividends, interest, rent, self-employment earnings etc. etc. without apportionment, which, according to both Pollock and Brushaber, still require apportionment.

5. As the Supreme Court ruled in *Brushaber* "The whole purpose of the (16th) Amendment was to relieve all income taxes when imposed from apportionment from A CONSIDERATION OF THE SOURCE whence the income was derived," by imposing on such "income" an EXCISE, since (as the court ruled at pages 16 and 17) an income tax "Was in its nature an excise entitled to be enforced as such." (emphasis added)

6. The meaning of "income" is not defined in the Internal Revenue Code (*United States v. Ballard*, 535 F2d. 400, 404), and "Congress cannot by any definition it may adopt conclude the matter, since it cannot by legislation alter the Constitution." *Eisner v. Macomber*, supra, at page 206. Thus, there can be no definition for "income" within the Internal Revenue Code.

7. The Supreme Court, therefore had to define "income," and it essentially defined it as "gains and profits" derived *from corporate activity.* "Whatever difficulty may be about a precise and scientific definition of 'income' it imports, as used here...the idea of *gain or increase arising from corporate activities.*" *Doyle v. Mitchell*, 247 U.S. 179 (1918). "Certainly the term 'income' has no broader meaning in the 1913 Act than in that of 1909 (See *Straton's Independence v. Howbert*, 231 U.S. 399, 416, 417) and ...*we assume that there is no difference in its meaning as used in the two acts.*" *Southern Pacific Co. v. John Z. Lowe, Jr.*, 247 U.S. 330, 335 (1918). And the most comprehensive and definitive definition of "income" will be found on pages 518 and 519 of *Merchant's Loan & Trust Co. v. Smientanka*, 255 U.S. 509, with the Supreme Court closing its, paragraph on the meaning of "income" with this observation:

There would seem to be no room for doubt that the word (income) *must be given the same meaning in all of the Income Tax Acts of Congress that was given to it in the Corporate Excise Tax Act* and that what that meaning is has now become definitely settled by decisions of this court." (emphases added)

8. So all three of these Supreme Court decisions clearly held that "income" was a derivative of corporate activity and that the word "income" had to be given the "same meaning" in all of the income tax acts of Congress as it had in the Corporate Excise Tax Act of 1909. And since none of the "income" alleged to have been received by petitioner in any of the years at issue would have been taxed as "income" pursuant to the Corporate Excise Tax Act of 1909 (since petitioner is not a corporation!), none of it can be subject to a MANDATORY income tax today - and EXTRACTED BY DISTRAINT.

9. In accordance with these Supreme Court decisions - and so as not to be held unconstitutional on these grounds - Section 61 of the Internal Revenue Code was careful not to define "income" (as "imposed" in Section 1 of the IR Code) , as being a tax ON ANYTHING, such as: a tax "on" wages; or "on" dividends; or "on" interest; or on "earnings" from self-employment, which is how the taxes at issue WERE IMPOSED ON PETITIONER. What Section 61 defines as "income" are "gains and profits" derived "from" (but not "on") those "sources" - and so, what is taxable as "income" can only be corporate profits. Since only when a "profit" is arrived at, are earnings "separated"

In addition, it was NEVER PETITIONER'S CLAIM that the "imposition" of the tax was not "validly enacted" - it was his claim that the ENFORCEMENT OF THAT "IMPOSITION" was done.IN VIOLATION OF: 1. its imposition, 2. the manner in which it was "enacted ...by Congress." and 3. the basis upon which it was held constitutional. And in addition, petitioner's appeal of this issue was based on ITS TOTAL MISREPRESENTATION by the trial court, and on the numerous misstatements of both law and fact made by that court to support it. For example, the trial court pretended to address this issue by initially stating that it, "Now turns to plaintiff's contention that the imposition of an income tax on plaintiff is unconstitutional." This was NOT THE "CONTENTION" raised by petitioner, as the following excerpts from his opening appeal brief make clear - at page 19.

The Government and Judge Eginton both avoided (as would the Second Circuit in its sustaining decision) addressing my actual claim because they knew they could not refute it - so they both contrived to change it. The subterfuge. ...took the following form. Both the Government in its Reply.at Segment II, and the trial court in its decision, at page 8, pretended that appellant's claim was that his income could not be constitutionally taxed. The Government even entitled its section ..."The Income Tax May Be Constitutionally Imposed Upon Schiff." Appellant (in his Reply Brief #2 at pages 37-43) immediately sought to expose the Government's false characterization...by stating, "Who said it couldn't be?" Appellant then went on to add that it was not his contention that an income tax could not be constitutionally imposed, but that it "Could not be SIMULTANEOUSLY imposed... pursuant to all three clauses of the Constitution as the United States CLAIMS TO HAVE IMPOSED IT - but without either apportioning the tax or imposing it as a duty, impost or excise."

The petitioner then devoted approximately 10 pages, refuting the trial court's claim that it was petitioner's claim that "The imposition of an income tax on plaintiff is unconstitutional" - a position adopted by the appeals court, nevertheless. And, of course, there is no mention in the trial court's decision that it was the Government's contention that it had imposed the income tax "pursuant to ALL THREE taxing clauses of the Constitution and the 16th Amendment." and the OBVIOUS UNCONSTITUTIONALITY OF ANY SUCH CLAIMED "IMPOSITION."

In addition on page 24 of petitioner's opening brief, he lists ALL SEVEN of the representations made by the trial court to support its FABRICATED CLAIM and then PROVED why each one of them MISREPRESENTED either a fact or the law -- such as its claim that "The 16th Amendment removed the limitation of Congress' authority to impose a direct tax only if proportioned among the States" (note 3) and the court's seventh claim, which was a restatement of its false claim that petitioner had contended "That his income cannot be constitutionally taxed."

Therefore, based upon: 1, the obvious misstatement of this issue by the trial court. 2, its refusal to deal with the constitutional implications inherent in the Government's claim that it imposed the income tax "Pursuant to all three taxing clauses of the Constitution and the 16th Amendment." 3, the numerous misstatements of both law and fact made by the trial court in addressing this issue - certainly

---

from their "sources," to become the "income" referred to in Section 61 and as referred to in Brushaber. However, since the taxes at issue were imposed DIRECTLY on the "sources" of petitioners earnings, they had to be imposed on the basis of apportionment, pursuant to both Pollock and Brushaber -BEFORE THEY COULD BE TAKEN BY DISTRAINT!

Based upon all of the above, there can be NO QUESTION that all of the funds at issue were taken by distraint in violation of:

a. all of the taxing clauses of the Constitution.

b. the 16th Amendment.

c. Section 61 of the Internal Revenue Code (along with numerous other sections of the Code), and

d. the Pollock, Brushaber, Baltic Mining Co., Eisner, and Smietanka Supreme Court decisions.

Therefore, when petitioner asked the Government to identify the taxing clause or clauses pursuant to which it had imposed the income tax, it should have honestly admitted that it imposed the tax pursuant to none of those clauses - since the tax is neither apportioned as a direct tax nor imposed as an excise tax on income separated from its source. as was the Corporate Excise Tax of 1909.

However, not wanting to admit that it had illegally EXTRACTED BY DISTRAINT a tax which it had was not imposed pursuant to any of the taxing clauses of the Constitution, it attempted to hide ITS THIEVERY by claiming to have imposed the tax pursuant to all three taxing clauses of the Constitution and the 16th Amendment - even though such a claim is so absurd, it can be of no help to the Government.

In any case, since the Government claimed to have imposed the income taxes at issue as a direct tax (though without apportion- ment), it certainly could not have imposed it as an excise tax separated from sources of "income" - which is the only way it can be lawfully imposed (without apportionment) as laid down in Brushaber, as cited above.

All of the above was explained to both courts - but apparently it went right over their heads: otherwise the Second Circuit could not have stated "We hold that all of (Schiff's) claims are completely lacking in merit" - and then immediately wrap up this entire issue in the following two sentences.

Initially, Schiff's contentions that the imposition of a validly enacted income tax by Congress violates the taxing clauses of the Constitution have been rejected previously. E.g., Brushaber v. Union Pacific R.R. Co., 240 U.S. 1., 19-20 (1916); Schiff v. Commissioner, supra, 751 F.2d at 117; Ficalora v. Commissioner, 751 F.2d 85, 87 (2 Cir. 1984); Cert. denied. 471 U.S. 1005 (1985).

The Second Circuit neglects to mention that "Schiff's contentions" were ACTUALLY based on the Government's claim that it had imposed the income tax pursuant "To the Constitution's three taxing clauses and the 16th Amendment" and my contention that such a claim was a CLEAR CUT ADMISSION BY THE GOVERNMENT that it had imposed the tax IN VIOLATION OF ALL THREE OF THOSE CLAUSES AND THE 16TH AMENDMENT - as claimed by petitioner in his complaint.

justified an appeal based just on this issue alone! So the claim by the Second Circuit (as quoted above) that petitioner's "claims are completely lacking in merit," is itself, obviously, "completely lacking in merit."

In Summation, therefore, petitioner would point out to this court that: 1. nowhere in the record is there any claim by petitioner that his "income" can not be constitutionally taxed; or that 2, petitioner believes that the income tax was "unconstitutionally imposed." What _is_ in the record is petitioner's contention that the income tax is constitutionally imposed because the law "as imposed":

1. is based on "voluntary" and not "compulsory" compliance," and voluntary "self-assessment."

2. contains no penalties for those who decline to "self-assess" themselves or pay the tax;

3. imposes no "liability" for the tax, nor authorizes the Government to estimate such a tax in the absence of a voluntary "self-assessment." and

4. does not authorize the collection of such a tax by distraint, as occurred in the instant case.

And all of the above were certainly recognized by this Court in _Laing v. United States_, 423 U.S. 161, 191 and in _Flora v. United States_, 262 U.S. 145, 176 in which both Court's held that the income tax is "Based upon voluntary assessment and payment, not upon distraint." However, in this case, the tax was extracted by DISTRAINT, in violation of both of these holdings. So it was petitioner's contention that even though the income tax was not imposed pursuant to any of the taxing clauses of the Constitution ITS 'IMPOSITION' WAS NOT UNCONSTITUTIONAL BECAUSE _PAYMENT OF THE TAX WAS NOT MADE COMPULSORY!_

However, the record will also show that its was petitioner's contention that since the funds at issue were _not voluntarily paid_ but taken by distraint, the tax was being enforced _IN VIOLATION OF ITS "IMPOSITION"_ and that if the Government wanted to make payment of income taxes _COMPULSORY_ as opposed to its being _VOLUNTARY,_ then the tax _had_ to be imposed either on the basis of apportionment or as an excise - as excises are required to be imposed, as explained on page 5 of the Congressional Research Service Report to Congress, which was attached to petitioner's Reply Brief to the appeals court as Exhibit J. That Report, which verified (at page 4) that the _Brushaber_ Court noted that the inherent character of an income tax was that of an indirect tax," was also ignored by the Second Circuit - along with everything else it ignored.

So, even though the Second Circuit HAD TO KNOW that the income tax is not imposed as the excise it was held to be in _Brushaber_ (as clearly acknowledged in the _CRS Report For Congress_), that court still _had_ the nerve to cite _Brushaber_ to support its claim. Therefore, petitioner is asking this Court to take JUDICIAL NOTICE of the fact that HE HAS A CONSTITUTIONAL RIGHT NOT TO BE COMPELLED BY THE UNITED STATES _to pay_ a FEDERAL TAX that does _not_ fall into _any of_ taxing clauses of the Constitution and since the income tax is not imposed pursuant to any of those clauses, ALL OF THE FUNDS AT ISSUE WERE UNCONSTITUTIONALLY DEPRIVED ON THIS BASIS ALONE - REGARDLESS OF ANY OTHER ISSUE RAISED BY PETITIONER IN THIS PETITION. If the Supreme Court does not reverse the Appellate Court's decision, and

order the United States to return FORTHWITH all the funds at issue (plus interest) then IT IS PETITIONER'S CLAIM, AS FULLY SUPPORTED HEREIN, THAT THE INCOME TAX IS BEING EXTRACTED UNCONSTITUTIONALLY - in violation of the Constitution's three taxing clauses, the 16th Amendment and the _Pollock_ and _Brushaber_ decisions.

D.

CAN THE IRS SEIZE PROPERTY IN PAYMENT OF A TAX FOR WHICH NO LAW MAKES PETITIONER "LIABLE"?

It is clear (as petitioner argued on page 49 of his appeal brief and as he contended in his complaint) that the Internal Revenue Code does not make petitioner "liable" for income taxes, as it makes the public liable for other taxes. And while Section 1 "imposes" an income tax, the Internal Revenue Code makes no one "liable" for the tax so "imposed," as, for example, Section 4401(c) makes persons "liable" for the wagering tax "imposed" in Section 4401(a) and Section 5005(a) makes the public "liable" for the taxes imposed... by section 5001(a)(1). Indeed the mere "imposition" of an income tax never made petitioner "liable" for the tax as clearly provided in Section 6001 which states that "Every person LIABLE for any tax imposed by this title...," while Section 6011 states that " When required...any person MADE LIABLE for any tax imposed by this title...". Since no Section of the Code makes petitioner "Liable" for income taxes, the IRS was not authorized by law to take the property at issue by distraint, because the existence of a tax "liability" is a condition precedent for 6331 seizures. Indeed, petitioner's footnote #17 on page 49 of petitioner's appeal brief, challenged the Second Circuit to cite the Code Section that made petitioner "liable" for income taxes, but it never cited any such Section in its decision. Thus, since the property at issue was seized pursuant to Code Section 6331, even though no Code section made plaintiff "liable" for the tax, all of the property at issue was deprived in violation of the "Due Process" Clause of the Constitution - overlooking all other considerations which made these deprivations unconstitutional.

OTHER ERRONEOUS HOLDINGS OF THE SECOND CIRCUIT

Since petitioner has now provided this court with more than enough reasons why the Second Circuit's decision must be reversed, petitioner does not believe that he needs to seriously deal with all of the other misstatements of law and fact contained in the Second Circuit's decision - especially since most of them are covered in petitioner's Motion to Reconsider, Exhibit B, and in his Reply Brief. However, to keep the record straight, petitioner will raise and comment on some of them here.

E

CAN THE IRS ASSESS INCOME TAXES WITHOUT HAVING ANY INCOME TAX RETURNS WHATSOEVER, EITHER ONES FILED BY TAXPAYERS OR ONES PREPARED BY THE SECRETARY PURSUANT TO CODE SECTION 6020(b) AS CLAIMED BY THE SECOND CIRCUIT

The claim by the Second Circuit, and as advanced by the Government, that income tax assessments can be made WITHOUT ANY income tax returns whatsoever, involves ignoring so many statutes and Treasury Regulations, that it literally takes ones breath away. Petitioner has, of course, dealt with this erroneous claim at some length in his Motion to Reconsider (pages 12-14) and in his Reply Brief (at pages 4 -16).

The claim by the Second Circuit that the Secretary can assess income taxes without tax returns, either ones prepared by taxpayers or ones prepared by the Secretary, immediately FLIES IN THE FACE of Code Sections 6201(1) and 6020(b),as well as Treasury Regulations 601.103(a), 601.103(b), 601.104(a), 301.6201-1(1) and 301.6203-1 and ALL OF THE PROCEDURES AND CLAIMS made by the Government (and the trial court in its decision) up until the Government's Reply Brief, where, for the first time, this NEW CLAIM WAS MADE. (Presumably, therefore, no "supporting" records are also not necessary, as provided for in Tres. Reg. 301.6203-1)

It is clear, however, that UNDER THE LAW as contained in Code Section 6201(1), no income tax assessments are possible WITHOUT RETURNS, since that Section clearly says:

"The Secretary shall assess all taxes as to which returns or lists ARE MADE under this title."

Petitioner would respectfully point out to this Court that there is no way that Section 6201(1) can be read to mean that, "The Secretary shall assess all taxes as to which returns or lists are made OR NOT MADE under this title." It is also clear that since "The Federal tax system is basically one of self assessment...a return...shows the facts upon which tax liability may be determined and assessed" (Treasury Reg. 601.103(a)); "AFTER RETURNS ARE FILED AND PROCESSED...some returns are selected for examination. If adjustments are proposed and...the taxpayer agrees to the proposed adjustments...and the tax involved is an income...the deficiency will be immediately assessed" (Treas. Reg. 601.103(b) emphasis added); "Generally, an internal revenue tax assessment is based upon a *RETURN* by law or regulations to be filed by the taxpayer ...If a taxpayer fails to make a *RETURN* it may be made for the taxpayer by a district director or other duly authorized officer or employee. *See section 6020 of the Code and the regulations thereunder.*" (Treas. Reg. 601.104(a), emphasis added): "The district director or the director ..shall assess all taxes determined by the taxpayer or by the district director... *DISCLOSED ON A RETURN OR LIST.*" and "The amount of the assessment shall, in the case of tax SHOWN ON A RETURN BY THE TAXPAYER, BE THE AMOUNT SO SHOWN, and in all other cases the amount of the assessment shall be the amount shown on the supporting list or record.." (Treas. Reg. 301.6201-1(1), emphasis added). It is clear from all of the above that the Secretary can not assess a tax not "disclosed on a return or list" and since income taxes are "disclosed" on returns - either ones prepared by the taxpayer or presumably ones prepared pursuant to Section 6020, as referred to in Treas. Reg. 601.104. (note #4) In view of all the above - and overlooking all other claims, the claim that income taxes can be assessed without returns is obviously without merit.

Further, in holding that the Government could make assessments without tax returns: either returns prepared by taxpayers, or by the Secretary pursuant to Section 6020(b); nor even "substitute," or "dummy returns", the Second Circuit, in reality, claimed that it was NOT NECESSARY for:

a. the IRS to have prepared the substitute returns which they did in this case, as shown in Exhibit M.

b. the IRS to have made the entries, "Substitute For Returns Prepared" which were the first entries on all of petitioner's Forms 4340s as shown in Exhibit M.

c. the Government to have claimed in discovery, that it made the assessment from returns prepared pursuant to Section 6020(b).

d. for the Government to have changed its claim, to that it made the assessments from "dummy returns." and

e. that the trial court erred in contending that the assessments were made from "dummy returns."

In view of all of the above - and overlooking all other considerations - the Second Circuit's claim that assessments can be made without returns is, obviously, contrary to all of the Government claims and procedures made prior to the appeal.

The Second Circuit based its claim on Roat v. Commissioner, 847 F.2d 1379, 1381(9 Cir. 1988), which based its erroneous conclusion on Treasury Regulation 301.6211-1(a) and the comment, in dicta in Laing v. United States, 423 U.S. 161, 174 in which the Supreme Court citing that Regulation stated "Where there has been no return filed, the deficiency is the amount of tax due. However, in making that statement, the Supreme Court (as noted in petitioner's Motion for Reconsideration, at page 14) never considered how the alleged "tax due" could be determined or on what basis it could be assessed!

Who would determine the "tax due" if no return is filed by a tax payer? Section 6201(2) only authorizes the Secretary to "estimate the amount of tax which has been omitted to be paid" BY STAMP, not "omitted" from a return. (This argument is fully addressed in pages 4 - 16 of petitioner's Reply Brief) And in addition, how can this "amount of tax due" be assessed - since the IRS would have no return from which to make the assessment? It is obvious that Treasury Regulation 301.6211-1(a) IS VOID as a matter of law, since it is contrary to the very statute (Code Section 6211) upon which it is based and would (as the Court has used it here) obliterate all of the other Regulations cited which call for .

And of course, Regulation 301.6211-1(a) would do away with the distinctions between "original" and "supplemental" assessments - as established in Code Sections 6201, 6204 and 6211 (as explained at pages 11 & 12 of petitioner's Reply Brief) and as explained in petitioners Motion for Summary Judgment. (Exhibit Q, p 7-11). It is clear that Treasury Regulation 301.6211-1(a) was deliberately written to provide the IRS with WHAT WOULD APPEAR TO BE A LAWFUL REGULATION. but which would allow it to UNLAWFULLY DEFEAT THE "SELF-ASSESSMENT" NATURE OF THE INCOME TAX. as provided for in ALL THE REST OF THE STATUTES AND REGULATIONS. What this Regulation 301.6211 states is as follows:

If no return is made, or if the return...does not show any tax. for the purpose of the deficiency "the amount shown as the tax by the taxpayer upon his return" shall be considered as zero. (emphasis added)

In addition, the Government could not produce one document that held that TD 1995 had been rescinded, or that Form 17 had been replaced by Form 3352. In addition petitioner produced for the court the "Catalog of Federal Tax Forms" (Exhibit G, petitioner's Reply Brief) in which form 3352 is identified as being a form which merely "request." not DEMANDS, payment - so. ADMITTEDLY, Form 3552 is NOT THE "DEMAND" CALLED FOR BY STATUTE - which was required to be served on petitioner before the IRS could take his property, by distraint, pursuant to Code Section 6331. Therefore, the claim by the trial and appeals courts that such a "Demand" WAS MADE on petitioner before the IRS seized his property, were both without merit.

G.

CAN THE IRS AND FEDERAL COURTS IGNORE CODE SECTION 6501(c)(3) IN
THE COLLECTION OF INCOME TAXES?

It is clear from all of petitioner's underlying briefs, that Code Section 6501(c)(3), required the Government, in this case, to bring "a proceeding in court." (since petitioner had not filed a return and no "original" assessment had been made) if the Government believed that petitioner owed any income taxes. However, the Commissioner sought to circumvent the law as contained in 6501(c)(3). by seeking to collect the tax by sending petitioner a fraudulent DEFICIENCY NOTICE. It is also clear that since neither the trial or appeals court WOULD EVEN ADDRESS THIS ISSUE, which petitioner had stressed in all of his briefs, both courts KNEW THAT SECTION 6501(c)(3) alone - and overlooking any other consideration - denied the Government the right to seize the property at issue in the manner it did. And the refusal by the Second Circuit to even ADDRESS THIS ISSUE is itself proof that the Second Circuit's claim that petitioner's appeal was frivolous was itself a frivolous claim.

H.

DO AMERICANS LOSE THEIR RIGHT TO JURY TRIALS IN DISTRICT COURT
AFTER SATISFYING THEIR ALLEGED DEFICIENCIES
BY EITHER VOLUNTARILY OR BY DISTRAINT
SIMPLY BECAUSE THEY REFUSE TO GO TO TAX COURT?

This is what the Second Circuit now contends in its instant decision. In support of this holding, the Second Circuit contends (at page 430) that :

The notice of deficiency sent to Schiff clearly informed him of his right to appeal to the Tax Court. Such an appeal would have provided Schiff with an opportunity to he heard and to contest the IRS's calculations. Schiff chose not to avail himself of that opportunity.

Thus, according to the Second Circuit - under no circumstances can individuals get a jury trial in district court (following payment of the deficiency) because...

1. It they go to tax court, the law bars them from getting a jury trial later, and

2. If they don't go to tax court, THE SECOND CIRCUIT CONTENDS that they have no right to a jury trial because they did not "avail themselves" of the "opportunity" to

While regulations are not laws those made pursuant to law and which do not "broaden or narrow the specific provisions" of the law are accorded the status of law -- but this regulation contradicts both law and fact. But assuming for the moment that this regulation is "law" (because that is how the Supreme Court in Laing treated it) - how can a law assume a fact that isn't so? What kind of law would assume a fact that isn't so? Laws tell you what you are required to do --they don't allege facts --especially false ones. So, how, if individuals do not file tax returns, can we have a law that 1) assumes they did and 2) further assumes that they showed zero amounts on the returns they didn't file?

However, if we compare Section 6211 with its Regulation, we see how lawless the Regulation is, since there is no provision anywhere in the law that would justify the absurd assumptions contained in the Regulation. The law is clear: it contemplates an assessment of "The amount shown as the tax by the taxpayer upon his return, if a return was made by the taxpayer and an amount was shown as the tax by the taxpayer." There is no suggestion anyplace in the "law" that anything not shown "as the tax by the taxpayer" can be assessed? Where does the law provide that the Government is free to make FILING ASSUMPTION against those parties who do not chose to make the returns THEY DIDN'T FILE?! And if the law contemplated any such ridiculous assumptions, it would have been contained in the law itself. Since the law specifically took into consideration "if a return was made," the law could have taken into consideration "if a return is not made, then the amount shown on the taxpayer's return will be considered to be zero" if that was what the law intended. But the law did not say, or even suggest any such thing! So, obviously, the Regulation was deliberately made TO SUBVERT THE LAW —which is what the Supreme Court has done by giving credence to it in Laing. And the Supreme Court most rectify THAT ERROR by disavowing its reference to Treasury Regulation 301.6211-1(a) in Laing —otherwise the Supreme Court will be encouraging Federal courts to disregard the law - as occurred in Roat. and in the instant case. Federal courts by claiming that the IRS can assess taxes without returns are creating "law" contrary to the laws passed by Congress (such as Section 6201) in violation of Article I, Section 1 of the Constitution. (SEE NOTE #5)

Therefore based upon all of the above, it is clear that the Second Circuit's claim that assessment's can be made without returns was totally without merit and is contradicted by every statute and every lawful Regulation bearing on the assessment of income taxes.

F.

DID THE IRS MAKE A LAWFUL DEMAND ON PETITIONER BY SENDING HIM A
FORM 3352?

It is clear from petitioner's Motion for Reconsideration (pages 14- 15) that the Second Circuit's claim that the IRS made a legitimate demand on petitioner by sending him a form 3352 was wholly without merit. Petitioner provided the court with Treasury Decision 1995 (Exhibit C of petitioner's opening appeal brief), which identifies Form 17 as the statutory Notice and Demand (Form 17) called for by such statutes as Code Section 6303, 6621 and 6331) as reproduced in U.S. V. Lehigh, 201 F. Supp. 224 (1961) (Exhibit D in that brief); and as identified in other case law. In so doing, petitioner exposed as a TOTAL FRAUD the Government's claim that Mertens had maintained that the Form 17 did not have to be employed.

go to Tax Court and so they have waived their right to a jury trial-in district court.

Since, I am sure, this is not the law in other circuits, the decision should be reviewed for this reason.

Petitioner would also like to point out to the Supreme Court that in reaching this legal conclusion, the Second Circuit would appear to have also lost sight of the following.

1. Since the U.S. Tax Court is actually a court in name only (since its "judges" have only "the same powers, tenure and jurisdiction as had been provided (to members) of the United States Board of Tax Appeals") its "judges" would not have the jurisdiction to address (let alone decide) the Constitutional issues raised by petitioner in this action.

2. Since no assessment was made prior to the Commissioner sending petitioner a DEFICIENCY NOTICE, there was no assessment that was "deficient" and thus no "deficiency" that was capable of being "redetermined" in Tax Court. Thus any petition to Tax Court would have been made from an invalid Deficiency Notice and the Tax Court would have had no jurisdiction to even consider petitioner's petition. (Scar v. C.I.R. 814 F.2d 1363. (9th Cr. 1987).

3. The holding of the Supreme Court in Phillips v. Commissioner, 283 U.S. 589, 597-599.

In Phillips, the Supreme Court clearly states that "Two alternative methods of eventual judicial review are available ..(petitioner) may contest his liability by bringing an action against the United States or the collector to recover the amount paid. This remedy is available where the transferee does not appeal from the determination of the Commissioner (i.e. elects not to go to Tax Court), and the latter makes an assessment an enforces payment by distraint." Thus according to the Supreme court in Phillips, petitioner had two alternatives - he could either go to Tax Court (where a jury trial is not available) or pay the tax (which he did by distraint) and get a jury trial in district court. However, in its decision, the Second Circuit ruled THAT petitioner COULD ONLY GO TO TAX COURT - because..

1. If he elected to go to Tax Court, he is bared by law from getting a jury trial in district court, and,

2. If he wanted a jury trial in district court BY NOT GOING to Tax Court, the Second Circuit has held that he can not get a jury trial in district court BECAUSE HE DID NOT GO TO TAX COURT.

Since petitioner has had no formal legal training, *he can not follow the Second Circuit's logic here* - but, in any case, it appears to be in conflict with Phillips and with what other circuits hold on this issue.

I

DID. AS THE APPEALS COURT CLAIMED TO HAVE DONE. "CONSIDER THE EVIDENCE IN THE LIGHT MOST FAVORABLE TO SCHIFF"?

It is obvious that even the members of the appeals panel do not believe that statement. It is perfectly obvious that in rendering

its decision, the Second Circuit decided every issue of law or fact in favor of the Government - EVEN IF IT HAD TO MAKE UP LAWS AND FACTS TO DO IT.

J.

COULD THE SECOND CIRCUIT HAVE HELD THAT THE GOVERNMENT COULD COLLECT. BY DISTRAINT. THE TAXES CLAIMED FOR 1976 EVEN THOUGH A GOVERNMENT DOCUMENT CLAIMED THAT THE STATUTE OF LIMITATIONS WITH RESPECT TO THEIR COLLECTION ENDED THREE YEARS BEFORE THE PROPERTY WAS SEIZED?

The Second Circuit's holding that the Government could collect by distraint the taxes allegedly owed by petitioner for 1976 without seeking to lift the three year bar that applies when returns are filed. without proving that the return petitioner filed for 1976 was fraudulent - is itself a totally frivolous claim (as fully supported in all of petitioner's briefs) and especially so. since the Second Circuit claimed to have "considered the evidence in the light most favorable to Schiff."

K

DID PETITIONER MERIT DOUBLE COSTS AND A $5,000 PENALTY FOR FILING THIS APPEAL?

As shown by all of the briefs filed in this case, if ever a district court decision warranted an appeal, this one did. It is clear that the Second Circuit imposed sanctions on petitioner to prevent him from appealing the district court's denial of his habeas corpus petition - and as such the penalty represented an "excessive" fine as barred by the 8th Amendment as well as "cruel and unusual punishment" since the sanctions were totally unwarranted and imposed purely to deny petitioner access to the appeals court, while the court's refusal to allow petitioner a jury trial in this matter was also a violation of petitioner's 7th Amendment Right.

L.

WHAT WILL BE THE EFFECT OF THE SUPREME COURT ALLOWING THIS DECISION TO STAND

Apart from converting America to a Fascist state. there will be other legal consequences if this decision is not reversed - two of which come immediately to mind.

1. The anti-injunction statute (Sect 7421) would become inoperable. and

2. "Concealment" of income or assets could no longer be regarded as an indicia of tax evasion - but would represent. in light of the Second Circuit's holding, a prudent course for Americans to follow.

When petitioner sought to enjoin the Government from seizing his assets pending a hearing on the merits. the district court ruled that the Anti-injunction Statute barred this form of relief and that petitioner's only legal remedy was to pay the taxes and penalties requested, and sue for a refund in district court. However, based upon the Second Circuit's instant ruling, persons who pay the taxes and penalties alleged to be due (either volun-tarily or, as in this case, by distraint), can still BE DENIED A HEARING IN A DISTRICT COURT on the merits of the Government's seizures! So, based on the this decision, there is NO LEGAL RELIEF FROM 6331 SEIZURES! Thus the anti-injunction statute can not be applied IN THE MANNER THAT IT WAS USED AGAINST PETITIONER.

In addition, if the Federal government can seize citizen property and never, as in the instant case, be required to give the party whose property it seized A HEARING IN A REAL COURT on the legality and/or the merits of its seizures - Americans would be WELL ADVISED to BEGIN CONCEALING THEIR ASSETS AND INCOME from the Federal government.

VI

CONCLUSION

THEREFORE, to prevent a substantial deviation from prior holdings of this Court; to prevent a substantial subversion of the United States Constitution; to prevent conflicts among the Circuits, and to prevent a FUNDAMENTAL CHANGE in the LEGAL CHARACTER of our Government, a writ of certiorari should issue to review the judgment and opinion of the United States Court of Appeals for the Second Circuit.

Respectfully submitted

[signature]
IRWIN A. SCHIFF, PRO SE

FOOT NOTES AS REFERRED TO IN THIS BRIEF

Note #1) It is clear that respondent induced Simon and Schuster to turn over the funds at issue (by using the intimidating power of the IRS) in violation of other provisions of Section 6331 as well. Such as, for example: 1. none of the finds were "seized" within the meaning of Section (b); 2. petitioner was not "liable" for the tax as provided for in Section (a); 3. no prior notice and demand (Form 17) was sent to petitioner as provide in section (a); 4. the funds did not represent the "accrued salary or wages of any...employee...of the United States." as provided in Section (a). Thus it is crystal clear that all of the funds at issue were extracted from Simon and Schuster by the United States in violation of *numerous provisions of Section 6331* - all of which *the Second Circuit disregarded in affirming a summary judgment given to the publisher* (no court hearings held) in Schiff v. Simon & Schuster, 780 F.2d 210, (1985). However, petitioner's illegal conviction to charges of tax evasion United States v. Schiff 801 F.2d 108 (2d Cir. 1986), cert. denied 480 U.S. 945 (1987) rendered him financially and mentally incapable of appealing this *lawless*, Second Circuit decision.

Note #2) On July 11, 1989 petitioner filed a Notice of Appeal in connection with a habeas corpus (2255) action. However, he had to pursue this appeal from imprisonment, since on August 8, 1989 - without any prior warning - he was incarcerated pursuant to false

allegations that he had violated the terms of his parole. (see Exhibits S & T). While incarcerated, the Second Circuit notified petitioner that it would not consider his 2255 appeal (which involved a supplemental instruction, in which the trial judge informed the jury that it could convict petitioner of income tax evasion even if he did not commit any affirmative act of tax evasion (as required by Spies and Sansone, see article from "The Journal of Taxation," Exhibit U), until petitioner proved he had paid an earlier sanction of $2,758.40. Not having the proof while incarcerated, petitioner provided the proof upon his release, and on October 19, 1990 filed a "Motion to Reinstate" his 2255 appeal. However, on December 3, the Second Circuit NOW refused to consider petitioner's appeal, until he paid the NEW SANCTIONS imposed on him on November 21, 1990 -or some 17 months after his habeas corpus appeal was initiated. but which he was unable to pursue because of the litigating problems caused by his incarceration and the earlier demand imposed upon him by the appeals court itself. Not having the money to pay the NEW SANCTIONS, petitioner filed a motion for reconsideration in which he submitted an Affidavit (Exhibit W) disclosing that he did not have the money to pay the NEW sanctions. However, the Second Circuit refused to reverse its decision. so petitioner was denied the ability to go forward with that appeal.

Note #3. Since the 16th Amendment gave the Government no new taxing powers, this claim by the trial court was totally erroneous as was fully supported by petitioner at pages 27 and 28 of his opening brief to the appeals court.

Note #4. Actually all references to Section 6020 (Exhibit E, in petitioner's Reply Brief) are designed to mislead the public to thinking that Section 6020 applies to income taxes - when it does not. Since income taxes are based on "self-assessment," there is no law that allows the Secretary to determine a total tax due, and assess it without a "self-assessment" being made by the taxpayer. So it is the Treasury's policy to mislead the public into THINKING that 6020 applies to income taxes - when it does not. That is why NO INCOME TAX RETURNS WERE PREPARED FOR PETITIONER IN THE INSTANT CASE - and that is why the IRS, the Government and the trial court had to FABRICATE the concept of "dummy returns" and that is why the appeals court had to switch to another fabrication when that one did not work!

NOTE #5. Indeed, Laing itself, refutes the definition it gives, on page 174, of a "deficiency" in its explanation (at pages 179 & 180) of how the word itself evolved. It first points out that in the United States' brief...

> Which set out the procedure for handling underpayments after returns have been filed:

> "If the amount already paid is less than that which should have been paid the difference...(hereinafter called "deficiency') ...shall be paid upon notice and demand

Thus it is admitted that deficiencies are based upon "returns (which have) been filed" and on amounts "already paid" which are less "than that which should have been paid." Well based upon this description alone there can be a "deficiency" unless a return "has been filed" and an "amount already paid" - and neither occurs when

United States Senate

DANIEL K. INOUYE
HAWAII

SUITE 722, HART SENATE BUILDING
WASHINGTON, DC 20510
(202) 224-3934
FAX (202) 224-6747

PRINCE KUHIO FEDERAL BUILDING
ROOM 7325, 300 ALA MOANA BOULEVAR
HONOLULU, HI 96850
(808) 541-2542
FAX (808) 541-2649

June 26, 1989

Mr. Fred M. Ortiz
Tax Consultant
73-4188 Eluna Street
Kailua-Kona, Hawaii 96740

Dear Mr. Ortiz:

On behalf of Senator Inouye, I am writing in further response to your inquiry regarding the precise provisions of the Internal Revenue Code (IRS) that render an individual liable for income taxes.

Based on the research performed by the Congressional Research Service, there is no provision which specifically and unequivocally requires an individual to pay income taxes. However, Article I, section 8 of the U.S. Constitution accords the Congress the "power to lay and collect Taxes...." Accordingly, the IRC need not specifically state that individuals shall be liable for income taxes because it is inferred from the Congress' authority to so levy and collect. This conclusion is further supported by I.R.S. Sec. 7201 et al. (1988) which sets forth the numerous penalties for failure to pay income taxes owed. I have enclosed a copy of these provisions for your information.

I am pleased to have had an opportunity to assist you in this matter.

Aloha,

MARK L. FORMAN
Legislative Correspondent

MLF:r
Enclosure

Page 25

returns are not filed. So, obviously, if "No tax return (has been) filed," the deficiency (can not be) the amount of tax due! The fact that a deficiency can only exist when returns are filed (as the statute itself makes clear) is developed further. "Since the reference (to deficiencies) Laing adds, "related only to money owed after a return had been filed and examined." So again we see that a "deficiency" can only occur "after a return has been filed and examined." Continuing with its explanation of "The use of the word "deficiency" the Court goes on to note that:

    was not formally defined (in the 1918 Act) but
    appeared in various provisions dealing with underpayments
    and overpayments.... "Deficiency" was used synonymously with
    the word "understatement."

    Laing goes on to point out that the 1921 Act replaced the word "understatement" with "deficiency." Thus it is clear from all of the above, that a "deficiency" is synonymous with an "understatement" of ones tax on a return and is related to an amount "already paid (which) is less than that which should have been paid." Since there are no "understatements" and no amounts "paid" when returns are not filed, there can be no "deficiency" based on this explanation of what a "deficiency" is - which is exactly what the statute itself says. So any claim that "Where there has been no tax return filed, the deficiency is the amount of tax due." is directly contradicted by the development of what the term really means. So the short, one line reference to a "deficiency" on page 174 of Laing is contradicted by the longer and more detailed description that appears on pages 179 and 180 of that decision.

    Further, the Second Circuit's claim that by not going to Tax Court, petitioner lost his right to the jury trial he had claimed - is also without merit, since the Supreme Court, in Laing, stated (on page 197-198):

    The choices the taxpayer makes, and the risks he assumes by (going to Tax Court), include the foregoing of trial of the factual issues by a jury, having his trial before a special judge not assigned to the taxpayer's local district...If he selects the other route, that is payment of the asserted deficiency, filing claim for refund, and suit. the taxpayer (if he chooses the district court rather than the Court of Claims) has his case tried before a United States district judge of his own district, WITH A JURY AVAILABLE, and it is the Government, not the taxpayer, that bears the burden of accruing interest.

    Thus it is clear, that the Second Circuit's argument that petitioner lost his right to the jury trial promised in Laing because he did not chose to "avail himself of (the) opportunity" to "contest the IRS' calculations" in Tax Court - was solely contrived TO DENY PETITIONER HIS RIGHT TO A JURY TRIAL and the due process this allegedly brings to 6331 seizures.

— *Reference Materials* —
Books, Reports & Tapes by Irwin Schiff

Books and Reports:

The Great Income Tax Hoax, by Irwin Schiff

It was the publication of this book in March, 1985 that caused the author's arrest in April of 1985. It contains the most comprehensive analysis of the income tax ever written, and uniquely explains why the income tax was declared unconstitutional in 1895, why the 16th Amendment was passed, and how that Amendment (which "amended" nothing) has been totally ignored by the government. The book thoroughly details the historic and constitutional development of the income tax from its earliest direct taxing roots, through the income tax passed during the Civil War, to its modern counterpart. It contains the only accurate description of the legal meaning of "income" ever to appear in print. In reviewing this book for the Copley News Service, Ralph de Toledano stated: "Puts to shame our economists, our legal profession, our great law schools, the federal judiciary, and the Justice Department ... should be in every university library and on the bookshelves of every senator and congressman." The book reveals how the Supreme Court has so emasculated the Constitution as to render that document practically meaningless today. Numerous tactics for frustrating the IRS and combatting its illegal procedures are presented. Extensive appendix material also provides an eye-opening understanding of the illegal nature of *all* U.S. coin and currency. Must reading. An indispensable companion to *The Federal Mafia.* Hardcover, 568 pages, index.   Ø17.95

How Anyone Can Stop Paying Income Taxes
by Irwin Schiff

Published in 1982, this book became an instant best seller which sold out its first printing of 30,000 in nine weeks. It was directly responsible for the many punitive provisions that were added to the Internal Revenue Code in 1983, as the government sought to prevent, punish and intimidate the public from using the lawful procedures presented in the book for stopping the voluntary payment of income taxes. While the book is more limited in scope than is *The Federal Mafia,* and while it duplicates a good deal of the material, it is still extremely readable and covers some aspects of the income tax and the author's battle against it, that were not covered in this book. It will also be helpful to those who want a more complete and thorough understanding of the subject. Hardcover, 179 pages, while supplies last.

Ø10.00

The Social Security Swindle—
How Anyone Can Drop Out, by Irwin Schiff

A comprehensive and extremely readable expose' of Social Security, the *biggest chain-letter* of them all. The book thoroughly refutes every actuarial, economic and social claim ever made for this socialistic scam, and reveals the absurdity of any belief that future Social Security "surpluses" will be able to pay future claims. The continual misrepresentation by the government, of the real Ponzi-like nature of this scam, is fully documented. The fraudulent basis upon which the Supreme Court upheld the constitutionality of this swindle (after it had been correctly held as being unconstitutional by the First Circuit Court of Appeals) is alone worth the price. Hardcover, 256 pages.

Ø13.00

The Biggest Con:
How The Government Is Fleecing You, by Irwin Schiff

Over 100,000 copies of Schiff's first book, an economic classic, are in print. The book will give you a thorough understanding of economics and is guaranteed to make you an expert on the subject—*even if you read nothing else!* It will convince you that most American "economists" don't know what they are talking about—which is why this country is in such deep economic and financial trouble. It provides irrefutable proof of how the federal government has been continually undermining the American economy and forcing a lower standard of living on us all. While the book covers many complex topics (such as: why all U.S. coin and currency is counterfeit, how the U.S. declared bankruptcy in 1971, how the government *hides* and *doesn't report* 90 percent of its debts, and the absurdity of its gross national product statistics), it does so in the humorous and entertaining style of Irwin Schiff. "The single most important book on the status of this nation I have ever read," said Howard Ruff, editor of *The Ruff Times.* Softcover, 359 pages, index.

Ø8.00

How An Economy Grows And Why It Doesn't
by Irwin Schiff with illustrations by Vic Lockman

Now there is *no excuse* for *anyone* not knowing the subject of economics. It should not take you more than 45 minutes to read this 108-page, fully illustrated book which will provide you with a thorough understanding of why some economies grow, and others do not. Although the book deals

with complex economic issues, such as: where capital comes from and how it is wasted and destroyed; the *sole* cause of inflation and why governments produce it; where credit comes from and how governments waste it; the basis of profit and how it benefits everyone—it does so in a way that any junior high school student will understand. Many an "economics" major will not have learned in four years what this book can teach any teenager in under an hour. Never again be intimidated by the mumbo-jumbo of economic "experts." Soft cover.
Ø7.00

The Schiff Audio Reports - Highly Recommended

These reports consist of a series of six 60-minute cassette tapes. Designed to be sent out over a six to 12-month period for the author to update the material in this book and communicate new and/or improved methods of dealing with the IRS and a corrupt court system. You will get a far more solid grasp of this material if it is drummed into your head while driving your car.

Audio Report #1 focuses on: establishing, in the order of their importance, the eight most important reasons why you are not required to file and pay income taxes; exposing the many erroneous theories that now abound in the tax rebellion movement; and how to beat the government at criminal trials. All aspects of such tax trials are examined, from the arraignment to closing argument, with many devastating defense tactics (which are almost never used) explained.   Ø65.00*

Audio Report #2 focuses on recently discovered material which reveals that all IRS liens are recorded in violation of both state and federal law. The author explains how this can be used to remove all IRS liens. In addition, author supplies statutory proof as to why no IRS agent can have delegated authority to interfere with anyone in connection with income taxes—an effective weapon in any confrontation you might have with the IRS. This series offers a new technique to stop banks from turning over your money to the IRS, and information on dealing with the U.S. Tax Court.   Ø65.00*

Put on Your Own Untax Seminars!

1. Get a VIDEO TAPE (three 2-hour cassettes) of the six-hour seminar put on by Irwin Schiff in Costa Mesa, California. Seminar comes with an index and the tape is coded so that you can fast-forward (or rewind) to specific areas of interest.   Ø65.00*

2. Get an AUDIO TAPE (two 60-minute tapes) of a three hour seminar put on by Irwin Schiff in Philadelphia.
Ø20.00*

Inquire about Irwin Schiff's **Freedom Package.** It includes all of his books and tapes and consulting services.   Ø385.00

Internal Revenue Code

Use *the law itself* against the IRS - color tabbed and highlighted. Tabs in five separate color groupings, and two pages of instructions allow you to use the **Code** in machine gun like fashion, to prove that, by law: no one is **"liable"** for income taxes, 2) no one is **required** to keep books and records for income tax purposes, and 3) that all IRS seizures for income taxes are **illegal.** 9,429 *riveting and suspenseful* pages!   Ø53.00

NOTE:

Prices are denoted by Ø which refers to Federal Reserve units—fiat currency now fraudulently circulating as U.S. dollars. All prices include postage and handling.

Please use the order form provided below and send all orders or inquiries to:

FREEDOM BOOKS
P.O. Box 5326
Evansville, IN 47716